# LEARNSMART ADVANTAGE WORKS

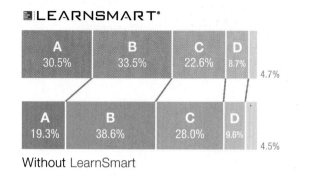

**LEARNSMART®**

| A | B | C | D | |
|---|---|---|---|---|
| 30.5% | 33.5% | 22.6% | 8.7% | 4.7% |

| A | B | C | D | |
|---|---|---|---|---|
| 19.3% | 38.6% | 28.0% | 9.6% | 4.5% |

Without LearnSmart

## More C students earn B's

*Study: 690 students / 6 institutions

## Over 20%
### more students pass the class with LearnSmart

*A&P Research Study

**LEARNSMART®** Pass Rate - 70%

Without LearnSmart Pass Rate - 57%

100% —
80% —
60% —
40% —
20% —
0 —

Jan–Dec 2011    Jan–Mar 2012

— Extremely

— Very

— Moderately

— Slightly
— Not at all

## More than 60%
of all students agreed LearnSmart was a very or extremely helpful learning tool

*Based on 750,000 student survey responses

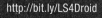

http://bit.ly/LS4Apple

http://bit.ly/LS4Droid

> *AVAILABLE* ON-THE-GO

How do you rank against your peers?

What you know (green) and what you still need to review (yellow), based on your answers.

Let's see how confident you are on the questions.

# COMPARE AND CHOOSE WHAT'S RIGHT FOR YOU

| | BOOK | LEARNSMART | ASSIGNMENTS | |
|---|:---:|:---:|:---:|---|
| **connect** (McGraw Hill Education) | ✓ | ✓ | ✓ | LearnSmart, assignments, and SmartBook—all in one digital product for maximum savings! |
| **connect** Looseleaf (McGraw Hill Education) | ✓ | ✓ | ✓ | Pop the pages into your own binder or carry just the pages you need. |
| **connect** Bound Book (McGraw Hill Education) | ✓ | ✓ | ✓ | The #1 Student Choice! |
| **LEARNSMART** Access Code | ✓ | ✓ | | The first and only book that adapts to you! |
| **LEARNSMART** ADVANTAGE Access Code | | ✓ | | The smartest way to get from a B to an A. |
| **CourseSmart** eBook | ✓ | | | Save some green and some trees! |
| **create** (McGraw Hill Education) | ✓ | ✓ | ✓ | Check with your instructor about a custom option for your course. |

> Buy directly from the source at http://shop.mheducation.com.

# Business

## A Changing World

# Business

## A Changing World

### tenth edition

**O.C. Ferrell**
University of New Mexico

**Geoffrey A. Hirt**
DePaul University

**Linda Ferrell**
University of New Mexico

BUSINESS: A CHANGING WORLD, TENTH EDITION

Published by McGraw-Hill Education, 2 Penn Plaza, New York, NY 10121. Copyright © 2016 by McGraw-Hill Education. All rights reserved. Printed in the United States of America. Previous edition © 2014, 2011 and 2009. No part of this publication may be reproduced or distributed in any form or by any means, or stored in a database or retrieval system, without the prior written consent of McGraw-Hill Education, including, but not limited to, in any network or other electronic storage or transmission, or broadcast for distance learning.

Some ancillaries, including electronic and print components, may not be available to customers outside the United States.

This book is printed on acid-free paper.

1 2 3 4 5 6 7 8 9 0 QVS/QVS 1 0 9 8 7 6 5

ISBN 978-1-259-17939-6
MHID 1-259-17939-7

Senior Vice President, Products & Markets: *Kurt L. Strand*
Vice President, General Manager, Products & Markets: *Marty Lange*
Vice President, Content Design & Delivery: *Kimberly Meriwether David*
Managing Director: *Paul Ducham*
Brand Manager: *Anke Weekes*
Director, Product Development: *Rose Koos*
Director of Development: *Ann Torbert*
Product Developer: *Gabriela Gonzalez*
Marketing Manager: *Michael Gedatus*
Director, Content Design & Delivery: *Linda Avenarius*
Executive Program Manager: *Faye Herrig*
Content Project Managers: *Heather Ervolino; Lisa Bruflodt; Mark Christianson; Judi David*
Buyer: *Debra R. Sylvester*
Design: *Debra Kubiak*
Content Licensing Specialists: *DeAnna Dausener; Shawntel Schmitt*
Cover Image: (top image) *Dougal Waters/Getty Images;* (bottom image) *Eva Serrabassa/Getty Images*
Compositor: *MPS Limited*
Typeface: *10.5/12 Times LT Std Roman*
Printer: *Quad/Graphics*

All credits appearing on page or at the end of the book are considered to be an extension of the copyright page.

**Library of Congress Cataloging-in-Publication Data**

Ferrell, O. C.
    Business : a changing world/O.C. Ferrell, University of New Mexico,
Geoffrey A. Hirt, DePaul University, Linda Ferrell, University of New Mexico.—Tenth edition.
    pages cm
    ISBN 978-1-259-17939-6 (alk. paper)
    1. Business. 2. Management—United States. I. Hirt, Geoffrey A. II.
Ferrell, Linda. III. Title.
HF1008.F47 2016
650—dc23
                              2014035249

The Internet addresses listed in the text were accurate at the time of publication. The inclusion of a website does not indicate an endorsement by the authors or McGraw-Hill Education, and McGraw-Hill Education does not guarantee the accuracy of the information presented at these sites.

www.mhhe.com

# Dedication

**To James Ferrell**

**To Linda Hirt**

**To George Ferrell**

# Authors

## O.C. FERRELL

O.C. Ferrell is University Distinguished Professor of Marketing and Bill Daniels Professor of Business Ethics in the Anderson School of Management at the University of New Mexico. He served as the Bill Daniels Distinguished Professor of Business Ethics at the University of Wyoming and the Chair of the Department of Marketing at Colorado State University. He also has held faculty positions at the University of Memphis, University of Tampa, Texas A&M University, Illinois State University, and Southern Illinois University, as well as visiting positions at Queen's University (Ontario, Canada), University of Michigan (Ann Arbor), University of Wisconsin (Madison), and University of Hannover (Germany). He has served as a faculty member for the Master's Degree Program in Marketing at Thammasat University (Bangkok, Thailand). Dr. Ferrell received his B.A. and M.B.A. from Florida State University and his Ph.D. from Louisiana State University. His teaching and research interests include business ethics, global business, and marketing.

Dr. Ferrell is widely recognized as a leading teacher and scholar in business. He has published more than 100 articles in leading journals. He has co-authored more than 20 books. In addition to *Business: A Changing World,* he has two other textbooks, *Marketing* and *Business Ethics: Ethical Decision Making and Cases,* that are market leaders in their respective areas. He also has co-authored other textbooks for marketing, management, business and society, and other business courses, as well as a trade book on business ethics. He chaired the American Marketing Association (AMA) ethics committee that developed its current code of ethics. He is past president of the Academic Council for the AMA. Currently he is Vice President of Publications for the Academy of Marketing Science and is a Distinguished Fellow with AMS and is the AMS, Cutco-Vector Distinguished Marketing Educator.

Dr. Ferrell's major focus is teaching and developing teaching resources for students and faculty to better understand the increasing complex global business environment. He has taught the introduction to business course using this textbook. This gives him the opportunity to develop, improve, and test the book and ancillary materials on a firsthand basis. He has traveled extensively to work with students and understands the needs of instructors of introductory business courses. He lives in Albuquerque, New Mexico, and enjoys skiing, golf, and international travel.

## GEOFFREY A. HIRT

Geoffrey A. Hirt of DePaul University previously taught at Texas Christian University and Illinois State University where he was Chairman of the Department of Finance and Law. At DePaul, he was Chairman of the Finance Department from 1987 to 1997 and held the title of Mesirow Financial Fellow. He developed the MBA program in Hong Kong and served as Director of International Initiatives for the College of Business, supervising overseas programs in Hong Kong, Prague, and Bahrain and was awarded the Spirit of St. Vincent DePaul award for his contributions to the university. Dr. Hirt directed the Chartered Financial Analysts (CFA) study program for the Investment Analysts Society of Chicago from 1987 to 2003. He has been a visiting professor at the University of Urbino in Italy, where he still maintains a relationship with the economics department. He received his Ph.D. in Finance from the University of Illinois at Champaign–Urbana, his M.B.A. at Miami University of Ohio, and his B.A. from Ohio Wesleyan University.

Dr. Hirt is currently on the Dean's Advisory Board and Executive Committee of DePaul's School of Music and is on the Board of the James Tyree Foundation. The Tyree Foundation funds innovative education programs in Chicago, and Dr. Hirt also serves on the Grant Committee. Dr. Hirt is past president and a current member of the Midwest Finance Association, a former editor of the *Journal of Financial Education,* and also a member of the Financial Management Association. He belongs to the Pacific Pension Institute, an organization of public pension funds, private equity firms, and international organizations such as the Asian Development Bank, the IMF, and the European Bank for Reconstruction and Development.

Dr. Hirt is widely known for his textbook *Foundations of Financial Management* published by McGraw-Hill/Irwin. This book in its fifteenth edition has been used in more than 31 countries and translated into more than 14 different languages. Additionally, Dr. Hirt is well known for his textbook, *Fundamentals of Investment Management,* also published by McGraw-Hill/Irwin and now in its tenth edition. Dr. Hirt enjoys golf, swimming, music, and traveling with his wife, who is a pianist and opera coach.

## LINDA FERRELL

Dr. Linda Ferrell is Professor of Marketing and Bill Daniels Professor of Business Ethics in the Anderson School of Management at the University of New Mexico. She completed her Ph.D. in Business Administration, with a concentration in management, at the University of Memphis. She has taught at the University of Tampa, Colorado State University, University of Northern Colorado, University of Memphis, and the University of Wyoming. She also team teaches a class at Thammasat University in Bangkok, Thailand, as well as an online Business Ethics Certificate course through the University of New Mexico.

Her work experience as an account executive for McDonald's and Pizza Hut's advertising agencies supports her teaching of advertising, marketing management, marketing ethics, and marketing principles. She has published in the *Journal of Public Policy & Marketing, Journal of Business Research, Journal of the Academy of Marketing Science, Journal of Business Ethics, AMS Review, Journal of Academic Ethics, Journal of Marketing Education, Marketing Education Review, Journal of Teaching Business Ethics,* and *Case Research Journal,* and is co-author of *Business Ethics: Ethical Decision Making and Cases* (10th edition) and *Business and Society* (5th edition). She co-leads the Daniels Fund business ethics initiative at the University of New Mexico.

Dr. Ferrell is the President of the Academy of Marketing Science and a past president for the Marketing Management Association. She is a member of the college advisory board for Cutco Vector. She is on the NASBA Center for the Public Trust Board of Directors, University of Central Florida-Nicholson School of Communication Board of Visitors, University of Tampa-Sykes College of Business, Board of Fellows, and the Direct Selling Education Foundation Board and Executive Committee. She frequently speaks to organizations on "Teaching Business Ethics," including the Direct Selling Education Foundation's training programs, Ethics & Compliance Officer Association, NASBA Center for the Public Trust Ethical Leadership Conference, as well as others. She has served as an expert witness in cases related to advertising, business ethics, and consumer protection.

# Welcome

The tenth edition provides a complete and integrated overview of the world of business. It is important for students to understand how the functional areas of business have to be coordinated as changes in the economy, technology, global competition, and consumer decision making continue to evolve. All of these changes are presented in concepts that entry-level students can understand. Our book contains all of the essentials that most students should learn in a semester. *Business: A Changing World* has, since its inception, been a concise presentation of the essential material needed to teach introduction to business. From our experience in teaching the course, we know that the most effective way to engage a student is by making business exciting, relevant, and up to date. Our teachable, from-the-ground-up approach involves a variety of media, application exercises, and subject matter, including up-to-date content supplements, boxed examples, video cases, PowerPoints, and testing materials that work for entry-level business students. We have worked hard to make sure that the content of this edition is as up to date as possible in order to best reflect today's dynamic world of business.

## The Tenth Edition

The tenth edition represents a complete revision. This is because so many recent events and changes in the environment relate to the foundational concepts in business. This means that an Introduction to Business textbook has to provide adequate coverage of dynamic changes in the economy as they relate to business decisions. We have listened to your feedback and incorporated needed changes in content, boxes, cases, exercises, and other features.

This is our third edition with a chapter on digital marketing and social networking in business. Since launching this chapter in the eighth edition, this dynamic area continues to change the face of business. Entrepreneurs and small businesses have to be able to increase sales and reduce costs by using social networking to communicate and develop relationships with customers. Because this area is a moving target, we have made substantial changes to the tenth edition of Chapter 13, Digital Marketing and Social Networking. Digital marketing has helped many entrepreneurs launch successful businesses.

While the title of our book remains *Business: A Changing World,* we could have changed the title to *Business: In a Green World.* Throughout the book, we recognize the importance of sustainability and "green" business. By using the philosophy *reduce, reuse, and recycle,* we believe every business can be more profitable and contribute to a better world through green initiatives. There is a new "Going Green" box in each chapter that covers these environmental changes. Our "Entrepreneurship in Action" boxes also discuss many innovations and opportunities to use sustainability for business success.

We have been careful to continue our coverage of global business, ethics and social responsibility, and information technology as it relates to the foundations important in an introduction to business course. Our co-author team has a diversity of expertise in these important areas. O.C. Ferrell and Linda Ferrell have been recognized as leaders in business ethics education, and their insights are reflected in every chapter and in the "Consider Ethics and Social Responsibility" boxes. In addition, they maintain a website, http://danielsethics.mgt.unm.edu/, that provides free resources such as PowerPoints and cases that can be used in the classroom. Geoff Hirt has a strong background in global business development, especially world financial markets and trade relationships.

The foundational areas of introduction to business, entrepreneurship, small business management, marketing, accounting, and finance have been completely revised. Examples have been provided to which students can easily relate. An understanding of core functional areas of business is presented so students get a holistic view of the world of business. Box examples related to "Responding to Business Challenges," "Entrepreneurship in Action," "Going Green," and "Consider Ethics and Social Responsibility" help provide real-world examples in these areas.

Our goal is to make sure that the content and teaching package for this book are of the highest quality possible. We wish to seize this opportunity to gain your trust, and we appreciate any feedback to help us continually improve these materials. We hope that the real beneficiary of all of our work will be well-informed students who appreciate the role of business in society and take advantage of the opportunity to play a significant role in improving our world. As students understand how our free enterprise system operates and how we fit into the global competitive environment, they will develop the foundation for creating their own success and improving our quality of life.

**O.C. Ferrell**
**Geoffrey A. Hirt**
**Linda Ferrell**

# Built from the Ground Up to Be Exciting, Applicable, and Happening!

The best-selling integrated text and digital resource package on the market, *Business: A Changing World* was built from the ground up—that is, developed and written expressly for faculty and students who value a brief, flexible, and affordable resource that is exciting, applicable, and happening!

What sets this fastest growing learning program apart from the competition? An unrivaled mixture of exciting content and resources, application-focused text and activities, and fresh topics and examples that show students what is happening in the world of business today!

## Built from the Ground Up

It's easy for students taking their first steps into business to become overwhelmed. Longer books try to solve this problem by chopping out examples or topics to make ad hoc shorter editions. *Business: A Changing World* carefully builds just the right mix of coverage and applications to give your students a firm grounding in business principles. Where other books have you sprinting through the semester to get everything in, Ferrell/Hirt/Ferrell allows you the breathing space to explore topics and incorporate other activities that are important to you and your students. The exceptional resources and the *Active Classroom Resource Manual* support you in this effort every step of the way.

## Exciting

It's exciting to see students succeed! It's exciting to see more As and Bs in a course without grade inflation. Ferrell/Hirt/Ferrell makes these results possible for your course with its integrated learning package that is proven effective, tailored to each individual student, and easy to use.

## Applicable

When students see how content applies to them, their life, their career, and the world around them, they are more engaged in the course. *Business: A Changing World* helps students maximize their learning efforts by setting clear objectives; delivering interesting cases and examples; focusing on core issues; and providing engaging activities to apply concepts, build skills, and solve problems.

## Happening!

Because it isn't tied to the revision cycle of a larger book, *Business: A Changing World* inherits no outdated or irrelevant examples or coverage. Everything in the tenth edition reflects the very latest developments in the business world—from the recent recession, high unemployment rates, and the financial instability in Europe, to the growth of digital marketing and social networking. In addition, ethics continues to be a key issue, and Ferrell/Hirt/Ferrell use "Consider Ethics and Social Responsibility" boxes to instill in students the importance of ethical conduct in business. To ensure you always know what's happening, join the author-led Facebook group page supporting this text.

Across the country, instructors and students continue to raise an important question: How can Introduction to Business courses further support students throughout the learning process to shape future business leaders? While there is no one solution, we see the impact of new learning technologies and innovative study tools that not only fully engage students in course material but also inform instructors of the students' skills and comprehension levels.

Interactive learning tools, including those offered through McGraw-Hill *Connect*, are being implemented to increase teaching effectiveness and learning efficiency in thousands of colleges and universities. By facilitating a stronger connection with the course and incorporating the latest technologies—such as McGraw-Hill LearnSmart, an adaptive learning program—these tools enable students to succeed in their college careers, which will ultimately increase the percentage of students completing their postsecondary degrees and create the business leaders of the future.

## McGraw-Hill Connect

*Connect* is an all-digital teaching and learning environment designed from the ground up to work with the way instructors and students think, teach, and learn. As a digital teaching, assignment, and assessment platform, *Connect* strengthens the link among faculty, students, and coursework, helping everyone accomplish more in less time.

## LearnSmart

### The smartest way to get from B to A

LearnSmart is the most widely used and intelligent adaptive learning resource. It is proven to strengthen memory recall, improve course retention, and boost grades by distinguishing between what students know and what they don't know and honing in on the concepts that they are most likely to forget. LearnSmart continuously adapts to each student's needs by building an individual learning path. As a result, students study smarter and retain more knowledge.

## SmartBook

### A revolution in reading

Fueled by LearnSmart, SmartBook is the first and only adaptive reading experience available today. SmartBook personalizes content for each student in a continuously adapting reading experience. Reading is no longer a passive and linear experience, but an engaging and dynamic one where students are more likely to master and retain important concepts, coming to class better prepared.

## LearnSmart Achieve

### Excel in your class

Accelerate student success with Learn-Smart Achieve™—the first and only

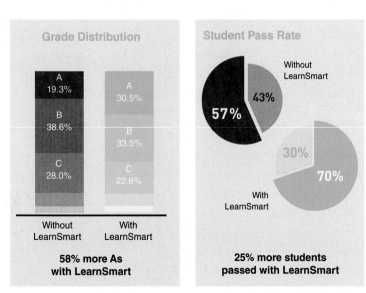

**Grade Distribution**

A 19.3%
B 38.6%
C 28.0%

A 30.5%
B 33.5%
C 22.6%

Without LearnSmart

With LearnSmart

**58% more As with LearnSmart**

**Student Pass Rate**

Without LearnSmart
43%
57%

30%
70%

With LearnSmart

**25% more students passed with LearnSmart**

adaptive study experience that pinpoints individual student knowledge gaps and provides targeted, interactive help at the moment of need.

## Interactive Applications

### A higher level of learning

These *exercises* require students to APPLY what they have learned in a real-world scenario. These online exercises will help students assess their understanding of the concepts.

## Videocases

### Real-world assignments

Industry-leading video support helps students understand concepts and see how real companies and professionals implement business principles in the workplace. The videocases highlight companies from a broad range of industries, sizes, and geographic locations, giving students a perspective from a variety of businesses.

### *iSee it!* Animated Video Explanations

What's the difference between *leadership* and *management?* What are line vs. staff employees? Topics such as these are often confused by students learning the language of business for the first time. What if you were able to convey important concepts in a fun, animated, and memorable way that explains the topic in a way students will quickly understand and remember? What if students could quickly access the clip while they are reading their *Connect* eBook. Instructors can access these clips in their Instructor Resource Library. They can also be assigned as Interactive Videocases.

### End-of-Chapter *"See for Yourself Videocase"* Clips

Videocases at the end of every chapter are supported by a stimulating mix of clips providing topical reinforcement and real-world insight to help students master the most challenging business topics—segments such as "Redbox Succeeds by Identifying Market Need" or "Groupon Masters Promotion to Become a Popular Daily Deal Site" or "Should Employees Use Social Media Sites at Work?" The videos can be found in the *Connect* eBook. Instructors can access these clips in their Instructor Resource Library.

### Manager's Hotseat

Short videocases show real managers applying their years of experience in confronting certain management and organizational behavior issues. Students assume the role of the manager as they watch the video and answer multiple choice questions that pop up during the segment, forcing them to make decisions on the spot. Students learn from the managers' unscripted mistakes and successes, and then do a report critiquing the managers' approach by defending their reasoning. Instructors can access these clips in their Instructor Resource Library. They can also be assigned as Interactive Videocases.

## Media Rich eBook

*Connect* provides students with a cost-saving alternative to the traditional textbook. A seamless integration of a media rich eBook features the following:
- A web-optimized eBook, allowing for anytime, anywhere online access to the textbook.
- Our iSeeit! animated video explanations of the most often confused topics.
- Powerful search function to pinpoint and connect key concepts in a snap.
- Highlighting and note-taking capabilities as well as access to shared instructors' notations.

# Applicable

## Chapter Objectives

These appear at the beginning of each chapter to provide goals for students to reach in their reading. The objectives are then used in the "Review Your Understanding," the summary at the end of each chapter, and help the students gauge whether they've learned and retained the material.

## Chapter Outlines

These provide a useful overview of all the topics covered in the chapter, giving students a sneak preview of what they'll be learning.

## Chapter-Opening Vignette

These anecdotes neatly illustrate the real-world implications of the business issues students will encounter in their reading. At the end of the chapter, students are asked to "Revisit the World of Business" and apply what they've learned throughout the chapter.

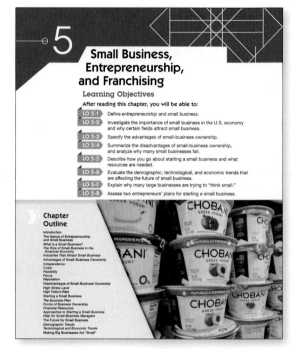

From page 144 of this text

## "So You Want a Job in . . ."

These end-of-chapter features offer valuable advice on a wide spectrum of business career choices.

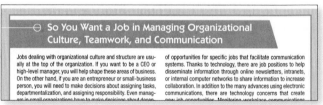

From page 225 of this text

## Spotlights on Business Issues

*Consider Ethics and Social Responsibility, Going Green, Responding to Business Challenges,* and *Entrepreneurship in Action* boxed features are placed liberally throughout the book to highlight important business issues in companies with which students are familiar.

# Application Exercises at the End of Every Chapter

Whether your students discover it on their own or you make it an integral part of your classroom and homework assignments, the end-of-chapter material provides a great opportunity to reinforce and expand upon the chapter content.

**Review Your Understanding** Are your students sometimes unsure whether they've properly absorbed the chapter material? This feature resummarizes the chapter objectives, leaving students in no doubt of what they're expected to remember.

**Revisit the World of Business** These exercises refer to the chapter opening vignettes and ask students to answer more in-depth questions using the knowledge they gained in their reading.

**Build Your Skills** These activities are designed to be carried out in teams, giving you a launching pad for a lively in-class discussion.

**Solve the Dilemma** These boxes give students an opportunity to think creatively in solving a realistic business situation.

**Build Your Business Plan** Written by Therese Maskulka of Walsh University, and used in her own classroom, the end-of-chapter feature "Build Your Business Plan" and Appendix A, "Guidelines for the Development of the Business Plan" help students through the steps of the business plan relating to each chapter. Additional information and resources can be found in the Instructor's Manual.

**See for Yourself Videocase** Stimulate your students with these engaging case videos.

**Team Exercise** Encourage your students to develop their teamwork and critical thinking skills while addressing real-world global business challenges.

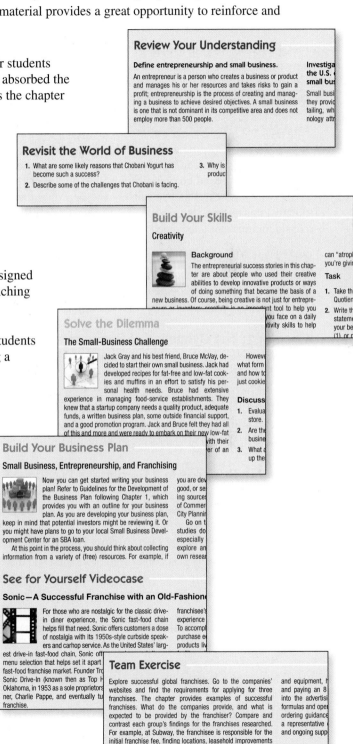

# Happening

**Facebook** Stay up to date! A lot changes in the business world, and on a daily basis, which is why the authors have created a Facebook page to stay connected with their readers from around the world and update them with relevant current events, study tips for students, and more. To join the community, please visit **www.bit.ly/FerrellFacebook.**

## Unique Chapter on Digital Marketing and Social Networking—

**Chapter 13** Digital media and digital marketing are recognized for their increasing value in strategic planning while adding new methods to the traditional marketing mix. Marketers' new ability to convert all types of communications into digital media has created efficient, inexpensive ways of connecting businesses and consumers and improves the flow and the usefulness of information. Additionally, this chapter describes how businesses use different types of social media and legal and ethical considerations marketers need to make.

**New to This Edition** As always, when revising this material for the current edition, all examples, figures, and statistics have been updated to incorporate the most recently published data and discuss any recent developments that affect the world of business. Additionally, content was updated to ensure the most pertinent topical coverage is provided. Here are the highlights for each chapter:

### Chapter 1: The Dynamics of Business and Economics
- New boxed features describing real-world business issues
- New examples of entrepreneurs

### Chapter 2: Business Ethics and Social Responsibility
- New examples of ethical issues facing today's businesses
- New "Consider Ethics and Social Responsibility" box in the appendix

### Chapter 3: Business in a Borderless World
- New examples of large multinational companies
- New content on opportunities for foreign investment in Mexico's oil industry

### Chapter 4: Options for Organizing Business
- New examples of companies with more than half their revenue generated outside the United States
- New boxed features describing current global issues

### Chapter 5: Small Business, Entrepreneurship, and Franchising
- New coverage of social entrepreneurship
- New examples of entrepreneurs
- New boxed features describing current business issues

### Chapter 6: The Nature of Management
- Expanded leadership section
- New *See for Yourself Videocase*—Ford Fusion

## Chapter 7: Organization, Teamwork, and Communication

- New content on Pepsi's global organizational structure
- New *See for Yourself Videocase*—Zappos

## Chapter 8: Managing Service and Manufacturing Operations

- New boxed features describing current business operational issues
- New *See for Yourself Videocase*—Home Run Inn

## Chapter 9: Motivating the Workforce

- New trend in businesses requiring their telecommuting workers to come back into the office
- New examples of companies with excellent motivational strategies

## Chapter 10: Managing Human Resources

- New updates on employee wages
- New graphic demonstrating perspectives regarding performance reviews

## Chapter 11: Customer-Driven Marketing

- New content on McDonald's emphasis on Millennials
- New boxed features describing customer-oriented marketing issues

## Chapter 12: Dimensions of Marketing Strategy

- Expanded content on reference pricing
- New examples of products in the life cycle

## Chapter 13: Digital Marketing and Social Networking

- Significant restructuring and rearrangement of material
- New information on Pinterest and Instagram
- New examples of Facebook tools
- New information on digital payment systems

## Chapter 14: Accounting and Financial Statements

- New information on the financial information and ratios of Microsoft
- Significant updates to industry analysis section
- More information on negative cash flow
- New information on types of Google stock

## Chapter 15: Money and the Financial System

- Additional information on deflation
- New section on shadow banking
- New boxed feature on Bitcoin

## Chapter 16: Financial Management and Securities Markets

- Description of beta as a financial term
- New content on electronic markets

## Appendix D: Personal Financial Planning

- New information on student debt
- New advice about how to borrow for educational purposes

# Exciting, Applicable, Happening: With the Best Instructor Support on the Market

**connect** |BUSINESS  McGraw-Hill strengthens the link between faculty, students, and coursework, helping everyone accomplish more in less time.

## Efficient Administrative Capabilities

*Connect* offers you, the instructor, auto-gradable material in an effort to facilitate teaching and learning.

| Reviewing Homework | Giving Tests or Quizzes | Grading |
|---|---|---|
|   |   |  |
| 60 minutes → 15 minutes | 60 minutes → 0 minutes | 60 minutes → 12 minutes |
| without Connect    with Connect | without Connect    with Connect | without Connect    with Connect |

## Student Progress Tracking

*Connect* keeps instructors informed about how each student, section, and class is performing, allowing for more productive use of lecture and office hours. The progress tracking function enables instructors to:

- View scored work immediately and track individual or group performance with assignment and grade reports.
- Access an instant view of student or class performance relative to learning objectives.
- Collect data and generate reports required by many accreditation organizations, such as AACSB.

**connect** INSIGHT

### Actionable Data

Connect Insight is a powerful data analytics tool that allows instructors to leverage aggregated information about their courses and students to provide a more personalized teaching and learning experience.

> *Connect* and LearnSmart allow students to present course material to students in more ways than just the explanations they hear from me directly. Because of this, students are processing the material in new ways, requiring them to think. I now have more students asking questions in class because the more we think, the more we question.
>
> *Instructor at Hinds Community College*

## Connect Instructor Library

*Connect*'s instructor library serves as a one-stop, secure site for essential course materials, allowing you to save prep time before class. The instructor resources found in the library include:

- **Instructor's Manual** The Instructor's Manual to accompany this text is an all-inclusive resource designed to support instructors in effectively teaching the Introduction to Business course. It includes learning objectives, lecture outlines, PowerPoint notes, supplemental lecture, answers to discussion questions and end-of-chapter exercises, notes for video cases, term paper and project topics, suggestions for guest speakers, and roles and options for implementing role-playing exercises.
- **Test Bank and EZ Test Online** The Test Bank offers more than 2,000 questions, which are categorized by topic, level of learning (knowledge, comprehension, or application), Learning Objectives, Bloom's Taxonomy, and accreditation standards (AACSB).
- **PowerPoint Presentations** The PowerPoint presentations feature slides that can be used and personalized by instructors to help present concepts to the students effectively. Each set of slides contains additional figures and tables from the text.
- **Videos** McGraw-Hill provides industry-leading video support to help students understand concepts and see how they apply in the real world.
- **A Guide for Introducing and Teaching Ethics in Introduction to Business** Written by O.C. Ferrell and Linda Ferrell, this is your one-stop guide for integrating this important issue into all aspects of your course. It helps you to demonstrate how business ethics leads to business success and offers a wide range of business ethics resources, including university centers, government resources, and corporate ethics programs.
- **Active Classroom Resource Guide** An additional collection of team projects, cases, and exercises that instructors can choose from to be used in class or out.

## Instructor's Resource CD (IRCD) ISBN 1259305635

This CD contains the Instructor's Manual, a Test Bank, and PowerPoint presentations.

## Create

Instructors can now tailor their teaching resources to match the way they teach! With McGraw-Hill Create, **www.mcgrawhillcreate.com,** instructors can easily rearrange chapters, combine material from other content sources, and quickly upload and integrate their own content, like course syllabi or teaching notes. Find the right content in Create by searching through thousands of leading McGraw-Hill textbooks. Arrange the material to fit your teaching style. Order a Create book and receive a complimentary print review copy in three to five business days or a complimentary electronic review copy via e-mail within one hour. Go to **www.mcgrawhillcreate.com** today and register.

## Tegrity Campus

Tegrity makes class time available 24/7 by automatically capturing every lecture in a searchable format for students to review when they study and complete assignments. With a simple one-click start-and-stop process, you capture all computer screens and corresponding audio. Students can replay any part of any class with easy-to-use browser-based viewing on a PC or Mac. Educators know that the more students can see, hear, and experience class resources, the better they learn. In fact, studies prove it. With patented Tegrity "search anything" technology, students instantly recall key class moments for replay online or on iPods and mobile devices. Instructors can help turn all their students' study time into learning moments immediately supported by their lecture. To learn more about Tegrity, watch a two-minute Flash demo at **http://tegritycampus.mhhe.com.**

## Blackboard® Partnership

McGraw-Hill Education and Blackboard have teamed up to simplify your life. Now you and your students can access *Connect* and Create right from within your Blackboard course—all with one single sign-on. The grade books are seamless, so when a student completes an integrated *Connect* assignment, the grade for that assignment automatically (and instantly) feeds your Blackboard grade center. Learn more at **www.domorenow.com.**

## McGraw-Hill Campus™

McGraw-Hill Campus is a new one-stop teaching and learning experience available to users of any learning management system. This institutional service allows faculty and students to enjoy single sign-on (SSO) access to all McGraw-Hill Education materials, including the award-winning McGraw-Hill *Connect* platform, from directly within the institution's website. With McGraw-Hill Campus, faculty receive instant access to teaching materials (e.g., eTextbooks, test banks, PowerPoint slides, animations, learning objects, etc.), allowing them to browse, search, and use any instructor ancillary content in our vast library at no additional cost to instructor or students.

## Course Design and Delivery

In addition, students enjoy SSO access to a variety of free content (e.g., quizzes, flash cards, narrated presentations, etc.) and subscription-based products (e.g., McGraw-Hill *Connect*). With McGraw-Hill Campus enabled, faculty and students will never need to create another account to access McGraw-Hill products and services. Learn more at **www.mhcampus.com.**

## Assurance of Learning Ready

Many educational institutions today focus on the notion of *assurance of learning,* an important element of some accreditation standards. *Business* is designed specifically to support instructors' assurance of learning initiatives with a simple yet powerful solution. Each test bank question for *Business* maps to a specific chapter learning objective listed in the text. Instructors can use our test bank software, EZ Test and EZ Test Online, to easily query for learning objectives that directly relate to the learning outcomes for their course. Instructors can then use the reporting features of EZ Test to aggregate student results in similar fashion, making the collection and presentation of assurance of learning data simple and easy.

## AACSB Tagging

McGraw-Hill Education is a proud corporate member of AACSB International. Understanding the importance and value of AACSB Accreditation, *Business* recognizes the curricula guidelines detailed in the AACSB standards for business accreditation by connecting selected questions in the text and the test bank to the six general knowledge and skill guidelines in the AACSB standards. The statements contained in *Business* are provided only as a guide for the users of this textbook. AACSB leaves content coverage and assessment within the purview of individual schools, the mission of the school, and the faculty. While the *Business* teaching package makes no claim of any specific AACSB qualification or evaluation, we have within *Business* labeled selected questions according to the six general knowledge and skills areas.

## McGraw-Hill Customer Experience Group Contact Information

At McGraw-Hill Education, we understand that getting the most from new technology can be challenging. That's why our services don't stop after you purchase our products. You can e-mail our Product Specialists 24 hours a day to get product training online. Or you can search our knowledge bank of Frequently Asked Questions on our support website. For Customer Support, call **800-331-5094** or visit **www.mhhe.com/support.** One of our Technical Support Analysts will be able to assist you in a timely fashion.

# Acknowledgments

The tenth edition of *Business: A Changing World* would not have been possible without the commitment, dedication, and patience of Jennifer Sawayda, Michelle Urban, and Danielle Jolley. Jennifer Sawayda provided oversight for editing and developing text content, cases, boxes, and the supplements. Michelle Urban assisted with editing, and Danielle Jolley and Michelle Urban assisted in developing some of the boxes in this edition. Brett Nafziger developed the PowerPoints, Test Bank, and Instructor's Manual. Anke Weekes, Senior Brand Manager, provided leadership and creativity in planning and implementing all aspects of the tenth edition. Gabriela Gonzalez, Product Developer, did an outstanding job of coordinating all aspects of the development and production process. Heather Ervolino was the Content Project Manager. Mark Christianson managed the technical aspects of Connect. Others important in this edition include Michael Gedatus (Marketing Manager) and Debra Kubiak (Designer). Michael Hartline developed the Personal Career Plan in Appendix C. Vickie Bajtelsmit developed Appendix D on personal financial planning. Eric Sandberg of Interactive Learning assisted in developing the interactive exercises. Many others have assisted us with their helpful comments, recommendations, and support throughout this and previous editions. We'd like to express our thanks to the reviewers who helped us shape the tenth edition:

**NaRita Gail Anderson**
*University of Central Oklahoma*

**Brenda Anthony**
*Delta College*

**Harvey S. Bronstein**
*Oakland Community College*

**Colin Brooks**
*University of New Orleans*

**Diana Carmel**
*Golden West College*

**Mark Lee Clark**
*Collin College*

**Deshaun H. Davis**
*Northern Virginia Community College*

**Bob Farris**
*Mt. San Antonio College*

**Connie Golden**
*Lakeland Community College*

**Terri Gonzales-Kreisman**
*Phoenix College*

**Carol Gottuso**
*Metropolitan Community College*

**Maurice P. Greene**
*Monroe College*

**Selina Andrea Griswold**
*University of Toledo*

**MaryAnne Holcomb**
*Antelope Valley College*

**Sandra Kana**
*Mid-Michigan Community College*

**Regina Korossy**
*Pepperdine University*

**Chris Mcnamara**
*Fingers Lake Community College*

**Lauren Paisley**
*Genesee Community College*

**Michael Quinn**
*James Madison University*

**Gregory J. Rapp**
*Portland Community College*

**Carol Rowey**
*Surry Community College*

**Greg Simpson**
*Blinn College*

**Lisa Strusowski**
*Tallahassee Community College*

**Bruce Yuille**
*Cornell University—Ithaca*

Linda Anglin, *Mankato State University*

Brenda Anthony, *Tallahassee Community College*

Phyllis Alderdice, *Jefferson Community College*

Vondra Armstrong, *Pulaski Tech College*

John Bajkowski, *American Association of Individual Investors*

Gene Baker, *University of North Florida*

Lia Barone, *Norwalk Community College*

James Bartlett, *University of Illinois*

Ellen Benowitz, *Mercer County Community College*

Stephanie Bibb, *Chicago State University*

Barbara Boyington, *Brookdale County College of Monmouth*

Suzanne Bradford, *Angelina College*

Alka Bramhandkar, *Ithaca College*

Dennis Brode, *Sinclair Community College*

Eric Brooks, *Orange County Community College*

Nicky Buenger, *Texas A&M University*

Anthony Buono, *Bentley College*

Tricia Burns, *Boise State University*

William Chittenden, *Texas Tech University*

Michael Cicero, *Highline Community College*

M. Lou Cisneros, *Austin Community College*

Margaret Clark, *Cincinnati State Tech & Community College*

Debbie Collins, *Anne Arundel Community College—Arnold*

Karen Collins, *Lehigh University*

Katherine Conway, *Borough of Manhattan Community College*

Rex Cutshall, *Vincennes University*

Dana D'Angelo, *Drexel University*

Laurie Dahlin, *Worcester State College*

Peter Dawson, *Collin County Community College—Plano*

John DeNisco, *Buffalo State College*

Tom Diamante, *Adelphi University*

Joyce Domke, *DePaul University*

Michael Drafke, *College of DuPage*

John Eagan, *Erie Community College/City Campus SUNY*

Glenda Eckert, *Oklahoma State University*

Thomas Enerva, *Lakeland Community College*

Robert Ericksen, *Craven Community College*

Donna Everett, *Santa Rosa Junior College*

Joe Farinella, *DePaul University*

Gil Feiertag, *Columbus State Community College*

James Ferrell, *R. G. Taylor, P.C.*

Art Fischer, *Pittsburg State University*

Jackie Flom, *University of Toledo*

Toni Forcino, *Montgomery College—Germantown*

Jennifer Friestad, *Anoka—Ramsey Community College*

Chris Gilbert, *Tacoma Community College/University of Washington*

Ross Gittell, *University of New Hampshire*

Frank Godfrey, *St. Augustine's College*

Kris Gossett, *Ivy Tech Community College of Indiana*

Bob Grau, *Cuyahoga Community College—Western Campus*

Gary Grau, *Northeast State Tech Community College*

Jack K. Gray, *Attorney-at-Law, Houston, Texas*

Catherine Green, *University of Memphis*

Claudia Green, *Pace University*

Phil Greenwood, *University of St. Thomas*

David Gribbin, *East Georgia College*

Peggy Hager, *Winthrop University*

Michael Hartline, *Florida State University*

Neil Herndon, *University of Missouri*

James Hoffman, *Borough of Manhattan Community College*

Joseph Hrebenak, *Community College of Allegheny County—Allegheny Campus*

Stephen Huntley, *Florida Community College*

Rebecca Hurtz, *State Farm Insurance Co.*

Roger Hutt, *Arizona State University—West*

Verne Ingram, *Red Rocks Community College*

Scott Inks, *Ball State University*

Steven Jennings, *Highland Community College*

Carol Jones, *Cuyahoga Community College—Eastern Campus*

Gilbert "Joe" Joseph, *University of Tampa*

Norm Karl, *Johnson County Community College*

Janice Karlan, *LaGuardia Community College*

Eileen Kearney, *Montgomery County Community College*

Craig Kelley, *California State University—Sacramento*

Susan Kendall, *Arapahoe Community College*

Ina Midkiff Kennedy, *Austin Community College*

Arbrie King, *Baton Rouge Community College*

John Knappenberger, *Mesa State College*

Gail Knell, *Cape Cod Community College*

Anthony Koh, *University of Toledo*

Velvet Landingham, *Kent State University—Geauga*

Daniel LeClair, *AACSB*

Frank Lembo, *North Virginia Community College*

Richard Lewis, *East Texas Baptist College*

Corinn Linton, *Valencia Community College*

Corrine Livesay, *Mississippi College*

Thomas Lloyd, *Westmoreland Community College*

Terry Loe, *Kennerow University*

Kent Lutz, *University of Cincinnati*

Scott Lyman, *Winthrop University*

Dorinda Lynn, *Pensacola Junior College*

Isabelle Maignan, *ING*

Larry Martin, *Community College of Southern Nevada—West Charles*

Therese Maskulka, *Youngstown State University*

Kristina Mazurak, *Albertson College of Idaho*

Debbie Thorne McAlister, *Texas State University—San Marcos*

John McDonough, *Menlo College*

Tom McInish, *University of Memphis*

Noel McDeon, *Florida Community College*

Mary Meredith, *University of Louisiana at Lafayette*

Michelle Meyer, *Joliet Junior College*

George Milne, *University of Massachusetts—Amherst*

Daniel Montez, *South Texas College*

Glynna Morse, *Augusta College*

Stephanie Narvell, *Wilmington College—New Castle*

Fred Nerone, *International College of Naples*

Laura Nicholson, *Northern Oklahoma College*

Stef Nicovich, *University of New Hampshire*

Michael Nugent, *SUNY—Stony Brook University New York*

Mark Nygren, *Brigham Young University—Idaho*

Wes Payne, *Southwest Tennessee Community College*

Dyan Pease, *Sacramento City College*

Constantine G. Petrides, *Borough of Manhattan Community College*

John Pharr, *Cedar Valley College*

Shirley Polejewski, *University of St. Thomas*

Daniel Powroznik, *Chesapeake College*

Krista Price, *Heald College*

Larry Prober, *Rider University*

Stephen Pruitt, *University of Missouri—Kansas City*

Kathy Pullins, *Columbus State Community College*

Charles Quinn, *Austin Community College*

Victoria Rabb, *College of the Desert*

Tom Reading, *Ivy Tech State College*

Delores Reha, *Fullerton College*

Susan Roach, *Georgia Southern University*

Dave Robinson, *University of California—Berkely*

Marsha Rule, *Florida Public Utilities Commission*

Carol A. Rustad, *Sylvan Learning*

Martin St. John, *Westmoreland Community College*

Don Sandlin, *East Los Angeles College*

Nick Sarantakes, *Austin Community College*

Andy Saucedo, *Dona Ana Community College—Las Cruces*

Elise "Pookie" Sautter, *New Mexico State University*

Dana Schubert, *Colorado Springs Zoo*

Marianne Sebok, *Community College of Southern Nevada—West Charles*

Jeffery L. Seglin, *Seglin Associates*

Daniel Sherrell, *University of Memphis*

Morgan Shepherd, *University of Colorado Elaine Simmons, Guilford Technical Community College*

Nicholas Siropolis, *Cuyahoga Community College*

Robyn Smith, *Pouder Valley Hospital*

Kurt Stanberry, *University of Houston Downtown*

Cheryl Stansfield, *North Hennepin Community College*

Ron Stolle, *Kent State University—Kent*

Jeff Strom, *Virginia Western Community College*

Scott Taylor, *Moberly Area Community College*

Wayne Taylor, *Trinity Valley Community College*

Ray Tewell, *American River College*

Evelyn Thrasher, *University of Mass—Dartmouth*

Steve Tilley, *Gainesville College*

Jay Todes, *Northlake College*

Amy Thomas, *Roger Williams University*

Kristin Trask, *Butler Community College*

Ted Valvoda, *Lakeland Community College*

Sue Vondram, *Loyola University*

Elizabeth Wark, *Springfield College*

Emma Watson, *Arizona State University—West*

Jerry E. Wheat, *Indiana University Southeast*

Frederik Williams, *North Texas State University*

Richard Williams, *Santa Clara University*

Pat Wright, *Texas A&M University*

Timothy Wright, *Lakeland Community College*

Lawrence Yax, *Pensacola Junior College—Warrington*

# Brief Contents

# Contents

## Part 2

## Starting and Growing a Business 113

....................................................

## CHAPTER 7

### Organization, Teamwork, and Communication   202

## CHAPTER 8

### Managing Service and Manufacturing Operations   230

## Part 4

## Creating the Human Resource Advantage   261

## CHAPTER 9

### Motivating the Workforce   262

## CHAPTER 10

### Managing Human Resources  286

## Part 5

## Marketing: Developing Relationships  327

## CHAPTER 11

### Customer-Driven Marketing  328

PART 1

# Business in a Changing World

# 1

# The Dynamics of Business and Economics

## Learning Objectives

### After reading this chapter, you will be able to:

**LO 1-1** Define basic concepts such as business, product, and profit.

**LO 1-2** Identify the main participants and activities of business and explain why studying business is important.

**LO 1-3** Define economics and compare the four types of economic systems.

**LO 1-4** Describe the role of supply, demand, and competition in a free-enterprise system.

**LO 1-5** Specify why and how the health of the economy is measured.

**LO 1-6** Trace the evolution of the American economy and discuss the role of the entrepreneur in the economy.

**LO 1-7** Evaluate a small-business owner's situation and propose a course of action.

## Chapter Outline

## Competition Is Good for Business

Mattel vs. Hasbro, Microsoft vs. Apple, Walmart vs. Target—the battles between these competitors are well known. Competition can be a strong motivator for business success. In a capitalist society, competition leads businesses to innovate and take risks. It is not uncommon for two or three key players to dominate an industry. These players often battle one another to provide the best product or experience for a customer, making it harder for new entrants to come in. It is essential that a business carefully monitor the progress of its primary competitor to maintain market share. However, sometimes the rivalry between businesses is so strong that their entire focus is on destroying the competition. When this occurs, businesses can fail to consider the threat of newer entrants and even face legal consequences because of anticompetitive actions.

Perhaps one of the largest business rivalries is between Coca-Cola and Pepsi. Seven years after Coca-Cola was launched, Pepsi was released. The two companies quickly became rivals, battling for shelf space and their quest to become the beverage of choice for consumers. For years, these two players dominated the industry. However, as soda sales began to flatten, competitors emerged to take advantage of new trends. Red Bull, for instance, tapped into the energy drink market.

Unlike Coca-Cola and Pepsi, Red Bull is not known for its good taste. Perhaps for this reason, its threat to the two beverage makers appeared minimal. Yet with its focus and branding on extreme sports, Red Bull surpassed Pepsi in brand value. The drink is now the third most valuable brand in the industry, after Coca-Cola and Diet Coke. While rivalry is a strong motivator, businesses must not get distracted from the possibility of newer competitors.[1]

# Introduction

We begin our study of business in this chapter by examining the fundamentals of business and economics. First, we introduce the nature of business, including its goals, activities, and participants. Next, we describe the basics of economics and apply them to the United States economy. Finally, we establish a framework for studying business in this text.

## LO 1-1

# The Nature of Business

**business**
individuals or organizations who try to earn a profit by providing products that satisfy people's needs

**product**
a good or service with tangible and intangible characteristics that provide satisfaction and benefits

A **business** tries to earn a profit by providing products that satisfy people's needs. The outcomes of its efforts are **products** that have both tangible and intangible characteristics that provide satisfaction and benefits. When you purchase a product, you are buying the benefits and satisfaction you think the product will provide. A Subway sandwich, for example, may be purchased to satisfy hunger, while a Honda Accord may be purchased to satisfy the need for transportation and the desire to present a certain image.

Most people associate the word *product* with tangible goods—an automobile, computer, phone, coat, or some other tangible item. However, a product can also be a service, which occurs when people or machines provide or process something of value to customers. Dry cleaning, a checkup by a doctor, a performance by a basketball player—these are examples of services. Some services, such as Flickr, an online photo management and sharing application, do not charge a fee for use but obtain revenue from ads on their sites. A product can also be an idea. Accountants and attorneys, for example, generate ideas for solving problems.

## The Goal of Business

**profit**
the difference between what it costs to make and sell a product and what a customer pays for it

**nonprofit organizations**
organizations that may provide goods or services but do not have the fundamental purpose of earning profits

The primary goal of all businesses is to earn a **profit,** the difference between what it costs to make and sell a product and what a customer pays for it. If a company spends $8.00 to manufacture, finance, promote, and distribute a product that it sells for $10.00, the business earns a profit of $2.00 on each product sold. Businesses have the right to keep and use their profits as they choose—within legal limits—because profit is the reward for the risks they take in providing products. Earning profits contributes to society by providing employment, which in turn provides money that is reinvested in the economy. In addition, profits must be earned in a responsible manner. Not all organizations are businesses, however. **Nonprofit organizations,** such as National Public Radio (NPR), Habitat for Humanity, and other charities and social causes, do not have the fundamental purpose of earning profits, although they may provide goods or services and engage in fund raising.

To earn a profit, a person or organization needs management skills to plan, organize, and control the activities of the business and to find and develop employees so that it can make products consumers will buy. A business also needs marketing expertise to learn what products consumers need and want and to develop, manufacture, price, promote, and distribute those products. Additionally, a business needs financial resources and skills to fund, maintain, and expand its operations. Other challenges for businesspeople include abiding by laws and government regulations; acting in an ethical and socially responsible manner; and adapting to economic, technological, political, and social changes. Even nonprofit organizations engage in management, marketing, and finance activities to help reach their goals.

To achieve and maintain profitability, businesses have found that they must produce quality products, operate efficiently, and be socially responsible and ethical in dealing with customers, employees, investors, government regulators, and the community.

Because these groups have a stake in the success and outcomes of a business, they are sometimes called **stakeholders.** Many businesses, for example, are concerned about how the production and distribution of their products affect the environment. Concerns about landfills becoming high-tech graveyards plague many electronics firms. Sprint became the first wireless company to institute a buyback program that encourages customers to turn in their used mobile devices in exchange for up to $300 in credit. The company cleans and updates the devices and sells them as refurbished phones at a lower cost. This initiative has reached developing markets because these devices are in high demand for an affordable price. Those devices that are unusable are sent to a certified third party for recycling. The Environmental Protection Agency has recognized the program as one of the best.[2] Others are concerned with promoting business careers among African American, Hispanic, and Native American students. The Diversity Pipeline Alliance is a network of national organizations that work toward preparing students and professionals of color for leadership and management in the 21st-century workforce. The Pipeline assists individuals in getting into the appropriate college, pursuing a career in business, or earning an advanced degree in business.[3] Other companies, such as Home Depot, have a long history of supporting natural disaster victims, relief efforts, and recovery.

Consumers are often willing to pay more for products they perceive as environmentally-friendly.

**stakeholders**
groups that have a stake in the success and outcomes of a business

## The People and Activities of Business

Figure 1.1 shows the people and activities involved in business. At the center of the figure are owners, employees, and customers; the outer circle includes the primary business activities—management, marketing, and finance. Owners have to put up resources—money or credit—to start a business. Employees are responsible for the work that goes on within a business. Owners can manage the business themselves or hire employees to accomplish this task. The president, CEO, and chairman of the board of Procter & Gamble, A.G. Lafley, does not own P&G, but is an employee who is responsible for managing all the other employees in a way that earns a profit for investors, who are the real owners. Finally, and most importantly, a business's major role is to satisfy the customers who buy its goods or services. Note also that people and forces beyond an organization's control—such as legal and regulatory forces, the economy, competition, technology, the political environment, and ethical and social concerns—all have an impact on the daily operations of businesses. You will learn more about these participants in business activities throughout this book. Next, we will examine the major activities of business.

**Management.**    Notice that in Figure 1.1 management and employees are in the same segment of the circle. This is because management involves coordinating employees' actions to achieve the firm's goals, organizing people to work efficiently, and motivating them to achieve the business's goals. Yang Yuanqing, CEO of Lenovo, recognizes the importance of management to company success. Under his

**FIGURE 1.1**
**Overview of the**
**Business World**

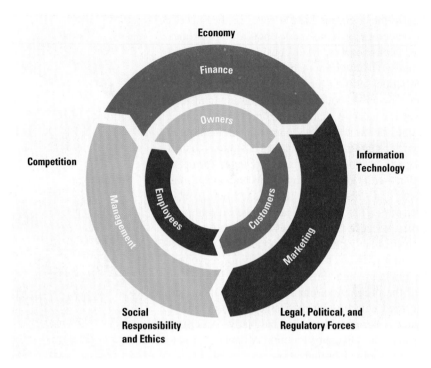

management, Lenovo has become one of the largest PC manufacturing businesses in the world, in addition to having a strong presence in other markets, such as mobile devices and servers. Their success is largely due to unique and efficient operations. All of the manufacturing activities are done in-house, allowing them to quickly adapt to changes in the market and consumer preferences.[4] Management is also concerned with acquiring, developing, and using resources (including people) effectively and efficiently. Amazon enlists workers and suppliers through its Vendor Flex Program to make distribution more efficient.[5]

Production and manufacturing is another element of management. Hershey, for example, invested $300 million in developing infrastructure and building a new manufacturing plant in Pennsylvania, which is equipped with production technology unprecedented in the candy industry. They are also extensively training 700 employees to manage the plant's operations.[6] In essence, managers plan, organize, staff, and control the tasks required to carry out the work of the company or nonprofit organization. We take a closer look at management activities in Parts 3 and 4 of this text.

**Marketing.**  Marketing and consumers are in the same segment of Figure 1.1 because the focus of all marketing activities is satisfying customers. Marketing includes all the activities designed to provide goods and services that satisfy consumers' needs and wants. Marketers gather information and conduct research to determine what customers want. Using information gathered from marketing research, marketers plan and develop products and make decisions about how much to charge for their products and when and where to make them available. They also analyze the marketing environment to see if products need to be modified. In response to First Lady Michelle Obama's campaign against childhood obesity, many companies announced they would begin offering products with reduced sugars, fats, and salts. Coca-Cola

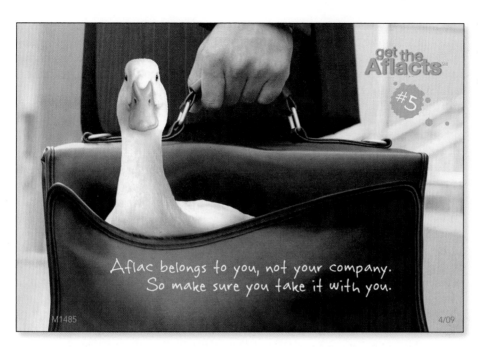

The Aflac duck advertisement uses humor to demonstrate that Aflac focuses on the individual rather than the company.

has launched an anti-obesity campaign with videos encouraging people to be more active and promising to clearly label its products with calorie counts. Such a response could be a smart move on Coca-Cola's part because sodas are often viewed as a main contributor to obesity. Several companies, including ConAgra Foods, Bumble Bee Foods, and General Mills, have all committed to reducing calories in their products. As a result, they have eliminated 6.4 trillion calories from grocery shelves since 2009.[7] Marketers use promotion—advertising, personal selling, sales promotion (coupons, games, sweepstakes, movie tie-ins), and publicity—to communicate the benefits and advantages of their products to consumers and increase sales. Nonprofit organizations also use promotion. For example, the National Fluid Milk Processor Promotion Board's "milk mustache" advertising campaign has featured Brooke Shields, Beyoncé Knowles, Sheryl Crow, Elizabeth Hurley, Serena Williams, and even animated "celebrities" such as Garfield.[8] We will examine marketing activities in Part 5 of this text.

**Finance.**    Owners and finance are in the same part of Figure 1.1 because, although management and marketing have to deal with financial considerations, it is the primary responsibility of the owners to provide financial resources for the operation of the business. Moreover, the owners have the most to lose if the business fails to make a profit. Finance refers to all activities concerned with obtaining money and using it effectively. People who work as accountants, stockbrokers, investment advisors, or bankers are all part of the financial world. Owners sometimes have to borrow money from banks to get started or attract additional investors who become partners or stockholders. Owners of small businesses in particular often rely on bank loans for funding. Part 6 of this text discusses financial management.

## Why Study Business?

Studying business can help you develop skills and acquire knowledge to prepare for your future career, regardless of whether you plan to work for a multinational *Fortune*

500 firm, start your own business, work for a government agency, or manage or volunteer at a nonprofit organization. The field of business offers a variety of interesting and challenging career opportunities throughout the world, such as marketing, human resources management, information technology, finance, production and operations, wholesaling and retailing, and many more.

Studying business can also help you better understand the many business activities that are necessary to provide satisfying goods and services—and that these activities carry a price tag. For example, if you buy a new compact disk, about half of the price goes toward activities related to distribution and the retailer's expenses and profit margins. The production (pressing) of the CD represents about $1, or a small percentage of its price. Most businesses charge a reasonable price for their products to ensure that they cover their production costs, pay their employees, provide their owners with a return on their investment, and perhaps give something back to their local communities. Bill Daniels founded Cablevision, building his first cable TV system in Casper, Wyoming, in 1953, and is now considered "the father of cable television." Prior to Daniels' passing in 2000, he had established a foundation that currently has funding of $1.1 billion and supports a diversity of causes from education to business ethics. During his career, Daniels created the Young Americans Bank, where children could create bank accounts and learn about financial responsibility, and this remains the world's only charter bank for young people. He created the Daniels College of Business through a donation of $20 million to the University of Denver. During his life, he affected many individuals and organizations, and his business success has allowed his legacy to be one of giving and impacting communities throughout the United States.[9] Thus, learning about business can help you become a well-informed consumer and member of society.

Business activities help generate the profits that are essential not only to individual businesses and local economies but also to the health of the global economy. Without profits, businesses find it difficult, if not impossible, to buy more raw materials, hire more employees, attract more capital, and create additional products that in turn make more profits and fuel the world economy. Understanding how our free-enterprise economic system allocates resources and provides incentives for industry and the workplace is important to everyone.

## The Economic Foundations of Business

To continue our introduction to business, it is useful to explore the economic environment in which business is conducted. In this section, we examine economic systems, the free-enterprise system, the concepts of supply and demand, and the role of competition. These concepts play important roles in determining how businesses operate in a particular society.

**Economics** is the study of how resources are distributed for the production of goods and services within a social system. You are already familiar with the types of resources available. Land, forests, minerals, water, and other things that are not made by people are **natural resources. Human resources,** or labor, refer to the physical and mental abilities that people use to produce goods and services. **Financial resources,** or capital, are the funds used to acquire the natural and human resources needed to provide products. Because natural, human, and financial resources are used to produce goods and services, they are sometimes called *factors of production*. The firm can also have intangible resources such as a good reputation for quality products or being socially responsible. The goal is to turn the factors of production and intangible resources into a competitive advantage.

**LO 1-3**

**economics**
the study of how resources are distributed for the production of goods and services within a social system

**natural resources**
land, forests, minerals, water, and other things that are not made by people

**human resources**
the physical and mental abilities that people use to produce goods and services; also called labor

## Economic Systems

An **economic system** describes how a particular society distributes its resources to produce goods and services. A central issue of economics is how to fulfill an unlimited demand for goods and services in a world with a limited supply of resources. Different economic systems attempt to resolve this central issue in numerous ways, as we shall see.

Although economic systems handle the distribution of resources in different ways, all economic systems must address three important issues:

1. What goods and services, and how much of each, will satisfy consumers' needs?
2. How will goods and services be produced, who will produce them, and with what resources will they be produced?
3. How are the goods and services to be distributed to consumers?

The Young Americans Bank in Denver was created by cable magnate Bill Daniels. It is the only chartered bank in the world that makes loans to children.

Communism, socialism, and capitalism, the basic economic systems found in the world today (Table 1.1), have fundamental differences in the way they address these issues. The factors of production in command economies are controlled by government planning. In many cases, the government owns or controls the production of goods and services. Communism and socialism are, therefore, considered command economies.

**Communism.** Karl Marx (1818–1883) first described **communism** as a society in which the people, without regard to class, own all the nation's resources. In his ideal political-economic system, everyone contributes according to ability and receives benefits according to need. In a communist economy, the people (through the government) own and operate all businesses and factors of production. Central government planning determines what goods and services satisfy citizens' needs, how the goods and services are produced, and how they are distributed. However, no true communist economy exists today that satisfies Marx's ideal.

On paper, communism appears to be efficient and equitable, producing less of a gap between rich and poor. In practice, however, communist economies have been marked by low standards of living, critical shortages of consumer goods, high prices, corruption, and little freedom. Russia, Poland, Hungary, and other eastern European nations have turned away from communism and toward economic systems governed by supply and demand rather than by central planning. However, their experiments with alternative economic systems have been fraught with difficulty and hardship. Cuba continues to apply communist principles to its economy, but Cuba is also experiencing economic and political change. Countries such as Venezuela have tried to incorporate communist economic principles. However, communism is declining and its future as an economic system is uncertain. When Fidel Castro stepped down as president of Cuba, his younger brother Raul formally assumed the role and eliminated many of the bans, including allowing the purchase of electric appliances, microwaves, computers, and cell phones. The communist country appears more open to free enterprise now.[10] There is a plan to shift hundreds of thousands of Cuban

**financial resources**
the funds used to acquire the natural and human resources needed to provide products; also called capital

**economic system**
a description of how a particular society distributes its resources to produce goods and services

**communism**
first described by Karl Marx as a society in which the people, without regard to class, own all the nation's resources

**TABLE 1.1**
**Comparison of Communism, Socialism, and Capitalism**

|  | Communism | Socialism | Capitalism |
|---|---|---|---|
| Business ownership | Most businesses are owned and operated by the government. | The government owns and operates major industries; individuals own small businesses. | Individuals own and operate all businesses. |
| Competition | None. The government owns and operates everything. | Restricted in major industries; encouraged in small business. | Encouraged by market forces and government regulations. |
| Profits | Excess income goes to the government. | Profits earned by small businesses may be reinvested in the business; profits from government-owned industries go to the government. | Individuals are free to keep profits and use them as they wish. |
| Product availability and price | Consumers have a limited choice of goods and services; prices are usually high. | Consumers have some choice of goods and services; prices are determined by supply and demand. | Consumers have a wide choice of goods and services; prices are determined by supply and demand. |
| Employment options | Little choice in choosing a career; most people work for government-owned industries or farms. | Some choice of careers; many people work in government jobs. | Unlimited choice of careers. |

Source: "Gross Domestic Product or Expenditure, 1930–2002," InfoPlease (n.d.), www.infoplease.com/ipa/A0104575.html (accessed February 16, 2004).

**■ connect**

▶ Need help understanding Basic Economic Systems? Visit your Connect ebook video tab for a brief animated explanation.

socialism
an economic system in which the government owns and operates basic industries but individuals own most businesses

workers from the public sector to the private sector. Similarly, China has become the first communist country to make strong economic gains by adopting capitalist approaches to business. The Chinese state is the largest shareholder among China's 150 largest companies and influences thousands of other businesses.[11] Economic prosperity has advanced in China with the government claiming to ensure market openness, equality, and fairness.[12]

**Socialism.**    **Socialism** is an economic system in which the government owns and operates basic industries—postal service, telephone, utilities, transportation, health care, banking, and some manufacturing—but individuals own most businesses. For example, in France the postal service industry La Poste is fully owned by the French government and makes a profit. Central planning determines what basic goods and services are produced, how they are produced, and how they are distributed. Individuals and small businesses provide other goods and services based on consumer demand and the availability of resources. Citizens are dependent on the government for many goods and services.

Most socialist nations, such as Sweden, India, and Israel, are democratic and recognize basic individual freedoms. Citizens can vote for political offices, but central government planners usually make decisions about what is best for the nation.

People are free to go into the occupation of their choice, but they often work in government-operated organizations. Socialists believe their system permits a higher standard of living than other economic systems, but the difference often applies to the nation as a whole rather than to its individual citizens. Socialist economies profess egalitarianism— equal distribution of income and social services. They believe their economies are more stable than those of other nations. Although this may be true, taxes and unemployment are generally higher in socialist countries. Perhaps as a result, many socialist countries have also experienced economic difficulties.

The Federal Trade Commission enforces antitrust laws and monitors businesses to ensure fair competition.

**Capitalism.**   **Capitalism,** or **free enterprise,** is an economic system in which individuals own and operate the majority of businesses that provide goods and services. Competition, supply, and demand determine which goods and services are produced, how they are produced, and how they are distributed. The United States, Canada, Japan, and Australia are examples of economic systems based on capitalism.

There are two forms of capitalism: pure capitalism and modified capitalism. In pure capitalism, also called a **free-market system,** all economic decisions are made without government intervention. This economic system was first described by Adam Smith in *The Wealth of Nations* (1776). Smith, often called the father of capitalism, believed that the "invisible hand of competition" best regulates the economy. He argued that competition should determine what goods and services people need. Smith's system is also called *laissez-faire* ("let it be") *capitalism* because the government does not interfere in business.

Modified capitalism differs from pure capitalism in that the government intervenes and regulates business to some extent. One of the ways in which the United States and Canadian governments regulate business is through laws. Laws such as the Federal Trade Commission Act, which created the Federal Trade Commission to enforce antitrust laws, illustrate the importance of the government's role in the economy. In the most recent recession, the government provided loans and took ownership positions in banks such as Citigroup, AIG (an insurance company), and General Motors. These actions were thought necessary to keep these firms from going out of business and creating a financial disaster for the economy.

**capitalism (free enterprise)**
an economic system in which individuals own and operate the majority of businesses that provide goods and services

**free-market system**
pure capitalism, in which all economic decisions are made without government intervention

**Mixed Economies.**   No country practices a pure form of communism, socialism, or capitalism, although most tend to favor one system over the others. Most nations operate as **mixed economies,** which have elements from more than one economic system. In socialist Sweden, most businesses are owned and operated by private individuals. In capitalist United States, an independent federal agency operates the postal service and another independent agency operates the Tennessee Valley Authority, an electric utility. In Great Britain and Mexico, the governments are attempting to sell many state-run businesses to private individuals and companies. In Germany, the Deutsche Post is privatized and trades on the stock market. In once-communist

**mixed economies**
economies made up of elements from more than one economic system

Russia, Hungary, Poland, and other eastern European nations, capitalist ideas have been implemented, including private ownership of businesses.

Countries such as China and Russia have used state capitalism to advance the economy. State capitalism tries to integrate the powers of the state with the advantages of capitalism. It is led by the government but uses capitalistic tools such as listing state-owned companies on the stock market and embracing globalization.[13] State capitalism includes some of the world's largest companies such as Russia's Gazprom, which is the largest natural gas company. China's ability to make huge investments to the point of creating entirely new industries puts many private industries at a disadavantage.[14]

## The Free-Enterprise System

Many economies—including those of the United States, Canada, and Japan—are based on free enterprise, and many communist and socialist countries, such as China and Russia, are applying more principles of free enterprise to their own economic systems. Free enterprise provides an opportunity for a business to succeed or fail on the basis of market demand. In a free-enterprise system, companies that can efficiently manufacture and sell products that consumers desire will probably succeed. Inefficient businesses and those that sell products that do not offer needed benefits will likely fail as consumers take their business to firms that have more competitive products.

A number of basic individual and business rights must exist for free enterprise to work. These rights are the goals of many countries that have recently embraced free enterprise.

1. Individuals must have the right to own property and to pass this property on to their heirs. This right motivates people to work hard and save to buy property.

2. Individuals and businesses must have the right to earn profits and to use the profits as they wish, within the constraints of their society's laws, principles, and values.

3. Individuals and businesses must have the right to make decisions that determine the way the business operates. Although there is government regulation, the philosophy in countries like the United States and Australia is to permit maximum freedom within a set of rules of fairness.

4. Individuals must have the right to choose what career to pursue, where to live, what goods and services to purchase, and more. Businesses must have the right to choose where to locate, what goods and services to produce, what resources to use in the production process, and so on.

Without these rights, businesses cannot function effectively because they are not motivated to succeed. Thus, these rights make possible the open exchange of goods and services. In the countries that favor free enterprise, such as the United States, citizens have the freedom to make many decisions about the employment they choose and create their own productivity systems. Many entrepreneurs are more productive in free-enterprise societies because personal and financial incentives are available that can aid in entrepreneurial success. For many entrepreneurs, their work becomes a part of their system of goals, values, and lifestyle. Consider the panelists ("sharks") on the ABC program *Shark Tank*. Panelists on *Shark Tank* give entrepreneurs a chance to receive funding to realize their dreams by deciding whether to invest in their projects. They include Barbara Corcoran, who built one of New York's largest real estate companies; Mark Cuban, founder of Broadcast.com and MicroSolutions; and Daymond John, founder of clothing company FUBU.[15]

## The Forces of Supply and Demand

In the United States and in other free-enterprise systems, the distribution of resources and products is determined by supply and demand. **Demand** is the number of goods and services that consumers are willing to buy at different prices at a specific time. From your own experience, you probably recognize that consumers are usually will-ing to buy more of an item as its price falls because they want to save money. Consider handmade rugs, for example. Consumers may be willing to buy six rugs at $350 each, four at $500 each, but only two at $650 each. The relationship between the price and the number of rugs consumers are willing to buy can be shown graphically with a *demand curve* (see Figure 1.2).

**Supply** is the number of products that businesses are willing to sell at different prices at a specific time. In general, because the potential for profits is higher, businesses are willing to supply more of a good or service at higher prices. For example, a company that sells rugs may be willing to sell six at $650 each, four at $500 each, but just two at $350 each. The relationship between the price of rugs and the quantity the company is willing to supply can be shown graphically with a *supply curve* (see Figure 1.2).

In Figure 1.2, the supply and demand curves intersect at the point where supply and demand are equal. The price at which the number of products that businesses are willing to supply equals the amount of products that consumers are willing to buy at a specific point in time is the **equilibrium price.** In our rug example, the company is willing to supply four rugs at $500 each, and consumers are willing to buy four rugs at $500 each. Therefore, $500 is the equilibrium price for a rug at that point in time, and most rug companies will price their rugs at $500. As you might imagine, a busi-ness that charges more than $500 (or whatever the current equilibrium price is) for its rugs will not sell many and might not earn a profit. On the other hand, a business that charges less than $500 accepts a lower profit per rug than could be made at the equilibrium price.

If the cost of making rugs goes up, businesses will not offer as many at the old price. Changing the price alters the supply curve, and a new equilibrium price results. This is an ongoing process, with supply and demand constantly changing in response to changes in economic conditions, availability of resources, and degree of competition. For example, the price of oil can change rapidly and has been be-tween $35 and $145 a barrel over the last five years. Prices for goods and ser-vices vary according to these changes in supply and demand. This concept is the force that drives the distribution of re-sources (goods and services, labor, and money) in a free-enterprise economy.

Critics of supply and demand say the system does not distribute re-sources equally. The forces of supply and demand prevent sellers who have to sell at higher prices (because their costs are high) and buyers who cannot afford to buy goods at the equilibrium price from participating in the market. According to critics, the wealthy can

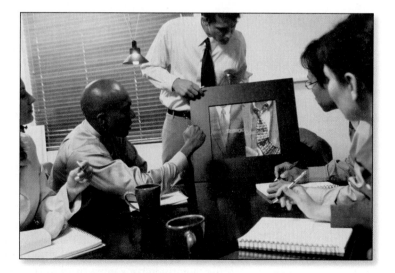

LO 1-4

**demand**
the number of goods and services that consumers are willing to buy at different prices at a specific time

**supply**
the number of products—goods and services—that businesses are willing to sell at different prices at a specific time

**equilibrium price**
the price at which the number of products that businesses are willing to supply equals the amount of products that consumers are willing to buy at a specific point in time

An entrepreneur presents his idea for a new product. Entrepreneurs are more productive in free-enterprise systems.

**FIGURE 1.2**
**Equilibrium Price of**
**Handmade Rugs**

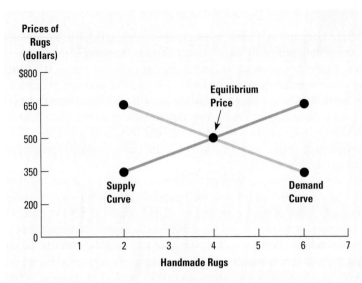

afford to buy more than they need, but the poor may be unable to buy enough of what they need to survive.

## The Nature of Competition

**Competition,** the rivalry among businesses for consumers' dollars, is another vital element in free enterprise. According to Adam Smith, competition fosters efficiency and low prices by forcing producers to offer the best products at the most reasonable price; those who fail to do so are not able to stay in business. Thus, competition should improve the quality of the goods and services available or reduce prices. Consider Marriott International, for example. It went from a small root beer stand in 1927 to its current status of 3,900 high-quality hotels in 72 countries. Marriott believed that if it treated its employees well, they in turn would provide good service to customers. Marriott has garnered a reputation as a high-quality hotel chain. It is now competing to attract younger travelers with reinvented lobbies filled with amenities and convenient ways to check in and out of a hotel, among other changes. It is also significantly expanding in Africa and Asia to capitalize on new market opportunities. The Marriott has been ranked as one of the leading hotel groups across the world. Competition and its drive to succeed have helped the firm achieve its current high status.[16]

Within a free-enterprise system, there are four types of competitive environments: pure competition, monopolistic competition, oligopoly, and monopoly.

**Pure competition** exists when there are many small businesses selling one standardized product, such as agricultural commodities like wheat, corn, and cotton. No one business sells enough of the product to influence the product's price. And, because there is no difference in the products, prices are determined solely by the forces of supply and demand.

**Monopolistic competition** exists when there are fewer businesses than in a pure-competition environment and the differences among the goods they sell is small. Aspirin, soft drinks, and vacuum cleaners are examples of such goods. These products differ slightly in packaging, warranty, name, and other characteristics, but all satisfy the same consumer need. Businesses have some power over the price they charge in

**connect**

Need help understanding Supply and Demand? Visit your Connect ebook video tab for a brief animated explanation.

**competition**
the rivalry among businesses for consumers' dollars

**pure competition**
the market structure that exists when there are many small businesses selling one standardized product

**monopolistic competition**
the market structure that exists when there are fewer businesses than in a pure-competition environment and the differences among the goods they sell are small

## Swatch Works to Restructure Company, Supply Less Parts to Competition

The Swatch Group SA is known for its beautifully elegant watches as well as its high-quality and precisely made internal movements and components. These internal parts have generated many sales for the company. At the same time, it has also generated a number of challenges. For several years, Swatch has been appealing to the Swiss Competition Commission to change regulation under the Swiss Cartel Act. The act mandates that Swatch supply movements and components of watches to other watchmakers. In other words, Swatch must provide supplies to its competitors in the watch industry. Swatch wants to stop supplying components to its rivals. Being the main supplier increases Swatch's expenses while allowing its competition to invest more money in advertising, thus stifling Swatch's sales. Repeatedly, the company's requests have been delayed or declined by the Swiss government because of the large market share that Swatch has in the industry.

Swatch and its subsidiaries provide approximately 70 percent of the movements and 90 percent of components to other domestic and foreign brands. Stopping the supply will have a tremendous effect on the entire industry. While the Swiss government has agreed to minimal reductions in Swatch's supplying of movements, cuts to the supply of components cannot be reduced.[17]

### Discussion Questions

1. Why does Swatch want to stop selling watch components?
2. Why is the Swiss government reluctant to allow Swatch to stop supplying components to its competitors?
3. Based on the large share of the watch movements and components industry that Swatch controls, which competitive environment do you think it operates in: pure competition, monopolistic competition, oligopoly, or monopoly?

---

monopolistic competition because they can make consumers aware of product differences through advertising. Jawbone, for example, differentiates its Jambox portable speakers through product design and quality. Consumers value some features more than others and are often willing to pay higher prices for a product with the features they want. For example, many consumers are willing to pay a higher price for organic fruits and vegetables rather than receive a bargain on nonorganic foods. The same holds true for non-genetically modified foods.

An **oligopoly** exists when there are very few businesses selling a product. In an oligopoly, individual businesses have control over their products' price because each business supplies a large portion of the products sold in the marketplace. Nonetheless, the prices charged by different firms stay fairly close because a price cut or increase by one company will trigger a similar response from another company. In the airline industry, for example, when one airline cuts fares to boost sales, other airlines quickly follow with rate decreases to remain competitive. On the other hand, airlines often raise prices at the same time. Oligopolies exist when it is expensive for new firms to enter the marketplace. Not just anyone can acquire enough financial capital to build an automobile production facility or purchase enough airplanes and related resources to build an airline.

**oligopoly**
the market structure that exists when there are very few businesses selling a product

When there is one business providing a product in a given market, a **monopoly** exists. Utility companies that supply electricity, natural gas, and water are monopolies. The government permits such monopolies because the cost of creating the good or supplying the service is so great that new producers cannot compete for sales. Government-granted monopolies are subject to government-regulated prices. Some monopolies exist because of technological developments that are protected by patent laws. Patent laws grant the developer of new technology a period of time (usually 20 years) during which no other producer can use the same technology without the

**monopoly**
the market structure that exists when there is only one business providing a product in a given market

agreement of the original developer. The United States granted its first patent in 1790. Now its patent office receives hundreds of thousands of patent applications a year, although Asian countries—including Japan, China, and South Korea—are not far behind.[18] This monopoly allows the developer to recover research, development, and production expenses and to earn a reasonable profit. An example of this type of monopoly is the dry-copier process developed by Xerox. Xerox's patents have expired, however, and many imitators have forced market prices to decline.

## Economic Cycles and Productivity

**economic expansion**
the situation that occurs when an economy is growing and people are spending more money; their purchases stimulate the production of goods and services, which in turn stimulates employment

**inflation**
a condition characterized by a continuing rise in prices

**economic contraction**
a slowdown of the economy characterized by a decline in spending and during which businesses cut back on production and lay off workers

**recession**
a decline in production, employment, and income

**unemployment**
the condition in which a percentage of the population wants to work but is unable to find jobs

**Expansion and Contraction.**   Economies are not stagnant; they expand and contract. **Economic expansion** occurs when an economy is growing and people are spending more money. Their purchases stimulate the production of goods and services, which in turn stimulates employment. The standard of living rises because more people are employed and have money to spend. Rapid expansions of the economy, however, may result in **inflation,** a continuing rise in prices. Inflation can be harmful if individuals' incomes do not increase at the same pace as rising prices, reducing their buying power. The worst case of hyperinflation occurred in Hungary in 1946. At one point, prices were doubling every 15.6 hours. One of the most recent cases of hyperinflation occurred in Zimbabwe.[19] Zimbabwe suffered from hyperinflation so severe that its inflation percentage rate rose into the hundreds of millions. With the elimination of the Zimbabwean dollar and certain price controls, the inflation rate began to decrease, but not before the country's economy was virtually decimated.[20]

**Economic contraction** occurs when spending declines. Businesses cut back on production and lay off workers, and the economy as a whole slows down. Contractions of the economy lead to **recession**—a decline in production, employment, and income. Recessions are often characterized by rising levels of **unemployment,** which is measured as the percentage of the population that wants to work but is unable to find jobs. Figure 1.3 shows the overall unemployment rate in the civilian labor force over the past 80 years. Rising unemployment levels tend to stifle demand for

**FIGURE 1.3**    **Annual Average Unemployment Rate, Civilian Labor Force, 16 Years and Over**

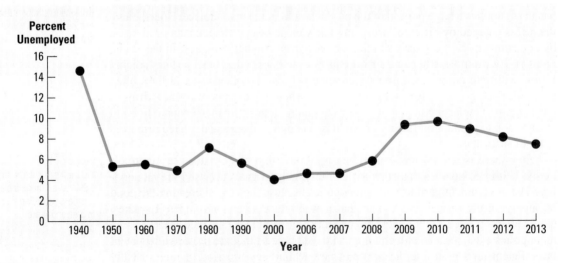

Sources: Bureau of Labor Statistics, "Household Data Annual Averages," ftp://ftp.bls.gov/pub/special.requests/lf/aa2010/pdf/cpsaat1.pdf (accessed February 20, 2014); Bureau of Labor Statistics, "Labor Force Statistics from the Current Population Survey, http://data.bls.gov/timeseries/LNS14000000 (accessed February 20, 2014).

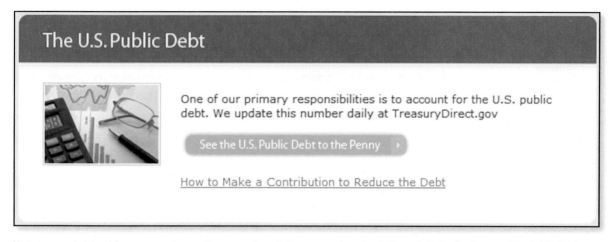

You can see what the U.S. government currently owes—down to the penny—by going to the website for the Bureau of the Public Debt, www.publicdebt.treas.gov/

goods and services, which can have the effect of forcing prices downward, a condition known as *deflation.* The United States has experienced numerous recessions, the most recent ones occurring in 1990–1991, 2002–2003, and 2008–2011. The most recent recession (or economic slowdown) was caused by the collapse in housing prices and consumers' inability to stay current on their mortgage and credit card payments. This caused a crisis in the banking industry, with the government bailing out banks to keep them from failing. This in turn caused a slowdown in spending on consumer goods and an increase in employment. Unemployment reached 10 percent of the labor force. Don't forget that personal consumption makes up almost 70 percent of gross domestic product, so consumer behavior is extremely important for economic activity. A severe recession may turn into a **depression,** in which unemployment is very high, consumer spending is low, and business output is sharply reduced, such as what occurred in the United States in the early 1930s. The most recent recession is often called the Great Recession because it was the longest and most severe economic decline since the Great Depression.

**depression**
a condition of the economy in which unemployment is very high, consumer spending is low, and business output is sharply reduced

Economies expand and contract in response to changes in consumer, business, and government spending. War also can affect an economy, sometimes stimulating it (as in the United States during World Wars I and II) and sometimes stifling it (as during the Vietnam, Persian Gulf, and Iraq wars). Although fluctuations in the economy are inevitable and to a certain extent predictable, their effects—inflation and unemployment—disrupt lives and thus governments try to minimize them.

**Measuring the Economy.**    Countries measure the state of their economies to determine whether they are expanding or contracting and whether corrective action is necessary to minimize the fluctuations. One commonly used measure is **gross domestic product (GDP)**—the sum of all goods and services produced in a country during a year. GDP measures only those goods and services made within a country and therefore does not include profits from companies' overseas operations; it does include profits earned by foreign companies within the country being measured. However, it does not take into account the concept of GDP in relation to population (GDP per capita). Figure 1.4 shows the increase in GDP over several years, while Table 1.2 compares a number of economic statistics for a sampling of countries.

**gross domestic product (GDP)**
the sum of all goods and services produced in a country during a year

## FIGURE 1.4
**Growth in U.S. Gross Domestic Product**

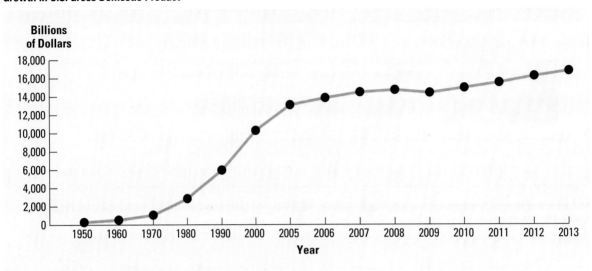

Source: U.S. Department of Commerce Bureau of Economic Analysis, "National Economic Accounts," www.bea.gov/national/index.htm#gdp (accessed February 20, 2014).

## TABLE 1.2
**Economic Indicators of Different Countries**

| Country | GDP (in billions of dollars) | GDP per Capita | Unemployment Rate (%) | Inflation Rate (%) |
|---|---|---|---|---|
| Argentina | 735.1 | 17,900 | 7.20 | 25.3 |
| Australia | 961 | 42,000 | 5.2 | 1.8 |
| Brazil | 2,330 | 11,700 | 5.5 | 5.4 |
| Canada | 1,474 | 42,300 | 7.3 | 1.5 |
| China | 12,260 | 9,100 | 6.5 | 2.6 |
| France | 2,238 | 35,300 | 9.8 | 2.2 |
| Germany | 3,167 | 38,700 | 5.5 | 2.1 |
| India | 4,716 | 3,800 | 8.5 | 9.7 |
| Israel | 260.9 | 33,900 | 6.9 | 1.7 |
| Japan | 4,576 | 35,900 | 4.4 | 0.0 |
| Mexico | 1,798 | 15,400 | 5.0 | 4.1 |
| Russia | 2,486 | 17,500 | 5.50 | 5.1 |
| South Africa | 576.1 | 11,300 | 25.1 | 5.7 |
| United Kingdom | 2,313 | 36,600 | 8.0 | 2.8 |
| United States | 16,803 | 51,700 | 7.4 | 2.1 |

Source: U.S. Department of Commerce Bureau of Economic Analysis, "National Economic Accounts," www.bea.gov/national/index.htm#gdp (accessed February 20, 2014); The CIA, The World Fact Book, www.cia.gov/library/publications/the-world-factbook/rankorder/rankorderguide.html (accessed February 20, 2014).

| Unit of Measure | Description |
|---|---|
| Trade balance | The difference between our exports and our imports. If the balance is negative, as it has been since the mid-1980s, it is called a trade deficit and is generally viewed as unhealthy for our economy. |
| Consumer Price Index | Measures changes in prices of goods and services purchased for consumption by typical urban households. |
| Per capita income | Indicates the income level of "average" Americans. Useful in determining how much "average" consumers spend and how much money Americans are earning. |
| Unemployment rate | Indicates how many working-age Americans are not working who otherwise want to work.* |
| Inflation | Monitors price increases in consumer goods and services over specified periods of time. Used to determine if costs of goods and services are exceeding worker compensation over time. |
| Worker productivity | The amount of goods and services produced for each hour worked. |

**TABLE 1.3**
**How Do We Evaluate Our Nation's Economy?**

*Americans who do not work in a traditional sense, such as househusbands/housewives, are not counted as unemployed.*

Another important indicator of a nation's economic health is the relationship between its spending and income (from taxes). When a nation spends more than it takes in from taxes, it has a **budget deficit.** In the 1990s, the U.S. government eliminated its long-standing budget deficit by balancing the money spent for social, defense, and other programs with the amount of money taken in from taxes.

In recent years, however, the budget deficit has reemerged and grown to record levels, partly due to defense spending in the aftermath of the terrorist attacks of September 11, 2001. Massive government stimulus spending during the most recent recession also increased the national debt. Because many Americans do not want their taxes increased and Congress has difficulty agreeing on appropriate tax rates, it is difficult to increase taxes and reduce the deficit. Like consumers and businesses, when the government needs money, it borrows from the public, banks, and even foreign investors. In 2013, the national debt (the amount of money the nation owes its lenders) exceeded $16 trillion, a new high.[21] This figure is especially worrisome because, to reduce the debt to a manageable level, the government either has to increase its revenues (raise taxes) or reduce spending on social, defense, and legal programs, neither of which is politically popular. The size of the national debt and little agreement on how to reduce the deficit caused the credit rating of the U.S. debt to go down in 2011. The national debt figure changes daily and can be seen at the Department of the Treasury, Bureau of the Public Debt, website. Table 1.3 describes some of the other ways we evaluate our nation's economy.

**budget deficit**
the condition in which a nation spends more than it takes in from taxes

## The American Economy

As we said previously, the United States is a mixed economy with a foundation based on capitalism. The answers to the three basic economic issues are determined primarily by competition and the forces of supply and demand, although the federal government does intervene in economic decisions to a certain extent. To understand the current state of the American economy and its effect on business practices, it is helpful to examine its history and the roles of the entrepreneur and the government.

LO 1-6

## Luxury Automakers Embracing Eco-Friendly Interiors

What type of car uses bamboo, eucalyptus, reclaimed logs, or old fence posts in its interior? The answer is luxury cars. Consumers of luxury cars prefer natural wood interiors rather than plastic or fiberglass. While exotic wood increases the luxury of the vehicle, the most valuable wood comes from old-growth forests and other vulnerable areas. Instead, automakers are turning to wood from reclaimed logs and bamboo. Using these woods allows luxury car makers to differentiate themselves from competitors and appeal to the eco-conscious consumer.

Electric vehicle company Fisker has incorporated three types of reclaimed wood into its Karma sedans, including wood collected from areas damaged by forest fires, wood fallen to the bottom of lakes, and wood that fell during storms. BMW announced that its electric vehicle, the i3 plug-in, will have a eucalyptus interior, a plant that grows back quickly. Ford is using the tropical kenaf plant to replace oil-based materials in its Ford Escape. With more consumers desiring sustainable products, using plant-based materials can increase perceptions of brand value.

There might also be another reason for using plant-based materials in car construction. In addition to being more sustainable, some of these materials are lighter than traditional materials. For instance, Ford states that using kenaf plants to replace oil-based resins inside its doors reduces door bolsters by 25 percent. Lighter cars are more fuel-efficient, which saves consumers money on gasoline.[22]

### Discussion Questions

1. Why might eco-friendly wood interior appeal to luxury car buyers?
2. What impact could using these plant-based materials have on the reputations of luxury automakers?
3. What are some benefits in using plant-based materials besides appealing to the luxury car buyer?

---

## A Brief History of the American Economy

**The Early Economy.** Before the colonization of North America, Native Americans lived as hunter/gatherers and farmers, with some trade among tribes. The colonists who came later operated primarily as an *agricultural economy*. People were self-sufficient and produced everything they needed at home, including food, clothing, and furniture. Abundant natural resources and a moderate climate nourished industries such as farming, fishing, shipping, and fur trading. A few manufactured goods and money for the colonies' burgeoning industries came from England and other countries.

As the nation expanded slowly toward the West, people found natural resources such as coal, copper, and iron ore and used them to produce goods such as horseshoes, farm implements, and kitchen utensils. Farm families who produced surplus goods sold or traded them for things they could not produce themselves, such as fine furniture and window glass. Some families also spent time turning raw materials into clothes and household goods. Because these goods were produced at home, this system was called the domestic system.

**The Industrial Revolution.** The 19th century and the Industrial Revolution brought the development of new technology and factories. The factory brought together all the resources needed to make a product—materials, machines, and workers. Work in factories became specialized as workers focused on one or two tasks. As work became more efficient, productivity increased, making more goods available at lower prices. Railroads brought major changes, allowing farmers to send their surplus crops and goods all over the nation for barter or for sale.

Factories began to spring up along the railways to manufacture farm equipment and a variety of other goods to be shipped by rail. Samuel Slater set up the first

American textile factory after he memorized the plans for an English factory and emigrated to the United States. Eli Whitney revolutionized the cotton industry with his cotton gin. Francis Cabot Lowell's factory organized all the steps in manufacturing cotton cloth for maximum efficiency and productivity. John Deere's farm equipment increased farm production and reduced the number of farmers required to feed the young nation. Farmers began to move to cities to find jobs in factories and a higher standard of living. Henry Ford developed the assembly-line system to produce automobiles. Workers focused on one part of an automobile and then pushed it to the next stage until it rolled off the assembly line as a finished automobile. Ford's assembly line could manufacture many automobiles efficiently, and the price of his cars was $200, making them affordable to many Americans.

**The Manufacturing and Marketing Economies.** Industrialization brought increased prosperity, and the United States gradually became a *manufacturing economy*—one devoted to manufacturing goods and providing services rather than producing agricultural products. The assembly line was applied to more industries, increasing the variety of goods available to the consumer. Businesses became more concerned with the needs of the consumer and entered the *marketing economy*. Expensive goods such as cars and appliances could be purchased on a time-payment plan. Companies conducted research to find out what products consumers needed and wanted. Advertising made consumers aware of products and important information about features, prices, and other competitive advantages.

Because these developments occurred in a free-enterprise system, consumers determined what goods and services were produced. They did this by purchasing the products they liked at prices they were willing to pay. The United States prospered, and American citizens had one of the highest standards of living in the world.

**The Service and New Digital Economy.** After World War II, with the increased standard of living, Americans had more money and more time. They began to pay others to perform services that made their lives easier. Beginning in the 1960s, more and more women entered the workforce. The United States began experiencing major shifts in the population. The U.S. population grew 9.7 percent in the past decade to about 316 million. This is the slowest pace of growth since the Great Depression, with the South leading the population gains. While the birth rate in the United States is declining, new immigrants help with population gains.[23] The profile of the family is also changing: Today there are more single-parent families and individuals living alone, and in two-parent families, both parents often work.

One result of this trend is that time-pressed Americans are increasingly paying others to do tasks they used to do at home, like cooking, laundry, landscaping, and child care. These trends have gradually changed the United States to a *service economy*—one devoted to the production of services that make life easier for busy consumers. Businesses increased their demand for services, especially in the areas of finance and information technology. Service industries such as restaurants, banking, health care, child care, auto repair, leisure-related industries, and even education are growing rapidly and may account for as much as 80 percent of the U.S. economy. These trends continue with advanced technology contributing to new service products based on technology and digital media that provide smart phones, social networking, and virtual worlds. Table 1.4 provides evidence that the new digital economy is changing how we use information and the service industry. More about the digital world, business, and new online social media can be found in Chapter 13.

**DID YOU KNOW?** Approximately 59 percent of adult women are engaged in the workforce.[24]

**TABLE 1.4**
**Cell Phone Activities**

| The % of cell phone owners who use their cell phone to ... | |
| --- | --- |
| 81 | send or receive text messages |
| 60 | access the Internet |
| 52 | send or receive email |
| 50 | download apps |
| 49 | get directions, recommendations, or other location-based information |
| 48 | listen to music |
| 21 | participate in a video call or video chat |
| 8 | "check in" or share your location |

Source: Pew Research Center's Internet & American Life Project Spring Tracking Survey, April 17–May 19, 2013. N = 2,076 cell phone owners. Interviews were conducted in English and Spanish and on landline and cell phones. The margin of error for results based on all cell phone owners is +/− 2.4 percentage points.

## The Role of the Entrepreneur

**entrepreneur**
an individual who risks his or her wealth, time, and effort to develop for profit an innovative product or way of doing something

An **entrepreneur** is an individual who risks his or her wealth, time, and effort to develop for profit an innovative product or way of doing something. Nick Woodman is a true American entrepreneur. At 26, Woodman—who was an avid surfer—identified the need to film events from the athlete's perspective. He developed GoPro Inc., which makes wearable cameras that are easily attachable to surfboards, ski helmets, and other equipment. Consumers who used a GoPro camera inundated YouTube with their own amateur videos, leading to strong word-of-mouth marketing. GoPro became so popular that Woodman and the company's backers want to take the firm public—at a valuation of more than $2.3 billion.[25]

The free-enterprise system provides the conditions necessary for entrepreneurs to succeed. In the past, entrepreneurs were often inventors who brought all the factors of production together to produce a new product. Thomas Edison, whose inventions include the record player and lightbulb, was an early American entrepreneur. Henry Ford was one of the first persons to develop mass assembly methods in the automobile industry. Other entrepreneurs, so-called captains of industry, invested in the country's growth. John D. Rockefeller built Standard Oil out of the fledgling oil industry, and Andrew Carnegie invested in railroads and founded the United States Steel Corporation. Andrew Mellon built the Aluminum Company of America and Gulf Oil. J.P. Morgan started financial institutions to fund the business activities of other entrepreneurs. Although these entrepreneurs were born in another century, their legacy to the American economy lives on in the companies they started, many of which still operate today. Colonel Eli Lilly in Indianapolis, Indiana, was continually frustrated with the quality of pharmaceutical products sold at the time. As a pharmaceutical chemist, he decided to start his own firm that would offer the highest-quality medicines. His firm, Eli Lilly and Company, would go on to make landmark achievements, including being one of the first pharmaceutical firms to mass-produce penicillin. Today, Eli Lilly is the 10th largest pharmaceutical firm in the world.[26]

Entrepreneurs are constantly changing American business practices with new technology and innovative management techniques. Bill Gates, for example, built

## Emeco Makes Indestructible Chairs

Electric Machine and Equipment Company (Emeco)
**Founder:** Wilton Carlyle Dinges
**Founded:** 1944, in Hanover, Pennsylannia
**Success:** Although it started out with the Navy as its only customer, Emeco's chair products are now common in businesses across the world.

Emeco was founded to make chairs for the Navy during World War II. The chairs had to meet certain specifications, such as the ability to withstand water, salt air, and sailors. The result was the virtually indestructible 1006, or the Navy Chair. It was made from aluminum and underwent a proprietary 77-step handmade process still used today.

After the war, however, Emeco faced difficulties. The indestructible nature of the chairs reduced the need for replacement orders. Then Emeco discovered that a designer named Philippe Starck was incorporating the chairs into his redesign of New York's Paramount Hotel. Emeco partnered with Starck to create redesigns that would appeal to more customers. This marked the beginning of a new personality for Emeco.

Over the years, Emeco has increased its clientele. Its chairs are commonly found in restaurants and airports and are even featured in movies. Coca-Cola has approached Emeco to create a version of the 1006 chair made from 111 recycled plastic bottles. Business markets appreciate the chairs' ability to withstand extreme pressure, while others enjoy the beautiful designs suitable for art gallery exhibits. Collaborating with designers has allowed Emeco to continue for more than 70 years.[27]

---

Microsoft, a software company whose products include Word and Windows, into a multibillion-dollar enterprise. Frederick Smith had an idea to deliver packages overnight, and now his FedEx Company plays an important role in getting documents and packages delivered all over the world for businesses and individuals. Steve Jobs co-founded Apple and turned the company into a successful consumer electronics firm that revolutionized many different industries, with products such as the iPod, iPhone, Mac computers, and iPad. The company went from near bankruptcy in the 1990s to become one of the most valuable brands in the entire world. Entrepreneurs have been associated with such uniquely American concepts as Dell Computers, Ben & Jerry's, Levi's, McDonald's, Dr Pepper, Apple, Google, Facebook, and Walmart. Walmart, founded by entrepreneur Sam Walton, was the first retailer to reach $100 billion in sales in one year and now routinely passes that mark, with more than $466 billion in 2013.[28] We will examine the importance of entrepreneurship further in Chapter 5.

## The Role of Government in the American Economy

The American economic system is best described as modified capitalism because the government regulates business to preserve competition and protect consumers and employees. Federal, state, and local governments intervene in the economy with laws and regulations designed to promote competition and to protect consumers, employees, and the environment. Many of these laws are discussed in Appendix B.

Additionally, government agencies such as the U.S. Department of Commerce measure the health of the economy (GDP, productivity, etc.) and, when necessary, take steps to minimize the disruptive effects of

Google Wallet is a mobile payments system that allows users to store their credit card or debit card information. When checking out at stores, users can bring up the app and use the information to pay for their purchases.

Many companies engage in socially responsible behavior to give back to their communities. Home Depot partners with Habitat for Humanity to build homes for disadvantaged families.

economic fluctuations and reduce unemployment. When the economy is contracting and unemployment is rising, the federal government through the Federal Reserve Board (see Chapter 15) tries to spur growth so that consumers will spend more money and businesses will hire more employees. To accomplish this, it may reduce interest rates or increase its own spending for goods and services. When the economy expands so fast that inflation results, the government may intervene to reduce inflation by slowing down economic growth. This can be accomplished by raising interest rates to discourage spending by businesses and consumers. Techniques used to control the economy are discussed in Chapter 15.

## The Role of Ethics and Social Responsibility in Business

In the past few years, you may have read about a number of scandals at a number of well-known corporations, including Enron, Countrywide Financial, BP, and even leading banks such as Bank of America and Citigroup. In many cases, misconduct by individuals within these firms had an adverse effect on current and retired employees, investors, and others associated with these firms. In some cases, individuals went to jail for their actions. Top executives like Enron's Jeffrey Skilling and Tyco's Dennis Kozlowski received long prison sentences for their roles in corporate misconduct. These scandals undermined public confidence in corporate America and sparked a new debate about ethics in business. Business ethics generally refers to the standards and principles used by society to define appropriate and inappropriate conduct in the workplace. In many cases, these standards have been codified as laws prohibiting actions deemed unacceptable.

Society is increasingly demanding that businesspeople behave ethically and socially responsibly toward not only their customers but also employees, investors, government regulators, communities, and the natural environment. No area is more debated as online piracy. Software, music, and film executives want to defend their intellectual property. On the other hand, companies such as Google are concerned that strict laws would stifle innovation and enable censorship.[29] When actions are heavily criticized, a balance is usually required to support and protect various stakeholders.

While one view is that ethics and social responsibility are a good supplement to business activities, there is an alternative viewpoint. Research has shown that ethical behavior can not only enhance a company's reputation but can also drive profits.[30] The ethical and socially responsible conduct of companies such as Whole Foods, Starbucks, and the hotel chain Marriott provides evidence that good ethics is good business. There is growing recognition that the long-term value of conducting business in an ethical and socially responsible manner that considers the interests of all stakeholders creates superior financial performance.[31]

To promote socially responsible and ethical behavior while achieving organizational goals, businesses can monitor changes and trends in society's values. Businesses should determine what society wants and attempt to predict the long-term effects of their decisions. While it requires an effort to address the interests of all stakeholders, businesses can prioritize and attempt to balance conflicting demands. The goal is to develop a solid reputation of trust and avoid misconduct to develop effective workplace ethics.

# Can You Learn Business in a Classroom?

Obviously, the answer is yes, or there would be no purpose for this textbook! To be successful in business, you need knowledge, skills, experience, and good judgment. The topics covered in this chapter and throughout this book provide some of the knowledge you need to understand the world of business. The opening vignette at the beginning of each chapter, boxes, examples within each chapter, and the case at the end of each chapter describe experiences to help you develop good business judgment. The "Build Your Skills" exercise at the end of each chapter and the "Solve the Dilemma" box will help you develop skills that may be useful in your future career. However, good judgment is based on knowledge and experience plus personal insight and understanding. Therefore, you need more courses in business, along with some practical experience in the business world, to help you develop the special insight necessary to put your personal stamp on knowledge as you apply it. The challenge in business is in the area of judgment, and judgment does not develop from memorizing an introductory business textbook. If you are observant in your daily experiences as an employee, as a student, and as a consumer, you will improve your ability to make good business judgments.

Figure 1.5 is an overview of how the chapters in this book are linked together and how the chapters relate to the participants, the activities, and the environmental factors found in the business world. The topics presented in the chapters that follow are those that will give you the best opportunity to begin the process of understanding the world of business.

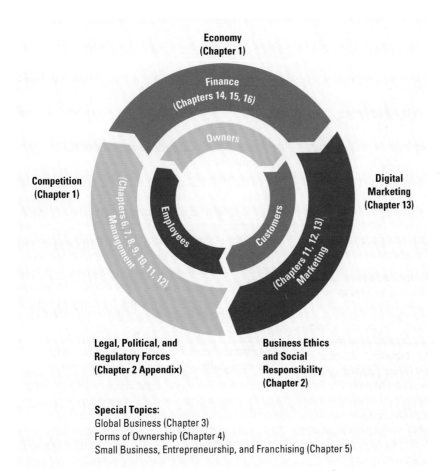

**FIGURE 1.5**
**The Organization of This Book**

**Special Topics:**
Global Business (Chapter 3)
Forms of Ownership (Chapter 4)
Small Business, Entrepreneurship, and Franchising (Chapter 5)

When most people think of a career in business, they see themselves entering the door to large companies and multinationals that they read about in the news and that are discussed in class. In a national survey, students indicated they would like to work for Google, Walt Disney, Apple, and Ernst & Young. In fact, most jobs are not with large corporations, but are in small companies, nonprofit organizations, government, and even self-employed individuals. There are nearly 22 million individuals who own their own businesses and have no employees. With more than 75 percent of the economy based on services, there are jobs available in industries, such as health care, finance, education, hospitality, entertainment, and transportation. The world is changing quickly and large corporations replace the equivalent of their entire workforce every four years.

The fast pace of technology today means that you have to be prepared to take advantage of emerging job opportunities and markets. You must also become adaptive and recognize that business is becoming more global, with job opportunities around the world. If you want to obtain such a job, you shouldn't miss a chance to spend some time overseas. To get you started on the path to thinking about job opportunities,

consider all of the changes in business today that might affect your possible long-term track and that could bring you lots of success. You may want to stay completely out of large organizations and corporations and put yourself in a position for an entrepreneurial role as a self-employed contractor or small-business owner. However, there are many who feel that experience in larger businesses is helpful to your success later as an entrepreneur.

You're on the road to learning the key knowledge, skills, and trends that you can use to be a star in business. Business's impact on our society, especially in the area of sustainability and improvement of the environment, is a growing challenge and opportunity. Green businesses and green jobs in the business world are provided to give you a glimpse at the possibilities. Along the way, we will introduce you to some specific careers and offer advice on developing your own job opportunities. Research indicates that you won't be that happy with your job unless you enjoy your work and feel that it has a purpose. Since you spend most of your waking hours every day at work, you need to seriously think about what is important to you in a job.[32]

# ⊖ Review Your Understanding

### Define basic concepts such as business, product, and profit.

A business is an organization or individual that seeks a profit by providing products that satisfy people's needs. A product is a good, service, or idea that has both tangible and intangible characteristics that provide satisfaction and benefits. Profit, the basic goal of business, is the difference between what it costs to make and sell a product and what a customer pays for it.

### Identify the main participants and activities of business and explain why studying business is important.

The three main participants in business are owners, employees, and customers, but others—government regulators, suppliers, social groups, etc.—are also important. Management involves planning, organizing, and controlling the tasks required to carry out the work of the company. Marketing refers to those activities—research, product development, promotion, pricing, and distribution—designed to provide goods and services that satisfy customers. Finance refers to activities concerned with funding a business and using its funds effectively. Studying business can help you prepare for a career and become a better consumer.

### Define economics and compare the four types of economic systems.

Economics is the study of how resources are distributed for the production of goods and services within a social system; an economic system describes how a particular society distributes its resources. Communism is an economic system in which the people, without regard to class, own all the nation's resources. In a socialist system, the government owns and operates basic industries, but individuals own most businesses. Under capitalism, individuals own and operate the majority of businesses that provide goods and services. Mixed economies have elements from more than one economic system; most countries have mixed economies.

### Describe the role of supply, demand, and competition in a free-enterprise system.

In a free-enterprise system, individuals own and operate the majority of businesses, and the distribution of resources is determined by competition, supply, and demand. Demand is the number of goods and services that consumers are willing to buy at different prices at a specific time. Supply is the number of goods or services that businesses are willing to sell at different prices at a specific time. The price at which the supply of a product equals demand at a specific point in time is the equilibrium price. Competition is the rivalry among businesses to convince consumers to buy goods or services. Four types of competitive environments are pure competition, monopolistic competition, oligopoly, and monopoly. These economic concepts determine how businesses may operate in a particular society and, often, how much they can charge for their products.

### Specify why and how the health of the economy is measured.

A country measures the state of its economy to determine whether it is expanding or contracting and whether the country needs to take steps to minimize fluctuations. One commonly used measure is gross domestic product (GDP), the sum of all goods and services produced in a country during a year. A budget deficit occurs when a nation spends more than it takes in from taxes.

### Trace the evolution of the American economy and discuss the role of the entrepreneur in the economy.

The American economy has evolved through several stages: the early economy, the Industrial Revolution, the manufacturing economy, the marketing economy, and the service and Internet-based economy of today. Entrepreneurs play an important role because they risk their time, wealth, and efforts to develop new goods, services, and ideas that fuel the growth of the American economy.

### Evaluate a small-business owner's situation and propose a course of action.

"Solve the Dilemma" on page 29 presents a problem for the owner of the firm. Should you, as the owner, raise prices, expand operations, or form a venture with a larger company to deal with demand? You should be able to apply your newfound understanding of the relationship between supply and demand to assess the situation and reach a decision about how to proceed.

## Revisit the World of Business

### Revisit the World of Business Questions

- Why is competition important in a capitalist economy?
- Why do businesses need to focus on both primary competitors and newer entrants?
- How was Red Bull able to become a major competitor in an industry dominated by two main players?

## Learn the Terms

budget deficit 19
business 4
capitalism (free enterprise) 11
communism 9
competition 14
demand 13
depression 17
economic contraction 16
economic expansion 16
economic system 9
economics 8

entrepreneur 22
equilibrium price 13
financial resources 9
free-market system 11
gross domestic product (GDP) 17
human resources 8
inflation 16
mixed economies 11
monopolistic competition 14
monopoly 15
natural resources 8

nonprofit organizations 4
oligopoly 15
product 4
profit 4
pure competition 14
recession 16
socialism 10
stakeholders 5
supply 13
unemployment 16

## Check Your Progress

1. What is the fundamental goal of business? Do all organizations share this goal?
2. Name the forms a product may take and give some examples of each.
3. Who are the main participants of business? What are the main activities? What other factors have an impact on the conduct of business in the United States?
4. What are four types of economic systems? Can you provide an example of a country using each type?

5. Explain the terms *supply, demand, equilibrium price,* and *competition.* How do these forces interact in the American economy?

6. List the four types of competitive environments and provide an example of a product of each environment.

7. List and define the various measures governments may use to gauge the state of their economies. If unemployment is high, will the growth of GDP be great or small?

8. Why are fluctuations in the economy harmful?

9. How did the Industrial Revolution influence the growth of the American economy? Why do we apply the term *service economy* to the United States today?

10. Explain the federal government's role in the American economy.

## Get Involved

1. Discuss the economic changes occurring in Russia and eastern European countries, which once operated as communist economic systems. Why are these changes occurring? What do you think the result will be?

2. Why is it important for the government to measure the economy? What kinds of actions might it take to control the economy's growth?

3. Is the American economy currently expanding or contracting? Defend your answer with the latest statistics on GDP, inflation, unemployment, and so on. How is the federal government responding?

## Build Your Skills

### The Forces of Supply and Demand

**Background**

WagWumps are a new children's toy with the potential to be a highly successful product. WagWumps are cute and furry, and their eyes glow in the dark. Each family set consists of a mother, a father, and two children. Wee-Toys' manufacturing costs are about $6 per set, with $3 representing marketing and distribution costs. The wholesale price of a WagWump family for a retailer is $15.75, and the toy carries a suggested retail price of $26.99.

**Task**

Assume you are a decision maker at a retailer, such as Target or Walmart, that must determine the price the stores in your district

**FIGURE 1.6**
**Equilibrium Price of WagWumps**

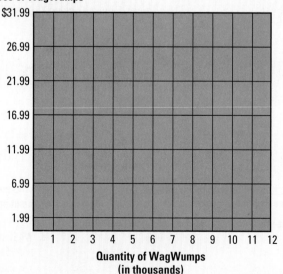

Prices of WagWumps

Quantity of WagWumps (in thousands)

should charge customers for the WagWump family set. From the information provided, you know that the SRP (suggested retail price) is $26.99 per set and that your company can purchase the toy set from your wholesaler for $15.75 each. Based on the following assumptions, plot your company's supply curve on the graph provided in Figure 1.6 and label it "supply curve."

| Quantity | Price |
|----------|--------|
| 3,000 | $16.99 |
| 5,000 | 21.99 |
| 7,000 | 26.99 |

Using the following assumptions, plot your customers' demand curve on Figure 1.6 and label it "demand curve."

| Quantity | Price |
|----------|--------|
| 10,000 | $16.99 |
| 6,000 | 21.99 |
| 2,000 | 26.99 |

For this specific time, determine the point at which the quantity of toys your company is willing to supply equals the quantity of toys the customers in your sales district are willing to buy and label that point "equilibrium price."

## Solve the Dilemma

### Mrs. Acres Homemade Pies

Shelly Acres, whose grandmother gave her a family recipe for making pies, loved to cook, and she decided to start a business she called Mrs. Acres Homemade Pies. The company produces specialty pies and sells them in local supermarkets and select family restaurants. In each of the first six months, Shelly and three part-time employees sold 2,000 pies for $4.50 each, netting $1.50 profit per pie. The pies were quite successful and Shelly could not keep up with demand. The company's success results from a quality product and productive employees who are motivated by incentives and who enjoy being part of a successful new business.

To meet demand, Shelly expanded operations, borrowing money and increasing staff to four full-time employees. Production and sales increased to 8,000 pies per month, and profits soared to $12,000 per month. However, demand for Mrs. Acres Homemade Pies continues to accelerate beyond what Shelly can supply. She has several options: (1) maintain current production levels and raise prices; (2) expand the facility and staff while maintaining the current price; or (3) contract the production of the pies to a national restaurant chain, giving Shelly a percentage of profits with minimal involvement.

#### Discussion Questions

1. Explain and demonstrate the relationship between supply and demand for Mrs. Acres Homemade Pies.

2. What challenges does Shelly face as she considers the three options?

3. What would you do in Shelly's position?

## Build Your Business Plan

### The Dynamics of Business and Economics

Have you ever thought about owning your business? If you have, how did your idea come about? Is it your experience with this particular field? Or might it be an idea that evolved from your desires for a particular good or service not being offered in your community? For example, perhaps you and your friends have yearned for a place to go have coffee, relax, and talk. Now is an opportunity to create the café bar you have been thinking of!

Whether you consider yourself a visionary or a practical thinker, think about your community. What needs are not being met? While it is tempting to suggest a new restaurant (maybe even one near campus), easier-to-implement business plans can range from a lawn care business or a designated driver business to a placement service agency for teenagers.

Once you have an idea for a business plan, think about how profitable this idea might be. Is there sufficient demand for this business? How large is the market for this particular business? What about competitors? How many are there?

To learn about your industry, you should do a thorough search of your initial ideas of a product on the Internet.

# See for Yourself Videocase

## Redbox Succeeds by Identifying Market Need

Redbox's tell-tale bright red kiosks in stores and fast-food restaurants across the country have become an image of what a great business model can accomplish. The company's ability to offer customers a convenient and inexpensive DVD rental option has allowed them to grow despite the widespread growth of streaming services such as Netflix and Amazon. In addition, Redbox has responded competitively by partnering with Verizon to offer their own streaming service in conjunction with DVD rentals. As one of the top rental companies in the United States, Redbox is a true entrepreneurial success story.

Building Redbox into a successful firm was not easy, however. It was fraught with challenges. Like most successful companies, Redbox started out by identifying a need. It recognized that consumers could not often find the movies they wanted in convenient locations. Like all good ideas, Redbox required funding to get started. This proved to be a major difficulty. Realizing that customers did not want to pay much for renting movies, Redbox decided to charge only one dollar. Yet the kiosks, which contain over 800 components, required a large amount of capital. The combination of the capital-intensive nature of the business and the low prices was not an attractive recipe for venture capital funding.

However, Redbox was certain that demand for its product offerings would exceed the costs. The company finally found a partner in the more established Outerwall, formerly known as Coinstar, which already had partnerships with many different retailers. The alliance opened the way for Redbox to begin installing kiosks at the front of stores.

Redbox did not immediately expand across the country. Instead, it took a cautious approach toward its business model. It began by focusing its efforts on making one kiosk profitable, then replicating this way of thinking regionally and nationally. In this way, Redbox was able to test its concept without taking the risk of widespread failure.

Even though it was expanding, it was some time before Redbox was able to earn a profit. Like all entrepreneurs, the founders of Redbox had to take many risks if they wanted the company to succeed. "The risks for starting Redbox were significant," said Marc Achler, vice president of new business, strategy, and innovation. "The first couple years we had some red ink. It took us a while before we turned profitable." Yet with persistence and continual relationship building with retailers, Redbox has been able to secure more than 50 percent of the DVD-rental market.

One way that Redbox has been able to secure such a large share of the market is by meeting the needs of a variety of stakeholders. Redbox views its customers as its first priority and has developed its kiosks and database to meet their needs. For instance, customers can reserve movies online and pick them up at their nearest kiosk. If a kiosk happens to be out of a particular movie, customers can search the Redbox database to locate the movie at a nearby kiosk. This combination of convenience and low prices has attracted customers who desire a simplified process to renting movies. The same is true for their streaming service, Redbox Instant by Verizon, which offers unlimited streaming for the same price as competitors and the option to purchase DVDs from the site.

Additionally, Redbox has created a process that also benefits the needs of its retail partners. Redbox kiosks help attract consumers to the store, where they may purchase additional products. Customers must come back the next day to return their movie, where they may once again purchase more products from the retailer. In this way, Redbox creates a win-win situation for both itself and its partners.

This is not to say that everything is easy for Redbox. For instance, it must continually safeguard against allowing underage children to rent inappropriate (rated-R) movies. And while Redbox has approached this changing and dynamic marketplace proactively, it must continue to do so in order to maintain its competitive position. The company's ability to price rentals and streaming services at 70 percent of the price of competitors and still make a 6 percent return is impressive, but this can easily change as competitors find ways to lower their prices or consumers' desires change.[33]

### Discussion Questions

1. Why are consumers so willing to rent from Redbox?

2. How was Redbox able to overcome some of its earliest challenges?

3. What are some recommendations for ways that Redbox can maintain its high market share?

**You can find the related video in the Video Library in Connect. Ask your instructor how you can access Connect.**

# Team Exercise

Major economic systems, including capitalism, socialism, and communism, as well as mixed economies, were discussed in this chapter. Assuming that you want an economic system that is best for the majority, not just a few members of society, defend one of the economic systems as the best system. Form groups and try to reach agreement on one economic system. Defend why you support the system that you advance.

# Guidelines for the Development of the Business Plan

These guidelines are for students to create a hypothetical business plan for a good/service/business of their choice. Students should assume to have $25,000 to start this new business in their community.

At the end of every chapter, there will be a section entitled "Build Your Business Plan" to assist you in the development of the business plan.

## Phase 1: Development of the Business Proposal

You are encouraged to submit your idea for approval to your instructor as soon as possible. This will eliminate wasted effort on an idea that is not feasible in the instructor's view. Business plan proposals will be evaluated based on their thoroughness and your ability to provide support for the idea.

The business proposal consists of the following elements.

**Business Description.** This consists of an overview of the existing good/service or the good/service/business you will be starting (manufacturer, merchandiser, or service provider). This includes developing a mission (reason for existence; overall purpose of the firm) and a rationale for why you believe this business will be a success. What is your vision for this proposed product/business?

**Brief Marketing Plan.** (The marketing plan will be further developed as the plan evolves.) A description of your business/product is required. Identify the target market and develop a strategy for appealing to it. Justify your proposed location for this business. Describe how you will promote the new business and provide a rationale for your pricing strategy. Select a name for this business. The name should be catchy yet relate to the competencies of the business.

**Competitive Analysis.** Identify the competition as broadly as possible. Indicate why this business will be successful given the market.

## Phase 2: Final Written Business Plan

**Executive Summary.** The executive summary appears first but should be written last.

**Business Description.** This section requires fleshing out the body of the business plan, including material from your revised preliminary proposal with more data, charts, and appendices. Include a description of the proposed form of organization, either a partnership or corporation, and the rationalization of the form chosen.

**Industry and Market Analysis.** An analysis of the industry including the growth rate of the industry and number of new entrants into this field is necessary. Identify uncontrollable variables within the industry. Determine an estimate of the proposed realistic size of the potential market. This will require interpretation of statistics from the U.S. census as well as from local sources such as the Chamber of Commerce.

**Competitive Analysis.** Include an exhaustive list of the primary and secondary competition, along with the competitive advantage of each.

**Marketing Strategy.** Target market specifics need to be developed.

Decisions on the marketing mix variables need to be made:

- Price (at the market, below market, above market)
- Promotion (sales associates, advertising budget, use of sales promotions, and publicity/goodwill)
- Distribution—Rationale of choice and level of distribution
- Product/Service—A detailed rationale of the perceived differential advantage of your product offering

**Operational Issues.** How will you make or provide your product? Location rationale, facility type, leasing considerations, and sources of suppliers need to be detailed. Software/hardware requirements necessary to maintain operations must be determined.

**Human Resources Requirement.** Number and description of personnel needed, including realistic required education and skills.

**Financial Projections.** Statement of cash flows must be prepared for the first 12 months of the business. This must include startup costs, opening expenses, and estimation of cash inflows and outflows. A breakeven analysis should be included and an explanation of your expected financial expenditures.

**Appendixes**

# Phase 3: Oral Presentation

Specific separate guidelines on the oral presentation will be provided.

# 2

# Business Ethics and Social Responsibility

## Learning Objectives

**After reading this chapter, you will be able to:**

**LO 2-1** Define business ethics and social responsibility and examine their importance.

**LO 2-2** Detect some of the ethical issues that may arise in business.

**LO 2-3** Specify how businesses can promote ethical behavior.

**LO 2-4** Explain the four dimensions of social responsibility.

**LO 2-5** Debate an organization's social responsibilities to owners, employees, consumers, the environment, and the community.

**LO 2-6** Evaluate the ethics of a business's decision.

## Chapter Outline

## Antibacterial Soap Faces Regulatory and Consumer Pressure

The soap industry is a strong business within the United States, amounting to more than $5 billion in sales of soaps, shower products, and body washes. However, the industry has come under scrutiny over product safety and validity of claims, which could lead to significant decreases in profits. If the soap is used too often, a chemical called triclosan—found in approximately 75 percent of antibacterial products—could lead to bacteria that are not only resistant to triclosan but to other antibiotics as well. Consumer advocates are also concerned that triclosan might interfere with hormones, making long-term use harmful for the body. In addition, critics claim that triclosan is not any more effective than regular soap and water. Studies have revealed the presence of triclosan in urine samples of 75 percent of respondents, suggesting that this chemical is highly present among the general population.

The Food and Drug Administration (FDA) has proposed that antibacterial soap and body wash manufacturers provide additional evidence that their products are more effective than comparable products and are safe for long-term use. If the proposal of the FDA goes through, it will have significant implications for soap manufacturers and other industries, such as cosmetics, that use triclosan in their products. If antibacterial soap manufacturers cannot prove their claims of effectiveness, they might have to relabel their products, reformulate them, or even remove them completely, which would be costly. Increased concern is causing some firms to begin to voluntarily remove triclosan. Johnson and Johnson and Reckitt Benckiser have begun phasing out triclosan from many of their products.[1]

## Introduction

Any organization, including nonprofits, has to manage the ethical behavior of employees and participants in the overall operations of the organization. Misconduct can take on many forms within the business environment, including deceptive business practices and the withholding of important information from investors or consumers. Wrongdoing by some businesses has focused public attention and government involvement on encouraging more acceptable business conduct. Any organizational decision may be judged as right or wrong, ethical or unethical, legal or illegal.

In this chapter, we take a look at the role of ethics and social responsibility in business decision making. First we define business ethics and examine why it is important to understand ethics' role in business. Next we explore a number of business ethics issues to help you learn to recognize such issues when they arise. Finally, we consider steps businesses can take to improve ethical behavior in their organizations. The second half of the chapter focuses on social responsibility and unemployment. We survey some important issues and detail how companies have responded to them.

**business ethics**
principles and standards that determine acceptable conduct in business

## Business Ethics and Social Responsibility

In this chapter, we define **business ethics** as the principles and standards that determine acceptable conduct in business organizations. Personal ethics, on the other hand, relates to an individual's values, principles, and standards of conduct. The acceptability of behavior in business is determined by not only the organization but also stakeholders such as customers, competitors, government regulators, interest groups, and the public, as well as each individual's personal principles and values. The publicity and debate surrounding highly visible legal and ethical issues at a number of well-known firms, including Diamond Foods, Target, and J.P. Morgan, highlight the need for businesses to integrate ethics and responsibility into all business decisions. For instance, Target was criticized for not having appropriate internal controls in place to prevent the theft of millions of their customers' credit and debit card accounts. Most unethical activities within organizations are supported by an organizational culture that encourages employees to bend the rules. On the other hand, trust in business is the glue that holds relationships together. In Figure 2.1, you can see that trust in banks is lower than in other industries, except for government.

Organizations that exhibit a high ethical culture encourage employees to act with integrity and adhere to business values. Many experts agree that ethical leadership, ethical values, and compliance are important in creating good business ethics. To truly create an ethical culture, however, managers must show a strong commitment to ethics and compliance. This "tone at the top" requires top managers to acknowledge their own role in supporting ethics and compliance, create strong relationships with the general counsel and the ethics and compliance department, clearly communicate company expectations for ethical behavior to all employees, educate all managers and supervisors in the business about the company's ethics policies, and train managers and employees on what to do if an ethics crisis occurs.[2]

**social responsibility**
a business's obligation to maximize its positive impact and minimize its negative impact on society

Many consumers and social advocates believe that businesses should not only make a profit but also consider the social implications of their activities. We define **social responsibility** as a business's obligation to maximize its positive impact and minimize its negative impact on society. Although many people use the terms *social responsibility* and *ethics* interchangeably, they do not mean the same thing. Business ethics relates to an *individual's* or a *work group's* decisions that society evaluates as right or

# Entrepreneurship in Action

## Listening for a Good Business Opportunity

**OrigAudio**
**Founders:** Jason Lucash and Mike Szymczak
**Founded:** 2009, in Costa Mesa, California
**Success:** OrigAudio released a recyclable foldable speaker that has helped the firm double its sales every year since its founding.

Jason Lucash and Mike Szymczak got the idea for their company from a Chinese food takeout box! This simple item inspired them to start OrigAudio and launch their first product: a set of portable speakers made out of recycled materials that can fold up! These speakers are made with 70 percent post-recycled materials and require no external power sources.

After being seen at a trade show by a QVC representative, the speakers were featured on the Home Shopping Network and sold more than $750,000 worth in two years. OrigAudio embraces simple products that make lives easier for consumers. For instance, it sells small devices that allow consumers to turn ordinary items into speakers. It also demonstrates social responsibility with its "Beet" product line. For every pair of Beets headphones it sells, OrigAudio donates a can of beets to the Second Harvest Food Bank of Orange County. To date, the company's recycled speakers and other items are sold on its website and in some well-known retail locations such as Bed, Bath, and Beyond.[3]

---

wrong, whereas social responsibility is a broader concept that concerns the impact of the *entire business's* activities on society. From an ethical perspective, for example, we may be concerned about a health care organization overcharging the government for Medicare services. From a social responsibility perspective, we might be concerned about the impact that this overcharging will have on the ability of the health care system to provide adequate services for all citizens. It would appear that such concern is warranted. In 2013, a Detroit-based oncologist was charged with purposefully misdiagnosing patients and then charging Medicaid for their treatment. Not only was this a serious case of health care fraud, it also endangered the safety of patients.[4]

The most basic ethical and social responsibility concerns have been codified by laws and regulations that encourage businesses to conform to society's standards, values, and attitudes. For example, after accounting scandals at a number of well-known firms in the

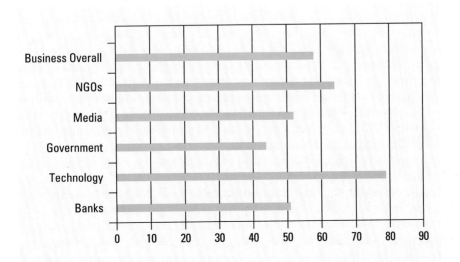

**FIGURE 2.1**
**Global Trust in Different Institutions**

Source: Edelman Trust Barometer: 2014 Annual Global Study, www.edelman.com/insights/intellectual-property/2014-edelman-trust-barometer/ (accessed February 21, 2014).

**TABLE 2.1**    **Timeline of Ethical and Socially Responsible Activities**

| 1960s | 1970s | 1980s | 1990s | 2000s |
|---|---|---|---|---|
| • Social issues | • Business ethics | • Standards for ethical conduct | • Corporate ethics programs | • Transparency in financial markets |
| • Consumer Bill of Rights | • Social responsibility | • Financial misconduct | • Regulation to support business ethics | • Corporate misconduct |
| • Disadvantaged consumer | • Diversity | • Self-regulation | • Health issues | • Intellectual property |
| • Environmental issues | • Bribery | • Codes of conduct | • Safe working conditions | • Regulation of accounting and finance |
| • Product safety | • Discrimination | • Ethics training | • Detecting misconduct | • Executive compensation |
| | • Identifying ethical issues | | | |

*Source: Adapted from "Business Ethics Timeline," copyright © 2003,* Ethics Resource Center *(n.d.), www.ethics.org, updated 2010.*

early 2000s shook public confidence in the integrity of corporate America, the reputations of every U.S. company suffered regardless of their association with the scandals.[5] To help restore confidence in corporations and markets, Congress passed the Sarbanes-Oxley Act, which criminalized securities fraud and stiffened penalties for corporate fraud. After the financial crisis occurred in the most recent recession, the Dodd-Frank Act was passed to reform the financial industry and offer consumers protection against complex and/or deceptive financial products. At a minimum, managers are expected to obey all laws and regulations. Most legal issues arise as choices that society deems unethical, irresponsible, or otherwise unacceptable. However, all actions deemed unethical by society are not necessarily illegal, and both legal and ethical concerns change over time (see Table 2.1). Business law refers to the laws and regulations that govern the conduct of business. Many problems and conflicts in business can be avoided if owners, managers, and employees knew more about business law and the legal system. Business ethics, social responsibility, and laws together act as a compliance system, requiring that businesses and employees act responsibly in society. In this chapter, we explore ethics and social responsibility; Appendix B addresses business law, including the Sarbanes-Oxley Act and the Dodd-Frank Act.

## The Role of Ethics in Business

You have only to pick up *The Wall Street Journal* or *USA Today* to see examples of the growing concern about legal and ethical issues in business. For example, the federal government launched an investigation into whether Avon had violated the Foreign Corrupt Practices Act by offering gifts or payments to foreign government officials to gain licenses. Because Avon wants to move on from the crisis, it is offering to settle the probe. Such a large settlement will result in a loss for the company.[6] Regardless of what an individual believes about a particular action, if society judges it to be unethical or wrong, whether correctly or not, that judgment directly affects the organization's ability to achieve its business goals.[7]

Well-publicized incidents of unethical and illegal activity—ranging from accounting fraud to using the Internet to steal another person's credit card number, from deceptive advertising of food and diet products to unfair competitive practices in the computer software industry—strengthen the public's perceptions that ethical standards and the level of trust in business need to be raised. Author David Callahan has commented, "Americans who wouldn't so much as shoplift a pack of chewing gum are committing felonies at tax time, betraying the trust of their patients, misleading investors, ripping off their insurance companies, lying to their clients, and much more."[8] Often, such charges start as ethical conflicts but evolve into legal disputes when cooperative conflict resolution cannot be accomplished. Headline-grabbing scandals like those associated with executive compensation and benefits packages create ethical concerns. It is estimated that the average CEO compensation is 204 times the amount paid to rank-and-file employees. This represents an increase in the compensation gap since 2009.[9] Consumer outrage over executive compensation is prompting companies to begin reevaluating how they compensate their CEOs relative to corporate performance. Walt Disney chairman and CEO Robert Iger saw a 15 percent drop in compensation after Disney failed to meet all its 2013 performance targets that the board had set.[10]

However, it is important to understand that business ethics goes beyond legal issues. Ethical conduct builds trust among individuals and in business relationships, which validates and promotes confidence in business relationships. Establishing trust and confidence is much more difficult in organizations that have reputations for acting unethically. If you were to discover, for example, that a manager had misled you about company benefits when you were hired, your trust and confidence in that company would probably diminish. And if you learned that a colleague had lied to you about something, you probably would not trust or rely on that person in the future.

Ethical issues are not limited to for-profit organizations either. Ethical issues include all areas of organizational activities, including government. In government, several politicians and some high-ranking officials have faced disciplinary actions over ethical indiscretions. For instance, former New Orleans mayor Ray Nagin was found guilty of 20 counts of corruption. Allegations claim that he accepted more than $500,000 in bribes.[11] Even sports can be subject to ethical lapses. New York Yankees third baseman Alex Rodriguez was suspended after he was accused of using illegal testosterone lozenges before baseball games. However, Rodriguez continues to maintain his innocence.[12] Thus, whether made in science, politics, sports, or business, most decisions are judged as right or wrong, ethical or unethical. Negative judgments can affect an organization's ability to build relationships with customers and suppliers, attract investors, and retain employees.[13]

Although we will not tell you in this chapter what you ought to do, others—your superiors, co-workers, and family—will make judgments about the ethics of your actions and decisions. Learning how to recognize and resolve ethical issues is a key step in evaluating ethical decisions in business.

Actor Derek Hough attends Blue Jeans Go Green celebration of 1 Million pieces of denim collected for recycling, hosted by Miles Teller at SkyBar at the Mondrian Los Angeles on November 6, 2013 in West Hollywood, California.

## Recognizing Ethical Issues in Business

Recognizing ethical issues is the most important step in understanding business ethics. An **ethical issue** is an identifiable problem, situation, or opportunity that requires a person to choose from among several actions that may be evaluated as right or wrong, ethical or unethical. In business, such a choice often involves weighing monetary profit against what a person considers appropriate conduct. The best way to judge the ethics of a decision is to look at a situation from a customer's or competitor's viewpoint: Should liquid-diet manufacturers make unsubstantiated claims about their products? Should an engineer agree to divulge her former employer's trade secrets to

**ethical issue**
an identifiable problem, situation, or opportunity that requires a person to choose from among several actions that may be evaluated as right or wrong, ethical or unethical

Ralph Lauren reported that its subsidiary had bribed foreign officials in Argentina. Because it took quick action to address the misconduct, the compay did not face charges.

**bribes**
payments, gifts, or special favors intended to influence the outcome of a decision

ensure that she gets a better job with a competitor? Should a salesperson omit facts about a product's poor safety record in his presentation to a customer? Such questions require the decision maker to evaluate the ethics of his or her choice.

Many business issues seem straightforward and easy to resolve on the surface, but are in reality very complex. A person often needs several years of experience in business to understand what is acceptable or ethical. For example, it is considered improper to give or accept **bribes,** which are payments, gifts, or special favors intended to influence the outcome of a decision. A bribe benefits an individual or a company at the expense of other stakeholders. Companies that do business overseas should be aware that bribes are a significant ethical issue and are, in fact, illegal in many countries. In the United States, the Foreign Corrupt Practices Act imposes heavy penalties on companies found guilty of bribery.

Ethics is also related to the culture in which a business operates. In the United States, for example, it would be inappropriate for a businessperson to bring an elaborately wrapped gift to a prospective client on their first meeting—the gift could be viewed as a bribe. In Japan, however, it is considered impolite *not* to bring a gift. Experience with the culture in which a business operates is critical to understanding what is ethical or unethical.

To help you understand ethical issues that perplex businesspeople today, we will take a brief look at some of them in this section. Ethical issues can be more complex now than in the past. The vast number of news-format investigative programs has increased consumer and employee awareness of organizational misconduct. In addition, the multitude of cable channels and Internet resources has improved the awareness of ethical problems among the general public.

One of the principal causes of unethical behavior in organizations is overly aggressive financial or business objectives. Many of these issues relate to decisions and concerns that managers have to deal with daily. It is not possible to discuss every issue, of course. However, a discussion of a few issues can help you begin to recognize the ethical problems with which businesspersons must deal. Many ethical issues in business can be categorized in the context of their relation with abusive and intimidating behavior, conflicts of interest, fairness and honesty, communications, misuse of company resources, and business associations. The National Business Ethics Survey found that workers witness many instances of ethical misconduct in their organizations (see Table 2.2).

**Misuse of Company Time.**    Theft of time is a common area of misconduct observed in the workplace.[14] One example of misusing time in the workplace is by engaging in activities that are not necessary for the job. For instance, many employees spend an average of one hour each day using social networking sites or watching YouTube. In this case, the employee is misusing not only time but also company resources by using the company's computer and Internet access for personal use.[15] Time theft costs can be difficult to measure but are estimated to cost companies hundreds of billions of dollars annually. It is widely believed that the average employee "steals" 4.5 hours a week with late arrivals, leaving early, long lunch breaks,

|  | 2011 (%) | 2013 (%) |
|---|---|---|
| Overall | 45 | 41 |
| Abusive behavior | 21 | 18 |
| Lying to employees | 20 | 17 |
| Conflict of interest | 15 | 12 |
| Violating company Internet use policies | 16 | 12 |
| Discrimination against employees | 15 | 12 |
| Violations of health or safety regulations | 13 | 10 |
| Lying to customers, vendors, the public | 12 | 10 |
| Retaliation against reporters of misconduct |  | 10 |
| Falsifying time reports/hours worked | 12 | 10 |
| Stealing or theft | 12 | 9 |

**TABLE 2.2**
**Percentage of U.S. Workforce Observing Specific Forms of Misconduct, 2011 and 2013**

*Source: Ethics Resource Center, 2013* National Business Ethics Survey® of the U.S. Workforce *(Arlington, VA: Ethics Resource Center, 2014), pp. 41–42.*

inappropriate sick days, excessive socializing, and engaging in personal activities such as online shopping and watching sports while on the job. All of these activities add up to lost productivity and profits for the employer—and relate to ethical issues in the area of time theft.

**Abusive and Intimidating Behavior.**   Abusive or intimidating behavior is the most common ethical problem for employees. These concepts can mean anything from physical threats, false accusations, profanity, insults, yelling, harshness, and unreasonableness to ignoring someone or simply being annoying; and the meaning of these words can differ by person—you probably have some ideas of your own. Abusive behavior can be placed on a continuum from a minor distraction to a disruption of the workplace. For example, what one person may define as yelling might be another's definition of normal speech. Civility in our society is a concern, and the workplace is no exception. The productivity level of many organizations has been diminished by the time spent unraveling abusive relationships.

Abusive behavior is difficult to assess and manage because of diversity in culture and lifestyle. What does it mean to speak profanely? Is profanity only related to specific words or other such terms that are common in today's business world? If you are using words that are normal in your language but that others consider to be profanity, have you just insulted, abused, or disrespected them?

Within the concept of abusive behavior, intent should be a consideration. If the employee was trying

The show *Undercover Boss* gives managers and business owners the chance to understand how their subordinates feel as they take on the responsibilities of their employees. Many bosses develop a stronger appreciation for their employees' challenging jobs, as Kat Cole, president of Cinnabon Inc., did after spending time undercover in the company's retail locations.

to convey a compliment but the comment was considered abusive, then it was probably a mistake. The way a word is said (voice inflection) can be important. Add to this the fact that we now live in a multicultural environment—doing business and working with many different cultural groups—and the businessperson soon realizes the depth of the ethical and legal issues that may arise. There are problems of word meanings by age and within cultures. For example, an expression such as "Did you guys hook up last night?" can have various meanings, including some that could be considered offensive in a work environment.

Bullying is associated with a hostile workplace when a person or group is targeted and is threatened, harassed, belittled, verbally abused, or overly criticized. Bullying may create what some consider a hostile environment, a term generally associated with sexual harassment. Although sexual harassment has legal recourse, bullying has little legal recourse at this time. Bullying is a widespread problem in the United States, and can cause psychological damage that can result in health-endangering consequences to the target. Surveys reveal that bullying in the workplace is on the rise.[16] As Table 2.3 indicates, bullying can use a mix of verbal, nonverbal, and manipulative threatening expressions to damage workplace productivity. One may wonder why workers tolerate such activities. The problem is that 81 percent of workplace bullies are supervisors. Additionally, bullying can occur in any type of business. A bullying scandal at the Miami Dolphins involved a player who abruptly left the team after a hazing incident. The player claimed he had been bullied mercilessly by three starters on the Dolphins' offensive line, which harmed his mental well-being.[17]

**Misuse of Company Resources.**   Misuse of company resources has been identified by the Ethics Resource Center as a leading issue in observed misconduct in organizations. Issues might include spending an excessive amount of time on personal e-mails, submitting personal expenses on company expense reports, or using the company copier for personal use. A senior administrative city government worker in New York was fired for misusing the company's work cell phone. It was estimated she spent an hour a day making personal calls, racketing up charges of $3,000.[18] While serious resource abuse can result in firing, some abuse can have legal repercussions.

**TABLE 2.3**
**Actions Associated with Bullies**

| |
|---|
| 1. Spreading rumors to damage others |
| 2. Blocking others' communication in the workplace |
| 3. Flaunting status or authority to take advantage of others |
| 4. Discrediting others' ideas and opinions |
| 5. Use of e-mails to demean others |
| 6. Failing to communicate or return communication |
| 7. Insults, yelling, and shouting |
| 8. Using terminology to discriminate by gender, race, or age |
| 9. Using eye or body language to hurt others or their reputation |
| 10. Taking credit for others' work or ideas |

*Source: © O. C. Ferrell, 2011.*

A man from Reddick, Florida, was arrested after misusing his company credit card at gas stations. Investigations revealed he had used the card to purchase other people's gas and then had them pay him a reduced charge to pocket.[19]

The most common way that employees abuse resources is by using company computers for personal use. Typical examples of using a computer for personal use include shopping on the Internet, downloading music, doing personal banking, surfing the Internet for entertainment purposes, or visiting Facebook. Some companies have chosen to block certain sites such as YouTube or Pandora from employees. However, other companies choose to take a more flexible approach. For example, many have instituted policies that allow for some personal computer use as long as the use does not detract significantly from the workday.

No matter what approach a business chooses to take, it must have policies in place to prevent company resource abuse. Because misuse of company resources is such a widespread problem, many companies, like Boeing, have implemented official policies delineating acceptable use of company resources. Boeing's policy states that use of company resources is acceptable when it does not result in "significant added costs, disruption of business processes, or any other disadvantage to the company." The policy further states that use of company resources for noncompany purposes is acceptable only when an employee receives explicit permission to do so. This kind of policy is in line with that of many companies, particularly large ones that can easily lose millions of dollars and thousands of hours of productivity to these activities.[20]

**Conflict of Interest.**   A conflict of interest, one of the most common ethical issues identified by employees, exists when a person must choose whether to advance his or her own personal interests or those of others. For example, a manager in a corporation is supposed to ensure that the company is profitable so that its stockholder-owners receive a return on their investment. In other words, the manager has a responsibility to investors. If she instead makes decisions that give her more power or money but do not help the company, then she has a conflict of interest—she is acting to benefit herself at the expense of her company and is not fulfilling her responsibilities as an employee. To avoid conflicts of interest, employees must be able to separate their personal financial interests from their business dealings. In the wake of the 2008 meltdown on Wall Street, stakeholders and legislators pushed for reform of the credit rating industry. Many cited rampant conflicts of interest between financial firms and the companies that rate them as part of the reason no one recognized the impending financial disaster. Conflict of interest has long been a serious problem in the financial industry because the financial companies pay the credit raters money in order to be rated. Because different rating companies exist, financial firms can also shop around for the best rating. There is no third-party mediator who oversees the financial industry and how firms are rated.[21]

Insider trading is an example of a conflict of interest. Insider trading is the buying or selling of stocks by insiders who possess material that is still not public. The Justice Department has taken an aggressive stance toward insider trading. For instance, SAC Capital Advisors LP settled with the Justice Department for $1.8 billion and agreed to close its investment advisory business after pleading guilty to insider trading. Several key executives at SAC Capital Advisors have been convicted of insider trading charges.[22] Bribery can also be a conflict of interest. While bribery is an increasing issue in many countries, it is more prevalent in some countries than in others. Transparency International has developed a Corruption Perceptions Index (Table 2.4). Note that there are 18 countries perceived as less corrupt than the United States.[23]

**TABLE 2.4**
**Least Corrupt Countries**

| Rank | Country | CPI Score* |
|------|---------|------------|
| 1. | Denmark/New Zealand | 91 |
| 3. | Finland/Sweden | 89 |
| 5. | Norway/Singapore | 86 |
| 7. | Switzerland | 85 |
| 8. | Netherlands | 83 |
| 9. | Australia/Canada | 81 |
| 11. | Luxembourg | 80 |
| 12. | Germany/Iceland | 78 |
| 14. | United Kingdom | 76 |
| 15. | Barbados/Belgium/Hong Kong | 75 |
| 18. | Japan | 74 |
| 19. | United States/Uruguay | 73 |

*Corruption Perceptions Index (CPI) score relates to perceptions of the degree of public sector corruption as seen by businesspeople and country analysts and ranges between 0 (highly corrupt) and 10 (very clean).

Source: Corruption Perceptions Index 2013, Copyright Transparency International 2013, http://cpi.transparency.org/cpi2013/results/ (accessed February 21, 2014).

## Fairness and Honesty

Fairness and honesty are at the heart of business ethics and relate to the general values of decision makers. At a minimum, businesspersons are expected to follow all applicable laws and regulations. But beyond obeying the law, they are expected not to harm customers, employees, clients, or competitors knowingly through deception, misrepresentation, coercion, or discrimination. Honesty and fairness can relate to how the employees use the resources of the organization. In contrast, dishonesty is usually associated with a lack of integrity, lack of disclosure, and lying. One common example of dishonesty is theft of office supplies. Fraud and theft occurs at approximately 35 percent of small businesses.[24] Although the majority of office supply thefts involve small things such as pencils or Post-it Notes, some workers admit to stealing more expensive equipment such as laptops, PDAs, and cell phones. Employees should be aware of policies on taking items and recognize how these decisions relate to ethical behavior.

One aspect of fairness relates to competition. Although numerous laws have been passed to foster competition and make monopolistic practices illegal, companies sometimes gain control over markets by using questionable practices that harm competition. Bullying can also occur between companies that are intense competitors. For example, European antitrust regulators alleged that some of the world's biggest banks—including Goldman Sachs, Morgan Stanley, and J.P. Morgan—collaborated with an industry association to prevent exchanges from offering and trading in credit derivatives. The allegations claim that the collusion was done to prevent banks from losing revenue in this profitable area. If true, the banks would be in violation of European laws dictating fair competition. The banks vehemently denied the accusations.[25] In many cases, the alleged misconduct not only can have monetary and legal implications but can also threaten reputation, investor confidence, and customer

Misuse of company time through the use of personal social media is very costly to businesses.

loyalty. At the minimum, a business found guilty of anticompetitive practices will be forced to stop such conduct. However, many companies end up paying millions in penalties to settle allegations.[26]

Another aspect of fairness and honesty relates to disclosure of potential harm caused by product use. For instance, the FDA has become increasingly concerned about the use of trans fats in food. The FDA believes that disclosing trans fats through labeling is no longer sufficient. Because trans fats are considered to be harmful, the FDA announced a proposal to phase out trans fats. If this proposal takes effect, food companies would have to eliminate trans fats from their ingredients or petition the agency and meet strong safety standards.[27]

Dishonesty has become a significant problem in the United States. A survey of 23,000 high school students reported that 51 percent of students admitted to cheating on an exam at least once in the past year, and 20 percent admitted to stealing. Perhaps even more disturbing, 93 percent of respondents stated that they were satisfied with their personal ethical character. If today's students are tomorrow's leaders, there is likely to be a correlation between acceptable behavior today and tomorrow. This adds to the argument that the leaders of today must be prepared for the ethical risks associated with this downward trend.[28]

Even military officers have felt the pressure to cheat. At one Air Force base in Montana, nearly half of the Air Force officers at the base cheated on a proficiency exam. Another investigation was launched shortly afterward to determine whether senior Navy enlistees in South Carolina cheated on an exam containing classified

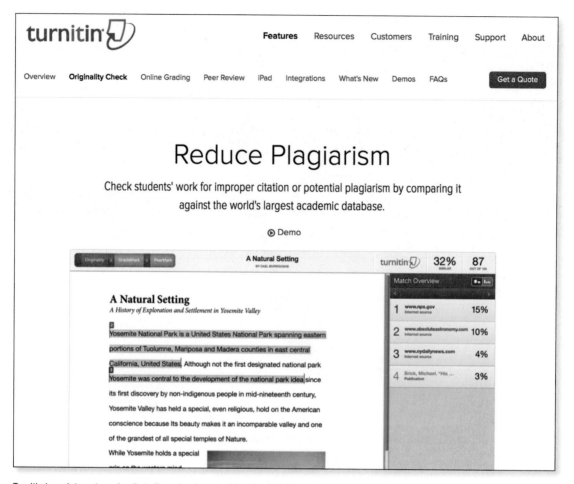

TrunItln is an Internet service that allows teachers to determine if their students have plagiarized content.

information. Another 800 soldiers in the Army were placed under criminal investigation for being involved in kickbacks to soldiers who recruited friends. As a result of these scandals, the military is increasing its ethics training.[29]

**Communications.**   Communications is another area in which ethical concerns may arise. False and misleading advertising, as well as deceptive personal-selling tactics, anger consumers and can lead to the failure of a business. Truthfulness about product safety and quality is also important to consumers. General Motors (GM) issued a recall on its 2005–2007 Chevrolet Cobalt vehicles, but not until at least six deaths were attributed to Cobalt car accidents where the airbags did not deploy due to switch failure. It has been alleged that a GM engineer had encountered the problem as early as 2004, but GM did not issue a recall. Rather, the company sent a service bulletin to its dealers advising them to install snap-on key covers that would fix the problem if customers complained. Many dealers did not install these key covers. A congressional hearing was ordered to investigate the situation, but before GM testified, it launched an additional recall of 1.5 million vehicles for electric power steering issues.[30]

Some companies fail to provide enough information for consumers about differences or similarities between products. For example, driven by high prices for medicines, many consumers are turning to Canadian, Mexican, and overseas Internet sources for drugs to treat a variety of illnesses and conditions. However, research suggests that a significant percentage of these imported pharmaceuticals may not actually contain the labeled drug, and the counterfeit drugs could even be harmful to those who take them.[31]

Another important aspect of communications that may raise ethical concerns relates to product labeling. This becomes an even greater concern with potentially harmful products like cigarettes. In Europe, at least 30 percent of the front side of cigarette packaging and 40 percent of the back needs to be taken up by the warning. The FDA passed similar rules for the United States, but its ruling was blocked until the lawsuit between the FDA and cigarette companies is resolved.[32] However, labeling of other products raises ethical questions when it threatens basic rights, such as freedom of speech and expression. This is the heart of the controversy surrounding the movement to require warning labels on movies and videogames, rating their content, language, and appropriate audience age. Although people in the entertainment industry claim that such labeling violates their First Amendment right to freedom of expression, other consumers—particularly parents—believe that labeling is needed to protect children from harmful influences. Similarly, alcoholic beverage and cigarette manufacturers have argued that a total ban on cigarette and alcohol advertisements violates the First Amendment. Internet regulation, particularly that designed to protect children and the elderly, is on the forefront in consumer protection legislation. Because of the debate surrounding the acceptability of these business activities, they remain major ethical issues.

New York Yankees third baseman Alex Rodriguez was suspended after evidence suggested he had been using performance-enhancing drugs.

**Business Relationships.**   The behavior of businesspersons toward customers, suppliers, and others in their workplace may also generate ethical concerns. Ethical behavior within a business involves keeping company secrets, meeting obligations and responsibilities, and avoiding undue pressure that may force others to act unethically.

Managers in particular, because of the authority of their position, have the opportunity to influence employees' actions. For example, a manager might influence employees to use pirated computer software to save costs. The use of illegal software puts the employee and the company at legal risk, but employees may feel pressured to do so by their superior's authority. The National Business Ethics Survey found that employees who feel pressured to compromise ethical standards view top and middle managers as the greatest source of such pressure.[33]

It is the responsibility of managers to create a work environment that helps the organization achieve its objectives and fulfill its responsibilities. However, the methods that managers use to enforce these responsibilities should not compromise employee rights. Organizational pressures may encourage a person to engage in activities that he or she might otherwise view as unethical, such as invading others' privacy or stealing a competitor's secrets. The firm may provide only vague or lax supervision on ethical issues, creating the opportunity for misconduct. Managers who offer no ethical direction to employees create many opportunities for manipulation, dishonesty, and conflicts of interest.

**TABLE 2.5**
**Questions to Consider in Determining Whether an Action Is Ethical**

| |
|---|
| Are there any potential legal restrictions or violations that could result from the action? |
| Does your company have a specific code of ethics or policy on the action? |
| Is this activity customary in your industry? Are there any industry trade groups that provide guidelines or codes of conduct that address this issue? |
| Would this activity be accepted by your co-workers? Will your decision or action withstand open discussion with co-workers and managers and survive untarnished? |
| How does this activity fit with your own beliefs and values? |

**plagiarism**
the act of taking someone else's work and presenting it as your own without mentioning the source

**Plagiarism**—taking someone else's work and presenting it as your own without mentioning the source—is another ethical issue. As a student, you may be familiar with plagiarism in school—for example, copying someone else's term paper or quoting from a published work or Internet source without acknowledging it. In business, an ethical issue arises when an employee copies reports or takes the work or ideas of others and presents it as his or her own. A manager attempting to take credit for a subordinate's ideas is engaging in another type of plagiarism.

## Making Decisions about Ethical Issues

Although we've presented a variety of ethical issues that may arise in business, it can be difficult to recognize specific ethical issues in practice. Whether a decision maker recognizes an issue as an ethical one often depends on the issue itself. Managers, for example, tend to be more concerned about issues that affect those close to them, as well as issues that have immediate rather than long-term consequences. Thus, the perceived importance of an ethical issue substantially affects choices. However, only a few issues receive scrutiny, and most receive no attention at all.[34]

Table 2.5 lists some questions you may want to ask yourself and others when trying to determine whether an action is ethical. Open discussion of ethical issues does not eliminate ethical problems, but it does promote both trust and learning in an organization.[35] When people feel that they cannot discuss what they are doing with their co-workers or superiors, there is a good chance that an ethical issue exists. Once a person has recognized an ethical issue and can openly discuss it with others, he or she has begun the process of resolving that issue.

**LO 2-3**

## Improving Ethical Behavior in Business

Understanding how people make ethical choices and what prompts a person to act unethically may reverse the current trend toward unethical behavior in business. Ethical decisions in an organization are influenced by three key factors: individual moral standards, the influence of managers and co-workers, and the opportunity to engage in misconduct (Figure 2.2). While you have great control over your personal ethics

**FIGURE 2.2**
**Three Factors That Influence Business Ethics**

| Individual Standards and Values | | Managers' and Co-workers' Influence | | Opportunity: Codes and Compliance Requirements | | Ethical/Unethical Choices in Business |
|---|---|---|---|---|---|---|
| | + | | + | | = | |

### Ralph Lauren Sets Example in FCPA Case

What does a company do when an internal audit finds that bribery has occurred? For Ralph Lauren Corporation, it turns itself in. The company discovered that from 2005 to 2009, bribes were paid to customs and government officials in Argentina in the form of cash, dresses, handbags, and perfume to expedite processes of merchandise in the South American country. This misconduct violates the Foreign Corrupt Practices Act (FCPA), which makes it illegal for companies with operations in the United States to bribe foreign officials.

When Ralph Lauren discovered the bribery, it immediately reported the misconduct to the Securities and Exchange Commission (SEC) and worked with government authorities in the investigation. The company agreed to pay $1.6 million to settle investigations. More than $700,000 of this payment covers the amount of the bribes paid to officials.

By turning itself in, Ralph Lauren received applause from several SEC officials, who deemed the company's actions ethical. The clothing retailer was able to resolve charges and sign nonprosecution agreements. This was the first such agreement in history related to the FCPA. This case demonstrates that it pays to comply with the law when misconduct is discovered. Not only can penalties be less severe, but Ralph Lauren's reputation as a company committed to doing the right thing will likely improve.[36]

**Discussion Questions**

1. How did Ralph Lauren violate the FCPA?
2. Why did Ralph Lauren receive less severe penalties for the misconduct?
3. How can the Ralph Lauren bribery case set a precedent for other firms when discovering misconduct?

---

outside the workplace, your co-workers and superiors exert significant control over your choices at work through authority and example. In fact, the activities and examples set by co-workers, along with rules and policies established by the firm, are critical in gaining consistent ethical compliance in an organization. If the company fails to provide good examples and direction for appropriate conduct, confusion and conflict will develop and result in the opportunity for misconduct. If your boss or co-workers leave work early, you may be tempted to do so as well. If you see co-workers engaged in personal activities such as shopping online or watching YouTube, then you may be more likely to do so also. In addition, having sound personal values contributes to an ethical workplace.

Because ethical issues often emerge from conflict, it is useful to examine the causes of ethical conflict. Business managers and employees often experience some tension between their own ethical beliefs and their obligations to the organizations in which they work. Many employees utilize different ethical standards at work than they do at home. This conflict increases when employees feel that their company is encouraging unethical conduct or exerting pressure on them to engage in it.

It is difficult for employees to determine what conduct is acceptable within a company if the firm does not have established ethics policies and standards. And without such policies and standards, employees may base decisions on how their peers and superiors behave. Professional **codes of ethics** are formalized rules and standards that describe what the company expects of its employees. Codes of ethics do not have to be so detailed that they take into account every situation, but they should provide guidelines and principles that can help employees achieve organizational objectives and address risks in an acceptable and ethical way. The development of a code of ethics should include not only a firm's executives and board of directors, but also legal staff and employees from all areas of a firm.[37] Table 2.6 lists some key things to consider when developing a code of ethics.

**codes of ethics**
formalized rules and standards that describe what a company expects of its employees

**TABLE 2.6**
**Key Things to Consider in Developing a Code of Ethics**

- Create a team to assist with the process of developing the code (include management and nonmanagement employees from across departments and functions).

- Solicit input from employees from different departments, functions, and regions to compile a list of common questions and answers to include in the code document.

- Make certain that the headings of the code sections can be easily understood by all employees.

- Avoid referencing specific U.S. laws and regulations or those of specific countries, particularly for codes that will be distributed to employees in multiple regions.

- Hold employee group meetings on a complete draft version (including graphics and pictures) of the text, using language that everyone can understand.

- Inform employees that they will receive a copy of the code during an introduction session.

- Let all employees know that they will receive future ethics training that will, in part, cover the important information contained in the code document.

Source: Adapted from William Miller, "Implementing an Organizational Code of Ethics," International Business Ethics Review 7 (Winter 2004), pp. 1, 6–10.

Codes of ethics, policies on ethics, and ethics training programs advance ethical behavior because they prescribe which activities are acceptable and which are not, and they limit the opportunity for misconduct by providing punishments for violations of the rules and standards. Codes and policies on ethics encourage the creation of an ethical culture in the company. According to the National Business Ethics Survey (NBES), employees in organizations that have written codes of conduct and ethics training, ethics offices or hotlines, and systems for reporting are more likely to report misconduct when they observe it. The survey found that a company's ethical culture is the greatest determinant of future misconduct.[38]

The enforcement of ethical codes and policies through rewards and punishments increases the acceptance of ethical standards by employees. For instance, Texas Instruments has a strong code of ethics and a culture of corporate citizenship that encourages employee participation. Every year, the firm releases an ethics and citizenship report and exercises transparency by making it easily accessible through its website. Texas Instruments posts periodic updates on its citizenship activities throughout the year, and a brochure featuring its values and ethical expectations can also be downloaded from its website. The company has been selected by the Ethisphere Institute as one of the world's most ethical companies for seven consecutive years.[39]

One of the most important components of an ethics program is a means through which employees can report observed misconduct anonymously. Although the risk of retaliation is still a major factor in whether an employee will report illegal conduct, the NBES found that whistleblowing has increased in the past few years. Approximately 63 percent of respondents said they reported misconduct when they observed it.[40] **Whistleblowing** occurs when an employee exposes an employer's wrongdoing to outsiders, such as the media or government regulatory agencies. However, more companies are establishing programs to encourage employees to report illegal or unethical practices internally so that they can take steps to remedy problems before they result in legal action or generate negative publicity.

**whistleblowing**
the act of an employee exposing an employer's wrongdoing to outsiders, such as the media or government regulatory agencies

Unfortunately, whistleblowers are often treated negatively in organizations. The government seeks to discourage this practice by rewarding firms that encourage employees to report misconduct—with reduced fines and penalties when violations occur. Congress has also taken steps to close a legislative loophole in whistleblowing legislation that has led to the dismissal of many whistleblowers. In 2010, Congress passed the Dodd-Frank Act, which includes a "whistleblower bounty program." The Securities and Exchange Commission can now award whistleblowers between 10 and 30 percent of monetary sanctions over $1 million. The hope is that incentives will encourage more people to come forward with information regarding corporate misconduct.

The current trend is to move away from legally based ethical initiatives in organizations to cultural- or integrity-based initiatives that make ethics a part of core organizational values. Organizations recognize that effective business ethics programs are good for business performance. Firms that develop higher levels of trust function more efficiently and effectively and avoid damaged company reputations and product images. Organizational ethics initiatives have been supportive of many positive and diverse organizational objectives, such as profitability, hiring, employee satisfaction, and customer loyalty.[41] Conversely, lack of organizational ethics initiatives and the absence of workplace values such as honesty, trust, and integrity can have a negative impact on organizational objectives and employee retention. According to one study, three of the most common factors that executives give for why turnover increases are employee loss of trust in the company, a lack of transparency among company leaders, and unfair employee treatment.[42]

## The Nature of Social Responsibility

LO 2-4

For the purposes of this book, we classify four stages of social responsibility: financial, legal compliance, ethics, and philanthropy (Table 2.7). Another way of categorizing these four dimensions of social responsibility: economic, legal, ethical, and voluntary (including philanthropic).[43] Earning profits is the economic foundation, and complying with the law is the next step. However, a business whose *sole* objective is to maximize profits is not likely to consider its social responsibility, although its activities will probably be legal. (We looked at ethical responsibilities in the first half of this chapter.) Finally, voluntary responsibilities are additional activities that may

| Stages | Examples |
|---|---|
| Stage 1: Financial Viability | Starbucks offers investors a healthy return on investment, including paying dividends. |
| Stage 2: Compliance with Legal and Regulatory Requirements | Starbucks specifies in its code of conduct that payments made to foreign government officials must be lawful according to the laws of the United States and the foreign country. |
| Stage 3: Ethics, Principles, and Values | Starbucks offers healthcare benefits to part-time employees and supports coffee growers by offering them fair prices. |
| Stage 4: Philanthropic Activities | Starbucks created the Starbucks Foundation to award grants to eligible nonprofits and to give back to their communities. |

**TABLE 2.7**
**Social Responsibility Requirements**

**corporate citizenship**
the extent to which businesses meet the legal, ethical, economic, and voluntary responsibilities placed on them by their stakeholders

not be required but which promote human welfare or goodwill. Legal and economic concerns have long been acknowledged in business, but voluntary and ethical issues are more recent concerns.

**Corporate citizenship** is the extent to which businesses meet the legal, ethical, economic, and voluntary responsibilities placed on them by their various stakeholders. It involves the activities and organizational processes adopted by businesses to meet their social responsibilities. A commitment to corporate citizenship by a firm indicates a strategic focus on fulfilling the social responsibilities expected of it by its stakeholders. For example, CVS is attempting to demonstrate corporate citizenship by eliminating tobacco products from its pharmacies. Although this will cost the firm $2 billion in sales, CVS believes it is contradictory to market itself as a health care services business while still selling a dangerous product.[44] Corporate citizenship involves action and measurement of the extent to which a firm embraces the corporate citizenship philosophy and then follows through by implementing citizenship and social responsibility initiatives. One of the major corporate citizenship issues is the focus on preserving the environment. The majority of people agree that climate change is a global emergency, but there is no agreement on how to solve the problem.[45] Another example of a corporate citizenship issue might be animal rights—an issue that is important to many stakeholders. As the organic and local foods movements grow and become more profitable, more and more stakeholders are calling for more humane practices in factory farms as well.[46] Large factory farms are where most Americans get their meat, but some businesses are looking at more animal-friendly options in response to public outcry.

Part of the answer to the climate change crisis is alternative energy such as solar, wind, bio-fuels, and hydro applications. The drive for alternative fuels such as ethanol from corn has added new issues such as food price increases and food shortages. More than 2 billion consumers earn less than $2 a day in wages. Sharply increased food costs have led to riots and government policies to restrict trade in basic commodities such as rice, corn, and soybeans.[47]

To respond to these developments, most companies are introducing eco-friendly products and marketing efforts. Netherlands-based Royal Philips has released its second generation of 75-watt and 100-watt LED equivalent light bulbs. To demonstrate their sustainability, these bulbs have been ENERGY STAR certified. LEDs are a more sustainable alternative to incandescent light bulbs, but they are more costly to the consumer. In its desires to make adoption easier for consumers, Philips offered rebates of up to $10 per light bulb.[48] However, although 69 percent of consumers say it is all right for a firm not to be environmentally perfect as long as it is honest, 78 percent claim that they will boycott firms caught making misleading environmental claims.[49] This is because many businesses are promoting themselves as green-conscious and concerned about the environment without actually making the necessary commitments to environmental health.

The Ethisphere Institute selects an annual list of the world's most ethical companies based on the following criteria: corporate citizenship and responsibility; corporate governance; innovation that contributes to the public well-being; industry leadership; executive leadership and tone from the top; legal, regulatory, and reputation track record; and internal systems and ethics/compliance program.[50] Table 2.8 shows 26 from that list.

Although the concept of social responsibility is receiving more and more attention, it is still not universally accepted. Table 2.9 lists some of the arguments for and against social responsibility.

**connect**

Need help Understanding Social Responsibility? Visit your Connect ebook video tab for a brief animated explanation.

| | |
|---|---|
| L'OREAL | eBay |
| Starbucks Coffee Company | Hospital Corporation of America (HCA) |
| Marks and Spencer | Xerox Corporation |
| General Electric Company | Eaton |
| T-Mobile USA Inc. | Cummins |
| PepsiCo | Ford Motor Company |
| ManpowerGroup | Google Inc. |
| Colgate-Palmolive Company | Gap, Inc. |
| International Paper | Texas Instruments Incorporated |
| Adobe Systems Incorporated | Waste Management |
| UPS | Kellogg Company |
| Accenture | Aflac Incorporated |
| Salesforce.com | Safeway Inc. |

**TABLE 2.8**
**A Selection of the World's Most Ethical Companies**

Source: "2014 World's Most Ethical Companies—Honorees," Ethisphere, *http://ethisphere.com/worlds-most-ethical/wme-honorees/ (accessed April 7, 2014).*

**TABLE 2.9**
**The Arguments For and Against Social Responsibility**

**For:**

1. Business helped to create many of the social problems that exist today, so it should play a significant role in solving them, especially in the areas of pollution reduction and cleanup.

2. Businesses should be more responsible because they have the financial and technical resources to help solve social problems.

3. As members of society, businesses should do their fair share to help others.

4. Socially responsible decision making by businesses can prevent increased government regulation.

5. Social responsibility is necessary to ensure economic survival: If businesses want educated and healthy employees, customers with money to spend, and suppliers with quality goods and services in years to come, they must take steps to help solve the social and environmental problems that exist today.

**Against:**

1. It sidetracks managers from the primary goal of business—earning profits. Every dollar donated to social causes or otherwise spent on society's problems is a dollar less for owners and investors.

2. Participation in social programs gives businesses greater power, perhaps at the expense of particular segments of society.

3. Some people question whether business has the expertise needed to assess and make decisions about social problems.

4. Many people believe that social problems are the responsibility of government agencies and officials, who can be held accountable by voters.

## Social Responsibility Issues

As with ethics, managers consider social responsibility on a daily basis. Among the many social issues that managers must consider are their firms' relations with owners and stockholders, employees, consumers, the environment, and the community. For example, Indra Nooyi, CEO of PepsiCo, believes that companies must embrace "purpose," not just for financial results, but also for the imprint they leave on society. She goes on to say that stakeholders, including employees, consumers, and regulators, "will leave no doubt that performance without purpose is not a long-term sustainable formula."[51]

Social responsibility is a dynamic area with issues changing constantly in response to society's demands. There is much evidence that social responsibility is associated with improved business performance. Consumers are refusing to buy from businesses that receive publicity about misconduct. A number of studies have found a direct relationship between social responsibility and profitability, as well as a link that exists between employee commitment and customer loyalty—two major concerns of any firm trying to increase profits.[52] This section highlights a few of the many social responsibility issues that managers face; as managers become aware of and work toward the solution of current social problems, new ones will certainly emerge.

**Relations with Owners and Stockholders.**    Businesses must first be responsible to their owners, who are primarily concerned with earning a profit or a return on their investment in a company. In a small business, this responsibility is fairly easy to fulfill because the owner(s) personally manages the business or knows the managers well. In larger businesses, particularly corporations owned by thousands of stockholders, ensuring responsibility becomes a more difficult task.

A business's obligations to its owners and investors, as well as to the financial community at large, include maintaining proper accounting procedures, providing all relevant information to investors about the current and projected performance of the firm, and protecting the owners' rights and investments. In short, the business must maximize the owners' investments in the firm.

**Employee Relations.**    Another issue of importance to a business is its responsibilities to employees. Without employees, a business cannot carry out its goals. Employees expect businesses to provide a safe workplace, pay them adequately for their work, and keep them informed of what is happening in their company. They want employers to listen to their grievances and treat them fairly. For instance, after months of negotiations, Safeway and Giant Food supermarkets agreed to a three-year agreement with the United Food & Commercial Workers union to continue providing health care benefits and pensions to workers. However, the decision did not come easily. The union nearly organized a worker strike when the stores could not agree on a new contract, especially as there was talk that the supermarkets were considering eliminating health care benefits for part-time workers and spouses. The agreement with the union will likely contribute to higher morale among employees.[53]

Congress has passed several laws regulating safety in the workplace, many of which are enforced by the Occupational Safety and Health Administration (OSHA). Labor unions have also made significant contributions to achieving safety in the workplace and improving wages and benefits. Most organizations now recognize that the safety and satisfaction of their employees are critical ingredients in their success, and many strive to go beyond what is legally expected of them. Healthy, satisfied employees also supply more than just labor to their employers. Employers are beginning to realize the importance of obtaining input from even the lowest-level employees to help the company reach its objectives.

A major social responsibility for business is providing equal opportunities for all employees regardless of their sex, age, race, religion, or nationality. Women and minorities have been slighted in the past in terms of education, employment, and advancement opportunities; additionally, many of their needs have not been addressed by business. Discrimination still occurs in business. The Equal Employment Opportunity Commission (EEOC) filed a class age discrimination lawsuit against Ruby Tuesday for discriminating against employees 40 years or older in several of its locations. Ruby Tuesday paid $575,000 and committed toward audits and better training as part of the settlement.[54] Women, who continue to bear most child-rearing responsibilities, often experience conflict between those responsibilities and their duties as employees. Consequently, day care has become a major employment issue for women, and more companies are providing day care facilities as part of their effort to recruit and advance women in the workforce. In addition, companies are considering alternative scheduling such as flex-time and job sharing to accommodate employee concerns. Telecommuting has grown significantly over the past 5 to 10 years as well. Many Americans today believe business has a social obligation to provide special opportunities for women and minorities to improve their standing in society.

**Consumer Relations.**    A critical issue in business today is business's responsibility to customers, who look to business to provide them with satisfying, safe products and to respect their rights as consumers. The activities that independent individuals, groups, and organizations undertake to protect their rights as consumers are known as **consumerism.** To achieve their objectives, consumers and their advocates write letters to companies, lobby government agencies, make public service announcements, and boycott companies whose activities they deem irresponsible.

**consumerism**
the activities that independent individuals, groups, and organizations undertake to protect their rights as consumers

Many of the desires of those involved in the consumer movement have a foundation in John F. Kennedy's 1962 consumer bill of rights, which highlighted four rights. The *right to safety* means that a business must not knowingly sell anything that could result in personal injury or harm to consumers. Defective or dangerous products erode public confidence in the ability of business to serve society. They also result in expensive litigation that ultimately increases the cost of products for all consumers. The right to safety also means businesses must provide a safe place for consumers to shop.

The *right to be informed* gives consumers the freedom to review complete information about a product before they buy it. This means that detailed information about ingredients, risks, and instructions for use are to be printed on labels and packages. When companies mislead consumers about the benefits of their products, then they infringe on consumers' rights to be informed. American Express Corporation paid $76 million to settle allegations that it had misled consumers about the benefits of its identity-theft protection add-on services.[55] The *right to choose* ensures that consumers have access to a variety of goods and services at competitive prices. The assurance of both satisfactory quality and service at a fair price is also a part of the consumer's right to choose. The *right to be heard* assures consumers that their interests will receive full and sympathetic consideration when the government formulates policy. It also ensures the fair treatment of consumers who voice complaints about a purchased product.

The role of the Federal Trade Commission's Bureau of Consumer Protection exists to protect consumers against unfair, deceptive, or fraudulent practices. The bureau, which enforces a variety of consumer protection laws, is divided into five divisions. The Division of Enforcement monitors legal compliance and investigates violations of

The National Hockey League's NHL Green iniatiative partners with organizations to contribute toward improving the environment.

laws, including unfulfilled holiday delivery promises by online shopping sites, employment opportunities fraud, scholarship scams, misleading advertising for health care products, and more.

**Sustainability Issues.**    Most people probably associate the term *environment* with nature, including wildlife, trees, oceans, and mountains. Until the 20th century, people generally thought of the environment solely in terms of how these resources could be harnessed to satisfy their needs for food, shelter, transportation, and recreation. As the earth's population swelled throughout the 20th century, however, humans began to use more and more of these resources and, with technological advancements, to do so with ever-greater efficiency. Although these conditions have resulted in a much-improved standard of living, they come with a cost. Plant and animal species, along with wildlife habitats, are disappearing at an accelerated rate, while pollution has rendered the atmosphere of some cities a gloomy haze. How to deal with these issues has become a major concern for business and society in the 21st century.

Although the scope of the word *sustainability* is broad, in this book we discuss the term from a strategic business perspective. Thus, we define **sustainability** as conducting activities in such a way as to provide for the long-term well-being of the natural environment, including all biological entities. Sustainability involves the interaction among nature and individuals, organizations, and business strategies and includes the assessment and improvement of business strategies, economic sectors, work practices, technologies, and lifestyles, so that they maintain the health of the natural environment. In recent years, business has played a significant role in adapting, using, and maintaining the quality of sustainability.

Environmental protection emerged as a major issue in the 20th century in the face of increasing evidence that pollution, uncontrolled use of natural resources, and population growth were putting increasing pressure on the long-term sustainability of these resources. Governments around the globe responded with environmental protection laws during the 1970s. In recent years, companies have been increasingly incorporating these issues into their overall business strategies. Some nonprofit organizations have stepped forward to provide leadership in gaining the cooperation of diverse groups in responsible environmental activities. For example, the Coalition for Environmentally Responsible Economies (CERES)—a union of businesses, consumer groups, environmentalists, and other stakeholders—has established a set of goals for environmental performance.

In the following section, we examine some of the most significant sustainability and environmental health issues facing business and society today, including pollution and alternative energy.

**sustainability**
conducting activities in a way that allows for the long-term well-being of the natural environment, including all biological entities. Sustainability involves the assessment and improvement of business strategies, economic sectors, work practices, technologies, and lifestyles so that they maintain the health of the natural environment.

**Pollution.**    A major issue in the area of environmental responsibility is pollution. Water pollution results from dumping toxic chemicals and raw sewage into rivers and oceans, oil spills, and the burial of industrial waste in the ground where it may filter into underground water supplies. Fertilizers and insecticides used in farming and grounds maintenance also run off into water supplies with each rainfall. Water pollution problems are especially notable in heavily industrialized areas. Medical waste—such as used syringes, vials of blood, and HIV-contaminated materials—has turned up on beaches in New York, New Jersey, and Massachusetts, as well as other places. Society is demanding that water supplies be clean and healthful to reduce the potential danger from these substances.

Air pollution is usually the result of smoke and other pollutants emitted by manufacturing facilities, as well as carbon monoxide and hydrocarbons emitted by motor vehicles. In addition to the health risks posed by air pollution, when some chemical compounds emitted by manufacturing facilities react with air and rain, acid rain results. Acid rain has contributed to the deaths of many forests and lakes in North America as well as in Europe. Air pollution may also contribute to global warming; as carbon dioxide collects in the earth's atmosphere, it traps the sun's heat and prevents the earth's surface from cooling. It is indisputable that the global surface temperature has been increasing over the past 35 years. Worldwide passenger vehicle ownership has been growing due to rapid industrialization and consumer purchasing power in China, India, and other developing countries with large populations. The most important way to contain climate change is to control carbon emissions. The move to green buildings, higher-mileage cars, and other emissions reductions resulting from better efficiency have the potential to generate up to 50 percent of the reductions needed to keep warming at no more than 28°C above present temperatures—considered the "safe" level.[56] The 2007 U.S. Federal Energy bill raised average fuel economy (CAFE) standards to 35 mpg for cars by 2020, while Europe has the goal of a 40 mpg standard by the same deadline. Because buildings create half of U.S. greenhouse emissions, there is tremendous opportunity to develop conservation measures. For example, some utilities charge more for electricity in peak demand periods, which encourages behavioral changes that reduce consumption. More and more consumers are recognizing the need to protect the planet. Figure 2.3 shows the conservation habits of consumers when they purchase, use, and dispose of products. Although most consumers admit that sustainable products are important and that they bear responsibility for properly using and disposing of the product, many admit that they fail to do this.

**FIGURE 2.3**   **Conservation Behaviors of Consumers**

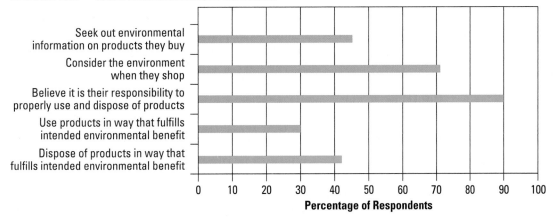

Online survey conducted March 7–10, 2013, by ORC International among a demographically representative sample of 1,068 adults, comprising 552 men and 516 women 18 years of age and older. The margin of error associated with a sample of this size is ±3% at a 95% level of confidence.

Source: Cone Communications, "Cone Releases 2013 Cone Communications Green Gap Trend Tracker," April 2, 2013, www.conecomm.com/2013-green-gap-trend-tracker-1 (accessed February 21, 2014).

## Sustainability Trade-offs: Lighter Vehicles and Higher Prices

As auto manufacturers focus on sustainability, vehicles are evolving into lighter versions of their old selves. Producing vehicles with materials such as aluminum, carbon fiber, and high-strength steel are decreasing the weight of vehicles by about 200 pounds, while still providing the same amount of strength and without increasing the retail price. It is estimated that a vehicle's weight accounts for two-thirds of the energy it uses, and lighter vehicles are expected to cut fuel usage in half. The use of lighter materials also allows for vehicles to be bound with structural adhesives and sealants, which can add rigidity to the body of the vehicle, absorb shock, and potentially provide a safer ride for the customer.

However, there is a downside. As cars become lighter, consumers face higher repair costs when it comes time to repair their environmentally friendly vehicles. These lighter materials are difficult to repair because welding and cutting weaken the surface. For example, customers may have to purchase an entire new panel for the damaged portion of the vehicle, which is more expensive than paying for repair work or replacement parts. Additionally, there have been cases wherein the auto adhesives have melted when reaching certain temperatures. These are some examples of the kinds of trade-offs companies and consumers are facing in the quest to be more sustainable.[57]

### Discussion Questions

1. Discuss some of the trade-offs of having lighter, more sustainable vehicles.
2. Discuss any ethical issues you can identify in this scenario.
3. In light of the negative consequences of producing these vehicles, do you think companies should continue to produce lighter-weight vehicles in the name of sustainability? Why or why not?

Land pollution is tied directly to water pollution because many of the chemicals and toxic wastes that are dumped on the land eventually work their way into the water supply. A study conducted by the Environmental Protection Agency found residues of prescription drugs, soaps, and other contaminants in virtually every waterway in the United States. Effects of these pollutants on humans and wildlife are uncertain, but there is some evidence to suggest that fish and other water-dwellers are starting to suffer serious effects.[58] Land pollution results from the dumping of residential and industrial waste, strip mining, forest fires, and poor forest conservation. In Brazil and other South American countries, rain forests are being destroyed—to make way for farms and ranches, at a cost of the extinction of the many animals and plants (some endangered species) that call the rain forest home. For example, annual deforestation in the Brazilian rainforest encompasses an area about the size of Delaware. The good news is that deforestation rates in Brazil may be decreasing due to new laws against illegal logging.[59] Large-scale deforestation also depletes the oxygen supply available to humans and other animals.

Related to the problem of land pollution is the larger issue of how to dispose of waste in an environmentally responsible manner. Americans discard nearly 7 million tons of plastic bags each year. Hawaii has banned plastic bag use, and California, Delaware, New York, Illinois, Maine, and Rhode Island have adopted reuse, relabel, or recycling programs for plastic bags.[60] Starting in 2014, Los Angeles also banned plastic bag use. Under the new law, shoppers will have to bring their own reusable bags or pay 10 cents for each paper bag. Los Angeles is the biggest city in the United States to ban plastic bag usage so far.[61]

**Alternative Energy.**   With ongoing plans to reduce global carbon emissions, countries and companies alike are looking toward alternative energy sources. Traditional fossil fuels are problematic because of their emissions, but also because stores have been greatly depleted. Foreign fossil fuels are often imported from politically and economically unstable regions, often making it unsafe to conduct business there. However, the United States is becoming an energy powerhouse with its ability to drill for natural gas in large shale reserves. This is allowing the United States to move forward on its goals to reach energy independence. On the other hand, concerns over how these drilling methods are affecting the environment make this a controversial topic.

Solar power is growing in popularity as an alternative to traditional fuel sources, as this solar-power race car demonstrates.

With global warming concerns and rising gas prices, the U.S. government has begun to recognize the need to look toward alternative forms of energy as a source of fuel and electricity. There have been many different ideas as to which form of alternative energy would best suit the United States' energy needs. These sources include wind power, solar power, nuclear power, biofuels, electric cars, and hydro- and geothermal power. As of yet, no "best" form of alternative fuel has been selected to replace gasoline. Additionally, there are numerous challenges with the economic viability of alternative energy sources. For instance, wind and solar power cost significantly more than traditional energy; watts from wind power are estimated to be 290 percent higher than from natural gas, and the costs of solar photovoltaic is estimated to be 230 percent more expensive. Alternative energy will likely require government subsidies to make any significant strides. However, the news for solar power might be getting brighter. First Solar, an Arizona-based manufacturer of solar photovoltaic modules, has rebounded. Heavy competition from Chinese solar manufacturers had eaten up some of First Solar's profits and bankrupted other American solar companies. Yet First Solar's growth prospects appear to be high, reflected in their climbing stock price.[62]

**Response to Environmental Issues.**    Partly in response to federal legislation such as the National Environmental Policy Act of 1969 and partly due to consumer concerns, businesses are responding to environmental issues. Many small and large companies, including Walt Disney Company, Chevron, and Scott Paper, have created an executive position—a vice president of environmental affairs—to help them achieve their business goals in an environmentally responsible manner. Some companies are finding that environmental consciousness can save them money. For example, one San Diego hotel saved more than $40,000 by changing how it uses energy and adopting more energy-saving devices.[63]

Many firms are trying to eliminate wasteful practices, the emission of pollutants, and/or the use of harmful chemicals from their manufacturing processes. Other companies are seeking ways to improve their products. Utility providers, for example, are increasingly supplementing their services with alternative energy sources, including solar, wind, and geothermal power. Environmentalists are concerned that some companies are merely *greenwashing,* or "creating a positive association with environmental issues for an unsuitable product, service, or practice."

In many places, local utility customers can even elect to purchase electricity from green sources—primarily wind power—for a few extra dollars a month. Austin Energy of Austin, Texas, has an award-winning GreenChoice program that includes many small and large businesses among its customers.[65] Indeed, a growing number of businesses and consumers are choosing green power sources where available. New Belgium Brewing Company, the third-largest craft brewer in the United States, is the first all-wind-powered brewery in the country. Many businesses have turned to *recycling,* the reprocessing of materials—aluminum, paper, glass, and some plastic—for reuse. Such efforts to make products, packaging, and processes more environmentally friendly have been labeled "green" business or marketing by the public and media. New Belgium, for instance, started selling aluminum cans of its beers because aluminum is easily recyclable and creates less waste. Lumber products at The Home Depot may carry a seal from the Forest Stewardship Council to indicate that they were harvested from sustainable forests using environmentally friendly methods.[66] Likewise, most Chiquita bananas are certified through the Better Banana Project as having been grown with more environmentally and labor-friendly practices.[67]

It is important to recognize that, with current technology, environmental responsibility requires trade-offs. Society must weigh the huge costs of limiting or eliminating pollution against the health threat posed by the pollution. Environmental responsibility imposes costs on both business and the public. Although people certainly do not want oil fouling beautiful waterways and killing wildlife, they insist on low-cost, readily available gasoline and heating oil. People do not want to contribute to the growing garbage-disposal problem, but they often refuse to pay more for "green" products packaged in an environmentally friendly manner, to recycle as much of their own waste as possible, or to permit the building of additional waste-disposal facilities (the "not in my backyard," or NIMBY, syndrome). Managers must coordinate environmental goals with other social and economic ones.

**Community Relations.**   A final, yet very significant, issue for businesses concerns their responsibilities to the general welfare of the communities and societies in which they operate. Many businesses simply want to make their communities better places for everyone to live and work. The most common way that businesses exercise their community responsibility is through donations to local and national charitable organizations. For example, General Electric employees hold fundraising efforts to raise money for the United Way. Additionally, GE donates 2 percent of its appliance sales from its online GE Appliance Outlet Store to the United Way.[68] Small businesses also give back to their communities. Chattanooga-based coffee retailer Blue Smoke Coffee donates 10 percent of its sales to environmental and humanitarian causes.[69] Even small companies participate in philanthropy through donations and volunteer support of local causes and national charities, such as the Red Cross and the United Way.

# Unemployment

After realizing that the current pool of prospective employees lacks many basic skills necessary to work, many companies have become concerned about the quality of education in the United States. Unemployment has become a significant problem since the onset of the financial crisis in 2008. In the years following, unemployment reached as high as 10 percent in the United States. Although it has fallen to about 7 percent since then, many consumers remain unemployed.[70]

Although most would argue that unemployment is an economic issue, it also carries ethical implications. Protests often occur in areas where unemployment is high, particularly when there seems to be a large gap between rich and poor. In Spain, high rates of unemployment caused unemployed citizens to arrange protests in the capital city of Madrid. Because Spain had received bailout money, international leaders have demanded steep spending cuts and tax rises. This has led to the unemployment of more than 6 million individuals. Spanish citizens protested the spending cuts imposed on them by other countries, feeling like they were unethical because they led to higher unemployment.[71]

Factory closures are another ethical issue because factories usually employ hundreds of workers. Sometimes it is necessary to close a plant due to economic reasons. However, factory closures not only affect individual employees, but their communities as well. When an Electrolux factory moved from Webster City, Iowa, to Juarez, Mexico, the city of 8,000 people lost its main employer. This is having repercussions on other businesses in the area because more unemployed people mean fewer sales.[72]

Thousands of jobs were lost after Blockbuster shuttered its stores.

Another criticism levied against companies involves hiring standards. Studies appear to show that while there are plenty of people unemployed, approximately 35 percent of companies cite employees' lack of experience as to why there are so many unfilled positions. Yet only about 28 percent are investing in more training and development for new hires. While it is important for employees to have certain skills, many feel that businesses must be willing to train employees if they want to fill their vacancies and decrease the unemployment rate.[73]

On the other hand, several businesses are working to reduce unemployment. After becoming frustrated with high unemployment rates, Starbucks founder and CEO Howard Schultz partnered with a national network of community lenders called Opportunity Network to develop Create Jobs for USA. This program provides funding for community businesses with the intent to reduce unemployment in their areas. Starbucks initially donated $5 million to the initiative. Other companies have also made significant contributions, including Banana Republic, Citi, Google Offers, and MasterCard.[74]

Additionally, businesses are beginning to take more responsibility for the hardcore unemployed. These are people who have never had a job or who have been unemployed for a long period of time. Some are mentally or physically handicapped; some are homeless. Organizations such as the National Alliance of Businessmen fund programs to train the hard-core unemployed so that they can find jobs and support themselves. Also, while numerous businesses laid off employees during the last recession, others were praised for their refusal to lay off workers. Boston Consulting Group (BCG), for instance, avoided laying off employees during the recession. As a result, employees at BCG are highly motivated and voted BCG as one of the best companies to work for.[75] Such commitment enhances self-esteem and helps people become productive members of society.

## So You Want a Job in Business Ethics and Social Responsibility

In the words of Kermit the Frog, "It's not easy being green." It may not be easy, but green business opportunities abound. A popular catch phrase, "Green is the new black," indicates how fashionable green business is becoming. Consumers are more in tune with and concerned about green products, policies, and behaviors by companies than ever before. Companies are looking for new hires to help them see their business creatively and bring insights to all aspects of business operations. The American Solar Energy Society estimates that the number of green jobs could rise to 40 million in the United States by 2030. Green business strategies not only give a firm a commercial advantage in the marketplace, but help lead the way toward a greener world. The fight to reduce our carbon footprint in an attempt against climate change has opened up opportunities for renewable energy, recycling, conservation, and increasing overall efficiency in the way resources are used. New businesses that focus on hydro, wind, and solar power are on the rise and will need talented businesspeople to lead them. Carbon emissions' trading is gaining popularity as large corporations and individuals alike seek to lower their footprints. A job in this growing field could be similar to that of a stock trader, or you could lead the search for carbon-efficient companies in which to invest.

In the ethics arena, current trends in business governance strongly support the development of ethics and compliance departments to help guide organizational integrity. This alone is a billion-dollar business, and there are jobs in developing organizational ethics programs, developing company policies, and training employees and management. An entry-level position might be as a communication specialist or trainer for programs in a business ethics department. Eventually there's an opportunity to become an ethics officer that would have typical responsibilities of meeting with employees, the board of directors, and top management to discuss and provide advice about ethics issues in the industry, developing and distributing a code of ethics, creating and maintaining an anonymous, confidential service to answer questions about ethical issues, taking actions on possible ethics code violations, and reviewing and modifying the code of ethics of the organization.

There are also opportunities to help with initiatives to help companies relate social responsibility to stakeholder interests and needs. These jobs could involve coordinating and implementing philanthropic programs that give back to others important to the organization or developing a community volunteering program for employees. In addition to the human relations function, most companies develop programs to assist employees and their families to improve their quality of life. Companies have found that the healthier and happier employees are the more productive they will be in the workforce.

Social responsibility, ethics, and sustainable business practices are not a trend, they are good for business and the bottom line. New industries are being created and old ones are adapting to the new market demands, opening up many varied job opportunities that will lead not only to a paycheck, but also to the satisfaction of making the world a better place.[76]

## Review Your Understanding

### Define business ethics and social responsibility and examine their importance.

Business ethics refers to principles and standards that define acceptable business conduct. Acceptable business behavior is defined by customers, competitors, government regulators, interest groups, the public, and each individual's personal moral principles and values. Social responsibility is the obligation an organization assumes to maximize its positive impact and minimize its negative impact on society. Socially responsible businesses win the trust and respect of their employees, customers, and society and, in the long run, increase profits. Ethics is important in business because it builds trust and confidence in business relationships. Unethical actions may result in negative publicity, declining sales, and even legal action.

### Detect some of the ethical issues that may arise in business.

An ethical issue is an identifiable problem, situation, or opportunity requiring a person or organization to choose from among several actions that must be evaluated as right or wrong. Ethical issues can be categorized in the context of their relation with conflicts of interest, fairness and honesty, communications, and business associations.

### Specify how businesses can promote ethical behavior by employees.

Businesses can promote ethical behavior by employees by limiting their opportunity to engage in misconduct. Formal codes of ethics, ethical policies, and ethics training programs reduce the incidence of unethical behavior by informing employees what is expected of them and providing punishments for those who fail to comply.

### Explain the four dimensions of social responsibility.

The four dimensions of social responsibility are economic or financial viability (being profitable), legal (obeying the law), ethical (doing what is right, just, and fair), and philanthropic, or voluntary (being a good corporate citizen).

**Debate an organization's social responsibilities to owners, employees, consumers, the environment, and the community.**

Businesses must maintain proper accounting procedures, provide all relevant information about the performance of the firm to investors, and protect the owners' rights and investments. In relations with employees, businesses are expected to provide a safe workplace, pay employees adequately for their work, and treat them fairly. Consumerism refers to the activities undertaken by independent individuals, groups, and organizations to protect their rights as consumers. Increasingly, society expects businesses to take greater responsibility for the environment, especially with regard to animal rights, as well as water, air, land, and noise pollution. Many businesses engage in activities to make the communities in which they operate better places for everyone to live and work.

**Evaluate the ethics of a business's decision.**

"Solve the Dilemma" on page 65 presents an ethical dilemma at Checkers Pizza. Using the material presented in this chapter, you should be able to analyze the ethical issues present in the dilemma, evaluate Barnard's plan, and develop a course of action for the firm.

## Revisit the World of Business

1. Describe the ethical issue.
2. What are some of the potential negative effects of triclosan?
3. What impact could the FDA's proposal have on soap manufacturers?

## Learn the Terms

| | | |
|---|---|---|
| bribes   40 | corporate citizenship   52 | sustainability   56 |
| business ethics   36 | ethical issue   39 | whistleblowing   50 |
| codes of ethics   49 | plagiarism   48 | |
| consumerism   55 | social responsibility   36 | |

## Check Your Progress

1. Define business ethics. Who determines whether a business activity is ethical? Is unethical conduct always illegal?
2. Distinguish between ethics and social responsibility.
3. Why has ethics become so important in business?
4. What is an ethical issue? What are some of the ethical issues named in your text? Why are they ethical issues?
5. What is a code of ethics? How can one reduce unethical behavior in business?
6. List and discuss the arguments for and against social responsibility by business (Table 2.9). Can you think of any additional arguments (for or against)?
7. What responsibilities does a business have toward its employees?
8. What responsibilities does business have with regard to the environment? What steps have been taken by some responsible businesses to minimize the negative impact of their activities on the environment?
9. What are a business's responsibilities toward the community in which it operates?

## Get Involved

1. Discuss some recent examples of businesses engaging in unethical practices. Classify these practices as issues of conflict of interest, fairness and honesty, communications, or business relationships. Why do you think the businesses chose to behave unethically? What actions might the businesses have taken?
2. Discuss with your class some possible methods of improving ethical standards in business. Do you think that business should regulate its own activities or that the federal government should establish and enforce ethical standards? How do you think businesspeople feel?
3. Find some examples of socially responsible businesses in newspapers or business journals. Explain why you believe their actions are socially responsible. Why do you think the companies chose to act as they did?

# Build Your Skills

## Making Decisions about Ethical Issues

### Background

The merger of Lockheed and Martin Marietta created Lockheed Martin, the number-one company in the defense industry—an industry that includes such companies as Raytheon and Northrop Grumman.

You and the rest of the class are managers at Lockheed Martin Corporation, Orlando, Florida. You are getting ready to do the group exercise in an ethics training session. The training instructor announces you will be playing *Gray Matters: The Ethics Game.* You are told that *Gray Matters,* which was prepared for your company's employees, is also played at 41 universities, including Harvard University, and at 65 other companies. Although there are 55 scenarios in *Gray Matters,* you will have time during this session to complete only the four scenarios that your group draws from the stack of cards.[77]

### Task

Form into groups of four to six managers and appoint a group leader who will lead a discussion of the case, obtain a consensus answer to the case, and be the one to report the group's answers to the instructor. You will have five minutes to reach each decision, after which time, the instructor will give the point values and rationale for each choice. Then you will have five minutes for the next case, etc., until all four cases have been completed. Keep track of your group's score for each case; the winning team will be the group scoring the most points.

Since this game is designed to reflect life, you may believe that some cases lack clarity or that some of your choices are not as precise as you would have liked. Also, some cases have only one solution, while others have more than one solution. Each choice is assessed to reflect which answer is the most correct. **Your group's task is to select only one option in each case.**

---

### 4

#### Mini-Case

For several months now, one of your colleagues has been slacking off, and you are getting stuck doing the work. You think it is unfair. What do you do?

#### Potential Answers

A. Recognize this as an opportunity for you to demonstrate how capable you are.

B. Go to your supervisor and complain about this unfair workload.

C. Discuss the problem with your colleague in an attempt to solve the problem without involving others.

D. Discuss the problem with the human resources department.

---

### 7

#### Mini-Case

You are aware that a fellow employee uses drugs on the job. Another friend encourages you to confront the person instead of informing the supervisor. What do you do?

#### Potential Answers

A. You speak to the alleged user and encourage him to get help.

B. You elect to tell your supervisor that you suspect an employee is using drugs on the job.

C. You confront the alleged user and tell him either to quit using drugs or you will "turn him in."

D. Report the matter to employee assistance.

---

### 36

#### Mini-Case

You work for a company that has implemented a policy of a smoke-free environment. You discover employees smoking in the restrooms of the building. You also smoke and don't like having to go outside to do it. What do you do?

#### Potential Answers

A. You ignore the situation.

B. You confront the employees and ask them to stop.

C. You join them, but only occasionally.

D. You contact your ethics or human resources representative and ask him or her to handle the situation.

---

### 40

#### Mini-Case

Your co-worker is copying company-purchased software and taking it home. You know a certain program costs $400, and you have been saving for a while to buy it. What do you do?

#### Potential Answers

A. You figure you can copy it too since nothing has ever happened to your co-worker.

B. You tell your co-worker he can't legally do this.

C. You report the matter to the ethics office.

D. You mention this to your supervisor.

## Solve the Dilemma

### Customer Privacy

 Checkers Pizza was one of the first to offer home delivery service, with overwhelming success. However, the major pizza chains soon followed suit, taking away Checkers's competitive edge. Jon Barnard, Checkers's founder and co-owner, needed a new gimmick to beat the competition. He decided to develop a computerized information database that would make Checkers the most efficient competitor and provide insight into consumer buying behavior at the same time. Under the system, telephone customers were asked their phone number; if they had ordered from Checkers before, their address and previous order information came up on the computer screen.

After successfully testing the new system, Barnard put the computerized order network in place in all Checkers outlets. After three months of success, he decided to give an award to the family that ate the most Checkers pizza. Through the tracking system, the company identified the biggest customer, who had ordered a pizza every weekday for the past three months (63 pizzas). The company put together a program to surprise the family with an award, free-food certificates, and a news story announcing the award. As Barnard began to plan for the event, however, he began to think that maybe the family might not want all the attention and publicity.

#### Discussion Questions

1.  What are some of the ethical issues in giving customers an award for consumption behavior without notifying them first?
2.  Do you see this as a potential violation of privacy? Explain.
3.  How would you handle the situation if you were Barnard?

## Build Your Business Plan

### Business Ethics and Social Responsibility

 Think about which industry you are considering competing in with your good/service. Is there any kind of questionable practices in the way the product has been traditionally sold? Produced? Advertised? Have there been any recent accusations regarding safety within the industry? What about any environmental concerns?

For example, if you are thinking of opening a lawn care business, you need to be thinking about what possible effects the chemicals you are using will have on the client and the environment. You have a responsibility to keep your customers safe and healthy. You also have the social responsibility to let the community know of any damaging effect you may be directly or indirectly responsible for.

## See for Yourself Videocase

### The Challenge of Building Trust in Business

 Corporate scandals, a growing awareness of environmental issues, and the last global recession have greatly altered the public's perspective of corporate America. Gone are the days in which consumers blindly trusted company publicity and rhetoric. The public's trust in business has been shattered, and many companies have a long way to go to earn it back.

The Arthur Page Society and the Business Roundtable Institute for Corporate Ethics are dedicated to corporate accountability and ethics. The organizations released a study addressing Americans' mistrust of business and how corporations can begin to win back the hearts and minds of consumers. The study, entitled "The Dynamics of Public Trust in Business—Emerging Opportunities for Leaders," shows that public trust in business has reached a low point. As the economy begins to recover, trust in business has increased. However, trust of business continues to be a serious challenge for businesses to overcome. This presents major difficulties for businesses because trust is the glue that holds relationships together.

A major issue appears to be the imbalance of power. Many consumers are still angry over business scandals and unemployment rates while corporate management still makes huge profits. The government defended corporate bailouts as a way to keep large companies from failing (which could have worsened the recession). Most of the money has since been paid back, and the government has made a profit. Unemployment has decreased in the last few years, although among young people it is still 15 percent. It is believed that if youth unemployment returned to pre-recession rates, the federal government would recoup $7.8 billion.

Distrust of business is not limited to the United States. According to the Edelman Trust Barometer, 54 percent of global consumers indicate that they trust business. Financial service institutions and banks have the lowest rankings in consumer trust worldwide, at 51 percent. More recent scandals at J.P. Morgan Stanley, HSBC, and British financial services firm Barclays continue to keep trust in this sector low.

Although the Arthur Page Society and the Business Roundtable see their report as a way to start a national dialogue, the report does offer a series of suggestions for businesses. First and foremost, the balance of power must be equalized. Companies must focus on creating mutual value and leaders must try to gain and retain trust. The study also suggests that corporations create quality goods/services, sell goods/services at fair prices, create and maintain positive employment practices, give investors a fair return, remain active in social responsibility, and create transparency.

Most firms have not been involved in scandals or misconduct. In fact, most companies operate in an ethical and socially responsible manner. Unfortunately, the public sees reports of misconduct in a few businesses and generalizes the misconduct to all businesses. Nevertheless, companies need to communicate their values and maintain responsible conduct. Another example involves the growing public concern regarding how businesses affect the environment—investors want details on a business's impact and what that business is doing to be more sustainable. As the public fights to make its desires known regarding business behavior, businesses that sincerely want to help the world are receiving some help. Maryland, Vermont, New York, California, and three other states have made "benefit corporations" legal. These corporations must make their values public, report yearly on their socially beneficial behavior, and agree to third-party audits of their social responsibility actions. Acquiring this designation requires the approval of more than half a company's shareholders. Companies may also establish themselves as B corporations, which certifies their socially responsible focus. It is entirely possible for businesses to regain public trust, but it means a change in values for many businesses in today's corporate America.[78]

### Discussion Questions

1. What are some of the reasons cited in the Arthur Page Society and the Business Roundtable Institute for Corporate Ethics report for public distrust of corporations?

2. What are some of the recommendations made by the report? Can you think of any other recommendations to give companies on how to behave more ethically?

3. What are the benefits of being perceived as an ethical company? What are the downsides of having a reputation for ethical misconduct?

**You can find the related video in the Video Library in Connect. Ask your instructor how you can access Connect.**

## Team Exercise

Sam Walton, founder of Walmart, had an early strategy for growing his business related to pricing. The "Opening Price Point" strategy used by Walton involved offering the introductory product in a product line at the lowest point in the market. For example, a minimally equipped microwave oven would sell for less than anyone else in town could sell the same unit. The strategy was that if consumers saw a product, such as the microwave, and saw it as a good value, they would assume that all of the microwaves were good values. Walton also noted that most people don't buy the entry-level product; they want more features and capabilities and often trade up.

Form teams and assign the role of defending this strategy or casting this strategy as an unethical act. Present your thoughts on either side of the issue.

carries the domestic firm's name. A joint venture is a partnership in which companies from different countries agree to share the costs and operation of the business. The purchase of overseas production and marketing facilities is direct investment. Outsourcing, a form of direct investment, involves transferring manufacturing to countries where labor and supplies are cheap. Offshoring is the relocation of business processes by a company or subsidiary to another country; it differs from outsourcing because the company retains control of the offshored processes. A multinational corporation is one that operates on a worldwide scale, without significant ties to any one nation or region.

### Contrast two basic strategies used in international business.

Companies typically use one of two basic strategies in international business. A multinational strategy customizes products, promotion, and distribution according to cultural, technological, regional, and national differences. A global strategy (globalization) standardizes products (and, as much as possible, their promotion and distribution) for the whole world, as if it were a single entity.

### Assess the opportunities and problems facing a small business that is considering expanding into international markets.

"Solve the Dilemma" on page 111 presents a small business considering expansion into international markets. Based on the material provided in the chapter, analyze the business's position, evaluating specific markets, anticipating problems, and exploring methods of international involvement.

## Revisit the World of Business

1. Why does Xiamoi appeal to the average Chinese consumer?

2. Why might Xiamoi's cool, hip image in China be tarnished if it goes global?

3. Describe the barriers Xiamoi will likely face as it expands into the United States.

## Learn the Terms

absolute advantage   85
Asia-Pacific Economic Cooperation (APEC)   99
Association of Southeast Asian Nations (ASEAN)   100
balance of payments   86
balance of trade   86
cartel   93
comparative advantage   85
contract manufacturing   104
countertrade agreements   102
direct investment   105
dumping   92
embargo   92

European Union (EU)   97
exchange controls   91
exchange rate   88
exporting   86
franchising   103
General Agreement on Tariffs and Trade (GATT)   95
global strategy (globalization)   107
import tariff   90
importing   86
infrastructure   88
international business   84
International Monetary Fund (IMF)   101
joint venture   105

licensing   103
multinational corporation (MNC)   105
multinational strategy   107
North American Free Trade Agreement (NAFTA)   96
offshoring   104
outsourcing   85
quota   91
strategic alliance   105
trade deficit   86
trading company   103
World Bank   101
World Trade Organization (WTO)   95

## Check Your Progress

1. Distinguish between an absolute advantage and a comparative advantage. Cite an example of a country that has an absolute advantage and one with a comparative advantage.

2. What effect does devaluation have on a nation's currency? Can you think of a country that has devaluated or revaluated its currency? What have been the results?

3. What effect does a country's economic development have on international business?

4. How do political issues affect international business?

5. What is an import tariff? A quota? Dumping? How might a country use import tariffs and quotas to control its balance of trade and payments? Why can dumping result in the imposition of tariffs and quotas?

6. How do social and cultural differences create barriers to international trade? Can you think of any additional social or cultural barriers (other than those mentioned in this chapter) that might inhibit international business?

7. Explain how a countertrade agreement can be considered a trade promoter. How does the World Trade Organization encourage trade?

8. At what levels might a firm get involved in international business? What level requires the least commitment of resources? What level requires the most?

9. Compare and contrast licensing, franchising, contract manufacturing, and outsourcing.

10. Compare multinational and global strategies. Which is better? Under what circumstances might each be used?

## Get Involved

1. If the United States were to impose additional tariffs on cars imported from Japan, what would happen to the price of Japanese cars sold in the United States? What would happen to the price of American cars? What action might Japan take to continue to compete in the U.S. automobile market?

2. Although NAFTA has been controversial, it has been a positive factor for U.S. firms desiring to engage in international business. What industries and specific companies have the greatest potential for opening stores in Canada and Mexico? What opportunities exist for small businesses that cannot afford direct investment in Mexico and Canada?

3. Identify a local company that is active in international trade. What is its level of international business involvement and why? Analyze the threats and opportunities it faces in foreign markets, as well as its strengths and weaknesses in meeting those challenges. Based on your analysis, make some recommendations for the business's future involvement in international trade. (Your instructor may ask you to share your report with the class.)

## Build Your Skills

### Global Awareness

**Background**

As American businesspeople travel the globe, they encounter and must quickly adapt to a variety of cultural norms quite different from the United States. When encountering individuals from other parts of the world, the best attitude to adopt is "Here is my way. Now what is yours?" The more you see that you are part of a complex world and that your culture is different from, not better than, others, the better you will communicate and the more effective you will be in a variety of situations. It takes time, energy, understanding, and tolerance to learn about and appreciate other cultures. Naturally you're more comfortable doing things the way you've always done them. Remember, however, that this fact will also be true of the people from other cultures with whom you are doing business.

**Task**

You will "travel the globe" by answering questions related to some of the cultural norms that are found in other countries. Form groups of four to six class members and determine the answers to the following questions. Your instructor has the answer key, which will allow you to determine your group's Global Awareness IQ, which is based on a maximum score of 100 points (10 points per question).

Match the country with the cultural descriptor provided.

| | |
|---|---|
| **A.** Saudi Arabia | **F.** China |
| **B.** Japan | **G.** Greece |
| **C.** Great Britain | **H.** Korea |
| **D.** Germany | **I.** India |
| **E.** Venezuela | **J.** Mexico |

_____ 1. When people in this country table a motion, they want to discuss it. In America, "to table a motion" means to put off discussion.

_____ 2. In this country, special forms of speech called *keigo* convey status among speakers. When talking with a person in this country, one should know the person's rank. People from this country will not initiate a conversation without a formal introduction.

_____ 3. People from this country pride themselves on enhancing their image by keeping others waiting.

_____ 4. When writing a business letter, people in this country like to provide a great deal of background information and detail before presenting their main points.

_____ 5. For a man to inquire about another man's wife (even a general question about how she is doing) is considered very offensive in this country.

**6.** When in this country, you are expected to negotiate the price on goods you wish to purchase.

**7.** While North Americans want to decide the main points at a business meeting and leave the details for later, people in this country need to have all details decided before the meeting ends to avoid suspicion and distrust.

**8.** Children in this country learn from a very early age to look down respectfully when talking to those of higher status.

**9.** In this country the husband is the ruler of the household, and the custom is to keep the women hidden.

**10.** Many businesspeople from the United States experience frustration because yes does not always mean the same thing in other cultures. For example, the word *yes* in this country means, "OK, I want to respect you and not offend you." It does not necessarily show agreement.

## Solve the Dilemma

### Global Expansion or Business as Usual?

 Audiotech Electronics, founded in 1959 by a father and son, currently operates a 35,000-square-foot factory with 75 employees. The company produces control consoles for television and radio stations and recording studios. It is involved in every facet of production—designing the systems, installing the circuits in its computer boards, and even manufacturing and painting the metal cases housing the consoles. The company's products are used by all the major broadcast and cable networks. The firm's newest products allow television correspondents to simultaneously hear and communicate with their counterparts in different geographic locations. Audiotech has been very successful meeting its customers' needs efficiently.

Audiotech sales have historically been strong in the United States, but recently, growth is stagnating. Even though Audiotech is a small, family-owned firm, it believes it should evaluate and consider global expansion.

### Discussion Questions

**1.** What are the key issues that need to be considered in determining global expansion?

**2.** What are some of the unique problems that a small business might face in global expansion that larger firms would not?

**3.** Should Audiotech consider a joint venture? Should it hire a sales force of people native to the countries it enters?

## Build Your Business Plan

### Business in a Borderless World

 Think about the good/service you are contemplating for your business plan. If it is an already established good or service, try to find out if the product is currently being sold internationally. If not, can you identify opportunities to do so in the future? What countries do you think would respond most favorably to your product? What problems would you encounter if you attempted to export your product to those countries?

If you are thinking of creating a new good or service for your business plan, think about the possibility of eventually marketing that product in another country. What countries or areas of the world do you think would be most responsive to your product?

Are there countries the United States has trade agreements or alliances with that would make your entry into the market easier? What would be the economic, social, cultural, and technological barriers you would have to recognize before entering the prospective country(ies)? Think about the specific cultural differences that would have to be taken into consideration before entering the prospective country.

# See for Yourself Videocase

## Walt Disney around the Globe

Mickey Mouse has been a beloved American icon since the 1930s. The success of this and other Disney characters helped to build Disney theme parks; first in Anaheim, California, in 1955 and then in Orlando, Florida, 16 years later. For decades, tourists from all over the globe traveled in droves to California or Florida to experience the "happiest place on earth." What could be more natural for Disney than to introduce Mickey around the globe with international parks?

Disneyland first opened on the international front in Tokyo, Japan, in 1983. Ten years later, Disney brought the magic to Paris, France. Finally, in 2005, Disneyland opened its gates in Hong Kong, China. Global expansion is tricky for any business. There are many challenges to overcome, such as economic, legal, political, social, and cultural barriers. While Mickey may be recognized and loved around the world, this does not mean that duplicating American parks in other countries will be a success.

Perhaps the greatest challenge for Disney when entering new international markets has been how to handle cultural differences. Euro Disney (later renamed Disneyland Resort Paris) opened near Paris, France, in 1992 to fanfare and problems. Many well-known French citizens and labor unions vocally opposed the park because they felt that it was wrong to allow a symbol of American culture to become a focal point in France. Attendance for the first three years was well below expectations, causing grave financial difficulties. Finally, in 1995, the park experienced a turnaround. Financial restructuring helped the park achieve profitability. New attractions, lower admission prices, renaming the park as Disneyland Paris, and a marketing campaign increased attendance. The park, now the number-one tourist attraction in Europe with nearly 15 million visitors per year, continues to expand in anticipation of future growth. The theme park has attracted more than 250 million visitors in its 20-year history.

Having learned from its experience in France, The Walt Disney Company entered its venture in Hong Kong with an eye to embracing and honoring local culture. The company had learned to be sensitive to cultural variations in events, trends, and cuisine. The parks must embrace local culture while staying true to the Disney message. To this end, Disney hired a feng shui consultant to assist with the layout of the Hong Kong park. The fourth floor was eliminated at all hotels because of the cultural belief that the number four is bad luck. One of the Hong Kong Disneyland ballrooms measures 888 square meters because eight signifies wealth in Chinese culture. Even with this attention to detail, Hong Kong Disneyland's first years have been rough, with attendance far below projections and protestors raising cultural and social objections. A major complaint among guests has been that the park is small. Over the next decade, the company plans to invest half a billion dollars in expansion efforts. Disney is also building another theme park in Shanghai, China. This park will be two to three times as large as Hong Kong Disney and is set to be completed in 2016.

While some locals continue to protest Disney's presence, there are benefits to allowing a global company like Disney to enter foreign markets. Disney theme parks attract both local and global tourists, which can be a major stimulus to the local economy. For example, Hong Kong expects that Hong Kong Disneyland will bring more than 50,000 jobs to the city between 2005 and 2025. Experts predict that the park will bring $19 billion (U.S.) to the local economy during the park's first 40 years. It is likely that, with expansion and further refinement, Hong Kong Disneyland will be a success in the long run. Problems in France and Hong Kong have not deterred The Walt Disney Company from further global expansion. Hopefully, the company has learned that it must pay close attention to cultural and social variances in global markets in order to succeed.[87]

### Discussion Questions

1.  What led The Walt Disney Company to believe that its theme parks would be successful internationally?

2.  What stumbling blocks did Disney encounter at their France and Hong Kong theme parks?

3.  What are some of the factors complicating international expansion of a brand like Disney? What can a multinational corporation do to mitigate these issues?

**You can find the related video in the Video Library in Connect. Ask your instructor how you can access Connect.**

# Team Exercise

Visit Transparency International's Country Corruption Index website: http://cpi.transparency.org/cpi2013/. Form groups and select two countries. Research some of the economic, ethical, legal, regulatory, and political barriers that would have an impact on international trade. Be sure to pair a fairly ethical country with a fairly unethical country (Sweden with Myanmar, Australia with Haiti). Report your findings.

# PART 2

# Starting and Growing a Business

# 4

# Options for Organizing Business

## Learning Objectives

**After reading this chapter, you will be able to:**

**LO 4-1** Define and examine the advantages and disadvantages of the sole proprietorship form of organization.

**LO 4-2** Identify two types of partnership and evaluate the advantages and disadvantages of the partnership form of organization.

**LO 4-3** Describe the corporate form of organization and cite the advantages and disadvantages of corporations.

**LO 4-4** Define and debate the advantages and disadvantages of mergers, acquisitions, and leveraged buyouts.

**LO 4-5** Propose an appropriate organizational form for a startup business.

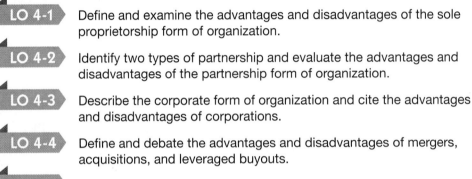

## Shareholder Activism

Corporations are owned by investors, who receive shares of stock and are called shareholders. Investors are increasingly clashing with board members of major corporations. Shareholder activism occurs when shareholders use their ownership to put pressure on management. The majority of activist campaigns are centered on getting corporations to increase dividends or change their boards of directors. Shareholders are also demanding more transparency about operations related to sustainability, human rights, and other social issues. Investors target firms with large cash reserves to release this cash in the form of preferred stock or dividends. Apple Inc. received a blow when investor David Einhorn filed a lawsuit demanding that Apple decrease its $137 billion cash stockpile by issuing preferred stock. Although the lawsuit was dropped, investor pressure on Apple continues.

Another reason for shareholder activism is dissatisfaction with the board. Proxy battles, in which shareholders use their proxy votes to change board members or managers, are increasing. Hess shareholder Elliot Management launched a large fight against the company, accusing its board of weak discipline and accountability. The battle ended when Hess agreed to give Elliot three board seats if the fund would support five of Hess's directors.

Shareholder activism can be beneficial and problematic. On the one hand, activism allows owners to participate in the company, and firms have acknowledged that activists sometimes have good ideas that benefit the firms. However, proxy battles and lawsuits cost money, and some managers claim they are spending more time with shareholders and less on managing.[1]

# Introduction

The legal form of ownership taken by a business is seldom of great concern to you as a customer. When you eat at a restaurant, you probably don't care whether the restaurant is owned by one person (a sole proprietorship), has two or more owners who share the business (a partnership), or is an entity owned by many stockholders (a corporation); all you want is good food. If you buy a foreign car, you probably don't care whether the company that made it has laws governing its form of organization that are different from those for businesses in the United States. You are buying the car because it is well made, fits your price range, or appeals to your sense of style. Nonetheless, a business's legal form of ownership affects how it operates, how much taxes it pays, and how much control its owners have.

This chapter examines three primary forms of business ownership—sole proprietorship, partnership, and corporation—and weighs the advantages and disadvantages of each. These forms are the most often used whether the business is a traditional bricks and mortar company, an online-only one, or a combination of both. We also take a look at S corporations, limited liability companies, and cooperatives and discuss some trends in business ownership. You may wish to refer to Table 4.1 to compare the various forms of business ownership mentioned in the chapter.

**Need help understanding Forms of Business Ownership? Visit your Connect ebook video tab for a brief animated explanation.**

**LO 4-1**

**sole proprietorships**
businesses owned and operated by one individual; the most common form of business organization in the United States

## Sole Proprietorships

**Sole proprietorships,** businesses owned and operated by one individual, are the most common form of business organization in the United States. Common examples include many restaurants, hair salons, flower shops, dog kennels, and independent grocery stores. Many sole proprietors focus on services—small retail stores, financial counseling, appliance repair, child care, and the like—rather than on the manufacture of goods, which often requires large sums of money not available to most small businesses. As you can see in Figure 4.1, proprietorships far outnumber corporations, but they net far fewer sales and less income.

**TABLE 4.1    Various Forms of Business Ownership**

| Structure | Ownership | Taxation | Liability | Use |
|---|---|---|---|---|
| Sole Proprietorship | One owner | Individual income taxed | Unlimited | Owned by a single individual and is the easiest way to conduct business |
| Partnership | Two or more owners | Individual owners' income taxed | Somewhat limited | Easy way for two individuals to conduct business |
| Corporation | Any number of shareholders | Corporate and shareholder taxed | Limited | A legal entity with shareholders or stockholders |
| S Corporation | Up to 100 shareholders | Taxed as a partnership | Limited | A legal entity with tax advantages for restricted number of shareholders |
| Limited Liability Company | Unlimited number of shareholders | Taxed as a partnership | Limited | Avoid personal lawsuits |

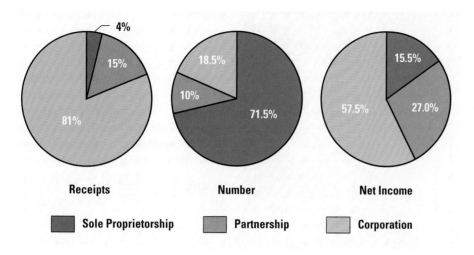

**FIGURE 4.1**

**Comparison of Sole Proprietorships, Partnerships, and Corporations**

Source: U.S. Bureau of the Census, *The 2012 Statistical Abstract*, www. census.gov/compendia/statab/2012/ tables/12s0744.pdf (accessed March 10, 2014).

Sole proprietorships are typically small businesses employing fewer than 50 people. (We'll look at small businesses in greater detail in Chapter 5.) Sole proprietorships constitute approximately three-fourths of all businesses in the United States. It is interesting to note that men are twice as likely as women to start their own business.[2] In many areas, small businesses make up the vast majority of the economy.

## Advantages of Sole Proprietorships

Sole proprietorships are generally managed by their owners. Because of this simple management structure, the owner/manager can make decisions quickly. This is just one of many advantages of the sole proprietorship form of business.

**Ease and Cost of Formation.**    Forming a sole proprietorship is relatively easy and inexpensive. In some states, creating a sole proprietorship involves merely announcing the new business in the local newspaper. Other proprietorships, such as barber shops and restaurants, may require state and local licenses and permits because of the nature of the business. The cost of these permits may run from $25 to $100. No lawyer is needed to create such enterprises, and the owner can usually take care of the required paperwork without outside assistance.

Of course, an entrepreneur starting a new sole proprietorship must find a suitable site from which to operate the business. Some sole proprietors look no farther than their garage or a spare bedroom when seeking a workshop or office. Among the more famous businesses that sprang to life in their founders' homes are Google, Walt Disney, Dell, eBay, Hewlett-Packard, Apple, and Mattel.[3] Computers, personal copiers, scanners, and other high-tech gadgets have been a boon for home-based businesses, permitting them to interact quickly with customers, suppliers, and others. Many independent salespersons and contractors can perform their work using a smartphone or tablet computer as they travel. E-mail and social networks have made it possible for many proprietorships to develop in the services area. Internet connections also allow small businesses to establish websites to promote their products and even to make low-cost long-distance phone calls with voice-over Internet protocol (VoIP) technology. One of the most famous services using VoIP is Skype, which allows people to make free calls over the Internet.

Many local restaurants are sole proprietorships.

**Secrecy.** Sole proprietorships make possible the greatest degree of secrecy. The proprietor, unlike the owners of a partnership or corporation, does not have to discuss publicly his or her operating plans, minimizing the possibility that competitors can obtain trade secrets. Financial reports need not be disclosed, as do the financial reports of publicly owned corporations.

**Distribution and Use of Profits.** All profits from a sole proprietorship belong exclusively to the owner. He or she does not have to share them with any partners or stockholders. The owner decides how to use the funds—for expansion of the business, or salary increases, for travel to purchase additional inventory, or to find new customers.

**Flexibility and Control of the Business.**    The sole proprietor has complete control over the business and can make decisions on the spot without anyone else's approval. This control allows the owner to respond quickly to competitive business conditions or to changes in the economy. The ability to quickly change prices or products can provide a competitive advantage for the business.

**Government Regulation.**    Sole proprietorships have the most freedom from government regulation. Many government regulations—federal, state, and local—apply only to businesses that have a certain number of employees, and securities laws apply only to corporations that issue stock. Nonetheless, sole proprietors must ensure that they follow all laws that do apply to their business. For example, sole proprietorships must be careful to obey employee and consumer protection regulation.

**Taxation.**    Profits from sole proprietorships are considered personal income and are taxed at individual tax rates. The owner, therefore, pays one income tax that includes the business and individual income. Another tax benefit is that a sole proprietor is allowed to establish a tax-exempt retirement account or a tax-exempt profit-sharing account. Such accounts are exempt from current income tax, but payments taken after retirement are taxed when they are received.

**Closing the Business.**    A sole proprietorship can be dissolved easily. No approval of co-owners or partners is necessary. The only legal condition is that all financial obligations must be paid or resolved.

## Disadvantages of Sole Proprietorships

What may be seen as an advantage by one person may turn out to be a disadvantage to another. For profitable businesses managed by capable owners, many of the following factors do not cause problems. On the other hand, proprietors starting out with little management experience and little money are likely to encounter many of the disadvantages.

**Unlimited Liability.**   The sole proprietor has unlimited liability in meeting the debts of the business. In other words, if the business cannot pay its creditors, the owner may be forced to use personal, nonbusiness holdings such as a car or a home to pay off the debts. There are only a few states in which houses and homesteads cannot be taken by creditors, even if the proprietor declares bankruptcy. The more wealth an individual has, the greater is the disadvantage of unlimited liability.

**Limited Sources of Funds.**   Among the relatively few sources of money available to the sole proprietorship are banks, friends, family, the Small Business Administration, or his or her own funds. The owner's personal financial condition determines his or her credit standing. Additionally, sole proprietorships may have to pay higher interest rates on funds borrowed from banks than do large corporations because they are considered greater risks. Often, the only way a sole proprietor can borrow for business purposes is to pledge a car, a house, other real estate, or other personal assets to guarantee the loan. If the business fails, the owner may lose the personal assets as well as the business. Publicly owned corporations, in contrast, can not only obtain funds from commercial banks but can sell stocks and bonds to the public to raise money. If a public company goes out of business, the owners do not lose personal assets.

Sole proprietorships often have greater difficulty attracting talented employees because of competition from larger companies.

**Limited Skills.**   The sole proprietor must be able to perform many functions and possess skills in diverse fields such as management, marketing, finance, accounting, bookkeeping, and personnel management. Specialized professionals, such as accountants or attorneys, can be hired by businesses for help or advice. Sometimes, sole proprietors need assistance with certain business functions. For instance, Barrett Business Services provides businesses with staffing and management consulting. The 50-year-old company has refined personnel placement skills, ensuring good matches between employee and employer, while having a strong management knowledge base that serves to strengthen the foundation of any business. Many businesses take advantage of these kinds of services to gain a competitive advantage.[4] In the end, however, it is up to the business owner to make the final decision in all areas of the business.

**Lack of Continuity.**   The life expectancy of a sole proprietorship is directly linked to that of the owner and his or her ability to work. The serious illness of the owner could result in failure of the business if competent help cannot be found.

It is difficult to arrange for the sale of a proprietorship and at the same time assure customers that the business will continue to meet their needs. For instance, how

### Smashing Its Way to Success: Smashburger

Smashburger
**Founder:** Tom Ryan
**Founded:** 2007, in Denver, Colorado
**Success:** Since its founding, Smashburger has opened 200 locations with annual profits of $250 million.

Smashburger differentiates itself from fast-food competitors with its unique approach to operations and service. When he opened Smashburger, founder Tom Ryan was aiming to create a "better burger" with fresh-quality ingredients and unique healthy options—including flash-fried green beans and carrot sticks—to appeal to all food lovers. To make Smashburger further stand out from competitors, stores have a gallery-like atmosphere complete with murals and real silverware. Local twists on certain product offerings inspire customer loyalty, such as the Brooklyn Burger offered in Brooklyn, New York.

A year after its creation, Smashburger was incorporated as a limited liability company. This means that the owners have limited liability for debt, but the organization is taxed like a partnership. Smashburger became a subsidiary of Burger Development LLC. It made the decision to become a franchise, allowing entrepreneurs to license the Smashburger name and open their own restaurants. According to Ryan, Smashburger views its franchisees as investors and important partners in the company. Strong partnership, quality food offerings, and customer engagement may be the edge Smashburger needs to propel it toward its goals and keep the competition at bay. The company has been included in *Inc.* magazine's 500 fastest-growing private companies.[5]

does one sell a veterinary practice? A veterinarian's major asset is patients. If the vet dies suddenly, the equipment can be sold, but the patients will not necessarily remain loyal to the office. On the other hand, a veterinarian who wants to retire could take in a younger partner and sell the practice to the partner over time. One advantage to the partnership is that some of the customers are likely to stay with the business, even if ownership changes.

**Lack of Qualified Employees.** It is usually difficult for a small sole proprietorship to match the wages and benefits offered by a large competing corporation because the proprietorship's profits may not be as high. In addition, there is little room for advancement within a sole proprietorship, so the owner may have difficulty attracting and retaining qualified employees. On the other hand, the trend of large corporations downsizing and outsourcing tasks has created renewed opportunities for small businesses to acquire well-trained employees.

**partnership**
a form of business organization defined by the Uniform Partnership Act as "an association of two or more persons who carry on as co-owners of a business for profit"

**Taxation.** Although we listed taxation as an advantage for sole proprietorships, it can also be a disadvantage, depending on the proprietor's income. Under current tax rates, sole proprietors pay a higher marginal tax rate than do small corporations on income of less than $75,000. However, sole proprietorships avoid the double taxation that occurs with corporations. The tax effect often determines whether a sole proprietor chooses to incorporate his or her business.

## Partnerships

One way to minimize the disadvantages of a sole proprietorship and maximize its advantages is to have more than one owner. Most states have a model law governing partnerships based on the Uniform Partnership Act. This law defines a **partnership** as "an association of two or more persons who carry on as co-owners of a business for

| |
|---|
| 1. Keep profit sharing and ownership at 50/50, or you have an employer/employee relationship. |
| 2. Partners should have different skill sets to complement one another. |
| 3. Honesty is critical. |
| 4. Must maintain face-to-face communication in addition to phone and e-mail. |
| 5. Maintain transparency, sharing more information over time. |
| 6. Be aware of funding constraints, and do not put yourself in a situation where neither you nor your partner can secure additional financial support. |
| 7. To be successful, you need experience. |
| 8. Whereas family should be a priority, be careful to minimize the number of associated problems. |
| 9. Do not become too infatuated with "the idea" as opposed to implementation. |
| 10. Couple optimism with realism in sales and growth expectations and planning. |

**TABLE 4.2**
**Keys to Success in Business Partnerships**

*Source: Abstracted from J. Watananbe, "14 Reasons Why 80% of New Business Partnerships Would Fail Within Their First 5 Years of Existence," http://ezinearticles.com/?14-Reasons-Why-80-Percent-Of-New-Business-Partnerships-Would-Fail-Within-Their-First-5-Years-Of-Exis&id=472498 (accessed March 16, 2010).*

profit." Partnerships are the least used form of business (see Figure 4.1). They are typically larger than sole proprietorships but smaller than corporations.

Partnerships can be a fruitful form of business, as long as you follow some basic keys to success, which are outlined in Table 4.2.

## Types of Partnership

There are two basic types of partnership: general partnership and limited partnership. A **general partnership** involves a complete sharing in the management of a business. In a general partnership, each partner has unlimited liability for the debts of the business. For example, Webco, a military retail service provider, is a general partnership that has four locations in the United States. These four locations are strategic business units that focus on many product categories at once. This strategy has allowed the company to become a leader in category management in the military retail market, sustaining its business for more than 50 years.[6] Professionals such as lawyers, accountants, and architects often join together in general partnerships.

A **limited partnership** has at least one general partner, who assumes unlimited liability, and at least one limited partner, whose liability is limited to his or her investment in the business. Limited partnerships exist for risky investment projects where the chance of loss is great. The general partners accept the risk of loss; the limited partners' losses are limited to their initial investment. Limited partners do not participate in the management of the business but share in the profits in accordance with the terms of a partnership agreement. Usually the general partner receives a larger share of the profits after the limited partners have received their initial investment back. Popular examples are oil-drilling partnerships and real estate partnerships.

## Articles of Partnership

**Articles of partnership** are legal documents that set forth the basic agreement between partners. Most states require articles of partnership, but even if they are not

**general partnership**
a partnership that involves a complete sharing in both the management and the liability of the business

**limited partnership**
a business organization that has at least one general partner, who assumes unlimited liability, and at least one limited partner, whose liability is limited to his or her investment in the business

**articles of partnership**
legal documents that set forth the basic agreement between partners

### Sustainably Organized: Crimson Renewable Energy

Crimson Midstream Limited Liability Corporation (LLC) is a holding company specializing in petroleum pipelines, the shipping of petro-chemicals, and specialty asphalt products. The LLC designation allows the company to have as many members or owners as it pleases of all different types (i.e., individuals, corporations, partnerships, and so on). It also gives the company the ability to choose how much and when to pay distributions to stockholders, giving it more control over its finances.

As a holding company, it is able to generate independent business units with slightly different functions within the same industry. Denver-based Crimson Renewable Energy Limited Partnership (LP) is one such business unit that produces oil and gas with a focus on biodiesel fuels. As an LP, Crimson Renewable Energy has limited its liability to its own business, while Crimson Midstream LLC serves as the general partner that holds unlimited liability for the LP.

Crimson Renewable Energy produces 25 million gallons of biodiesel per year. It invests heavily in its ability to transform natural materials such as used cooking oil waste, vegetable oils, algae oils, animal fats, and waste corn oil derived from ethanol production into biofuels. With more than 20 years of experience, the firm oversees the quality of its operations in-house through testing and has the capacity to customize fuel for customers to meet certain price points, function requirements, or climate considerations. Crimson Renewable Energy's supply chain consists of those who are dedicated to sustainable practices. The company also sources locally when possible.[7]

#### Discussion Questions

1. Crimson Midstream organized as a limited liability corporation. What are some of the advantages of an LLC?
2. What protections does Crimson Renewable receive by organizing as a limited partnership?
3. What does it mean that Crimson Midstream holds unlimited liability for Crimson Renewable LP?

required, it makes good sense for partners to draw them up. Articles of partnership usually list the money or assets that each partner has contributed (called *partnership capital*), state each partner's individual management role or duty, specify how the profits and losses of the partnership will be divided among the partners, and describe how a partner may leave the partnership as well as any other restrictions that might apply to the agreement. Table 4.3 lists some of the issues and provisions that should be included in articles of partnership.

In 1996, Stanford students Sergey Brin and Larry Page partnered to form the search engine Google as part of a research project. The company was incorporated in 1998 and is now the world's top search engine.

### Advantages of Partnerships

Law firms, accounting firms, and investment firms with several hundred partners have partnership agreements that are quite complicated in comparison with the partnership agreement among two or three people owning a computer repair shop. The advantages must be compared with those offered by other forms of business organization, and not all apply to every partnership.

**Ease of Organization.** Starting a partnership requires little more than drawing up articles of partnership. No legal charters have to be granted, but the name of the business should be registered with the state.

| |
|---|
| 1. Name, purpose, location |
| 2. Duration of the agreement |
| 3. Authority and responsibility of each partner |
| 4. Character of partners (i.e., general or limited, active or silent) |
| 5. Amount of contribution from each partner |
| 6. Division of profits or losses |
| 7. Salaries of each partner |
| 8. How much each partner is allowed to withdraw |
| 9. Death of partner |
| 10. Sale of partnership interest |
| 11. Arbitration of disputes |
| 12. Required and prohibited actions |
| 13. Absence and disability |
| 14. Restrictive covenants |
| 15. Buying and selling agreements |

**TABLE 4.3**
**Issues and Provisions in Articles of Partnership**

**Availability of Capital and Credit.**   When a business has several partners, it has the benefit of a combination of talents and skills and pooled financial resources. Partnerships tend to be larger than sole proprietorships and therefore have greater earning power and better credit ratings. Because many limited partnerships have been formed for tax purposes rather than for economic profits, the combined income of all U.S. partnerships is quite low, as shown in Figure 4.1. Nevertheless, the professional partnerships of many lawyers, accountants, and banking firms make quite large profits. For instance, the partners in the international law firm Davis Polk & Wardwell LLP take home an average of nearly $3 million a year.[8]

**Combined Knowledge and Skills.**   Partners in the most successful partnerships acknowledge each other's talents and avoid confusion and conflict by specializing in a particular area of expertise such as marketing, production, accounting, or service. The diversity of skills in a partnership makes it possible for the business to be run by a management team of specialists instead of by a generalist sole proprietor. Co-founders Justin Wetherill, Edward Trujillo, and David Reiff credit diversity as being a key component to the success of their company uBreakiFix, an iPhone repair service. In just six years, the startup has grown to 47 locations, generating $8.5 million in revenue. They have also embarked upon a franchising strategy, which is sure to spur further growth.[9] Service-oriented partnerships in fields such as law, financial planning, and accounting may attract customers because clients may think that the service offered by a diverse team is of higher quality than that provided by one person. Larger law firms, for example, often have individual partners who specialize in certain areas of the law—such as family, bankruptcy, corporate, entertainment, and criminal law.

**Decision Making.**    Small partnerships can react more quickly to changes in the business environment than can large partnerships and corporations. Such fast reactions are possible because the partners are involved in day-to-day operations and can make decisions quickly after consultation. Large partnerships with hundreds of partners in many states are not common. In those that do exist, decision making is likely to be slow. However, some partnerships have been successful despite their large size. The accounting firm PricewaterhouseCoopers LLP (PwC) is the third largest accounting and advisory firm in the United States with more than 9,500 partners and principals and more than 174,000 personnel. The company has gross revenues of more than $32 billion. Some have attributed PwC's success to its strong diversification techniques and the ability to operate in different market niches.[10]

**Regulatory Controls.**    Like a sole proprietorship, a partnership has fewer regulatory controls affecting its activities than does a corporation. A partnership does not have to file public financial statements with government agencies or send out quarterly financial statements to several thousand owners, as do corporations such as Apple and Ford Motor Co. A partnership does, however, have to abide by all laws relevant to the industry or profession in which it operates as well as state and federal laws relating to hiring and firing, food handling, and so on, just as the sole proprietorship does.

## Disadvantages of Partnerships

Partnerships have many advantages compared to sole proprietorships and corporations, but they also have some disadvantages. Limited partners have no voice in the management of the partnership, and they may bear most of the risk of the business while the general partner reaps a larger share of the benefits. There may be a change in the goals and objectives of one partner but not the other, particularly when the partners are multinational organizations. This can cause friction, giving rise to an enterprise that fails to satisfy both parties or even forcing an end to the partnership. Many partnership disputes wind up in court or require outside mediation. A partnership can be jeopardized when two business partners cannot resolve disputes. For instance, Evan Spiegel and Bobby Murphy, co-founders of photo sharing mobile application Snapchat, are being sued by an earlier founder, Reggie Brown, for one-third of the value of the company. Brown claims that the business is founded on his idea, which Spiegel and Murphy stole from him. Despite a few settlement talks, an agreement is still pending at this time.[11] In some cases, the ultimate solution may be dissolving the partnership. Major disadvantages of partnerships include the following.

**Unlimited Liability.**    In general partnerships, the general partners have unlimited liability for the debts incurred by the business, just as the sole proprietor has unlimited liability for his or her business. Such unlimited liability can be a distinct disadvantage to one partner if his or her personal financial resources are greater than those of the others. A potential partner should check to make sure that all partners have comparable resources to help the business in time of trouble. This disadvantage is eliminated for limited partners, who can lose only their initial investment.

**Business Responsibility.**    All partners are responsible for the business actions of all others. Partners may have the ability to commit the partnership to a contract without approval of the other partners. A bad decision by one partner may put the other partners' personal resources in jeopardy. Personal problems such as a divorce can eliminate a significant portion of one partner's financial resources and weaken the financial structure of the whole partnership.

**Life of the Partnership.**   A partnership is terminated when a partner dies or withdraws. In a two-person partnership, if one partner withdraws, the firm's liabilities would be paid off and the assets divided between the partners. Obviously, the partner who wishes to continue in the business would be at a serious disadvantage. The business could be disrupted, financing would be reduced, and the management skills of the departing partner would be lost. The remaining partner would have to find another or reorganize the business as a sole proprietorship. In very large partnerships such as those found in law firms and investment banks, the continuation of the partnership may be provided for in the articles of partnership. The provision may simply state the terms for a new partnership agreement among the remaining partners. In such cases, the disadvantage to the other partners is minimal.

Selling a partnership interest has the same effect as the death or withdrawal of a partner. It is difficult to place a value on a partner's share of the partnership. No public value is placed on the partnership, as there is on publicly owned corporations. What is a law firm worth? What is the local hardware store worth? Coming up with a fair value that all partners can agree to is not easy. Selling a partnership interest is easier if the articles of partnership specify a method of valuation. Even if there is not a procedure for selling one partner's interest, the old partnership must still be dissolved and a new one created. In contrast, in the corporate form of business, the departure of owners has little effect on the financial resources of the business, and the loss of managers does not cause long-term changes in the structure of the organization.

**Distribution of Profits.**   Profits earned by the partnership are distributed to the partners in the proportions specified in the articles of partnership. This may be a disadvantage if the division of the profits does not reflect the work each partner puts into the business. You may have encountered this disadvantage while working on a student group project: You may have felt that you did most of the work and that the other students in the group received grades based on your efforts. Even the perception of an unfair profit-sharing agreement may cause tension between the partners, and unhappy partners can have a negative effect on the profitability of the business.

**Limited Sources of Funds.**   As with a sole proprietorship, the sources of funds available to a partnership are limited. Because no public value is placed on the business (such as the current trading price of a corporation's stock), potential partners do not know what one partnership share is worth. Moreover, because partnership shares cannot be bought and sold easily in public markets, potential owners may not want to tie up their money in assets that cannot be readily sold on short notice. Accumulating enough funds to operate a national business, especially a business requiring intensive investments in facilities and equipment, can be difficult. Partnerships also may have to pay higher interest rates on funds borrowed from banks than do large corporations because partnerships may be considered greater risks.

## Taxation of Partnerships

Partnerships are quasi-taxable organizations. This means that partnerships do not pay taxes when submitting the partnership tax return to the Internal Revenue Service. The tax return simply provides information about the profitability of the organization and the distribution of profits among the partners. Partners must report their share of profits on their individual tax returns and pay taxes at the income tax rate for individuals.

**corporation**
a legal entity, created by the state, whose assets and liabilities are separate from its owners

# Corporations

When you think of a business, you probably think of a huge corporation such as General Electric, Procter & Gamble, or Sony because a large portion of your consumer dollars go to such corporations. A **corporation** is a legal entity, created by the state, whose assets and liabilities are separate from its owners. As a legal entity, a corporation has many of the rights, duties, and powers of a person, such as the right to receive, own, and transfer property. Corporations can enter into contracts with individuals or with other legal entities, and they can sue and be sued in court.

Corporations account for the majority of all U.S. sales and income. Thus, most of the dollars you spend as a consumer probably go to incorporated businesses (see Figure 4.1). Most corporations are not mega-companies like General Mills or Ford Motor Co.; even small businesses can incorporate. As we shall see later in the chapter, many smaller firms elect to incorporate as "S Corporations," which operate under slightly different rules and have greater flexibility than do traditional "C Corporations" like General Mills.

**stock**
shares of a corporation that may be bought or sold

Corporations are typically owned by many individuals and organizations who own shares of the business, called **stock** (thus, corporate owners are often called *shareholders* or *stockholders*). Stockholders can buy, sell, give or receive as gifts, or inherit their shares of stock. As owners, the stockholders are entitled to all profits that are left after all the corporation's other obligations have been paid. These profits may be distributed in the form of cash payments called **dividends.** For example, if a corporation earns $100 million after expenses and taxes and decides to pay the owners $40 million in dividends, the stockholders receive 40 percent of the profits in cash dividends. However, not all after-tax profits are paid to stockholders in dividends. Some corporations may retain profits to expand the business. For example, Berkshire Hathaway has always retained its earnings and reinvested them for the shareholders. This has resulted in an average 20 percent increase in per share investment over a 40-year period.[12]

**dividends**
profits of a corporation that are distributed in the form of cash payments to stockholders

## Creating a Corporation

A corporation is created, or incorporated, under the laws of the state in which it incorporates. The individuals creating the corporation are known as *incorporators*. Each state has a specific procedure, sometimes called *chartering the corporation,* for incorporating a business. Most states require a minimum of three incorporators; thus, many small businesses can be and are incorporated. Another requirement is that the new corporation's name cannot be similar to that of another business. In most states, a corporation's name must end in "company," "corporation," "incorporated," or "limited" to show that the owners have limited liability. (In this text, however, the word *company* means any organization engaged in a commercial enterprise and can refer to a sole proprietorship, a partnership, or a corporation.)

The incorporators must file legal documents generally referred to as *articles of incorporation* with the appropriate state office (often the secretary of state). The articles of incorporation contain basic information about the business. The following 10 items are found in the Model Business Corporation Act, issued by the American Bar Association, which is followed by most states:

1. Name and address of the corporation.
2. Objectives of the corporation.
3. Classes of stock (common, preferred, voting, nonvoting) and the number of shares for each class of stock to be issued.

4. Expected life of the corporation (corporations are usually created to last forever).

5. Financial capital required at the time of incorporation.

6. Provisions for transferring shares of stock between owners.

7. Provisions for the regulation of internal corporate affairs.

8. Address of the business office registered with the state of incorporation.

9. Names and addresses of the initial board of directors.

10. Names and addresses of the incorporators.

Based on the information in the articles of incorporation, the state issues a **corporate charter** to the company. After securing this charter, the owners hold an organizational meeting at which they establish the corporation's bylaws and elect a board of directors. The bylaws might set up committees of the board of directors and describe the rules and procedures for their operation.

**corporate charter**
a legal document that the state issues to a company based on information the company provides in the articles of incorporation

## Types of Corporations

If the corporation does business in the state in which it is chartered, it is known as a *domestic corporation.* In other states where the corporation does business, it is known as a *foreign corporation.* If a corporation does business outside the nation in which it is incorporated, it is called an *alien corporation.* A corporation may be privately or publicly owned.

A **private corporation** is owned by just one or a few people who are closely involved in managing the business. These people, often a family, own all the corporation's stock, and no stock is sold to the public. Many corporations are quite large, yet remain private, including Cargill, a farm products business. It is the nation's largest private corporation with annual revenues of well over $100 billion. Founded at the end of the Civil War, descendents of the original founder have owned equity in the company for more than 140 years.[13] The fifth largest privately held company in the United States is Mars, founded by Frank C. Mars, who spent time in Switzerland learning to create chocolate confectionaries. Mars grew significantly through the acquisition of the Wm. Wrigley Jr. Company. Founded in Tacoma, Washington, in 1911, Mars is now the world's leading confectionary company and a leader in pet care products with Pedigree and Whiskas.[14] The business was successful early on because it paid employees three times the normal wage for the time. The company remains successful to this day, largely because of its established brands, such as M&Ms, and healthy snack lines for kids, like Generation Max.[15] Other well-known privately held companies include HJ Heinz, Publix Supermarkets, Toys 'R' Us, and Amway.[16] Privately owned corporations are not required to disclose financial information publicly, but they must, of course, pay taxes.

**private corporation**
a corporation owned by just one or a few people who are closely involved in managing the business

A **public corporation** is one whose stock anyone may buy, sell, or trade. Table 4.4 lists 10 U.S. corporations with more than half of their revenue coming from outside of the United States. Despite its high revenue, Amazon had negative profits in 2013.[17] Thousands of smaller public corporations in the United States have sales under $10 million. In large public corporations such as AT&T, the stockholders are often far removed from the management of the company. In other public corporations, the managers are often the founders and the major shareholders. Moelis & Co., for example, became a public corporation under the terms that the founder, chairman, and CEO would remain in his position and control more than 50 percent of the company.[18] *Forbes'* Global 2000 companies generate around $38 trillion in revenues, $2.4 trillion

**public corporation**
a corporation whose stock anyone may buy, sell, or trade

**TABLE 4.4**
**American Companies with More than Half of Their Revenues from Outside the United States**

| Company | Description |
|---|---|
| Caterpillar Inc. | Designs, manufactures, markets, and sells machinery, engines, and financial products |
| Dow Chemical | Manufactures chemicals, with products including plastics, oil, and crop technology |
| General Electric | Operates in the technology infrastructure, energy, capital finance, and consumer and industrial fields, with products including appliances, locomotives, weapons, lighting, and gas |
| General Motors | Sells automobiles with brands including Chevrolet, Buick, Cadillac, and Isuzu |
| IBM | Conducts technological research, develops intellectual property including software and hardware, and offers consulting services |
| Intel | Manufactures and develops semiconductor chips and microprocessors |
| McDonald's | Operates second-largest chain of fast-food restaurants worldwide after Subway |
| Nike | Designs, develops, markets, and sells athletic shoes and clothing |
| Procter & Gamble | Sells consumer goods with brands including Tide, Bounty, Crest, and Iams |
| Yum! Brands | Operates and licenses restaurants including Taco Bell, Kentucky Fried Chicken, and Pizza Hut |

in profits, and $159 trillion in assets. They are worth $39 trillion in market value.[19] Asia-Pacific companies account for the majority of the Global 2000 companies, but other nations are catching up. The rankings of the Global 2000 span across 63 countries.[20] Publicly owned corporations must disclose financial information to the public under specific laws that regulate the trade of stocks and other securities.

A private corporation that needs more money to expand or to take advantage of opportunities may have to obtain financing by "going public" through an **initial public offering (IPO),** that is, becoming a public corporation by selling stock so that it can be traded in public markets. Digital media companies are leading a surge in initial public offerings. Twitter, Marketo (a cloud-based marketing services company), Rocket Fuel (a digital advertising company), and Veeva Systems (an enterprise cloud provider for life sciences companies) all released IPOs in 2013.[21]

Also, privately owned firms are occasionally forced to go public with stock offerings when a major owner dies and the heirs have large estate taxes to pay. The tax payment may only be possible with the proceeds of the sale of stock. This happened to the brewer Adolph Coors Inc. After Adolph Coors died, the business went public and his family sold shares of stock to the public in order to pay the estate taxes.

On the other hand, public corporations can be "taken private" when one or a few individuals (perhaps the management of the firm) purchase all the firm's stock so that it can no longer be sold publicly. Taking a corporation private may be desirable

**initial public offering (IPO)** selling a corporation's stock on public markets for the first time

when owners want to exert more control over the firm or they want the flexibility to make decisions for restructuring operations. For example, Michael Dell took his company private in order to set a new direction as PC sales continue to decline. Becoming a private company again allows Mr. Dell to focus on the needs of the company more fully than having to worry about the stock price for investors.[22] Taking a corporation private is also one technique for avoiding a takeover by another corporation.

Quasi-public corporations and nonprofits are two types of public corporations. **Quasi-public corporations** are owned and operated by the federal, state, or local government. The focus of these entities is to provide a service to citizens, such as mail delivery, rather than earning a profit. Indeed, many quasi-public corporations operate at a loss. Examples of quasi-public corporations include the National Aeronautics and Space Administration (NASA) and the U.S. Postal Service.

Like quasi-public corporations, **nonprofit corporations** focus on providing a service rather than earning a profit, but they are not owned by a government entity. Organizations such as the Sesame Workshop, the Elks Clubs, the American Lung Association, the American Red Cross, museums, and private schools provide services without a profit motive. To fund their operations and services, nonprofit organizations solicit donations from individuals and companies and grants from the government and other charitable foundations.

## Elements of a Corporation

**The Board of Directors.**   A **board of directors,** elected by the stockholders to oversee the general operation of the corporation, sets the long-range objectives of the corporation. It is the board's responsibility to ensure that the objectives are achieved on schedule. Board members are legally liable for the mismanagement of the firm or for any misuse of funds. An important duty of the board of directors is to hire corporate officers, such as the president and the chief executive officer (CEO), who are responsible to the directors for the management and daily operations of the firm. The role and expectations of the board of directors took on greater significance after the accounting scandals of the early 2000s and the passage of the Sarbanes-Oxley Act.[23] As a result, most corporations have restructured how they compensate board directors for their time and expertise.

However, some experts now speculate that Sarbanes-Oxley did little to motivate directors to increase company oversight. Founder and former chairman of Best Buy Richard Schulze found this out firsthand. He resigned after a probe revealed he had known about an inappropriate relationship between the Best Buy CEO and an employee but failed to inform the board. Schulze later returned to Best Buy under a new title, chairman emeritus.[24] At the same time, the pay rate of directors is rising. On average, corporate directors are paid around $250,000. Over the past several years, the trend of increasing directors' pay continues to reach higher and higher limits. Although such pay is meant to attract top-quality directors, concerns exist over whether excessive pay will have unintended consequences. Some believe that this trend is contributing to the declining effectiveness in corporate governance.[25]

Directors can be employees of the company (*inside directors*) or people unaffiliated with the company (*outside directors*). Inside directors are usually the officers responsible for running the company. Outside directors are often top executives from other companies, lawyers, bankers, even professors. Directors today are increasingly chosen

**quasi-public corporations**
corporations owned and operated by the federal, state, or local government

**nonprofit corporations**
corporations that focus on providing a service rather than earning a profit but are not owned by a government entity

**board of directors**
a group of individuals, elected by the stockholders to oversee the general operation of the corporation, who set the corporation's long-range objectives

for their expertise, competence, and ability to bring diverse perspectives to strategic discussions. Outside directors are also thought to bring more independence to the monitoring function because they are not bound by past allegiances, friendships, a current role in the company, or some other issue that may create a conflict of interest. Many of the corporate scandals uncovered in recent years might have been prevented if each of the companies' boards of directors had been better qualified, more knowledgeable, and more independent.

There is a growing shortage of available and qualified board members. Boards are increasingly telling their own CEOs that they should be focused on serving their company, not serving on outside boards. Because of this, the average CEO sits on less than one outside board. This represents a decline from a decade ago when the average was two. Because many CEOs are turning down outside positions, many companies have taken steps to ensure that boards have experienced directors. They have increased the mandatory retirement age to 72 or older, and some have raised it to 75 or even older. Minimizing the amount of overlap between directors sitting on different boards helps to limit conflicts of interest and provides for independence in decision making.

**preferred stock**
a special type of stock whose owners, though not generally having a say in running the company, have a claim to profits before other stockholders do

**common stock**
stock whose owners have voting rights in the corporation, yet do not receive preferential treatment regarding dividends

**Stock Ownership.**     Corporations issue two types of stock: preferred and common. Owners of **preferred stock** are a special class of owners because, although they generally do not have any say in running the company, they have a claim to profits before any other stockholders do. Other stockholders do not receive any dividends unless the preferred stockholders have already been paid. Dividend payments on preferred stock are usually a fixed percentage of the initial issuing price (set by the board of directors). For example, if a share of preferred stock originally cost $100 and the dividend rate was stated at 7.5 percent, the dividend payment will be $7.50 per share per year. Dividends are usually paid quarterly. Most preferred stock carries a cumulative claim to dividends. This means that if the company does not pay preferred-stock dividends in one year because of losses, the dividends accumulate to the next year. Such dividends unpaid from previous years must also be paid to preferred stockholders before other stockholders can receive any dividends.

Although owners of **common stock** do not get such preferential treatment with regard to dividends, they do get some say in the operation of the corporation. Their ownership gives them the right to vote for members of the board of directors and on other important issues. Common stock dividends may vary according to the profitability of the business, and some corporations do not issue dividends at all, but instead plow their profits back into the company to fund expansion.

Owners of preferred stock have first claim to profits.

Common stockholders are the voting owners of a corporation. They are usually entitled to one vote per share of common stock. During an annual stockholders' meeting, common stockholders elect a board of directors. Some boards find it easier than others to attract high profile individuals. For example, the board of Procter & Gamble consists of Ernesto Zedillo, former president of Mexico; Kenneth I. Chenault, CEO of the American Express Company; Scott D. Cook, founder of Intuit Inc.; Patricia A. Woerte, CEO of Archer Daniels Midland; W. James McNerney Jr., CEO of Boeing; Margaret C. Whitman, CEO of Hewlett-Packard; and a few others.[26] Because they can choose the board of directors, common stockholders have some say in how the company will operate. Common stockholders may vote by *proxy,* which is a written authorization by which stockholders assign their voting privilege to someone else, who then votes for his or her choice at the stockholders' meeting. It is a normal practice for management to request proxy statements from shareholders who are not planning to attend the annual meeting. Most owners do not attend annual meetings of the very large companies, such as Westinghouse or Boeing, unless they live in the city where the meeting is held.

Common stockholders have another advantage over preferred shareholders. In most states, when the corporation decides to sell new shares of common stock in the marketplace, common stockholders have the first right, called a *preemptive right,* to purchase new shares of the stock from the corporation. A preemptive right is often included in the articles of incorporation. This right is important because it allows stockholders to purchase new shares to maintain their original positions. For example, if a stockholder owns 10 percent of a corporation that decides to issue new shares, that stockholder has the right to buy enough of the new shares to retain the 10 percent ownership.

## Advantages of Corporations

Because a corporation is a separate legal entity, it has some very specific advantages over other forms of ownership. The biggest advantage may be the limited liability of the owners.

**Limited Liability.** Because the corporation's assets (money and resources) and liabilities (debts and other obligations) are separate from its owners', in most cases the stockholders are not held responsible for the firm's debts if it fails. Their liability or potential loss is limited to the amount of their original investment. Although a creditor can sue a corporation for not paying its debts, even forcing the corporation into bankruptcy, it cannot make the stockholders pay the corporation's debts out of their personal assets. Occasionally, the owners of a private corporation may pledge personal assets to secure a loan for the corporation; this would be most unusual for a public corporation.

**Ease of Transfer of Ownership.** Stockholders can sell or trade shares of stock to other people without causing the termination of the corporation, and they can do this without the prior approval of other shareholders. The transfer of ownership (unless it is a majority position) does not affect the daily or long-term operations of the corporation.

**Perpetual Life.** A corporation usually is chartered to last forever unless its articles of incorporation stipulate otherwise. The existence of the corporation is unaffected by the death or withdrawal of any of its stockholders. It survives until

Volkswagen is the eighth-largest corporation in the world.

the owners sell it or liquidate its assets. However, in some cases, bankruptcy ends a corporation's life. Bankruptcies occur when companies are unable to compete and earn profits. Eventually, uncompetitive businesses must close or seek protection from creditors in bankruptcy court while the business tries to reorganize.

**External Sources of Funds.**   Of all the forms of business organization, the public corporation finds it easiest to raise money. When a corporation needs to raise more money, it can sell more stock shares or issue bonds (corporate "IOUs," which pledge to repay debt), attracting funds from anywhere in the United States and even overseas. The larger a corporation becomes, the more sources of financing are available to it. We take a closer look at some of these in Chapter 15.

**Expansion Potential.**   Because large public corporations can find long-term financing readily, they can easily expand into national and international markets. And, as a legal entity, a corporation can enter into contracts without as much difficulty as a partnership.

## Disadvantages of Corporations

Corporations have some distinct disadvantages resulting from tax laws and government regulation.

**Double Taxation.**   As a legal entity, the corporation must pay taxes on its income just like you do. When after-tax corporate profits are paid out as dividends to the stockholders, the dividends are taxed a second time as part of the individual owner's income. This process creates double taxation for the stockholders of dividend paying corporations. Double taxation does not occur with the other forms of business organization.

**Forming a Corporation.**   The formation of a corporation can be costly. A charter must be obtained, and this usually requires the services of an attorney and payment of legal fees. Filing fees ranging from $25 to $150 must be paid to the state that awards the corporate charter, and certain states require that an annual fee be paid to maintain the charter. Today, a number of Internet services such as LegalZoom.com and Business.com make it easier, quicker, and less costly to form a corporation. However, in making it easier for people to form businesses without expert consultation, these services have increased the risk that people will not choose the kind of organizational form that is right for them. Sometimes, one form works better than another. The business's founders may fail to take into account disadvantages, such as double taxation with corporations.

**Disclosure of Information.**    Corporations must make information available to their owners, usually through an annual report to shareholders. The annual report contains financial information about the firm's profits, sales, facilities and equipment, and debts, as well as descriptions of the company's operations, products, and plans for the future. Public corporations must also file reports with the Securities and Exchange Commission (SEC), the government regulatory agency that regulates securities such as stocks and bonds. The larger the firm, the more data the SEC requires. Because all reports filed with the SEC are available to the public, competitors can access them. Additionally, complying with securities laws takes time.

> **DID YOU KNOW?**  The first corporation with a net income of more than $1 billion in one year was General Motors, with a net income in 1955 of $1,189,477,082.[27]

**Employee–Owner Separation.**    Many employees are not stockholders of the company for which they work. This separation of owners and employees may cause employees to feel that their work benefits only the owners. Employees without an ownership stake do not always see how they fit into the corporate picture and may not understand the importance of profits to the health of the organization. If managers are part owners but other employees are not, management–labor relations take on a different, sometimes difficult, aspect from those in partnerships and sole proprietorships. However, this situation is changing as more corporations establish employee stock ownership plans (ESOPs), which give shares of the company's stock to its employees. Such plans build a partnership between employee and employer and can boost productivity because they motivate employees to work harder so that they can earn dividends from their hard work as well as from their regular wages.

# Other Types of Ownership

In this section we take a brief look at joint ventures, S corporations, limited liability companies, and cooperatives—businesses formed for special purposes.

### Joint Ventures

A **joint venture** is a partnership established for a specific project or for a limited time. The partners in a joint venture may be individuals or organizations, as in the case of the international joint ventures discussed in Chapter 3. Control of a joint venture may be shared equally, or one partner may control decision making. Joint ventures are especially popular in situations that call for large investments, such as extraction of natural resources and the development of new products. Joint ventures are especially popular in situations that call for large investments and can even take place between businesses and governments. For example, Samsung and Venezuela formed a joint venture for the purpose of manufacturing electronics and appliances in the country. This partnership also serves to limit the amount of price manipulation that occurs in the country by smaller companies that import items and mark them up.[28]

**joint venture**
a partnership established for a specific project or for a limited time

### S Corporations

An **S corporation** is a form of business ownership that is taxed as though it were a partnership. Net profits or losses of the corporation pass to the owners, thus

**S corporation**
corporation taxed as though it were a partnership with restrictions on shareholders

REI is organized as a consumer cooperative.

eliminating double taxation. The benefit of limited liability is retained. Formally known as Subchapter S Corporations, they have become a popular form of business ownership for entrepreneurs and represent almost half of all corporate filings.[29] Vista Bank Texas is an S corporation, and the owners get the benefits of tax advantages and limited liability. Advantages of S corporations include the simple method of taxation, the limited liability of shareholders, perpetual life, and the ability to shift income and appreciation to others. Disadvantages include restrictions on the number (75) and types (individuals, estates, and certain trusts) of shareholders and the difficulty of formation and operation.

## Limited Liability Companies

**limited liability company (LLC)**
form of ownership that provides limited liability and taxation like a partnership but places fewer restrictions on members

A **limited liability company (LLC)** is a form of business ownership that provides limited liability, as in a corporation, but is taxed like a partnership. Although relatively new in the United States, LLCs have existed for many years abroad. Professionals such as lawyers, doctors, and engineers often use the LLC form of ownership. Many consider the LLC a blend of the best characteristics of corporations, partnerships, and sole proprietorships. One of the major reasons for the LLC form of ownership is to protect the members' personal assets in case of lawsuits. LLCs are flexible, simple to run, and do not require the members to hold meetings, keep minutes, or make resolutions, all of which are necessary in corporations. For example, Domino's Pizza, which sells and delivers pizza, is a limited liability company.[30]

## Cooperatives

**cooperative (co-op)**
an organization composed of individuals or small businesses that have banded together to reap the benefits of belonging to a larger organization

Another form of organization in business is the **cooperative** or **co-op,** an organization composed of individuals or small businesses that have banded together to reap the benefits of belonging to a larger organization. ARISE Food Co-op, for example, is a food cooperative based in Massachusetts;[31] Ocean Spray is a cooperative of cranberry farmers. REI operates a bit differently because it is owned by consumers rather than farmers or small businesses. A co-op is set up not to make money as an entity. It exists so that its members can become more profitable or save money. Co-ops are generally expected to operate without profit or to create only enough profit to maintain the co-op organization.

Many cooperatives exist in small farming communities. The co-op stores and markets grain; orders large quantities of fertilizer, seed, and other supplies at discounted prices; and reduces costs and increases efficiency with good management. A co-op can purchase supplies in large quantities and pass the savings on to its members. It

### The Evolution of Sears Holdings Company

Sears Holdings began as a sole proprietorship in 1886 known as R.W. Sears Watch Company in Minneapolis. As the name suggests, founder Richard W. Sears sold only watches. Sears wanted to establish his company in Chicago and needed a partner to do so. He put an advertisement in the local paper, and Alvah C. Roebuck responded. Together, they formed Sears, Roebuck, and Co. as a corporation and expanded the business's to offer more product lines through mail order catalogs.

Sears became a public corporation in 1901 to secure financing for growth. To manage its growth, the company developed a time scheduling system that ensured orders were accurate and shipped on time. Expansion continued with the introduction of retail stores in 1925. The company's Craftsman and Kenmore brands became popular, and soon retail sales outperformed mail order sales. Sears even sold arts and crafts

for assembly on the customer's property. Foreign expansion, the building of the famous Sears Tower, and the installation of Sears.com solidified the retailer as a household name.

However, success can often breed complacency that results in a business' decline. Lack of investment has resulted in less-than-pristine retail locations that customers no longer frequent. In 2004, Kmart acquired Sears for $11 billion and adopted the name Sears Holdings Company. The merged company continues to struggle with losses and is selling off its best-known business units and underperforming stores.[32]

#### Discussion Questions

1. Why did Sears become a public corporation? What benefits does this form of organization have to offer Sears?
2. Describe some reasons for why the firm is struggling.
3. What is Sears doing to bounce back from its losses?

---

also can help distribute the products of its members more efficiently than each could on an individual basis. A cooperative can advertise its members' products and thus generate demand. Ace Hardware, a cooperative of independent hardware store owners, allows its members to share in the savings that result from buying supplies in large quantities; it also provides advertising, which individual members might not be able to afford on their own.

# Trends in Business Ownership: Mergers and Acquisitions

Companies large and small achieve growth and improve profitability by expanding their operations, often by developing and selling new products or selling current products to new groups of customers in different geographic areas. Such growth, when carefully planned and controlled, is usually beneficial to the firm and ultimately helps it reach its goal of enhanced profitability. But companies also grow by merging with or purchasing other companies.

A **merger** occurs when two companies (usually corporations) combine to form a new company. An **acquisition** occurs when one company purchases another, generally by buying most of its stock. The acquired company may become a subsidiary of the buyer, or its operations and assets may be merged with those of the buyer. The government sometimes scrutinizes mergers and acquisitions in an attempt to protect customers from monopolistic practices. For example, the decision to authorize Whole Foods' acquisition of Wild Oats was carefully analyzed, as was the merger of Sirius and XM Satellite Radio. In 2013, Google paid $3.2 billion for smart home company, Nest Labs.[33] The company was just one of many that Google acquired

**merger**
the combination of two companies (usually corporations) to form a new company

**acquisition**
the purchase of one company by another, usually by buying its stock

**TABLE 4.5**    Major Mergers and Acquisitions Worldwide 2000–2010

| Rank | Year | Acquirer | Target | Transaction Value (in millions of U.S. dollars) |
|---|---|---|---|---|
| 1 | 2000 | America Online Inc. (AOL) (*Merger*) | Time Warner | $164,747 |
| 2 | 2000 | Glaxo Wellcome Plc. | SmithKline Beecham Plc. | 75,961 |
| 3 | 2004 | Royal Dutch Petroleum Co. | Shell Transport & Trading Co. | 74,559 |
| 4 | 2006 | AT&T Inc. | BellSouth Corporation | 72,671 |
| 5 | 2001 | Comcast Corporation | AT&T Broadband & Internet Svcs. | 72,041 |
| 6 | 2004 | JP Morgan Chase & Co. | Bank One Corporation | 58,761 |
| 7 | 2013 | American Airlines | U.S. Airways | 11,000 |
| 8 | 2008 | Bank of America | Countrywide | 4,000 |
| 9 | 2008 | JP Morgan Chase & Co. | Bear Stearns Companies Inc. | 1,100 |
| 10 | 2011 | Southwest Airlines | AirTran Holdings | 1,000 |

Unless noted, deal was an acquisition.

*Sources: Institute of Mergers, Acquisitions and Alliances Research,* Thomson Financial, *www.imaa-institute.org/en/publications+mergers+acquisitions+m&a. php#Reports (accessed March 16, 2010); "JPMorgan Chase Completes Bear Stearns Acquisition,"* JPMorganChase News Release, May 31, 2008, www.bearstearns.com/ includes/pdfs/PressRelease_BSC_31May08.pdf *(accessed March 1, 2010); "Southwest Completes Purchase of Orlando-Based AirTran,"* Orlando Sentinel, May 2, 2011, *http://articles.orlandosentinel.com/2011-05-02/business/os-southwest-airtran-reuters-update2-20110502_1_southwest-executive-vice-president-southwest-brand-airtran-holdings (accessed January 27, 2012).*

during the year. While these acquisitions have the potential to diversify Google's service offerings and benefit it financially, some believe that Google might be investing in companies of which it has little knowledge. In these cases, acquisitions could end up harming the acquiring company.[34] Acquisitions sometimes involve the purchase of a division or some other part of a company rather than the entire company. The late 1990s saw a merger and acquisition frenzy, which is slowing in the 21st century (see Table 4.5).

When firms that make and sell similar products to the same customers merge, it is known as a *horizontal merger,* as when Martin Marietta and Lockheed, both defense contractors, merged to form Lockheed Martin. Horizontal mergers, however, reduce the number of corporations competing within an industry, and for this reason they are usually reviewed carefully by federal regulators before the merger is allowed to proceed.

When companies operating at different but related levels of an industry merge, it is known as a *vertical merger.* In many instances, a vertical merger results when one corporation merges with one of its customers or suppliers. For example, if Burger King were to purchase a large Idaho potato farm—to ensure a ready supply of potatoes for its french fries—a vertical merger would result.

A *conglomerate merger* results when two firms in unrelated industries merge. For example, the purchase of Sterling Drug, a pharmaceutical firm, by Eastman Kodak, best-known for its films and cameras, represents a conglomerate merger because the two companies are of different industries. (Kodak later sold Sterling Drug to a pharmaceutical company.)

When a company (or an individual), sometimes called a *corporate raider,* wants to acquire or take over another company, it first offers to buy some or all of the other company's stock at a premium over its current price in a *tender offer.* Most such offers are "friendly," with both groups agreeing to the proposed deal, but some are "hostile," when the second company does not want to be taken over. News Corp. adopted a poison pill plan to discourage challenges to Rupert Murdoch's family-controlled media empire, which split into two businesses. (A poison pill is an attempt to make a takeover less attractive to a potential acquirer.) News Corp.'s plan is set to go off if an outside company buys 15 percent or more of the companies' Class B voting shares. In this case, shareholders would have the option to buy new shares at a 50 percent discount. Because the Murdoch family owns many of the shares, this plan is a good way to maintain control of the firm.[35]

Eli Lilly purchased Novartis' animal health unit for $5.4 billion.

To head off a hostile takeover attempt, a threatened company's managers may use one or more of several techniques. They may ask stockholders not to sell to the raider; file a lawsuit in an effort to abort the takeover; institute a *poison pill* (in which the firm allows stockholders to buy more shares of stock at prices lower than the current market value) or *shark repellant* (in which management requires a large majority of stockholders to approve the takeover); or seek a *white knight* (a more acceptable firm that is willing to acquire the threatened company). In some cases, management may take the company private or even take on more debt so that the heavy debt obligation will "scare off" the raider.

In a **leveraged buyout (LBO),** a group of investors borrows money from banks and other institutions to acquire a company (or a division of one), using the assets of the purchased company to guarantee repayment of the loan. In some LBOs, as much as 95 percent of the buyout price is paid with borrowed money, which eventually must be repaid.

**leveraged buyout (LBO)** a purchase in which a group of investors borrows money from banks and other institutions to acquire a company (or a division of one), using the assets of the purchased company to guarantee repayment of the loan

Because of the explosion of mergers, acquisitions, and leveraged buyouts in the 1980s and 1990s, financial journalists coined the term *merger mania.* Many companies joined the merger mania simply to enhance their own operations by consolidating them with the operations of other firms. Mergers and acquisitions enabled these companies to gain a larger market share in their industries, acquire valuable assets such as new products or plants and equipment, and lower their costs. Mergers also represent a means of making profits quickly, as was the case during the 1980s when many companies' stock was undervalued. Quite simply, such companies represent a bargain to other companies that can afford to buy them. Additionally, deregulation of some industries has permitted consolidation of firms within those industries for the first time, as is the case in the banking and airline industries.

Some people view mergers and acquisitions favorably, pointing out that they boost corporations' stock prices and market value, to the benefit of their stockholders. In many instances, mergers enhance a company's ability to meet foreign competition in an increasingly global marketplace. Additionally, companies that are victims of hostile takeovers generally streamline their operations, reduce unnecessary staff, cut costs, and otherwise become more efficient with their operations, which benefits their stockholders whether or not the takeover succeeds.

Critics, however, argue that mergers hurt companies because they force managers to focus their efforts on avoiding takeovers rather than managing effectively and profitably. Some companies have taken on a heavy debt burden to stave off a takeover, later to be forced into bankruptcy when economic downturns left them unable to handle the debt. Mergers and acquisitions also can damage employee morale and productivity, as well as the quality of the companies' products.

Many mergers have been beneficial for all involved; others have had damaging effects for the companies, their employees, and customers. No one can say whether mergers will continue to slow, but many experts say the utilities, telecommunications, financial services, natural resources, computer hardware and software, gaming, managed health care, and technology industries are likely targets.

## ⊖ So You'd Like to Start a Business

If you have a good idea and want to turn it into a business, you are not alone. Small businesses are popping up all over the United States, and the concept of entrepreneurship is hot. Entrepreneurs seek opportunities and creative ways to make profits. Business emerges in a number of different organizational forms, each with its own advantages and disadvantages. Sole proprietorships are the most common form of business organization in the United States. They tend to be small businesses and can take pretty much any form—anything from a hair salon to a scuba shop, from an organic produce provider to a financial advisor. Proprietorships are everywhere serving consumers' wants and needs. Proprietorships have a big advantage in that they tend to be simple to manage—decisions get made quickly when the owner and the manager are the same person and they are fairly simple and inexpensive to set up. Rules vary by state, but at most all you will need is a license from the state.

Many people have been part of a partnership at some point in their life. Group work in school is an example of a partnership. If you ever worked as a DJ on the weekend with your friend and split the profits, then you have experienced a partnership. Partnerships can be either general or limited. General partners have unlimited liability and share completely in the management, debts, and profits of the business. Limited partners, on the other hand, consist of at least one general partner and one or more limited partners who do not participate in the management of the company but share in the profits. This form of partnership is used more often in risky investments where the limited partner stands only to lose his or her initial investment. Real estate limited partnerships are an example

of how investors can minimize their financial exposure, given the poor performance of the real estate market in recent years. Although it has its advantages, partnership is the least utilized form of business. Part of the reason is that all partners are responsible for the actions and decisions of all other partners, whether or not all of the partners were involved. Usually, partners will have to write up an Articles of Partnership that outlines respective responsibilities in the business. Even in states where it is not required, it is a good idea to draw up this document as a way to cement each partner's role and hopefully minimize conflict. Unlike a corporation, proprietorships and partnerships both expire upon the death of one or more of those involved.

Corporations tend to be larger businesses, but do not need to be. A corporation can consist of nothing more than a small group of family members. In order to become a corporation, you will have to file in the state under which you wish to incorporate. Each state has its own procedure for incorporation, meaning there are no general guidelines to follow. You can make your corporation private or public, meaning the company issues stocks, and shareholders are the owners. While incorporating is a popular form of organization because it gives the company an unlimited lifespan and limited liability (meaning that if your business fails, you cannot lose personal funds to make up for losses), there is a downside. You will be taxed as a corporation and as an individual, resulting in double taxation. No matter what form of organization suits your business idea best, there is a world of options out there for you if you want to be or experiment with being an entrepreneur.

# Review Your Understanding

### Define and examine the advantages and disadvantages of the sole proprietorship form of organization.

Sole proprietorships—businesses owned and managed by one person—are the most common form of organization. Their major advantages are the following: (1) They are easy and inexpensive to form, (2) they allow a high level of secrecy, (3) all profits belong to the owner, (4) the owner has complete control over the business, (5) government regulation is minimal, (6) taxes are paid only once, and (7) the business can be closed easily. The disadvantages include: (1) The owner may have to use personal assets to borrow money, (2) sources of external funds are difficult to find, (3) the owner must have many diverse skills, (4) the survival of the business is tied to the life of the owner and his or her ability to work, (5) qualified employees are hard to find, and (6) wealthy sole proprietors pay a higher tax than they would under the corporate form of business.

### Identify two types of partnership and evaluate the advantages and disadvantages of the partnership form of organization.

A partnership is a business formed by several individuals; a partnership may be general or limited. Partnerships offer the following advantages: (1) They are easy to organize, (2) they may have higher credit ratings because the partners possibly have more combined wealth, (3) partners can specialize, (4) partnerships can make decisions faster than larger businesses, and (5) government regulations are few. Partnerships also have several disadvantages: (1) General partners have unlimited liability for the debts of the partnership, (2) partners are responsible for each other's decisions, (3) the death or termination of one partner requires a new partnership agreement to be drawn up, (4) it is difficult to sell a partnership interest at a fair price, (5) the distribution of profits may not correctly reflect the amount of work done by each partner, and (6) partnerships cannot find external sources of funds as easily as can large corporations.

### Describe the corporate form of organization and cite the advantages and disadvantages of corporations.

A corporation is a legal entity created by the state, whose assets and liabilities are separate from those of its owners. Corporations are chartered by a state through articles of incorporation. They have a board of directors made up of corporate officers or people from outside the company. Corporations, whether private or public, are owned by stockholders. Common stockholders have the right to elect the board of directors. Preferred stockholders do not have a vote but get preferential dividend treatment over common stockholders.

Advantages of the corporate form of business include: (1) The owners have limited liability, (2) ownership (stock) can be easily transferred, (3) corporations usually last forever, (4) raising money is easier than for other forms of business, and (5) expansion into new businesses is simpler because of the ability of the company to enter into contracts. Corporations also have disadvantages: (1) The company is taxed on its income, and owners pay a second tax on any profits received as dividends; (2) forming a corporation can be expensive; (3) keeping trade secrets is difficult because so much information must be made available to the public and to government agencies; and (4) owners and managers are not always the same and can have different goals.

### Define and debate the advantages and disadvantages of mergers, acquisitions, and leveraged buyouts.

A merger occurs when two companies (usually corporations) combine to form a new company. An acquisition occurs when one company buys most of another company's stock. In a leveraged buyout, a group of investors borrows money to acquire a company, using the assets of the purchased company to guarantee the loan. They can help merging firms to gain a larger market share in their industries, acquire valuable assets such as new products or plants and equipment, and lower their costs. Consequently, they can benefit stockholders by improving the companies' market value and stock prices. However, they also can hurt companies if they force managers to focus on avoiding takeovers at the expense of productivity and profits. They may lead a company to take on too much debt and can harm employee morale and productivity.

### Propose an appropriate organizational form for a startup business.

After reading the facts in "Solve the Dilemma" on page 141 and considering the advantages and disadvantages of the various forms of business organization described in this chapter, you should be able to suggest an appropriate form for the startup nursery.

# Revisit the World of Business

1. What are some of the major reasons for shareholder activism?

2. Do you feel that large shareholders such as David Einhorn are justified in filing lawsuits against corporations sitting on large cash reserves?

3. What are some of the benefits of shareholder activism? Disadvantages?

# Learn the Terms

acquisition  135
articles of partnership  121
board of directors  129
common stock  130
cooperative (co-op)  134
corporate charter  127
corporation  126
dividends  126

general partnership  121
initial public offering (IPO)  128
joint venture  133
leveraged buyout (LBO)  137
limited liability company (LLC)  134
limited partnership  121
merger  135
nonprofit corporations  129

partnership  120
preferred stock  130
private corporation  127
public corporation  127
quasi-public corporations  129
S corporation  133
sole proprietorships  116
stock  126

# Check Your Progress

1. Name five advantages of a sole proprietorship.

2. List two different types of partnerships and describe each.

3. Differentiate among the different types of corporations. Can you supply an example of each type?

4. Would you rather own preferred stock or common stock? Why?

5. Contrast how profits are distributed in sole proprietorships, partnerships, and corporations.

6. Which form of business organization has the least government regulation? Which has the most?

7. Compare the liability of the owners of partnerships, sole proprietorships, and corporations.

8. Why would secrecy in operating a business be important to an owner? What form of organization would be most appropriate for a business requiring great secrecy?

9. Which form of business requires the most specialization of skills? Which requires the least? Why?

10. The most common example of a cooperative is a farm co-op. Explain the reasons for this and the benefits that result for members of cooperatives.

# Get Involved

1. Select a publicly owned corporation and bring to class a list of its subsidiaries. These data should be available in the firm's corporate annual report, *Standard & Poor's Corporate Records,* or *Moody Corporate Manuals.* Ask your librarian for help in finding these resources.

2. Select a publicly owned corporation and make a list of its outside directors. Information of this nature can be found in several places in your library: the company's annual report, its list of corporate directors, and various financial sources. If possible, include each director's title and the name of the company that employs him or her on a full-time basis.

## Build Your Skills  LO 4-5

### Selecting a Form of Business

**Background**

Ali Bush sees an opportunity to start her own website development business. Ali has just graduated from the University of Mississippi with a master's degree in computer science. Although she has many job opportunities outside the Oxford area, she wishes to remain there to care for her aging parents. She already has most of the computer equipment necessary to start the business, but she needs additional software. She is considering the purchase of a server to maintain websites for small businesses. Ali feels she has the ability to take this start-up firm and create a long-term career opportunity for herself and others. She knows she can hire Ole Miss students to work on a part-time basis to support her business. For now, as she starts the business, she can work out of the extra bedroom of her apartment. As the business grows, she'll hire the additional full- and/or part-time help needed and reassess the location of the business.

**Task**

1. Using what you've learned in this chapter, decide which form of business ownership is most appropriate for Ali. Use the tables provided to assist you in evaluating the advantages and disadvantages of each decision.

| Sole Proprietorships | |
| --- | --- |
| Advantages | Disadvantages |
| • | • |
| • | • |
| • | • |
| • | • |
| • | • |
| • | • |

| Corporation | |
| --- | --- |
| Advantages | Disadvantages |
| • | • |
| • | • |
| • | • |
| • | • |
| • | • |
| • | • |
| • | • |

| Limited Liability Company | |
| --- | --- |
| Advantages | Disadvantages |
| • | • |
| • | • |
| • | • |
| • | • |
| • | • |
| • | • |

## Solve the Dilemma

### To Incorporate or not to Incorporate

Thomas O'Grady and Bryan Rossisky have decided to start a small business buying flowers, shrubs, and trees wholesale and re-selling them to the general public. They plan to contribute $5,000 each in startup capital and lease a 2.5-acre tract of land with a small, portable sales office.

Thomas and Bryan are trying to decide what form of organization would be appropriate. Bryan thinks they should create a corporation because they would have limited liability and the image of a large organization. Thomas thinks a partnership would be easier to start and would allow them to rely on the combination of their talents and financial resources. In addition, there might be fewer reports and regulatory controls to cope with.

## Discussion Questions

1. What are some of the advantages and disadvantages of Thomas and Bryan forming a corporation?

2. What are the advantages and disadvantages of their forming a partnership?

3. Which organizational form do you think would be best for Thomas and Bryan's company and why?

# Build Your Business Plan

## Options for Organizing Business

Your team needs to think about how you should organize yourselves that would be most efficient and effective for your business plan. The benefits of having partners include having others to share responsibilities with and to toss ideas off of each other. As your business evolves, you will have to decide whether one or two members will manage the business while the other members are silent partners. Or perhaps you will all decide on working in the business to keep costs down, at least initially. However you decide on team member involvement in the business, it is imperative to have a written agreement so that all team members understand what their responsibilities are and what will happen if the partnership dissolves.

It is not too soon for you and your partners to start thinking about how you might want to find additional funding for your business. Later on in the development of your business plan, you might want to show your business plan to family members. Together, you and your partners will want to develop a list of potential investors in your business.

# See for Yourself Videocase

## PODS Excels at Organizing a Business

What happens when homeowners need to store their belongings temporarily? Before 1998, people would choose to either rent storage space, which can be costly and inconvenient, or store their belongings in their front yards. Yet, starting in 1998, another option was introduced: PODS.

PODS, short for Portable On Demand Storage, was founded after a group of firemen noticed the difficulties that many people faced when they needed to store their belongings for a short period. PODS delivers storage containers and leaves them in front of a house or business. A specially made hydraulic lift called Podzilla is able to place the container on ground level, which makes it easier for owners to store their belongings inside the container. PODS will then pick up the containers and move them to either its warehouses for storage or to anywhere else in the country.

When PODS was first started, banks and financial institutions were uncertain about how successful the moving and storage services company would be. Another issue was the expense of the actual containers. PODS containers, made of plywood over steel frames, cost between $2,200 and $2,500 each. If the company failed, the banks could repossess the containers. However, because PODS was a first-mover and there were no other comparable companies around, the banks feared that they would not be able to resell the containers. The risk for banks and financial institutions was high. This meant that PODS initially depended on venture capitalists for funding.

Once the company got started, however, PODS proved it was well worth the investment. More than a decade later, PODS can be found on three continents and has more than 200 million customers across the United States, Canada, the United Kingdom, and Australia. In addition to its convenience, PODS has also become known for its high-quality services and social responsibility. For instance, the company provided PODS containers to help recovery efforts in Hurricane Katrina. In 2011, PODS became a finalist in the National Association of Professional Organizers award for best service provider.

As PODS has expanded, its business organization has also undergone changes. Originally, PODS was formed as a sole proprietorship. Many businesses start off as sole proprietorships because of the benefits involved, such as ease of formation and greater control over operations. PODS's initial name was PODS LLC, meaning that it was a limited liability company. Limited liability companies provide more protection to owners so that their personal belongings will not be seized to pay the company's debts. It also frees owners from some of the restrictions that exist for corporations.

However, as businesses grow nationally, they become much more difficult for one or two individuals to handle. PODS soon realized that its rapid expansion required a new form of business organization. PODS decided to become a private corporation and renamed itself PODS Enterprises Inc. Although more people became involved in the ownership of the company, a small group of individuals maintains control over much of the general corporate operations. PODS stock is not issued publicly.

Eventually, PODS also decided to adopt a franchise model. The corporation began to allow other entrepreneurs, called franchisees, to license its name and products for a fee. This provided PODS with additional funding as well as the opportunity to expand into more areas. Because PODS is already successful, franchisees have a lower failure rate than starting their own businesses from scratch. Franchisees also understand their particular markets better than a corporation can.

"Franchisees bring another advantage, though, and that is their knowledge and connections in the local market, so they can take advantage of particularities in a market," said Ann Lehman, senior vice president of Franchise Operations. This increases PODS's adaptability when it expands into other areas.

On the other hand, because corporations are able to bring together several knowledgeable individuals, PODS corporate headquarters finds that it is better able to handle larger markets such as Los Angeles and Chicago. With this business model, PODS has figured out how to meet the needs of both local markets, through franchisees, and larger markets. Because of PODS's ability to understand the best ways of organizing its business, the company has been able to reap the benefits from all types of market sizes.[36]

### Discussion Questions

1.  What are some advantages of sole proprietorships for PODS? What are some disadvantages?

2.  What are some advantages of private corporations for PODS? What are some disadvantages?

3.  How has adopting a franchise model made PODS more adaptable?

**You can find the related video in the Video Library in Connect. Ask your instructor how you can access Connect.**

## Team Exercise

Form groups and find examples of mergers and acquisitions. Mergers can be broken down into traditional mergers, horizontal mergers, and conglomerate mergers. When companies are found, note how long the merger or acquisition took, if there were any requirements by the government before approval of the merger or acquisition, and if any failed mergers or acquisitions were found that did not achieve government approval. Report your findings to the class, and explain what the companies hoped to gain from the merger or acquisition.

# 5

# Small Business, Entrepreneurship, and Franchising

## Learning Objectives

**After reading this chapter, you will be able to:**

**LO 5-1** Define *entrepreneurship* and *small business*.

**LO 5-2** Investigate the importance of small business in the U.S. economy and why certain fields attract small business.

**LO 5-3** Specify the advantages of small-business ownership.

**LO 5-4** Summarize the disadvantages of small-business ownership, and analyze why many small businesses fail.

**LO 5-5** Describe how you go about starting a small business and what resources are needed.

**LO 5-6** Evaluate the demographic, technological, and economic trends that are affecting the future of small business.

**LO 5-7** Explain why many large businesses are trying to "think small."

**LO 5-8** Assess two entrepreneurs' plans for starting a small business.

## Chapter Outline

## Chobani Yogurt Fights for Dominance in the Yogurt Market

For the founder of Chobani Yogurt, it took more than a good idea to propel the company into what it is today. It was almost by chance that Hamdi Ulukaya made it into the billion-dollar venture it is now. At one time, Greek yogurt accounted for less than 1 percent of the yogurt market in the United States; it now makes up 50 percent. With the help of a Small Business Administration loan, Ulukaya purchased a small yogurt plant Kraft was selling. Ulukaya decided to sell Greek yogurt, a product he knew was popular in other parts of the world.

When Chobani yogurt hit shelves in 2007, the product was an immediate success. Unlike his contemporaries, Ulukaya does not outsource but maintains control of the entire manufacturing process. Under his leadership, the company has become a challenger to the top yogurt makers in the industry in only a matter of years. It is for this reason that Hamdi Ulukaya has been nicknamed the "Steve Jobs of yogurt." Today, Chobani Yogurt is netting more than $1 billion in sales and controls 17 percent of the yogurt market.

Chobani Yogurt has recently faced some challenges. For instance, in fall 2013 the company had to recall its yogurt after reports that mold growing in the yogurt made consumers sick. Later that year, Whole Foods decided to drop Chobani Yogurt from its shelves. Chobani is also facing increased competition from more established rivals such as Danone's Oikos brand and Yoplait Greek.[1]

## Introduction

Although many business students go to work for large corporations upon graduation, others may choose to start their own business or to find employment opportunities in small organizations with 500 or fewer employees. Small businesses employ about half of all private-sector employees.[2] Each small business represents the vision of its owners to succeed through providing new or better products. Small businesses are the heart of the U.S. economic and social system because they offer opportunities and demonstrate the freedom of people to make their own destinies. Today, the entrepreneurial spirit is growing around the world, from Russia and China to India, Germany, Brazil, and Mexico. For instance, within eastern Europe, approximately 24 percent of the population is engaged in entrepreneurial activities. Within the BRIC countries (Brazil, Russia, India, and China), the average is only slightly less at 21 percent.[3]

This chapter surveys the world of entrepreneurship and small business. First we define entrepreneurship and small business and examine the role of small business in the American economy. Then we explore the advantages and disadvantages of small-business ownership and analyze why small businesses succeed or fail. Next, we discuss how an entrepreneur goes about starting a business and the challenges facing small businesses today. Finally, we look at entrepreneurship in larger organizations.

**LO 5-1**

## The Nature of Entrepreneurship and Small Business

In Chapter 1, we defined an entrepreneur as a person who risks his or her wealth, time, and effort to develop for profit an innovative product or way of doing something. **Entrepreneurship** is the process of creating and managing a business to achieve desired objectives. Many large businesses you may recognize (Levi Strauss and Co., Procter & Gamble, McDonald's, Dell Computers, Microsoft, and Google) all began as small businesses based on the visions of their founders. Some entrepreneurs who start small businesses have the ability to see emerging trends; in response, they create a company to provide a product that serves customer needs. For example, rather than inventing a major new technology, an innovative company may take advantage of technology to create new markets, such as Amazon.com. Or they may offer a familiar product that has been improved or placed in a unique retail environment, such as Starbucks and its coffee shops. A company may innovate by focusing on a particular market segment and delivering a combination of features that consumers in that segment could not find anywhere else. Tweezerman, which manufactures beauty tools, became successful after its founder, Dal LaMagna, developed diamond tweezers directed specifically for beauty salons. For many years, the company only sold tweezers but has since expanded to encompass a range of other beauty tools.[4]

Of course, smaller businesses do not have to evolve into such highly visible companies to be successful, but those entrepreneurial efforts that result in rapidly growing businesses gain visibility along with success. Entrepreneurs who have achieved success, like Michael Dell (Dell Computers), Bill Gates (Microsoft), Larry Page and Sergey Brin (Google), and the late Steve Jobs (Apple) are some of the most well known. Table 5.1 lists some of the greatest entrepreneurs of the past few decades.

The entrepreneurship movement is accelerating, and many new, smaller businesses are emerging. Technology once available only to the largest firms can now

**enterpreneurship**
the process of creating and managing a business to achieve desired objectives

| Company | Entrepreneur |
|---|---|
| Hewlett-Packard | Bill Hewlett, David Packard |
| Walt Disney Productions | Walt Disney |
| Starbucks | Howard Schultz |
| Amazon.com | Jeff Bezos |
| Dell | Michael Dell |
| Microsoft | Bill Gates |
| Apple | Steve Jobs |
| Walmart | Sam Walton |
| Google | Larry Page, Sergey Brin |
| Ben & Jerry's | Ben Cohen, Jerry Greenfield |
| Ford | Henry Ford |
| General Electric | Thomas Edison |

**TABLE 5.1**
**Great Entrepreneurs of Innovative Companies**

be obtained by a small business. Websites, podcasts, online videos, social media, cellular phones, and even expedited delivery services enable small businesses to be more competitive with today's giant corporations. Small businesses can also form alliances with other companies to produce and sell products in domestic and global markets.

Another growing trend among small businesses is social entrepreneurship. *Social entrepreneurs* are individuals who use entrepreneurship to address social problems. They operate by the same principles as other entrepreneurs but view their organizations as vehicles to create social change. Although these entrepreneurs often start their own nonprofit organizations, they can also operate for-profit organizations committed to solving social issues. CEO of TOMS Shoes Blake Mycoskie is an example of a social entrepreneur who founded the firm with the purpose of donating one pair of shoes to a child in need for every pair of shoes sold to consumers. Muhammad Yunus, founder of micro-lending organization Grameen Bank, is another example of a social entrepreneur. Yunus seeks to combat poverty by providing small loans to low-income individuals to start their own businesses.

## What Is a Small Business?

This question is difficult to answer because smallness is relative. In this book, we will define a **small business** as any independently owned and operated business that is not dominant in its competitive area and does not employ more than 500 people. A local Mexican restaurant may be the most patronized Mexican restaurant in your community, but because it does not dominate the restaurant industry as a whole, the restaurant can be considered a small business. This definition is similar to the one used by the **Small Business Administration (SBA),** an independent agency of the federal government that offers managerial and financial assistance to small businesses. On its website, the SBA outlines the first steps in starting a small business and offers a wealth of information to current and potential small-business owners.

**small business**
any independently owned and operated business that is not dominant in its competitive area and does not employ more than 500 people

**Small Business Administration (SBA)**
an independent agency of the federal government that offers managerial and financial assistance to small businesses

**TABLE 5.2**
**Importance of Small Businesses to Our Economy**

| |
|---|
| Small firms represent 99.7 percent of all employer firms. |
| Small firms have generated 63 percent of net new jobs. |
| Small firms hire approximately 37 percent of high-tech workers (such as scientists, engineers, computer programmers, and others). |
| Small firms produce 16 times more patents per employee than large patenting firms. |
| Small firms employ nearly half of all private-sector employees. |
| Small firms pay 42 percent of the total U.S. private payroll. |

Source: Small Business Administration Department of Advocacy, "Frequently Asked Questions," March 2014, www.sba.gov/sites/default/files/FAQ_March_2014_0.pdf (accessed April 10, 2014).

## The Role of Small Business in the American Economy

No matter how you define a small business, one fact is clear: They are vital to the American economy. As you can see in Table 5.2, more than 99 percent of all U.S. firms are classified as small businesses, and they employ about half of private workers. Small firms are also important as exporters, representing 98 percent of U.S. exporters of goods and contributing 33 percent of the value of exported goods.[5] In addition, small businesses are largely responsible for fueling job creation and innovation. Small businesses also provide opportunities for minorities and women to succeed in business. Women-owned businesses are responsible for employing 7.7 million workers and contribute $1.3 trillion in sales. Women own more than 8 million businesses nationwide, with great success in the professional services, retail, communication, and administrative services areas.[6] Minority-owned businesses have been growing faster than other classifiable firms as well, representing 21.3 percent of all small businesses.[7] One successful business was started by a refugee from Belgrade, Serbia (formerly Yugoslavia). Although Marie Gray's early life was filled with hardship in WWII Yugoslavia, she immigrated to the United States and later used her passion for clothing to develop the women's dressmaker brand, St. John. Today, the company earns $346 million in annual revenue.[8]

**Job Creation.**    The energy, creativity, and innovative abilities of small-business owners have resulted in jobs for many people. About 63 percent of net new jobs annually were created by small businesses.[9] Table 5.3 indicates that 99.7 percent of all businesses employ fewer than 500 people. Businesses employing 19 or fewer people account for 89.8 percent of all businesses.[10]

Many small businesses today are being started because of encouragement from larger ones. Many new jobs are also created by big-company/small-company alliances. Whether through formal joint ventures, supplier relationships, or product or marketing cooperative projects, the rewards of collaborative relationships are creating many jobs for small-business owners and their employees. In India, many small information technology (IT) firms provide IT services to global markets. Because of lower costs, international companies often can find Indian businesses to provide their information processing solutions.[11]

**Innovation.**    Perhaps one of the most significant strengths of small businesses is their ability to innovate and to bring significant benefits to customers. Small firms produce more than half of all innovations. Among the important 20th-century innovations

| Firm Size | Number of Firms | Percentage of All Firms |
|---|---|---|
| 0–19 employees | 5,104,014 | 89.8 |
| 20–99 employees | 481,496 | 8.5 |
| 100–499 employees | 81,243 | 1.4 |
| 500+ employees | 17,671 | 0.3 |

**TABLE 5.3**
**Number of Firms by Employment Size**

*Source: "Statistics of U.S. Businesses (SUSB)," Statistics of U.S. Businesses, www.census.gov/econ/susb/index.html (accessed April 10, 2014).*

by U.S. small firms are the airplane, the audio tape recorder, fiber-optic examining equipment, the heart valve, the optical scanner, the pacemaker, the personal computer, soft contact lenses, the Internet, and the zipper. For instance, the founder and CEO of the small firm UniKey, Phil Dumas, invented a new way for consumers to keep their doors locked. Dumas invented Kevo, a motorized deadbolt lock that links to users' iPhones. With just the touch of a finger, consumers can lock and unlock their doors from remote locations. UniKey distributes products in major retailers such as Lowe's and Home Depot. This is just one example of a small company with the ability to innovate and contribute to the benefit of customers.[12]

The innovation of successful firms take many forms. For instance, small firms make up approximately 52 percent of home-based businesses and 2 percent of franchises. Many of today's largest businesses started off as small firms that used innovation to achieve success.[13] Small businessman Ray Kroc found a new way to sell hamburgers and turned his ideas into one of the most successful fast-food franchises in the world— McDonald's. Small businesses have become an integral part of our lives. J. Darius Bikoff founded Glaceau in 1996 to market enhanced water drinks. He built his small

Jeffrey Lubell founded premium apparel company True Religion in 2002. It has gone on to be listed among *Forbes'* best publicly traded small companies in America.

business offering slightly flavored drinks in health food stores into a nationally recognized company that Coca-Cola acquired in 2006. Its brands—including VitaminWater and SmartWater—are still popular today.[14] Travis Kalanick co-launched the successful company Uber, an app-based car service company rapidly growing in cities throughout the world. The Uber app allows consumers to rent a car or driver on demand. The cars arrive within a few minutes of the order. Much like Ray Kroc, Kalanick's innovative concept has the potential to change its industry—its low cost and convenience is making it a major player in the transportation rivaling traditional cab companies.[15] Entrepreneurs provide fresh ideas and usually have greater flexibility to change than do large companies.

## Industries That Attract Small Business

Small businesses are found in nearly every industry, but retailing and wholesaling, services, manufacturing, and high technology are especially attractive to entrepreneurs. These fields are relatively easy to enter and require low initial financing. Small-business owners in these industries also find it easier to focus on specific groups of consumers; new firms in these industries initially suffer less from heavy competition than do established firms.

The retailing industry is particularly attractive to entrepreneurs. Pike's Perk Coffee & Tea House is a small locally owned coffee shop in Colorado Springs, Colorado.

**Retailing and Wholesaling.** Retailers acquire goods from producers or wholesalers and sell them to consumers. Main streets and shopping centers and malls are generally lined with independent music stores, sporting-goods stores, dry cleaners, boutiques, drugstores, restaurants, caterers, service stations, and hardware stores that sell directly to consumers. Retailing attracts entrepreneurs because gaining experience and exposure in retailing is relatively easy. Additionally, an entrepreneur opening a new retail store does not have to spend the large sums of money for the equipment and distribution systems that a manufacturing business requires. All that a new retailer needs is a lease on store space, merchandise, money to sustain the business, knowledge about prospective customers' needs and desires, and basic management and marketing skills. However, it is important for entrepreneurs to anticipate the costs of opening a retail or wholesale business beforehand. When Patrick Leon Esquerré decided to open up a French bakery, he invested $100,000 into the bakery—all the money he had. He was able to raise more money from friends in France and Texas and opened up his first bakery, La Madeleine. After guests started asking for food, Esquerré used his mother's recipes to expand the menu. Eventually, the company began selling its products through stores such as Sam's Club. Esquerré's initial $100,000 investment has led to 63 restaurant locations today.[16]

### From Farmer's Market to Franchiser: Auntie Anne's Soft Pretzels

**Auntie Anne's Soft Pretzels**
**Founder:** Anne Beiler
**Founded:** 1988, in Downingtown, Pennsylvania
**Success:** Auntie Anne's is the largest soft pretzel franchise in the world with sales of $410 million.

Auntie Anne's Soft Pretzels began as a weekend operation at a farmer's market in Downingtown, Pennsylvania, in February 1988. Founder Anne Beiler received a $6,000 loan from her husband's parents to buy a pretzel stand at the farmer's market. In the first weekend, the business earned close to $1,000. Beiler experimented with the pretzel recipes, and the final product was twice as profitable as the original. She bought more ovens, hired more employees, and was soon making $2,000 each weekend. The company used sampling to market the product.

In July 1988, Beiler opened a store in Harrisburg, Pennsylvania, and by the end of the year made approximately $100,000. Beiler received repeated requests from people wanting to sell her product, so she decided to allow friends and family to open 10 new stores under a licensing agreement. By 1990, there were 75 locations in several states. Now owned by Focus Brands, Auntie Anne's is the largest soft pretzel franchise in the world with 1,200 shops in 26 countries.[17]

Wholesalers supply products to industrial, retail, and institutional users for resale or for use in making other products. Wholesaling activities range from planning and negotiating for supplies, promoting, and distributing (warehousing and transporting) to providing management and merchandising assistance to clients. Wholesalers are extremely important for many products, especially consumer goods, because of the marketing activities they perform. Although it is true that wholesalers themselves can be eliminated, their functions must be passed on to some other organization such as the producer, or another intermediary, often a small business. Frequently, small businesses are closer to the final customers and know what it takes to keep them satisfied. Some smaller businesses start out manufacturing, but find their real niche as a supplier or distributor of larger firms' products.

**Services.** The service sector includes businesses that do not actually produce tangible goods. The service sector accounts for 80 percent of U.S. jobs, excluding farmworkers. Real-estate, insurance and personnel agencies, barbershops, banks, television and computer repair shops, copy centers, dry cleaners, and accounting firms are all service businesses. Services also attract individuals—such as beauticians, morticians, jewelers, doctors, and veterinarians—whose skills are not usually required by large firms. Many of these service providers are retailers who provide their services to ultimate consumers.

**Manufacturing.** Manufacturing goods can provide unique opportunities for small businesses. Consider Nashville-based specialty chocolate company Olive & Sinclair. Within four years of its founding, the company was selling chocolates in the United States, London, Singapore, and Japan. The manufacturing of the chocolate is distinctively "southern" in nature. Its varieties include two ingredients—buttermilk and brown sugar—commonly associated with the South and a grinding process used to make Southern-style grits. This association appeals to global consumers. Today, Olive & Sinclair manufactures 1,500 chocolate bars each day.[18] Small businesses sometimes have an advantage over large firms because they can customize products to meet specific customer needs and wants. Such products include custom artwork, jewelry, clothing, and furniture.

**High Technology.**  *High technology* is a broad term used to describe businesses that depend heavily on advanced scientific and engineering knowledge. People who were able to innovate or identify new markets in the fields of computers, biotechnology, genetic engineering, robotics, and other markets have become today's high-tech giants. One innovative technology was developed by a teenager interested in virtual reality. Only a few years ago, virtual reality was considered a dead technology past its prime. However, when 19-year-old Palmer Luckey developed a virtual gaming headset, it caught the attention of programmer John Carmack. Together, they brought virtual reality to a new level for gamers. The company, Oculus Rift, was sold to Facebook for $2 billion.[20] In general, high-technology businesses require greater capital and have higher initial startup costs than do other small businesses. Many of the biggest, nonetheless, started out in garages, basements, kitchens, and dorm rooms.

**LO 5-3**

# Advantages of Small-Business Ownership

There are many advantages to establishing and running a small business. These can be categorized into personal advantages and business advantages. Table 5.4 lists some of the traits that can help entrepreneurs succeed.

## Independence

Independence is probably one of the leading reasons that entrepreneurs choose to go into business for themselves. Being a small-business owner means being your own boss. Many people start their own businesses because they believe they will do better for themselves than they could do by remaining with their current employer or by changing jobs. They may feel stuck on the corporate ladder and that no business would take them seriously enough to fund their ideas. Sometimes people who venture forth to start their own small business are those who simply cannot work for someone else. Such people may say that they just do not fit the "corporate mold."

More often, small-business owners just want the freedom to choose whom they work with, the flexibility to pick where and when to work, and the option of working in a family setting. The availability of the computer, copy machine, fax, and Internet has permitted many people to work at home. In the past, most of them would have needed the support that an office provides.

**TABLE 5.4**
**10 Successful Traits of Young Entrepreneurs**

| | |
|---|---|
| Intuitive | Persistent |
| Creative | Innovative |
| Productive | Frugal |
| Patient | Friendly |
| Charismatic | Fearless |

*Source: Yan Susanto, "10 Successful Traits of Young Entrepreneurs," Retire @ 21, April 10, 2009, www.retireat21.com/blog/10-successful-traits-of-young-entrepreneurs (accessed March 17, 2011).*

## Costs

As already mentioned, small businesses often require less money to start and maintain than do large ones. Obviously, a firm with just 25 people in a small factory spends less money on wages and salaries, rent, utilities, and other expenses than does a firm employing tens of thousands of people in several large facilities. Rather than maintain the expense of keeping separate departments for accounting, advertising, and legal counseling, small businesses often hire other firms (sometimes small businesses themselves) to supply these services as they are needed. Additionally, small-business owners can sometimes rely on friends and family members to help them save money by volunteering to work on a difficult project.

## Flexibility

With small size comes the flexibility to adapt to changing market demands. Small businesses usually have only one layer of management—the owners. Decisions therefore can be made and executed quickly. In larger firms, decisions about even routine matters can take weeks because they must pass through multiple levels of management before action is authorized. When Taco Bell introduces a new product, for example, it must first research what consumers want, then develop the product and test it before introducing it nationwide—a process that sometimes takes years. An independent snack shop, however, can develop and introduce a new product (perhaps to meet a customer's request) in a much shorter time.

## Focus

Small firms can focus their efforts on a precisely defined market niche—that is, a specific group of customers. Many large corporations must compete in the mass market or for large market segments. Smaller firms can develop products for particular groups of customers or to satisfy a need that other companies have not addressed. For example, Hampton Creek, based in San Francisco, focuses on using technology to produce sustainable protein products. The company developed a new type of egg substitute made from plant materials. This concept is likely to attract vegetarians and consumers concerned with sustainability, but founder and CEO Josh Tetrick has bigger plans. His concept is not to focus solely on a niche industry; he believes the solutions discovered at Hampton Creek will eventually help solve food shortages through alternatives that do not place a strain on the environment.[21] By targeting small niches or product needs, businesses can sometimes avoid competition from larger firms, helping them to grow into stronger companies.

## Reputation

Small firms, because of their capacity to focus on narrow niches, can develop enviable reputations for quality and service. A good example of a small business with a formidable reputation is W. Atlee Burpee and Co., which has the country's premier bulb and seed catalog. Burpee has an unqualified returns policy (complete satisfaction or your money back) that demonstrates a strong commitment to customer satisfaction.

# Disadvantages of Small-Business Ownership     LO 5-4

The rewards associated with running a small business are so enticing that it's no wonder many people dream of it. However, as with any undertaking, small-business ownership has its disadvantages.

## High Stress Level

A small business is likely to provide a living for its owner, but not much more (although there are exceptions as some examples in this chapter have shown). There are ongoing worries about competition, employee problems, new equipment, expanding inventory, rent increases, or changing market demand. In addition to other stresses, small-business owners tend to be victims of physical and psychological stress. The small-business person is often the owner, manager, sales force, shipping and receiving clerk, bookkeeper, and custodian. Having to multitask can result in long hours for most small-business owners. Many creative persons fail, not because of their business concepts, but rather because of difficulties in managing their business.

## High Failure Rate

Despite the importance of small businesses to our economy, there is no guarantee of success. Half of all new employer firms fail within the first five years.[22] Restaurants are a case in point. Look around your own neighborhood, and you can probably spot the locations of several restaurants that are no longer in business.

   Small businesses fail for many reasons (see Table 5.5). A poor business concept—such as insecticides for garbage cans (research found that consumers are not concerned with insects in their garbage)—will produce disaster nearly every time. Expanding a hobby into a business may work if a genuine market niche exists, but all too often people start such a business without identifying a real need for the goods or services. Other notable causes of small-business failure include the burdens imposed by government regulation, insufficient funds to withstand slow sales, and vulnerability to competition from larger companies. However, three major causes of small-business failure deserve a close look: undercapitalization, managerial inexperience or incompetence, and inability to cope with growth.

Entrepreneurs experience a great deal of independence but also a great deal of stress. Many fail.

| |
|---|
| 1. Underfunded (not providing adequate startup capital) |
| 2. Not understanding your competitive niche |
| 3. Lack of effective utilization of websites and social media |
| 4. Lack of a marketing and business plan |
| 5. If operating a retail store, poor site selection |
| 6. Pricing mistakes—too high or too low |
| 7. Underestimating the time commitment for success |
| 8. Not finding complementary partners to bring in additional experience |
| 9. Not hiring the right employees and/or not training them properly |
| 10. Not understanding legal and ethical responsibilities |

**TABLE 5.5**
**Challenges in Starting a New Business**

**Undercapitalization.**    The shortest path to failure in business is **undercapitalization,** the lack of funds to operate a business normally. Too many entrepreneurs think that all they need is enough money to get started, that the business can survive on cash generated from sales soon thereafter. But almost all businesses suffer from seasonal variations in sales, which make cash tight, and few businesses make money from the start. Many small rural operations cannot obtain financing within their own communities because small rural banks often lack the necessary financing expertise or assets sizable enough to counter the risks involved with small-business loans. Without sufficient funds, the best small-business idea in the world will fail.

*undercapitalization* the lack of funds to operate a business normally

**Managerial Inexperience or Incompetence.**    Poor management is the cause of many business failures. Just because an entrepreneur has a brilliant vision for a small business does not mean he or she has the knowledge or experience to manage a growing business effectively. A person who is good at creating great product ideas and marketing them may lack the skills and experience to make good management decisions in hiring, negotiating, finance, and control. Moreover, entrepreneurs may neglect those areas of management they know little about or find tedious, at the expense of the business's success.

**Inability to Cope with Growth.**    Sometimes, the very factors that are advantages for a small business turn into serious disadvantages when the time comes to grow. Growth often requires the owner to give up a certain amount of direct authority, and it is frequently hard for someone who has called all the shots to give up control. It has often been said that the greatest impediment to the success of a business is the entrepreneur. Similarly, growth requires specialized management skills in areas such as credit analysis and promotion—skills that the founder may lack or not have time to apply. The founders of many small businesses, including Dell Computers, found that they needed to bring in more experienced managers to help manage their companies through growing pains.

Poorly managed growth probably affects a company's reputation more than anything else, at least initially. And products that do not arrive on time or goods that are poorly made can quickly reverse a success. The principal immediate threats to small and mid-sized businesses include rising inflation, energy and other supply shortages or cost escalations, and excessive household and/or corporate debt.

### The Differences between Successful Entrepreneurs and Fraudsters

What do Steve Jobs and Bernie Madoff have in common? One is a highly admired entrepreneur responsible for creating one of the most valuable brands in the world. The other is a criminal guilty of operating the largest Ponzi scheme in the United States. The outcomes of the two men could not be more different. However, there are surprising similarities in the characteristics of famous entrepreneurs and fraudsters.

For instance, fraudsters tend to be intelligent, creative, persuasive, and seemingly confident—all characteristics of many successful entrepreneurs. Bernie Madoff built his enterprise from the ground-up, much like Oprah Winfrey, Bill Gates, and Steve Jobs. Successful entrepreneurs and fraudsters often display what has been termed "fearless dominance." Those that display fearless dominance demonstrate boldness, grace under pressure, charisma, and intelligence.

If fraudsters and entrepreneurs share so many characteristics, then what keeps entrepreneurs from becoming fraudsters? One trait is empathy. Being able to sympathize and care about others' well-being is lacking among fraudsters. Al Dunlap, former CEO of Sunbeam, was known for firing people and taking an aggressive approach to business. He was later implicated in accounting fraud. Another major characteristic is the ability to bounce back from failure. When Steve Jobs was ousted from Apple, he went on to found Pixar and later returned to save Apple from bankruptcy. When Bernie Madoff encountered financial difficulties, he covered them up through fraud.[23]

#### Discussion Questions

1. What characteristics do fraudsters and successful entrepreneurs share?
2. What are some major differences in the personalities of fraudsters and successful entrepreneurs?
3. Why is a lack of empathy fairly common among fraudsters?

---

## Starting a Small Business

We've told you how important small businesses are, and why they succeed and fail, but *how do you go about* starting your own business in the first place? To start any business, large or small, you must have some kind of general idea. Sam Walton, founder of Walmart stores, had a vision of a discount retailing enterprise that spawned the world's largest retailing empire and changed the way companies look at business. Next, you need to devise a strategy to guide planning and development in the business. Finally, you must make decisions about form of ownership, the financial resources needed, and whether to acquire an existing business, start a new one, or buy a franchise.

### The Business Plan

**business plan**
a precise statement of the rationale for a business and a step-by-step explanation of how it will achieve its goals

A key element of business success is a **business plan**—a precise statement of the rationale for the business and a step-by-step explanation of how it will achieve its goals. The business plan should include an explanation of the business, an analysis of the competition, estimates of income and expenses, and other information. It should also establish a strategy for acquiring sufficient funds to keep the business going. Many financial institutions decide whether to loan a small business money based on its business plan. A good business plan should act as a guide and reference document—not a shackle that limits the business's flexibility and decision-making ability. The business plan must be revised periodically to ensure that the firm's goals and strategies adapt to changes in the environment. Business plans allow companies to assess market potential, determine price and manufacturing requirements, identify optimal distribution channels, and refine product selection. Two college students had an innovative idea that prompted them to create a business plan. They recognized a need for people to get a hold of their personal medical information. The two developed the concept for a medical management company that helps clients locate their records and pitched it in the Rutgers Business Plan Competition. After winning the first prize of $20,000, the students launched Opcura.com, started hiring employees, and began promoting their business.[24] The SBA website provides an overview of a plan for small businesses to use to gain financing. Appendix A presents a comprehensive business plan.

## Forms of Business Ownership

After developing a business plan, the entrepreneur has to decide on an appropriate legal form of business ownership—whether it is best to operate as a sole proprietorship, partnership, or corporation—and to examine the many factors that affect that decision, which we explored in Chapter 4.

## Financial Resources

The expression "it takes money to make money" holds especially true in developing a business enterprise. To make money from a small business, the owner must first provide or obtain money (capital) to get started and to keep it running smoothly. Even a small retail store will probably need at least $50,000 in initial financing to rent space, purchase or lease necessary equipment and furnishings, buy the initial inventory, and provide working capital. Often, the small-business owner has to put up a significant percentage of the necessary capital. Few new business owners have a large amount of their own capital and must look to other sources for additional financing.

**Equity Financing.**   The most important source of funds for any new business is the owner. Many owners include among their personal resources ownership of a home, the accumulated value in a life-insurance policy, or a savings account. A new business owner may sell or borrow against the value of such assets to obtain funds to operate a business. Additionally, the owner may bring useful personal assets—such as a computer, desks and other furniture, a car or truck—as part of his or her ownership interest in the firm. Such financing is referred to as *equity financing* because the owner uses real personal assets rather than borrowing funds from outside sources to get started in a new business. The owner can also provide working capital by reinvesting profits into the business or simply by not drawing a full salary.

Small businesses can also obtain equity financing by finding investors for their operations. They may sell stock in the business to family members, friends, employees, or other investors. For example, Harvard alumnus Katrina Lake created a website called Stitch Fix that uses algorithms and personal stylists

Small-business owners often use debt financing from banks or the Small Business Administration to start their own organization.

Some of the advantages of small businesses include flexibility, lower startup costs, and perhaps most desirable, the ability to be your own boss.

**venture capitalists**
persons or organizations that agree to provide some funds for a new business in exchange for an ownership interest or stock

to develop sets, or "fixes," of clothes based upon the consumer's individual tastes. The fixes are mailed to the consumer, who pays for what she wants to keep and mails the rest back. Stich Fix is meant to appeal to consumers who want to keep shopping simple and are turned off by the large number of choices on websites such as Amazon.com. Despite high shipping costs, Stich Fix received $12 million from a venture-capital firm. These investors believe Stitch Fix has significant potential to expand and be successful.[25] **Venture capitalists** are persons or organizations that agree to provide some funds for a new business in exchange for an owner-ship interest or stock. Venture capitalists hope to purchase the stock of a small business at a low price and then sell the stock for a profit after the business has grown successful. Although these forms of equity financing have helped many small businesses, they require that the small-business owner share the profits of the business—and sometimes control, as well—with the investors.

**Debt Financing.**    New businesses sometimes borrow more than half of their financial resources. Banks are the main suppliers of external financing to small businesses. On the federal level, the SBA offers financial assistance to qualifying businesses. They can also look to family and friends as sources for long-term loans or other assets, such as computers or an automobile, that are exchanged for an owner-ship interest in a business. In such cases, the business owner can usually structure a favorable repayment schedule and sometimes negotiate an interest rate below current bank rates. If the business goes bad, however, the emotional losses for all concerned may greatly exceed the money involved. Anyone lending a friend or family member money for a venture should state the agreement clearly in writing before any money changes hands.

The amount a bank or other institution is willing to loan depends on its assessment of the venture's likelihood of success and of the entrepreneur's ability to repay the loan. The bank will often require the entrepreneur to put up *collateral,* a financial interest in the property or fixtures of the business, to guarantee payment of the debt. Additionally, the small-business owner may have to provide personal property as col-lateral, such as his or her home, in which case the loan is called a *mortgage.* If the small business fails to repay the loan, the lending institution may eventually claim and sell the collateral or mortgage to recover its loss.

Banks and other financial institutions can also grant a small business a *line of credit*—an agreement by which a financial institution promises to lend a business a predetermined sum on demand. A line of credit permits an entrepreneur to take quick advantage of opportunities that require external funding. Small businesses may obtain funding from their suppliers in the form of a *trade credit*—that is, suppliers allow the business to take possession of the needed goods and services and pay for them at a later date or in installments. Occasionally, small businesses engage in *bartering*—trading their own products for the goods and services offered by other businesses. For example, an accountant may offer accounting services to an office supply firm in exchange for office supplies and equipment.

### ReFleece: A Simple but Sustainable Product

Sam Palmer and Jennifer Feller took a risk with their idea for a sustainable iPad case. They refinanced their home and took out a home equity loan for $150,000 to found ReFleece in 2012, a business that uses up-cycled fleece as material for tablet cases. *Up-cycling* refers to reusing material without compromising its quality. Equipped with design experience and a concern for sustainability, Palmer and Feller partnered with Patagonia's Common Threads Initiative that brings in old consumer fleece to be recycled. ReFleece gets most of its raw materials from this program. The only new materials on these tablet cases are thread, snaps, and elastic. These sustainable tablet cases are manufactured in the United States, which helps the company save on costs. ReFleece is sold on Amazon, in Patagonia stores, and on refleece.com for $25 to $32, depending on the size of the case.

The entrepreneurs have been praised for their ability to create a useful product from old materials as well as for their commitment toward social responsibility. The company is a member of 1 percent for the Planet, donating 1 percent of its profits toward environmental nonprofits. ReFleece expects to earn $150,000 in sales of sustainable tablet cases.[26]

#### Discussion Questions

1. Why do you think a simple concept such as a tablet case made from up-cycled material became successful?
2. How were the ReFleece founders able to fund their startup company? What risks did they accept to make their idea into a reality?
3. How has the partnership with Patagonia likely affected ReFleece's sales?

---

Additionally, some community groups sponsor loan funds to encourage the development of particular types of businesses. State and local agencies may guarantee loans, especially to minority business people or for development in certain areas.

## Approaches to Starting a Small Business

**Starting from Scratch versus Buying an Existing Business.** Although entrepreneurs often start new small businesses from scratch much the way we have discussed in this section, they may elect instead to buy an existing business. This has the advantage of providing a built-in network of customers, suppliers, and distributors and reducing some of the guesswork inherent in starting a new business from the ground up. However, an entrepreneur who buys an existing business also takes on any problems the business already has.

**Franchising.** Many small-business owners find entry into the business world through franchising. A license to sell another's products or to use another's name in business, or both, is a **franchise.** The company that sells a franchise is the **franchiser.** Dunkin' Donuts, Subway, and Jiffy Lube are well-known franchisers with national visibility. The purchaser of a franchise is called a **franchisee.**

The franchisee acquires the rights to a name, logo, methods of operation, national advertising, products, and other elements associated with the franchiser's business in return for a financial commitment and the agreement to conduct business in accordance with the franchiser's standard of operations. The initial fee to join a franchise varies greatly. In addition, franchisees buy equipment, pay for training, and obtain a mortgage or lease. The franchisee also pays the franchiser a monthly or annual fee based on a percentage of sales or profits. In return, the franchisee often receives building specifications and designs, site recommendations, management and accounting support, and perhaps most importantly, immediate name recognition. Visit the website of the International Franchise Association to learn more on this topic.

**franchise**
a license to sell another's products or to use another's name in business, or both

**franchiser**
the company that sells a franchise

**franchisee**
the purchaser of a franchise

**TABLE 5.6**
**Fastest Growing and Hottest New Franchises**

| Top 10 Fastest Growing Franchises | Top 10 Hottest New Franchises |
|---|---|
| Subway | Kona Ice |
| Jan-Pro Franchising Int'l. Inc. | Menchie's |
| 7-Eleven Inc. | Orange Leaf Frozen Yogurt |
| Vanguard Cleaning Systems | ShelfGenie Franchise Systems LLC |
| Liberty Tax Service | Bricks 4 Kidz |
| Chester's | Smashburger Franchising LLC |
| Jazzercise Inc. | Game Truck Licensing LLC |
| Jimmy John's Gourmet Sandwiches | Paul Davis Emergency Services |
| Dunkin' Donuts | Signal 88 Security |
| Anago Cleaning Systems | Mac Tools |

Sources: "2013 Fastest-Growing Franchise Rankings," Entrepreneur, www.entrepreneur.com/franchises/rankings/
fastestgrowing-115162/2013,-1.html# (accessed April 10, 2014); "2013 New Franchise Rankings," Entrepreneur, www.entrepreneur.
com/franchises/rankings/topnew-115520/2013,-1.html (accessed April 10, 2014).

The practice of franchising first began in the United States in the 19th century when Singer used it to sell sewing machines. The method of goods distribution soon became commonplace in the automobile, gasoline, soft drink, and hotel industries. The concept of franchising grew especially rapidly during the 1960s, when it expanded to diverse industries. Table 5.6 shows the 10 fastest growing franchises and the top 10 new franchises.

The entrepreneur will find that franchising has both advantages and disadvantages. Franchising allows a franchisee the opportunity to set up a small business relatively quickly, and because of its association with an established brand, a franchise outlet often reaches the break-even point faster than an independent business would. Franchisees commonly report the following advantages:

- Management training and support.
- Brand-name appeal.
- Standardized quality of goods and services.
- National and local advertising programs.
- Financial assistance.
- Proven products and business formats.
- Centralized buying power.
- Site selection and territorial protection.
- Greater chance for success.[27]

However, the franchisee must sacrifice some freedom to the franchiser. Some shortcomings experienced by franchisees include:

- Franchise fees and profit sharing with the franchiser.
- Strict adherence to standardized operations.
- Restrictions on purchasing.

- Limited product line.
- Possible market saturation.
- Less freedom in business decisions.[28]

Strict uniformity is the rule rather than the exception. Entrepreneurs who want to be their own bosses are often frustrated with the restrictions of a franchise.

## Help for Small-Business Managers

Because of the crucial role that small business and entrepreneurs play in the U.S. economy, a number of organizations offer programs to improve the small-business owner's ability to compete. These include entrepreneurial training programs and programs sponsored by the SBA. Such programs provide small-business owners with invaluable assistance in managing their businesses, often at little or no cost to the owner.

Entrepreneurs can learn critical marketing, management, and finance skills in seminars and college courses. In addition, knowledge, experience, and judgment are necessary for success in a new business. While knowledge can be communicated and some experiences can be simulated in the classroom, good judgment must be developed by the entrepreneur. Local chambers of commerce and the U.S. Department of Commerce offer information and assistance helpful in operating a small business. National publications such as *Inc.* and *Entrepreneur* share statistics, advice, tips, and success/failure stories. Additionally, most urban areas have weekly business journals/newspapers that provide stories on local businesses as well as on business techniques that a manager or small business can use.

The SBA offers many types of management assistance to small businesses, including counseling for firms in difficulty, consulting on improving operations, and training for owner/managers and their employees. Among its many programs, the SBA funds Small Business Development Centers (SBDCs). These are business clinics, usually located on college campuses, that provide counseling at no charge and training at only a nominal charge. SBDCs are often the SBA's principal means of providing direct management assistance.

The Service Corps of Retired Executives (SCORE) and the Active Corps of Executives (ACE) are volunteer agencies funded by the SBA to provide advice for owners of small firms. Both are staffed by experienced managers whose talents and experience the small firms could not ordinarily afford. SCORE has more than 13,000 volunteers at 354 locations in the United States and has served more than 8.5 million small businesses.[29] The SBA also has organized Small Business Institutes (SBIs) on almost 500 university and college campuses in the United States. Seniors, graduate students, and faculty at each SBI provide onsite management counseling.

Finally, the small-business owner can obtain advice from other small-business owners, suppliers, and even customers. A customer may approach a small business it frequents with a request for a new product, for example, or a supplier may offer suggestions for improving a manufacturing process. Networking—building relationships and sharing information with colleagues—is vital for any businessperson, whether you work for a huge corporation or run your own small business. Communicating with other business owners is a great way to find ideas for dealing with employees and government regulation, improving processes, or solving problems. New technology is making it easier to network. For example, some states are establishing social networking sites for the use of their businesses to network and share ideas.

## The Future for Small Business[30]

Although small businesses are crucial to the economy, their size and limited resources can make them more vulnerable to turbulence and change in the marketplace than large businesses. Next, we take a brief look at the demographic, technological, and economic trends that will have the most impact on small business in the future.

### Demographic Trends

America's baby boom started in 1946 and ended in 1964. Many boomers are over 50, and in the next few years, millions more will pass that mark. The baby boomer generation represents 26 percent of Americans.[31] This segment of the population is wealthy, but many small businesses do not actively pursue it. Some exceptions, however, include Gold Violin, which sells designer canes and other products online and through a catalog, and LifeSpring, which delivers nutritional meals and snacks directly to the customer. Industries such as travel, financial planning, and health care will continue to grow as boomers age. Many experts believe that the boomer demographic is the market of the future.

Another market with huge potential for small business is the echo boomers, also called millennials or Generation Y. Millennials number around 75 million and possess a number of unique characteristics. Born between the early 1980s and the early 2000s, this cohort is not solely concerned about money. Those that fall into this group are also concerned with advancement, recognition, and improved capabilities. They need direct, timely feedback and frequent encouragement and recognition. Millennials do well when training sessions combine entertainment with learning. Working remotely is more acceptable to this group than previous generations, and virtual communication may become as important as face-to-face meetings.[32]

The Latino population is the biggest and fastest growing minority segment in the United States—and a lucrative market for businesses looking for ways to meet the segment's many needs.

| |
|---|
| 1. Austin, Texas |
| 2. Virginia Beach, Virginia |
| 3. Houston, Texas |
| 4. Colorado Springs, Colorado |
| 5. San Antonio, Texas |
| 6. Nashville, Tennessee |
| 7. Dallas-Fort Worth, Texas |
| 8. Raleigh-Durham, North Carolina |

**TABLE 5.7**
**Most Business-Friendly Cities**

*Source: "8 most business-friendly cities," CNN Money, 2013, http://money.cnn.com/gallery/smallbusiness/2013/06/18/best-places-launch-cities/index.html (accessed April 10, 2014).*

Yet another trend is the growing number of immigrants living in the United States, who now represent about 16 percent of the population. If this trend continues, by 2050 nearly one in five Americans will be classified as immigrants. The Latino population, the nation's largest minority group, is expected to triple in size by 2050.[33]

This vast group provides still another greatly untapped market for small businesses. Retailers who specialize in ethnic products, and service providers who offer bi- or multilingual employees, will find a large amount of business potential in this market. Table 5.7 ranks top cities in the United States for small businesses and startups.

## Technological and Economic Trends

Advances in technology have opened up many new markets to small businesses. Undoubtedly, the Internet will continue to provide new opportunities for small businesses. Imgur is a photo-sharing hub filled with trivial and humorous photos. It has become popular as a meme site. The company generates income by posting display advertisements from movie studios and videogame publishers. It charges users of the site $24 a year if they want features like unlimited data storage. Users do not have to register to show approval or disapproval of a photo. The company's users upload 1.5 million images every day and is becoming one of the most traveled to sites in the world—despite the fact that it only has 11 employees.[34]

Technological advances and an increase in service exports have created new opportunities for small companies to expand their operations abroad. Changes in communications and technology can allow small companies to customize their services quickly for international customers. Also, free trade agreements and trade alliances are helping to create an environment in which small businesses have fewer regulatory and legal barriers.

In recent years, economic turbulence has provided both opportunities and threats for small businesses. As large information technology companies such as Cisco, Oracle, and Sun Microsystems had to recover from an economic slowdown and an oversupply of Internet infrastructure products, some smaller firms found new niche markets. Smaller companies can react quickly to change and can stay close to their customers. While well-funded dot-coms were failing, many small businesses were learning how to use the Internet to promote themselves and sell products online. For example, arts and crafts dealers and makers of specialty products found they could sell their wares on existing websites, such as eBay. Service providers related to tourism, real estate, and construction also found they could reach customers through their own or existing websites.

Deregulation of the energy market and interest in alternative fuels and in fuel conservation have spawned many small businesses. Southwest Windpower Inc. manufactures and markets small wind turbines for producing electric power for homes, sailboats, and telecommunications. Solar Attic Inc. has developed a process to recover heat from home attics to use in heating water or swimming pools. As entrepreneurs begin to realize that worldwide energy markets are valued in the hundreds of billions of dollars, the number of innovative companies entering this market will increase. In addition, many small businesses have the desire and employee commitment to purchase such environmentally friendly products. New Belgium Brewing Company received the U.S. Environmental Protection Agency and Department of Energy Award for leadership in conservation for making a 10-year commitment to purchase wind energy. The company's employees unanimously agreed to cover the increased costs of wind-generated electricity from the employee profit-sharing program.

The future for small business remains promising. The opportunities to apply creativity and entrepreneurship to serve customers are unlimited. While large organizations such as Walmart, which has more than 2.1 million employees, typically must adapt to change slowly, a small business can adapt immediately to customer and community needs and changing trends. This flexibility provides small businesses with a definite advantage over large companies.

## LO 5-7

## Making Big Businesses Act "Small"

The continuing success and competitiveness of small businesses through rapidly changing conditions in the business world have led many large corporations to take a closer look at what makes their smaller rivals tick. More and more firms are emulating small businesses in an effort to improve their own bottom line. Beginning in the 1980s and continuing through the present, the buzzword in business has been to *downsize* or *right-size* to reduce management layers, corporate staff, and work tasks in order to make the firm more flexible, resourceful, and innovative. Many well-known U.S. companies, including IBM, Ford, Apple Computer, General Electric, Xerox, and 3M, have downsized to improve their competitiveness, as have German, British, and Japanese firms. Other firms have sought to make their businesses "smaller" by making their operating units function more like independent small businesses, each responsible for its profits, losses, and resources. Of course, some large corporations, such as Southwest Airlines, have acted like small businesses from their inception, with great success.

Trying to capitalize on small-business success in introducing innovative new products, more and more companies are attempting to instill a spirit of entrepreneurship into even the largest firms. In major corporations, **intrapreneurs,** like entrepreneurs, take responsibility for, or "champion," the development of innovations of any kind *within* the larger organization.[35] Often, they use company resources and time to develop a new product for the company.

**intrapreneurs**
individuals in large firms who take responsibility for the development of innovations within the organizations

## So You Want to Be an Entrepreneur or Small-Business Owner

In times when jobs are scarce, many people turn to entrepreneurship as a way to find employment. As long as there are unfulfilled needs from consumers, there will be a demand for entrepreneurs and small businesses. Entrepreneurs and small-business owners have been, and will continue to be, a vital part of the U.S. economy, whether in retailing, wholesaling, manufacturing, technology, or services. Creating a business around your idea has a lot of advantages. For many people, independence is the biggest advantage of forming their own small business, especially for those who do not work well in a corporate setting and like to call their own shots. Smaller businesses are also cheaper to start up than large ones in terms of salaries, infrastructure, and equipment. Smallness also provides a lot of flexibility to change with the times. If consumers suddenly start demanding new and different products, a small business is more likely to deliver quickly.

Starting your own business is not easy, especially in slow economic times. Even in a good economy, taking an idea and turning it into a business has a very high failure rate. The possibility of failure can increase even more when money is tight. Reduced revenues and expensive materials can hurt a small business more than a large one because small businesses have fewer resources. When people are feeling the pinch from rising food and fuel prices, they tend to cut back on other expenditures—which could potentially harm your small business. The increased cost of materials will also affect your bottom line. However, several techniques can help your company survive:

- Set clear payment schedules for all clients. Small businesses tend to be worse about collecting payments than large ones, especially if the clients are acquaintances. However, you need to keep cash flowing into the company in order to keep business going.

- Take the time to learn about tax breaks. A lot of people do not realize all of the deductions they can claim on items such as equipment and health insurance.

- Focus on your current customers, and don't spend a lot of time looking for new ones. It is far less expensive for a company to keep its existing customers happy.

- Although entrepreneurs and small-business owners are more likely to be friends with their customers, do not let this be a temptation to give things away for free. Make it clear to your customers what the basic price is for what you are selling and charge for extra features, extra services, etc.

- Make sure the office has the conveniences employees need—like a good coffee maker and other drinks and snacks. This will not only make your employees happy, but it will also help maintain productivity by keeping employees closer to their desks.

- Use your actions to set an example. If money is tight, show your commitment to cutting costs and making the business work by doing simple things like taking the bus to work or bringing a sack lunch every day.

- Don't forget to increase productivity in addition to cutting costs. Try not to focus so much attention on cost cutting that you don't try to increase sales.

In unsure economic times, these measures should help new entrepreneurs and small-business owners sustain their businesses. Learning how to run a business on a shoestring is a great opportunity to cut the fat and to establish lean, efficient operations.[36]

## Review Your Understanding

### Define entrepreneurship and small business.

An entrepreneur is a person who creates a business or product and manages his or her resources and takes risks to gain a profit; entrepreneurship is the process of creating and managing a business to achieve desired objectives. A small business is one that is not dominant in its competitive area and does not employ more than 500 people.

### Investigate the importance of small business in the U.S. economy and why certain fields attract small business.

Small businesses are vital to the American economy because they provide products, jobs, innovation, and opportunities. Retailing, wholesaling, services, manufacturing, and high technology attract small businesses because these industries are relatively easy to enter, require relatively low initial financing, and may experience less heavy competition.

### Specify the advantages of small-business ownership.

Small-business ownership offers some personal advantages, including independence, freedom of choice, and the option of working at home. Business advantages include flexibility, the ability to focus on a few key customers, and the chance to develop a reputation for quality and service.

### Summarize the disadvantages of small-business ownership, and analyze why many small businesses fail.

Small businesses have many disadvantages for their owners such as expense, physical and psychological stress, and a high failure rate. Small businesses fail for many reasons: undercapitalization, management inexperience or incompetence, neglect, disproportionate burdens imposed by government regulation, and vulnerability to competition from larger companies.

### Describe how you go about starting a small business and what resources are needed.

First, you must have an idea for developing a small business. Next, you need to devise a business plan to guide planning and development of the business. Then you must decide what form of business ownership to use: sole proprietorship, partnership, or corporation. Small-business owners are expected to provide some of the funds required to start their businesses, but funds also can be obtained from friends and family, financial institutions, other businesses in the form of trade credit, investors (venture capitalists), state and local organizations, and the Small Business Administration. In addition to loans, the Small Business Administration and other organizations offer counseling, consulting, and training services. Finally, you must decide whether to start a new business from scratch, buy an existing one, or buy a franchise operation.

### Evaluate the demographic, technological, and economic trends that are affecting the future of small business.

Changing demographic trends that represent areas of opportunity for small businesses include more elderly people as baby boomers age, a large group in the 11 to 28 age range known as echo boomers, millennials, or Generation Y, and an increasing number of immigrants to the United States. Technological advances and an increase in service exports have created new opportunities for small companies to expand their operations abroad, while trade agreements and alliances have created an environment in which small business has fewer regulatory and legal barriers. Economic turbulence presents both opportunities and threats to the survival of small businesses.

### Explain why many large businesses are trying to "think small."

More large companies are copying small businesses in an effort to make their firms more flexible, resourceful, and innovative, and generally to improve their bottom line. This effort often involves downsizing (reducing management layers, laying off employees, and reducing work tasks) and intrapreneurship, when an employee takes responsibility for (champions) developing innovations of any kind within the larger organization.

### Assess two entrepreneurs' plans for starting a small business.

Based on the facts given in "Solve the Dilemma" on page 168 and the material presented in this chapter, you should be able to assess the feasibility and potential success of Gray and McVay's idea for starting a small business.

## Revisit the World of Business

1. What are some likely reasons that Chobani Yogurt has become such a success?

2. Describe some of the challenges that Chobani is facing.

3. Why is it such an issue when a major retailer drops a product from its shelves?

## Learn the Terms

business plan  156
entrepreneurship  146
franchise  159
franchisee  159

franchiser  159
intrapreneurs  164
small business  147
Small Business Administration (SBA)  147

undercapitalization  155
venture capitalists  158

## Check Your Progress

1. Why are small businesses so important to the U.S. economy?

2. Which fields tend to attract entrepreneurs the most? Why?

3. What are the advantages of starting a small business? The disadvantages?

4. What are the principal reasons for the high failure rate among small businesses?

5. What decisions must an entrepreneur make when starting a small business?

6. What types of financing do small entrepreneurs typically use? What are some of the pros and cons of each?

7. List the types of management and financial assistance that the Small Business Administration offers.

8. Describe the franchising relationship.

9. What demographic, technological, and economic trends are influencing the future of small business?

10. Why do large corporations want to become more like small businesses?

## Get Involved

1. Interview a local small-business owner. Why did he or she start the business? What factors have led to the business's success? What problems has the owner experienced? What advice would he or she offer a potential entrepreneur?

2. Using business journals, find an example of a company that is trying to emulate the factors that make small businesses flexible and more responsive. Describe and evaluate the company's activities. Have they been successful? Why or why not?

3. Using the business plan outline in Appendix A, create a business plan for a business idea that you have. (A man named Fred Smith once did a similar project for a business class at Yale. His paper became the basis for the business he later founded: Federal Express!)

## Build Your Skills

### Creativity

**Background**

The entrepreneurial success stories in this chapter are about people who used their creative abilities to develop innovative products or ways of doing something that became the basis of a new business. Of course, being creative is not just for entrepreneurs or inventors; creativity is an important tool to help you find the optimal solutions to the problems you face on a daily basis. Employees rely heavily on their creativity skills to help them solve daily workplace problems.

According to brain experts, the right-brain hemisphere is the source of creative thinking; and the creative part of the brain can "atrophy" from lack of use. Let's see how much "exercise" you're giving your right-brain hemisphere.

**Task**

1. Take the following self-test to check your Creativity Quotient.[37]

2. Write the appropriate number in the box next to each statement according to whether the statement describes your behavior always (3), sometimes (2), once in a while (1), or never (0).

| | Always 3 | Sometimes 2 | Once in a While 1 | Never 0 |
|---|---|---|---|---|
| 1. I am a curious person who is interested in other people's opinions. | | | | |
| 2. I look for opportunities to solve problems. | | | | |
| 3. I respond to changes in my life creatively by using them to redefine my goals and revising plans to reach them. | | | | |
| 4. I am willing to develop and experiment with ideas of my own. | | | | |
| 5. I rely on my hunches and insights. | | | | |
| 6. I can reduce complex decisions to a few simple questions by seeing the "big picture." | | | | |
| 7. I am good at promoting and gathering support for my ideas. | | | | |
| 8. I think further ahead than most people I associate with by thinking long term and sharing my vision with others. | | | | |
| 9. I dig out research and information to support my ideas. | | | | |
| 10. I am supportive of the creative ideas from my peers and subordinates and welcome "better ideas" from others. | | | | |
| 11. I read books and magazine articles to stay on the "cutting edge" in my areas of interest. I am fascinated by the future. | | | | |
| 12. I believe I am creative and have faith in my good ideas. | | | | |
| Subtotal for each column | | | | |
| Grand Total | | | | |

3. Check your score using the following scale:

30–36  High creativity. You are giving your right-brain hemisphere a regular workout.

20–29  Average creativity. You could use your creativity capacity more regularly to ensure against "creativity atrophy."

10–19  Low creativity. You could benefit by reviewing the questions you answered "never" in the above assessment and selecting one or two of the behaviors that you could start practicing.

0–9  Undiscovered creativity. You have yet to uncover your creative potential.

## Solve the Dilemma

### The Small-Business Challenge

Jack Gray and his best friend, Bruce McVay, decided to start their own small business. Jack had developed recipes for fat-free and low-fat cookies and muffins in an effort to satisfy his personal health needs. Bruce had extensive experience in managing food-service establishments. They knew that a startup company needs a quality product, adequate funds, a written business plan, some outside financial support, and a good promotion program. Jack and Bruce felt they had all of this and more and were ready to embark on their new low-fat cookie/muffin store. Each had $35,000 to invest and with their homes and other resources, they had borrowing power of an additional $125,000.

However, they still have many decisions to make, including what form or organization to use, how to market their product, and how to determine exactly what products to sell—whether just cookies and muffins or additional products.

### Discussion Questions

1. Evaluate the idea of a low-fat cookie and muffin retail store.

2. Are there any concerns in connection with starting a small business that Jack and Bruce have not considered?

3. What advice would you give Jack and Bruce as they start up their business?

## Build Your Business Plan

### Small Business, Entrepreneurship, and Franchising

Now you can get started writing your business plan! Refer to Guidelines for the Development of the Business Plan following Chapter 1, which provides you with an outline for your business plan. As you are developing your business plan, keep in mind that potential investors might be reviewing it. Or you might have plans to go to your local Small Business Development Center for an SBA loan.

At this point in the process, you should think about collecting information from a variety of (free) resources. For example, if you are developing a business plan for a local business, product good, or service, you might want to check out any of the following sources for demographic information: your local Chamber of Commerce, Economic Development office, census bureau, or City Planning office.

Go on the Internet and see if there have been any recent studies done or articles on your specific type of business, especially in your area. Remember, you always want to explore any secondary data before trying to conduct your own research.

## See for Yourself Videocase

### Sonic—A Successful Franchise with an Old-Fashioned Drive-In Experience

For those who are nostalgic for the classic drive-in diner experience, the Sonic fast-food chain helps fill that need. Sonic offers customers a dose of nostalgia with its 1950s-style curbside speakers and carhop service. As the United States' largest drive-in fast-food chain, Sonic offers a unique and diverse menu selection that helps set it apart from a highly competitive fast-food franchise market. Founder Troy Smith launched the first Sonic Drive-In (known then as Top Hat Drive-In) in Shawnee, Oklahoma, in 1953 as a sole proprietorship. He later added a partner, Charlie Pappe, and eventually turned the business into a franchise.

Despite its traditional feel, the company has seized upon new trends and opportunities to secure more business. Customers at Sonic frequently eat in their cars or at tables outside the restaurant. However, Sonic has begun building indoor dining prototypes in colder areas to test whether this will entice more customers to eat at its locations. The prototype still makes use of the restaurant's traditional patio but encloses it to protect customers from the elements. So far, prototypes have been set up in 10 locations. Each of these restaurants maintains its carhop and drive-thru features in order to retain the "Sonic experience."

Today, Sonic is a publicly traded company and ranks as the 10th largest fast-food franchise in terms of sales revenue. Franchising is an appealing option for entrepreneurs looking to begin businesses without creating them from scratch. In the case of Sonic, when a franchisee purchases a franchise, he or she is getting a business that already has a national reputation and a national advertising campaign. The company also offers its franchisees tremendous support and training. As a pioneer, Troy Smith was required to innovate; as a Sonic franchisee, one steps into an already proven system.

That being said, successfully running a franchise is not easy. One entrepreneur who owns 22 Sonic franchises says the franchisee's job is to ensure that each customer has the best experience possible, thereby making repeat visits more likely. To accomplish this, a franchisee must build his or her locations, purchase equipment, hire excellent employees, make certain the products live up to Sonic's reputation, maintain a clean, inviting facility, and much more. In order to run 22 franchises, the entrepreneur runs his locations as limited partnerships, ensuring that a managing partner is on site at each location to keep day-to-day operations running smoothly.

Some of Sonic's success may be attributed to its stringent requirements for selecting franchisees. Although franchisees must have excellent financial credentials and prior restaurant/entrepreneurial experience, the most important factor is that each franchisee fit into the Sonic culture. Sonic offers two types of franchises. The traditional franchise, which includes the full restaurant set-up, requires a total investment of between $1.1 million and $3 million. Franchisees are required to pay 2 to 5 percent in ongoing royalty fees and a franchise fee of $45,000. A Sonic in a travel plaza, a mall food court, or a college campus are all examples of the nontraditional model. Because these set-ups do not include the drive-in and carhop features, initial investment is less. However, royalty and advertising fees still apply.

For entrepreneurs looking for limited risk, franchises like Sonic are great options. The advantages are abundant, as discussed earlier. There is a high failure rate among small businesses. Entering into a successful franchise significantly cuts down on the risk of failure, although a franchisee does have to watch for market saturation, poor location choice, and other determining factors. However, there are also disadvantages; chiefly, franchisees are often required to follow a strict model set by the franchiser. For instance, in addition to prior restaurant experience, Sonic requires its franchisees to be financially and operationally able to open two or more drive-ins. These types of requirements may make it difficult for entrepreneurs who want to set their own terms. However, with Sonic's successful business model and brand equity, there is no shortage of individuals who would like to operate a Sonic franchise.[38]

### Discussion Questions

1.  What is Sonic's competitive advantage over other fast-food franchises?

2.  What are the advantages of becoming a Sonic franchisee?

3.  What are the disadvantages of buying into the Sonic franchise?

**You can find the related video in the Video Library in Connect. Ask your instructor how you can access Connect.**

## Team Exercise

Explore successful global franchises. Go to the companies' websites and find the requirements for applying for three franchises. The chapter provides examples of successful franchises. What do the companies provide, and what is expected to be provided by the franchiser? Compare and contrast each group's findings for the franchises researched. For example, at Subway, the franchisee is responsible for the initial franchise fee, finding locations, leasehold improvements and equipment, hiring employees and operating restaurants, and paying an 8 percent royalty to the company and a fee into the advertising fund. The company provides access to formulas and operational systems, store design and equipment ordering guidance, a training program, an operations manual, a representative on-site during opening, periodic evaluations and ongoing support, and informative publications.

PART 3

# Managing for Quality and Competitiveness

# 6

# The Nature of Management

## Learning Objectives

**After reading this chapter, you will be able to:**

**LO 6-1** Define *management,* and explain its role in the achievement of organizational objectives.

**LO 6-2** Describe the major functions of management.

**LO 6-3** Distinguish among three levels of management and the concerns of managers at each level.

**LO 6-4** Specify the skills managers need in order to be successful.

**LO 6-5** Summarize the systematic approach to decision making used by many business managers.

**LO 6-6** Recommend a new strategy to revive a struggling business.

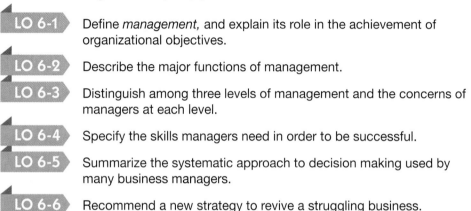

## Chapter Outline

## The Importance of Middle Managers

Middle managers are responsible for tactical planning and implementing top management's guidelines. Middle managers are expected to work across departments, put in long hours, and often remain available outside of work. Unfortunately, many middle managers feel that while they have much responsibility, they have very little authority. When cutbacks occur within an organization, middle managers are often the ones who are eliminated. Today there are 10.8 million middle managers in the United States, or 7.6 percent of the workforce.

As the major contact person between front-line employees and top managers, middle managers are required to have strong people skills and good communication. Middle managers have the responsibility of managing their teams while creating a positive influence on the company. Despite their often hectic work schedules, 44 percent of middle managers in one study reported that they were satisfied with their work/life balance, compared with 70 percent of nonmanagers.

There are different steps middle managers can take to improve their careers and move into top leadership positions. Suggestions include thinking big, asking for input, being flexible to new situations, clearly communicating between front-line employees and managers, and showing empathy for employees. Companies are also beginning to realize the benefit of middle managers when it comes to leadership. Half of mid-level executives receive leadership training. Although it is possible to eliminate the middle manager position, it is impossible to eliminate their functions—including communication, team building, and tactical planning—which are essential to leading the firm to success.[1]

## Introduction

For any organization—small or large, for profit or nonprofit—to achieve its objectives, it must have equipment and raw materials to turn into products to market, employees to make and sell the products, and financial resources to purchase additional goods and services, pay employees, and generally operate the business. To accomplish this, it must also have one or more managers to plan, organize, staff, direct, and control the work that goes on.

This chapter introduces the field of management. It examines and surveys the various functions, levels, and areas of management in business. The skills that managers need for success and the steps that lead to effective decision making are also discussed.

**LO 6-1**

**management**
a process designed to achieve an organization's objectives by using its resources effectively and efficiently in a changing environment

**managers**
those individuals in organizations who make decisions about the use of resources and who are concerned with planning, organizing, staffing, directing, and controlling the organization's activities to reach its objectives

## The Importance of Management

**Management** is a process designed to achieve an organization's objectives by using its resources effectively and efficiently in a changing environment. *Effectively* means having the intended result; *efficiently* means accomplishing the objectives with a minimum of resources. **Managers** make decisions about the use of the organization's resources and are concerned with planning, organizing, staffing, directing, and controlling the organization's activities so as to reach its objectives. The decision to introduce new products in order to reach objectives is often a key management duty. For instance, Samsung managers were involved in the decision to introduce their new line of curved televisions with Ultra High Definition to rejuvenate sales. The curved screen increases the clarity of viewing from all angles and has proportions similar to movie theater screens, making this an attractive alternative to going to movie theaters.[2] Management is universal. It takes place not only in business, but also in government, the military, labor unions, hospitals, schools, and religious groups—any organization requiring the coordination of resources.

Every organization must acquire resources (people, raw materials and equipment, money, and information) to effectively pursue its objectives and coordinate their use to turn out a final good or service. Employees are one of the most important resources in helping a business attain its objectives. Successful companies recruit, train, compensate, and provide benefits (such as shares of stock and health insurance) to foster employee loyalty. Acquiring suppliers is another important part of managing resources and ensuring that products are made available to customers. As firms reach global markets, companies such as Walmart, Corning, and Charles Schwab enlist hundreds of diverse suppliers that provide goods and services to support operations. A good supplier maximizes efficiencies and provides creative solutions to help the company reduce expenses and reach its objectives. Finally, the manager needs adequate financial resources to pay for essential activities. Primary funding comes from owners and shareholders, as well as banks and other financial institutions. All these resources and activities must be coordinated and controlled if the company is to earn a profit. Organizations must also have adequate supplies of resources of all types, and managers must carefully coordinate their use if they are to achieve the organization's objectives.

Mary Barra, the CEO of General Motors, must lead the company through a recall crisis involving faulty ignition switches.

# Management Functions

To harmonize the use of resources so that the business can develop, produce, and sell products, managers engage in a series of activities: planning, organizing, staffing, directing, and controlling (Figure 6.1). Although this book discusses each of the five functions separately, they are interrelated; managers may perform two or more of them at the same time.

## Planning

**Planning,** the process of determining the organization's objectives and deciding how to accomplish them, is the first function of management. Planning is a crucial activity, for it designs the map that lays the groundwork for the other functions. It involves forecasting events and determining the best course of action from a set of options or choices. The plan itself specifies what should be done, by whom, where, when, and how. For example, Toys "R" Us implemented a plan to refresh operations, strengthen customer experience, and improve its image. The plan—called "Tru Transformation"—is based on consumer research and vendor feedback. It aims to simplify stores and bring them back to profitability. The three major components of the plan are customers, inventory management, and cost management tactics. Stores will be redesigned with self-checkout lanes, wider aisles, and knowledgeable salespeople; product life-cycle management initiatives have begun allowing inventory to move more quickly; and pricing, discount, and promotional activities are being simplified and more targeted.[3] All businesses—from the smallest restaurant to the largest multinational corporation—need to develop plans for achieving success. But before an organization can plan a course of action, it must first determine what it wants to achieve.

**planning**
the process of determining the organization's objectives and deciding how to accomplish them; the first function of management

**Mission.**    A **mission,** or mission statement, is a declaration of an organization's fundamental purpose and basic philosophy. It seeks to answer the question: "What business are we in?" Good mission statements are clear and concise statements that explain the organization's reason for existence. A well-developed mission statement, no matter what the industry or size of business, will answer five basic questions:

**mission**
the statement of an organization's fundamental purpose and basic philosophy

1.  Who are we?
2.  Who are our customers?
3.  What is our operating philosophy (basic beliefs, values, ethics, etc.)?
4.  What are our core competencies and competitive advantages?
5.  What are our responsibilities with respect to being a good steward of environmental, financial, and human resources?

**FIGURE 6.1**
**The Functions of Management**

Private-equity firms Apollo Global Management and Metropoulos made the strategic plan to purchase the Hostess snack business after the firm declared bankruptcy.

A mission statement that delivers a clear answer to these questions provides the foundation for the development of a strong organizational culture, a good marketing plan, and a coherent business strategy. Sustainable cleaning products company Seventh Generation states that its mission is to "inspire a revolution that nurtures the health of the next seven generations."[4]

**Goals.** A goal is the result that a firm wishes to achieve. A company almost always has multiple goals, which illustrates the complex nature of business. A goal has three key components: an attribute sought, such as profits, customer satisfaction, or product quality; a target to be achieved, such as the volume of sales or extent of management training to be achieved; and a time frame, which is the time period in which the goal is to be achieved. CVS Caremark, under CEO Larry J. Merlo, set the goal of becoming a health care provider. As a result, the organization announced it would no longer sell cigarettes because it fundamentally conflicts with the company's goal. Electronic cigarettes are also not sold at CVS because the harm they may cause consumers is still to be determined. To be successful, company goals should be specific. This allows for better decision making in organizations.[5] To be successful at achieving goals, it is necessary to know what is to be achieved, how much, when, and how succeeding at a goal is to be determined.

**Objectives.** Objectives, the ends or results desired by an organization, derive from the organization's mission. A business's objectives may be elaborate or simple. Common objectives relate to profit, competitive advantage, efficiency, and growth. The principal difference between goals and objectives is that objectives are generally stated in such a way that they are measurable. Organizations with profit as an objective want to have money and assets left over after paying off business expenses. Objectives regarding competitive advantage are generally stated in terms of percentage of sales increase and market share, with the goal of increasing those figures. Efficiency objectives involve making the best use of the organization's resources. Dalhousie University has developed energy calculators for small and medium-sized businesses to help them become more aware of their energy usage and to reduce their energy expenditure. Growth objectives relate to an organization's ability to adapt and to get new products to the marketplace in a timely fashion. One of the most important objectives for businesses is sales. Nike, for example, has set its sales objectives for 2017 to reach $36 billion. In order to do this, it is putting effort into direct-to-consumer sales channels and using brick-and-mortar locations for testing new products.[6] Objectives provide direction for all managerial decisions; additionally, they establish criteria by which performance can be evaluated.

Herbalife does businesses in 90 countries, and contingency plans must often be made for fluctuating exchange rates.

**Plans.**    There are three general types of plans for meeting objectives—strategic, tactical, and operational. A firm's highest managers develop its **strategic plans,** which establish the long-range objectives and overall strategy or course of action by which the firm fulfills its mission. Strategic plans generally cover periods ranging from one year or longer. They include plans to add products, purchase companies, sell unprofitable segments of the business, issue stock, and move into international markets. For example, Sony decided to sell its unprofitable personal computer unit in order to mitigate against projected losses of up to $1.1 billion. Companies have been known to close U.S. plants and move manufacturing activities overseas when faced with stiff competition, rising costs, and slowing sales. However, many companies, including General Electric, Ford, and Whirlpool, are moving these activities back to the United States (an activity known as re-shoring) as transportation costs and wages in Asian countries rise.[7] Strategic plans must take into account the organization's capabilities and resources, the changing business environment, and organizational objectives. Plans should be market-driven, matching customers' desire for value with operational capabilities, processes, and human resources.[8]

**strategic plans**
those plans that establish the long-range objectives and overall strategy or course of action by which a firm fulfills its mission

   **Tactical plans** are short range and designed to implement the activities and objectives specified in the strategic plan. These plans, which usually cover a period of one year or less, help keep the organization on the course established in the strategic plan. Because tactical plans allow the organization to react to changes in the environment while continuing to focus on the company's overall strategy, management must periodically review and update them. Declining performance or failure to meet objectives set out in tactical plans may be one reason for revising them. The Michigan Department of Natural Resources Fisheries division developed a strategic plan to run through 2017. To implement this strategic plan, the department constructed a tactical plan with about 100 tasks to complete. For instance, a major goal of the tactical plan is to prevent the introduction of aquatic invasive species.[9] The differences between the two types of planning result in different activities in the short term versus the

**tactical plans**
short-range plans designed to implement the activities and objectives specified in the strategic plan

long term. For instance, a strategic plan might include the use of social media to reach consumers. A tactical plan could involve finding ways to increase traffic to the site or promoting premium content to those who visit the site. A fast-paced and ever-changing market requires companies to develop short-run or tactical plans to deal with the changing environment.

A retailing organization with a five-year strategic plan to invest $5 billion in 500 new retail stores may develop five tactical plans (each covering one year) specifying how much to spend to set up each new store, where to locate, and when to open each new store. Tactical plans are designed to execute the overall strategic plan. Because of their short-term nature, they are easier to adjust or abandon if changes in the environment or the company's performance so warrant.

**operational plans**
very short-term plans that specify what actions individuals, work groups, or departments need to accomplish in order to achieve the tactical plan and ultimately the strategic plan

**Operational plans** are very short term and specify what actions specific individuals, work groups, or departments need to accomplish in order to achieve the tactical plan and ultimately the strategic plan. They apply to details in executing activities in one month, week, or even day. For example, a work group may be assigned a weekly production quota to ensure there are sufficient products available to elevate market share (tactical goal) and ultimately help the firm be number one in its product category (strategic goal). Returning to our retail store example, operational plans may specify the schedule for opening one new store, hiring and training new employees, obtaining merchandise, and opening for actual business.

**crisis management (contingency planning)**
an element in planning that deals with potential disasters such as product tampering, oil spills, fire, earthquake, computer virus, or airplane crash

Another element of planning is **crisis management** or **contingency planning,** which deals with potential disasters such as product tampering, oil spills, fire, earthquake, computer viruses, or even a reputation crisis due to unethical or illegal conduct by one or more employees. Unfortunately, many businesses do not have updated contingency plans to handle the types of crises that their companies might encounter. Approximately 51 percent of companies have outdated disaster recovery and business continuity plans.[10] Businesses that have correct and well-thought-out contingency plans tend to respond more effectively when problems occur than do businesses who lack such planning.

Many companies, including Ashland Oil, H. J. Heinz, and Johnson & Johnson, have crisis management teams to deal specifically with problems, permitting other managers to continue to focus on their regular duties. Some companies even hold periodic disaster drills to ensure that their employees know how to respond when a crisis does occur. After the horrific earthquake in Japan, many companies in U.S. earthquake zones reevaluated their crisis management plans. Crisis management plans generally cover maintaining business operations throughout a crisis and communicating with the public, employees, and officials about the nature of and the company's response to the problem. Communication is especially important to minimize panic and damaging rumors; it also demonstrates that the company is aware of the problem and plans to respond.

Sometimes disasters occur that no one can anticipate, but companies can still plan for how to react to the disaster. The investment company Fred Alger Management Inc. was one company that displayed exemplary disaster recovery planning. When the company's core investment team—including its president—was killed during the September 11 attacks (the office was located in the World Trade Center), the firm relied upon its employee assistance programs and a recovery office located in New Jersey to help weather the emergency. Ten years later, the successful company continues to maintain disaster recovery plans, such as an unoccupied office for emergencies and the use of vendors to back up essential data in case the company's own data are destroyed.[11] Incidents such as this highlight the importance of planning for crises and the need to respond publicly and quickly when a disaster occurs.

## Organizing

Rarely are individuals in an organization able to achieve common goals without some form of structure. **Organizing** is the structuring of resources and activities to accomplish objectives in an efficient and effective manner. Managers organize by reviewing plans and determining what activities are necessary to implement them; then, they divide the work into small units and assign it to specific individuals, groups, or departments. As companies reorganize for greater efficiency, more often than not, they are organizing work into teams to handle core processes such as new product development instead of organizing around traditional departments such as marketing and production. Organizing occurs continuously because change is inevitable.

Organizing is important for several reasons. It helps create synergy, whereby the effect of a whole system equals more than that of its parts. It also establishes lines of authority, improves communication, helps avoid duplication of resources, and can improve competitiveness by speeding up decision making. When Japanese consumer electronics firm Panasonic decided to reorganize its business, it reduced its workforce, formed overseas alliances to expand into new product areas such as industrial-use solar systems, and stopped investing in less profitable areas. Although eliminating jobs was a difficult move, Panasonic believed that it must reduce redundancies and streamline operations to create a more efficient business.[12] Because organizing is so important, we'll take a closer look at it in Chapter 7.

**organizing**
the structuring of resources and activities to accomplish objectives in an efficient and effective manner

## Staffing

Once managers have determined what work is to be done and how it is to be organized, they must ensure that the organization has enough employees with appropriate skills to do the work. Hiring people to carry out the work of the organization is known as **staffing.** Beyond recruiting people for positions within the firm, managers must determine what skills are needed for specific jobs, how to motivate and train employees, how much to pay, what benefits to provide, and how to prepare employees for higher-level jobs in the firm at a later date. These elements of staffing will be explored in detail in Chapters 9 and 10.

**staffing**
the hiring of people to carry out the work of the organization

Another aspect of staffing is **downsizing,** the elimination of significant numbers of employees from an organization, which has been a pervasive and much-talked-about trend. Staffing can be outsourced to companies that focus on hiring and managing employees. For instance, Collabera provides IT staffing and a range of services to both *Fortune* 500 companies and mid-sized companies across the globe. The company has also been named "Best Staffing Firm to Work For" for three consecutive years, citing excellence in teamwork, trust, effectiveness, and compensation and benefits.[13] Many firms downsize by outsourcing production, sales, and technical positions to companies in other countries with lower labor costs. Downsizing has helped numerous firms reduce costs quickly and become more profitable (or become profitable after lengthy losses) in a short period of time. Whether it is called downsizing, rightsizing, trimming the fat, or the new reality in business, the implications of downsizing have been dramatic. During the recent economic recession, many companies laid off workers to cut costs. The nationwide unemployment rate climbed above 10 percent, but after the recovery, unemployment dropped significantly.[14]

**downsizing**
the elimination of a significant number of employees from an organization

Downsizing and outsourcing, however, have painful consequences. Obviously, the biggest casualty is those who lose their jobs, along with their incomes, insurance, and pensions. Some find new jobs quickly; others do not. Another victim is the morale of the remaining employees at downsized firms. Those left behind often feel insecure,

Some companies choose to recruit people to hire through online job websites such as Monster.com. Monster.com is one of the world's largest employment websites. Using websites like Monster.com falls under the staffing function of management.

angry, and sad, and their productivity may decline as a result, the opposite of the effect sought. Studies have found that firms that lay off more than 10 percent of their surviving workforce can expect to see turnover increase to 15.5 percent versus 10.4 percent at firms that do not have layoffs.[15]

After a downsizing situation, an effective manager will promote optimism and positive thinking and minimize criticism and fault-finding. Management should also build teamwork and encourage positive group discussions. Honest communication is important during a time of change and will lead to trust. In reality, when departments are downsized, the remaining employees end up working harder to fill the gaps left by layoffs. Truthfulness about what has happened and about future expectations is essential.

## Directing

**directing**
motivating and leading employees to achieve organizational objectives

Once the organization has been staffed, management must direct the employees. **Directing** is motivating and leading employees to achieve organizational objectives. Good directing involves telling employees what to do and when to do it through the implementation of deadlines, and then encouraging them to do their work. For example, as a sales manager, you would need to learn how to motivate salespersons; provide leadership; teach sales teams to be responsive to customer needs; and manage organizational issues as well as evaluate sales results. Finally, directing also involves determining and administering appropriate rewards and recognition. All managers are involved in directing, but it is especially important for lower-level managers who interact daily with the employees operating the organization. For example, an assembly-line supervisor for Frito-Lay must ensure that her workers know how to use their equipment properly and have the resources needed to carry out their jobs safely and efficiently, and she must motivate her workers to achieve their expected output of packaged snacks.

Managers may motivate employees by providing incentives—such as the promise of a raise or promotion—for them to do a good job. But most workers want more than money from their jobs: They need to know that their employer values their ideas and input. Managers should give younger employees some decision-making authority as soon as possible. Smart managers, therefore, ask workers to contribute ideas for reducing costs, making equipment more efficient, improving customer service, or even developing new products. For example, Rackspace, an IT hosting company, has made employee engagement a top priority to bring customer service to the highest level.[16] This participation makes workers feel important, and

### Ken Grossman's Management of Sierra Nevada's Growth

Ken Grossman, founder and CEO of Sierra Nevada Brewing Co., is familiar with the management challenges that accompany growth. Founded in 1980 in Chico, California, Sierra Nevada is now building another brewery in Mills River, North Carolina. This is a challenge to Grossman's management style because he is very involved in the day-to-day operations of the brewery. Walking around, talking to the company's 650 employees every day, and ensuring the quality of the brews are just a few of his managerial responsibilities.

Grossman also had to make the managerial decision to expand operations. The decision to expand was not merely driven by economic impetus, but also by environmental concerns. The new brewery will reduce the emissions the company creates in distribution. In addition, Grossman has installed 10,000 solar panels on the brewery in Chico, the largest private installation in the country, which accounts for 80 percent of its energy usage.

It is not all business for Grossman, however. He encourages employees to think like owners and takes a group of employees out to lunch with him every other week. This allows him to know people in the company on a personal level and establishes a mutual loyalty. Employees also receive subsidized meals at the brewery restaurant and day care, as well as a free health clinic for employees and their families.[17]

#### Questions for Discussion

1. Describe some of the managerial skills that Ken Grossman possesses in successfully leading Sierra Nevada.
2. How are the breweries increasing the firm's sustainability?
3. How does Ken Grossman motivate his employees?

---

the company benefits. Recognition and appreciation are often the best motivators. Employees who understand more about their effect on the financial success of the company may be induced to work harder for that success, and managers who understand the needs and desires of workers can encourage their employees to work harder and more productively. The motivation of employees is discussed in detail in Chapter 9.

## Controlling

Planning, organizing, staffing, and directing are all important to the success of an organization, whether its objective is earning a profit or something else. But what happens when a firm fails to reach its goals despite a strong planning effort? **Controlling** is the process of evaluating and correcting activities to keep the organization on course. Control involves five activities: (1) measuring performance, (2) comparing present performance with standards or objectives, (3) identifying deviations from the standards, (4) investigating the causes of deviations, and (5) taking corrective action when necessary.

Controlling and planning are closely linked. Planning establishes goals and standards. By monitoring performance and comparing it with standards, managers can determine whether performance is on target. When performance is substandard, management must determine why and take appropriate actions to get the firm back on course. In short, the control function helps managers assess the success of their plans. You might relate this to your performance in this class. If you did not perform as well on early projects or exams, you must take corrective action such as increasing studying or using website resources to achieve your overall objective of getting an A or B in the course. When the outcomes of plans do not meet expectations, the control process facilitates revision of the plans. Control can take many forms such as visual inspections, testing, and statistical modeling processes. The basic idea is to ensure that operations meet requirements and are satisfactory to reach objectives.

**controlling**
the process of evaluating and correcting activities to keep the organization on course

The control process also helps managers deal with problems arising outside the firm. For example, if a firm is the subject of negative publicity, management should use the control process to determine why and to guide the firm's response.

## Types of Management

LO 6-3

All managers—whether the sole proprietor of a jewelry store or the hundreds of managers of a large company such as Paramount Pictures—perform the five functions just discussed. In the case of the jewelry store, the owner handles all the functions, but in a large company with more than one manager, responsibilities must be divided and delegated. This division of responsibility is generally achieved by establishing levels of management and areas of specialization—finance, marketing, and so on.

**top managers**
the president and other top executives of a business, such as the chief executive officer (CEO), chief financial officer (CFO), and chief operations officer (COO), who have overall responsibility for the organization

### Levels of Management

As we have hinted, many organizations have multiple levels of management—top management, middle management, and first-line, or supervisory management. These levels form a pyramid, as shown in Figure 6.2. As the pyramid shape implies, there are generally more middle managers than top managers, and still more first-line managers. Very small organizations may have only one manager (typically, the owner), who assumes the responsibilities of all three levels. Large businesses have many managers at each level to coordinate the use of the organization's resources. Managers at all three levels perform all five management functions, but the amount of time they spend on each function varies, as we shall see (Figure 6.3).

**Top Management.**    In businesses, **top managers** include the president and other top executives, such as the chief executive officer (CEO), chief financial officer (CFO), and chief operations officer (COO), who have overall responsibility for the organization. For example, Mark Zuckerberg, CEO and founder of Facebook, manages the overall strategic direction of the company and plays a key role in representing the company to stakeholders. Sheryl Sandberg, Facebook's chief operating officer, is responsible for the daily operation of the company. The COO reports to the CEO and is often considered to be number two in command. In public corporations, even chief executive officers have a boss—the firm's board of directors. With technological advances accelerating and privacy concerns increasing, some companies are adding a new top management position—chief privacy officer (CPO). The position of privacy officer has grown so widespread that the International Association of Privacy Professionals boasts 14,000 members in 83 countries.[18] In government, top management refers to the president, a governor, or a mayor or city manager; in education, a chancellor of a university or a superintendent of education.

John Hammergren, CEO of McKesson, is the highest paid CEO at $131.2 million.

**FIGURE 6.2**

**Levels of Management**

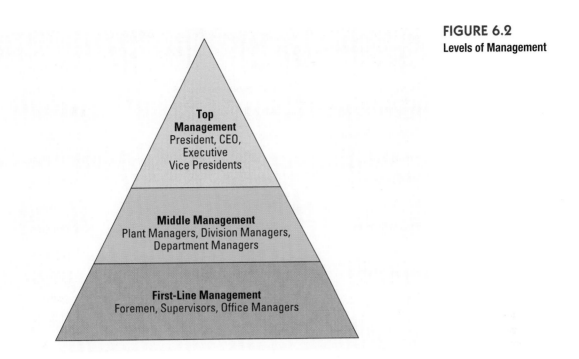

Top-level managers spend most of their time planning. They make the organization's strategic decisions, decisions that focus on an overall scheme or key idea for using resources to take advantage of opportunities. They decide whether to add products, acquire companies, sell unprofitable business segments, and move into foreign markets. Top managers also represent their company to the public and to government regulators.

**DID YOU KNOW?**  Only 4.6 percent of *Fortune* 500 CEOs are women.[19]

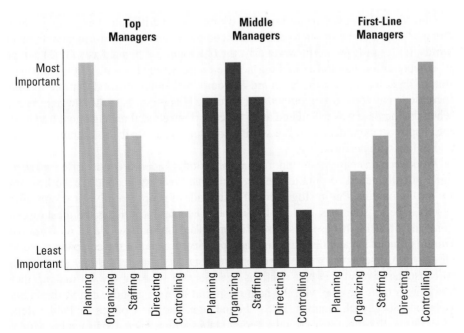

**FIGURE 6.3**

**Importance of Management Functions to Managers in Each Level**

**TABLE 6.1**
**The Highest Paid CEOs**

| CEO | Company | Compensation* |
|-----|---------|---------------|
| Larry Ellison | Oracle | $78.4 million |
| Robert Iger | Walt Disney Productions | $34.3 million |
| Kenneth I. Chenault | American Express | $24.4 million |
| Randall L. Stephenson | Apple | $20.6 million |
| Muhtar Kent | Coca-Cola | $20.4 million |
| James P. Gorman | Morgan Stanley | $18 million |
| Meg Whitman | Hewlett-Packard | $17.6 million |
| Virginia Rometty | IBM | $13.97 million |
| Jeff Bezos | Amazon | $1.68 million |
| Warren Buffett | Berkshire Hathaway | $485,606 |

*2013 compensation results compiled from publicly available data.*

Given the importance and range of top managements' decisions, top managers generally have many years of varied experience and command top salaries. In addition to salaries, top managers' compensation packages typically include bonuses, long-term incentive awards, stock, and stock options. Table 6.1 lists the compensation packages of different CEOs. Top management may also get perks and special treatment that is criticized by stakeholders.

Compensation committees are increasingly working with boards of directors and CEOs to attempt to keep pay in line with performance in order to benefit stockholders and key stakeholders. The majority of major companies cite their concern about attracting capable leadership for the CEO and other top executive positions in their organizations. However, many firms are trying to curb criticism of excessive executive compensation by trying to align CEO compensation with performance. In other words, if the company performs poorly, the CEO will not be paid as well. This type of compensation method is making a difference. An analysis of CEO compensation of 46 companies in the Standard & Poor's 500 Index showed that the median increase in pay for 2013 amounted to 1 percent. This is compared to the year before when the increase was calculated at 15 percent.[20] Successful management translates into happy stockholders who are willing to compensate their top executives fairly and in line with performance.

Workforce diversity is an important issue in today's corporations. Effective managers at enlightened corporations have found that diversity is good for workers and for the bottom line. Putting together different kinds of people to solve problems often results in better solutions. Sodexo Inc. topped DiversityInc's list as the most diverse company of 2014. It has consistently been ranked on the list due to its corporate culture of inclusion and diversity and their priority as a part of the company's overall strategy.[21] A diverse workforce is better at making decisions regarding issues related to consumer diversity. Public relations agencies are working toward making their workforces more diverse with the help of special interest groups such as the Public Relations Society of America, PRSA Foundation, and the Council of Public Relations Firms. Reaching fast-growing demographic groups such as Hispanics, African

| Rule | Action |
|------|--------|
| 1. Get everyone involved. | Educate all employees on the tangible benefits of diversity recruiting to garner support and enthusiasm for those initiatives. |
| 2. Showcase your diversity. | Prospective employees are not likely to become excited about joining your company just because you say that your company is diversity-friendly; they need to see it. |
| 3. Work with diversity groups within your community. | By supporting community-based diversity organizations, your company will generate the priceless word-of-mouth publicity that will lead qualified diversity candidates to your company. |
| 4. Spend money. | If you are serious about diversity recruiting, you will need to spend some money getting your message out to the right places. |
| 5. Sell, sell, sell—and measure your return on investment. | Employers need to sell their company to prospective diversity employees and present them with a convincing case as to why their company is a good fit for the diversity candidate. |

**TABLE 6.2**
**Five Rules of Successful Diversity Recruiting**

Source: Adapted from Juan Rodriguez, "The Five Rules of Successful Diversity Recruiting," Diversityjobs.com, www.diversityjobs.com/Rules-of-Successful-Diversity-Recruiting (accessed February 25, 2010).

Americans, Asian Americans, and others will be beneficial to large companies as they begin to target these markets.[22] Managers from companies devoted to workforce diversity devised five rules that make diversity recruiting work (see Table 6.2). Diversity is explored in greater detail in Chapter 10.

**Middle Management.**    Rather than making strategic decisions about the whole organization, **middle managers** are responsible for tactical planning that will implement the general guidelines established by top management. Thus, their responsibility is more narrowly focused than that of top managers. Middle managers are involved in the specific operations of the organization and spend more time organizing than other managers. In business, plant managers, division managers, and department managers make up middle management. The product manager for laundry detergent at a consumer products manufacturer, the department chairperson in a university, and the head of a state public health department are all middle managers. The ranks of middle managers have been shrinking as more and more companies downsize to be more productive.

**First-Line Management.**    Most people get their first managerial experience as **first-line managers,** those who supervise workers and the daily operations of the organization. They are responsible for implementing the plans established by middle management and directing workers' daily performance on the job. They spend most of their time directing and controlling. Common titles for first-line managers are foreman, supervisor, and office service manager.

## Areas of Management

At each level, there are managers who specialize in the basic functional areas of business: finance, production and operations, human resources (personnel), marketing, and administration.

**middle managers** those members of an organization responsible for the tactical planning that implements the general guidelines established by top management

**first-line managers** those who supervise both workers and the daily operations of an organization

**financial managers** those who focus on obtaining needed funds for the successful operation of an organization and using those funds to further organizational goals

**production and operations managers** those who develop and administer the activities involved in transforming resources into goods, services, and ideas ready for the marketplace

**human resources managers** those who handle the staffing function and deal with employees in a formalized manner

**marketing managers** those who are responsible for planning, pricing, and promoting products and making them available to customers through distribution

**information technology (IT) managers** those who are responsible for implementing, maintaining, and controlling technology applications in business, such as computer networks

# Entrepreneurship in Action

## Philip Pillsbury: The Entrepreneur behind the Billion-Dollar Brand

Pillsbury Company
**Founder:** Charles A. Pillsbury and John S. Pillsbury
**Founded:** 1872, in Minneapolis, Minnesota
**Success:** In its transition from commodities to consumer products, the Pillsbury Company became so successful that it was purchased by General Mills in 2001 for $10.5 billion.

Although Charles Pillsbury co-founded the successful Pillsbury Company, it was his grandson who led the company toward its status as a billion-dollar brand. In 1940, Philip Pillsbury became president of his grandfather's flour milling company. He had worked as a miller early in life and knew the industry. As the markets changed, Pillsbury's entrepreneurial instinct and management skills allowed him to transform the company's direction from commodities to consumer products.

Pillsbury was a visionary with strong conceptual skills who recognized growing opportunities in the consumer market. He targeted this market by investing in product research and development, resulting in product lines such as cake mixes and refrigerated rolls, biscuits, and cookies. He also infused the company's marketing with the Grand National Recipe & Baking Contest, which later became known as the annual Pillsbury Bake-Off. Influential judges—including Eleanor Roosevelt—drew the attention of 700,000 new customers. International expansion was also part of Pillsbury's strategy, and he implemented it with global acquisitions. By 1974, Pillsbury had increased the company's sales by seven times the 1940 level to $315 million.[23]

---

**administrative managers** those who manage an entire business or a major segment of a business; they are not specialists but coordinate the activities of specialized managers

Each of these management areas is important to a business's success. For instance, a firm cannot survive without someone obtaining needed financial resources (financial managers) or staff (human resources managers). While larger firms will most likely have all of these managers, and even more depending upon that particular firm's needs, in smaller firms these important tasks may fall onto the owner or a few employees. Yet whether or not companies have managers for specific areas, every company must have someone responsible for obtaining financial resources, transforming resources into finished products for the marketplace, hiring and/or dealing with staff, marketing products, handling the firm's information technology resources, and managing a business segment or the overall business. These different types of managers are discussed in more detail in Table 6.3.

**TABLE 6.3** **Areas of Management**

| Manager | Function |
| --- | --- |
| **Financial manager** | Focus on obtaining the money needed for the successful operation of the organization and using that money in accordance with organizational goals. |
| **Production and operations manager** | Develop and administer the activities involved in transforming resources into goods, services, and ideas ready for the marketplace. |
| **Human resources manager** | Handle the staffing function and deals with employees in a formalized manner. |
| **Marketing manager** | Responsible for planning, pricing, and promoting products and making them available to customers through distribution. |
| **Information technology (IT) manager** | Responsible for implementing, maintaining, and controlling technology applications in business, such as computer networks. |
| **Administrative manager** | Manage an entire business or a major segment of a business; do not specialize in a particular function. |

TABLE 6.4    **Managerial Roles**

| Type of Role | Specific Role | Examples of Role Activities |
|---|---|---|
| Decisional | Entrepreneur | Commit organizational resources to develop innovative goods and services; decide to expand internationally to obtain new customers for the organization's products. |
| | Disturbance handler | Move quickly to take corrective action to deal with unexpected problems facing the organization from the external environment, such as a crisis like an oil spill, or from the internal environment, such as producing faulty goods or services. |
| | Resource allocator | Allocate organizational resources among different functions and departments of the organization; set budgets and salaries of middle and first-level managers. |
| | Negotiator | Work with suppliers, distributors, and labor unions to reach agreements about the quality and price of input, technical, and human resources; work with other organizations to establish agreements to pool resources to work on joint projects. |
| Informational | Monitor | Evaluate the performance of managers in different functions and take corrective action to improve their performance; watch for changes occurring in the external and internal environment that may affect the organization in the future. |
| | Disseminator | Inform employees about changes taking place in the external and internal environment that will affect them and the organization; communicate to employees the organization's vision and purpose. |
| | Spokesperson | Launch a national advertising campaign to promote new goods and services; give a speech to inform the local community about the organization's future intentions. |
| Interpersonal | Figurehead | Outline future organizational goals to employees at company meetings; open a new corporate headquarters building; state the organization's ethical guidelines and the principles of behavior employees are to follow in their dealings with customers and suppliers. |
| | Leader | Provide an example for employees to follow; give direct commands and orders to subordinates; make decisions concerning the use of human and technical resources; mobilize employee support for specific organizational goals. |
| | Liaison | Coordinate the work of managers in different departments; establish alliances between different organizations to share resources to produce new goods and services. |

Source: Gareth R. Jones and Jennifer M. George, Essentials of Contemporary Management (Burr Ridge, IL: McGraw-Hill/Irwin, 2007, 3rd edition), p. 14.

# Skills Needed by Managers

Managers are typically evaluated using the metrics of how effective and efficient they are. Managing effectively and efficiently requires certain skills—technical expertise, conceptual skills, analytical skills, human relations skills and leadership. Table 6.4 describes some of the roles managers may fulfill.

**LO 6-4**

## Technical Expertise

Managers need **technical expertise,** the specialized knowledge and training required to perform jobs related to their area of management. Accounting managers need to be able to perform accounting jobs, and production managers need to be able to perform production jobs. Although a production manager may not actually perform a job, he or she needs technical expertise to train employees, answer questions, provide guidance, and solve problems. Technical skills are most needed by first-line managers and are least critical to top-level managers.

**technical expertise**
the specialized knowledge and training needed to perform jobs that are related to particular areas of management

This financial manager of a city hedge fund analyzes data from financial charts. Financial managers are responsible for obtaining the necessary funding for organizations to succeed, both in the short term and in the long term.

## Conceptual Skills

**Conceptual skills,** the ability to think in abstract terms, and to see how parts fit together to form the whole, are needed by all managers, but particularly top-level managers. Top management must be able to evaluate continually where the company will be in the future. Conceptual skills also involve the ability to think creatively. Recent scientific research has revealed that creative thinking, which is behind the development of many innovative products and ideas, including fiber optics and compact disks, can be learned. As a result, IBM, AT&T, GE, Hewlett-Packard, Intel, and other top U.S. firms hire creative consultants to teach their managers how to think creatively.

## Analytical Skills

**Analytical skills** refer to the ability to identify relevant issues and recognize their importance, understand the relationships between them, and perceive the underlying causes of a situation. When managers have identified critical factors and causes, they can take appropriate action. All managers need to think logically, but this skill is probably most important to the success of top-level managers. To be analytical, it is necessary to think about a broad range of issues and to weigh different options before taking action. Because analytical skills are so important, questions that require analytical skills are often a part of job interviews. Questions such as "Tell me how you would resolve a problem at work if you had access to a large amount of data?" may be part of the interview process. The answer would require the interviewee to try to explain how to sort data to find relevant facts that could resolve the issue. Analytical thinking is required in complex or difficult situations where the solution is often not clear. Resolving ethical issues often requires analytical skills.

## Human Relations Skills

People skills, or **human relations skills,** are the ability to deal with people, both inside and outside the organization. Those who can relate to others, communicate well with others, understand the needs of others, and show a true appreciation for others are generally more successful than managers who lack such skills. People skills are especially important in hospitals, airline companies, banks, and other organizations that provide services. For example, Southwest Airlines places great value on its employees. New hires go through extensive training to teach employees about the airline and its reputation for impeccable customer service. All employees in management positions at Southwest take mandatory leadership classes that address skills related to listening, staying in touch with employees, and handling change without compromising values.

# Leadership

**Leadership** is the ability to influence employees to work toward organizational goals. Strong leaders manage and pay attention to the culture of their organizations and the needs of their customers. Table 6.5 offers some tips for successful leadership.

**conceptual skills**
the ability to think in abstract terms and to see how parts fit together to form the whole

**analytical skills**
the ability to identify relevant issues, recognize their importance, understand the relationships between them, and perceive the underlying causes of a situation

**human relations skills**
the ability to deal with people, both inside and outside the organization

**leadership**
the ability to influence employees to work toward organizational goals

Howard Schultz, CEO of Starbucks, has great human relations skills and leadership abilities, as demonstrated by his ability to relate to others. Under his leadership, Starbucks decided to offer health insurance to its part-time workers.

Managers often can be classified into three types based on their leadership style. *Autocratic leaders* make all the decisions and then tell employees what must be done and how to do it. They generally use their authority and economic rewards to get employees to comply with their directions. Martha Stewart is an example of an autocratic leader. She built up her media empire by paying close attention to every detail.[24] *Democratic leaders* involve their employees in decisions. The manager presents a

| **TABLE 6.5**<br>**Seven Tips for Successful Leadership** |
| --- |
| • Build effective and responsive interpersonal relationships. |
| • Communicate effectively—in person, print, e-mail, etc. |
| • Build the team and enable employees to collaborate effectively. |
| • Understand the financial aspects of the business. |
| • Know how to create an environment in which people experience positive morale and recognition. |
| • Lead by example. |
| • Help people grow and develop. |

*Source: Susan M. Heathfield, "Seven Tips About Successful Management," About.com, http://humanresources.about.com/cs/ managementissues/qt/mgmtsuccess.htm (accessed February 25, 2010)*

situation and encourages his or her subordinates to express opinions and contribute ideas. The manager then considers the employees' points of view and makes the decision. Herb Kelleher, co-founder of Southwest Airlines, had a democratic leadership style. Under his leadership, employees were encouraged to discuss concerns and provide input.[25] *Free-rein leaders* let their employees work without much interference. The manager sets performance standards and allows employees to find their own ways to meet them. For this style to be effective, employees must know what the standards are, and they must be motivated to attain them. The free-rein style of leadership can be a powerful motivator because it demonstrates a great deal of trust and confidence in the employee. Warren Buffett, CEO of Berkshire Hathaway, exhibits free-rein leadership among the managers who run the company's various businesses.

The effectiveness of the autocratic, democratic, and free-rein styles depends on several factors. One consideration is the type of employees. An autocratic style of leadership is generally best for stimulating unskilled, unmotivated employees; highly skilled, trained, and motivated employees may respond better to democratic or free-rein leadership styles. Employees who have been involved in decision making generally require less supervision than those not similarly involved. Other considerations are the manager's abilities and the situation itself. When a situation requires quick decisions, an autocratic style of leadership may be best because the manager does not have to consider input from a lot of people. If a special task force must be set up to solve a quality-control problem, a normally democratic manager may give free rein to the task force.

Many managers, however, are unable to use more than one style of leadership. Some are incapable of allowing their subordinates to participate in decision making, let alone make any decisions. Thus, what leadership style is "best" depends on specific circumstances, and effective managers will strive to adapt their leadership style as circumstances warrant. Many organizations offer programs to develop goal leadership skills. When plans fail, very often leaders are held responsible for what goes wrong. For example, JCPenney Co.'s CEO Ron Johnson was booted out of the position after an unsuccessful attempt at turning the struggling company around. This came only 17 months after the company hired him to lead the company after a successful run at Apple.[26]

Another type of leadership style that has been gaining in popularity is authentic leadership. Authentic leadership is a bit different from the other three leadership styles because it is not exclusive. Both democratic and free-rein leaders could qualify as authentic leaders depending upon how they conduct themselves among stakeholders. Authentic leaders are passionate about the goals and mission of the company, display corporate values in the workplace, and form long-term relationships with stakeholders.[27] Kim Jordan of New Belgium Brewing is an authentic leader. As co-founder of the company, she helped develop the firm's core values and has ensured that everything New Belgium does aligns with these values.

While leaders might incorporate different leadership styles depending on the business and the situation, all leaders must be able to align employees behind a common vision to be effective.[28] Strong leaders also realize the value that employees can provide by participating in the firm's corporate culture. It is important that companies develop leadership training programs for employees. Because managers cannot oversee everything that goes on in the company, empowering employees to take more responsibility for their decisions can aid in organizational growth and productivity. Leadership training also enables a smooth transition when an executive or manager leaves the organization. For instance, when CEO Jim Skinner of McDonald's retired, he made sure the current chief operating officer had enough leadership experience to take over the position of CEO. While it is common for stock prices to drop whenever an effective leader leaves the organization, in this case investors seemed so reassured that the new leader was up to the task that stock prices hardly dropped when Skinner's resignation was announced.[29]

### Employee Empowerment

Businesses are increasingly realizing the benefits of participative corporate cultures characterized by employee empowerment. **Employee empowerment** occurs when employees are provided with the ability to take on responsibilities and make decisions about their jobs. Employee empowerment does not mean that managers are not needed. Managers are important for guiding employees, setting goals, making major decisions, and other responsibilities emphasized throughout this chapter. However, companies that have a participative corporate culture have been found to be beneficial because employees feel like they are taking an active role in the firm's success.

**employee empowerment** when employees are provided with the ability to take on responsibilities and make decisions about their jobs

Leaders who wish to empower employees must adopt systems that support an employee's ability to provide input and feedback on company decisions. Employees must be encouraged to actively participate in decision making. While this might be simpler for some employees, other employees might find it difficult if they come from more of an autocratic or authoritarian background, where lower-level employees were discouraged from speaking up. Managers also might find it difficult to support a participative culture if they come from similar backgrounds. One of the best ways to overcome these challenges is through employee and managerial training. As mentioned earlier, employees should be trained in leadership skills, including teamwork, conflict resolution, and decision making. Managers should also be trained in ways to empower employees to make decisions while also guiding employees to challenging situations in which the right decision might not be so clear.[30]

A section on leadership would not be complete without a discussion of leadership in teams. In today's business world, decisions made by teams are becoming the norm. Employees at Zappos, for instance, often work in teams and are encouraged to make decisions that they believe will reinforce the company's mission and values. Teamwork has often been an effective way for encouraging employee empowerment. Although decision making in teams is collective, the most effective teams are those in which all employees are encouraged to contribute their ideas and recommendations. Because each employee can bring in his or her own unique insights, teams often result in innovative ideas or decisions that would not have been reached by only one or two people. However, truly empowering employees in team decision making can be difficult. It is quite common for more outspoken employees to dominate the team and engage in groupthink, in which team members go with the majority rather than what they think is the right decision. Training employees how to listen to one another and provide relevant feedback can help to prevent these common challenges. Another way is to rotate the team leader so that no one person can assume dominancy.[31]

# Decision Making

LO 6-5

Managers make many different kinds of decisions, such as the hours in a workday, which employees to hire, what products to introduce, and what price to charge for a product. Decision making is important in all management functions and at all levels, whether the decisions are on a strategic, tactical, or operational level.

### Managers Discover Benefits of Feminine Traits for Leadership

The collective idea of what it means to be a great leader is changing. In the past, successful leadership has often been associated with authoritative traits such as decisiveness, resilience, and confidence. These leaders tend to exude confidence and charisma, resulting in admiration and a desire to follow. However, over the past several years, the leadership landscape has been changing. Recurring scandals involving leaders and the widespread use of technology has increased the need for leadership traits such as integrity. Employees as well as consumers are placing a major emphasis on the values of leaders.

One study showed that traits increasingly desired in leaders include patience, flexibility, empathy, vulnerability, inclusiveness, generosity, and balance. Interestingly, all of these characteristics are generally considered to be feminine. While assertiveness and ambition—considered more masculine traits—remain important, leaders who have an emotional connection to their work, good listening

skills, and generosity are now thought to be important for a successful firm. For instance, Oprah Winfrey, who has been described as a demanding but caring boss, and Whole Foods CEO John Mackey, who donates $100,000 every year toward a fund to help employees with personal struggles, have come to be highly admired. Leaders who exhibit these traits have been found to make more thoughtful decisions and have better relationships with their employees and customers, often resulting in successful company operations and profits.[32]

#### Discussion Questions

1. Why are some characteristics traditionally associated as feminine considered important for leadership?
2. Why might a lack of empathy create a significant disadvantage in leadership?
3. Describe ways in which Oprah Winfrey and John Mackey of Whole Foods demonstrate strong leadership characteristics.

A systematic approach using the following six steps usually leads to more effective decision making: (1) recognizing and defining the decision situation, (2) developing options to resolve the situation, (3) analyzing the options, (4) selecting the best option, (5) implementing the decision, and (6) monitoring the consequences of the decision (Figure 6.4).

### Recognizing and Defining the Decision Situation

The first step in decision making is recognizing and defining the situation. The situation may be negative—for example, huge losses on a particular product—or positive—for example, an opportunity to increase sales.

Situations calling for small-scale decisions often occur without warning. Situations requiring large-scale decisions, however, generally occur after some warning signs.

**FIGURE 6.4**

**Steps in the Decision-Making Process**

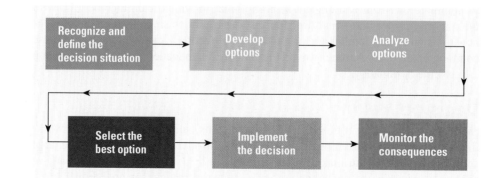

Effective managers pay attention to such signals. Declining profits, small-scale losses in previous years, inventory buildup, and retailers' unwillingness to stock a product are signals that may foreshadow huge losses to come. If managers pay attention to such signals, problems can be contained.

Once a situation has been recognized, management must define it. Losses reveal a problem—for example, a failing product. One manager may define the situation as a product quality problem; another may define it as a change in consumer preference. These two viewpoints may lead to vastly different solutions. The first manager, for example, may seek new sources of raw materials of better quality. The second manager may believe that the product has reached the end of its lifespan and decide to discontinue it. This example emphasizes the importance of carefully defining the problem rather than jumping to conclusions.

## Developing Options

Once the decision situation has been recognized and defined, the next step is to develop a list of possible courses of action. The best lists include both standard and creative plans. As a general rule, more time and expertise are devoted to the development stage of decision making when the decision is of major importance. When the decision is of less importance, less time and expertise will be spent on this stage. Options may be developed individually, by teams, or through analysis of similar situations in comparable organizations. Creativity is a very important part of selecting the most viable option. Creativity depends on new and useful ideas, regardless of where they originate or the method used to create them. The best option can range from a required solution to an identified problem or a volunteered solution, to an observed problem by an outside work group member.[33]

## Analyzing Options

After developing a list of possible courses of action, management should analyze the practicality and appropriateness of each option. An option may be deemed impractical because of a lack of financial resources, legal restrictions, ethical and social responsibility considerations, authority constraints, technological constraints, economic limitations, or simply a lack of information and expertise. For example, a small computer manufacturer may recognize an opportunity to introduce a new type of computer but lack the financial resources to do so. Other options may be more practical for the computer company: It may consider selling its technology to another computer company that has adequate resources, or it may allow itself to be purchased by a larger company that can introduce the new technology.

When assessing appropriateness, the decision maker should consider whether the proposed option adequately addresses the situation. When analyzing the consequences of an option, managers should consider its impact on the situation and on the organization as a whole. For example, when considering a price cut to boost sales, management must think about the consequences of the action on the organization's cash flow and consumers' reaction to the price change.

Technology can help managers maintain an agenda, analyze options, and make decisions.

## Selecting the Best Option

When all courses of action have been analyzed, management must select the best one. Selection is often a subjective procedure because many situations do not lend themselves to quantitative analysis. Of course, it is not always necessary to select only one option and reject all others; it may be possible to select and use a combination of several options. William Wrigley Jr. made a decision to sell his firm to Mars for $23 billion. The firm was founded by his great-grandfather in 1891, but hard times forced Wrigley to take what was considered to be the best option. This option was to create the Mars-Wrigley firm, currently the world's largest confectionary company with a distribution network in 180 countries.[34] A different set of choices would have been available to the company had it been able to purchase Hershey for $12 billion a few years earlier.

## Implementing the Decision

To deal with the situation at hand, the selected option or options must be put into action. Implementation can be fairly simple or very complex, depending on the nature of the decision. Effective implementation of a decision to abandon a product, close a plant, purchase a new business, or something similar requires planning. For example, when a product is dropped, managers must decide how to handle distributors and customers and what to do with the idle production facility. Additionally, they should anticipate resistance from people within the organization. (People tend to resist change because they fear the unknown.) Finally, management should be ready to deal with the unexpected consequences. No matter how well planned implementation is, unforeseen problems will arise. Management must be ready to address these situations when they occur.

## Monitoring the Consequences

After managers have implemented the decision, they must determine whether it has accomplished the desired result. Without proper monitoring, the consequences of decisions may not be known quickly enough to make efficient changes. If the desired result is achieved, management can reasonably conclude that it made a good choice. If the desired result is not achieved, further analysis is warranted. Was the decision simply wrong, or did the situation change? Should some other option have been implemented?

If the desired result is not achieved, management may discover that the situation was incorrectly defined from the beginning. That may require starting the decision-making process all over again. Finally, management may determine that the decision was good even though the desired results have not yet shown up, or it may determine a flaw in the decision's implementation. In the latter case, management would not change the decision but would change the way in which it is implemented.

# Management in Practice

Management is not a cut-and-dried process. There is no mathematical formula for managing an organization and achieving organizational goals, although many managers passionately wish for one! Managers plan, organize, staff, direct, and control, but management expert John P. Kotter says even these functions can be boiled down to two basic activities:

1. Figuring out what to do despite uncertainty, great diversity, and an enormous amount of potentially relevant information, and

2. Getting things done through a large and diverse set of people despite having little direct control over most of them.[35]

Managers spend as much as 75 percent of their time working with others—not only with subordinates but with bosses, people outside their hierarchy at work, and people outside the organization itself. In these interactions, they discuss anything and everything remotely connected with their business.

Managers spend a lot of time establishing and updating an agenda of goals and plans for carrying out their responsibilities. An **agenda** contains both specific and vague items, covering short-term goals and long-term objectives. Like a calendar, an agenda helps the manager figure out what must be done and how to get it done to meet the objectives set by the organization. Technology tools such as smartphones can help managers manage their agendas, contacts, communications, and time.

Managers also spend a lot of time **networking**—building relationships and sharing information with colleagues who can help them achieve the items on their agendas. Managers spend much of their time communicating with a variety of people and participating in activities that on the surface do not seem to have much to do with the goals of their organization. Nevertheless, these activities are crucial to getting the job done. Networks are not limited to immediate subordinates and bosses; they include other people in the company as well as customers, suppliers, and friends. These contacts provide managers with information and advice on diverse topics. Managers ask, persuade, and even intimidate members of their network in order to get information and to get things done. Networking helps managers carry out their responsibilities. Social media sites have increased the ability of both managers and subordinates to network. Internal social networks such as Yammer allow employees to connect with one another, while social networks such as Facebook or Twitter enable managers to connect with customers. Sales managers are even using social networks to communicate with their distributors. LinkedIn has been used for job networking and is gaining in popularity among the younger generation as an alternative to traditional job hunting. Some speculate that social networks might eventually replace traditional résumés and job boards.[36]

Finally, managers spend a great deal of time confronting the complex and difficult challenges of the business world today. Some of these challenges relate to rapidly changing technology (especially in production and information processing), increased scrutiny of individual and corporate ethics and social responsibility, the impact of social media, the changing nature of the workforce, new laws and regulations, increased global competition and more challenging foreign markets, declining educational standards (which may limit the skills and knowledge of the future labor and customer pool), and time itself—that is, making the best use of it. But such diverse issues cannot simply be plugged into a computer program that supplies correct, easy-to-apply solutions. It is only through creativity and imagination that managers can make effective decisions that benefit their organizations.

**agenda**
a calendar, containing both specific and vague items, that covers short-term goals and long-term objectives

**networking**
the building of relationships and sharing of information with colleagues who can help managers achieve the items on their agendas

Websites like LinkedIn are helping managers and employees network with one another to achieve their professional goals.

## What Kind of Manager Do You Want to Be?

Managers are needed in a wide variety of organizations. Experts suggest that employment will increase by millions of jobs by 2016. But the requirements for the jobs become more demanding with every passing year—with the speed of technology and communication increasing by the day, and the stress of global commerce increasing pressures to perform. However, if you like a challenge and if you have the right kind of personality, management remains a viable field. Even as companies are forced to restructure, management remains a vital role in business. In fact, the Bureau of Labor Statistics predicts that management positions in public relations, marketing, and advertising are set to increase around 12 percent overall between 2006 and 2016. Financial managers will be in even more demand, with jobs increasing 13 percent in the same time period. Computer and IT managers will continue to be in strong demand, with the number of jobs increasing 16 percent between 2006 and 2016.[37]

Salaries for managerial positions remain strong overall. While pay can vary significantly depending on your level of experience, the firm where you work, and the region of the country where you live, below is a list of the nationwide average incomes for a variety of different managers:

Chief executive: $178,400
Computer and IT manager: $132,570
Marketing manager: $133,700
Financial manager: $126,660
General and operations manager: $116,090
Medical/health services manager: $101,340
Administrative services manager: $90,190
Human resources manager: $111,180
Sales manager: $123,150[38]

In short, if you want to be a manager, there are opportunities in almost every field. There may be fewer middle management positions available in firms, but managers remain a vital part of most industries and will continue to be long into the future—especially as navigating global business becomes ever more complex.

## Review Your Understanding

### Define management, and explain its role in the achievement of organizational objectives.

Management is a process designed to achieve an organization's objectives by using its resources effectively and efficiently in a changing environment. Managers make decisions about the use of the organization's resources and are concerned with planning, organizing, staffing, directing, and controlling the organization's activities so as to reach its objectives.

### Describe the major functions of management.

Planning is the process of determining the organization's objectives and deciding how to accomplish them. Organizing is the structuring of resources and activities to accomplish those objectives efficiently and effectively. Staffing obtains people with the necessary skills to carry out the work of the company. Directing is motivating and leading employees to achieve organizational objectives. Controlling is the process of evaluating and correcting activities to keep the organization on course.

### Distinguish among three levels of management and the concerns of managers at each level.

Top management is responsible for the whole organization and focuses primarily on strategic planning. Middle management develops plans for specific operating areas and carries out the general guidelines set by top management. First-line, or supervisory, management supervises the workers and day-to-day operations. Managers can also be categorized as to their area of responsibility: finance, production and operations, human resources, marketing, or administration.

### Specify the skills managers need in order to be successful.

To be successful, managers need leadership skills (the ability to influence employees to work toward organizational goals), technical expertise (the specialized knowledge and training needed to perform a job), conceptual skills (the ability to think in abstract terms and see how parts fit together to form the whole), analytical skills (the ability to identify relevant issues and recognize their importance, understand the relationships between issues, and perceive the underlying causes of a situation), and human relations (people) skills.

### Summarize the systematic approach to decision making used by many business managers.

A systematic approach to decision making follows these steps: recognizing and defining the situation, developing options, analyzing options, selecting the best option, implementing the decision, and monitoring the consequences.

**Recommend a new strategy to revive a struggling business.**

Using the decision-making process described in this chapter, analyze the struggling company's problems described in "Solve the Dilemma" on page 199 and formulate a strategy to turn the company around and aim it toward future success.

## Revisit the World of Business

1. What are the challenges middle managers commonly face?

2. What are some good characteristics for effective middle managers to have?

3. Why are the job functions of middle management important to organizational success?

## Learn the Terms

administrative managers  186
agenda  195
analytical skills  188
conceptual skills  188
controlling  181
crisis management or contingency planning  178
directing  180
downsizing  179
employee empowerment  191
financial managers  186

first-line managers  185
human relations skills  188
human resources managers  186
information technology (IT) managers  186
leadership  188
management  174
managers  174
marketing managers  186
middle managers  185
mission  175

networking  195
operational plans  178
organizing  179
planning  175
production and operations managers  186
staffing  179
strategic plans  177
tactical plans  177
technical expertise  187
top managers  182

## Check Your Progress

1. Why is management so important, and what is its purpose?

2. Explain why the American Heart Association would need management, even though its goal is not profit related.

3. Why must a company have financial resources before it can use human and physical resources?

4. Name the five functions of management, and briefly describe each function.

5. Identify the three levels of management. What is the focus of managers at each level?

6. In what areas can managers specialize? From what area do top managers typically come?

7. What skills do managers need? Give examples of how managers use these skills to do their jobs.

8. What are three styles of leadership? Describe situations in which each style would be appropriate.

9. Explain the steps in the decision-making process.

10. What is the mathematical formula for perfect management? What do managers spend most of their time doing?

## Get Involved

1. Give examples of the activities that each of the following managers might be involved in if he or she worked for the Coca-Cola Company:

   Financial manager
   Production and operations manager

   Personnel manager
   Marketing manager
   Administrative manager
   Information technology manager
   Foreman

**2.** Interview a small sample of managers, attempting to include representatives from all three levels and all areas of management. Discuss their daily activities and relate these activities to the management functions of planning, organizing, staffing, directing, and controlling. What skills do the managers say they need to carry out their tasks?

**3.** You are a manager of a firm that manufactures conventional ovens. Over the past several years, sales of many of your products have declined; this year, your losses may be quite large. Using the steps of the decision-making process, briefly describe how you arrive at a strategy for correcting the situation.

## Build Your Skills

### Functions of Management

**Background**

Although the text describes each of the five management functions separately, you learned that these five functions are interrelated, and managers sometimes perform two or more of them at the same time. Here you will broaden your perspective of how these functions occur simultaneously in management activities.

### Task

1. Imagine that you are the manager in each scenario described in the following table and you have to decide which management function(s) to use in each.

2. Mark your answers using the following codes:

| Codes | Management Functions |
|-------|----------------------|
| P | Planning |
| O | Organizing |
| S | Staffing |
| D | Directing |
| C | Controlling |

| No. | Scenario | Answer(s) |
|-----|----------|-----------|
| 1 | Your group's work is centered on a project that is due in two months. Although everyone is working on the project, you have observed your employees involved in what you believe is excessive socializing and other time-filling behaviors. You decide to meet with the group to have them help you break down the project into smaller subprojects with mini-deadlines. You believe this will help keep the group members focused on the project and that the quality of the finished project will then reflect the true capabilities of your group. | |
| 2 | Your first impression of the new group you'll be managing is not too great. You tell your friend at dinner after your first day on the job: "Looks like I got a baby sitting job instead of a management job." | |
| 3 | You call a meeting of your work group and begin it by letting them know that a major procedure used by the work group for the past two years is being significantly revamped, and your department will have to phase in the change during the next six weeks. You proceed by explaining to them the reasoning your boss gave you for this change. You then say, "Let's take the next 5 to 10 minutes to let you voice your reactions to this change." After 10 minutes elapse with the majority of comments being critical of the change, you say: "I appreciate each of you sharing your reactions; and I, too, recognize that *all* change creates problems. The way I see it, however, is that we can spend the remaining 45 minutes of our meeting focusing on why we don't want the change and why we don't think it's necessary; or we can work together to come up with viable solutions to solve the problems that implementing this change will most likely create." After about five more minutes of comments being exchanged, the consensus of the group is that the remainder of the meeting needs to be focused on how to deal with the potential problems the group anticipates having to deal with as the new procedure is implemented. | |
| 4 | You are preparing for the annual budget allocation meetings to be held in the plant manager's office next week. You are determined to present a strong case to support your department getting money for some high-tech equipment that will help your employees do their jobs better. You will stand firm against any suggestions of budget cuts in your area. | |

| 5 | Early in your career, you learned an important lesson about employee selection. One of the nurses on your floor unexpectedly quit. The other nurses were putting pressure on you to fill the position quickly because they were overworked even before the nurse left, and then things were really bad. After a hasty recruitment effort, you made a decision based on insufficient information. You ended up regretting your quick decision during the three months of problems that followed until you finally had to discharge the new hire. Since then, you have never let anybody pressure you into making a quick hiring decision. | |

## Solve the Dilemma  LO 6-6

### Making Infinity Computers Competitive

Infinity Computers Inc. produces notebook computers, which it sells through direct mail catalog companies under the Infinity name and in some retail computer stores under their private brand names. Infinity's products are not significantly different from competitors', nor do they have extra product-enhancing features, although they are very price competitive. The strength of the company has been its CEO and president, George Anderson, and a highly motivated, loyal workforce. The firm's weakness is having too many employees and too great a reliance on one product. The firm switched to computers with the Intel Core i5 processors after it saw a decline in its netbook computer sales.

Recognizing that the strategies that initially made the firm successful are no longer working effectively, Anderson wants to reorganize the company to make it more responsive and competitive and to cut costs. The threat of new technological developments and current competitive conditions could eliminate Infinity.

### Discussion Questions

1. Evaluate Infinity's current situation and analyze its strengths and weaknesses.

2. Evaluate the opportunities for Infinity, including using its current strategy, and propose alternative strategies.

3. Suggest a plan for Infinity to compete successfully over the next 10 years.

## Build Your Business Plan

### The Nature of Management

The first thing you need to be thinking about is "What is the mission of your business? What is the shared vision your team members have for this business? How do you know if there is demand for this particular business?" Remember, you need to think about the customer's *ability and willingness* to try this particular product.

Think about the various processes or stages of your business in the creation and selling of your good, or service. What functions need to be performed for these processes to be completed? These functions might include buying, receiving, selling, customer service, and/or merchandising.

Operationally, if you are opening up a retail establishment, how do you plan to provide your customers with superior customer service? What hours will your customers expect you to be open? At this point in time, how many employees are you thinking you will need to run your business? Do you (or one of your partners) need to be there all the time to supervise?

# See for Yourself Videocase

## Planning Drives the Success of Ford Fusion

 The release of the Ford Fusion was the culmination of six years of planning, implementation, and monitoring. Before the process began, top managers established the mission for the new vehicle as "the most talked about car of 2012." This guided the strategic plan during various levels of the project. The three goals for driving this strategy were to (1) become the company's highest volume car in order to gain market share, (2) offer customers unparalleled levels of choice, and (3) have green offerings.

When Alan Mulally became CEO, he instituted the One Ford Strategy. The One Ford Strategy unites the operations of the company through four clear objectives. The first objective involves having the ability to adapt to the current status of demand and change the model mix to achieve operational profitability. The second focuses on the rate of new product development while keeping customers' wants and values in mind. The third objective aims toward the improvement of financial planning. The final objective is focused on teamwork. This plan has helped the company focus their efforts and work together through a single approach toward the same goals. The plan also encourages measuring activities based on customer satisfaction and the happiness of employees and business partners. This allows the company to create high-quality, environmentally friendly, safe, and smart vehicles; create a durable and stable business; and contribute to the improvement of the world through sustainability efforts.

The One Ford Plan facilitated the collaboration between marketing and product development for the Ford Fusion project. This ensured the final product was cohesive both in design and market positioning. This collaboration was especially important to the execution of tactical plans for this project. The tactical plans focused on suppliers, design, parts needed, and marketing plans (channels that would be used, which audience would be targeted, and the determination of communication objectives). Furthermore, the team developed plans for potential capacity issues such as shutdowns or ramp-ups, as well as for scenarios in which there would be an over- or undersupply.

It is not enough to simply create plans—measuring the effects of a plan is imperative to successful execution. Ford uses a system called Launch Readiness, which began about two years before the launch with phase 1 or LR1. For example, Ford's marketing department measured consumer interest months before the Fusion was introduced onto the market by holding events and using "Build and Price" on Ford.com. This allowed customers to log on to the website and choose features, colors, and prices of the new vehicle. The company measured customer interest by determining how many people logged onto to the website and used Build and Price. The Fusion generated 1.6 million interactions, which was significantly more interest than any other vehicle generated. This phase also measured the various aspects of quality present in suppliers, design, and parts.

The operational part of planning is encompassed by LR2, the next phase in Launch Readiness. This phase focuses on execution and is informed by the previous phase. Details on the specifics of plans are established and refined, such as what events the company will attend and how they will use Facebook. This phase precedes the Final Status Review. Each of these phases serves as an overall control process for the entire project, and all phases are considered to be milestones that determine the project's progress.

The results of the Ford Fusion launch exceeded the company's aggressive expectations, and these significant results can be attributed to the level of planning the company engaged in. The Ford Fusion became one of the company's best-selling vehicles, second only to the popular F-150 pickup truck. The company also achieved another one of its goals by gaining two points in market share as a result of its new product launch. This is especially significant as a successful gain in market share in the automobile industry is one-tenth of a percentage point.

The Ford Fusion became one of the most popular vehicles in the mid-sized sedan segment because it offered consumers more luxury and choices than were previously available. They were able to choose from four different types of engines and two types of transmissions (6-speed automatic or manual). The Fusion also propelled the company toward one of its long-term strategic goals to offer economically friendly vehicles, which Ford has continued to introduce to the market.[39]

### Discussion Questions

1. How did Ford use strategic and tactical planning in its launch of the Ford Fusion?

2. How did the companywide One Ford Plan contribute to the project-specific Launch Readiness plan?

3. What was the role of implementation in the success of the Ford Fusion?

You can find the related video in the Video Library in Connect. Ask your instructor how you can access Connect.

## Team Exercise

Form groups and assign the responsibility of locating examples of crisis management implementation for companies dealing with natural disasters (explosions, fires, earthquakes, etc.), technology disasters (viruses, plane crashes, compromised customer data, etc.), or ethical or legal disasters. How did these companies communicate with key stakeholders? What measures did the company take to provide support to those involved in the crisis? Report your findings to the class.

# 7

# Organization, Teamwork, and Communication

## Learning Objectives

**After reading this chapter, you will be able to:**

**LO 7-1** Define organizational structure, and relate how organizational structures develop.

**LO 7-2** Describe how specialization and departmentalization help an organization achieve its goals.

**LO 7-3** Determine how organizations assign responsibility for tasks and delegate authority.

**LO 7-4** Compare and contrast some common forms of organizational structure.

**LO 7-5** Distinguish between groups and teams, and identify the types of groups that exist in organizations.

**LO 7-6** Describe how communication occurs in organizations.

**LO 7-7** Analyze a business's use of teams.

## CarMax Uses Decentralized Structure to Support Teamwork

In 1991, some executives from Circuit City decided to test-launch a new business idea for a used car company termed Project X. Two years later, CarMax was officially launched. CarMax makes it a priority to develop satisfied employees. The company has a decentralized structure where employees are encouraged to submit recommendations and develop leadership skills. Over the past 20 years, CarMax has grown to 119 stores with 18,000 employees. In 2013, CarMax was listed as one of *Fortune's* Best Companies to Work For.

CarMax uses RFID technology to track how long cars sit in the lot, extensive sales data to determine inventory needs accurately, and a flat commission compensation system so salespeople will promote the cars that best meet customer needs rather than trying to sell the most expensive car.

Tom Folliard, the CEO of CarMax, learned that developing a decentralized corporate culture focusing on teamwork and employee empowerment generates positive results. CarMax prides itself on being founded on fundamental principles that every store must abide by. Values include respect, communication, customer focus, and teamwork. CarMax believes that employees who work together are able to place the customer first and serve their best interests. Folliard stays accessible for employees through town hall meetings and steak cookouts.

With this type of company culture, employees are able to feel a sense of ownership and high levels of contribution to the company. This allows for employees to hold themselves to higher standards, resulting in higher work performance. In an industry that has a certain stigma about car salespeople, CarMax's focus of empowering employees to provide quality customer service and take ownership of the company has revolutionized the used car industry.[1]

# Introduction

An organization's structure determines how well it makes decisions and responds to problems, and it influences employees' attitudes toward their work. A suitable structure can minimize a business's costs and maximize its efficiency. Even companies that operate within the same industry may utilize different organizational structures. For example, in the consumer electronics industry, Samsung is organized as a conglomerate with separate business units or divisions. Samsung is largely decentralized. Apple, under CEO Tim Cook, has moved from a hierarchical structure to a more collaborative approach between divisions.[2]

Because a business's structure can so profoundly affect its success, this chapter will examine organizational structure in detail. First, we discuss how an organization's culture affects its operations. Then we consider the development of structure, including how tasks and responsibilities are organized through specialization and departmentalization. Next, we explore some of the forms organizational structure may take. Finally, we consider communications within business.

# Organizational Culture

One of the most important aspects of organizing a business is determining its **organizational culture,** a firm's shared values, beliefs, traditions, philosophies, rules, and role models for behavior. Also called corporate culture, an organizational culture exists in every organization, regardless of size, organizational type, product, or profit objective. Sometimes behaviors, programs, and policies enhance and support the organizational culture. Netflix, for example, established a "freedom and responsibility culture," which has become a culture code many Silicon Valley companies have used as a template for establishing their organizational cultures. One way Netflix expresses this culture is by not having a vacation policy. Employees are expected to be responsible and disciplined while working, and in exchange, they are allowed the freedom to take vacation when they like and for as long as they like.[3] A firm's culture may be expressed formally through its mission statement, codes of ethics, memos, manuals, and ceremonies, but it is more commonly expressed informally. Examples of informal expressions of culture include dress codes (or the lack thereof), work habits, extracurricular activities, and stories. Employees often learn the accepted standards through discussions with co-workers.

TOMS Shoes' organizational culture is determined by the founder's desire to provide as many shoes as possible to children in developing countries (where shoeless children walk for miles to get water, food, and medical care). Blake Mycoskie gives hundreds of thousands of shoes to children around the world each year, creating a strong organizational culture of giving back and corporate social responsibility. His company operates with a program that for every pair of shoes purchased, a pair will be donated to children in need.[4] Disneyland/DisneyWorld and McDonald's have organizational cultures focused on cleanliness, value, and service. The company Zappos. com created a culture of "fun and a little weirdness." The company has a flexible work environment with very few rules, and employees are encouraged to socialize and engage in unique activities (such as ringing cowbells when visitors arrive). Zappos' goal is to make both employees and customers feel good. Customer service is such a must at Zappos that new hires must work for one month at a call center, even if the new employees are not going to be interacting with customers normally.[5] When such values

**organizational culture**
a firm's shared values, beliefs, traditions, philosophies, rules, and role models for behavior

### Companies Embracing Greater Employee Interaction

Getting rid of cubicles, creating inconvenient work spaces, and eliminating work-from-home programs are some of the methods being used by companies to increase collaboration, communication, and teamwork. Yahoo! and Best Buy, for example, have eliminated their work-from-home programs to increase face-to-face interaction among employees. Studies have shown that employee interaction leads to more innovative ideas.

Google and Zappos are among those companies taking the lead in using their space to encourage collaboration and innovation. Both are designing new buildings with smaller workspaces and break rooms and narrower hallways so employees will see each other more often and have more opportunity for chance discussions. Zappos CEO Tony Hsieh is purposefully designing inconvenience into the new Zappos headquarters so that employees will have to interact with one another. Campbell's Soup is removing cubicles and installing more common spaces to increase employee teamwork and problem-solving.

Other companies are installing interactive devices in elevators where silence is usually the norm. Salesforce.com is installing a lunch button kiosk. Employees can push a button on the kiosk, and the kiosk matches a fellow co-worker that shares a common interest with the employee. The employee can then invite that person to lunch—and a new relationship is formed. This increase in interaction is anticipated to improve communication and relationships in companies.[6]

### Discussion Questions

1. Describe methods some companies are using to increase employee interaction.
2. Why is it important that employees interact with one another?
3. Do you feel that the disadvantages of work-from-home programs are higher than their benefits?

---

and philosophies are shared by all members of an organization, they will be expressed in its relationships with stakeholders. However, organizational cultures that lack such positive values may result in employees who are unproductive and indifferent and have poor attitudes, which will be reflected externally to customers. The corporate culture may have contributed to the misconduct at a number of well-known companies. A survey found that executives in financial and technology companies are mostly cut-throat in collecting intelligence about competition, creating a corporate culture in which unethical acts might be tolerated if it means beating the competition.[7]

Organizational culture helps ensure that all members of a company share values and suggests rules for how to behave and deal with problems within the organization. Table 7.1 confirms that executives in this study believe that corporate culture has a significant impact on organizational performance and the ability to retain good employees. The key to success in any organization is satisfying stakeholders, especially customers. Establishing a positive organizational culture sets the tone for all other decisions, including building an efficient organizational structure.

The organizational structure at TOMS Shoes consists of two parts. The for-profit component of the company manages overall operations. Its nonprofit component, Friends of TOMS, is responsible for volunteer activities and shoe donations.

**TABLE 7.1**
**Attitudes and Behaviors
Associated with Corporate
Cultures**

| | Employees Who View Their Culture Negatively | Employees Who View Their Culture Positively |
|---|---|---|
| Committed toward organization | 17% | 86% |
| Satisfied with organization | 13 | 87 |
| Likely to recommend their organization to others | 13 | 88 |
| Intend to leave the organizations | 63 | 10 |
| Alignment with leadership | 8 | 59 |

*N = 236 management and human resources professionals from U.S. companies with more than 100 employees.*

*Source: Survey conducted by Critical Metrics LLC, CR Magazine 3, June 2012, www.thecro.com/content/quantifying-corporate-culture.*

**structure**
the arrangement or
relationship of positions
within an organization

# Developing Organizational Structure

**Structure** is the arrangement or relationship of positions within an organization. Rarely is an organization, or any group of individuals working together, able to achieve common objectives without some form of structure, whether that structure is explicitly defined or only implied. A professional baseball team such as the Colorado Rockies is a business organization with an explicit formal structure that guides the team's activities so that it can increase game attendance, win games, and sell souvenirs such as T-shirts. But even an informal group playing softball for fun has an organization that specifies who will pitch, catch, bat, coach, and so on. Governments and nonprofit organizations also have formal organizational structures to facilitate the achievement of their objectives. Getting people to work together efficiently and coordinating the skills of diverse individuals require careful planning. Developing appropriate organizational structures is therefore a major challenge for managers in both large and small organizations.

An organization's structure develops when managers assign work tasks and activities to specific individuals or work groups and coordinate the diverse activities required to reach the firm's objectives. When Macy's, for example, has a sale, the store manager must work with the advertising department to make the public aware of the sale, with department managers to ensure that extra salespeople are scheduled to handle the increased customer traffic, and with merchandise buyers to ensure that enough sale merchandise is available to meet expected consumer demand. All the people occupying these positions must work together to achieve the store's objectives.

**organizational chart**
a visual display of the
organizational structure,
lines of authority (chain of
command), staff relationships,
permanent committee
arrangements, and lines of
communication

The best way to begin to understand how organizational structure develops is to consider the evolution of a new business such as a clothing store. At first, the business is a sole proprietorship in which the owner does everything—buys, prices, and displays the merchandise; does the accounting and tax records; and assists customers. As the business grows, the owner hires a salesperson and perhaps a merchandise buyer to help run the store. As the business continues to grow, the owner hires more salespeople. The growth and success of the business now require the owner to be away from the store frequently, meeting with suppliers, engaging in public relations, and attending trade shows. Thus, the owner must designate someone to manage the salespeople and maintain the accounting, payroll, and tax functions. If the owner decides to expand by opening more stores, still more managers will be needed. Figure 7.1 shows these stages of growth with three **organizational charts** (visual displays of organizational structure, chain of command, and other relationships).

**FIGURE 7.1**    **The Evolution of a Clothing Store, Phases 1, 2, and 3**

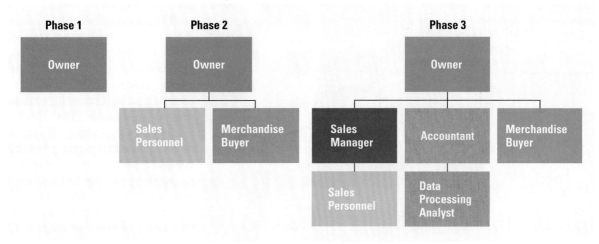

Growth requires organizing—the structuring of human, physical, and financial resources to achieve objectives in an effective and efficient manner. Growth necessitates hiring people who have specialized skills. With more people and greater specialization, the organization needs to develop a formal structure to function efficiently. Imagine the various organizational changes that Nokia has undergone. It was founded in 1865 as a paper mill in Finland and has become a global telecommunications company serving more than 1 billion customers. During its history, the company has transformed itself various times—including as a rubber company, television maker, and a cable company—each time changing the organizational structure to accommodate its business.[8] As we shall see, structuring an organization requires that management assign work tasks to specific individuals and departments and assign responsibility for the achievement of specific organizational objectives.

# Assigning Tasks

LO 7-2

For a business to earn profits from the sale of its products, its managers must first determine what activities are required to achieve its objectives. At Celestial Seasonings, for example, employees must purchase herbs from suppliers, dry the herbs and place them in tea bags, package and label the tea, and then ship the packages to grocery stores around the country. Other necessary activities include negotiating with supermarkets and other retailers for display space, developing new products, planning advertising, managing finances, and managing employees. All these activities must be coordinated, assigned to work groups, and controlled. Two important aspects of assigning these work activities are specialization and departmentalization.

## Specialization

After identifying all activities that must be accomplished, managers then break these activities down into specific tasks that can be handled by individual employees. This division of labor into small, specific tasks and the assignment of employees to do a single task is called **specialization.**

**specialization**
the division of labor into small, specific tasks and the assignment of employees to do a single task

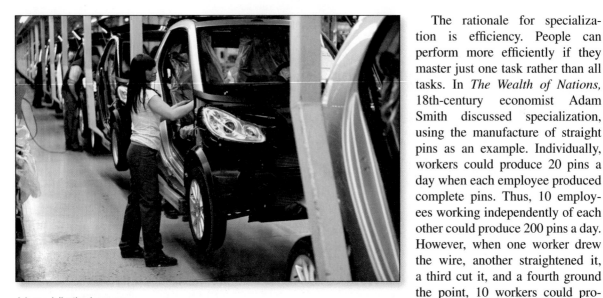

Job specialization is common in automobile manufacturing. By dividing work into smaller specialized tasks, employees can perform their work more quickly and efficiently.

The rationale for specialization is efficiency. People can perform more efficiently if they master just one task rather than all tasks. In *The Wealth of Nations,* 18th-century economist Adam Smith discussed specialization, using the manufacture of straight pins as an example. Individually, workers could produce 20 pins a day when each employee produced complete pins. Thus, 10 employees working independently of each other could produce 200 pins a day. However, when one worker drew the wire, another straightened it, a third cut it, and a fourth ground the point, 10 workers could produce 48,000 pins per day.[9] To save money and achieve the benefits of specialization, some companies outsource and hire temporary workers to provide key skills. Many highly skilled, diverse, experienced workers are available through temp agencies.

Specialization means workers do not waste time shifting from one job to another, and training is easier. However, efficiency is not the only motivation for specialization. Specialization also occurs when the activities that must be performed within an organization are too numerous for one person to handle. Recall the example of the clothing store. When the business was young and small, the owner could do everything; but when the business grew, the owner needed help waiting on customers, keeping the books, and managing other business activities.

Overspecialization can have negative consequences. Employees may become bored and dissatisfied with their jobs, and the result of their unhappiness is likely to be poor quality work, more injuries, and high employee turnover. In extreme cases, employees in crowded specialized electronic plants are unable to form working relationships with one another. At Foxconn, a multinational electronics manufacturing firm and one of the suppliers of Apple iPhones and iPads, lack of working relationships, long work hours, low pay, and other conditions resulted in employee dissatisfaction and, tragically, depression and even suicide.[10] This is why some manufacturing firms allow job rotation so that employees do not become dissatisfied and leave. Although some degree of specialization is necessary for efficiency, because of differences in skills, abilities, and interests, all people are not equally suited for all jobs. We examine some strategies to overcome these issues in Chapter 9.

## Departmentalization

**departmentalization**
the grouping of jobs into working units usually called departments, units, groups, or divisions

After assigning specialized tasks to individuals, managers next organize workers doing similar jobs into groups to make them easier to manage. **Departmentalization** is the grouping of jobs into working units usually called departments, units, groups, or divisions. As we shall see, departments are commonly organized by function, product, geographic region, or customer (Figure 7.2). Most companies use more than one departmentalization plan to enhance productivity. For instance, many consumer

**FIGURE 7.2**    **Departmentalization**

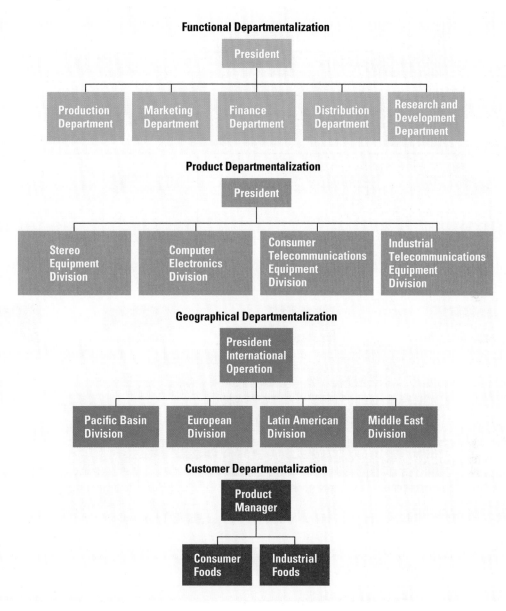

goods manufacturers have departments for specific product lines (beverages, frozen dinners, canned goods, and so on) as well as departments dealing with legal, purchasing, finance, human resources, and other business functions. For smaller companies, accounting can be set up online, almost as an automated department. Accounting software can handle electronic transfers so you never have to worry about a late bill. Many city governments also have departments for specific services (e.g., police, fire, waste disposal) as well as departments for legal, human resources, and other business functions. Figure 7.3 depicts the organizational chart for the city of Corpus Christi, Texas, showing these departments.

**FIGURE 7.3**     **An Organizational Chart for the City of Corpus Christi**

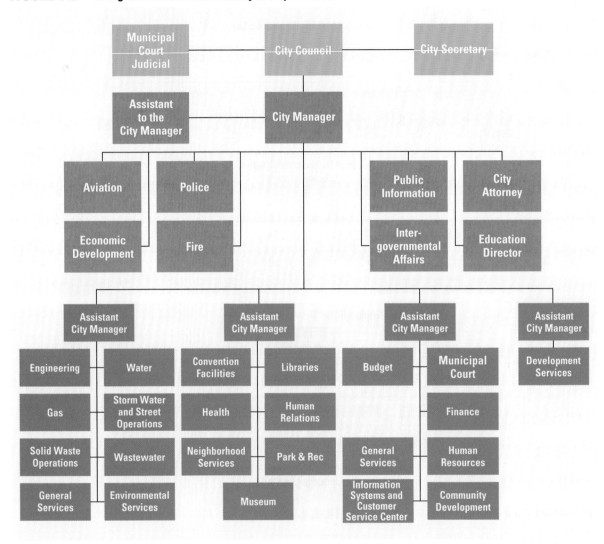

Source: "City of Corpus Christi Organizational Chart," City of Corpus Christi www.cctexas.com/files/g5/cityorgchart.pdf (accessed February 11, 2010).

**functional departmentalization**
the grouping of jobs that perform similar functional activities, such as finance, manufacturing, marketing, and human resources

**Functional Departmentalization.** **Functional departmentalization** groups jobs that perform similar functional activities, such as finance, manufacturing, marketing, and human resources. Each of these functions is managed by an expert in the work done by the department—an engineer supervises the production department; a financial executive supervises the finance department. This approach is common in small organizations. Green Mountain Coffee is departmentalized into six functions: sales and marketing, operations, human resources, finance, information systems, and social responsibility. A weakness of functional departmentalization is that, because it tends to emphasize departmental units rather than the organization as a whole, decision making that involves more than one department may be slow, and it requires greater coordination. Thus, as businesses grow, they tend to adopt other approaches to organizing jobs.

### Product Departmentalization.

**Product departmentalization,** as you might guess, organizes jobs around the products of the firm. Unilever has global units, including personal care, foods, refreshment, and home care.[11] Each division develops and implements its own product plans, monitors the results, and takes corrective action as necessary. Functional activities—production, finance, marketing, and others—are located within each product division. Consequently, organizing by products duplicates functions and resources and emphasizes the product rather than achievement of the organization's overall objectives. However, it simplifies decision making and helps coordinate all activities related to a product or product group. PepsiCo Inc. is organized into four business units: (1) PepsiCo Americas Foods, which includes brands such as Frito-Lay North America, Quaker Foods North America, and all of its Latin American food and snack businesses; (2) PepsiCo Americas Beverages, which includes the Mountain Dew, Lipton, and Tropicana brands; (3) PepsiCo Europe, which includes regional brands like Wimm-Bill-Dann and Marbo as well as all beverage, food, and snack businesses in Europe and South Africa; and (4) PepsiCo Asia, Middle East and Africa, which includes all beverage, food, and snack businesses in these regions. PepsiCo has actually adopted a combination of two types of departmentalization. While it clearly separates foods from beverages in the Americas, the company chooses to divide its segments into geographic regions—a type of geographic departmentalization.[12]

**product departmentalization** the organization of jobs in relation to the products of the firm

### Geographical Departmentalization.

**Geographical departmentalization** groups jobs according to geographic location, such as a state, region, country, or continent. Diageo, the premium beverage company known for brands such as Johnny Walker and Tanqueray, is organized into five geographic regions, allowing the company to get closer to its customers and respond more quickly and efficiently to regional competitors.[13] Multinational corporations often use a geographical approach because of vast differences between different regions. Coca-Cola, General Motors, and Caterpillar are organized by region. However, organizing by region requires a large administrative staff and control system to coordinate operations, and tasks are duplicated among the different regions.

**geographical departmentalization** the grouping of jobs according to geographic location, such as state, region, country, or continent

### Customer Departmentalization.

**Customer departmentalization** arranges jobs around the needs of various types of customers. Proctor & Gamble, for example, recently restructured their business divisions according to types of customers: global baby, feminine and family care; global beauty; global health and grooming; and global fabric and home care. This allows the company to address the unique requirements of each group.[14] Airlines, such as British Airways and Delta, provide prices and services customized for either business/frequent travelers or infrequent/vacationing customers. Customer departmentalization, like geographical departmentalization, does not focus on the organization as a whole and therefore requires a large administrative staff to coordinate the operations of the various groups.

**customer departmentalization** the arrangement of jobs around the needs of various types of customers

## Assigning Responsibility

After all workers and work groups have been assigned their tasks, they must be given the responsibility to carry them out. Management must determine to what extent it will delegate responsibility throughout the organization and how many employees will report to each manager.

## Delegation of Authority

**delegation of authority**
giving employees not only tasks, but also the power to make commitments, use resources, and take whatever actions are necessary to carry out those tasks

**Delegation of authority** means not only giving tasks to employees but also empowering them to make commitments, use resources, and take whatever actions are necessary to carry out those tasks. Let's say a marketing manager at Nestlé has assigned an employee to design a new package that is less wasteful (more environmentally responsible) than the current package for one of the company's frozen dinner lines. To carry out the assignment, the employee needs access to information and the authority to make certain decisions on packaging materials, costs, and so on. Without the authority to carry out the assigned task, the employee would have to get the approval of others for every decision and every request for materials.

As a business grows, so do the number and complexity of decisions that must be made; no one manager can handle them all. Nordstrom delegates authority to its customer service personnel by telling them to use their best judgment when dealing with customers. This allows employees to offer the best tailored service to each individual customer and is one reason the retailer is known for its superior customer service.[15] Delegation of authority frees a manager to concentrate on larger issues, such as planning or dealing with problems and opportunities.

**responsibility**
the obligation, placed on employees through delegation, to perform assigned tasks satisfactorily and be held accountable for the proper execution of work

Delegation also gives a **responsibility,** or obligation, to employees to carry out assigned tasks satisfactorily and holds them accountable for the proper execution of their assigned work. The principle of **accountability** means that employees who accept an assignment and the authority to carry it out are answerable to a superior for the outcome. Returning to the Nestlé example, if the packaging design prepared by the employee is unacceptable or late, the employee must accept the blame. If the new design is innovative, attractive, and cost-efficient, as well as environmentally responsible, or is completed ahead of schedule, the employee will accept the credit.

**accountability**
the principle that employees who accept an assignment and the authority to carry it out are answerable to a superior for the outcome

The process of delegating authority establishes a pattern of relationships and accountability between a superior and his or her subordinates. The president of a firm delegates responsibility for all marketing activities to the vice president of marketing. The vice president accepts this responsibility and has the authority to obtain all relevant information, make certain decisions, and delegate any or all activities to his or her subordinates. The vice president, in turn, delegates all advertising activities to the advertising manager, all sales activities to the sales manager, and so on. These managers then delegate specific tasks to their subordinates. However, the act of delegating authority to a subordinate does not relieve the superior of accountability for the delegated job. Even though the vice president of marketing delegates work to subordinates, he or she is still ultimately accountable to the president for all marketing activities.

## Degree of Centralization

The extent to which authority is delegated throughout an organization determines its degree of centralization.

**centralized organization**
a structure in which authority is concentrated at the top, and very little decision-making authority is delegated to lower levels

**Centralized Organizations.**    In a **centralized organization,** authority is concentrated at the top, and very little decision-making authority is delegated to lower levels. Although decision-making authority in centralized organizations rests with top levels of management, a vast amount of responsibility for carrying out daily and routine procedures is delegated to even the lowest levels of the organization. Many government organizations, including the U.S. Army, the Postal Service, and the IRS, are centralized.

Businesses tend to be more centralized when the decisions to be made are risky and when low-level managers are not highly skilled in decision making. In the banking

### Forming a Successful New Business: Group Collaboration

**Nota Bene**
**Founders:** Amy Bass and Evvy Diamond
**Founded:** 2007, in Aspinwall, Pennsylvania
**Success:** Through intense teamwork and collaboration, Nota Bene has become a successful stationery business with $500,000 in annual revenues.

The stationery shop Nota Bene was founded through the collaboration between the skills and interests of two friends, Amy Bass and Evvy Diamond. Diamond, who had had a life-long attraction to stationery, started designing note cards when her children left for college. After an unsuccessful effort to sell her craft at a stationery show, she realized she needed a different outlet and a significant investment in order to properly sell her designs. Diamond sparked the interest of her friend Amy, who had business experience, and together they invested their money and started the business full-time in 2007. They formed a group with complementary skills in business and design and differentiated themselves from their competition by offering original designs, customization, and in-depth personal interaction with their customers. For instance, the entrepreneurs frequently meet with brides after-hours to go over their needs for wedding announcements. Five years after its creation, the company is generating $500,000 in annual revenues despite intense online competition.[16]

industry, for example, authority to make routine car loans is given to all loan managers, while the authority to make high-risk loans, such as for a large residential development, may be restricted to upper-level loan officers.

Overcentralization can cause serious problems for a company, in part because it may take longer for the organization as a whole to implement decisions and to respond to changes and problems on a regional scale. McDonald's, for example, was one of the last chains to introduce a chicken sandwich because of the amount of research, development, test marketing, and layers of approval the product had to go through.

**Decentralized Organizations.** A **decentralized organization** is one in which decision-making authority is delegated as far down the chain of command as possible. Decentralization is characteristic of organizations that operate in complex, unpredictable environments. Businesses that face intense competition often decentralize to improve responsiveness and enhance creativity. Lower-level managers who interact with the external environment often develop a good understanding of it and thus are able to react quickly to changes. Johnson & Johnson has a very decentralized, flat organizational structure.

Delegating authority to lower levels of managers may increase the organization's productivity. Decentralization requires that lower-level managers have strong decision-making skills. In recent years, the trend has been toward more decentralized organizations, and some of the largest and most successful companies, including GE, IBM, Google, and Nike, have decentralized decision-making authority. McDonald's, Taco Bell, and Pizza Hut have established themselves in the growing Indian market by decentralizing operations by varying products in specific markets to better meet customer demands. McDonald's, for example, has implemented spicy and vegetarian menu options in India to appeal to the native tastes. Becoming decentralized can be difficult for a fast-food restaurant that relies on standardized processes and core products. Burger King's core offering, the Whopper, will not likely be well accepted in India because beef is rarely eaten. Some suggest the chain should offer vegetarian pizza since it is popular in India. Diversity and decentralization are the keys to being better, not just bigger.[17] Nonprofit organizations benefit from decentralization as well.

**decentralized organization**
an organization in which decision-making authority is delegated as far down the chain of command as possible

## Span of Management

How many subordinates should a manager manage? There is no simple answer. Experts generally agree, however, that top managers should not directly supervise more than four to eight people, while lower-level managers who supervise routine tasks are capable of managing a much larger number of subordinates. For example, the manager of the finance department may supervise 25 employees, whereas the vice president of finance may supervise only five managers. **Span of management** refers to the number of subordinates who report to a particular manager. A *wide span of management* exists when a manager directly supervises a very large number of employees. A *narrow span of management* exists when a manager directly supervises only a few subordinates (Figure 7.4). At Whole Foods, the best employees are recruited and placed in small teams. Employees are empowered to discount, give away, and sample products, as well as to assist in creating a respectful workplace where goals are achieved, individual employees succeed, and customers are core in business decisions. Whole Foods teams get to vote on new employee hires as well. This approach allows Whole Foods to offer unique and "local market" experiences in each of its stores. This level of customization is in contrast to more centralized national supermarket chains such as Kroger, Safeway, and Publix.[18]

Should the span of management be wide or narrow? To answer this question, several factors need to be considered. A narrow span of management is appropriate when superiors and subordinates are not in close proximity, the manager has many responsibilities in addition to the supervision, the interaction between superiors and subordinates is frequent, and problems are common. However, when superiors and subordinates are located close to one another, the manager has few responsibilities other than supervision, the level of interaction between superiors and subordinates is low, few problems arise, subordinates are highly competent, and a set of specific operating procedures governs the activities of managers and their subordinates, a wide span of management will be more appropriate. Narrow spans of management are typical in centralized organizations, while wide spans of management are more common in decentralized firms.

**span of management**
the number of subordinates who report to a particular manager

## Organizational Layers

Complementing the concept of span of management is **organizational layers,** the levels of management in an organization. A company with many layers of managers is considered tall; in a tall organization, the span of management is narrow (see Figure 7.4). Because each manager supervises only a few subordinates, many

**organizational layers**
the levels of management in an organization

**FIGURE 7.4**
**Span of Management: Wide Span and Narrow Span**

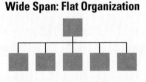

Wide Span: Flat Organization          Narrow Span: Tall Organization

layers of management are necessary to carry out the operations of the business. McDonald's, for example, has a tall organization with many layers, including store managers, district managers, regional managers, and functional managers (finance, marketing, and so on), as well as a chief executive officer and many vice presidents. Because there are more managers in tall organizations than in flat organizations, administrative costs are usually higher. Communication is slower because information must pass through many layers.

Organizations with few layers are flat and have wide spans of management. When managers supervise a large number of employees, fewer management layers are needed to conduct the organization's activities. Managers in flat organizations typically perform more administrative duties than managers in tall organizations because there are fewer of them. They also spend more time supervising and working with subordinates.

Many of the companies that have decentralized also flattened their structures and widened their spans of management, often by eliminating layers of middle management. As mentioned earlier in this chapter, Johnson & Johnson has both a decentralized and flat organizational structure. Other corporations, including Avon, AT&T, and Ford Motor Company, embraced a more decentralized structure to reduce costs, speed up decision making, and boost overall productivity.

# Forms of Organizational Structure                    LO 7-4

Along with assigning tasks and the responsibility for carrying them out, managers must consider how to structure their authority relationships—that is, what structure the organization itself will have and how it will appear on the organizational chart. Common forms of organization include line structure, line-and-staff structure, multidivisional structure, and matrix structure.

## Line Structure

The simplest organizational structure, **line structure,** has direct lines of authority that extend from the top manager to employees at the lowest level of the organization. For example, a convenience store employee at 7-Eleven may report to an assistant manager, who reports to the store manager, who reports to a regional manager, or, in an independent store, directly to the owner (Figure 7.5). This structure has a clear chain of command, which enables managers to make decisions quickly. A mid-level manager facing a decision must consult only one person, his or her immediate supervisor. However, this structure requires that managers possess a wide range of knowledge and skills. They are responsible for a variety of activities and must be knowledgeable about them all. Line structures are most common in small businesses.

**line structure**
the simplest organizational structure, in which direct lines of authority extend from the top manager to the lowest level of the organization

**FIGURE 7.5   Line Structure**

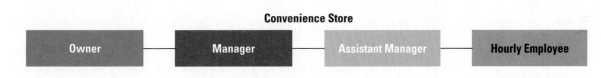

**Convenience Store**

| Owner | Manager | Assistant Manager | Hourly Employee |

**FIGURE 7.6**
**Line-and-Staff Structure**

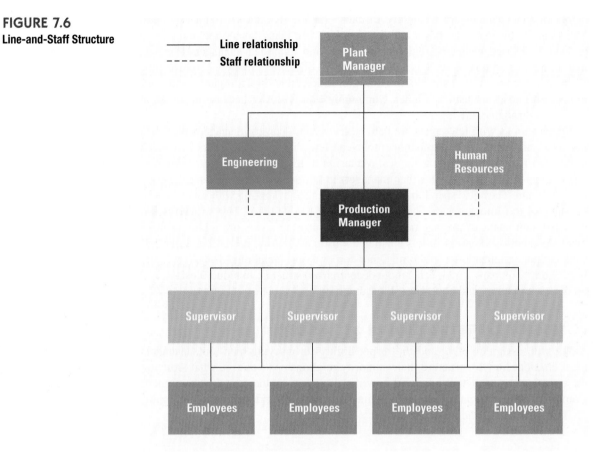

Line relationship
Staff relationship

Plant Manager

Engineering

Human Resources

Production Manager

Supervisor

Supervisor

Supervisor

Supervisor

Employees

Employees

Employees

Employees

## Line-and-Staff Structure

**line-and-staff structure**
a structure having a traditional line relationship between superiors and subordinates and also specialized managers—called staff managers—who are available to assist line managers

The **line-and-staff structure** has a traditional line relationship between superiors and subordinates, and specialized managers—called staff managers—are available to assist line managers (Figure 7.6). Line managers can focus on their area of expertise in the operation of the business, while staff managers provide advice and support to line departments on specialized matters such as finance, engineering, human resources, and the law. In the city of Corpus Christi (refer back for Figure 7.3), for example, assistant city managers are line managers who oversee groups of related departments. However, the city attorney, police chief, and fire chief are effectively staff managers who report directly to the city manager (the city equivalent of a business chief executive officer). Staff managers do not have direct authority over line managers or over the line manager's subordinates, but they do have direct authority over subordinates in their own departments. However, line-and-staff organizations may experience problems with overstaffing and ambiguous lines of communication. Additionally, employees may become frustrated because they lack the authority to carry out certain decisions.

## Multidivisional Structure

As companies grow and diversify, traditional line structures become difficult to coordinate, making communication difficult and decision making slow. When the weaknesses of the structure—the "turf wars," miscommunication, and working at cross-purposes—exceed the benefits, growing firms tend to restructure, often into the

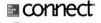 connect

Need help understanding Line vs. Staff Employees? Visit your Connect ebook video tab for a brief animated explanation.

divisionalized form. A **multidivisional structure** organizes departments into larger groups called divisions. Just as departments might be formed on the basis of geography, customer, product, or a combination of these, so too divisions can be formed based on any of these methods of organizing. Within each of these divisions, departments may be organized by product, geographic region, function, or some combination of all three. Indra Nooyi, CEO of PepsiCo, rearranged the company's organizational structure. Prior to her tenure, PepsiCo was organized geographically. She created new units—PepsiCo Americas Foods (PAF), PepsiCo Americas Beverages (PAB), PepsiCo Europe, and PepsiCo Asia, Middle East & Africa—that span international boundaries and make it easier for employees in different geographic regions to share business practices.[19]

Multidivisional structures permit delegation of decision-making authority, allowing divisional and department managers to specialize. They allow those closest to the action to make the decisions that will affect them. Delegation of authority and divisionalized work also mean that better decisions are made faster, and they tend to be more innovative. Most importantly, by focusing each division on a common region, product, or customer, each is more likely to provide products that meet the needs of its particular customers. However, the divisional structure inevitably creates work duplication, which makes it more difficult to realize the economies of scale that result from grouping functions together.

**multidivisional structure** a structure that organizes departments into larger groups called divisions

## Matrix Structure

Another structure that attempts to address issues that arise with growth, diversification, productivity, and competitiveness, is the matrix. A **matrix structure,** also called a project management structure, sets up teams from different departments, thereby creating two or more intersecting lines of authority (Figure 7.7). One of the first

**matrix structure** a structure that sets up teams from different departments, thereby creating two or more intersecting lines of authority; also called a project-management structure

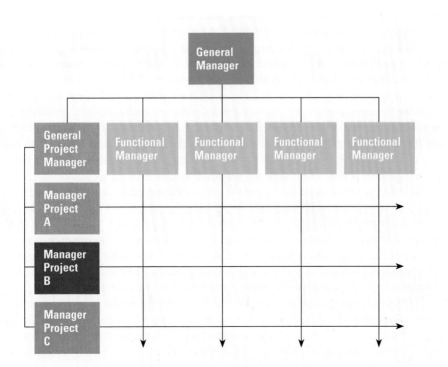

**FIGURE 7.7**
**Matrix Structure**

organizations to design and implement a matrix structure was the National Aeronautics and Space Administration (NASA) for the space program because it needed to coordinate different projects at the same time. The matrix structure superimposes project-based departments on the more traditional, function-based departments. Project teams bring together specialists from a variety of areas to work together on a single project, such as developing a new fighter jet. In this arrangement, employees are responsible to two managers—functional managers and project managers. Matrix structures are usually temporary: Team members typically go back to their functional or line department after a project is finished. However, more firms are becoming permanent matrix structures, creating and dissolving project teams as needed to meet customer needs. The aerospace industry was one of the first to apply the matrix structure, but today it is used by universities and schools, accounting firms, banks, and organizations in other industries.

Matrix structures provide flexibility, enhanced cooperation, and creativity, and they enable the company to respond quickly to changes in the environment by giving special attention to specific projects or problems. However, they are generally expensive and quite complex, and employees may be confused as to whose authority has priority—the project manager's or the immediate supervisor's.

**LO 7-5**

# The Role of Groups and Teams in Organizations

Regardless of how they are organized, most of the essential work of business occurs in individual work groups and teams, so we'll take a closer look at them now. Although some experts do not make a distinction between groups and teams, in recent years there has been a gradual shift toward an emphasis on teams and managing them to enhance individual and organizational success. Some experts now believe that highest productivity results only when groups become teams.[20]

**group**
two or more individuals who communicate with one another, share a common identity, and have a common goal

Traditionally, a **group** has been defined as two or more individuals who communicate with one another, share a common identity, and have a common goal. A **team** is a small group whose members have complementary skills; have a common purpose, goals, and approach; and hold themselves mutually accountable.[21] All teams are groups, but not all groups are teams. Table 7.2 points out some important differences between them. Work groups emphasize individual work products, individual accountability, and even individual leadership. Salespeople working independently for the same company could be a work group. In contrast, work teams share leadership roles, have both individual and mutual accountability, and create collective work products. In other words, a work group's performance depends on what its members do as individuals, while a team's performance is based on creating a knowledge center and a competency to work together to accomplish a goal. On the other hand, it is also important for team members to retain their individuality and avoid becoming just "another face in the crowd." According to former corporate lawyer and negotiations consultant Susan Cain, the purpose of teams should be toward collaboration versus collectivism. Although the team is working toward a common goal, it is important that all team members actively contribute their ideas and work together to achieve this common goal.[22]

**team**
a small group whose members have complementary skills; have a common purpose, goals, and approach; and hold themselves mutually accountable

The type of groups an organization establishes depends on the tasks it needs to accomplish and the situation it faces. Some specific kinds of groups and teams include committees, task forces, project teams, product-development teams, quality-assurance teams, and self-directed work teams. All of these can be *virtual teams*—employees in

| Working Group | Team |
|---|---|
| Has strong, clearly focused leader | Has shared leadership roles |
| Has individual accountability | Has individual and group accountability |
| Has the same purpose as the broader organizational mission | Has a specific purpose that the team itself delivers |
| Creates individual work products | Creates collective work products |
| Runs efficient meetings | Encourages open-ended discussion and active problem-solving meetings |
| Measures its effectiveness indirectly by its effects on others (e.g., financial performance of the business) | Measures performance directly by assessing collective work products |
| Discusses, decides, and delegates | Discusses, decides, and does real work together |

**TABLE 7.2**
**Differences between Groups and Teams**

Source: Robert Gatewood, Robert Taylor, and O. C. Ferrell, Management: Comprehension Analysis and Application, 1995, p. 427. Copyright © 1995 Richard D. Irwin, a Times Mirror Higher Education Group, Inc., company. Reproduced with permission of the McGraw-Hill Companies.

different locations who rely on e-mail, audio conferencing, fax, Internet, videoconferencing, or other technological tools to accomplish their goals. Virtual teams are becoming a part of everyday business, with the number of employees working remotely from their employer increasing more than 80 percent in the last several years.[23] Virtual teams have also opened up opportunities for different companies. Not only does Cisco Systems Inc. work in virtual teams, but the company makes networking technology to support video conferencing. At Cisco Europe, 10,000 employees across 21 countries developed a set of team operating principles to aid team collaboration.[24]

## Committees

A **committee** is usually a permanent, formal group that does some specific task. For example, many firms have a compensation or finance committee to examine the effectiveness of these areas of operation as well as the need for possible changes. Ethics committees are formed to develop and revise codes of ethics, suggest methods for implementing ethical standards, and review specific issues and concerns.

**committee**
a permanent, formal group that performs a specific task

## Task Forces

A **task force** is a temporary group of employees responsible for bringing about a particular change. They typically come from across all departments and levels of an organization. Task force membership is usually based on expertise rather than organizational position. Occasionally, a task force may be formed from individuals outside a company. Coca-Cola has often used task forces to address problems and provide recommendations for improving company practices or products. While some task forces might last a few months, others last for years. When Coca-Cola faced lawsuits alleging discrimination practices in hiring and promotion, it developed a five-year task force to examine pay and promotion practices among minority employees. Its experiences helped Coca-Cola realize the advantages of having a cross-functional task force made up of employees from different departments, and it continued to use task forces to

**task force**
a temporary group of employees responsible for bringing about a particular change

At Google, small teams work on research and engineering projects that often last 6–12 months.

tackle major company issues. Other companies that have also recognized the benefits of task forces include IBM, Prudential, and General Electric.[25]

## Teams

Teams are becoming far more common in the U.S. workplace as businesses strive to enhance productivity and global competitiveness. In general, teams have the benefit of being able to pool members' knowledge and skills and make greater use of them than can individuals working alone. Team building is becoming increasingly popular in organizations, with around half of executives indicating their companies had team-building training. Teams require harmony, cooperation, synchronized effort, and flexibility to maximize their contribution.[26] Teams can also create more solutions to problems than can individuals. Furthermore, team participation enhances employee acceptance of, understanding of, and commitment to team goals. Teams motivate workers by providing internal rewards in the form of an enhanced sense of accomplishment for employees as they achieve more, and external rewards in the form of praise and certain perks. Consequently, they can help get workers more involved. They can help companies be more innovative, and they can boost productivity and cut costs.

According to psychologist Ivan Steiner, team productivity peaks at about five team members. People become less motivated and group coordination becomes more difficult after this size. Jeff Bezos, Amazon.com CEO, says that he has a "two-pizza rule": If a team cannot be fed by two pizzas, it is too large. Keep teams small enough where everyone gets a piece of the action.[27]

**project teams**
groups similar to task forces that normally run their operation and have total control of a specific work project

**Project Teams.**    **Project teams** are similar to task forces, but normally they run their operation and have total control of a specific work project. Like task forces, their membership is likely to cut across the firm's hierarchy and be composed of people from different functional areas. They are almost always temporary, although a large project, such as designing and building a new airplane at Boeing Corporation, may last for years.

**product-development teams**
a specific type of project team formed to devise, design, and implement a new product

**Product-development teams** are a special type of project team formed to devise, design, and implement a new product. Sometimes product-development teams exist within a functional area—research and development—but now they more frequently include people from numerous functional areas and may even include customers to help ensure that the end product meets the customers' needs. Intel informs their product development process through indirect input from customers. They have a social scientist on staff who leads a research team on how customers actually use products. This is done mainly by observation and asking questions. Once enough information is gathered, it is relayed to the product-development team and incorporated into their designs.[28]

**quality-assurance teams (or quality circles)**
small groups of workers brought together from throughout the organization to solve specific quality, productivity, or service problems

**Quality-Assurance Teams.**    **Quality-assurance teams,** sometimes called **quality circles,** are fairly small groups of workers brought together from throughout the organization to solve specific quality, productivity, or service problems. Although the *quality circle* term is not as popular as it once was, the concern about quality is stronger than ever. Companies such as IBM and Xerox as well as companies in the

### Numi Organic Tea Utilizes Teamwork to Increase Sustainability Initiatives

Numi Organic Tea was organized as a Benefit (B) corporation in 1999 in Oakland, California. This benefit status is a certification that implies the company adheres to strict environmental and socially responsible standards. Numi, a dried lime that can be brewed as tea, is a staple in Iraq, the native home of the founders: brother-and-sister team Ahmed and Reem Rahim. The company incorporates the quadruple bottom line (people, planet, product, and profit) into their business model with organic tea that is completely natural and ethically and environmentally sourced. In reaching their shared goals, the founders quickly learned that effective communication is a vital component. Having different communication styles, Ahmed taught Reem to be more outspoken with her ideas and criticisms, while Reem taught Ahmed the value of listening to others and considering their opinions.

They translated these lessons externally to build partnerships with various Fair Trade organizations to extend their reach. As a result, Numi became one of the world's leaders in importing Fair Trade–certified organic tea and achieved annual sales of more than $20 million with a presence in almost 40 countries. Face-to-face communication is heavily emphasized by the company. The founders frequently travel to the farms where the tea leaves are sourced to make sure farmers are receiving competitive compensation and Fair Trade standards are met.

Their values are also apparent in their packaging. Numi became the first company to receive verification of its packaging and tea bags by the Non-GMO Project with its all-natural, completely recyclable, and biodegradable hemp-based tea bags that are printed with soy-based inks. Many companies, especially in the United States, make packaging and tea bags from genetically modified materials such as genetically modified corn and petroleum-based nylon.[29]

---

automobile industry have used quality circles to shift the organization to a more participative culture. The use of teams to address quality issues will no doubt continue to increase throughout the business world.

**Self-directed Work Teams.** A **self-directed work team (SDWT)** is a group of employees responsible for an entire work process or segment that delivers a product to an internal or external customer.[30] SDWTs permit the flexibility to change rapidly to meet the competition or respond to customer needs. The defining characteristic of an SDWT is the extent to which it is empowered or given authority to make and implement work decisions. Thus, SDWTs are designed to give employees a feeling of "ownership" of a whole job. Employees at 3M as well as an increasing number of companies encourage employees to be active to perform a function or operational task. With shared team responsibility for work outcomes, team members often have broader job assignments and cross-train to master other jobs, thus permitting greater team flexibility.

> **self-directed work team (SDWT)**
> a group of employees responsible for an entire work process or segment that delivers a product to an internal or external customer

## Communicating in Organizations

LO 7-6

Communication within an organization can flow in a variety of directions and from a number of sources, each using both oral and written forms of communication. The success of communication systems within the organization has a tremendous effect on the overall success of the firm. Communication mistakes can lower productivity and morale.

Alternatives to face-to-face communications—such as meetings—are growing, thanks to technology such as voice-mail, e-mail, social media, and online newsletters. Many companies use internal networks called intranets

> **DID YOU KNOW?** A survey of managers and executives found that they feel 28 percent of meetings are a waste of time and that information could be communicated more effectively using other methods.[31]

Yammer is a social network that companies can use to connect employees with one another.

to share information with employees. Intranets increase communication across different departments and levels of management and help with the flow of everyday business activities. Another innovative approach is cloud computing. Rather than using physical products, companies using cloud computing technology can access computing resources and information over a network. Cloud computing allows companies to have more control over computing resources and can be less expensive than hardware or software. Salesforce.com uses cloud computing in its customer relationship management solutions.[32] Companies can even integrate aspects of social media into their intranets, allowing employees to post comments and pictures, participate in polls, and create group calendars. However, increased access to the Internet at work has also created many problems, including employee abuse of company email and Internet access.[33]

## Formal Communication

Formal channels of communication are intentionally defined and designed by the organization. They represent the flow of communication within the formal organizational structure, as shown on organizational charts. Traditionally, formal communication patterns were classified as vertical and horizontal, but with the increased use of teams and matrix structures, formal communication may occur in a number of patterns (Figure 7.8).

*Upward communication* flows from lower to higher levels of the organization and includes information such as progress reports, suggestions for improvement, inquiries, and grievances. *Downward communication* refers to the traditional flow of

**FIGURE 7.8**
**The Flow of Communication in an Organizational Hierarchy**

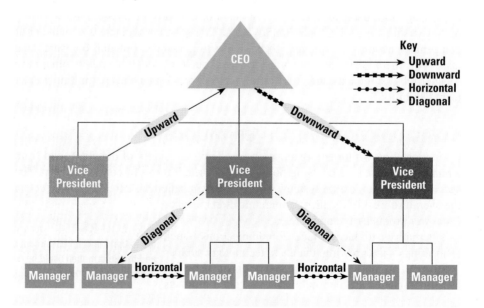

information from upper organizational levels to lower levels. This type of communication typically involves directions, the assignment of tasks and responsibilities, performance feedback, and certain details about the organization's strategies and goals. Speeches, policy and procedures manuals, employee handbooks, company leaflets, telecommunications, and job descriptions are examples of downward communication.

*Horizontal communication* involves the exchange of information among colleagues and peers on the same organizational level, such as across or within departments. Horizontal information informs, supports, and coordinates activities both within the department and with other departments. At times, the business will formally require horizontal communication among particular organizational members, as is the case with task forces or project teams.

With more and more companies downsizing and increasing the use of self-managed work teams, many workers are being required to communicate with others in different departments and on different levels to solve problems and coordinate work. When these individuals from different units and organizational levels communicate, it is *diagonal communication.*

## Informal Communication Channels

Along with the formal channels of communication shown on an organizational chart, all firms communicate informally as well. Communication between friends, for instance, cuts across department, division, and even management–subordinate boundaries. Such friendships and other nonwork social relationships comprise the *informal organization* of a firm, and their impact can be great.

The most significant informal communication occurs through the **grapevine,** an informal channel of communication, separate from management's formal, official communication channels. Grapevines exist in all organizations. Information passed along the grapevine may relate to the job or organization, or it may be gossip and rumors unrelated to either. The accuracy of grapevine information has been of great concern to managers.

Additionally, managers can turn the grapevine to their advantage. Using it as a "sounding device" for possible new policies is one example. Managers can obtain valuable information from the grapevine that could improve decision making. Some organizations use the grapevine to their advantage by floating ideas, soliciting feedback, and reacting accordingly. People love to gossip, and managers need to be aware that grapevines exist in every organization. Managers who understand how the grapevine works also can use it to their advantage by feeding it facts to squelch rumors and incorrect information.

**grapevine**
an informal channel of communication, separate from management's formal, official communication channels

## Monitoring Communications

Technological advances and the increased use of electronic communication in the workplace have made monitoring its use necessary for most companies. Failing to monitor employees' use of e-mail, social media, and the Internet can be costly. Many companies require that employees sign and follow a policy on appropriate Internet use. These agreements often require that employees will use corporate computers only for work-related activities. Additionally, several companies use software programs to monitor employee computer usage.[34] Instituting practices that show respect for employee privacy but do not abdicate employer responsibility are increasingly necessary in today's workplace. Several websites provide model policies and detailed guidelines for conducting electronic monitoring, including the Model Electronic Privacy Act on the American Civil Liberties Union site.

## Improving Communication Effectiveness

Without effective communication, the activities and overall productivity of projects, groups, teams, and individuals will be diminished. Communication is an important area for a firm to address at all levels of management. Apple supplier Foxconn is one example of how essential communication is to a firm. Despite criticisms of unfair labor conditions, the Fair Labor Association determined that Foxconn had formal procedures in place at its factories to prevent many major accidents. However, it concluded that the firm had a communication problem. These procedures were not being communicated to the factory workers, contributing to unsafe practices and two tragic explosions.[35]

One of the major issues of effective communication is in obtaining feedback. If feedback is not provided, then communication will be ineffective and can drag down overall performance. Managers should always encourage feedback, including concerns and challenges about issues. Listening is a skill that involves hearing, and most employees listen much more than they actively communicate to others. Therefore, managers should encourage employees to provide feedback—even if it is negative. This will allow the organization to identify strengths and weaknesses and make adjustments when needed. At the same time, strong feedback mechanisms help to empower employees as they feel that their voices are being heard.

Interruptions can be a serious threat to effective communication. Various activities can interrupt the message. For example, interjecting a remark can create discontinuance in the communication process or disrupt the uniformity of the message. Even small interruptions can be a problem if the messenger cannot adequately understand or interpret the communicator's message. One suggestion is to give the communicator space or time to make another statement rather than quickly responding or making your own comment.

Strong and effective communication channels are a requirement for companies to distribute information to different levels of the company. Businesses have several channels for communication, including face-to-face, e-mail, phone, and written communication (for example, memos). Each channel has advantages and disadvantages, and some are more appropriate to use than others. For instance, a small task requiring little instruction might be communicated through a short memo or e-mail. An in-depth task would most likely require a phone conversation or face-to-face contact. E-mail has become especially helpful for businesses, and both employees and managers are increasingly using e-mail rather than memos or phone conversations. However, it is important that employees use e-mail correctly. It is quite easy to send the wrong e-mail to the wrong person, and messages sent over e-mail can be misinterpreted. Inappropriate e-mails can be forwarded without a second thought, and employees have gotten in trouble for sending personal e-mails in the workplace. It is therefore important for companies to communicate their e-mail policies throughout the organization. Communicators using e-mail, whether managers or employees, must exert caution before pushing that "Send" button.

Communication is necessary in helping every organizational member understand what is expected of him or her. Many business problems can be avoided if clear communication exists within the company. Even the best business strategies are of little use if those who will oversee them cannot understand what is intended. Communication might not seem to be as big of a concern to management as finances, human resources, and marketing, but in reality it can make the difference between successful implementation of business activities or failure.

Jobs dealing with organizational culture and structure are usually at the top of the organization. If you want to be a CEO or high-level manager, you will help shape these areas of business. On the other hand, if you are an entrepreneur or small-business person, you will need to make decisions about assigning tasks, departmentalization, and assigning responsibility. Even managers in small organizations have to make decisions about decentralization, span of management, and forms of organizational structure. While these decisions may be part of your job, there are usually no job titles dealing with these specific areas. Specific jobs that attempt to improve organizational culture could include ethics and compliance positions as well as those who are in charge of communicating memos, manuals, and policies that help establish the culture. These positions will be in communications, human resources, and positions that assist top organizational managers.

Teams are becoming more common in the workplace, and it is possible to become a member of a product development group or quality assurance team. There are also human resource positions that encourage teamwork through training activities. The area of corporate communications provides lots of opportunities for specific jobs that facilitate communication systems. Thanks to technology, there are job positions to help disseminate information through online newsletters, intranets, or internal computer networks to share information to increase collaboration. In addition to the many advances using electronic communications, there are technology concerns that create new job opportunities. Monitoring workplace communications such as the use of e-mail and the Internet has created new industries. There have to be internal controls in the organization to make sure that the organization does not engage in any copyright infringement. If this is an area of interest, there are specific jobs that provide an opportunity to use your technological skills to assist in maintaining appropriate standards in communicating and using technology.

If you go to work for a large company with many divisions, you can expect a number of positions dealing with the tasks discussed here. If you go to work for a small company, you will probably engage in most of these tasks as a part of your position. Organizational flexibility requires individual flexibility, and those employees willing to take on new domains and challenges will be the employees who survive and prosper in the future.

## Review Your Understanding

### Define organizational structure, and relate how organizational structures develop.

Structure is the arrangement or relationship of positions within an organization; it develops when managers assign work activities to work groups and specific individuals and coordinate the diverse activities required to attain organizational objectives. Organizational structure evolves to accommodate growth, which requires people with specialized skills.

### Describe how specialization and departmentalization help an organization achieve its goals.

Structuring an organization requires that management assign work tasks to specific individuals and groups. Under specialization, managers break labor into small, specialized tasks and assign employees to do a single task, fostering efficiency. Departmentalization is the grouping of jobs into working units (departments, units, groups, or divisions). Businesses may departmentalize by function, product, geographic region, or customer, or they may combine two or more of these.

### Distinguish between groups and teams, and identify the types of groups that exist in organizations.

A group is two or more persons who communicate, share a common identity, and have a common goal. A team is a small group whose members have complementary skills, a common purpose, goals, and approach and who hold themselves mutually accountable. The major distinction is that individual performance is most important in groups, while collective work group performance counts most in teams. Special kinds of groups include task forces, committees, project teams, product-development teams, quality-assurance teams, and self-directed work teams.

### Determine how organizations assign responsibility for tasks and delegate authority.

Delegation of authority means assigning tasks to employees and giving them the power to make commitments, use resources, and take whatever actions are necessary to accomplish the tasks. It lays responsibility on employees to carry out assigned tasks satisfactorily and holds them accountable to a superior for the proper execution of their assigned work. The extent to which authority is delegated throughout an organization determines its degree of centralization. Span of management refers to the number of subordinates who report to a particular manager. A wide span of management occurs in flat organizations; a narrow one exists in tall organizations.

### Compare and contrast some common forms of organizational structure.

Line structures have direct lines of authority that extend from the top manager to employees at the lowest level of the organization. The line-and-staff structure has a traditional line relationship between superiors and subordinates, and specialized staff managers are available to assist line managers. A multidivisional structure gathers departments into larger groups called divisions. A matrix, or project-management, structure sets up

teams from different departments, thereby creating two or more intersecting lines of authority.

### Describe how communication occurs in organizations.

Communication occurs both formally and informally in organizations. Formal communication may be downward, upward, horizontal, and even diagonal. Informal communication takes place through friendships and the grapevine.

### Analyze a business's use of teams.

"Solve the Dilemma" on page 228 introduces a firm attempting to restructure to a team environment. Based on the material presented in this chapter, you should be able to evaluate the firm's efforts and make recommendations for resolving the problems that have developed.

## Revisit the World of Business

1. How does CarMax encourage employees to put customer needs first?

2. How has CarMax developed a decentralized culture?

3. Describe some ways that CarMax empowers its employees.

## Learn the Terms

accountability 212
centralized organization 212
committee 219
customer departmentalization 211
decentralized organization 213
delegation of authority 212
departmentalization 208
functional departmentalization 210
geographical departmentalization 211
grapevine 223

group 218
line-and-staff structure 216
line structure 215
matrix structure 217
multidivisional structure 217
organizational chart 206
organizational culture 204
organizational layers 214
product departmentalization 211
product-development teams 220

project teams 220
quality-assurance teams (or quality circles) 220
responsibility 212
self-directed work team (SDWT) 221
span of management 214
specialization 207
structure 206
task force 219
team 218

## Check Your Progress

1. Identify four types of departmentalization and give an example of each type.

2. Explain the difference between groups and teams.

3. What are self-managed work teams and what tasks might they perform that traditionally are performed by managers?

4. Explain how delegating authority, responsibility, and accountability are related.

5. Distinguish between centralization and decentralization. Under what circumstances is each appropriate?

6. Define span of management. Why do some organizations have narrow spans and others wide spans?

7. Discuss the different forms of organizational structure. What are the primary advantages and disadvantages of each form?

8. Discuss the role of the grapevine within organizations. How can managers use it to further the goals of the firm?

9. How have technological advances made electronic oversight a necessity in many companies?

10. Discuss how an organization's culture might influence its ability to achieve its objectives. Do you think that managers can "manage" the organization's culture?

## Get Involved

1. Explain, using a specific example (perhaps your own future business), how an organizational structure might evolve. How would you handle the issues of specialization, delegation of authority, and centralization? Which structure would you use? Explain your answers.

2. Interview the department chairperson in charge of one of the academic departments in your college or university. Using Table 7.2 as a guideline, explore whether the professors function more like a group or a team. Contrast what you find here with what you see on your school's basketball, football, or baseball team.

## Build Your Skills

### Teamwork

**Background**

Think about all the different kinds of groups and teams you have been a member of or been involved with. Here's a checklist to help you remember them—with "Other" spaces to fill in ones not listed. Check all that apply.

**School Groups/Teams**
- ☐ Sports teams
- ☐ Cheerleading squads
- ☐ Musical groups
- ☐ Hobby clubs
- ☐ Foreign language clubs
- ☐ Study groups
- ☐ Other _____

**Community Groups/Teams**
- ☐ Fund-raising groups
- ☐ Religious groups
- ☐ Sports teams
- ☐ Political groups
- ☐ Boy/Girl Scout troops
- ☐ Volunteer organizations
- ☐ Other _____

**Employment Groups/Teams**
- ☐ Problem-solving teams
- ☐ Work committees
- ☐ Project teams
- ☐ Labor union groups
- ☐ Work crews
- ☐ Other _____

### Task

1. Of those you checked, circle those that you would categorize as a "really great team."

2. Examine the following table[36] and circle those characteristics from columns two and three that were represented in your "really great" team experiences.

| Indicator | Good Team Experience | Not-So-Good Team Experience |
|---|---|---|
| Members arrive on time? | Members are prompt because they know others will be. | Members drift in sporadically, and some leave early. |
| Members prepared? | Members are prepared and know what to expect. | Members are unclear what the agenda is. |
| Meeting organized? | Members follow a planned agenda. | The agenda is tossed aside, and free-wheeling discussion ensues. |
| Members contribute equally? | Members give each other a chance to speak; quiet members are encouraged. | Some members always dominate the discussion; some are reluctant to speak their minds. |
| Discussions help members make decisions? | Members learn from others' points of view, new facts are discussed, creative ideas evolve, and alternatives emerge. | Members reinforce their belief in their own points of view, or their decisions were made long before the meeting. |

| Indicator | Good Team Experience | Not-So-Good Team Experience |
|---|---|---|
| Any disagreement? | Members follow a conflict-resolution process established as part of the team's policies. | Conflict turns to argument, angry words, emotion, blaming. |
| More cooperation or more conflict? | Cooperation is clearly an important ingredient. | Conflict flares openly, as well as simmering below the surface. |
| Commitment to decisions? | Members reach consensus before leaving. | Compromise is the best outcome possible; some members don't care about the result. |
| Member feelings after team decision? | Members are satisfied and are valued for their ideas. | Members are glad it's over, not sure of results or outcome. |
| Members support decision afterward? | Members are committed to implementation. | Some members second-guess or undermine the team's decision. |

3.  What can you take with you from your positive team experiences and apply to a work-related group or team situation in which you might be involved?    _____
   _____
   _____

## Solve the Dilemma — LO 7-7

### Quest Star in Transition

Quest Star (QS), which manufactures quality stereo loudspeakers, wants to improve its ability to compete against Japanese firms. Accordingly, the company has launched a comprehensive quality-improvement program for its Iowa plant. The QS Intracommunication Leadership Initiative (ILI) has flattened the layers of management. The program uses teams and peer pressure to accomplish the plant's goals instead of multiple management layers with their limited opportunities for communication. Under the initiative, employees make all decisions within the boundaries of their responsibilities, and they elect team representatives to coordinate with other teams. Teams are also assigned tasks ranging from establishing policies to evaluating on-the-job safety.

However, employees who are not self-motivated team players are having difficulty getting used to their peers' authority within this system. Upper-level managers face stress and frustration because they must train workers to supervise themselves.

### Discussion Questions

1.  What techniques or skills should an employee have to assume a leadership role within a work group?
2.  If each work group has a team representative, what problems will be faced in supervising these representatives?
3.  Evaluate the pros and cons of the system developed by QS.

## Build Your Business Plan

### Organization, Teamwork, and Communication

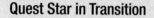

Developing a business plan as a team is a deliberate move of your instructor to encourage you to familiarize yourself with the concept of teamwork. You need to realize that you are going to spend a large part of your professional life working with others. At this point in time, you are working on the business plan for a grade, but after graduation, you will be "teaming" with coworkers and the success of your endeavor may determine whether you get a raise or a bonus. It is important that you be comfortable as soon as possible with working with others and holding them accountable for their contributions.

Some people are natural "leaders," and leaders often feel that if team members are not doing their work, they take it upon themselves to "do it all." This is not leadership, but rather micro-managing.

Leadership means holding members accountable for their responsibilities. Your instructor may provide ideas on how this could be implemented, possibly by utilizing peer reviews. Remember, you are not doing a team member a favor by doing their work for them.

If you are a "follower" (someone who takes directions well) rather than a leader, try to get into a team where others are hard workers and you will rise to their level. There is nothing wrong with being a follower; not everyone can be a leader!

# See for Yourself Videocase

## Zappos Creates Organizational Structure and Culture with Teams

Zappos began in 1999 as an online shoe retailer but has expanded into many product categories since then. The company has always taken pride in its focus on employees and customers and, as a result, has adopted a team structure to reinforce the kind of organizational culture for which it aims. Jeanne Markel, the director of the Downtown Team, states that the managerial goal "is to drive the culture within Zappos." As Zappos began incorporating more product categories, the teams grew both in size and number. This helped to reduce the complexity of company growth and establish a basis for success. Many companies utilize functional departmentalization as a structure to organize their activities. Zappos' many teams serve this same purpose but are described as teams rather than departments. This means that there is a team for each function under each product category, and if the product category is large enough, there will be teams for product subcategories.

While the company is run by teams in every department, one of the most important teams is the merchandising team, because team members are responsible for purchasing all inventory on the Zappos website. This team has approximately 200 people and is led by the Vice President of Merchandising. Under the VP is a Senior Director of Clothing and a General Manager of Footwear, who lead the directors responsible for each purchasing category, including clothing, fashion, and couture and accessories, as well as private-label, performance, and casual lifestyle categories. A team that encompasses such a large and integral responsibility to Zappos' business model will likely change structure to accommodate growth. For example, over the course of seven years, Jeanne Markel saw her team grow from 4 people to 27.

Each purchasing category is composed of its own team as well. The casual lifestyle category, for instance, is led by the Director of Merchandising, who manages four directors responsible for separate subcategories, including kids, comfort, size and width, and home and luggage. There is also a Lead Buyer for each subcategory. From here, the subcategories are divided into further categories. The kids category has a kids footwear merchandising team. The structure of this team begins with entry level Merchandising Assistants, who work closely with the next level of Assistant Buyers to learn the industry and the trade. Assistant Buyers are responsible for mentoring Merchandising Assistants as well as handling up to 15 brands and making decisions on purchases. The next level consists of Buyers, who manage the Assistant Buyers and govern a group of brands. As an employee reaches higher levels in the team, his or her responsibility shifts more from buying activities to mentoring, training, and building the team. This is a core characteristic of Zappos' structure. The company strives to empower employees from the bottom up so that when they are hired as an entry-level employee, within five to seven years they have the opportunity to move up to leadership positions. The top-level positions on this team are the Lead Buyers, who manage the largest one or two brands on the team or on the company's website, and the Director, who rarely ever buys and only mentors and manages.

Because Zappos is an online company, most of the communication that occurs is via e-mail. However in order to ensure that teams function properly and work to reinforce their strong organizational culture, the company encourages face-to-face meetings. Formal meetings between the directors and the various levels on their teams will occur once per month. CEO Tony Hsieh also calls for directors to spend 20 percent of their time with their teams outside of work and gives them an allowance of $50 per month in order to do this. These kinds of activities strengthen the teams by making them more invested in collaboration and instilling trust among team members, as well as with other teams outside of their specific functional area. This serves as a valuable relationship building activity that allows entry-level employees to engage with all levels of the company in a casual manner, promotes brainstorming that results in creative solutions to challenges the team might be facing, and offers all employees a different perspective of their team members and the company they work for.

The most recent development the company has made in terms of organizational structure and teamwork is the adoption of Holacracy. This is a management structure that focuses on the type and amount of work that needs to be accomplished rather than on titles and hierarchy. This seems to be a natural transition for a company whose structure is highlighted by the use of teams and was instituted to avoid rigid structure that leads to inflexibility. The effects of this emerging management style are not fully known; however, it leaves Zappos with an opportunity to show others how it can be successful.[37]

### Discussion Questions

1. Why do companies like Zappos incorporate the use of teams into their organizational structure?

2. How does the use of teams contribute to the organizational culture?

3. How does a focus on the work to be accomplished versus the institution of titles relate to the concept of teamwork?

You can find the related video in the Video Library in Connect. Ask your instructor how you can access Connect.

# Team Exercise

Assign the responsibility of providing the organizational structure for a company one of your team members has worked for. Was your organization centralized or decentralized in terms of decision making? Would you consider the span of control to be wide or narrow? Were any types of teams, committees, or task forces utilized in the organization? Report your work to the class.

# 8

# Managing Service and Manufacturing Operations

## Learning Objectives

### After reading this chapter, you will be able to:

**LO 8-1** Define operations management, and differentiate between operations and manufacturing.

**LO 8-2** Explain how operations management differs in manufacturing and service firms.

**LO 8-3** Describe the elements involved in planning and designing an operations system.

**LO 8-4** Specify some techniques managers may use to manage the logistics of transforming inputs into finished products.

**LO 8-5** Assess the importance of quality in operations management.

**LO 8-6** Evaluate a business's dilemma and propose a solution.

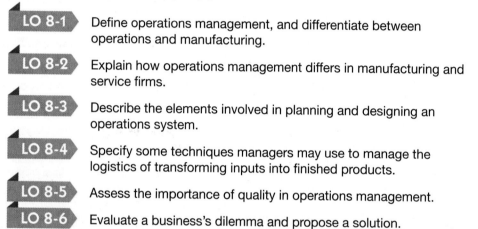

## Manufacturers Use Remote Monitoring Systems to Detect Problems

When something breaks at a manufacturing plant, an engineer or manager comes in to fix the problem. Often, these problems happen after work hours, including the middle of the night. Loss of sleep and stress can profoundly affect these employees, particularly as factories are facing a shortage of skilled workers to handle manufacturing malfunctions. This has created an opportunity for global suppliers of factory automation equipment to expand into remote monitoring.

For instance, ABB Ltd. works with Bayer AG to remotely monitor equipment at its plant in Berkeley, California, for signs that would indicate a problem with Bayer's equipment. This monitoring helps factory employees detect a potential problem and correct it before it becomes an issue. ABB's factory-automation gear also creates greater efficiencies, removing the likelihood for error. International Paper has a similar system with Rockwell Automation. Rockwell monitors International Paper's factory in Ticonderoga, New York, from its location in Cleveland. If a problem is detected at International Paper's factory, Rockwell engineers will contact International Paper and provide recommendations on how to fix the problem.

Some organizations have found it beneficial to offer 24-hour monitoring services. Mitsubishi Power Systems, for instance, provides 24-hour remote monitoring services for turbine operators. Eaton technicians use a remote monitoring system to detect issues with the battery systems of clients. However, there are risks associated with allowing an outside supplier complete access to information about manufacturing processes. Protecting their manufacturing processes is important for manufacturers to retain their competitive advantage. For this reason, some organizations such as Bayer are allowing remote monitoring of its systems only when the company requires help fixing problems.[1]

# Introduction

All organizations create products—goods, services, or ideas—for customers. Thus, organizations as diverse as Toyota, Campbell Soup, UPS, and a public hospital share a number of similarities relating to how they transform resources into the products we consume. Most hospitals use similar admission procedures, while online social media companies, like Facebook and Twitter, use their technology and operating systems to create social networking opportunities and sell advertising. Such similarities are to be expected. But even organizations in unrelated industries take similar steps in creating goods or services. The check-in procedures of hotels and commercial airlines are comparable, for example. The way Subway assembles a sandwich and the way GMC assembles a truck are similar (both use automation and an assembly line). These similarities are the result of operations management, the focus of this chapter.

Here, we discuss the role of production or operations management in acquiring and managing the resources necessary to create goods and services. Production and operations management involves planning and designing the processes that will transform those resources into finished products, managing the movement of those resources through the transformation process, and ensuring that the products are of the quality expected by customers.

# The Nature of Operations Management

**operations management (OM)** the development and administration of the activities involved in transforming resources into goods and services

**manufacturing** the activities and processes used in making tangible products; also called production

**production** the activities and processes used in making tangible products; also called manufacturing

**operations** the activities and processes used in making both tangible and intangible products

**Operations management (OM),** the development and administration of the activities involved in transforming resources into goods and services, is of critical importance. Operations managers oversee the transformation process and the planning and designing of operations systems, managing logistics, quality, and productivity. Quality and productivity have become fundamental aspects of operations management because a company that cannot make products of the quality desired by consumers, using resources efficiently and effectively, will not be able to remain in business. OM is the "core" of most organizations because it is responsible for the creation of the organization's goods and services. Some organizations like General Motors produce tangible products, but service is an important part of the total product for the customer.

Historically, operations management has been called "production" or "manufacturing" primarily because of the view that it was limited to the manufacture of physical goods. Its focus was on methods and techniques required to operate a factory efficiently. The change from "production" to "operations" recognizes the increasing importance of organizations that provide services and ideas. Additionally, the term *operations* represents an interest in viewing the operations function as a whole rather than simply as an analysis of inputs and outputs.

Today, OM includes a wide range of organizational activities and situations outside of manufacturing, such as health care, food service, banking, entertainment, education, transportation, and charity. Thus, we use the terms **manufacturing** and **production** interchangeably to represent the activities and processes used in making *tangible* products, whereas we use the broader term **operations** to describe those processes used in the making of *both tangible and intangible products*. Manufacturing provides tangible products such as Hewlett-Packard's latest printer, and operations provides intangibles such as a stay at Wyndham Hotels and Resorts.

## The Transformation Process

At the heart of operations management is the transformation process through which **inputs** (resources such as labor, money, materials, and energy) are converted into **outputs** (goods, services, and ideas). The transformation process combines inputs in predetermined ways using different equipment, administrative procedures, and technology to create a product (Figure 8.1). To ensure that this process generates quality products efficiently, operations managers control the process by taking measurements (feedback) at various points in the transformation process and comparing them to previously established standards. If there is any deviation between the actual and desired outputs, the manager may take some sort of corrective action. All adjustments made to create a satisfying product are a part of the transformation process.

Transformation may take place through one or more processes. In a business that manufactures oak furniture, for example, inputs pass through several processes before being turned into the final outputs—furniture that has been designed to meet the desires of customers (Figure 8.2). The furniture maker must first strip the oak trees of their bark and saw them into appropriate sizes—one step in the transformation process. Next, the firm dries the strips of oak lumber, a second form of transformation. Third, the dried wood is routed into its appropriate shape and made smooth. Fourth, workers assemble and treat the wood pieces, then stain or varnish the piece of assembled furniture. Finally, the completed piece of furniture is stored until it can be shipped to customers at the appropriate time. Of course, many businesses choose to eliminate some of these stages by purchasing already processed materials—lumber, for example—or outsourcing some tasks to third-party firms with greater expertise.

## Operations Management in Service Businesses

Different types of transformation processes take place in organizations that provide services, such as airlines, colleges, and most nonprofit organizations. An airline transforms inputs such as employees, time, money, and equipment through processes such as booking flights, flying airplanes, maintaining equipment, and training crews. The

---

**inputs**
the resources—such as labor, money, materials, and energy—that are converted into outputs

**outputs**
the goods, services, and ideas that result from the conversion of inputs

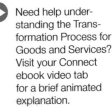

Need help understanding the Transformation Process for Goods and Services? Visit your Connect ebook video tab for a brief animated explanation.

 LO 8-2

---

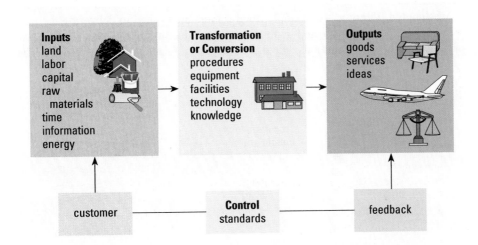

customer ——— **Control** standards ——— feedback

**FIGURE 8.1**
**The Transformation Process of Operations Management**

### Celebrity Auto Group Provides Unique Service—Matching Customized Cars to Celebrities

**Celebrity Auto Group**
**Founder:** Conor Delaney
**Founded:** 2006, in Sarasota, Florida
**Success:** With annual revenue of $16 million, Celebrity Auto Group has grown 4,745 percent in the last three years.

Conor Delaney learned from his days as a professional tennis athlete that celebrities, especially professional basketball players, buy about 2 to 12 cars every year at an average price of $150,000 each. They usually customize their vehicles by style, features, or comfort. This inspired Delaney to retire from tennis and open Celebrity Auto Group—a service operation that finds cars for celebrities, customizes them, transports them, and sells them when the celebrities no longer

want them. Customization is an important component in attracting celebrities. For instance, one of its cars included a Rolls-Royce Phantom with built-in iPads.

Delaney has been successful because of his personal involvement and the trust he has built with clients. Delaney promises never to reveal the names of the celebrities. Because he does not reveal the identity of the previous owner, Delaney sells the vehicles for less than he would be able to if he disclosed this information. This kind of trust allows Delaney to create and maintain long-term relationships with customers. Their loyalty is reinforced because Delaney sells them vehicles for less than other dealers.[2]

output of these processes is flying passengers and/or packages to their destinations. In a nonprofit organization like Habitat for Humanity, inputs such as money, materials, information, and volunteer time and labor are used to transform raw materials into homes for needy families. In this setting, transformation processes include fundraising and promoting the cause in order to gain new volunteers and donations of supplies, as well as pouring concrete, raising walls, and setting roofs. Transformation processes occur in all organizations, regardless of what they produce or their objectives. For most organizations, the ultimate objective is for the produced outputs to be worth more than the combined costs of the inputs.

Unlike tangible goods, services are effectively actions or performances that must be directed toward the consumers who use them. Thus, there is a significant customer-contact component to most services. Examples of high-contact services include health care, real estate, tax preparation, and food service. At the Inn at Little Washington in Washington, Virginia, for example, food servers are critical to delivering the perfect dining experience expected by the most discriminating diners. Wait staff are expected not only to be courteous, but also to demonstrate a detailed knowledge of the

**FIGURE 8.2**

**Inputs, Outputs, and Transformation Processes in the Manufacture of Oak Furniture**

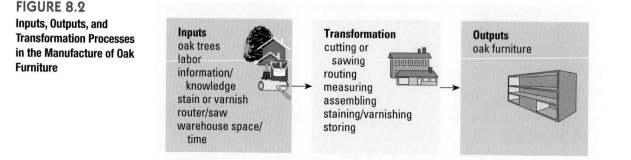

restaurant's offerings, and even to assess the mood of guests in order to respond to diners appropriately.[3] Low-contact services, such as online auction services like eBay, often have a strong high-tech component.

Regardless of the level of customer contact, service businesses strive to provide a standardized process, and technology offers an interface that creates an automatic and structured response. The ideal service provider will be high-tech and high-touch. JetBlue, for example, strives to maintain an excellent website; friendly, helpful customer contact; and satellite TV service at every seat on each plane. Thus, service organizations must build their operations around good execution, which comes from hiring and training excellent employees, developing flexible systems, customizing services, and maintaining adjustable capacity to deal with fluctuating demand.[4]

Another challenge related to service operations is that the output is generally intangible and even perishable. Few services can be saved, stored, resold, or returned.[5] A seat on an airline or a table in a restaurant, for example, cannot be sold or used at a later date. Because of the perishability of services, it can be extremely difficult for service providers to accurately estimate the demand in order to match the right supply of a service. If an airline overestimates demand, for example, it will still have to fly each plane even with empty seats. The flight costs the same regardless of whether it is 50 percent full or 100 percent full, but the former will result in much higher costs per passenger. If the airline underestimates demand, the result can be long lines of annoyed customers or even the necessity of bumping some customers off of an overbooked flight.

Businesses that manufacture tangible goods and those that provide services or ideas are similar yet different. For example, both types of organizations must make design and operating decisions. Most goods are manufactured prior to purchase, but most services are performed after purchase. Flight attendants at Southwest Airlines, hotel service personnel, and even the New York Giants football team engage in performances that are a part of the total product. Though manufacturers and service providers often perform similar activities, they also differ in several respects. We can classify these differences in five basic ways.

**Nature and Consumption of Output.**   First, manufacturers and service providers differ in the nature and consumption of their output. For example, the term *manufacturer* implies a firm that makes tangible products. A service provider, on the other hand, produces more intangible outputs such as U.S. Postal Service delivery of priority mail or a business stay in a Hyatt hotel. As mentioned earlier, the very nature of the service provider's product requires a higher degree of customer contact. Moreover, the actual performance of the service typically occurs at the point of consumption. At the Hyatt, the business traveler may evaluate in-room communications and the restaurant. Automakers, on the other hand, can separate the production of a car from its actual use, but the service dimension requires closer contact with the consumer. Manufacturing, then, can occur in an isolated environment, away from the customer. However, service providers, because of their need for customer contact, are often more limited than manufacturers in selecting work methods, assigning jobs, scheduling work, and exercising control over operations. For this reason, Freddie Mac implemented the Quality Control Information Manager (QCIM) system, a secure, web-based system that allows lenders access to the status of quality control loan file requests. The system makes it easier to control this important aspect of lending.[6] The quality of the service experience is often controlled by a service contact employee. However, some hospitals are studying the manufacturing processes and quality control mechanisms applied in

Subway's inputs are sandwich components such as bread, tomatoes, and lettuce, while its outputs are customized sandwiches.

the automotive industry in an effort to improve their service quality. By analyzing work processes to find unnecessary steps to eliminate and using teams to identify and address problems as soon as they occur, these hospitals are slashing patient waiting times, decreasing inventories of wheelchairs, readying operating rooms sooner, and generally moving patients through their hospital visit more quickly, with fewer errors, and at a lower cost.[7]

**Uniformity of Inputs.**   A second way to classify differences between manufacturers and service providers has to do with the uniformity of inputs. Manufacturers typically have more control over the amount of variability of the resources they use than do service providers. For example, each customer calling Fidelity Investments is likely to require different services due to differing needs, whereas many of the tasks required to manufacture a Ford Focus are the same across each unit of output. Consequently, the products of service organizations tend to be more "customized" than those of their manufacturing counterparts. Consider, for example, a haircut versus a bottle of shampoo. The haircut is much more likely to incorporate your specific desires (customization) than is the bottle of shampoo.

**Uniformity of Output.**   Manufacturers and service providers also differ in the uniformity of their output, the final product. Because of the human element inherent in providing services, each service tends to be performed differently. Not all grocery checkers, for example, wait on customers in the same way. If a barber or stylist performs 15 haircuts in a day, it is unlikely that any two of them will be exactly the same. Consequently, human and technological elements associated with a service can result in a different day-to-day or even hour-to-hour performance of that service. The service experience can even vary at McDonald's or Burger King despite the fact that the two chains employ very similar procedures and processes. Moreover, no two customers are exactly alike in their perception of the service experience. Health care offers another excellent example of this challenge. Every diagnosis, treatment, and surgery varies because every individual is different. In manufacturing, the high degree of automation available allows manufacturers to generate uniform outputs and, thus, the operations are more effective and efficient. For example, we would expect every TAG Heuer or Rolex watch to maintain very high standards of quality and performance.

**Labor Required.**   A fourth point of difference is the amount of labor required to produce an output. Service providers are generally more labor-intensive (require more labor) because of the high level of customer contact, perishability of the output (must be consumed immediately), and high degree of variation of inputs and outputs (customization). For example, Adecco provides temporary support personnel. Each temporary worker's performance determines Adecco's product quality. A manufacturer, on the other hand, is likely to be more capital-intensive because of the machinery and technology used in the mass production of highly similar goods. For instance, it would take a considerable investment for Ford to make an electric car that has batteries with a longer life.

**Measurement of Productivity.**   The final distinction between service providers and manufacturers involves the measurement of productivity for each output produced. For manufacturers, measuring productivity is fairly straightforward because of the tangibility of the output and its high degree of uniformity. For the service provider, variations in demand (for example, higher demand for air travel in some seasons than in others), variations in service requirements from job to job, and the intangibility of the product make productivity measurement more difficult. Consider, for example, how much easier it is to measure the productivity of employees involved in the production of Intel computer processors as opposed to serving the needs of Prudential Securities' clients.

It is convenient and simple to think of organizations as being either manufacturers or service providers as in the preceding discussion. In reality, however, most organizations are a combination of the two, with both tangible and intangible qualities embodied in what they produce. For example, Porsche provides customer services such as toll-free hotlines and warranty protection, while banks may sell checks and other tangible products that complement their primarily intangible product offering. Thus, we consider "products" to include both tangible physical goods and intangible service offerings. It is the level of tangibility of its principal product that tends to classify a company as either a manufacturer or a service provider. From an OM standpoint, this level of tangibility greatly influences the nature of the company's operational processes and procedures.

# Planning and Designing Operations Systems

Before a company can produce any product, it must first decide what it will produce and for what group of customers. It must then determine what processes it will use to make these products as well as the facilities it needs to produce them. These decisions comprise operations planning. Although planning was once the sole realm of the production and operations department, today's successful companies involve all departments within an organization, particularly marketing and research and development, in these decisions.

## Planning the Product

Before making any product, a company first must determine what consumers want and then design a product to satisfy that want. Most companies use marketing research (discussed in Chapter 11) to determine the kinds of goods and services to provide and the features they must possess. Twitter and Facebook provide new opportunities for businesses to discover what consumers want, then design the product accordingly. For instance, the hamburger restaurant chain Red Robin used the social network Yammer to solicit customer and employee feedback. It has become extremely popular among employees and restaurant owners. When Red Robin introduced its new Tavern Double Burger, restaurant servers and regional managers posted comments they had heard from customers. Based on these comments, Red Robin was able to make immediate changes to its recipe to satisfy its customer needs. This process, which traditionally takes 6 to 12 months, took four weeks using social media.[8] Marketing research can also help gauge the demand for a product and how much consumers are willing to pay for it. But when a market's environment changes, firms have to be flexible.

Developing a product can be a lengthy, expensive process. For example, in the automobile industry, developing the new technology for night vision, parking assist systems, and a satellite service that locates and analyzes car problems has been a lengthy, expensive process. Most companies work to reduce development time and costs. The University of Leicester and Polytec UK joined together to build the Advanced Structural Dynamics Evaluation Centre (ASDEC), which reduces new product development time for the automotive and engineered systems industries.[9] Once management has developed an idea for a product that customers will buy, it must then plan how to produce the product.

Within a company, the engineering or research and development department is charged with turning a product idea into a workable design that can be produced economically. In smaller companies, a single individual (perhaps the owner) may be solely responsible for this crucial activity. Regardless of who is responsible for product design, planning does not stop with a blueprint for a product or a description of a service; it must also work out efficient production of the product to ensure that enough is available to satisfy consumer demand. How does a lawn mower company transform steel, aluminum, and other materials into a mower design that satisfies consumer and environmental requirements? Operations managers must plan for the types and quantities of materials needed to produce the product, the skills and quantity of people needed to make the product, and the actual processes through which the inputs must pass in their transformation to outputs.

## Designing the Operations Processes

Before a firm can begin production, it must first determine the appropriate method of transforming resources into the desired product. Often, consumers' specific needs and desires dictate a process. Customer needs, for example, require that all 3/4-inch bolts have the same basic thread size, function, and quality; if they did not, engineers and builders could not rely on 3/4-inch bolts in their construction projects. A bolt manufacturer, then, will likely use a standardized process so that every 3/4-inch bolt produced is like every other one. On the other hand, a bridge often must be customized so that it is appropriate for the site and expected load; furthermore, the bridge must be constructed on site rather than in a factory. Typically, products are designed to be manufactured by one of three processes: standardization, modular design, or customization.

**standardization**
the making of identical interchangeable components or products

**Standardization.**　Most firms that manufacture products in large quantities for many customers have found that they can make them cheaper and faster by standardizing designs. **Standardization** is making identical, interchangeable components or even complete products. With standardization, a customer may not get exactly what he or she wants, but the product generally costs less than a custom-designed product. Television sets, ballpoint pens, and tortilla chips are standardized products; most are manufactured on an assembly line. Standardization speeds up production and quality control and reduces production costs. And, as in the example of the 3/4-inch bolts, standardization provides consistency so that customers who need certain products to function uniformly all the time will get a product that meets their expectations. Standardization becomes more complex on a global scale because different countries have different standards for quality. To help solve this problem, the International Organization for Standardization (ISO) has developed a list of global standards that companies can adopt to assure stakeholders that they are complying with the highest quality, environmental, and managerial guidelines.

**modular design**
the creation of an item in self-contained units, or modules, that can be combined or interchanged to create different products

**Modular Design.**　**Modular design** involves building an item in self-contained units, or modules, that can be combined or interchanged to create different products. IKEA furniture, for example, embodies a modular design with several components.

This allows for customers to mix and match components for customized design. Because many modular components are produced as integrated units, the failure of any portion of a modular component usually means replacing the entire component. Modular design allows products to be repaired quickly, thus reducing the cost of labor, but the component itself is expensive, raising the cost of repair materials. Many automobile manufacturers use modular design in the production process. Manufactured homes are built on a modular design and often cost about one-fourth the cost of a conventionally built house.

**Customization.** **Customization** is making products to meet a particular customer's needs or wants. Products produced in this way are generally unique. Such products include repair services, photocopy services, custom artwork, jewelry, and furniture, as well as large-scale products such as bridges, ships, and computer software. For instance, bicycles are popular products to customize. A company called Breadwinner Cycles designs eight models of bicycles in such a way that riders can customize various features and sizes to fit their specific needs.[10] Mass customization relates to making products that meet the needs or wants of a large number of individual customers. The customer can select the model, size, color, style, or design of the product. Dell can customize a computer with the exact configuration that fits a customer's needs. Services such as fitness programs and travel packages can also be custom designed for a large number of individual customers. For both goods and services, customers get to make choices and have options to determine the final product.

> **customization**
> making products to meet a particular customer's needs or wants

## Planning Capacity

Planning the operational processes for the organization involves two important areas: capacity planning and facilities planning. The term **capacity** basically refers to the maximum load that an organizational unit can carry or operate. The unit of measurement may be a worker or machine, a department, a branch, or even an entire plant. Maximum capacity can be stated in terms of the inputs or outputs provided. For example, an electric plant might state plant capacity in terms of the maximum number of kilowatt-hours that can be produced without causing a power outage, while a restaurant might state capacity in terms of the maximum number of customers who can be effectively—comfortably and courteously—served at any one particular time.

> **capacity**
> the maximum load that an organizational unit can carry or operate

Efficiently planning the organization's capacity needs is an important process for the operations manager. Capacity levels that fall short can result in unmet demand, and consequently, lost customers. On the other hand, when there is more capacity available than needed, operating costs are driven up needlessly due to unused and often expensive resources. To avoid such situations, organizations must accurately forecast demand and then plan capacity based on these forecasts. Another reason for the importance of efficient capacity planning has to do with long-term commitment of resources. Often, once a capacity decision—such as factory size—has been implemented, it is very difficult to change the decision without incurring substantial costs. Large companies have come to realize that although change can be expensive, not adjusting to future demand and stakeholder desires will be more expensive in the long run. For this reason, Honda has begun to adopt ISO 14001 guidelines for environmental management systems in its factories. These systems help firms monitor their impact on the environment. Thirteen of Honda's 14 North American factories have received certification.[12]

**DID YOU KNOW?** Hershey's has the production capacity to make more than 80 million chocolate kisses per day.[11]

## Planning Facilities

Once a company knows what process it will use to create its products, it then can design and build an appropriate facility in which to make them. Many products are manufactured in factories, but others are produced in stores, at home, or where the product ultimately will be used. Companies must decide where to locate their operations facilities, what layout is best for producing their particular product, and even what technology to apply to the transformation process.

Many firms are developing both a traditional organization for customer contact and a virtual organization. Charles Schwab Corporation, a securities brokerage and investment company, maintains traditional offices and has developed complete telephone and Internet services for customers. Through its website, investors can obtain personal investment information and trade securities over the Internet without leaving their home or office.

**Facility Location.**    Where to locate a firm's facilities is a significant question because, once the decision has been made and implemented, the firm must live with it due to the high costs involved. When a company decides to relocate or open a facility at a new location, it must pay careful attention to factors such as proximity to market, availability of raw materials, availability of transportation, availability of power, climatic influences, availability of labor, community characteristics (quality of life),

Apple stores are designed to make the most efficient use of space. The layout of the stores allows customers to test its products before purchasing.

and taxes and inducements. Inducements and tax reductions have become an increasingly important criterion in recent years. To increase production and to provide incentives for small startups, many states are offering tax inducements for solar companies. State governments are willing to forgo some tax revenue in exchange for job growth, getting in on a burgeoning industry as well as the good publicity generated by the company. In a very solar-friendly state like Colorado, companies may get tax reductions for starting production, and consumers receive additional rebates for installing solar systems in their homes and businesses.[13] Apple has followed the lead of other major companies by locating its manufacturing facilities in Asia to take advantage of lower labor and production costs. The facility-location decision is complex because it involves the evaluation of many factors, some of which cannot be measured with precision. Because of the long-term impact of the decision, however, it is one that cannot be taken lightly.

**Facility Layout.** Arranging the physical layout of a facility is a complex, highly technical task. Some industrial architects specialize in the design and layout of certain types of businesses. There are three basic layouts: fixed-position, process, and product.

A company using a **fixed-position layout** brings all resources required to create the product to a central location. The product—perhaps an office building, house, hydroelectric plant, or bridge—does not move. A company using a fixed-position layout may be called a **project organization** because it is typically involved in large, complex projects such as construction or exploration. Project organizations generally make a unique product, rely on highly skilled labor, produce very few units, and have high production costs per unit.

Firms that use a **process layout** organize the transformation process into departments that group related processes. A metal fabrication plant, for example, may have a cutting department, a drilling department, and a polishing department. A hospital may have an X-ray unit, an obstetrics unit, and so on. These types of organizations are sometimes called **intermittent organizations,** which deal with products of a lesser magnitude than do project organizations, and their products are not necessarily unique but possess a significant number of differences. Doctors, makers of custom-made cabinets, commercial printers, and advertising agencies are intermittent organizations because they tend to create products to customers' specifications and produce relatively few units of each product. Because of the low level of output, the cost per unit of product is generally high.

The **product layout** requires that production be broken down into relatively simple tasks assigned to workers, who are usually positioned along an assembly line. Workers remain in one location, and the product moves from one worker to another. Each person in turn performs his or her required tasks or activities. Companies that use assembly lines are usually known as **continuous manufacturing organizations,** so named because once they are set up, they run continuously, creating products with many similar characteristics. Examples of products produced on assembly lines are automobiles, television sets, vacuum cleaners, toothpaste, and meals from a cafeteria. Continuous manufacturing organizations using a product layout are characterized by the standardized product they produce, the large number of units produced, and the relatively low unit cost of production.

Many companies actually use a combination of layout designs. For example, an automobile manufacturer may rely on an assembly line (product layout) but may also use a process layout to manufacture parts.

**fixed-position layout**
a layout that brings all resources required to create the product to a central location

**project organization**
a company using a fixed-position layout because it is typically involved in large, complex projects such as construction or exploration

**process layout**
a layout that organizes the transformation process into departments that group related processes

**intermittent organizations**
organizations that deal with products of a lesser magnitude than do project organizations; their products are not necessarily unique but possess a significant number of differences

**product layout**
a layout requiring that production be broken down into relatively simple tasks assigned to workers, who are usually positioned along an assembly line

**continuous manufacturing organizations**
companies that use continuously running assembly lines, creating products with many similar characteristics

**Technology.**    Every industry has a basic, underlying technology that dictates the nature of its transformation process. The steel industry continually tries to improve steelmaking techniques. The health care industry performs research into medical technologies and pharmaceuticals to improve the quality of health care service. Two developments that have strongly influenced the operations of many businesses are computers and robotics.

Computers have been used for decades and on a relatively large scale since IBM introduced its 650 series in the late 1950s. The operations function makes great use of computers in all phases of the transformation process. **Computer-assisted design (CAD),** for example, helps engineers design components, products, and processes on the computer instead of on paper. CAD is used in 3D printing. CAD software is used to develop a 3D image. Then, the CAD file is sent to the printer. The printer is able to use layers of liquid, powder, paper, or metal to construct a 3D model.[14] **Computer-assisted manufacturing (CAM)** goes a step further, employing specialized computer systems to actually guide and control the transformation processes. Such systems can monitor the transformation process, gathering information about the equipment used to produce the products and about the product itself as it goes from one stage of the transformation process to the next. The computer provides information to an operator who may, if necessary, take corrective action. In some highly automated systems, the computer itself can take corrective action. At Dell's OptiPlex Plant, electronic instructions are sent to double-decker conveyor belts that speed computer components to assembly stations. Two-member teams are told by computers which PC or server to build, with initial assembly taking only three to four minutes. Then more electronic commands move the products to a finishing area to be customized, boxed, and sent to waiting delivery trucks.

Using **flexible manufacturing,** computers can direct machinery to adapt to different versions of similar operations. For example, with instructions from a computer, one machine can be programmed to carry out its function for several different versions of an engine without shutting down the production line for refitting.

Robots are also becoming increasingly useful in the transformation process. These "steel-collar" workers have become particularly important in industries such as nuclear power, hazardous-waste disposal, ocean research, and space construction and maintenance, in which human lives would otherwise be at risk. Robots are used in numerous applications by companies around the world. Many assembly operations— cars, television sets, telephones, stereo equipment, and numerous other products— depend on industrial robots. The Robotic Industries Association estimates that about 228,000 robots are now at work in U.S. factories, making the United States one of the two largest users of robotics, second only to Japan. Researchers continue to make more sophisticated robots, extending their use beyond manufacturing and space programs to various industries, including laboratory research, education, medicine, and household activities. Projections for the next few years indicate that these emerging markets will account for the use of 22 million robots. There are many advantages in using robotics, such as more successful surgeries, re-shoring manufacturing activities back to America, energy conservation, and safer work practices.[15]

When all these technologies—CAD/CAM, flexible manufacturing, robotics, computer systems, and more—are integrated, the result is **computer-integrated manufacturing (CIM),** a complete system that designs products, manages machines and materials, and controls the operations function. Companies adopt CIM to boost productivity and quality and reduce costs. Such technology, and computers in particular, will continue to make strong inroads into operations on two fronts—one dealing with

**computer-assisted design (CAD)**
the design of components, products, and processes on computers instead of on paper

**computer-assisted manufacturing (CAM)**
manufacturing that employs specialized computer systems to actually guide and control the transformation processes

**flexible manufacturing**
the direction of machinery by computers to adapt to different versions of similar operations

**computer-integrated manufacturing (CIM)**
a complete system that designs products, manages machines and materials, and controls the operations function

### Lenovo Gains a Competitive Advantage through Manufacturing

Lenovo, a Chinese computer company and one of the largest PC manufacturers in the world, has defied the state of the personal computer market by experiencing rapid growth and increase in market share. In 2013, the company completed a 240,000-square-foot manufacturing facility in Whitsett, North Carolina, where it previously had a logistics center, customer solutions center, and national returns center. This expansion will enable it to become even larger, which is necessary for its next venture.

While the company specializes in PCs, Lenovo is preparing to enter the U.S. mobile phone market. The market is highly competitive, with Apple and Samsung holding 70 percent of the market. Despite the intense competition, however, Lenovo's manufacturing plant could help it gain a competitive advantage. For instance, the manufacturing plant could be used to increase the range of Lenovo's product lines. The company also achieves efficiencies in manufacturing that

may help it save costs and meet changing market conditions. Lenovo sets itself apart from others in the industry by having all parts of the production process in-house. It does not outsource any activities, unlike many other companies in the industry. This allows the firm to keep up with the changes in innovation by better understanding and controlling inventory, matching supply with demand, and handling fast inventory turnover.[16]

#### Discussion Questions

1. Despite the decline in PCs, Lenovo has surpassed most of its competitors in the computer market. Do you think it can do the same in the mobile phone industry?
2. Describe some of the ways Lenovo sets itself apart from competitors.
3. How might keeping the production process in-house help Lenovo?

---

the technology involved in manufacturing and one dealing with the administrative functions and processes used by operations managers. The operations manager must be willing to work with computers and other forms of technology and to develop a high degree of computer literacy.

## Sustainability and Manufacturing

Manufacturing and operations systems are moving quickly to establish environmental sustainability and minimize negative impact on the natural environment. Sustainability deals with conducting activities in such a way as to provide for the long-term well-being of the natural environment, including all biological entities. Sustainability issues are becoming increasingly important to stakeholders and consumers, as they pertain to the future health of the planet. Some sustainability issues include pollution of the land, air, and water, climate change, waste management, deforestation, urban sprawl, protection of biodiversity, and genetically modified foods.

For example, Biogen Idec, the world's oldest biotechnology company, set a goal in 2009 to increase sustainability of operations in water, energy, and materials usage by 15 percent in 2015. The company reached this goal in 2012 by using an internally developed tool called Risk-Weighted Environmental Index to measure the impact of its operations on the environment. As a result, the company was awarded a spot on the Dow Jones Sustainability World Index. Biogen Idec is the first American biotechnology company to be awarded this honor.[17]

New Belgium Brewing is another company that illustrates green initiatives in operations and manufacturing. New Belgium was the first brewery to adopt 100 percent wind-powered electricity, reducing carbon emissions by 1,800 metric tons a year. It uses a steam condenser to capture hot water to be reused for boiling the next batch of barley and hops. Then the steam is redirected to heat the floor tiles and de-ice the loading docks

The outdoor clothing company Patagonia is always looking for a greener way to design, produce, and recycle its products. The company's mission statement: *Build the best product, cause no unnecessary harm, and use business to inspire and implement solutions to the environmental crisis.*

in cold Colorado weather. Used barley and hops are given to local farmers to feed cattle. The company is moving to aluminum cans because they can be recycled an infinite number of times, and recycling one can save enough electricity to run a television for three hours or save a half gallon of gasoline.

Biogen Idec and New Belgium Brewing demonstrate that reducing waste, recycling, conserving, and using renewable energy not only protect the environment, but can also gain the support of stakeholders. Green operations and manufacturing can improve a firm's reputation along with customer and employee loyalty, leading to improved profits.

Much of the movement to green manufacturing and operations is the belief that global warming and climate change must decline. The McKinsey Global Institute (MGI) says that just by investing in existing technologies, the world's energy use could be reduced by 50 percent by the year 2020. Creating green buildings and higher mileage cars could yield $900 billion in savings per year by 2020.[18] Companies like General Motors and Ford are adapting to stakeholder demands for greater sustainability by producing smaller and more fuel-efficient cars. Tesla has taken sustainability even further by making a purely electric vehicle that also ranks at the top in safety. The company also makes sure that its manufacturing facilities operate sustainably by installing solar panels and other renewable sources of energy. Green products produced through green operations and manufacturing are our future. A report authored by the Center for American Progress cites ways that cities and local governments can play a role. For example, Los Angeles plans to save the city utility costs by retrofitting hundreds of city buildings while creating a green careers training program for low-income residents. Newark, New Jersey, and Richmond, California, also have green jobs training programs.[19] Government initiatives provide space for businesses to innovate their green operations and manufacturing.

## Managing the Supply Chain

**supply chain management**
connecting and integrating all parties or members of the distribution system in order to satisfy customers

A major function of operations is **supply chain management,** which refers to connecting and integrating all parties or members of the distribution system in order to satisfy customers.[20] Also called logistics, supply chain management includes all the activities involved in obtaining and managing raw materials and component parts, managing finished products, packaging them, and getting them to customers. UPS implemented a cloud-based supply chain management system to better control international operations. This allowed for more accuracy and on-time delivery of shipments, better management and coordination of suppliers, and real-time shipment status of packages.[21] The supply chain integrates firms such as raw material suppliers, manufacturers, retailers, and ultimate consumers into a seamless flow of information and products.[22] Some aspects of logistics (warehousing, packaging, distributing) are so closely linked with marketing that we will discuss them in Chapter 12. In this section, we look at purchasing, managing inventory, outsourcing, and scheduling, which are vital tasks in the transformation of raw materials into finished goods. To illustrate logistics, consider a hypothetical small business—we'll call it Rushing Water Canoes Inc.—that manufactures aluminum canoes, which it sells primarily to sporting goods stores and river-rafting expeditions. Our company also makes paddles and helmets, but the focus of the following discussion is the manufacture of the company's quality canoes as they proceed through the logistics process.

## Purchasing

**Purchasing,** also known as procurement, is the buying of all the materials needed by the organization. The purchasing department aims to obtain items of the desired quality in the right quantities at the lowest possible cost. Rushing Water Canoes, for example, must procure not only aluminum and other raw materials, and various canoe parts and components, but also machines and equipment, manufacturing supplies (oil, electricity, and so on), and office supplies in order to make its canoes. People in the purchasing department locate and evaluate suppliers of these items. They must constantly be on the lookout for new materials or parts that will do a better job or cost less than those currently being used. The purchasing function can be quite complex and is one area made much easier and more efficient by technological advances.

Not all companies purchase all of the materials needed to create their products. Oftentimes, they can make some components more economically and efficiently than can an outside supplier. Zara, a Spanish fast fashion retailer, manufactures the majority of the clothes it sells.[23] On the other hand, firms sometimes find that it is uneconomical to make or purchase an item, and instead arrange to lease it from another organization. Some airlines, for example, lease airplanes rather than buy them. Whether to purchase, make, or lease a needed item generally depends on cost, as well as on product availability and supplier reliability.

**purchasing**
the buying of all the materials needed by the organization; also called procurement

## Managing Inventory

Once the items needed to create a product have been procured, some provision has to be made for storing them until they are needed. Every raw material, component, completed or partially completed product, and piece of equipment a firm uses—its **inventory**—must be accounted for, or controlled. There are three basic types of inventory. *Finished-goods inventory* includes those products that are ready for sale, such as a fully assembled automobile ready to ship to a dealer. *Work-in-process inventory* consists of those products that are partly completed or are in some stage of the transformation process. At McDonald's, a cooking hamburger represents work-in-process inventory because it must go through several more stages before it can be sold to a customer. *Raw materials inventory* includes all the materials that have been purchased to be used as inputs for making other products. Nuts and bolts are raw materials for an automobile manufacturer, while hamburger patties, vegetables, and buns are raw materials for the fast-food restaurant. Our fictional Rushing Water Canoes has an inventory of materials for making canoes, paddles, and helmets, as well as its inventory of finished products for sale to consumers. **Inventory control** is the process of determining how many supplies and goods are needed and keeping track of quantities on hand, where each item is, and who is responsible for it.

Operations management must be closely coordinated with inventory control. The production of televisions, for example, cannot be planned without some knowledge of the availability of all the necessary materials—the chassis, picture tubes, color guns,

**inventory**
all raw materials, components, completed or partially completed products, and pieces of equipment a firm uses

**inventory control**
the process of determining how many supplies and goods are needed and keeping track of quantities on hand, where each item is, and who is responsible for it

Operations managers are concerned with managing inventory to ensure that there is enough inventory in stock to meet demand.

and so forth. Also, each item held in inventory—any type of inventory—carries with it a cost. For example, storing fully assembled televisions in a warehouse to sell to a dealer at a future date requires not only the use of space, but also the purchase of insurance to cover any losses that might occur due to fire or other unforeseen events.

Inventory managers spend a great deal of time trying to determine the proper inventory level for each item. The answer to the question of how many units to hold in inventory depends on variables such as the usage rate of the item, the cost of maintaining the item in inventory, future costs of inventory and other procedures associated with ordering or making the item, and the cost of the item itself. For example, the price of copper has fluctuated between $1.50 and $3 a pound over the past five years.[24] Firms using copper wiring for construction, copper pipes for plumbing, and other industries requiring copper have to analyze the trade-offs between inventory costs and expected changes in the price of copper. Several approaches may be used to determine how many units of a given item should be procured at one time and when that procurement should take place.

**The Economic Order Quantity Model.**   To control the number of items maintained in inventory, managers need to determine how much of any given item they should order. One popular approach is the **economic order quantity (EOQ) model,** which identifies the optimum number of items to order to minimize the costs of managing (ordering, storing, and using) them.

**economic order quantity (EOQ) model**
a model that identifies the optimum number of items to order to minimize the costs of managing (ordering, storing, and using) them

**just-in-time (JIT) inventory management**
a technique using smaller quantities of materials that arrive "just in time" for use in the transformation process and therefore require less storage space and other inventory management expense

**Just-in-Time Inventory Management.**   An increasingly popular technique is **just-in-time (JIT) inventory management,** which eliminates waste by using smaller quantities of materials that arrive "just in time" for use in the transformation process and therefore require less storage space and other inventory management expense. JIT minimizes inventory by providing an almost continuous flow of items from suppliers to the production facility. Many U.S. companies, including Hewlett-Packard, IBM, and Harley Davidson, have adopted JIT to reduce costs and boost efficiency.

Let's say that Rushing Water Canoes uses 20 units of aluminum from a supplier per day. Traditionally, its inventory manager might order enough for one month at a time: 440 units per order (20 units per day times 22 workdays per month). The expense of such a large inventory could be considerable because of the cost of insurance coverage, recordkeeping, rented storage space, and so on. The just-in-time approach would reduce these costs because aluminum would be purchased in smaller quantities, perhaps in lot sizes of 20, which the supplier would deliver once a day. Of course, for such an approach to be effective, the supplier must be extremely reliable and relatively close to the production facility.

On the other hand, there are some downsides to just-in-time inventory management that marketers must take into account. When the earthquake and tsunami hit Japan, resulting in a nuclear reactor crisis, several Japanese companies halted their operations. Some multinationals relied so much upon their Japanese suppliers that their supply chains were also affected. In the case of natural disasters, having only enough inventory to meet current needs could create delays in production and hurt the company's bottom line. For this reason, many economists suggest that businesses store components that are essential for production and diversify their supply chains. That way, if a natural disaster knocks out a major supplier, the company can continue to operate.[25]

**Material-requirements Planning.**   Another inventory management technique is **material-requirements planning (MRP),** a planning system that schedules the precise quantity of materials needed to make the product. The basic components of MRP are a master production schedule, a bill of materials, and an inventory status file. At Rushing Water Canoes, for example, the inventory-control manager will look at the production schedule to determine how many canoes the company plans to make. He or she will then prepare a bill of materials—a list of all the materials needed to make that quantity of canoes. Next, the manager will determine the quantity of these items that RWC already holds in inventory (to avoid ordering excess materials) and then develop a schedule for ordering and accepting delivery of the right quantity of materials to satisfy the firm's needs. Because of the large number of parts and materials that go into a typical production process, MRP must be done on a computer. It can be, and often is, used in conjunction with just-in-time inventory management.

**material-requirements planning (MRP)**
a planning system that schedules the precise quantity of materials needed to make the product

## Outsourcing

Increasingly, outsourcing has become a component of supply chain management in operations. As we mentioned in Chapter 3, outsourcing refers to the contracting of manufacturing or other tasks to independent companies, often overseas. Many companies elect to outsource some aspects of their operations to companies that can provide these products more efficiently, at a lower cost, and with greater customer satisfaction. Globalization has put pressure on supply chain managers to improve speed and balance resources against competitive pressures. Companies outsourcing to China, in particular, face heavy regulation, high transportation costs, inadequate facilities, and unpredictable supply chain execution. Therefore, suppliers need to provide useful, timely, and accurate information about every aspect of the quality requirements, schedules, and solutions to dealing with problems. Companies that hire suppliers must also make certain that their suppliers are following company standards; failure to do so could lead to criticism of the parent company. For example, Tesco, a British grocery chain, had to reevaluate its supply chain after some meat sold in its stores was found to have traces of horse meat. Some changes include sourcing meat from closer locations and conducting DNA testing on meat.[26]

Many high-tech firms have outsourced the production of chips, computers, and telecom equipment to Asian companies. The hourly labor costs in countries such as China, India, and Vietnam are far less than in the United States, Europe, or even Mexico. These developing countries have improved their manufacturing capabilities, infrastructure, and technical and business skills, making them more attractive regions for global sourcing. For instance, Nike outsources almost all of its production to Asian countries such as China and Vietnam. On the other hand, the cost of outsourcing halfway around the world must be considered in decisions. While information technology

## Automakers Look toward Hydrogen Fuel Vehicles

In order to meet the California government's clean air requirements, automakers have been investing millions of dollars into research and development for clean vehicle technology. Electric vehicles are becoming more popular, but a lack of infrastructure, the range of charge, and high prices are impacting widespread adoption. Automakers are investigating other forms of cleaner energy, including hydrogen fuel.

Investments into hydrogen fuel-cell technology have proved promising as the costs have significantly fallen and vehicles can travel 250 miles on a single tank. However, there is still the service problem due to lack of infrastructure. Extracting hydrogen can be a difficult and time-consuming process. Additionally, hydrogen vehicles will require cities to build hydrogen fueling stations. Hydrogen fuel cars require high capital costs, which have led many automakers to conclude that wide-scale manufacturing of these cars will not be feasible until about 2020.

On the other hand, Toyota is not allowing these challenges to hinder its production. Toyota plans to release its first hydrogen fuel car in 2015. Honda has already begun selling hydrogen-fuel electric cars in California. Additionally, California announced plans to install 68 hydrogen fueling stations by the end of 2015. Whether automakers plan to introduce hydrogen fuel-cell vehicles in a few years or in another decade, it seems clear that auto companies are very interested in this alternative fuel technology.[27]

### Discussion Questions

1. Why are automakers attempting to develop more eco-friendly vehicles?
2. What are some of the challenges in the manufacturing and adoption of hydrogen fuel cars?
3. Why do you think Toyota is willing to expend resources in developing hydrogen vehicles despite the high costs of capital involved?

---

is often outsourced today, transportation, human resources, services, and even marketing functions can be outsourced. Our hypothetical Rushing Water Canoes might contract with a local janitorial service to clean its offices and with a local accountant to handle routine bookkeeping and tax-preparation functions.

Outsourcing, once used primarily as a cost-cutting tactic, has increasingly been linked with the development of competitive advantage through improved product quality, speeding up the time it takes products to get to the customer, and overall supply-chain efficiencies. Table 8.1 provides the world's top five outsourcing providers that assist mainly in information technology. Outsourcing allows companies to free up time and resources to focus on what they do best and to create better opportunities to focus on customer satisfaction. Many executives view outsourcing as an innovative way to boost productivity and remain competitive against low-wage offshore factories. However, outsourcing may create conflict with labor and negative public opinion when it results in U.S. workers being replaced by lower-cost workers in other countries.

**TABLE 8.1**
**The World's Top Five Outsourcing Providers**

| Company | Services |
|---|---|
| ISS | Facility services |
| Accenture | Management consulting, technology, and outsourcing |
| Wipro | Global information technology, consulting, and outsourcing |
| CBRE | Commercial real estate services |
| Infosys | Business consulting, IT services, and product engineering |

*Source: International Association of Outsourcing, "The 2013 Global Outsourcing 100," www.iaop.org/Content/19/165/3612 (accessed April 24, 2014).*

## Routing and Scheduling

After all materials have been procured and their use determined, managers must then consider the **routing,** or sequence of operations through which the product must pass. For example, before employees at Rushing Water Canoes can form aluminum sheets into a canoe, the aluminum must be cut to size. Likewise, the canoe's flotation material must be installed before workers can secure the wood seats. The sequence depends on the product specifications developed by the engineering department of the company.

routing
the sequence of operations through which the product must pass

Once management knows the routing, the actual work can be scheduled. **Scheduling** assigns the tasks to be done to departments or even specific machines, workers, or teams. At Rushing Water, cutting aluminum for the company's canoes might be scheduled to be done by the "cutting and finishing" department on machines designed especially for that purpose.

scheduling
the assignment of required tasks to departments or even specific machines, workers, or teams

Many approaches to scheduling have been developed, ranging from simple trial and error to highly sophisticated computer programs. One popular method is the *Program Evaluation and Review Technique (PERT),* which identifies all the major activities or events required to complete a project, arranges them in a sequence or path, determines the critical path, and estimates the time required for each event. Producing a McDonald's Big Mac, for example, involves removing meat, cheese, sauce, and vegetables from the refrigerator; grilling the hamburger patties; assembling the ingredients; placing the completed Big Mac in its package; and serving it to the customer (Figure 8.3). The cheese, pickles, onions, and sauce cannot be put on before the hamburger patty is completely grilled and placed on the bun. The path that requires the longest time from start to finish is called the *critical path* because it determines the minimum amount of time in which the process can be completed. If any of the activities on the critical path for production of the Big Mac fall behind schedule, the sandwich will not be completed on time, causing customers to wait longer than they usually would.

**FIGURE 8.3   A Hypothetical PERT Diagram for a McDonald's Big Mac**

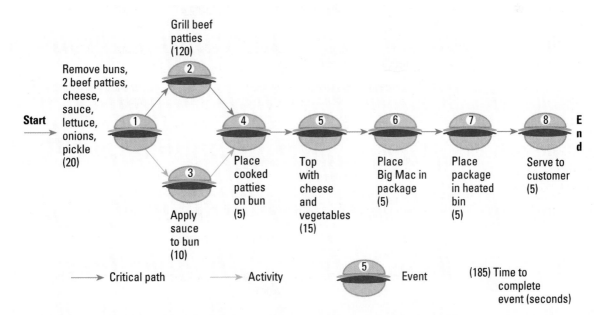

## Managing Quality

Quality, like cost and efficiency, is a critical element of operations management, for defective products can quickly ruin a firm. Quality reflects the degree to which a good or service meets the demands and requirements of customers. Customers are increasingly dissatisfied with the quality of service provided by many airlines. Table 8.2 gives the rankings of U.S. airlines in certain operational areas. Determining quality can be difficult because it depends on customers' perceptions of how well the product meets or exceeds their expectations. For example, customer satisfaction on airlines can vary wildly depending on individual customers' perspectives. However, the airline industry is notorious for its dissatisfied customers. Flight delays are a common complaint from airline passengers; 30 percent of all flights arrive late. However, most passengers do not select an airline based on how often flights arrive on time.[28]

The fuel economy of an automobile or its reliability (defined in terms of frequency of repairs) can be measured with some degree of precision. Although automakers rely on their own measures of vehicle quality, they also look to independent sources such as the J.D. Power & Associates annual initial quality survey for confirmation of their quality assessment as well as consumer perceptions of quality for the industry, as indicated in Figure 8.4.

It is especially difficult to measure quality characteristics when the product is a service. A company has to decide exactly which quality characteristics it considers important and then define those characteristics in terms that can be measured. The inseparability of production and consumption and the level of customer contact

**TABLE 8.2**
**2013 Airline Scorecard (Best to Worst)**

| Rank | Overall Rank | On-Time Arrival | Cancelled Flights | Baggage Handling | Bumping Passengers | Customer Complaints |
|---|---|---|---|---|---|---|
| 1 | Alaska | Alaska | Delta | Virgin America | JetBlue | Southwest |
| 2 | Delta | Delta | Frontier | JetBlue | Virgin America | Alaska |
| 3 | Virgin America | Virgin America | Virgin America | Delta | Alaska | Delta |
| 4 | Southwest | US Airways | Alaska | Frontier | American Airlines | JetBlue |
| 5 | JetBlue | United | Southwest | US Airways | US Airways | Virgin America |
| 6 | US Airways | American Airlines | JetBlue | Alaska | Delta | US Airways |
| 7 | Frontier | Southwest | US Airways | American Airlines | Frontier | American Airlines |
| 8 | American Airlines | JetBlue | United | United | Southwest | United |
| 9 | United | Frontier | American Airlines | Southwest | United | Frontier |

*Sources: FlightStats; U.S. Department of Transportation.*

**FIGURE 8.4**

**J.D. Power and Associates Initial Automobile Quality Study**

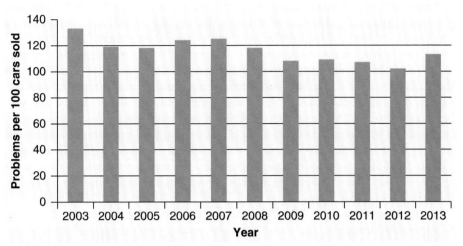

Source: J.D. Power and Associates, "2013 U.S. Initial Quality Study," June 19, 2013, http://autos.jdpower.com/content/press-release/3WScQEz/2013-j-d-power-initial-quality-study.htm (accessed April 24, 2014).

influence the selection of characteristics of the service that are most important. Employees in high-contact services such as hairstyling, education, legal services, and even the barista at Starbucks are an important part of the product.

The Malcolm Baldrige National Quality Award is given each year to companies that meet rigorous standards of quality. The Baldrige criteria are (1) leadership, (2) information and analysis, (3) strategic planning, (4) human resource development and management, (5) process management, (6) business results, and (7) customer focus and satisfaction. The criteria have become a worldwide framework for driving business improvement. Three organizations won the award in 2013, representing two different categories: Pewaukee School District, Pewaukee, Wisconsin (education); Baylor Regional Medical Center at Plano, Plano, Texas (health care); and Sutter Davis Hospital, Davis, California (health care).[29]

Quality is so important that we need to examine it in the context of operations management. **Quality control** refers to the processes an organization uses to maintain its established quality standards. Kia recognized the importance of quality control when it sought to revamp its image. For years, Kia vehicles were seen as low quality. To change consumer perceptions of the Kia brand, the company had its quality-control managers provide final approval for its products instead of sales executives, implemented benchmarks for improving product quality, developed strong marketing campaigns promoting the brand, and cut dealers that they did not feel were supporting the Kia franchise. Kia's quality efforts were largely successful; its overall sales grew 27 percent in a one-year period.[30] Quality has become a major concern in many organizations, particularly in light of intense foreign competition and increasingly demanding customers. To regain a competitive edge, a number of firms have adopted a total quality management approach. **Total quality management (TQM)** is a philosophy that uniform commitment to quality in all areas of the organization will promote a culture that meets customers' perceptions of quality. It involves coordinating efforts to improve customer satisfaction, increasing employee participation, forming and strengthening supplier partnerships, and facilitating an organizational culture of continuous quality improvement. TQM requires constant improvements in all areas of the company as well as employee empowerment.

**quality control**
the processes an organization uses to maintain its established quality standards

**total quality management (TQM)**
a philosophy that uniform commitment to quality in all areas of an organization will promote a culture that meets customers' perceptions of quality

Continuous improvement of an organization's goods and services is built around the notion that quality is free; by contrast, *not* having high-quality goods and services can be very expensive, especially in terms of dissatisfied customers.[31] A primary tool of the continuous improvement process is *benchmarking,* the measuring and evaluating of the quality of the organization's goods, services, or processes as compared with the quality produced by the best-performing companies in the industry.[32] Benchmarking lets the organization know where it stands competitively in its industry, thus giving it a goal to aim for over time. Now that online digital media are becoming more important in businesses, companies such as Compuware Corporation offer benchmarking tools so companies can monitor and compare the success of their websites. Such tools allow companies to track traffic to the site versus competitors' sites. Studies have shown a direct link between website performance and online sales, meaning this type of benchmarking is important.[33]

Companies employing TQM programs know that quality control should be incorporated throughout the transformation process, from the initial plans to the development of a specific product through the product and production-facility design processes to the actual manufacture of the product. In other words, they view quality control as an element of the product itself, rather than as simply a function of the operations process. When a company makes the product correctly from the outset, it eliminates the need to rework defective products, expedites the transformation process itself, and allows employees to make better use of their time and materials. One method through which many companies have tried to improve quality is **statistical process control,** a system in which management collects and analyzes information about the production process to pinpoint quality problems in the production system.

**statistical process control**
a system in which management collects and analyzes information about the production process to pinpoint quality problems in the production system

## International Organization for Standardization (ISO)

Regardless of whether a company has a TQM program for quality control, it must first determine what standard of quality it desires and then assess whether its products meet that standard. Product specifications and quality standards must be set so the company can create a product that will compete in the marketplace. Rushing Water Canoes, for example, may specify that each of its canoes has aluminum walls of a specified uniform thickness, that the front and back be reinforced with a specified level of steel, and that each contain a specified amount of flotation material for safety. Production facilities must be designed that can produce products with the desired specifications.

Intel has adopted ISO 9000 quality standards to ensure consistent quality throughout its global operations.

Quality standards can be incorporated into service businesses as well. A hamburger chain, for example, may establish standards relating to how long it takes to cook an order and serve it to customers, how many fries are in each order, how thick the burgers are, or how many customer complaints might be acceptable. Once the desired quality characteristics, specifications, and standards have been stated in measurable terms, the next step is inspection.

The International Organization for Standardization (ISO) has created a series of quality management standards—**ISO 9000**—designed to ensure the customer's quality standards are met. The standards provide a framework for documenting how a certified business keeps records, trains employees, tests products, and fixes defects. To obtain ISO 9000 certification, an independent auditor must verify that a business's factory, laboratory, or office meets the quality standards spelled out by the International Organization for Standardization. The certification process can require significant investment, but for many companies, the process is essential to being able to compete. Thousands of companies have been certified, including General Electric Analytical Instruments, which has applied ISO standards to everything from the design to the manufacturing practices of its global facilities.[34] Certification has become a virtual necessity for doing business in Europe in some high-technology businesses. ISO 9002 certification was established for service providers. **ISO 14000** is a comprehensive set of environmental standards that encourages a cleaner and safer world. ISO 14000 is a valuable standard because currently considerable variation exists between the regulations in different nations, and even regions within a nation. These variations make it difficult for organizations committed to sustainability to find acceptable global solutions to problems. The goal of the ISO 14000 standards is to promote a more uniform approach to environmental management and to help companies attain and measure improvements in their environmental performance.

**ISO 9000**
a series of quality assurance standards designed by the International Organization for Standardization (ISO) to ensure consistent product quality under many conditions

**ISO 14000**
a comprehensive set of environmental standards that encourages companies to conduct business in a cleaner, safer, and less wasteful way; ISO 14000 provides a uniform set of standards globally

## Inspection

Inspection reveals whether a product meets quality standards. Some product characteristics may be discerned by fairly simple inspection techniques—weighing the contents of cereal boxes or measuring the time it takes for a customer to receive his or her hamburger. As part of the ongoing quality assurance program at Hershey Foods, all wrapped Hershey Kisses are checked, and all imperfectly wrapped kisses are rejected. Other inspection techniques are more elaborate. Automobile manufacturers use automated machines to open and close car doors to test the durability of latches and hinges. The food-processing and pharmaceutical industries use various chemical tests to determine the quality of their output. Rushing Water Canoes might use a special device that can precisely measure the thickness of each canoe wall to ensure that it meets the company's specifications.

Organizations normally inspect purchased items, work-in-process, and finished items. The inspection of purchased items and finished items takes place after the fact; the inspection of work-in-process is preventive. In other words, the purpose of inspection of purchased items and finished items is to determine what the quality level is. For items that are being worked on—an automobile moving down the assembly line or a canoe being assembled—the purpose of the inspection is to find defects before the product is completed so that necessary corrections can be made.

## Sampling

An important question relating to inspection is how many items should be inspected. Should all canoes produced by Rushing Water be inspected or just some of them? Whether to inspect 100 percent of the output or only part of it is related to the cost of the inspection process, the destructiveness of the inspection process (some tests last until the product fails), and the potential cost of product flaws in terms of human lives and safety.

Some inspection procedures are quite expensive, use elaborate testing equipment, destroy products, and/or require a significant number of hours to complete. In such cases, it is usually desirable to test only a sample of the output. If the sample passes inspection, the inspector may assume that all the items in the lot from which the sample was drawn would also pass inspection. By using principles of statistical inference, management can employ sampling techniques that ensure a relatively high probability of reaching the right conclusion—that is, rejecting a lot that does not meet standards and accepting a lot that does. Nevertheless, there will always be a risk of making an incorrect conclusion—accepting a population that *does not* meet standards (because the sample was satisfactory) or rejecting a population that *does* meet standards (because the sample contained too many defective items).

Sampling is likely to be used when inspection tests are destructive. Determining the life expectancy of lightbulbs by turning them on and recording how long they last would be foolish: There is no market for burned-out lightbulbs. Instead, a generalization based on the quality of a sample would be applied to the entire population of lightbulbs from which the sample was drawn. However, human life and safety often depend on the proper functioning of specific items, such as the navigational systems installed in commercial airliners. For such items, even though the inspection process is costly, the potential cost of flawed systems—in human lives and safety—is too great not to inspect 100 percent of the output.

## Integrating Operations and Supply Chain Management

Managing operations and supply chains can be complex and challenging due to the number of independent organizations that must perform their responsibilities in creating product quality. Managing supply chains requires constant vigilance and the ability to make quick tactical changes. Even Apple Inc., the most admired company in the world, has had supply chain problems. Reports of forced overtime, underage workers, and dangerous conditions at its Chinese supplier factories have resulted in negative publicity for the company.[35] Therefore, managing the various partners involved in supply chains and operations is important because many stakeholders hold the firm responsible for appropriate conduct related to product quality. This requires that the company exercise oversight over all suppliers involved in producing a product. Encouraging suppliers to report problems, issues, or concerns requires excellent communication systems to obtain feedback. Ideally, suppliers will report potential problems before they reach the next level of the supply chain, which reduces damage.

Despite the challenges of monitoring global operations and supply chains, there are steps businesses can take to manage these risks. All companies who work with global suppliers should adopt a Global Supplier Code of Conduct and ensure that it is effectively communicated. Additionally, companies should encourage compliance and procurement employees to work together to find ethical suppliers at reasonable costs. Those in procurement are concerned with the costs of obtaining materials for the company. As a result, supply chain and procurement managers must work together to make operational decisions to ensure the selection of the best suppliers from an ethical and cost-effective standpoint. Businesses must also work to make certain that their supply chains are diverse. Having only a few suppliers in one area can disrupt operations should a disaster strike. Finally, companies must perform regular audits on its suppliers and take action against those found to be in violation of company standards.[36]

While you might not have been familiar with terms such as *supply chain* or *logistics* or *total quality management* before taking this course, careers abound in the operations management field. You will find these careers in a wide variety of organizations—manufacturers, retailers, transportation companies, third-party logistics firms, government agencies, and service firms. Approximately $1.3 trillion is spent on transportation, inventory, and related logistics activities, and logistics alone accounts for more than 9.5 percent of U.S. gross domestic product.[37] Closely managing how a company's inputs and outputs flow from raw materials to the end consumer is vital to a firm's success. Successful companies also need to ensure that quality is measured and actively managed at each step.

Supply chain managers have a tremendous impact on the success of an organization. These managers are engaged in every facet of the business process, including planning, purchasing, production, transportation, storage and distribution, customer service, and more. Their performance helps organizations control expenses, boost sales, and maximize profits.

Warehouse managers are a vital part of manufacturing operations. A typical warehouse manager's duties include overseeing and recording deliveries and pickups, maintaining inventory records and the product tracking system, and adjusting inventory levels to reflect receipts and disbursements. Warehouse managers also have to keep in mind customer service and employee issues. Warehouse managers can earn up to $60,000 in some cases.

Operations management is also required in service businesses. With more than 80 percent of the U.S. economy in services, jobs exist for services operations. Many service contact operations require standardized processes that often use technology to provide an interface that provides an automatic quality performance. Consider jobs in health care, the travel industry, fast food, and entertainment. Think of any job or task that is a part of the final product in these industries. Even an online retailer such as Amazon.com has a transformation process that includes information technology and human activities that facilitate a transaction. These services have a standardized process and can be evaluated based on their level of achieved service quality.

Total quality management is becoming a key attribute for companies to ensure that quality pervades all aspects of the organization. Quality assurance managers make a median salary of $79,500. These managers monitor and advise on how a company's quality management system is performing and publish data and reports regarding company performance in both manufacturing and service industries.[38]

# Review Your Understanding

### Define operations management, and differentiate between operations and manufacturing.

Operations management (OM) is the development and administration of the activities involved in transforming resources into goods and services. Operations managers oversee the transformation process and the planning and designing of operations systems, managing logistics, quality, and productivity. The terms *manufacturing* and *production* are used interchangeably to describe the activities and processes used in making tangible products, whereas *operations* is a broader term used to describe the process of making both tangible and intangible products.

### Explain how operations management differs in manufacturing and service firms.

Manufacturers and service firms both transform inputs into outputs, but service providers differ from manufacturers in several ways: They have greater customer contact because the service typically occurs at the point of consumption; their inputs and outputs are more variable than manufacturers', largely because of the human element; service providers are generally more labor intensive; and their productivity measurement is more complex.

### Describe the elements involved in planning and designing an operations system.

Operations planning relates to decisions about what product(s) to make, for whom, and what processes and facilities are needed to produce them. OM is often joined by marketing and research and development in these decisions. Common facility layouts include fixed-position layouts, process layouts, or product layouts. Where to locate operations facilities is a crucial decision that depends on proximity to the market, availability of raw materials, availability of transportation, availability of power, climatic influences, availability of labor, and community characteristics. Technology is also vital to operations, particularly computer-assisted design, computer-assisted manufacturing, flexible manufacturing, robotics, and computer-integrated manufacturing.

**Specify some techniques managers may use to manage the logistics of transforming inputs into finished products.**

Logistics, or supply chain management, includes all the activities involved in obtaining and managing raw materials and component parts, managing finished products, packaging them, and getting them to customers. The organization must first make or purchase (procure) all the materials it needs. Next, it must control its inventory by determining how many supplies and goods it needs and keeping track of every raw material, component, completed or partially completed product, and piece of equipment, how many of each are on hand, where they are, and who has responsibility for them. Common approaches to inventory control include the economic order quantity (EOQ) model, the just-in-time (JIT) inventory concept, and material-requirements planning (MRP). Logistics also includes routing and scheduling processes and activities to complete products.

**Assess the importance of quality in operations management.**

Quality is a critical element of OM because low-quality products can hurt people and harm the business. Quality control refers to the processes an organization uses to maintain its established quality standards. To control quality, a company must establish what standard of quality it desires and then determine whether its products meet that standard through inspection.

**Evaluate a business's dilemma and propose a solution.**

Based on this chapter and the facts presented in "Solve the Dilemma" on page 258, you should be able to evaluate the business's problem and propose one or more solutions for resolving it.

## Revisit the World of Business

1. Describe how suppliers of factory automation equipment are helping manufacturers to solve or prevent factory malfunctions.

2. How might these remote monitoring systems create greater efficiencies at factories?

3. What are some of the risks associated with continual monitoring by a third-party supplier?

## Learn the Terms

capacity  239
computer-assisted design (CAD)  242
computer-assisted manufacturing (CAM)  242
computer-integrated manufacturing (CIM)  242
continuous manufacturing organizations  241
customization  239
economic order quantity (EOQ) model  246
fixed-position layout  241
flexible manufacturing  242
inputs  233

intermittent organizations  241
inventory  245
inventory control  245
ISO 9000  253
ISO 14000  253
just-in-time (JIT) inventory management  246
manufacturing  232
material-requirements planning (MRP)  247
modular design  238
operations  232
operations management (OM)  232

outputs  233
process layout  241
product layout  241
production  232
project organization  241
purchasing  245
quality control  251
routing  249
scheduling  249
standardization  238
statistical process control  252
supply chain management  244
total quality management (TQM)  251

## Check Your Progress

1. What is operations management?

2. Differentiate among the terms *operations, production,* and *manufacturing.*

3. Compare and contrast a manufacturer versus a service provider in terms of operations management.

4. Who is involved in planning products?

5. In what industry would the fixed-position layout be most efficient? The process layout? The product layout? Use real examples.

6. What criteria do businesses use when deciding where to locate a plant?

7. What is flexible manufacturing? How can it help firms improve quality?

8. Define supply chain management and summarize the activities it involves.

9. Describe some of the methods a firm may use to control inventory.

10. When might a firm decide to inspect a sample of its products rather than test every product for quality?

## Get Involved

1. Compare and contrast OM at McDonald's with that of Honda of America. Compare and contrast OM at McDonald's with that of a bank in your neighborhood.

2. Find a real company that uses JIT, either in your local community or in a business journal. Why did the company decide to use JIT? What have been the advantages and disadvantages of using JIT for that particular company?

What has been the overall effect on the quality of the company's goods or services? What has been the overall effect on the company's bottom line?

3. Interview someone from your local Chamber of Commerce and ask him or her what incentives the community offers to encourage organizations to locate there. (See if these incentives relate to the criteria firms use to make location decisions.)

## Build Your Skills

### Reducing Cycle Time

#### Background

An important goal of production and operations management is reducing cycle time—the time it takes to complete a task or process. The goal in cycle time reduction is to reduce costs and/or increase customer service.[39] Many experts believe that the rate of change in our society is so fast that a firm must master speed and connectivity.[40] Connectivity refers to a seamless integration of customers, suppliers, employees, and organizational, production, and operations management. The use of the Internet and other telecommunications systems helps many organizations connect and reduce cycle time.

#### Task

Break up into pairs throughout the class. Select two businesses (local restaurants, retail stores, etc.) that both of you frequent, are employed by, and/or are fairly well acquainted with. For the first business, one of you will role-play the "manager" and the other will role-play the "customer." Reverse roles for the second business you have selected. As managers at your respective businesses, you are to prepare a list of five questions you will ask the customer during the role-play. The questions you prepare should be designed to get the customer's viewpoint on how good the cycle time is at your business. If one of the responses leads to a problem area, you may need to ask a follow-up question to determine the nature of the dissatisfaction. Prepare one

main question and a follow-up, if necessary, for each of the five dimensions of cycle time:

1. **Speed**—the delivery of goods and services in the minimum time; efficient communications; the elimination of wasted time.

2. **Connectivity**—all operations and systems in the business appear connected with the customer.

3. **Interactive relationships**—a continual dialog exists among operations units, service providers, and customers that permits the exchange of feedback on concerns or needs.

4. **Customization**—each product is tailored to the needs of the customer.

5. **Responsiveness**—the willingness to make adjustments and be flexible to help customers and to provide prompt service when a problem develops.

Begin the two role-plays. When it is your turn to be the manager, listen carefully when your partner answers your prepared questions. You need to elicit information on how to improve the cycle time at your business. You will achieve this by identifying the problem areas (weaknesses) that need attention.

After completing both role-play situations, fill out the form on the next page for the role-play when you were the manager. You may not have gathered enough information to fill in all the boxes.

For example, for some categories, the customer may have had only good things to say; for others, the comments may all be negative. Be prepared to share the information you gain with the rest of the class.

I role-played the manager at (business). After listening carefully to the customer's responses to my five questions, I determined the following strengths and weaknesses as they relate to the cycle time at my business:

| Dimension | Strength | Weakness |
|---|---|---|
| Speed | | |
| Connectivity | | |
| Interactive relationships | | |
| Customization | | |
| Responsiveness | | |

## Solve the Dilemma

### Planning for Pizza

McKing Corporation operates fast-food restaurants in 50 states, selling hamburgers, roast beef and chicken sandwiches, french fries, and salads. The company wants to diversify into the growing pizza business. Six months of tests revealed that the ideal pizza to sell was a 16-inch pie in three varieties: cheese, pepperoni, and deluxe (multiple toppings). Research found the size and toppings acceptable to families as well as to individuals (single buyers could freeze the leftovers), and the price was acceptable for a fast-food restaurant ($7.99 for cheese, $8.49 for pepperoni, and $9.99 for deluxe).

Marketing and human resources personnel prepared training manuals for employees, advertising materials, and the rationale to present to the restaurant managers (many stores are franchised). Store managers, franchisees, and employees are excited about the new plan. There is just one problem:

The drive-through windows in current restaurants are too small for a 16-inch pizza to pass through. The largest size the present windows can accommodate is a 12-inch pie. The managers and franchisees are concerned that if this aspect of operations has been overlooked, perhaps the product is not ready to be launched. Maybe there are other problems yet to be uncovered.

### Discussion Questions

1. What mistake did McKing make in approaching the introduction of pizza?

2. How could this product introduction have been coordinated to avoid the problems that were encountered?

3. If you were an executive at McKing, how would you proceed with the introduction of pizza into the restaurants?

## Build Your Business Plan

### Managing Service and Manufacturing Operations

For your business, you need to determine if you are providing raw materials that will be used in further production, or if you are a reseller of goods and services, known as a retailer. If you are the former, you need to determine what processes you go through in making your product.

The text provides ideas of breaking the process into inputs, transformation processes, and outputs. If you are a provider of a service or a link in the supply chain, you need to know exactly what your customer expectations are. Services are intangible, so it is all the more important to better understand what exactly the customer is looking for in resolving a problem or filling a need.

# See for Yourself Videocase

## Home Run Inn's Operational Excellence Propels It to Top Spot

It's not often that frozen pizza is compared favorably with fresh pizzas served in restaurants. Home Run Inn is the exception to the rule. Home Run Inn's frozen cheese pizza is considered tastier than the fresh deep dish and original pizzas from Domino's and Pizza Hut. In 2013, *Consumer Reports* named Home Run Inn as number one in the frozen pizza category. Its popularity is evident as it has become one of the fastest-growing frozen pizza companies in the nation. Today, Home Run Inn distributes pizza in 28 states and sells almost as much as DiGiorno and Tombstone brands combined.

Home Run Inn is a family-run business with headquarters in Chicago. The inspiration for the name happened after a baseball from a nearby sandlot crashed through Mary and Vincent Grittani's window of their new restaurant in 1923. More than 20 years later, in 1947 the Grittanis' son-in-law Nick Perinno partnered with Mary Grittani to develop the recipe for the company's all-natural Home Run Inn pizza. This pizza would place the restaurant on the map.

During the 1950s, the business chose to expand into the frozen pizza business. In the 1980s, Nick's son Joe Perrino, currently the president and CEO of the business, realized that they needed to expand if they wanted to grow. He began to look at ways to improve the organization's operations through automation. "We started very basically with conveyers and ovens, and we then proceeded with different presses," he said.

Soon, demand for Home Run Inn pizzas began to eclipse supply. Home Run Inn was unable to meet this demand with its current capacity due to manufacturing limitations. Cooking the pizzas and freezing them with conventional freezing methods was complex and placed constraints on how much the company could produce. As a result, Perrino decided to purchase a cryogenic freezer that freezes using $CO_2$ gas. The equipment cost $250,000, which was approximately what it would cost to purchase a restaurant. However, the result was far worth the money spent. Perrino states, "We were able to produce pizzas three, four times as fast as we were currently doing with fewer people, so that really set a light bulb off in our heads."

Two years later, the company built a new facility to keep up with demand. The major reason for this high demand is the quality of the pizza. Home Run Inn guarantees that its frozen pizzas are just as good as the pizzas it serves in its restaurants (it currently has nine restaurant locations). The company does this by controlling quality in-house. Home Run Inn pizza uses all-natural ingredients and its homemade sauce, sausage, and cheese. These all-natural ingredients have enabled the company to differentiate its products, allowing it to have higher prices compared to competitors and still retain high demand.

In 2002, Home Run Inn decided to go a step further. The company partnered with former Kraft CEO Jay Williams to self-distribute its pizzas. Until then, Home Run Inn frozen pizzas were stored in warehouses and then distributed to retailers. Self-distribution required the company to have its own fleet of trucks to deliver the pizzas to the retailers. This requires Home Run Inn to keep careful track of inventory in the stores. It was a significant investment for Home Run Inn, but it also allowed the company to control its supply chain and ensure that quality was maintained from manufacturing all the way to the finished product on the shelf. According to Perrino, this move helped the firm grow from 8 percent market share to 28 percent market share.

Thanks to quality operation processes, strong supply chain control, and careful monitoring of inventory, Home Run Inn pizza has secured its place as a top-quality frozen pizza business. Despite its high price compared to rivals, customers are eager to purchase Home Run Inn frozen pizza because they know the value is worth the price.[41]

### Discussion Questions

1. Describe how taking risks to increase its operational capacity turned Home Run Inn pizza into the top player in the frozen pizza industry.

2. Why is Home Run Inn able to compete at prices higher than its rivals'?

3. Why has self-distribution been so beneficial for Home Run Inn? Do you think it would be successful for every manufacturing company?

**You can find the related video in the Video Library in Connect. Ask your instructor how you can access Connect.**

# Team Exercise

Form groups and assign the responsibility of finding companies that outsource their production to other countries. What are the key advantages of this outsourcing decision? Do you see any drawbacks or weaknesses in this approach?

Why would a company not outsource when such a tactic can be undertaken to cut manufacturing costs? Report your findings to the class.

# PART 4

# Creating the Human Resource Advantage

# 9

# Motivating the Workforce

## Learning Objectives

**After reading this chapter, you will be able to:**

**LO 9-1**    Define human relations, and determine why its study is important.

**LO 9-2**    Summarize early studies that laid the groundwork for understanding employee motivation.

**LO 9-3**    Compare and contrast the human-relations theories of Abraham Maslow and Frederick Herzberg.

**LO 9-4**    Investigate various theories of motivation, including theories X, Y, and Z; equity theory; and expectancy theory.

**LO 9-5**    Describe some of the strategies that managers use to motivate employees.

**LO 9-6**    Critique a business's program for motivating its sales force.

## Chapter Outline

## Mars, Incorporated: Where Employees Love to Work

The 70,000 employees working at Mars Inc. look forward to going to work in the morning. Mars is the third largest private company in the United States that is 100 percent family owned. The company specializes in six brand areas: chocolate, pet care, Wrigley, food, drinks, and symbioscience. While the company is known for products such as Pedigree pet care, M&Ms, and Wrigley gum, it has also become known for its motivational corporate culture. Mars has consistently made the list of *Fortune*'s "Best Companies to Work for."

Mars aims to provide a positive work environment that motivates employees to strive for excellence and provide exceptional products for consumers everywhere. To do this, Mars has stayed a private company and has no plans to go public. This keeps the company from having to answer to stockholders regarding every decision and motivates employees to develop and test new ideas. Employees fondly dub themselves "Martians" and abide by the company's Five Principles of Mars embedded on the walls of the company's offices. These principles are quality, responsibility, mutuality, efficiency, and freedom.

Employee perks at Mars are various. Employees have access to vending machines that dispense free candy, the ability to grow within the company, and the opportunity to receive bonuses from 10 to 100 percent of their salaries. Employees of the company's pet care division are encouraged to bring their dogs to work. Monitors display sales and financial updates of the company, which motivate employees to strive for success. The company has been known to employ generations of families within the firm. As a result of its motivational environment, the company boosts a low 5 percent turnover rate.[1]

# Introduction

Because employees do the actual work of the business and influence whether the firm achieves its objectives, most top managers agree that employees are an organization's most valuable resource. To achieve organizational objectives, employees must have the motivation, ability (appropriate knowledge and skills), and tools (proper training and equipment) to perform their jobs. Chapter 10 covers topics related to managing human resources, such as those listed earlier. This chapter focuses on how to motivate employees.

We examine employees' needs and motivation, managers' views of workers, and several strategies for motivating employees. Managers who understand the needs of their employees can help them reach higher levels of productivity and thus contribute to the achievement of organizational goals.

# Nature of Human Relations

**human relations**
the study of the behavior of individuals and groups in organizational settings

What motivates employees to perform on the job is the focus of **human relations,** the study of the behavior of individuals and groups in organizational settings. In business, human relations involves motivating employees to achieve organizational objectives efficiently and effectively. The field of human relations has become increasingly important over the years as businesses strive to understand how to boost workplace morale, maximize employees' productivity and creativity, and motivate their ever more diverse employees to be more effective.

**motivation**
an inner drive that directs a person's behavior toward goals

**Motivation** is an inner drive that directs a person's behavior toward goals. A goal is the satisfaction of some need, and a need is the difference between a desired state and an actual state. Both needs and goals can be motivating. Motivation explains why people behave as they do; similarly, a lack of motivation explains, at times, why people avoid doing what they should do. Motivating employees to do the wrong things or for the wrong reasons can be problematic, however. Encouraging employees to take excessive risks through high compensation, for example, led to the downfall of AIG and most major U.S. banks. Also, encouraging employees to lie to customers or to create false documentation is unethical and could even have legal ramifications. A person who recognizes or feels a need is motivated to take action to satisfy the need and achieve a goal (Figure 9.1). Consider a person who takes a job as a salesperson. If his or her performance is far below other salespeople's, he or she will likely recognize a need to increase sales. To satisfy that need and achieve success, the person may try to acquire new insights from successful salespeople or obtain additional training to improve sales skills. In addition, a sales manager might try different means to motivate the salesperson to work harder and to improve his or her skills. Human relations is concerned with the needs of employees, their goals and how they try to achieve them, and the impact of those needs and goals on job performance.

Many companies offer onsite day care as a benefit for employees who have children. Company benefits such as these tend to increase employee satisfaction and motivation.

Effectively motivating employees helps keep them engaged in their work. Engagement involves emotional involvement and commitment. Being engaged

**FIGURE 9.1**
**The Motivation Process**

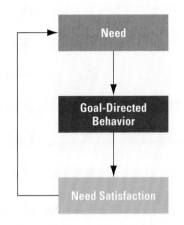

results in carrying out the expectations and obligations of employment. Many employees are actively engaged in their jobs, while others are not. Some employees do the minimum amount of work required to get by, and some employees are completely disengaged. Motivating employees to stay engaged is a key responsibility of management. For example, to test if his onsite production managers were fully engaged in their jobs, former Van Halen frontman David Lee Roth placed a line in the band's rider asking for a bowl of M&Ms with the brown ones removed. It was a means for the band to test local stage production crews' attention to detail. Because their shows were highly technical, David Lee Roth would demand a complete recheck of everything if he found brown M&Ms in the bowl.[2]

One prominent aspect of human relations is **morale**—an employee's attitude toward his or her job, employer, and colleagues. High morale contributes to high levels of productivity, high returns to stakeholders, and employee loyalty. Conversely, low morale may cause high rates of absenteeism and turnover (when employees quit or are fired and must be replaced by new employees). Google recognizes the value of happy, committed employees and strives to engage in practices that will minimize turnover. Employees have access to onsite medical care, travel and emergency insurance, educational reimbursements, and many more incentives that keep employees' morale in good condition.[3]

Employees are motivated by their perceptions of extrinsic and intrinsic rewards. An **intrinsic reward** is the personal satisfaction and enjoyment that you feel from attaining a goal. For example, in this class you may feel personal enjoyment in learning how business works and aspire to have a career in business or to operate your own business one day. **Extrinsic rewards** are benefits and/or recognition that you receive from someone else. In this class, your grade is extrinsic recognition of your efforts and success in the class. In business, praise and recognition, pay increases, and bonuses are extrinsic rewards. If you believe that your job provides an opportunity to contribute to society or the environment, then that aspect would represent an intrinsic reward. Both intrinsic and extrinsic rewards contribute to motivation that stimulates employees to do their best in contributing to business goals.

Even small symbols of recognition, such as an "Employee of the Month" parking space, can serve as strong motivators for employees.

morale
an employee's attitude toward his or her job, employer, and colleagues

intrinsic rewards
the personal satisfaction and enjoyment felt after attaining a goal

extrinsic rewards
benefits and/or recognition received from someone else

**TABLE 9.1**
**How to Retain Good Employees**

| |
|---|
| 1. Challenge your employees. |
| 2. Provide adequate incentives. |
| 3. Don't micromanage. |
| 4. Create a work-friendly environment. |
| 5. Provide opportunities for employee growth. |

Source: Adapted from Geoff Williams, "Retaining Employees: 5 Things You Need to Know," The Huffington Post, February 2, 2012, www.huffingtonpost.com/2012/02/01/retaining-employees-5-things-you-need-to-know_n_976767.html (accessed April 24, 2014).

Respect, involvement, appreciation, adequate compensation, promotions, a pleasant work environment, and a positive organizational culture are all morale boosters. Table 9.1 lists some ways to retain good employees. Costco Wholesale, the second largest retailer in America, knows how to retain happy employees. The company pays an average annual rate of $20.89 per hour plus overtime, gives five weeks of vacation per year, and matches 401(k) contributions; in addition, almost 90 percent of employees are covered by company-sponsored health insurance. The retail industry is peppered with unhappy employees and dwindling profits, but Costco's efforts result in happy workers. The company was even able to give raises when the economic recession hit. In addition, the company has not experienced any major labor disputes in its more than 30 years of existence.[5] Many companies offer a diverse array of benefits designed to improve the quality of employees' lives and increase their morale and satisfaction. Some of the "best companies to work for" offer onsite day care, concierge services (e.g., dry cleaning, shoe repair, prescription renewal), domestic partner benefits to same-sex couples, and fully paid sabbaticals. Table 9.2 offers suggestions as to how leaders can motivate employees on a daily basis.

**DID YOU KNOW?**  Absenteeism can cost a company as much as 36 percent of payroll.[4]

**TABLE 9.2**
**How to Motivate Employees**

| |
|---|
| 1. Interact with employees in a friendly and open manner. |
| 2. Equitably dispense rewards and other incentives. |
| 3. Create a culture of collaboration. |
| 4. Provide both positive and negative feedback and constructive criticism. |
| 5. Make employees feel as if they are partners rather than workers. |
| 6. Handle conflicts in an open and professional manner. |
| 7. Provide continuous opportunities for improvement and employee growth. |
| 8. Encourage creativity in problem solving. |
| 9. Recognize employees for jobs well done. |
| 10. Allow employees to make mistakes, as these become learning opportunities. |

# Historical Perspectives on Employee Motivation

Throughout the 20th century, researchers have conducted numerous studies to try to identify ways to motivate workers and increase productivity. From these studies have come theories that have been applied to workers with varying degrees of success. A brief discussion of two of these theories—the classical theory of motivation and the Hawthorne studies—provides a background for understanding the present state of human relations.

## Classical Theory of Motivation

The birth of the study of human relations can be traced to time and motion studies conducted at the turn of the century by Frederick W. Taylor and Frank and Lillian Gilbreth. Their studies analyzed how workers perform specific work tasks in an effort to improve the employees' productivity. These efforts led to the application of scientific principles to management.

According to the **classical theory of motivation,** money is the sole motivator for workers. Taylor suggested that workers who were paid more would produce more, an idea that would benefit both companies and workers. To improve productivity, Taylor thought that managers should break down each job into its component tasks (specialization), determine the best way to perform each task, and specify the output to be achieved by a worker performing the task. Taylor also believed that incentives would motivate employees to be more productive. Thus, he suggested that managers link workers' pay directly to their output. He developed the piece-rate system, under which employees were paid a certain amount for each unit they produced; those who exceeded their quota were paid a higher rate per unit for all the units they produced.

**classical theory of motivation**
theory suggesting that money is the sole motivator for workers

We can still see Taylor's ideas in practice today in the use of financial incentives for productivity. Moreover, companies are increasingly striving to relate pay to performance at both the hourly and managerial level. Incentive planners choose an individual incentive to motivate and reward their employees. In contrast, team incentives are used to generate partnership and collaboration to accomplish organizational goals. Boeing develops sales teams for most of its products, including commercial airplanes. The team dedicated to each product shares in the sales incentive program.

More and more corporations are tying pay to performance in order to motivate—even up to the CEO level. The topic of executive pay has become controversial in recent years, and many corporate boards of directors have taken steps to link executive compensation more closely to corporate performance. Despite these changes, many top executives still receive large compensation packages. Larry Ellison, CEO of Oracle, earns $96.2 million in annual compensation.[6]

Like most managers of the early 20th century, Taylor believed that satisfactory pay and job security would motivate employees to work hard. However, later studies showed that other factors are also important in motivating workers.

## The Hawthorne Studies

Elton Mayo and a team of researchers from Harvard University wanted to determine what physical conditions in the workplace—such as light and noise levels—would stimulate employees to be most productive. From 1924 to 1932, they studied a group of workers at the Hawthorne Works Plant of the Western Electric Company and measured their productivity under various physical conditions.

## Wegmans Motivates Employees and Excels in Sustainability

Wegmans, a small grocery chain along the Atlantic region, is keen on motivating its more than 42,000 employees. The 96-year-old grocer offers benefits such as flexible scheduling, employee scholarship programs, and a 66 percent rate of internal promotions to empower and motivate its workforce to optimal levels. The company generated $6.7 billion in revenue in 2013 and has been consistently ranked as one of *Fortune*'s top five best companies to work for since the list began in 1998.

Wellness programs for employees, which include free monthly health screenings, blood pressure and nutrition coaching, and onsite yoga and Zumba classes, are a priority for the chain. It will also subsidize other health programs that employees find more effective. The result is highly energized, healthy, and happy employees who feel invested in the company. Employees undergo 40 hours of training before interacting with customers and are given the opportunity to travel in order to become experts in the store's products.

Sustainability is another investment Wegmans values, and it encourages employees to feel the same. The company uses paper boats for sampling rather than plastic cups and grocery bags made from 40 percent recycled material. Wegmans retreaded the tires on its trucks rather than purchase new tires, saving more than 30,000 gallons of oil. Additionally, Greenpeace recently ranked the company number one in seafood sustainability.[7]

### Discussion Questions

1. How does Wegmans empower employees?
2. Describe the employee benefits Wegmans offers and how this motivates them to offer better customer service.
3. How might Wegmans' sustainability endeavors influence employees to be more sustainable in their own lives?

Some companies let people bring their pets to work as an added incentive to make the workplace seem more friendly.

What the researchers discovered was quite unexpected and very puzzling: Productivity increased regardless of the physical conditions. This phenomenon has been labeled the Hawthorne effect. When questioned about their behavior, the employees expressed satisfaction because their co-workers in the experiments were friendly and, more importantly, because their supervisors had asked for their help and cooperation in the study. In other words, they were responding to the attention they received, not the changing physical work conditions. The researchers concluded that social and psychological factors could significantly affect productivity and morale. The United Services Automobile Association (USAA) has a built-in psychological factor that influences employee morale. The work of the financial services company serves military and veteran families, which enlivens employees. Genentech, a biotechnology company, also knows how to inspire employees through the development of medications that better the lives of patients. Patients have been known to share their stories with employees, and in one instance, employees put in extra hours to ship breast cancer medication to a hospital when they discovered three patients were awaiting treatment. This shows how important it is for employees to feel like their work matters.[8] Figure 9.2 indicates aspects of the job that appear to be most important for job satisfaction.

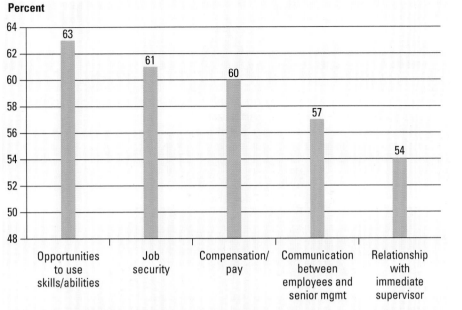

**Percent**

**FIGURE 9.2**

**Job Aspects Important to Employee Satisfaction**

Source: Society for Human Resource Management, 2012 *Employee Job Satisfaction and Engagement: A Research Report by SHRM,* www.shrm.org/LegalIssues/ StateandLocalResources/ StateandLocalStatutesandRegulations/ Documents/12-0537%202012_ JobSatisfaction_FNL_online.pdf (accessed May 5, 2014).

The Hawthorne experiments marked the beginning of a concern for human relations in the workplace. They revealed that human factors do influence workers' behavior and that managers who understand the needs, beliefs, and expectations of people have the greatest success in motivating their workers.

# Theories of Employee Motivation

The research of Taylor, Mayo, and many others has led to the development of a number of theories that attempt to describe what motivates employees to perform. In this section, we will discuss some of the most important of these theories. The successful implementation of ideas based on these theories will vary, of course, depending on the company, its management, and its employees. It should be noted, too, that what worked in the past may no longer work today. Good managers must have the ability to adapt their ideas to an ever-changing, diverse group of employees.

### Maslow's Hierarchy of Needs

Psychologist Abraham Maslow theorized that people have five basic needs: physiological, security, social, esteem, and self-actualization. **Maslow's hierarchy** arranges these needs into the order in which people strive to satisfy them (Figure 9.3).

   **Physiological needs,** the most basic and first needs to be satisfied, are the essentials for living—water, food, shelter, and clothing. According to Maslow, humans devote all their efforts to satisfying physiological needs until they are met. Only when these needs are met can people focus their attention on satisfying the next level of needs—security.

   **Security needs** relate to protecting yourself from physical and economic harm. Actions that may be taken to achieve security include reporting a dangerous workplace

**Maslow's hierarchy**
a theory that arranges the five basic needs of people—physiological, security, social, esteem, and self-actualization—into the order in which people strive to satisfy them

**physiological needs**
the most basic human needs to be satisfied—water, food, shelter, and clothing

**security needs**
the need to protect oneself from physical and economic harm

**FIGURE 9.3**
**Maslow's Hierarchy of Needs**

Source: Adapted from Abraham H. Maslow, "A Theory of Human Motivation," *Psychology Review* 50 (1943), pp. 370–396. American Psychology Association.

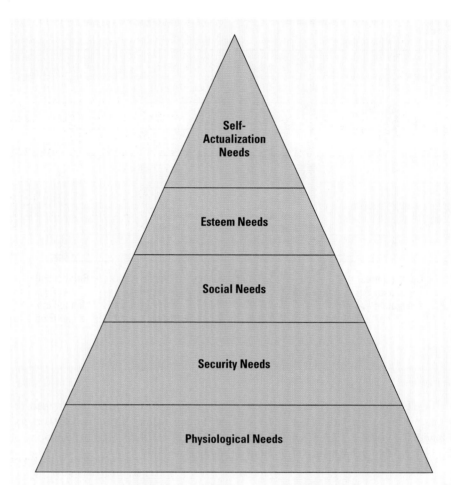

condition to management, maintaining safety equipment, and purchasing insurance with income protection in the event you become unable to work. Once security needs have been satisfied, people may strive for social goals.

**social needs**
the need for love, companionship, and friendship—the desire for acceptance by others

**Social needs** are the need for love, companionship, and friendship—the desire for acceptance by others. To fulfill social needs, a person may try many things: making friends with a co-worker, joining a group, volunteering at a hospital, throwing a party, and so on. Once their social needs have been satisfied, people attempt to satisfy their need for esteem.

**esteem needs**
the need for respect—both self-respect and respect from others

**Esteem needs** relate to respect—both self-respect and respect from others. One aspect of esteem needs is competition—the need to feel that you can do something better than anyone else. Competition often motivates people to increase their productivity. Esteem needs are not as easily satisfied as the needs at lower levels in Maslow's hierarchy because they do not always provide tangible evidence of success. However, these needs can be realized through rewards and increased involvement in organizational activities. Until esteem needs are met, people focus their attention on achieving respect. When they feel they have achieved some measure of respect, self-actualization becomes the major goal of life.

**Self-actualization needs,** at the top of Maslow's hierarchy, mean being the best you can be. Self-actualization involves maximizing your potential. A self-actualized person feels that she or he is living life to its fullest in every way. For Stephen King, self-actualization might mean being praised as the best fiction writer in the world; for actress Halle Berry, it might mean winning an Oscar.

Maslow's theory maintains that the more basic needs at the bottom of the hierarchy must be satisfied before higher-level goals can be pursued. Thus, people who are hungry and homeless are not concerned with obtaining respect from their colleagues. Only when physiological, security, and social needs have been more or less satisfied do people seek esteem. Maslow's theory also suggests that if a low-level need is suddenly reactivated, the individual will try to satisfy that need rather than higher-level needs. Many laid off workers probably shift their focus from high-level esteem needs to the need for security. Managers should learn from Maslow's hierarchy that employees will be motivated to contribute to organizational goals only if they are able to first satisfy their physiological, security, and social needs through their work.

## Herzberg's Two-Factor Theory

In the 1950s, psychologist Frederick Herzberg proposed a theory of motivation that focuses on the job and on the environment where work is done. Herzberg studied various factors relating to the job and their relation to employee motivation and concluded that they can be divided into hygiene factors and motivational factors (Table 9.3).

**Hygiene factors,** which relate to the work setting and not to the content of the work, include adequate wages, comfortable and safe working conditions, fair company policies, and job security. These factors do not necessarily motivate employees to excel, but their absence may be a potential source of dissatisfaction and high turnover. Employee safety and comfort are clearly hygiene factors.

Many people feel that a good salary is one of the most important job factors, even more important than job security and the chance to use one's mind and abilities. Salary and security, two of the hygiene factors identified by Herzberg, make it possible for employees to satisfy the physiological and security needs identified by Maslow. However, the presence of hygiene factors is unlikely to motivate employees to work harder. For example, many people do not feel motivated to pursue a career as a gastroenterologist (doctors who specialize in the digestive system). Although the job is important and pays more than $250,000 on average, the tasks are routine and most patients are not looking forward to their appointments.[9]

**self-actualization needs**
the need to be the best one can be; at the top of Maslow's hierarchy

**connect**

▶ Need help understanding Maslow's Hierarchy? Visit your Connect ebook video tab for a brief animated explanation.

**hygiene factors**
aspects of Herzberg's theory of motivation that focus on the work setting and not the content of the work; these aspects include adequate wages, comfortable and safe working conditions, fair company policies, and job security

**TABLE 9.3**
**Herzberg's Hygiene and Motivational Factors**

| Hygiene Factors | Motivational Factors |
|---|---|
| Company policies | Achievement |
| Supervision | Recognition |
| Working conditions | Work itself |
| Relationships with peers, supervisors, and subordinates | Responsibility |
| Salary | Advancement |
| Security | Personal growth |

**motivational factors**
aspects of Herzberg's theory of motivation that focus on the content of the work itself; these aspects include achievement, recognition, involvement, responsibility, and advancement

**Motivational factors,** which relate to the content of the work itself, include achievement, recognition, involvement, responsibility, and advancement. The absence of motivational factors may not result in dissatisfaction, but their presence is likely to motivate employees to excel. Many companies are beginning to employ methods to give employees more responsibility and control and to involve them more in their work, which serves to motivate them to higher levels of productivity and quality. Hotels are adopting more customer-centric processes in order to better their experiences. Doubletree, a franchise owned by Hilton Hotels and Resorts, has created a CARE committee for each of its locations. The committee is composed of employees from all departments so that they can ensure maximum operational performance and customer satisfaction. Marriott International employees leave personal notes for guests, and their loyalty program is above comparison.[10]

Herzberg's motivational factors and Maslow's esteem and self-actualization needs are similar. Workers' low-level needs (physiological and security) have largely been satisfied by minimum-wage laws and occupational-safety standards set by various government agencies and are therefore not motivators. Consequently, to improve productivity, management should focus on satisfying workers' higher-level needs (motivational factors) by providing opportunities for achievement, involvement, and advancement and by recognizing good performance.

## McGregor's Theory X and Theory Y

In *The Human Side of Enterprise,* Douglas McGregor related Maslow's ideas about personal needs to management. McGregor contrasted two views of management—the traditional view, which he called Theory X, and a humanistic view, which he called Theory Y.

**Theory X**
McGregor's traditional view of management whereby it is assumed that workers generally dislike work and must be forced to do their jobs

According to McGregor, managers adopting **Theory X** assume that workers generally dislike work and must be forced to do their jobs. They believe that the following statements are true of workers:

1. The average person naturally dislikes work and will avoid it when possible.
2. Most workers must be coerced, controlled, directed, or threatened with punishment to get them to work toward the achievement of organizational objectives.
3. The average worker prefers to be directed and to avoid responsibility, has relatively little ambition, and wants security.[11]

Managers who subscribe to the Theory X view maintain tight control over workers, provide almost constant supervision, try to motivate through fear, and make decisions in an autocratic fashion, eliciting little or no input from their subordinates. The Theory X style of management focuses on physiological and security needs and virtually ignores the higher needs discussed by Maslow. Foxconn, a manufacturing company that creates components for tech products such as the Apple iPad, is a company that had adopted the Theory X perspective. In China, Foxconn workers live in crowded dorms and often work more than 60 hours per week.

**Theory Y**
McGregor's humanistic view of management whereby it is assumed that workers like to work and that under proper conditions employees will seek out responsibility in an attempt to satisfy their social, esteem, and self-actualization needs

The Theory X view of management does not take into account people's needs for companionship, esteem, and personal growth, whereas Theory Y, the contrasting view of management, does. Managers subscribing to the **Theory Y** view assume that workers like to work and that under proper conditions employees will seek out responsibility in an attempt to satisfy their social, esteem, and self-actualization needs. McGregor describes the assumptions behind Theory Y in the following way:

### The Stein Mart Culture Is a Key Ingredient for Success

**Stein Mart**
**Founder:** Sam Stein
**Founded:** 1908, in Greenville, Mississippi
**Success:** Stein Mart has 263 retail stores in 29 states and earns more than $1 billion in total revenue.

Sam Stein couldn't have known that his small merchandise store in 1908 would one day grow into a thriving discount apparel chain helmed by his grandson. When Sam Stein's son took over, he shifted the emphasis to apparel and renamed the store. Today, grandson Jay Stein runs the company. While other regional, discount, and high-end retailers have struggled through the economic downturn, Stein Mart has maintained a strong presence in the market. Its competitive

advantage is its pricing strategy—it offers quality goods at the prices of a discount retailer. Stein Mart does this by purchasing unsold merchandise from high-end retailers such as Saks Fifth Avenue and Neiman Marcus.

Stein's emphasis on customers and employees contributes to the personal culture of the company. Employees can receive health benefits, paid time off, and 25 percent discounts. Stein himself travels to stores weekly to meet and thank employees for their work. He also models good customer service by giving out thank-you notes to customers when they make purchases. These types of incentives add a personal touch absent from other retailers, resulting in high employee empowerment.[12]

---

1. The expenditure of physical and mental effort in work is as natural as play or rest.

2. People will exercise self-direction and self-control to achieve objectives to which they are committed.

3. People will commit to objectives when they realize that the achievement of those goals will bring them personal reward.

4. The average person will accept and seek responsibility.

5. Imagination, ingenuity, and creativity can help solve organizational problems, but most organizations do not make adequate use of these characteristics in their employees.

6. Organizations today do not make full use of workers' intellectual potential.[13]

Obviously, managers subscribing to the Theory Y philosophy have a management style very different from managers subscribing to the Theory X philosophy. Theory Y managers maintain less control and supervision, do not use fear as the primary motivator, and are more democratic in decision making, allowing subordinates to participate in the process. Theory Y managers address the high-level needs in Maslow's hierarchy as well as physiological and security needs. For instance, the Virgin Group, which is a conglomerate of various businesses in many industries, allows CEOs and managers to run their locations as they see fit. This also applies to complicated expansion measures such as opening foreign locations, which can become very complex. The company has achieved success by empowering employees to make their own decisions and follow their passions.[14] Today, Theory Y enjoys widespread support and may have displaced Theory X.

## Theory Z

**Theory Z** is a management philosophy that stresses employee participation in all aspects of company decision making. It was first described by William Ouchi in his book *Theory Z—How American Business Can Meet the Japanese Challenge.* Theory Z incorporates many elements associated with the Japanese approach to

**Theory Z**
a management philosophy that stresses employee participation in all aspects of company decision making

**TABLE 9.4    Comparison of American, Japanese, and Theory Z Management Styles**

| | American | Japanese | Theory Z |
|---|---|---|---|
| **Duration of employment** | Relatively short term; workers subject to layoffs when business slows | Lifelong; no layoffs | Long term; layoffs rare |
| **Rate of promotion** | Rapid | Slow | Slow |
| **Amount of specialization** | Considerable; worker develops expertise in one area only | Minimal; worker develops expertise in all aspects of the organization | Moderate; worker learns all aspects of the organization |
| **Decision making** | Individual | Consensual; input from all concerned parties is considered | Consensual; emphasis on quality |
| **Responsibility** | Assigned to the individual | Shared by the group | Assigned to the individual |
| **Control** | Explicit and formal | Less explicit and less formal | Informal but with explicit performance measures |
| **Concern for workers** | Focus is on work only | Focus extends to worker's whole life | Focus includes worker's life and family |

*Source: Adapted from William Ouchi,* Theory Z—How American Business Can Meet the Japanese Challenge, *p. 58. © 1981 by Addison-Wesley Publishing Company, Inc.*

management, such as trust and intimacy, but Japanese ideas have been adapted for use in the United States. In a Theory Z organization, managers and workers share responsibilities; the management style is participative; and employment is long term and often lifelong. Japan has faced a significant period of slowing economic progress and competition from China and other Asian nations. This has led to experts questioning Theory Z, particularly at firms such as Sony and Toyota. Theory Z results in employees feeling organizational ownership. Research has found that such feelings of ownership may produce positive attitudinal and behavioral effects for employees.[15] In a Theory Y organization, managers focus on assumptions about the nature of the worker. The two theories can be seen as complementary. Table 9.4 compares the traditional American management style, the Japanese management style, and Theory Z (the modified Japanese management style).

**equity theory**
an assumption that how much people are willing to contribute to an organization depends on their assessment of the fairness, or equity, of the rewards they will receive in exchange

## Equity Theory

According to **equity theory,** how much people are willing to contribute to an organization depends on their assessment of the fairness, or equity, of the rewards they will receive in exchange. In a fair situation, a person receives rewards proportional to the contribution he or she makes to the organization. However, in practice, equity is a subjective notion. Each worker regularly develops a personal input-output ratio by taking stock of his or her contribution (inputs) to the organization in time, effort, skills, and experience and assessing the rewards (outputs) offered by the organization in pay, benefits, recognition, and promotions. The worker compares his or her ratio to the input-output ratio of some other person—a "comparison other," who may be a co-worker, a friend working in another organization, or an "average" of several people working in the organization. If the two ratios are close, the individual will feel that he or she is being treated equitably.

Let's say you have a high-school education and earn $25,000 a year. When you compare your input-output ratio with that of a co-worker who has a college degree and makes $35,000 a year, you will probably feel that you are being paid fairly. However, if you perceive that your personal input-output ratio is lower than that of your college-educated co-worker, you may feel that you are being treated unfairly and be motivated to seek change. Or if you learn that your co-worker who makes $35,000 has only a high-school diploma, you may feel cheated by your employer. To achieve equity, you could try to increase your outputs by asking for a raise or promotion. You could also try to have your co-worker's inputs increased or his or her outputs decreased. Failing to achieve equity, you may be motivated to look for a job at a different company.

Equity theory might explain why many consumers are upset about CEO compensation. Although the job of the CEO can be incredibly stressful, the fact that they take home millions in compensation, bonuses, and stock options has been questioned. The high unemployment rate coupled with the misconduct that occurred at some large corporations prior to the recession contributed largely to the Occupy Wall Street protests. To counter this perception of pay inequality, several corporations have now begun to tie CEO compensation with company performance. If the company performs poorly for the year, then firms such as Goldman Sachs will cut bonuses and other compensation.[16] While lower compensation rates might appease the general public, some companies are worried that lower pay might deter talented individuals from wanting to assume the position of CEO at their firms.

Because almost all the issues involved in equity theory are subjective, they can be problematic. Author David Callahan has argued that feelings of inequity may underlie some unethical or illegal behavior in business. For example, due to employee theft and shoplifting, Walmart experiences billions in inventory losses every year. Some employees may take company resources to restore what they perceive to be equity. Theft of company resources is a major ethical issue, based on a survey by the Ethics Resource Center.[17] Callahan believes that employees who do not feel they are being treated equitably may be motivated to equalize the situation by lying, cheating, or otherwise "improving" their pay, perhaps by stealing.[18] Managers should try to avoid equity problems by ensuring that rewards are distributed on the basis of performance and that all employees clearly understand the basis for their pay and benefits.

**expectancy theory**
the assumption that motivation depends not only on how much a person wants something but also on how likely he or she is to get it

## Expectancy Theory

Psychologist Victor Vroom described **expectancy theory,** which states that motivation depends not only on how much a person wants something but also on the person's perception of how likely he or she is to get it. A person who wants something and has reason to be optimistic will be strongly motivated. For example, say you really want a promotion. And let's say because you have taken some night classes to improve your skills, and moreover, have just made a large, significant sale, you feel confident that you are qualified and able to handle the new position. Therefore, you are motivated to try to get the promotion. In contrast, if you do not believe you are likely to get what you want, you may not be motivated to try to get it, even though you really want it.

Your motivation depends not only on how much you want something, but also on how likely you are to get it.

# Strategies for Motivating Employees

Based on the various theories that attempt to explain what motivates employees, businesses have developed several strategies for motivating their employees and boosting morale and productivity. Some of these techniques include behavior modification and job design, as well as the already described employee involvement programs and work teams.

## Behavior Modification

**behavior modification** changing behavior and encouraging appropriate actions by relating the consequences of behavior to the behavior itself

**Behavior modification** involves changing behavior and encouraging appropriate actions by relating the consequences of behavior to the behavior itself. The concept of behavior modification was developed by psychologist B. F. Skinner, who showed that there are two types of consequences that can modify behavior—reward and punishment. Skinner found that behavior that is rewarded will tend to be repeated, while behavior that is punished will tend to be eliminated. For example, employees who know that they will receive a bonus such as an expensive restaurant meal for making a sale over $2,000 may be more motivated to make sales. Workers who know they will be punished for being tardy are likely to make a greater effort to get to work on time.

However, the two strategies may not be equally effective. Punishing unacceptable behavior may provide quick results but may lead to undesirable long-term side effects, such as employee dissatisfaction and increased turnover. In general, rewarding appropriate behavior is a more effective way to modify behavior.

## Job Design

Herzberg identified the job itself as a motivational factor. Managers have several strategies that they can use to design jobs to help improve employee motivation. These include job rotation, job enlargement, job enrichment, and flexible scheduling strategies.

**job rotation** movement of employees from one job to another in an effort to relieve the boredom often associated with job specialization

**Job Rotation.**   **Job rotation** allows employees to move from one job to another in an effort to relieve the boredom that is often associated with job specialization. Businesses often turn to specialization in hopes of increasing productivity, but there is a negative side effect to this type of job design: Employees become bored and dissatisfied, and productivity declines. Job rotation reduces this boredom by allowing workers to undertake a greater variety of tasks and by giving them the opportunity to learn new skills. With job rotation, an employee spends a specified amount of time performing one job and then moves on to another, different job. The worker eventually returns to the initial job and begins the cycle again.

Job rotation is a good idea, but it has one major drawback. Because employees may eventually become bored with all the jobs in the cycle, job rotation does not totally eliminate the problem of boredom. Job rotation is extremely useful, however, in situations where a person is being trained for a position that requires an understanding of various units in an organization. Eli Lilly is a strong believer in the benefits of job rotation. The company leaves employees in their current jobs and asks them to take on short-term assignments outside their field of expertise or interest. The results of the process have been positive, and Nokia is trying the same process with similar outcomes.[19] Many executive training programs require trainees to spend time learning a variety of specialized jobs. Job rotation is also used to cross-train today's self-directed work teams.

**Job Enlargement.**  **Job enlargement** adds more tasks to a job instead of treating each task as separate. Like job rotation, job enlargement was developed to overcome the boredom associated with specialization. The rationale behind this strategy is that jobs are more satisfying as the number of tasks performed by an individual increases. Employees sometimes enlarge, or craft, their jobs by noticing what needs to be done and then changing tasks and relationship boundaries to adjust. Individual orientation and motivation shape opportunities to craft new jobs and job relationships. Job enlargement strategies have been more successful in increasing job satisfaction than have job rotation strategies. IBM, AT&T, and Maytag are among the many companies that have used job enlargement to motivate employees.

**job enlargement**
the addition of more tasks to a job instead of treating each task as separate

**Job Enrichment.**  **Job enrichment** incorporates motivational factors such as opportunity for achievement, recognition, responsibility, and advancement into a job. It gives workers not only more tasks within the job, but more control and authority over the job. Job enrichment programs enhance a worker's feeling of responsibility and provide opportunities for growth and advancement when the worker is able to take on the more challenging tasks. Hyatt Hotels Corporation and Clif Bar use job enrichment to improve the quality of work life for their employees. The potential benefits of job enrichment are great, but it requires careful planning and execution.

**job enrichment**
the incorporation of motivational factors, such as opportunity for achievement, recognition, responsibility, and advancement, into a job

**Flexible Scheduling Strategies.**  Many U.S. workers work a traditional 40-hour workweek consisting of five 8-hour days with fixed starting and ending times. Facing problems of poor morale and high absenteeism as well as a diverse workforce with changing needs, many managers have turned to flexible scheduling strategies such as flextime, compressed workweeks, job sharing, part-time work, and telecommuting. A survey by WorldatWork showed that 88 percent of businesses offer some sort of telecommuting work. Employees have shown greater commitment to these organizations, reducing turnover and increasing job satisfaction.[20]

**Flextime** is a program that allows employees to choose their starting and ending times, as long as they are at work during a specified core period (Figure 9.4). It does not reduce the total number of hours that employees work; instead, it gives employees more flexibility in choosing which hours they work. A firm may specify that employees must be present from 10:00 a.m. to 3:00 p.m. One employee may choose to come in at 7:00 a.m. and leave at the end of the core time, perhaps to attend classes at a nearby college after work. Another employee, a mother who lives in the suburbs, may

**flextime**
a program that allows employees to choose their starting and ending times, provided that they are at work during a specified core period

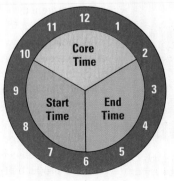

**FIGURE 9.4**
**Flextime, Showing Core and Flexible Hours**

come in at 9:00 a.m. in order to have time to drop off her children at a day-care center and commute by public transportation to her job. Flextime provides many benefits, including improved ability to recruit and retain workers who wish to balance work and home life. Customers can be better served by allowing more coverage of customers over longer hours, workstations and facilities can be better utilized by staggering employee use, and rush hour traffic may be reduced. In addition, flexible schedules have been associated with an increase in healthy behaviors on the part of employees. More flexible schedules are associated with healthier lifestyle choices such as increased physical activity and healthier sleep habits.[21]

Related to flextime are the scheduling strategies of the compressed workweek and job sharing. The **compressed workweek** is a four-day (or shorter) period in which an employee works 40 hours. Under such a plan, employees typically work 10 hours per day for four days and have a three-day weekend. The compressed workweek reduces the company's operating expenses because its actual hours of operation are reduced. It is also sometimes used by parents who want to have more days off to spend with their families. The U.S. Bureau of Labor Statistics notes that the following career options provide greater flexibility in scheduling: medical transcriptionist, financial manager, nurse, database administrator, accountant, software developer, physical therapist assistant, paralegal, graphic designer, and private investigator.[22]

**compressed workweek**
a four-day (or shorter) period during which an employee works 40 hours

**Job sharing** occurs when two people do one job. One person may work from 8:00 a.m. to 12:30 p.m.; the second person comes in at 12:30 p.m. and works until 5:00 p.m. Job sharing gives both people the opportunity to work as well as time to fulfill other obligations, such as parenting or school. With job sharing, the company has the benefit of the skills of two people for one job, often at a lower total cost for salaries and benefits than one person working eight hours a day would be paid.

**job sharing**
performance of one full-time job by two people on part-time hours

Two other flexible scheduling strategies attaining wider use include allowing full-time workers to work part time for a certain period and allowing workers to work at home either full or part time. Employees at some firms may be permitted to work part time for several months in order to care for a new baby or an elderly parent or just to slow down for a little while to "recharge their batteries." When the employees return to full-time work, they are usually given a position comparable to their original full-time position. Other firms are allowing employees to telecommute or telework (work at home a few days of the week), staying connected via computers, modems, and telephones. Most telecommuters tend to combine going into the office with working from home. Only about 3.3 million employees (not including entrepreneurs) cite the home as their primary workplace.[23]

Working from home is becoming increasingly common. Telecommuting, job sharing, and flextime can be beneficial for employees who cannot work normal work hours.

Although many employees ask for the option of working at home to ease the responsibilities of caring for family members, some have discovered that they are more productive at home without the distractions of the workplace. PGi conducted a survey on telecommuting and found that telecommuters experienced a decrease in stress and absenteeism and an increase in morale and productivity. Perhaps due to the positive morale that telecommuting can create, many

## The Pros and Cons of Working from Home

Allowing employees to work from home, known as telecommuting, has become a controversial topic for managers and human resources departments. With the advancement of technology, telecommuting has become easier and a part of many companies' cultures. It has been reported that 80 percent of companies listed on *Fortune*'s "Best Companies to Work For" offer employees the opportunity to work from home. Telecommuting has become a major benefit for employees. However, working from home has many challenges, and some firms are reversing their companies' work-from-home policies. Yahoo! CEO Marissa Mayer declared that the majority of Yahoo! employees would no longer be allowed to work from home because she believes employees need to interact with one another to improve productivity and cohesiveness. Bank of America and Best Buy have also reduced or eliminated work-from-home programs.

For many employees, working from home provides the benefit of achieving a work/life balance. Studies have shown that working from home can provide a happier environment and foster stronger loyalty from employees. This idea can be used as a motivational tool for employees if proper communication is provided linking employees to their businesses.

However, some employers believe that telecommuting is allowing collaboration among employees to suffer. By working from home, employees are becoming independent and potentially isolated, creating disconnections within the company. Also, employers are questioning whether employees abuse this privilege and are less efficient than they would be in an office environment. The question of whether telecommuting is productive and beneficial for the company remains a center of debate.[24]

### Discussion Questions

1. What are the advantages of using work-from-home policies to motivate employees?
2. What are the disadvantages of using work-from-home policies to motivate employees?
3. What impact do you feel reversing a firm's work-from-home policies will have on employee motivation?

---

*Fortune* 500 companies—including Apple, Google, and J. P. Morgan Chase—offer several types of telecommuting positions.[25] Other employees, however, have discovered that they are not suited for working at home. For telecommuting to work, it must be a feasible alternative and must not create significant costs for the company.[26] Bank of America, Yahoo!, and Best Buy are all eliminating their work-from-home programs as they feel that being present in the workplace increases collaboration and productivity. Still, work-at-home programs can help reduce overhead costs for businesses. For example, some companies used to maintain a surplus of office space but have reduced the surplus through employee telecommuting, "hoteling" (being assigned to a desk through a reservation system), and "hot-desking" (several people using the same desk but at different times).

Companies are turning to flexible work schedules to provide more options to employees who are trying to juggle their work duties with other responsibilities and needs. Preliminary results indicate that flexible scheduling plans increase job satisfaction, which, in turn, leads to increases in productivity. Some recent research, however, has indicated there are potential problems with telecommuting. Some managers are reluctant to adopt the practice because the pace of change in today's workplace is faster than ever, and telecommuters may be left behind or actually cause managers more work in helping them stay abreast of changes. Some employers also worry that telecommuting workers create a security risk by creating more opportunities for computer hackers or equipment thieves. Some employees have found that working outside the office may hurt career advancement opportunities, and some report that instead of helping them balance work and family responsibilities, telecommuting increases the strain by blurring the barriers between the office and home. Co-workers call at all

Businesses have come up with different ways to motivate employees, including rewards such as trophies and plaques to show the company's appreciation.

hours, and telecommuters are apt to continue to work when they are not supposed to (after regular business hours or during vacation time).

## Importance of Motivational Strategies

Motivation is more than a tool that managers can use to foster employee loyalty and boost productivity. It is a process that affects all the relationships within an organization and influences many areas such as pay, promotion, job design, training opportunities, and reporting relationships. Employees are motivated by the nature of the relationships they have with their supervisors, by the nature of their jobs, and by characteristics of the organization. Table 9.5 shows companies with excellent motivational strategies, along with the types of strategies they use to motivate employees. Even the economic environment can change an employee's motivation. In a slow growth or recession economy, sales can flatten or decrease and morale can drop because of the need to cut jobs. In the most recent recession, many workers feared losing their jobs and increased the amount they were

**TABLE 9.5    Companies with Excellent Motivational Strategies**

| Company | Motivational Strategies |
|---------|-------------------------|
| 3M | Gives employees 15–20 percent of their time to pursue on projects |
| Google | Perks include a massage every other week, free gourmet lunches, tuition reimbursement, a volleyball court, and time to work on own projects |
| Whole Foods | Employees receive 20 percent discounts on company products, the opportunity to gain stock options, and the ability to make major decisions in small teams |
| Patagonia | Provides areas for yoga and aerobics, in-house child care services, organic food in its café, and opportunities to go surfing during the day |
| The Container Store | Provides more than 260 hours of employee training and hosts "We Love Our Employees" Day |
| Southwest Airlines | Gives employees permission to interact with passengers as they see fit, provides free or discounted flights, and hosts the "Adopt-a-Pilot" program to connect pilots with students across the nation |
| Nike | Offers tuition assistance, product discounts, onsite fitness centers, and the ability for employees to give insights on how to improve the firm |
| Apple | Creates a fast-paced, innovative work environment where employees are encouraged to debate ideas |
| Marriott | Offers discounts at hotels across the world as well as free hotel stays and travel opportunities for employees with exceptional service |
| Zappos | Creates a fun, zany work environment for employees and empowers them to take as much times as needed to answer customer concerns |

saving. The firm may have to work harder to keep good employees and to motivate all employees to work to overcome obstacles. In good economic times, employees may be more demanding and be on the lookout for better opportunities. New rewards or incentives may help motivate workers in such economies. Motivation tools, then, must be varied as well. Managers can further nurture motivation by being honest, supportive, empathic, accessible, fair, and open. Motivating employees to increase satisfaction and productivity is an important concern for organizations seeking to remain competitive in the global marketplace.

## ⊖ So You Think You May Be Good at Motivating a Workforce

If you are good at mediation, smoothing conflict, and have a good understanding of motivation and human relations theories, then you might be a good leader, human resource manager, or training expert. Most organizations, especially as they grow, will need to implement human relations programs. These are necessary to teach employees about sensitivity to other cultures, religions, and beliefs, as well as for teaching the workforce about the organization so that they understand how they fit in the larger picture. Employees need to appreciate the benefits of working together to make the firm run smoothly, and they also need to understand how their contributions help the firm. To stay motivated, most employees need to feel like what they do each day contributes something of value to the firm. Disclosing information and including employees in decision-making processes will also help employees feel valuable and wanted within the firm.

There are many different ways employers can reward and encourage employees. However, employers must be careful when considering what kinds of incentives to use. Different cultures value different kinds of incentives more highly than others. For example, a Japanese worker would probably not like it if she were singled out from the group and given a large cash bonus as reward for her work. Japanese workers tend to be more group oriented, and therefore anything that singles out individuals would not be an effective way of rewarding and motivating. American workers, on the other hand, are very individualistic, and a raise and public praise might be more effective. However, what might motivate a younger employee (bonuses, raises, and perks) may not be the same as what motivates a more seasoned, experienced, and financially successful employee (recognition, opportunity for greater influence, and increased training). Motivation is not an easy thing to understand, especially as firms become more global and more diverse.

Another important part of motivation is enjoying where you work and your career opportunities. Here is a list of the best places to do business and start careers in the United States, according to *Forbes* magazine. Chances are, workers who live in these places have encountered fewer frustrations than those places at the bottom of the list and, therefore, would probably be more content with where they work.[27]

Best Places for Businesses and Careers[28]

| Rank | Metro Area | Gross Metro Product* | Metro Population |
|------|-----------|---------------------|------------------|
| 1. | Des Moines, Iowa | $37 billion | 589,500 |
| 2. | Provo, Utah | $18 billion | 552,800 |
| 3. | Raleigh, North Carolina | $58 billion | 1,194,100 |
| 4. | Lincoln, Nebraska | $17 billion | 310,700 |
| 5. | Nashville, Tennessee | $83 billion | 1,647,200 |
| 6. | Denver, Colorado | $153 billion | 2,649,400 |
| 7. | Fort Collins, Colorado | $15 billion | 311,300 |
| 8. | Oklahoma City, Oklahoma | $59 billion | 1,297,900 |
| 9. | Seattle, Washington | $203 billion | 2,744,100 |
| 10. | Durham, North Carolina | $34 billion | 523,600 |

*Gross metro product is the market value of all products produced within a metropolitan area in a given time period; similar to GDP but on a metropolitan area.

# Review Your Understanding

### Define human relations, and determine why its study is important.

Human relations is the study of the behavior of individuals and groups in organizational settings. Its focus is what motivates employees to perform on the job. Human relations is important because businesses need to understand how to motivate their increasingly diverse employees to be more effective, boost workplace morale, and maximize employees' productivity and creativity.

### Summarize studies that laid the groundwork for understanding employee motivation.

Time and motion studies by Frederick Taylor and others helped them analyze how employees perform specific work tasks in an effort to improve their productivity. Taylor and the early practitioners of the classical theory of motivation felt that money and job security were the primary motivators of employees. However, the Hawthorne studies revealed that human factors also influence workers' behavior.

### Compare and contrast the human-relations theories of Abraham Maslow and Frederick Herzberg.

Abraham Maslow defined five basic needs of all people and arranged them in the order in which they must be satisfied: physiological, security, social, esteem, and self-actualization. Frederick Herzberg divided characteristics of the job into hygiene factors and motivational factors. Hygiene factors relate to the work environment and must be present for employees to remain in a job. Motivational factors—recognition, responsibility, and advancement—relate to the work itself. They encourage employees to be productive. Herzberg's hygiene factors can be compared to Maslow's physiological and security needs; motivational factors may include Maslow's social, esteem, and self-actualization needs.

### Investigate various theories of motivation, including theories X, Y, and Z; equity theory; and expectancy theory.

Douglas McGregor contrasted two views of management: Theory X (traditional) suggests workers dislike work, while theory Y (humanistic) suggests that workers not only like work but seek out responsibility to satisfy their higher-order needs. Theory Z stresses employee participation in all aspects of company decision making, often through participative management programs and self-directed work teams. According to equity theory, how much people are willing to contribute to an organization depends on their assessment of the fairness, or equity, of the rewards they will receive in exchange. Expectancy theory states that motivation depends not only on how much a person wants something but also on the person's perception of how likely he or she is to get it.

### Describe some of the strategies that managers use to motivate employees.

Strategies for motivating workers include behavior modification (changing behavior and encouraging appropriate actions by relating the consequences of behavior to the behavior itself) and job design. Among the job design strategies businesses use are job rotation (allowing employees to move from one job to another to try to relieve the boredom associated with job specialization), job enlargement (adding tasks to a job instead of treating each task as a separate job), job enrichment (incorporating motivational factors into a job situation), and flexible scheduling strategies (flextime, compressed workweeks, job sharing, part-time work, and telecommuting).

### Critique a business's program for motivating its sales force.

Using the information presented in the chapter, you should be able to analyze and defend Eagle Pharmaceutical's motivation program in "Solve the Dilemma" on page 284, including the motivation theories the firm is applying to boost morale and productivity.

# Revisit the World of Business

1.  Why do you think that Mars Inc. refuses to become a public company?

2.  How does Mars Inc. motivate its employees?

3.  How does employee motivation at Mars Inc. contribute to the firm's success?

# Learn the Terms

| | | |
|---|---|---|
| behavior modification   276 | flextime   277 | job sharing   278 |
| classical theory of motivation   267 | human relations   264 | Maslow's hierarchy   269 |
| compressed workweek   278 | hygiene factors   271 | morale   265 |
| equity theory   274 | intrinsic rewards   265 | motivation   264 |
| esteem needs   270 | job enlargement   277 | motivational factors   272 |
| expectancy theory   275 | job enrichment   277 | physiological needs   269 |
| extrinsic rewards   265 | job rotation   276 | security needs   269 |

## Check Your Progress

1. Why do managers need to understand the needs of their employees?
2. Describe the motivation process.
3. What was the goal of the Hawthorne studies? What was the outcome of those studies?
4. Explain Maslow's hierarchy of needs. What does it tell us about employee motivation?
5. What are Herzberg's hygiene and motivational factors? How can managers use them to motivate workers?

6. Contrast the assumptions of theory X and theory Y. Why has theory Y replaced theory X in management today?
7. What is theory Z? How can businesses apply theory Z to the workplace?
8. Identify and describe four job-design strategies.
9. Name and describe some flexible scheduling strategies. How can flexible schedules help motivate workers?
10. Why are motivational strategies important to both employees and employers?

## Get Involved

1. Consider a person who is homeless: How would he or she be motivated and what actions would that person take? Use the motivation process to explain. Which of the needs in Maslow's hierarchy are likely to be most important? Least important?

2. View the video *Cheaper by the Dozen* (1950) and report on how the Gilbreths tried to incorporate their passion for efficiency into their family life.

3. What events and trends in society, technology, and economics do you think will shape human relations management theory in the future?

## Build Your Skills

### Motivating

#### Background

Do you think that, if employers could make work more like play, employees would be as enthusiastic about their jobs as they are about what they do in their leisure time? Let's see where this idea might take us.

#### Task

After reading the "Characteristics of PLAY," place a √ in column one for those characteristics you have experienced in your leisure time activities. Likewise, check column three for those "Characteristics of WORK" you have experienced in any of the jobs you've held.

| All That Apply | Characteristics of PLAY | All That Apply | Characteristics of WORK |
|---|---|---|---|
| | 1. New games can be played on different days. | | 1. Job enrichment, job enlargement, or job rotation. |
| | 2. Flexible duration of play. | | 2. Job sharing. |
| | 3. Flexible time of when to play. | | 3. Flextime, telecommuting. |
| | 4. Opportunity to express oneself. | | 4. Encourage and implement employee suggestions. |
| | 5. Opportunity to use one's talents. | | 5. Assignment of challenging projects. |
| | 6. Skillful play brings applause, praise, and recognition from spectators. | | 6. Employee-of-the-month awards, press releases, employee newsletter announcements. |
| | 7. Healthy competition, rivalry, and challenge exist. | | 7. Production goals with competition to see which team does best. |
| | 8. Opportunity for social interaction. | | 8. Employee softball or bowling teams. |
| | 9. Mechanisms for scoring one's performance are available (feedback). | | 9. Profit sharing; peer performance appraisals. |
| | 10. Rules ensure basic fairness and justice. | | 10. Use tactful and consistent discipline. |

## Discussion Questions

1. What prevents managers from making work more like play?

2. Are these forces real or imagined?

3. What would be the likely (positive and negative) results of making work more like play?

4. Could others in the organization accept such creative behaviors?

## Solve the Dilemma  LO 9-6

### Motivating to Win

 Eagle Pharmaceutical has long been recognized for its innovative techniques for motivating its salesforce. It features the salesperson who has been the most successful during the previous quarter in the company newsletter, "Touchdown." The salesperson also receives a football jersey, a plaque, and $1,000 worth of Eagle stock. Eagle's "Superbowl Club" is for employees who reach or exceed their sales goal, and a "Heisman Award," which includes a trip to the Caribbean, is given annually to the top 20 salespeople in terms of goal achievement.

Eagle employs a video conference hookup between the honored salesperson and four regional sales managers to capture some of the successful tactics and strategies the winning salesperson uses to succeed. The managers summarize these ideas and pass them along to the salespeople they manage. Sales managers feel strongly that programs such as this are important and that, by sharing strategies and tactics with one another, they can be a successful team.

### Discussion Questions

1. Which motivational theories are in use at Eagle?

2. What is the value of getting employees to compete against a goal instead of against one another?

3. Put yourself in the shoes of one of the four regional sales managers and argue against potential cutbacks to the motivational program.

## Build Your Business Plan

### Motivating the Workforce

 As you determine the size of your workforce, you are going to face the reality that you cannot provide the level of financial compensation that you would like to your employees, especially when you are starting your business.

Many employees are motivated by other things than money. Knowing that they are appreciated and doing a good job can bring great satisfaction to employees. Known as "stroking," it can provide employees with internal gratification that can be valued even more than financial incentives. Listening to your employees' suggestions, involving them in discussions about future growth, and valuing their input can go a long way toward building loyal employees and reducing employee turnover.

Think about what you could do in your business to motivate your employees without spending much money. Maybe you will have lunch brought in once a week or offer tickets to a local sporting event to the employee with the most sales. Whatever you elect to do, you must be consistent and fair with all your employees.

## See for Yourself Videocase

### The Container Store's Secret to Success: Employee Satisfaction

 Can you form a successful company by selling containers, boxes, and other storage products? The Container Store has shown that the answer is yes. With more than 10,000 products available, The Container Store sells items such as hanging bins, drawers, trash cans, and other items to help make a hectic life more organized. While there might have been skeptics in the beginning, particularly as the firm started out in a small 1,600 square-foot store, the idea quickly caught on with consumers.

"Word of mouth spread incredibly. It was just the oddest collection of merchandising anybody had ever seen to organize your home and to organize your life. A week into it, we knew we had something," co-founder and CEO Kip Tindell said.

Yet in addition to its unusual product mix, The Container Store is also unique for its dedication to employees. The retail world can be difficult for employees because of high turnover, different hours every week, lower benefits, and constant interaction with people. The turnover rate in the retail industry is about 100 percent. This increases training costs, which can cause companies to decrease the amount of training offered.

This trend is reversed at The Container Store. First-year full-time employees receive 263 hours of training, much higher than the industry average of 10 hours. Employees receive 50 percent more pay than at other retail establishments. Employee turnover at The Container Store is a low 10 percent. For more than a decade, The Container Store has been elected as one of the top 100 companies to work for by *Fortune* magazine.

Yet, the satisfaction that employees feel toward the company is not solely a result of higher pay. According to Frederick Herzberg's two-factor theory, good workplace conditions can prevent dissatisfaction but do not motivate the employee to go above and beyond what is required of them. As CEO of the company, Kip Tindell realizes that the amount of time and effort an employee gives to the company will determine productivity.

"The first 25 percent for any employee is mandatory. If they don't do that, they're going to get fired. But the next 75 percent of an employee's productivity for any business in the world, I believe, is more or less voluntary. You do more or less of it depending upon how you feel about your boss and your product and your company."

Therefore, to enhance productivity, the firm has made employee satisfaction a priority. Employees come first, followed by customers and then shareholders. One of the ways that The Container Store motivates its employees is by creating an open communication culture. Employees are encouraged to approach their managers on any topic. This causes employees to feel as if the organization cares about them enough to take their concerns seriously. The Container Store also holds several events to show their appreciation of employee efforts. For instance, every February 14, The Container Store holds its "We Love Our Employees" day. At one of the events, the company announced the establishment of an emergency fund for employees. The

company contributed $100,000 for unexpected costs that employees may find themselves having to pay for due to natural disasters, terrorist attacks, or significant medical issues.

Employees also receive many perks for working at The Container Store, and even part-time employees are eligible for health care benefits. Because employees take precedence at The Container Store, the company bases its decisions on what is best for employees even during hard times. During the recession, for instance, The Container Store refused to lay off employees. In addition to benefits, employees have access to all company data, including financial reports.

Does this mean that The Container Store ignores its customers for the sake of its employees? The high-quality customer service that The Container Store offers suggests just the opposite. In fact, the extensive employee training and the company's values demonstrate its high commitment to customer satisfaction. According to Tindell, the key to great customer service, however, is highly motivated employees.

"We believe that if you take better care of your employees than anybody else, they'll take better care of the customer than anybody else, and if those two guys are ecstatic, ironically enough, your shareholder's going to be ecstatic too."[29]

### Discussion Questions

1. Name some of the hygiene factors at The Container Store.
2. Name some of the ways that The Container Store motivates its employees.
3. Do you believe Tindell's statement that highly satisfied employees will lead to highly satisfied customers and shareholders?

**You can find the related video in the Video Library in Connect. Ask your instructor how you can access Connect.**

## Team Exercise

Form groups and outline a compensation package that you would consider ideal in motivating an employee, recognizing performance, and assisting the company in attaining its cost-to-performance objectives. Think about the impact of intrinsic and extrinsic motivation and recognition. How can flexible scheduling strategies be used effectively to motivate employees? Report your compensation package to the class.

# 10

# Managing Human Resources

## Learning Objectives

**After reading this chapter, you will be able to:**

**LO 10-1** Define human resources management, and explain its significance.

**LO 10-2** Summarize the processes of recruiting and selecting human resources for a company.

**LO 10-3** Discuss how workers are trained and their performance appraised.

**LO 10-4** Identify the types of turnover companies may experience, and explain why turnover is an important issue.

**LO 10-5** Specify the various ways a worker may be compensated.

**LO 10-6** Discuss some of the issues associated with unionized employees, including collective bargaining and dispute resolution.

**LO 10-7** Describe the importance of diversity in the workforce.

**LO 10-8** Assess an organization's efforts to reduce its workforce size and manage the resulting effects.

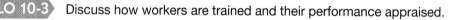

## The Recruitment Process of Cirque du Soleil

Cirque du Soleil is known for its fanciful shows and for being the only circus that does not use animals. It uses a blend of circus arts and street entertainment to entertain guests. This unique organization requires a unique hiring process. The company holds recruiting events on different continents to recruit the best talent. Yet, the hiring process is based on the creative capacity of applicants more than their current skills or past experience. People from various ethnic backgrounds and professional careers submit their applications through different categories called pools. Recruiters go through these pools to find the applicants they think will be a good fit for the company. About one-third of new hires come from these pools.

Cirque du Soleil requires the recruiter to look not only at skills and accomplishments, but also to foresee what the applicant could become if chosen to be part of the team. Transformation, creativity, and openness are crucial to the success of Cirque du Soleil productions and must be manifested in potential performers. Interviewers will often ask unusual questions to see what kinds of creative responses they get. The diversity of applicants requires that recruiters are sensitive to various ways of interacting with potential employees. For example, some applicants are athletes who are contracted with their government, some are from circus families, and others are represented through agencies. Cirque du Soleil attracts a number of people with unique talents, from athletic skills to pick-pocketing as a part of the show. In each of these instances, there are different protocols and customs that must be observed. While looking for people with skill sets of high quality, the recruiters must also make sure that the applicants are open to becoming a true performer.[1]

# Introduction

If a business is to achieve success, it must have sufficient numbers of employees who are qualified and motivated to perform the required duties. Thus, managing the quantity (from hiring to firing) and quality (through training, compensating, and so on) of employees is an important business function. Meeting the challenge of managing increasingly diverse human resources effectively can give a company a competitive edge in a global marketplace.

This chapter focuses on the quantity and quality of human resources. First we look at how human resources managers plan for, recruit, and select qualified employees. Next we look at training, appraising, and compensating employees, aspects of human resources management designed to retain valued employees. Along the way, we'll also consider the challenges of managing unionized employees and workplace diversity.

**human resources management (HRM)**
all the activities involved in determining an organization's human resources needs, as well as acquiring, training, and compensating people to fill those needs

LO 10-1

# The Nature of Human Resources Management

Chapter 1 defined human resources as labor, the physical and mental abilities that people use to produce goods and services. **Human resources management (HRM)** refers to all the activities involved in determining an organization's human resources needs, as well as acquiring, training, and compensating people to fill those needs. Human resources managers are concerned with maximizing the satisfaction of employees and motivating them to meet organizational objectives productively. In some companies, this function is called personnel management.

HRM has increased in importance over the past few decades, in part because managers have developed a better understanding of human relations through the work of Maslow, Herzberg, and others. Moreover, the human resources themselves are changing. Employees today are concerned not only about how much a job pays; they are concerned also with job satisfaction, personal performance, recreation, benefits, the work environment, and their opportunities for advancement. Once dominated by white men, today's workforce includes significantly more women, African Americans, Hispanics, and other minorities, as well as disabled and older workers. Human resources managers must be aware of these changes and leverage them to increase the productivity of their employees. Every manager practices some of the functions of human resources management at all times.

Today's organizations are more diverse, with a greater range of women, minorities, and older workers.

# Planning for Human Resources Needs

When planning and developing strategies for reaching the organization's overall objectives, a company must consider whether it will have the human resources necessary to carry out its plans. After determining how many employees and what skills are needed to satisfy the overall plans, the human resources department (which may range from the owner in a small business to hundreds of people in a large corporation) ascertains how many employees the company currently has and how many will be retiring or otherwise leaving the organization during the planning period. With this information, the human resources manager can then forecast how many more employees the company will need to hire and what qualifications they must have, or determine if layoffs are required to

**connect**

Need help understanding the Five Steps of Human Resource Planning? Visit your Connect ebook video tab for a brief animated explanation.

meet demand more efficiently. HRM planning also requires forecasting the availability of people in the workforce who will have the necessary qualifications to meet the organization's future needs. The human resources manager then develops a strategy for satisfying the organization's human resources needs. As organizations strive to increase efficiency through outsourcing, automation, or learning to effectively use temporary workers, hiring needs can change dramatically.

Next, managers analyze the jobs within the organization so that they can match the human resources to the available assignments. **Job analysis** determines, through observation and study, pertinent information about a job—the specific tasks that comprise it; the knowledge, skills, and abilities necessary to perform it; and the environment in which it will be performed. Managers use the information obtained through a job analysis to develop job descriptions and job specifications.

A **job description** is a formal, written explanation of a specific job that usually includes job title, tasks to be performed (for instance, waiting on customers), relationship with other jobs, physical and mental skills required (such as lifting heavy boxes or calculating data), duties, responsibilities, and working conditions. Job seekers might turn to online websites or databases to help find job descriptions for specific occupations. For instance, the Occupational Information Network has an online database with hundreds of occupational descriptors. These descriptors describe the skills, knowledge, and education needed to fulfill a particular occupation (e.g., human resources).[2] A **job specification** describes the qualifications necessary for a specific job, in terms of education (some jobs require a college degree), experience, personal characteristics (ads frequently request outgoing, hardworking persons), and physical characteristics. Both the job description and job specification are used to develop recruiting materials such as newspapers, trade publications, and online advertisements.

**job analysis**
the determination, through observation and study, of pertinent information about a job—including specific tasks and necessary abilities, knowledge, and skills

**job description**
a formal, written explanation of a specific job, usually including job title, tasks, relationship with other jobs, physical and mental skills required, duties, responsibilities, and working conditions

**job specification**
a description of the qualifications necessary for a specific job, in terms of education, experience, and personal and physical characteristics

# Recruiting and Selecting New Employees

After forecasting the firm's human resources needs and comparing them to existing human resources, the human resources manager should have a general idea of how many new employees the firm needs to hire. With the aid of job analyses, management can then recruit and select employees who are qualified to fill specific job openings.

LO 10-2

## Recruiting

**Recruiting** means forming a pool of qualified applicants from which management can select employees. There are two sources from which to develop this pool of applicants—internal and external.

Internal sources of applicants include the organization's current employees. Many firms have a policy of giving first consideration to their own employees—or promoting from within. The cost of hiring current employees to fill job openings is inexpensive when compared with the cost of hiring from external sources, and it is good for employee morale. However, hiring from within creates another job vacancy to be filled.

External sources of applicants consist of advertisements in newspapers and professional journals, employment agencies, colleges, vocational schools, recommendations from current employees, competing firms, unsolicited applications, online websites, and social networking sites such as LinkedIn. Internships are also a good way to solicit for potential employees. Many companies hire college students or recent graduates to low-paying internships that give them the opportunity to get hands-on experience on the job. If the intern proves to be a good fit, an organization may

**recruiting**
forming a pool of qualified applicants from which management can select employees

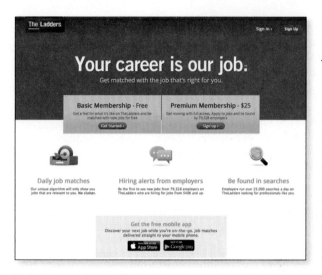

TheLadders.com is a website that targets career-driven professionals.

then hire the intern as a full-time worker. There are also hundreds of websites where employers can post job openings and job seekers can post their résumés, including Monster.com, USAJobs, Simply Hired, SnagaJob, and CareerBuilder.com. TheLadders.com is a website that focuses on career-driven professionals who make salaries of $40,000 or more. Employers looking for employees for specialized jobs can use more focused sites such as computerwork.com. Increasingly, companies can turn to their own websites for potential candidates: Nearly all of the *Fortune* 500 firms provide career websites where they recruit, provide employment information, and take applications. Using these sources of applicants is generally more expensive than hiring from within, but it may be necessary if there are no current employees who meet the job specifications or there are better-qualified people outside of the organization.

Recruiting for entry-level managerial and professional positions is often carried out on college and university campuses. For managerial or professional positions above the entry level, companies sometimes depend on employment agencies or executive search firms, sometimes called *headhunters,* which specialize in luring qualified people away from other companies. Employers are also increasingly using professional social networking sites such as LinkedIn and Viadeo as recruitment tools. Figure 10.1 shows some ways that recruiters use social media to recruit and hire job candidates.

## FIGURE 10.1
### Recruiting through Social Networking

Online survey conducted June 2013 with 1,600 recruiting and human resources professionals.

Source: Jobvite, *Social Survey Recruiting Results 2013,* http://web.jobvite.com/rs/jobvite/images/Jobvite_2013_SocialRecruitingSurveyResults.pdf (accessed May 2, 2014).

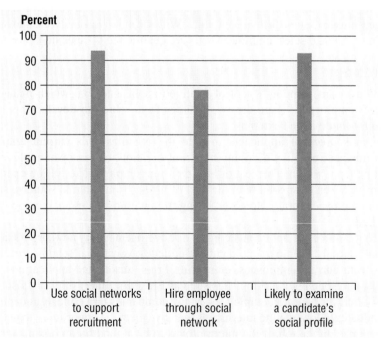

## Selection

**Selection** is the process of collecting information about applicants and using that information to decide which ones to hire. It includes the application itself, as well as interviewing, testing, and reference checking. This process can be quite lengthy and expensive. Procter & Gamble, for example, offers online applications for jobs in approximately 100 countries. The first round of evaluation involves assessment, and if this stage goes well, the candidate interviews in the region or country to which the applicant applied.[3] Such rigorous scrutiny is necessary to find those applicants who can do the work expected and fit into the firm's structure and culture. If an organization finds the "right" employees through its recruiting and selection process, it will not have to spend as much money later in recruiting, selecting, and training replacement employees.

**selection**
the process of collecting information about applicants and using that information to make hiring decisions

**The Application.**   In the first stage of the selection process, the individual fills out an application form and perhaps has a brief interview. The application form asks for the applicant's name, address, telephone number, education, and previous work experience. The goal of this stage of the selection process is to get acquainted with the applicants and to weed out those who are obviously not qualified for the job. For employees with work experience, most companies ask for the following information before contacting a potential candidate: current salary, reason for seeking a new job, years of experience, availability, and level of interest in the position. In addition to identifying obvious qualifications, the application can provide subtle clues about whether a person is appropriate for a particular job. For instance, an applicant who gives unusually creative answers may be perfect for a position at an advertising agency; a person who turns in a sloppy, hurriedly scrawled application probably would not be appropriate for a technical job requiring precise adjustments. Most companies now accept online applications. The online application for Target is designed not only to collect biographical data on the applicant, but also to create a picture of the applicant and how that person might contribute to the company. The completion of the survey takes about 15–45 minutes, depending on the position. To get a better view of the fit between the applicant and the company, the online application contains a questionnaire that asks applicants more specific questions, from how they might react in a certain situation to personality attributes like self-esteem or ability to interact with people.

**The Interview.**   The next phase of the selection process involves interviewing applicants. Table 10.1 provides some insights on finding the right work environment. Interviews allow management to obtain detailed information about the applicant's experience and skills, reasons for changing jobs, attitudes toward the job, and an idea of whether the person would fit in with the company. Table 10.2 lists some of the most common questions asked by interviewers while Table 10.3 reveals some common

**TABLE 10.1**
**Interviewing Tips**

1. Evaluate the work environment. Do employees seem to get along and work well in teams?
2. Evaluate the attitude of employees. Are employees happy, tense, or overworked?
3. Are employees enthusiastic and excited about their work?
4. What is the organizational culture, and would you feel comfortable working there?

*Source: Adapted from "What to Look for During Office Visits," http://careercenter.tamu.edu/guides/interviews/lookforinoffice.cfm?sn=parents (accessed April 23, 2012).*

**TABLE 10.2**
**Most Common Questions Asked during the Interview**

| |
|---|
| 1. Tell me about yourself. |
| 2. Why should I hire you? |
| 3. Please tell me about your future objectives. |
| 4. Has your education prepared you for your career? |
| 5. Have you been a team player? |
| 6. Did you encounter any conflict with your previous professors or employer? What are the steps that you have taken to resolve this issue? |
| 7. What is your biggest weakness? |
| 8. How would your professors describe you? |
| 9. What are the qualities that a manager should possess? |
| 10. If you could turn back time, what would you change? |

Source: "Job Interview Skills Training: Top Ten Interview Questions for College Graduates," February 17, 2010, www.articlesbase.com/business-articles/job-interview-skills-training-top-ten-interview-questions-for-college-graduates-1871741.html (accessed April 13, 2011).

**TABLE 10.3**
**Mistakes Made in Interviewing**

| |
|---|
| 1. Not taking the interview seriously. |
| 2. Not dressing appropriately (dressing down). |
| 3. Not appropriately discussing experience, abilities, and education. |
| 4. Being too modest about your accomplishments. |
| 5. Talking too much. |
| 6. Too much concern about compensation. |
| 7. Speaking negatively of a former employer. |
| 8. Not asking enough or appropriate questions. |
| 9. Not showing the proper enthusiasm level. |
| 10. Not engaging in appropriate follow-up to the interview. |

Source: "Avoid the Top 10 Job Interview Mistakes," All Business, www.allbusiness.com/human-resources/careers-job-interview/1611-1.html (accessed April 23, 2012).

mistakes candidates make in interviewing. Furthermore, the interviewer can answer the applicant's questions about the requirements for the job, compensation, working conditions, company policies, organizational culture, and so on. A potential employee's questions may be just as revealing as his or her answers. Today's students might be surprised to have an interviewer ask them, "What's on your Facebook account?" or have them show the interviewer their Facebook accounts. Currently, these are legal questions for an interviewer to ask.

**Testing.**    Another step in the selection process is testing. Ability and performance tests are used to determine whether an applicant has the skills necessary for the job.

Aptitude, IQ, or personality tests may be used to assess an applicant's potential for a certain kind of work and his or her ability to fit into the organization's culture. One of the most commonly used tests is the Myers-Briggs Type Indicator. The Myers-Briggs Type Indicator Test is used worldwide by millions of people each year. Although polygraph ("lie detector") tests were once a common technique for evaluating the honesty of applicants, in 1988 their use was restricted to specific government jobs and those involving security or access to drugs. Applicants may also undergo physical examinations to determine their suitability for some jobs, and many companies require applicants to be screened for illegal drug use. Illegal drug use and alcoholism can be particularly damaging to businesses. It has been estimated that 8.4 percent of full-time employees engage in illicit drug use, while 29.7 percent engage in binge drinking and 8.5 percent are considered to be heavy drinkers.[4] Small businesses may have a higher percentage of these employees because they do not engage in systematic drug testing. If you employ a drug or alcohol abuser, you can expect a 33 percent loss in productivity from this employee. Loss in productivity from alcohol abuse alone costs companies $134 billion each year. Health care costs are also more expensive for those who abuse alcohol—twice as more than those for employees who do not abuse alcohol.[5]

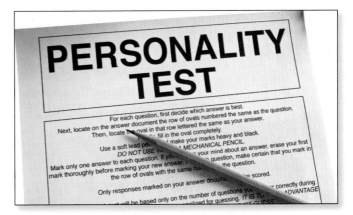

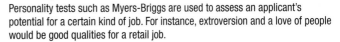

Personality tests such as Myers-Briggs are used to assess an applicant's potential for a certain kind of job. For instance, extroversion and a love of people would be good qualities for a retail job.

Because computer knowledge is a requirement for many jobs today, certain companies also require an applicant to take a typing test or tests to determine their knowledge of MS Word, Excel, PowerPoint, and/or other necessary programs. Like the application form and the interview, testing serves to eliminate those who do not meet the job specifications.

**Reference Checking.**    Before making a job offer, the company should always check an applicant's references. Reference checking usually involves verifying educational background and previous work experience. An Internet search is often done to determine social media activities or other public activities. While public Internet searches are usually deemed acceptable, asking for private information—while legal—is deemed to be intrusive by many job seekers.[6] Many states are already taking legislative action to ban this practice.[7] Public companies are likely to do more extensive background searches to make sure applicants are not misrepresenting themselves.

Background checking is important because applicants may misrepresent themselves on their applications or résumés. Matthew Martoma, a trader for SAC Capital Advisors, was convicted of conspiracy and securities fraud. Court testimony revealed that he had been expelled from Harvard after forging a transcript for an application and creating an elaborate cover-up. Research has shown that those who are willing to exaggerate or lie on their résumés are more likely to engage in unethical behaviors.[8] As Table 10.4 illustrates, some of the most common types of résumé lies include the faking of credentials, overstatements of skills or accomplishments, lies concerning education/degrees, omissions of past employment, and the falsification of references.[9]

**TABLE 10.4**
**Top 10 Résumé Lies**

| |
|---|
| 1. Stretching dates of employment |
| 2. Inflating past accomplishments and skills |
| 3. Enhancing job titles and responsibilities |
| 4. Education exaggeration and fabricating degrees |
| 5. Unexplained gaps and periods of "self employment" |
| 6. Omitting past employment |
| 7. Faking credentials |
| 8. Fabricating reasons for leaving previous job |
| 9. Providing fraudulent references |
| 10. Misrepresenting military record |

*Source: Christopher T. Marquet and Lisa J. B. Peterson, "Résumé Fraud: The Top 10 Lies," www.marquetinternational.com/pdf/Resume%20Fraud-Top%20Ten%20Lies.pdf (accessed April 13, 2011).*

Reference checking is a vital, albeit often overlooked, stage in the selection process. Managers charged with hiring should be aware, however, that many organizations will confirm only that an applicant is a former employee, perhaps with beginning and ending work dates, and will not release details about the quality of the employee's work.

## Legal Issues in Recruiting and Selecting

Legal constraints and regulations are present in almost every phase of the recruitment and selection process, and a violation of these regulations can result in lawsuits and fines. Therefore, managers should be aware of these restrictions to avoid legal problems. Some of the laws affecting human resources management are discussed here.

Because one law pervades all areas of human resources management, we'll take a quick look at it now. **Title VII of the Civil Rights Act** of 1964 prohibits discrimination in employment. It also created the Equal Employment Opportunity Commission (EEOC), a federal agency dedicated to increasing job opportunities for women and minorities and eliminating job discrimination based on race, religion, color, sex, national origin, or handicap. As a result of Title VII, employers must not impose sex distinctions in job specifications, job descriptions, or newspaper advertisements. In 2013, workplace discrimination charges filed with the EEOC were 93,727. The EEOC received more than 7,200 charges of sexual harassment. Sexual harassment often makes up the largest number of claims the EEOC encounters each day.[10] The Civil Rights Act of 1964 also outlaws the use of discriminatory tests for applicants. Aptitude tests and other indirect tests must be validated; in other words, employers must be able to demonstrate that scores on such tests are related to job performance, so that no one race has an advantage in taking the tests or is alternatively discriminated against. Although many hope for improvements in organizational diversity, only 4.4 percent of *Fortune* 500 companies are run by people of color. Despite the low

**Title VII of the Civil Rights Act**
prohibits discrimination in employment and created the Equal Employment Opportunity Commission

number, this is an improvement from the mid-1990s when no *Fortune* 500 company had a person of color as a CEO. Additionally, 13.3 percent of board seats are now held by racial minorities.[11]

Other laws affecting HRM include the Americans with Disabilities Act (ADA), which prevents discrimination against disabled persons. It also classifies people with AIDS as handicapped and, consequently, prohibits using a positive AIDS test as reason to deny an applicant employment. The Age Discrimination in Employment Act specifically outlaws discrimination based on age. Its focus is banning hiring practices that discriminate against people 40 years and older. Generally, when companies need employees, recruiters head to college campuses, and when downsizing is necessary, many older workers are offered early retirement. Forced retirement based on age, however, is generally considered to be illegal in the United States, although claims of forced retirement still abound. Until recently, employees in the United Kingdom could be forced to retire at age 65. However, a new law abolished the default retirement age.[12] Indeed there are

Title VII of the Civil Rights Act prohibits discrimination in employment. People who feel they have been discriminated against can file a formal complaint with the Equal Employment Opportunity Commission.

many benefits that companies are realizing in hiring older workers. Some of these benefits include the fact that they are more dedicated, punctual, honest, and detail-oriented; are good listeners; take pride in their work; exhibit good organizational skills; are efficient and confident; are mature; can be seen as role models; have good communication skills; and offer an opportunity for a reduced labor cost because of already having insurance plans.[13] Figure 10.2 shows the age ranges of employed workers in the United States.

The Equal Pay Act mandates that men and women who do equal work must receive the same wage. Wage differences are acceptable only if they are attributed to seniority, performance, or qualifications. In the United States, the typical full-time female employee earns 17.2 percent less than the average full-time employee.[14] In a study by PayScale, gender pay gaps can be found in positions such as chief executive (women earn 87 percent of what men earn), software architect (women earn 88 percent of what men earn), and executive chef (women earn 91 percent of what men earn).[15] Performance quality in these jobs is relatively subjective. Jobs like engineers, actuaries, or electricians, where the performance evaluation is more objective, result in greater salary parity between men and women.[16] However, despite the wage inequalities that still exist, women in the workplace are becoming increasingly accepted among both genders. The working mother is no longer a novelty; in fact, many working mothers seek the same amount of achievement as working men and women who are not mothers.

**FIGURE 10.2**
**U.S. Population Employed by Age Group (in thousands)**

Source: Bureau of Labor Statistics, labor force statistics from the *Current Population Survey,* www.bls.gov/cps/cpsaat03.pdf (accessed May 2, 2014).

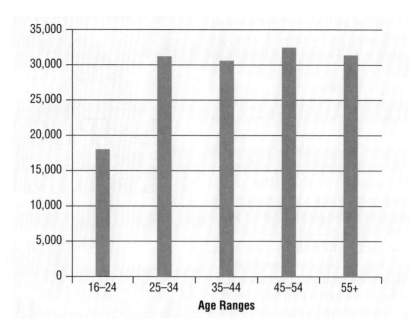

# Developing the Workforce

**orientation**
familiarizing newly hired employees with fellow workers, company procedures, and the physical properties of the company

Once the most qualified applicants have been selected, have been offered positions, and have accepted their offers, they must be formally introduced to the organization and trained so they can begin to be productive members of the workforce. **Orientation** familiarizes the newly hired employees with fellow workers, company procedures, and the physical properties of the company. It generally includes a tour of the building; introductions to supervisors, co-workers, and subordinates; and the distribution of organizational manuals describing the organization's policy on vacations, absenteeism, lunch breaks, company benefits, and so on. Orientation also involves socializing the new employee into the ethics and culture of the new company. Many larger companies now show videotapes of procedures, facilities, and key personnel in the organization to help speed the adjustment process.

## Training and Development

**training**
teaching employees to do specific job tasks through either classroom development or on-the-job experience

Although recruiting and selection are designed to find employees who have the knowledge, skills, and abilities the company needs, new employees still must undergo **training** to learn how to do their specific job tasks. *On-the-job training* allows workers to learn by actually performing the tasks of the job, while *classroom training* teaches employees with lectures, conferences, videotapes, case studies, and web-based training. For instance, McDonald's trains those interested in company operations and leadership development at the Fred L. Turner Training Center, otherwise known as Hamburger University. Hamburger University employs full-time professors to train students in a variety of topics, including crew development, restaurant management, middle management, and executive development. Training includes classroom instruction, hands-on instruction, and computer e-learning.[17] **Development** is training that augments the skills and knowledge of managers and professionals. Training and development are also used to improve the skills of employees in their present positions and to prepare them for increased responsibility and job promotions. Training

**development**
training that augments the skills and knowledge of managers and professionals

is therefore a vital function of human resources management. At the Container Store, for example, first-year sales personnel receive 263 hours of training about the company's products.[18] Companies are engaging in more experiential and involvement-oriented training exercises for employees. Use of role-plays, simulations, and online training methods are becoming increasingly popular in employee training.

## Assessing Performance

Assessing an employee's performance—his or her strengths and weaknesses on the job—is one of the most difficult tasks for managers. However, performance appraisal is crucial because it gives employees feedback on how they are doing and what they need to do to improve. It also provides a basis for determining how to compensate

McDonald's has expanded its famous Hamburger University into China. This branch of Hamburger University will train a new generation of Chinese students in such areas as restaurant management, leadership development, and other skills.

and reward employees, and it generates information about the quality of the firm's selection, training, and development activities. Table 10.5 identifies 16 characteristics that may be assessed in a performance review.

| |
| --- |
| • **Productivity**—rate at which work is regularly produced |
| • **Quality**—accuracy, professionalism, and deliverability of produced work |
| • **Job knowledge**—understanding of the objectives, practices, and standards of work |
| • **Problem solving**—ability to identify and correct problems effectively |
| • **Communication**—effectiveness in written and verbal exchanges |
| • **Initiative**—willingness to identify and address opportunities for improvement |
| • **Adaptability**—ability to become comfortable with change |
| • **Planning and organization skills**—reflected through the ability to schedule projects, set goals, and maintain organizational systems |
| • **Teamwork and cooperation**—effectiveness of collaborations with co-workers |
| • **Judgment**—ability to determine appropriate actions in a timely manner |
| • **Dependability**—responsiveness, reliability, and conscientiousness demonstrated on the job |
| • **Creativity**—extent to which resourceful ideas, solutions, and methods for task completion are proposed |
| • **Sales**—demonstrated through success in selling products, services, yourself, and your company |
| • **Customer service**—ability to communicate effectively with customers, address problems, and offer solutions that meet or exceed their expectations |
| • **Leadership**—tendency and ability to serve as a doer, guide, decision maker, and role model |
| • **Financial management**—appropriateness of cost controls and financial planning within the scope defined by the position |

**TABLE 10.5**
**Performance Characteristics**

Performance appraisals are important because they provide employees with feedback on how well they are doing as well as areas for improvement.

Performance appraisals may be objective or subjective. An objective assessment is quantifiable. For example, a Westinghouse employee might be judged by how many circuit boards he typically produces in one day or by how many of his boards have defects. A Century 21 real estate agent might be judged by the number of houses she has shown or the number of sales she has closed. A company can also use tests as an objective method of assessment. Whatever method they use, managers must take into account the work environment when they appraise performance objectively.

When jobs do not lend themselves to objective appraisal, the manager must relate the employee's performance to some other standard. One popular tool used in subjective assessment is the ranking system, which lists various performance factors on which the manager ranks employees against each other. Although used by many large companies, ranking systems are unpopular with many employees. Qualitative criteria, such as teamwork and communication skills, used to evaluate employees are generally hard to gauge. Such grading systems have triggered employee lawsuits that allege discrimination in grade/ranking assignments. For example, one manager may grade a company's employees one way, while another manager grades a group more harshly depending on the managers' grading style. If layoffs occur, then employees graded by the second manager may be more likely to lose their jobs. Other criticisms of grading systems include unclear wording or inappropriate words that a manager may unintentionally write in a performance evaluation, like *young* or *pretty* to describe an employee's appearance. These liabilities can all be fodder for lawsuits should employees allege that they were treated unfairly. It is therefore crucial that managers use clear language in performance evaluations and be consistent with all employees. Several employee grading computer packages have been developed to make performance evaluations easier for managers and clearer for employees.[19] Figure 10.3 demonstrates that employers are more likely to believe that performance reviews improve employee performance than employees do.

Another performance appraisal method used by many companies is the 360-degree feedback system, which provides feedback from a panel that typically includes superiors, peers, and subordinates. Because of the tensions it may cause, peer appraisal appears to be difficult for many. However, companies that have success with 360-degree feedback tend to be open to learning and willing to experiment and are led by executives who are direct about the expected benefits as well as the challenges.[20] Managers and leaders with a high emotional intelligence (sensitivity to their own as well as others' emotions) assess and reflect upon their interactions with colleagues on a daily basis. In addition,

**FIGURE 10.3**    **Performance Reviews: Those Who Believe Reviews Improve Employees' Performance**

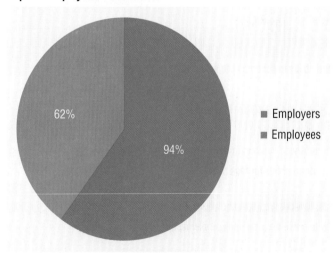

- Employers
- Employees

Robert Half survey of 1,400 chief financial officers and 422 workers, 2012. Survey developed by Accountemps.

Source: Accountemps, "Mixed Review for the Employee Review," July 12, 2012, http://accountemps.rhi.mediaroom.com/performance-review (accessed May 5, 2014).

they conduct follow-up analysis on their projects, asking the right questions and listening carefully to responses without getting defensive of their actions.[21]

Whether the assessment is objective or subjective, it is vital that the manager discuss the results with the employee, so that the employee knows how well he or she is doing the job. The results of a performance appraisal become useful only when they are communicated, tactfully, to the employee and presented as a tool to allow the employee to grow and improve in his or her position and beyond. Performance appraisals are also used to determine whether an employee should be promoted, transferred, or terminated from the organization.

## Turnover

**Turnover,** which occurs when employees quit or are fired and must be replaced by new employees, results in lost productivity from the vacancy, costs to recruit replacement employees, management time devoted to interviewing, training, and socialization expenses for new employees. However, some companies have created innovative solutions for reducing turnover. Accenture, a global management consulting firm, has 275,000 employees around the world who travel frequently. Because of the hectic pace of the job and constant traveling, the company has instituted a unique wellness program offered to its on-the-go employees to encourage them to take care of their health while getting their jobs done. This program is personalized to the lifestyles of the employees and offers health tips and exercises that are effective but not time consuming. Accenture employees have rated this program as fun and relevant to their lives, resulting in higher job satisfaction. Job satisfaction is one of the best ways of reducing turnover.[22] Part of the reason for turnover may be overworked employees as a result of downsizing and a lack of training and advancement opportunities.[23] Of course, turnover is not always an unhappy occasion when it takes the form of a promotion or transfer.

A **promotion** is an advancement to a higher-level job with increased authority, responsibility, and pay. In some companies and most labor unions, seniority—the length of time a person has been with the company or at a particular job classification—is the key issue in determining who should be promoted. Most managers base promotions on seniority only when they have candidates with equal qualifications: Managers prefer to base promotions on merit.

A **transfer** is a move to another job within the company at essentially the same level and wage. Transfers allow workers to obtain new skills or to find a new position within an organization when their old position has been eliminated because of automation or downsizing.

**Separations** occur when employees resign, retire, are terminated, or are laid off. Employees may be terminated, or fired, for poor performance, violation of work rules, absenteeism, and so on. Businesses have traditionally been able to fire employees *at will,* that is, for any reason other than for race, religion, sex, or age, or because an employee is a union organizer. However, recent legislation and court decisions now require that companies fire employees fairly, for just cause only. Managers must take care, then, to warn employees when their performance is unacceptable and may lead to dismissal, elevating the importance of performance evaluations. They should also document all problems and warnings in employees' work records. To avoid the possibility of lawsuits from individuals who may feel they

**turnover**
occurs when employees quit or are fired and must be replaced by new employees

 **LO 10-4**

**promotion**
an advancement to a higher-level job with increased authority, responsibility, and pay

**transfer**
a move to another job within the company at essentially the same level and wage

**separations**
employment changes involving resignation, retirement, termination, or layoff

Many companies in recent years are choosing to downsize by eliminating jobs. Reasons for downsizing might be due to financial constraints or the need to become more productive and competitive.

**TABLE 10.6**
**What You Should Not Do When You Are Terminated**

| |
|---|
| 1. Do not tell off your boss and co-workers, even if you think they deserve it. |
| 2. Do not damage company property or steal something. |
| 3. Do not forget to ask for a reference. |
| 4. Do not badmouth your employer or any of your co-workers to your replacement. |
| 5. Do not badmouth your employer to a prospective employer when you go on a job interview. |

*Source: Dawn Rosenberg McKay, "Five Things Not to Do When You Leave Your Job," http://careerplanning.about.com/od/jobseparation/a/leave_mistakes.htm (accessed April 13, 2011).*

have been fired unfairly, employers should provide clear, business-related reasons for any firing, supported by written documentation if possible. Employee disciplinary procedures should be carefully explained to all employees and should be set forth in employee handbooks. Table 10.6 illustrates what *not* to do when you are terminated.

Many companies have downsized in recent years, laying off tens of thousands of employees in their effort to become more productive and competitive. For example, Radio Shack had to lay off workers after it decided to close more than 1,000 stores in the United State. The electronics retailer suffered declining sales as consumers increasingly purchase such items online.[24] Layoffs are sometimes temporary; employees may be brought back when business conditions improve. When layoffs are to be permanent, employers often help employees find other jobs and may extend benefits while the employees search for new employment. Such actions help lessen the trauma of the layoffs. Fortunately, there are several business areas that are choosing not to downsize.

A well-organized human resources department strives to minimize losses due to separations and transfers because recruiting and training new employees is very expensive. Note that a high turnover rate in a company may signal problems with the selection and training process, the compensation program, or even the type of company. To help reduce turnover, companies have tried a number of strategies, including giving employees more interesting job responsibilities (job enrichment), allowing for increased job flexibility, and providing more employee benefits.

## Compensating the Workforce

People generally don't work for free, and how much they are paid for their work is a complicated issue. Also, designing a fair compensation plan is an important task because pay and benefits represent a substantial portion of an organization's expenses. Wages that are too high may result in the company's products being priced too high, making them uncompetitive in the market. Wages that are too low may damage employee morale and result in costly turnover. Remember that compensation is one of the hygiene factors identified by Herzberg.

Designing a fair compensation plan is a difficult task because it involves evaluating the relative worth of all jobs within the business while allowing for individual efforts. Compensation for a specific job is typically determined through a **wage/salary survey,** which tells the company how much compensation comparable firms are paying for specific jobs that the firms have in common. Compensation for individuals within a specific job category depends on both the compensation for that job and the individual's productivity. Therefore, two employees with identical jobs may not receive exactly the same pay because of individual differences in performance.

**wage/salary survey**
a study that tells a company how much compensation comparable firms are paying for specific jobs that the firms have in common

## Sustainability Job Opportunities

As businesses become more focused on their environmental impact, job opportunities in sustainability are increasing. These positions, while present in some small businesses, are more common in larger organizations that use a lot of energy and generally have a larger impact on the environment. They exist in both the public and private sectors. Because these positions are becoming more important, sometimes employees—if savvy and persuasive enough—can create a sustainability position or department within the companies at which they currently work.

Some positions in this field require strong leadership and communication skills over technical knowledge in sustainability practices. People in this area generally create an atmosphere of sustainability as an institutional goal, bring employees and departments together to define and meet short-term goals, ensure communication channels around sustainability are open, and compile sustainability reports.

Other positions require knowledge in life-cycle and supply chain operations and management. These people are generally inclined toward more quantitative responsibilities in engineering, finance, and technical project management and support the activities of energy systems and building maintenance requirements. Finally, sustainability positions can be found in planning and design. Employees in these positions engage in the development of transportation avenues, protection of forests and open spaces, and the incorporation of green attributes to new and existing structures.[25]

### Discussion Questions

1. Why are sustainability job opportunities increasing in the business field?
2. Why might a large organization want to adopt a sustainability position or department?
3. Describe the responsibilities for different jobs in sustainability.

## Financial Compensation

Financial compensation falls into two general categories—wages and salaries. **Wages** are financial rewards based on the number of hours the employee works or the level of output achieved. Wages based on the number of hours worked are called time wages. The federal minimum wage increased to $7.25 per hour in 2009 for covered nonexempt workers.[26] However, Congress is expected to vote on whether to increase the minimum wage to $10.10. If passed, the minimum wage would increase over the next few years. Many members of Congress want to increase the minimum wage to $15 per hour.[27] Tipped wages must be $2.13 per hour as long as tips plus the wage of $2.13 per hour equal the minimum wage of $7.25 per hour.[28] Many states also mandate minimum wages; in the case where the two wages are in conflict, the higher of the two wages prevails. There may even be differences between city and state minimum wages. In New Mexico, the minimum wage is $7.50, whereas in the state capitol of Santa Fe, the minimum wage is $10.66, due to a higher cost of living. When Santa Fe went to $10.66 per hour on March 1, 2014, this became the third highest minimum wage in the United States after Seattle-Tacoma, Washington, at $15 per hour and San Francisco at $10.74 per hour.[29] Table 10.7 compares wages and other information for Costco and Walmart, two well-known discount chains. Time wages are appropriate when employees are continually interrupted and when quality is more important than quantity. Assembly-line workers, clerks, and maintenance personnel are commonly paid on a time-wage basis. The advantage of time wages is the ease of computation. The disadvantage is that time wages provide no incentive to increase productivity. In fact, time wages may encourage employees to be less productive.

To overcome these disadvantages, many companies pay on an incentive system, using piece wages or commissions. Piece wages are based on the level of output achieved. A major advantage of piece wages is that they motivate employees to

**wages**
financial rewards based on the number of hours the employee works or the level of output achieved

**TABLE 10.7**
**Costco versus Walmart**

|  | Costco | Walmart |
|---|---|---|
| Number of employees | 185,000+ | 2,200,000 |
| Revenues | $99.1 billion | $469.2 billion |
| Average pay per hour | $21 | $12.83 |
| World's most admired ranking | 12 | 28 |
| Strengths | Management quality; financial soundness; people management | Management quality; financial soundness; global competitiveness |

Sources: "Fortune Global 500," CNN Money, 2014, http://money.cnn.com/magazines/fortune/global500/2013/full_list/?iid=G500_sp_full (accessed May 5, 2014); "Fortune World's Most Admired Rankings," CNN Money, 2014, http://money.cnn.com/magazines/fortune/most-admired/2014/list/?iid=wma14_sp_full (accessed May 5, 2014); Costco Wholesale, "Investor Relations," http://phx.corporate-ir.net/phoenix.zhtml?c=83830&p=irol-homeprofile (accessed May 5, 2014); Kevin Short, "11 Reasons to Love Costco That Have Nothing to Do with Shopping," Huffington Post, November 19, 2013, www.huffingtonpost.com/2013/11/19/reasons-love-costco_n_4275774.html (accessed May 5, 2014); "Wal-Mart," NY JobSource, January 26, 2014, http://nyjobsource.com/walmart.html (accessed May 5, 2014).

**commission**
an incentive system that pays a fixed amount or a percentage of the employee's sales

**salary**
a financial reward calculated on a weekly, monthly, or annual basis

**bonuses**
monetary rewards offered by companies for exceptional performance as incentives to further increase productivity

**profit sharing**
a form of compensation whereby a percentage of company profits is distributed to the employees whose work helped to generate them

supervise their own activities and to increase output. Skilled craftworkers are often paid on a piece-wage basis.

The other incentive system, **commission,** pays a fixed amount or a percentage of the employee's sales. Kele & Co Jewelers in Plainfield, Illinois, make sterling silver jewelry and offer semi-precious stones and gemstones at affordable prices. Their handcrafted jewelry is sold through the Internet (www.keleonline.com) and through independent sales representatives (ISRs) all over the country. The unique aspect of Kele's sales process is their innovative sales and commission structure. ISRs have no minimum sales quotas, sales are shared among team members during training and after being promoted, and there is no requirement to purchase inventory as jewelry is shipped from Kele headquarters. ISRs receive a 30 to 50 percent commission on sales. The goal is to increase the profit margin and earning potential of the salespeople. The company's goal is to become the largest direct sales company in the industry.[30] This method motivates employees to sell as much as they can. Some companies also combine payment based on commission with time wages or salaries.

A **salary** is a financial reward calculated on a weekly, monthly, or annual basis. Salaries are associated with white-collar workers such as office personnel, executives, and professional employees. Although a salary provides a stable stream of income, salaried workers may be required to work beyond usual hours without additional financial compensation.

In addition to the basic wages or salaries paid to employees, a company may offer **bonuses** for exceptional performance as an incentive to increase productivity further. Many workers receive a bonus as a "thank you" for good work and an incentive to continue working hard. Many owners and managers are recognizing that simple bonuses and perks foster happier employees and reduce turnover. Bonuses are especially popular among Wall Street firms. In 2014, Wall Street disbursed more than $26 billion in bonuses to more than 165,000 employees. This amount is 15 percent more than the year before and is the third largest bonus sum ever given out.[31]

Another form of compensation is **profit sharing,** which distributes a percentage of company profits to the employees whose work helped to generate those profits. Some profit-sharing plans involve distributing shares of company stock to employees.

Usually referred to as *ESOPs*—employee stock ownership plans—they have been gaining popularity in recent years. One reason for the popularity of ESOPs is the sense of partnership that they create between the organization and employees. Profit sharing can also motivate employees to work hard, because increased productivity and sales mean that the profits or the stock dividends will increase. Many organizations offer employees a stake in the company through stock purchase plans, ESOPs, or stock investments through 401(k) plans. Employees below senior management levels rarely received stock options until recently. Companies are adopting broad-based stock option plans to build a stronger link between employees' interests and the organization's interests. ESOPs have met with enormous success over the years, and employee-owned stock has even outperformed the stock market during certain periods. Many businesses have found employee stock options a great way to boost productivity and increase morale. As of 2014, there were nearly 12,000 ESOPs in the United States.[32]

## Benefits

**Benefits** are nonfinancial forms of compensation provided to employees, such as pension plans for retirement; health, disability, and life insurance; holidays and paid days off for vacation or illness; credit union membership; health programs; child care; elder care; assistance with adoption; and more. According to the Bureau of Labor Statistics, employer costs for employee compensation for civilian workers in the United States average $29.63 per hour worked. Wages and salaries account for approximately 70.1 percent of those costs, while benefits account for 29.9 percent of the cost. Legally required benefits (Social Security, Medicare, federal and state employment insurance, and workers' compensation) account for 8.2 percent of total compensation.[33] Such benefits increase employee security and, to a certain extent, their morale and motivation.

**benefits**
nonfinancial forms of compensation provided to employees, such as pension plans, health insurance, paid vacation and holidays, and the like

Table 10.8 lists some of the benefits Internet search engine Google offers its employees. Although health insurance is a common benefit for full-time employees, rising health care costs have forced a growing number of employers to trim this benefit. Even government workers, whose wages and benefits used to be virtually guaranteed safe, have seen reductions in health care and other benefits. Surveys have revealed that with the decrease in benefits comes a decrease in employee loyalty. Only 42 percent of employees say they feel a strong sense of loyalty to their employers. However, more than half of respondents indicated that employee benefits were important in decisions to stay with the company. Benefits are particularly important to younger generations of employees.[34] Starbucks recognizes the importance of how benefits can significantly impact an employee's health and well-being. As a result, it is the only fast-food company to offer its part-time employees health insurance.

A benefit increasingly offered is the employee assistance program (EAP). Each company's EAP is different, but most offer counseling for and assistance with those employees' personal problems that might hurt

An onsite fitness center is just one of the benefits that large companies have begun to offer employees. Such onsite benefits like fitness centers and child care are particularly important for employees who work long hours or who struggle to maintain a healthy work-life balance.

**TABLE 10.8**
**Google's Employees' Benefits**

| |
|---|
| • Health insurance: |
| – Employee medical insurance |
| – Dental insurance |
| – Vision insurance |
| • Vacation (15 days per year for one–three years' employment; 20 days off for four–five years' employment; 25 days for more than six years' employment) |
| • Twelve paid holidays/year |
| • Savings plans |
| – 401(k) retirement plan, matched by Google |
| – Flexible spending accounts |
| • Disability and life insurance |
| • Employee Assistance Program |
| • Free lunches and snacks |
| • Massages, gym membership, hair stylist, fitness class, and bike repair |
| • Weekly activities |
| • Maternity leave |
| • Adoption assistance |
| • Tuition reimbursement |
| • Employee referral plan |
| • Onsite doctor |
| • Backup child care |
| • Holiday parties, health fair, credit union, roller hockey, outdoor volleyball court, discounts for local attractions |

Source: "Google Benefits," www.google.com/about/careers/lifeatgoogle/benefits/ (accessed May 27, 2014).

their job performance if not addressed. The most common counseling services offered include drug- and alcohol-abuse treatment programs, fitness programs, smoking cessation clinics, stress-management clinics, financial counseling, family counseling, and career counseling. Lowe's, for example, offers work/life seminars, smoking cessation clinics, and other assistance programs for its employees.[35] EAPs help reduce costs associated with poor productivity, absenteeism, and other workplace issues by helping employees deal with personal problems that contribute to these issues. For example, exercise and fitness programs reduce health insurance costs by helping employees stay healthy. Family counseling may help workers trying to cope with a divorce or other personal problems to better focus on their jobs.

Companies try to provide the benefits they believe their employees want, but diverse people may want different things. In recent years, some single workers have felt that co-workers with spouses and children seem to get "special breaks" and extra time off to deal with family issues. Some companies use flexible benefit programs to allow employees to choose the benefits they would like, up to a specified amount.

### Urban Lending Solutions Hires Outside the Box

Urban Lending Solutions
    **Founders:** Charles and Elisa Sanders
    **Founded:** 2002, in Pittsburg, Pennsylvania
    **Success:** Urban Lending Solutions generated revenue of $183.1 million in 2012.

In 2002, former professional athlete Charles Sanders and his wife, Elisa, founded Urban Lending Solutions (ULS), a real estate company in Pittsburg, Pennsylvania. The real estate industry is highly competitive and especially vulnerable to changes in the market. Because of this volatility in the market, Charles Sanders, who serves as CEO, takes a different approach to hiring employees. While other real estate companies focus on hiring seasoned professionals, Sanders looks for intellect and ambition in potential hires regardless of their experience. He has hired people ranging from managers at fast-food restaurants to the newly graduated. As a result, ULS has grown to more than 1,500 employees, a 257 percent increase since 2009.

ULS believes in the importance of employee training. It established its training program, called Urban University, to offer 15 courses meant to teach new hires everything they need to know, while preparing them to become adaptable when market conditions change. ULS's training and hiring approach has allowed the company to expand its services across the nation, retain valuable employees, and successfully respond to the difficulties of the latest housing market crash.[36]

---

Fringe benefits include sick leave, vacation pay, pension plans, health plans, and any other extra compensation. Soft benefits include perks that help balance life and work. They include onsite child care, spas, food service, and even laundry services and hair salons. These soft benefits motivate employees and give them more time to focus on their job.

Cafeteria benefit plans provide a financial amount to employees so that they can select the specific benefits that fit their needs. The key is making benefits flexible, rather than giving employees identical benefits. As firms go global, the need for cafeteria or flexible benefit plans becomes even more important. For some employees, benefits are a greater motivator and differentiator in jobs than wages. For many Starbucks employees who receive health insurance when working part time, this benefit could be the most important compensation.

Over the past two decades, the list of fringe benefits has grown dramatically, and new benefits are being added every year.

## Managing Unionized Employees

Employees who are dissatisfied with their working conditions or compensation have to negotiate with management to bring about change. Dealing with management on an individual basis is not always effective, however, so employees may organize themselves into **labor unions** to deal with employers and to achieve better pay, hours, and working conditions. Organized employees are backed by the power of a large group that can hire specialists to represent the entire union in its dealings with management. Union workers make significantly more than nonunion employees. The United States has a roughly 11.3 percent unionization rate. Figure 10.4 displays unionization rates by state. On average, the median usual weekly earnings of unionized full-time and salary workers are about $200 more than their non-union counterparts.[37]

However, union growth has slowed in recent years, and prospects for growth do not look good. One reason is that most blue-collar workers, the traditional members

**labor unions**
employee organizations formed to deal with employers for achieving better pay, hours, and working conditions

**FIGURE 10.4**     **Union Membership Rates by State**

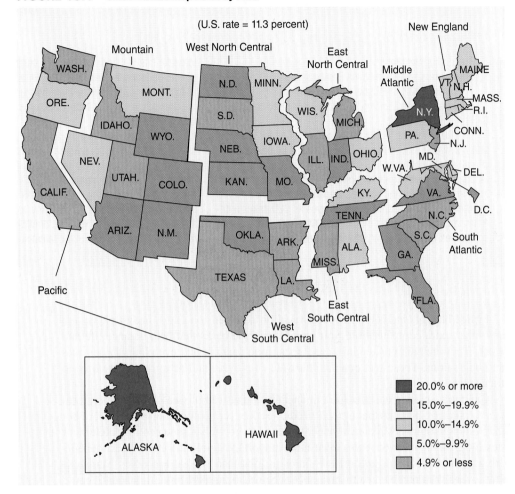

Source: Bureau of Labor Statistics, "Union Members—2013," January 24, 2014, www.bls.gov/news.release/pdf/union2.pdf (accessed May 7, 2014).

of unions, have already been organized. Factories have become more automated and need fewer blue-collar workers. The United States has shifted from a manufacturing to a service economy, further reducing the demand for blue-collar workers. Moreover, in response to foreign competition, U.S. companies are scrambling to find ways to become more productive and cost efficient. Job enrichment programs and participative management have blurred the line between management and workers. Because workers' say in the way plants are run is increasing, their need for union protection is decreasing.

Nonetheless, labor unions have been successful in organizing blue-collar manufacturing, government, and health care workers, as well as smaller percentages of employees in other industries. Consequently, significant aspects of HRM, particularly compensation, are dictated to a large degree by union contracts at many companies. Therefore, we'll take a brief look at collective bargaining and dispute resolution in this section.

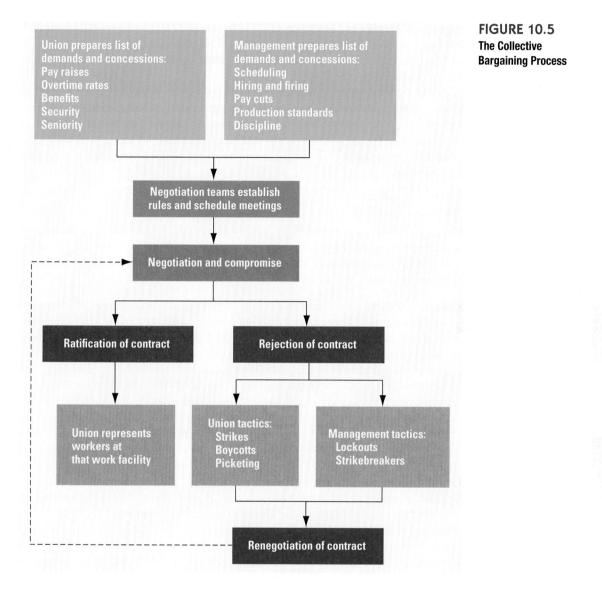

FIGURE 10.5
The Collective
Bargaining Process

## Collective Bargaining

**Collective bargaining** is the negotiation process through which management and unions reach an agreement about compensation, working hours, and working conditions for the bargaining unit (Figure 10.5). The objective of negotiations is to reach agreement about a **labor contract,** the formal, written document that spells out the relationship between the union and management for a specified period of time, usually two or three years.

In collective bargaining, each side tries to negotiate an agreement that meets its demands; compromise is frequently necessary. Management tries to negotiate a labor contract that permits the company to retain control over things like work schedules; the hiring and firing of workers; production standards; promotions, transfers, and separations; the span of management in each department; and discipline. Unions tend

**collective bargaining**
the negotiation process through which management and unions reach an agreement about compensation, working hours, and working conditions for the bargaining unit

**labor contract**
the formal, written document that spells out the relationship between the union and management for a specified period of time—usually two or three years

to focus on contract issues such as magnitude of wages; better pay rates for overtime, holidays, and undesirable shifts; scheduling of pay increases; and benefits. These issues will be spelled out in the labor contract, which union members will vote to either accept (and abide by) or reject.

Many labor contracts contain a *cost-of-living escalator* (or *adjustment*) *(COLA) clause,* which calls for automatic wage increases during periods of inflation to protect the "real" income of the employees. During tough economic times, unions may be forced to accept *givebacks*—wage and benefit concessions made to employers to allow them to remain competitive or, in some cases, to survive and continue to provide jobs for union workers.

## Resolving Disputes

Sometimes, management and labor simply cannot agree on a contract. Most labor disputes are handled through collective bargaining or through grievance procedures. When these processes break down, however, either side may resort to more drastic measures to achieve its objectives.

**picketing**
a public protest against management practices that involves union members marching and carrying antimanagement signs at the employer's plant or work site

**Labor Tactics.**    **Picketing** is a public protest against management practices and involves union members marching (often waving antimanagement signs and placards) at the employer's plant or work site. Picketing workers hope that their signs will arouse sympathy for their demands from the public and from other unions. Picketing may occur as a protest or in conjunction with a strike.

**strikes**
employee walkouts; one of the most effective weapons of labor unions

**Strikes** (employee walkouts) are one of the most effective weapons labor has. By striking, a union makes carrying out the normal operations of a business difficult at best and impossible at worst. Strikes receive widespread publicity, but they remain a weapon of last resort. However, in extreme cases, workers may organize a strike with the help of unions and coalitions to which they do not yet belong. Walmart employees, who are not unionized in the United States, held a series of strikes to voice concerns over low wages and poor working conditions. The situation escalated when the company fired 9 workers and disciplined 18 others after one of the protests. This led to the intervention of the U.S. Labor Board by filing a complaint alleging violations of labor laws. While it is mostly the case that the mere threat of a strike is enough to make management back down, there are times when the issues are heatedly debated and regulatory agencies become involved.[38]

**boycott**
an attempt to keep people from purchasing the products of a company

A **boycott** is an attempt to keep people from purchasing the products of a company. In a boycott, union members are asked not to do business with the boycotted organization. Some unions may even impose fines on members who ignore the boycott. To gain further support for their objectives, a union involved in a boycott may also ask the public—through picketing and advertising—not to purchase the products of the picketed firm.

**lockout**
management's version of a strike, wherein a work site is closed so that employees cannot go to work

**Management Tactics.**    Management's version of a strike is the **lockout;** management actually closes a work site so that employees cannot go to work. Lockouts are used, as a general rule, only when a union strike has partially shut down a plant and it seems less expensive for the plant to close completely. Kellogg locked out workers from its Memphis cereal plant for three months due to failure to reach a negotiating agreement on employees' wages and benefits. The situation escalated, with the company deciding to cut off the employees' health insurance for the duration of the strike.[39]

**Strikebreakers,** called "scabs" by striking union members, are people hired by management to replace striking employees. Managers hire strikebreakers to continue operations and reduce the losses associated with strikes—and to show the unions that they will not bow to their demands. Strikebreaking is generally a last-resort measure for management because it does great damage to the relationship between management and labor.

**strikebreakers**
people hired by management to replace striking employees; called "scabs" by striking union members

**Outside Resolution.**    Management and union members normally reach mutually agreeable decisions without outside assistance. Sometimes though, even after lengthy negotiations, strikes, lockouts, and other tactics, management and labor still cannot resolve a contract dispute. In such cases, they have three choices: conciliation, mediation, and arbitration. **Conciliation** brings in a neutral third party to keep labor and management talking. The conciliator has no formal power over union representatives or over management. The conciliator's goal is to get both parties to focus on the issues and to prevent negotiations from breaking down. Like conciliation, **mediation** involves bringing in a neutral third party, but the mediator's role is to suggest or propose a solution to the problem. The Association of Mineworkers and Construction Union (AMCU) and platinum workers had to meet with South African state mediators in order to resolve a $36 million per day dispute.[40] Mediators have no formal power over either labor or management. With **arbitration,** a neutral third party is brought in to settle the dispute, but the arbitrator's solution is legally binding and enforceable. Chevron won an arbitration case against the country of Ecuador regarding an ongoing 20-year dispute over pollution. The international arbitration panel ruled that the original case did not consider the fact that Ecuador had released the company from liability in the 1990s. Chevron was able to avoid a $19 billion penalty as a result.[41] Generally, arbitration takes place on a voluntary basis—management and labor must agree to it, and they usually split the cost (the arbitrator's fee and expenses) between them. Occasionally, management and labor submit to *compulsory arbitration,* in which an outside party (usually the federal government) requests arbitration as a means of eliminating a prolonged strike that threatens to disrupt the economy.

**conciliation**
a method of outside resolution of labor and management differences in which a third party is brought in to keep the two sides talking

**mediation**
a method of outside resolution of labor and management differences in which the third party's role is to suggest or propose a solution to the problem

**arbitration**
settlement of a labor/management dispute by a third party whose solution is legally binding and enforceable

# The Importance of Workforce Diversity

Customers, employees, suppliers—all the participants in the world of business—come in different ages, genders, races, ethnicities, nationalities, and abilities, a truth that business has come to label **diversity.** Understanding this diversity means recognizing and accepting differences as well as valuing the unique perspectives such differences can bring to the workplace.

**diversity**
the participation of different ages, genders, races, ethnicities, nationalities, and abilities in the workplace

## The Characteristics of Diversity

When managers speak of diverse workforces, they typically mean differences in gender and race. While gender and race are important characteristics of diversity, others are also important. We can divide these differences into primary and secondary characteristics of diversity. In the lower segment of Figure 10.6, age, gender, race, ethnicity, abilities, and sexual orientation represent *primary characteristics* of diversity that are inborn and cannot be changed. In the upper section of Figure 10.6 are eight *secondary characteristics* of diversity—work background, income, marital status, military experience, religious beliefs, geographic location, parental status, and education—which *can* be changed. We acquire, change, and discard them as we progress through our lives.

Need help understanding Mediation vs. Arbitration? Visit your Connect ebook video tab for a brief animated explanation.

**FIGURE 10.6**

**Characteristics of Diversity**

Source: Marilyn Loden and Judy B. Rosener, *Workforce America! Managing Employee Diversity as a Vital Resource*, 1991, p. 20. Used with permission. Copyright © 1991 The McGraw-Hill Companies.

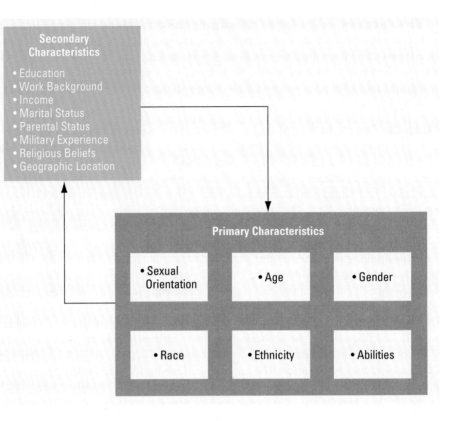

Defining characteristics of diversity as either primary or secondary enhances our understanding, but we must remember that each person is defined by the interrelation of all characteristics. In dealing with diversity in the workforce, managers must consider the complete person—not one or a few of a person's differences.

## Why Is Diversity Important?

The U.S. workforce is becoming increasingly diverse. Once dominated by white men, today's workforce includes significantly more women, African Americans, Hispanics, and other minorities, as well as disabled and older workers. The census bureau has predicted that by 2042, minorities will make up more than 50 percent of the U.S. population.[42] These groups have traditionally faced discrimination and higher unemployment rates and have been denied opportunities to assume leadership roles in corporate America. Consequently, more and more companies are trying to improve HRM programs to recruit, develop, and retain more diverse employees to better serve their diverse customers. Some firms are providing special programs such as sponsored affinity groups, mentoring programs, and special career

Some of the major benefits of diversity include a wider range of employee perspectives, greater innovaiton and creativity, and the ability to target a diverse customer base more effectively.

development opportunities. Kaiser Permanente has incorporated diversity into its goals and corporate strategies. More than half of the company's board of directors consists of minorities, while 60 percent are women. This level of diversity has earned Kaiser Permanente fourth place on Diversity Inc.'s Top 50 Companies for Diversity list.[43] Diversity and equal rights is so important to Kaiser Permanente that it has established the Institute for Culturally Competent Care and the nine Centers of Excellence to pave the way for equal health care for all, including minorities, immigrants, and those with disabilities.[44] Table 10.9 shows the top companies for minorities according to a study by DiversityInc. Effectively managing diversity in the workforce involves cultivating and valuing its benefits and minimizing its problems.

**TABLE 10.9**
**Top 50 Companies for Diversity**

| | |
|---|---|
| 1. Novartis Pharmaceuticals Corporation | 26. BASF |
| 2. Sodexo | 27. Eli Lilly and Company |
| 3. Ernst & Young | 28. Northrop Grumman |
| 4. Kaiser Permanente | 29. WellPoint |
| 5. PricewaterhouseCoopers | 30. Colgate-Palmolive |
| 6. MasterCard Worldwide | 31. Kellogg Company |
| 7. Procter & Gamble | 32. Dell |
| 8. Prudential Financial | 33. The Coca-Cola Company |
| 9. Johnson & Johnson | 34. The Walt Disney Company |
| 10. AT&T | 35. Kraft Foods Group |
| 11. Deloitte | 36. TIAA-CREF |
| 12. Accenture | 37. Allstate Insurance Company |
| 13. Abbott | 38. Toyota Motor North America |
| 14. Merck & Co | 39. Wyndham Worldwide |
| 15. Cummins | 40. Rockwell Collins |
| 16. Marriott International | 41. Medtronic |
| 17. Wells Fargo | 42. Time Warner |
| 18. Cox Communications | 43. Verizon Communications |
| 19. Aetna | 44. Comcast |
| 20. General Mills | 45. TD Bank |
| 21. KPMG | 46. Monsanto |
| 22. Target | 47. KeyCorp |
| 23. IBM | 48. JCPenney |
| 24. ADP | 49. AbbVie |
| 25. New York Life | 50. Nielsen |

Source: "The 2014 DiversityInc Top 50 Companies for Diversity," DiversityInc, 2014, www.diversityinc.com/the-diversityinc-top-50-companies-for-diversity-2014/ (accessed May 12, 2014).

## The Benefits of Workforce Diversity

There are a number of benefits to fostering and valuing workforce diversity, including the following:

1. More productive use of a company's human resources.
2. Reduced conflict among employees of different ethnicities, races, religions, and sexual orientations as they learn to respect each other's differences.
3. More productive working relationships among diverse employees as they learn more about and accept each other.
4. Increased commitment to and sharing of organizational goals among diverse employees at all organizational levels.
5. Increased innovation and creativity as diverse employees bring new, unique perspectives to decision-making and problem-solving tasks.
6. Increased ability to serve the needs of an increasingly diverse customer base.[45]

Companies that do not value their diverse employees are likely to experience greater conflict, as well as prejudice and discrimination. Among individual employees, for example, racial slurs and gestures, sexist comments, and other behaviors by co-workers harm the individuals at whom such behavior is directed. The victims of such behavior may feel hurt, depressed, or even threatened and suffer from lowered self-esteem, all of which harm their productivity and morale. In such cases, women and minority employees may simply leave the firm, wasting the time, money, and other resources spent on hiring and training them. When discrimination comes from a supervisor, employees may also fear for their jobs. A discriminatory atmosphere not only can harm productivity and increase turnover, but it may also subject a firm to costly lawsuits and negative publicity.

Astute businesses recognize that they need to modify their human resources management programs to target the needs of *all* their diverse employees as well as the needs of the firm itself. They realize that the benefits of diversity are long term in nature and come only to those organizations willing to make the commitment. Most importantly, as workforce diversity becomes a valued organizational asset, companies spend less time managing conflict and more time accomplishing tasks and satisfying customers, which is, after all, the purpose of business.

## Affirmative Action

**affirmative action programs**
legally mandated plans that try to increase job opportunities for minority groups by analyzing the current pool of workers, identifying areas where women and minorities are underrepresented, and establishing specific hiring and promotion goals, with target dates, for addressing the discrepancy

Many companies strive to improve their working environment through **affirmative action programs,** legally mandated plans that try to increase job opportunities for minority groups by analyzing the current pool of workers, identifying areas where women and minorities are underrepresented, and establishing specific hiring and promotion goals along with target dates for meeting those goals to resolve the discrepancy. Affirmative action began in 1965 as Lyndon B. Johnson issued the first of a series of presidential directives. It was designed to make up for past hiring and promotion prejudices, to overcome workplace discrimination, and to provide equal employment opportunities for blacks and whites. Since then, minorities have made solid gains.

Legislation passed in 1991 reinforces affirmative action but prohibits organizations from setting hiring quotas that might result in reverse discrimination. Reverse discrimination occurs when a company's policies force it to consider only minorities or women instead of concentrating on hiring the person who is best qualified. More companies are arguing that affirmative action stifles their ability to hire the best

### Employee Privacy or Employer Vulnerability: The Role of Social Media in the Financial Industry

Since the advent of social media in the workplace, many states have begun passing legislation to prevent employers from monitoring their employees' social media activities. This is done to protect employee privacy. However, the Financial Industry Regulatory Authority and Wall Street are asking regulators to make an exception for employees in the financial industry. Worries of insider trading, potential Ponzi schemes, and influencing stock activity on the market are at the heart of this request. For instance, one CFO was fired after venting on social media using confidential financial information. Such information could negatively affect the firm if released early.

Regulators allow financial firms to communicate information through social media outlets as long as they disclose to the investor where, when, and how they plan to divulge this information. This could lead employees to believe it is also all right to discuss nonpublic information on social media. Financial firms are concerned that by protecting employee's privacy on social media, they become vulnerable to potential scandals involving the misappropriation of financial information, which could harm investors. While the requested amendment to the privacy laws will only be put to use if an employee is suspected of releasing unwarranted information, critics believe that such an exception will erode employee privacy altogether.[46]

#### Discussion Questions

1. What are advantages of laws forbidding employers from accessing employees' social media activities?
2. What are disadvantages of laws forbidding employers from accessing employees' social media activities?
3. Is there anything firms can do to keep employees from releasing nonpublic information over social media without infringing on their privacy?

---

employees, regardless of their minority status. Because of these problems, affirmative action became politically questionable.

## Trends in Management of the Workforce

As unemployment reached 10 percent during the last recession, businesses laid off almost 9 million employees. Even after the recession and financial crisis, many firms reduced hiring and pushed workers to spend more time on the job for the same or less pay. Because of the economic uncertainty, this post-recession austerity has pervaded the workplace and inflated U.S. productivity. While companies are squeezing workers to cut costs, they are also drawing clear lines between workers and managers and are reducing privileges and benefits.

Many employees are developing grievances, claiming that they are being overworked. The number of lawsuits filed by employees against their employers continues to rise. Many of the claims include working overtime without being appropriately compensated, being overworked to the point of physical injury, and not being compensated for time waiting for company mandated security checks.[47]

The nature of the workplace is changing as well. The increasing use of smart phones and tablet computers are blurring the lines between leisure and work time, with some employers calling employees after hours.[48] Employees themselves are mixing work and personal time by using social media in the office. In fact, theft of time is a major form of misconduct in the workplace. This is requiring companies to come up with new policies that limit how employees can use social media in the workplace. Clearly, technology is changing the dynamics of the workplace in both positive and negative ways.

It is important for human resources managers to be aware of legal issues regarding worker rights. Strict criteria—such as having management responsibilities, having advanced degrees, or making more than $455 a week—determine whether an employee is exempt from overtime pay.[49] Interestingly, although it might currently be legal for employers to request an applicant's Facebook password, employees who "rant" about their employers on Facebook can receive some form of legal protection. Under the National Labor Relations Act of 1935, certain private-sector employees are allowed to complain about working conditions and pay—which seems to apply to social media sites as well. Threats, on the other hand, are not protected.[50] Hence, human resources managers should understand these issues to ensure that an employee is not wrongfully terminated.

Despite the grim outlook of the past few years, hiring trends appear to be on the rise. Companies are finding that as consumer demands rise, their current employees are hitting the limits of productivity, requiring firms to hire more workers.[51] This will require firms to not only know about relevant employee laws, but also to understand how benefits and employee morale can contribute to overall productivity. Many of the most successful firms have discovered ways to balance costs with the well-being of their employees.

Managing human resources is a challenging and creative facet of a business. It is the department that handles the recruiting, hiring, training, and firing of employees. Because of the diligence and detail required in hiring and the sensitivity required in firing, human resources managers have a broad skill set. Human resources, therefore, is vital to the overall functioning of the business because without the right staff a firm will not be able to effectively carry out its plans. Like in basketball, a team is only as strong as its individual players, and those players must be able to work together and to enhance strengths and downplay weaknesses. In addition, a good human resources manager can anticipate upcoming needs and changes in the business, hiring in line with the dynamics of the market and organization.

Once a good workforce is in place, human resources managers must ensure that employees are properly trained and oriented and that they clearly understand some elements of what the organization expects. Hiring new people is expensive, time consuming, and turbulent; thus, it is imperative that all employees are carefully selected, trained, and motivated so that they will remain committed and loyal to the company. This is not an easy task, but it is one of the responsibilities of the human resources manager. Because even with references, a résumé, background checks, and an interview, it can be hard to tell how a person will fit in the organization—the HR manager needs to have skills to be able to anticipate how every individual will "fit in." Human resources jobs include compensation, labor relations, benefits, training, ethics, and compliance managers. All of the tasks associated with the interface with hiring, developing, and maintaining employee motivation come into play in human resources management. Jobs are diverse and salaries will depend on responsibilities, education, and experience.

One of the major considerations for an HR manager is workforce diversity. A multicultural, multiethnic workforce consisting of men and women will help to bring a variety of viewpoints and improve the quality and creativity of organizational decision making. Diversity is an asset and can help a company from having blindspots or harmony in thought, background, and perspective, which stifles good team decisions. However, a diverse workforce can present some management challenges. Human resources management is often responsible for managing diversity training and compliance to make sure employees do not violate the ethical culture of the organization or break the law. Different people have different goals, motivations, and ways of thinking about issues that are informed by their culture, religion, and the people closest to them. No one way of thinking is more right or more wrong than others, and they are all valuable. A human resources manager's job can become very complicated, however, because of diversity. To be good at human resources, you should be aware of the value of differences, strive to be culturally sensitive, and ideally should have a strong understanding and appreciation of different cultures and religions. Human resources managers' ability to manage diversity and those differences will affect their overall career success.

## ⊖ Review Your Understanding

### Define human resources management, and explain its significance.

Human resources, or personnel, management refers to all the activities involved in determining an organization's human resources needs and acquiring, training, and compensating people to fill those needs. It is concerned with maximizing the satisfaction of employees and improving their efficiency to meet organizational objectives.

### Summarize the processes of recruiting and selecting human resources for a company.

First, the human resources manager must determine the firm's future human resources needs and develop a strategy to meet them. Recruiting is the formation of a pool of qualified applicants from which management will select employees; it takes place both internally and externally. Selection is the process of collecting information about applicants and using that information to decide which ones to hire; it includes the application, interviewing, testing, and reference checking.

### Discuss how workers are trained and their performance appraised.

Training teaches employees how to do their specific job tasks; development is training that augments the skills and knowledge of managers and professionals, as well as current employees. Appraising performance involves identifying an employee's strengths and weaknesses on the job. Performance appraisals may be subjective or objective.

### Identify the types of turnover companies may experience, and explain why turnover is an important issue.

A promotion is an advancement to a higher-level job with increased authority, responsibility, and pay. A transfer is a move to another job within the company at essentially the same level and wage. Separations occur when employees resign, retire, are terminated, or are laid off. Turnovers due to separation are expensive because of the time, money, and effort required to select, train, and manage new employees.

## Specify the various ways a worker may be compensated.

Wages are financial compensation based on the number of hours worked (time wages) or the number of units produced (piece wages). Commissions are a fixed amount or a percentage of a sale paid as compensation. Salaries are compensation calculated on a weekly, monthly, or annual basis, regardless of the number of hours worked or the number of items produced. Bonuses and profit sharing are types of financial incentives. Benefits are nonfinancial forms of compensation, such as vacation, insurance, and sick leave.

## Discuss some of the issues associated with unionized employees, including collective bargaining and dispute resolution.

Collective bargaining is the negotiation process through which management and unions reach an agreement on a labor contract—the formal, written document that spells out the relationship written between the union and management. If labor and management cannot agree on a contract, labor union members may picket, strike, or boycott the firm, while management may lock out striking employees, hire strikebreakers, or form employers' associations. In a deadlock, labor disputes may be resolved by a third party—a conciliator, mediator, or arbitrator.

## Describe the importance of diversity in the workforce.

When companies value and effectively manage their diverse workforces, they experience more productive use of human resources, reduced conflict, better work relationships among workers, increased commitment to and sharing of organizational goals, increased innovation and creativity, and enhanced ability to serve diverse customers.

## Assess an organization's efforts to reduce its workforce size and manage the resulting effects.

Based on the material in this chapter, you should be able to answer the questions posed in "Solve the Dilemma" on page 319 and evaluate the company's efforts to manage the human consequences of its downsizing.

# Revisit the World of Business

1. Describe Cirque du Soleil's recruitment and interview process.

2. Why is creativity of new hires important to Cirque du Soleil?

3. What are some of the difficulties in hiring such a diverse group of performers?

# Learn the Terms

# Check Your Progress

1. Distinguish among job analysis, job descriptions, and job specifications. How do they relate to planning in human resources management?

2. What activities are involved in acquiring and maintaining the appropriate level of qualified human resources? Name the stages of the selection process.

3. What are the two types of training programs? Relate training to kinds of jobs.

4. What is the significance of performance appraisal? How do managers appraise employees?

5. Why does turnover occur? List the types of turnover. Why do businesses want to reduce turnover due to separations?

6. Relate wages, salaries, bonuses, and benefits to Herzberg's distinction between hygiene and motivation factors. How does the form of compensation relate to the type of job?

7. What is the role of benefits? Name some examples of benefits.

8. Describe the negotiation process through which management and unions reach an agreement on a contract.

9. Besides collective bargaining and the grievance procedures, what other alternatives are available to labor and management to handle labor disputes?

10. What are the benefits associated with a diverse workforce?

# Get Involved

1. Although many companies screen applicants and test employees for illegal drug use, such testing is somewhat controversial. Find some companies in your community that test applicants and/or employees for drugs. Why do they have such a policy? How do the employees feel about it? Using this information, debate the pros and cons of drug testing in the workplace.

2. If collective bargaining and the grievance procedures have not been able to settle a current labor dispute, what tactics would you and other employees adopt? Which tactics would be best for which situations? Give examples.

3. Find some examples of companies that value their diverse workforces, perhaps some of the companies mentioned in the chapter. In what ways have these firms derived benefits from promoting cultural diversity? How have they dealt with the problems associated with cultural diversity?

# Build Your Skills

## Appreciating and Valuing Diversity

### Background

Here's a quick self-assessment to get you to think about diversity issues and evaluate the behaviors you exhibit that reflect your level of appreciation of other cultures:

| Do you . . . | Regularly | Sometimes | Never |
|---|---|---|---|
| 1. Make a conscious effort not to think stereotypically? | | | |
| 2. Listen with interest to the ideas of people who don't think like you do? | | | |
| 3. Respect other people's opinions, even when you disagree? | | | |
| 4. Spend time with friends who are not your age, race, gender, or the same economic status and education? | | | |

*continued*

| Do you . . . | Regularly | Sometimes | Never |
|---|---|---|---|
| 5.  Believe your way is *not* the only way? | | | |
| 6.  Adapt well to change and new situations? | | | |
| 7.  Enjoy traveling, seeing new places, eating different foods, and experiencing other cultures? | | | |
| 8.  Try not to offend or hurt others? | | | |
| 9.  Allow extra time to communicate with someone whose first language is not yours? | | | |
| 10. Consider the effect of cultural differences on the messages you send and adjust them accordingly? | | | |

Scoring

Number of **Regularly** checks     \_\_\_\_\_  multiplied by 5 = \_\_\_\_\_
Number of **Sometimes** checks     \_\_\_\_\_  multiplied by 3 = \_\_\_\_\_
Number of **Never** checks         \_\_\_\_\_  multiplied by 0 = \_\_\_\_\_
                                            TOTAL \_\_\_\_\_

Indications from score

40–50     You appear to understand the importance of valuing diversity and exhibit behaviors that support your appreciation of diversity.

6–39      You appear to have a basic understanding of the importance of valuing diversity and exhibit some behaviors that support that understanding.

13–5      You appear to lack a thorough understanding of the importance of valuing diversity and exhibit only some behaviors related to valuing diversity.

0–1       You appear to lack an understanding of valuing diversity and exhibit few, if any, behaviors of an individual who appreciates and values diversity.

Task

In a small group or class discussion, share the results of your assessment. After reading the following list of ways you can increase your knowledge and understanding of other cultures, select one of the items that you have done and share how it helped you learn more about another culture. Finish your discussion by generating your own ideas on other ways you can learn about and understand other cultures and fill in those ideas on the blank lines on page 319.

- Be alert to and take advantage of opportunities to talk to and get to know people from other races and ethnic groups. You can find them in your neighborhood, in your classes, at your fitness center, at a concert or sporting event—just about anywhere you go. Take the initiative to strike up a conversation and show a genuine interest in getting to know the other person.

- Select a culture you're interested in and immerse yourself in that culture. Read novels, look at art, take courses, see plays.

- College students often have unique opportunities to travel inexpensively to other countries—for example, as a member of a performing arts group, with a humanitarian mission group, or as part of a college course studying abroad. Actively seek out travel opportunities that will expose you to as many cultures as possible during your college education.

- Study a foreign language.

- Expand your taste buds. The next time you're going to go to a restaurant, instead of choosing that old familiar favorite, find a restaurant that serves ethnic food you've never tried before.

- Many large metropolitan cities sponsor ethnic festivals, particularly in the summertime, where you can go and take in the sights and sounds of other cultures. Take advantage of these opportunities to have a fun time learning about cultures that are different from yours.

- _____
  _____

- _____
  _____

## Solve the Dilemma — LO 10-8

### Morale among the Survivors

Medallion Corporation manufactures quality carpeting and linoleum for homes throughout the United States. A recession and subsequent downturn in home sales has sharply cut the company's sales. Medallion found itself in the unenviable position of having to lay off hundreds of employees in the home office (the manufacturing facilities) as well as many salespeople. Employees were called in on Friday afternoon and told about their status in individual meetings with their supervisors. The laid-off employees were given one additional month of work and a month of severance pay, along with the opportunity to sign up for classes to help with the transition, including job search tactics and résumé writing.

Several months after the cutbacks, morale was at an all-time low for the company, although productivity had improved. Medallion brought in consultants, who suggested that the leaner, flatter organizational structure would be suitable for more team activities. Medallion therefore set up task forces and teams to deal with employee concerns, but the diversity of the workforce led to conflict and misunderstandings among team members. Medallion is evaluating how to proceed with this new team approach.

#### Discussion Questions

1.  What did Medallion's HRM department do right in dealing with the employees who were laid off?

2.  What are some of the potential problems that must be dealt with after an organization experiences a major trauma such as massive layoffs?

3.  What can Medallion do to make the team approach work more smoothly? What role do you think diversity training should play?

## Build Your Business Plan

### Managing Human Resources

Now is the time to start thinking about the employees you will need to hire to implement your business plan. What kinds of background/skills are you going to look for in potential employees? Are you going to require a certain amount of work experience?

When you are starting a business, you are often only able to hire part-time employees because you cannot afford to pay the benefits for a full-time employee. Remember at the end of the last chapter we discussed how important it is to think of ways to motivate your employees when you cannot afford to pay them what you would like.

You need to consider how you are going to recruit your employees. When you are first starting your business, it is often a good idea to ask people you respect (and not necessarily members of your family) for any recommendations of potential employees they might have. You probably won't be able to afford to advertise in the classifieds, so announcements in sources such as church bulletins or community bulletin boards should be considered as an excellent way to attract potential candidates with little, if any, investment.

Finally, you need to think about hiring employees from diverse backgrounds, especially if you are considering targeting diverse segments. The more diverse your employees, the greater the chance you will be able to draw in diverse customers.

# See for Yourself Videocase

## The Importance of Hollywood Labor Unions

 You might be familiar with unions for teachers or autoworkers. But what about unions for actors, radio artists, and screenwriters? Because we tend to view Hollywood as a glamorous place, we are tempted to view unions as unnecessary for these types of professions. Yet Hollywood unions were, and continue to be, important players in the careers of Hollywood artists.

When actors first became mainstream in the early 20th century, working conditions for the industry included long work weeks and low pay. Studios essentially "owned" their artists, which meant that rival studios would not hire actors or actresses once their contracts ended. Actors were forced to work for the same studio to advance their careers. Negotiations with studios often proved fruitless.

Because strikes can be so disruptive and risky, they are often used as a last resort. Yet, in 1919 the Actors' Equity Association, a union for theatrical performers, and the American Federation of Labor staged a Broadway strike to protest harsh working conditions. The strike resulted in a five-year contract and promises to improve labor conditions. Although the event happened off Broadway and not in Hollywood, it would inspire other artists to begin forming their own unions.

Working conditions might have improved somewhat for theatrical actors, but radio artists, film actors, and screenwriters still had to bear with hard conditions. For instance, radio artists might do an entire show and then receive only a dollar. Film actors would work around the clock with few (if any) breaks. Screenwriters experienced salary cuts. As individuals, these artists did not have much bargaining power with studios. Realizing that banding together could improve conditions, the Masquers Club (later the Screen Actors Guild of America) was created in 1925. It was followed by the Screenwriters Guild (later renamed the Writers Guild of America) in 1933 and the American Federation of Radio Artists in 1937.

It would take lawsuits, strikes, and hardline negotiations for Hollywood artists to receive more rights. This often required artists to take risks such as suspensions or firings in the hope of better treatment. In 1988, the Writers Guild of America organized the longest strike in Hollywood history after disagreements with producers over payments and creative rights. The strike, which lasted five months, was estimated to cost the industry $500 million.

Now that working conditions seem to have improved, it might be tempting to discard Hollywood unions as no longer useful. Yet, even today, conflicts often occur between artists and studios. For instance, the Screen Actors Guild of America (SAG) watches to make sure that low-budget actors know their rights and are not exploited by producers. Unequal treatment still happens in the entertainment industry. For instance, minorities and female actors/actresses still tend to be paid less than Caucasian and male actors. The introduction of new media venues, particularly the Internet, may also warrant additional negotiations.

To address these challenges, many unions are banding together to address mutual concerns in the industry. In 2012, SAG united with the American Federation of Television and Radio Artists (AFTRA). This increases the bargaining power of the combined union. Additionally, Hollywood unions work closely with the American Federation of Labor and Congress of Industrial Organizations (AFL-CIO), which represents a federation of labor unions. The merger between SAG and AFTRA creates solidarity in the industry's unions through the formation of an Industry Coordinating Committee. This allows for coordination of activity among 10 or 12 major unions within the industry.

Although these unions are for movie stars and other artists, the goal is much the same as for other unions across the nation. As the industry expands, Hollywood unions feel that they must work together to secure benefits for their members while striving to arrive at mutually beneficial agreements with studios, producers, and other stakeholders in the entertainment industry.[52]

### Discussion Questions

1. Why are Hollywood labor unions considered necessary?

2. Why is striking often avoided if possible?

3. Why do you think unions in the entertainment industry are banding together?

**You can find the related video in the Video Library in Connect. Ask your instructor how you can access Connect.**

# Team Exercise

Form groups and go to monster.com and look up job descriptions for positions in business (account executive in advertising, marketing manager, human resource director, production supervisor, financial analyst, bank teller, etc.). What are the key requirements for the position that you have been assigned (education, work experience, language/computer skills, etc.)? Does the position announcement provide a thorough understanding of the job? Was any key information that you would have expected omitted? Report your findings to the class.

# Appendix C

# Personal Career Plan

The tools and techniques used in creating a business plan are just as useful in designing a plan to help sell yourself to potential employers. The outline in this appendix is designed to assist you in writing a personalized plan that will help you achieve your career goals. While this outline follows the same general format found in Appendix A, it has been adapted to be more relevant to career planning. Answering the questions presented in this outline will enable you to:

1. Organize and structure the data and information you collect about job prospects, the overall job market, and your competition.
2. Use this information to better understand your own personal strengths and weaknesses, as well as recognize the opportunities and threats that exist in your career development.
3. Develop goals and objectives that will capitalize on your strengths.
4. Develop a personalized strategy that will give you a competitive advantage.
5. Outline a plan for implementing your personalized strategy.

As you work through the following outline, it is very important that you be honest with yourself. If you do not possess a strength in a given area, it is important to recognize that fact. Similarly, do not overlook your weaknesses. The viability of your SWOT analysis and your strategy depend on how well you have identified all of the relevant issues in an honest manner.

## I. Summary
If you choose to write a summary, do so after you have written the entire plan. It should provide a brief overview of the strategy for your career. State your career objectives and what means you will use to achieve those objectives.

## II. Situation Analysis
### A. The External Environment
#### 1. Competition
a. Who are your major competitors? What are their characteristics

(number and growth in the number of graduates, skills, target employers)? Competitors to consider include peers at the same college or in the same degree field, peers at different colleges or in different degree fields, and graduates of trade, technical, or community colleges.
b. What are the key strengths and weaknesses of the total pool of potential employees (or recent college graduates)?
c. What are other college graduates doing in terms of developing skills, networking, showing a willingness to relocate, and promoting themselves to potential employers?
d. What are the current trends in terms of work experience versus getting an advanced degree?
e. Is your competitive set likely to change in the future? If so, how? Who are these new competitors likely to be?

#### 2. Economic conditions
a. What are the general economic conditions of the country, region, state, and local area in which you live or in which you want to relocate?
b. Overall, are potential employers optimistic or pessimistic about the economy?
c. What is the overall outlook for major job/career categories? Where do potential employers seem to be placing their recruitment and hiring emphasis?
d. What is the trend in terms of starting salaries for major job/career categories?

**3. Political trends**

    **a.** Have recent elections changed the political landscape so that certain industries or companies are now more or less attractive as potential employers?

**4. Legal and regulatory factors**

    **a.** What changes in international, federal, state, or local laws and regulations are being proposed that would affect your job/career prospects?

    **b.** Have recent court decisions made it easier or harder for you to find employment?

    **c.** Have global trade agreements changed in any way that makes certain industries or companies more or less attractive as potential employers?

**5. Changes in technology**

    **a.** What impact has changing technology had on potential employers in terms of their need for employees?

    **b.** What technological changes will affect the way you will have to work and compete for employment in the future?

    **c.** What technological changes will affect the way you market your skills and abilities to potential employers?

    **d.** How do technological advances threaten to make your skills and abilities obsolete?

**6. Cultural trends**

    **a.** How are society's demographics and values changing? What effect will these changes have on your:

        (1) Skills and abilities:

        (2) Career/lifestyle choices:

        (3) Ability to market yourself:

        (4) Willingness to relocate:

        (5) Required minimum salary:

    **b.** What problems or opportunities are being created by changes in the cultural diversity of the labor pool and the requirements of potential employers?

    **c.** What is the general attitude of society regarding the particular skills, abilities, and talents that you possess and the career/lifestyle choices that you have made?

**B. The Employer Environment**

**1. Who are your potential employers?**

    **a.** Identify characteristics: industry, products, size, growth, profitability, hiring practices, union/nonunion, employee needs, etc.

    **b.** Geographic characteristics: home office, local offices, global sites, expansion, etc.

    **c.** Organizational culture: mission statement, values, priorities, employee training, etc.

    **d.** In each organization, who is responsible for recruiting and selecting new employees?

**2. What do your potential employers look for in new employees?**

    **a.** What are the basic or specific skills and abilities that employers are looking for in new employees?

    **b.** What are the basic or specific needs that are fulfilled by the skills and abilities that you *currently* possess and that other potential employees currently possess?

    **c.** How well do your skills and abilities (and those of your competitors) currently meet the needs of potential employers?

    **d.** How are the needs of potential employers expected to change in the future?

**3. What are the recent hiring practices of your potential employers?**

    **a.** How many employees are being hired? What combination of skills and abilities do these new hires possess?

    **b.** Is the growth or decline in hiring related to the recent expansion or downsizing of markets and/or territories? Changes in technology?

    **c.** Are there major hiring differences between large and small companies? If so, why?

4. **Where and how do your potential employers recruit new employees?**

   a. Where do employers make contact with potential employees?
      (1) College placement offices:
      (2) Job/career fairs:
      (3) Internship programs:
      (4) Headhunting firms:
      (5) Unsolicited applications:
      (6) The Internet:
   b. Do potential employers place a premium on experience or are they willing to hire new graduates without experience?

5. **When do your potential employers recruit new employees?**

   a. Does recruiting follow a seasonal pattern or do employers recruit new employees on an ongoing basis?

C. **Personal Assessment**

1. **Review of personal goals, objectives, and performance**

   a. What are your personal goals and objectives in terms of employment, career, lifestyle, geographic preferences, etc.?
   b. Are your personal goals and objectives consistent with the realities of the labor market? Why or why not?
   c. Are your personal goals and objectives consistent with recent changes in the external or employer environments? Why or why not?
   d. How are your current strategies for success working in areas such as course performance, internships, networking, job leads, career development, interviewing skills, etc.?
   e. How does your current performance compare to that of your peers (competitors)? Are they performing well in terms of course performance, internships, networking, job leads, career development, interviewing skills, etc.?

   f. If your performance is improving, what actions can you take to ensure that your performance continues in this direction?

2. **Inventory of personal skills and resources**

   a. What do you consider to be your marketable skills? This list should be as comprehensive as possible and include areas such as interpersonal skills, organizational skills, technological skills, communication skills (oral and written), networking/teambuilding skills, etc.
   b. Considering the current and future needs of your potential employers, what important skills are you lacking?
   c. Other than personal skills, what do you consider to be your other career-enhancing resources? This list should be as comprehensive as possible and include areas such as financial resources (to pay for additional training, if necessary), personal contacts or "connections" with individuals who can assist your career development, specific degrees or certificates you hold, and intangible resources (family name, prestige of your educational institution, etc.).
   d. Considering the current and future needs of your potential employers, what important resources are you lacking?

III. **SWOT Analysis (your personal strengths and weaknesses and the opportunities and threats that may impact your career)**

   A. **Personal Strengths**

   1. Three key strengths
      a. Strength 1:
      b. Strength 2:
      c. Strength 3:
   2. How do these strengths allow you to meet the needs of your potential employers?
   3. How do these strengths compare to those of your peers/competitors? Do these strengths give you an advantage relative to your peers/competitors?

**B. Personal Weaknesses**

    **1.** Three key weaknesses

        **a.** Weakness 1:

        **b.** Weakness 2:

        **c.** Weakness 3:

    **2.** How do these weaknesses cause you to fall short of meeting the needs of your potential employers?

    **3.** How do these weaknesses compare to those of your peers/competitors? Do these weaknesses put you at a disadvantage relative to your peers/competitors?

**C. Career Opportunities**

    **1.** Three key career opportunities

        **a.** Opportunity 1:

        **b.** Opportunity 2:

        **c.** Opportunity 3:

    **2.** How are these opportunities related to serving the needs of your potential employers?

    **3.** What actions must be taken to capitalize on these opportunities in the short term? In the long term?

**D. Career Threats**

    **1.** Three key career threats

        **a.** Threat 1:

        **b.** Threat 2:

        **c.** Threat 3:

    **2.** How are these threats related to serving the needs of your potential employers?

    **3.** What actions must be taken to prevent these threats from limiting your capabilities in the short term? In the long term?

**E. The SWOT Matrix**

**F. Matching, Converting, Minimizing, and Avoiding Strategies**

    **1.** How can you match your strengths to your opportunities to better serve the needs of your potential employers?

    **2.** How can you convert your weaknesses into strengths?

    **3.** How can you convert your threats into opportunities?

    **4.** How can you minimize or avoid those weaknesses and threats that cannot be converted successfully?

**IV. Resources**

    **A. Financial**

        **1.** Do you have the financial resources necessary to undertake and successfully complete this plan (that is, preparation/ duplication/mailing of a résumé; interviewing costs, including proper attire; etc.)?

    **B. Human**

        **1.** Is the industry in which you are interested currently hiring? Are companies in your area currently hiring?

    **C. Experience and Expertise**

        **1.** Do you have experience from either part-time or summer employment that could prove useful in your current plan?

        **2.** Do you have the required expertise or skills to qualify for a job in your desired field? If not, do you have the resources to obtain them?

**V. Strategies**

    **A. Objective(s)**

        **1.** Potential employer A:

            **a.** Descriptive characteristics:

            **b.** Geographic locations:

            **c.** Culture/values/mission:

            **d.** Basic employee needs:

            **e.** Recruiting/hiring practices:

            **f.** Employee training/compensation practices:

            **g.** Justification for selection:

        **2.** Potential employer B:

            **a.** Descriptive characteristics:

            **b.** Geographic locations:

            **c.** Culture/values/mission:

            **d.** Basic employee needs:

            **e.** Recruiting/hiring practices:

            **f.** Employee training/compensation practices:

            **g.** Justification for selection:

    **B. Strategy(ies) for Using Capabilities and Resources**

        **1.** Strategy A (to meet the needs of potential employer A)

            **a.** Personal skills, abilities, and resources

                (1) Description of your skills and abilities:

(2) Specific employer needs that your skills/abilities can fulfill:

(3) Differentiation relative to peers/competitors (why should *you* be hired?):

(4) Additional resources that you have to offer:

(5) Needed or expected starting salary:

(6) Expected employee benefits:

(7) Additional employer-paid training that you require:

(8) Willingness to relocate:

(9) Geographic areas to target:

(10) Corporate divisions or offices to target:

(11) Summary of overall strategy:

(12) Tactics for standing out among the crowd of potential employees:

(13) Point of contact with potential employer:

(14) Specific elements

   *(a)* Résumé:

   *(b)* Internships:

   *(c)* Placement offices:

   *(d)* Job fairs:

   *(e)* Personal contacts:

   *(f)* Unsolicited:

(15) Specific objectives and budget:

2. Strategy B (to meet the needs of potential employer B)

   a. Personal skills, abilities, and resources

      (1) Description of your skills and abilities:

      (2) Specific employer needs that your skills/abilities can fulfill:

      (3) Differentiation relative to peers/competitors (why should *you* be hired?):

      (4) Additional resources that you have to offer:

      (5) Needed or expected starting salary:

      (6) Expected employee benefits:

      (7) Additional employer-paid training that you require:

      (8) Willingness to relocate:

      (9) Geographic areas to target:

(10) Corporate divisions or offices to target:

(11) Summary of overall strategy:

(12) Tactics for standing out among the crowd of potential employees:

(13) Point of contact with potential employer:

(14) Specific elements

   *(a)* Résumé:

   *(b)* Internships:

   *(c)* Placement offices:

   *(d)* Job fairs:

   *(e)* Personal contacts:

   *(f)* Unsolicited:

(15) Specific objectives and budget:

**C. Strategy Summary**

1. How does strategy A (B) give you a competitive advantage in serving the needs of potential employer A (B)?

2. Is this competitive advantage sustainable? Why or why not?

## VI. Financial Projections and Budgets

A. Do you have a clear idea of your budgetary requirements (for example, housing, furnishings, clothing, transportation, food, other living expenses)?

B. Will the expected salaries/benefits from potential employers meet these requirements? If not, do you have an alternative plan (that is, a different job choice, a second job, requesting a higher salary)?

## VII. Controls and Evaluation

**A. Performance Standards**

1. What do you have to offer? Corrective actions that can be taken if your skills, abilities, and resources do not match the needs of potential employers:

2. Are you worth it? Corrective actions that can be taken if potential employers do not think your skills/abilities are worth your asking price:

3. Where do you want to go? Corrective actions that can be taken if potential employers do not offer you

a position in a preferred geographic location:

4. How will you stand out among the crowd?

Corrective actions that can be taken if your message is not being heard by potential employers or is not reaching the right people:

## B. Monitoring Procedures

1. What types and levels of formal control mechanisms are in place to ensure the proper implementation of your plan?
   a. Are your potential employers hiring?
   b. Do you need additional training/education?
   c. Have you allocated sufficient time to your career development?
   d. Are your investments in career development adequate?
      (1) Training/education:
      (2) Networking/making contacts:
      (3) Wardrobe/clothing:
      (4) Development of interviewing skills:
   e. Have you done your homework on potential employers?
   f. Have you been involved in an internship program?
   g. Have you attended job/career fairs?
   h. Are you using the resources of your placement center?
   i. Are you committed to your career development?

## C. Performance Analysis

1. Number/quality/potential of all job contacts made:
2. Number of job/career fairs attended and quality of the job leads generated:
3. Number of résumés distributed:
   a. Number of potential employers who responded:
   b. Number of negative responses:
4. Number of personal interviews:
5. Number/quality of job offers:

PART 5

# Marketing: Developing Relationships

# 11

# Customer-Driven Marketing

## Chapter Outline

## Banana Republic Uses Marketing to Bring Brand to Life

Banana Republic owes its success to marketing. The international firm was founded in 1978 by Mel and Patricia Ziegler as a safari- and travel-themed clothing company. Mel and Patricia desired to produce eccentric, high-end apparel from exotic locations to appeal to customers looking for clothing with meaning behind the designs. Creating value and satisfying consumers followed several attempts to find the right target market.

The idea came after the couple designed shirts and tried to sell them at a flea market. When the products did not sell, they altered their strategy, increasing the price and renaming the shirts Short-Armed Spanish Paratrooper shirts. The strategy was a success, and the two found that creating a visual story for customers appealed more to them than an average product. This form of customer-driven marketing helped propel the brand to profitability through discovering the right market segment. The couple released catalogs with scenes of jungles and safaris to provide a back story to their apparel.

Banana Republic also implemented themed decorations in its stores, incorporating authentic elements to aid in creating its brand. Sales grew. After being acquired by Gap, Banana Republic took a different approach to its clothes. Today's Banana Republic does not look like it did when it was founded, but it often continues to incorporate "stories" that create the brand image to differentiate its products. For instance, the company made a deal with the popular TV show *Mad Men* allowing Banana Republic to develop a collection dedicated to classic designs from the vintage era. This showcases the company's desire to use creativity to bring consumers into the stores.[1]

# Introduction

Marketing involves planning and executing the development, pricing, promotion, and distribution of ideas, goods, and services to create exchanges that satisfy individual and organizational goals. These activities ensure that the products consumers want to buy are available at a price they are willing to pay and that consumers are provided with information about product features and availability. Organizations of all sizes and objectives engage in these activities.

In this chapter, we focus on the basic principles of marketing. First we define and examine the nature of marketing. Then we look at how marketers develop marketing strategies to satisfy the needs and wants of their customers. Next we discuss buying behavior and how marketers use research to determine what consumers want to buy and why. Finally, we explore the impact of the environment on marketing activities.

# Nature of Marketing

**marketing**
a group of activities designed to expedite transactions by creating, distributing, pricing, and promoting goods, services, and ideas

A vital part of any business undertaking, **marketing** is a group of activities designed to expedite transactions by creating, distributing, pricing, and promoting goods, services, and ideas. These activities create value by allowing individuals and organizations to obtain what they need and want. A business cannot achieve its objectives unless it provides something that customers value. But just creating an innovative product that meets many users' needs isn't sufficient in today's volatile global marketplace. Products must be conveniently available, competitively priced, and uniquely promoted.

Marketing is an important part of a firm's overall strategy. Other functional areas of the business—such as operations, finance, and all areas of management—must be coordinated with marketing decisions. Marketing has the important function of providing revenue to sustain a firm. Only by creating trust and effective relationships with customers can a firm succeed in the long run. Businesses try to respond to consumer wants and needs and to anticipate changes in the environment. Unfortunately, it is difficult to understand and predict what consumers want: Motives are often unclear; few principles can be applied consistently; and markets tend to fragment, each desiring customized products, new value, or better service.

It is important to note what marketing is not: It is not manipulating consumers to get them to buy products they do not want. It is not just selling and advertising; it is a systematic approach to satisfying consumers. Marketing focuses on the many activities—planning, pricing, promoting, and distributing products—that foster exchanges. Unfortunately, the mass media and movies sometimes portray marketing as unethical or as not adding value to business. In this chapter, we point out that marketing is essential and provides important benefits in making products available to consumers.

## The Exchange Relationship

**exchange**
the act of giving up one thing (money, credit, labor, goods) in return for something else (goods, services, or ideas)

At the heart of all business is the **exchange,** the act of giving up one thing (money, credit, labor, goods) in return for something else (goods, services, or ideas). Businesses exchange their goods, services, or ideas for money or credit supplied by customers in a voluntary *exchange relationship,* illustrated in Figure 11.1. The buyer must feel good about the purchase, or the exchange will not continue. If your cell phone service works everywhere, you will probably feel good about using its services. But if you have a lot of dropped calls, you will probably use another phone service next time.

For an exchange to occur, certain conditions are required. As indicated by the arrows in Figure 11.1, buyers and sellers must be able to communicate about the

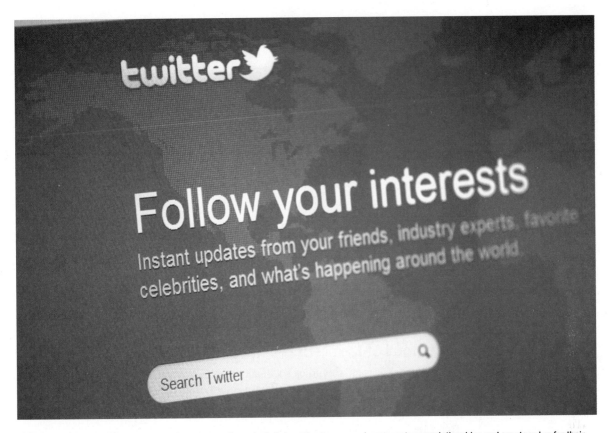

Companies find that communicating with customers through digital media sites can enhance customer relationships and create value for their brands.

"something of value" available to each. An exchange does not necessarily take place just because buyers and sellers have something of value to exchange. Each participant must be willing to give up his or her respective "something of value" to receive the "something" held by the other. You are willing to exchange your "something of value"—your money or credit—for soft drinks, football tickets, or new shoes because you consider those products more valuable or more important than holding on to your cash or credit potential.

When you think of marketing products, you may think of tangible things—cars, MP3 players, or books, for example. What most consumers want, however, is a way to get a job done, solve a problem, or gain some enjoyment. You may purchase a Hoover vacuum cleaner not because you want a vacuum cleaner but because you want clean carpets. Starbucks serves coffee drinks at a premium price, providing convenience, quality, and an inviting environment. Therefore, the tangible product itself may not be as important as the image or the benefits associated with the product. This intangible "something of value" may be capability gained from using a product or the image evoked by it, or even the brand name. Good examples of brand names that are easy to remember include Avon's Skin So Soft, Tide detergent, and the Ford Mustang. The label or brand name may also offer the added bonus of being a conversation piece in a social environment, such as Dancing Bull or Smoking Loon wine.

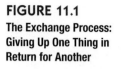

**FIGURE 11.1**

**The Exchange Process: Giving Up One Thing in Return for Another**

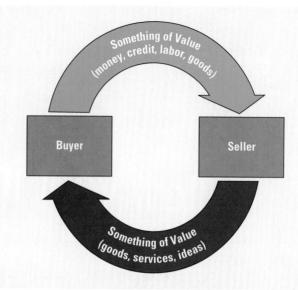

## Functions of Marketing

Marketing focuses on a complex set of activities that must be performed to accomplish objectives and generate exchanges. These activities include buying, selling, transporting, storing, grading, financing, marketing research, and risk taking.

**Buying.**    Everyone who shops for products (consumers, stores, businesses, governments) decides whether and what to buy. A marketer must understand buyers' needs and desires to determine what products to make available.

**Selling.**    The exchange process is expedited through selling. Marketers usually view selling as a persuasive activity that is accomplished through promotion (advertising, personal selling, sales promotion, publicity, and packaging).

**Transporting.**    Transporting is the process of moving products from the seller to the buyer. Marketers focus on transportation costs and services.

**Storing.**    Like transporting, storing is part of the physical distribution of products and includes warehousing goods. Warehouses hold some products for lengthy periods in order to create time utility. Time utility has to do with being able to satisfy demand in a timely manner. This especially pertains to a seasonal good such as orange juice. Fresh oranges are only available for a few months annually, but consumers demand juice throughout the entire year. Sellers must arrange for cold storage of orange juice concentrate so that they can maintain a steady supply all of the time.

**Grading.**    Grading refers to standardizing products by dividing them into subgroups and displaying and labeling them so that consumers clearly understand their nature and quality. Many products, such as meat, steel, and fruit, are graded according to a set of standards that often are established by the state or federal government.

**Financing.**    For many products, especially large items such as automobiles, refrigerators, and new homes, the marketer arranges credit to expedite the purchase.

**Marketing Research.**   Through research, marketers ascertain the need for new goods and services. By gathering information regularly, marketers can detect new trends and changes in consumer tastes.

**Risk Taking.**   Risk is the chance of loss associated with marketing decisions. Developing a new product creates a chance of loss if consumers do not like it enough to buy it. Spending money to hire a sales force or to conduct marketing research also involves risk. The implication of risk is that most marketing decisions result in either success or failure.

## Creating Value with Marketing[2]

Value is an important element of managing long-term customer relationships and implementing the marking concept. We view **value** as a customer's subjective assessment of benefits relative to costs in determining the worth of a product (customer value = customer benefits − customer costs).

> **value**
> a customer's subjective assessment of benefits relative to costs in determining the worth of a product

Customer benefits include anything a buyer receives in an exchange. Hotels and motels, for example, basically provide a room with a bed and bathroom, but each firm provides a different level of service, amenities, and atmosphere to satisfy its guests. Hampton Inn offers the minimum services necessary to maintain a quality, efficient, low-price overnight accommodation. In contrast, the Ritz-Carlton provides every imaginable service a guest might desire and strives to ensure that all service is of the highest quality. Customers judge which type of accommodation offers them the best value according to the benefits they desire and their willingness and ability to pay for the costs associated with the benefits.

Customer costs include anything a buyer must give up to obtain the benefits the product provides. The most obvious cost is the monetary price of the product, but nonmonetary costs can be equally important in a customer's determination of value. Two nonmonetary costs are the time and effort customers expend to find and purchase desired products. To reduce time and effort, a company can increase product availability, thereby making it more convenient for buyers to purchase the firm's products. Another nonmonetary cost is risk, which can be reduced by offering good basic warranties for an additional charge. Another risk-reduction strategy is increasingly popular in today's catalog/telephone/Internet shopping environment. L.L. Bean, for example, uses a guarantee to reduce the risk involved in ordering merchandise from its catalogs.

In developing marketing activities, it is important to recognize that customers receive benefits based on their experiences. For example, many computer buyers consider services such as fast delivery, ease of installation, technical advice, and training assistance to be important elements of the product. Customers also derive benefits from the act of shopping and selecting products. These benefits can be affected by the atmosphere or environment of a store, such as Red Lobster's nautical/seafood theme.

## The Marketing Concept

LO 11-3

A basic philosophy that guides all marketing activities is the **marketing concept,** the idea that an organization should try to satisfy customers' needs through coordinated activities that also allow it to achieve its own goals. According to the marketing concept, a business must find out what consumers desire and then develop the good, service, or idea that fulfills their needs or wants. The business must then get the product to the customer. In addition, the business must continually alter, adapt, and develop products to keep pace with changing consumer needs and wants. For instance,

> **marketing concept**
> the idea that an organization should try to satisfy customers' needs through coordinated activities that also allow it to achieve its own goals

### It'Sugar: Novelty Candy Emporium

It'Sugar

**Founder:** Jeff Rubin

**Founded:** 2006, in south Florida

**Success:** It'Sugar is the fastest-growing candy chain in the world, with 45 global stores and 30 outposts within department stores.

Imagine a place where you are encouraged to cheat—on your diet that is. It'Sugar is a novelty candy emporium founded by CEO Jeff Rubin, after a revolutionary idea hit him when visiting the candy aisle of a drugstore. He knew that children did not really care about novelty candy combinations, but he recognized that an older demographic could be attracted to a store with products tailored specifically toward them. Rubin found the right target market in the 19-year-old female demographic as his single market segment. He realized that if he could attract this demographic, he could also simultaneously attract their boyfriends, pre-teens, and older women longing for their younger days.

The candy found at It'Sugar is not found at other candy stores. Products include the world's largest box of Nerd's candy, Marilyn Monroe Gummy Lips, lingerie made of candy, and a Laffy Taffy leather jacket with Swarovski crystals priced at $2,499. These unique items have made a splash with consumers, so much so that a store was recently opened at the Venetian hotel in Las Vegas.[3]

---

Domino's has announced that it will begin to offer pizza with a gluten-free crust. With 6 to 8 percent of consumers on a gluten-free diet, many restaurants and fast-food companies are developing new food products to meet the needs of this growing segment.[4] To remain competitive, companies must be prepared to add to or adapt their product lines to satisfy customers' desires for new fads or changes in eating habits. Each business must determine how best to implement the marketing concept, given its own goals and resources.

Trying to determine customers' true needs is increasingly difficult because no one fully understands what motivates people to buy things. However, Estée Lauder, founder of her namesake cosmetics company, had a pretty good idea. When a prestigious store in Paris rejected her perfume in the 1960s, she "accidentally" dropped a bottle on the floor where nearby customers could get a whiff of it. So many asked about the scent that Galeries Lafayette was obliged to place an order. Lauder ultimately built an empire using then-unheard-of tactics like free samples and gifts with purchases to market her "jars of hope."[5]

Trader Joe's, which sells many lines of organic and natural food products, is often thought to have better deals than some of its competitors. The grocery chain attempts to meet consumer demands for high-quality food at reasonable prices.

Although customer satisfaction is the goal of the marketing concept, a business must also achieve its own objectives, such as boosting productivity, reducing costs, or achieving a percentage of a specific market. If it does not, it will not survive. For example, Lenovo could sell computers for $50 and give customers a lifetime guarantee, which would be great for customers but not so great for Lenovo. Obviously, the company must strike a balance between achieving organizational objectives and satisfying customers.

To implement the marketing concept, a firm must have good information about what consumers want, adopt a consumer orientation, and coordinate its efforts throughout the entire organization; otherwise, it may be awash with goods, services, and ideas that consumers do not want or need. Successfully implementing the marketing concept requires that a business view the customer's perception of value as the ultimate measure of work performance and improving value, and the rate at which this is done, as the measure of success.[6] Everyone in the organization who interacts with customers—*all* customer-contact employees— must know what customers want. They are selling ideas, benefits, philosophies, and experiences—not just goods and services.

Someone once said that if you build a better mousetrap, the world will beat a path to your door. Suppose you do build a better mousetrap. What will happen? Actually, consumers are not likely to beat a path to your door because the market is so competitive. A coordinated effort by everyone involved with the mousetrap is needed to sell the product. Your company must reach out to customers and tell them about your mousetrap, especially how your mousetrap works better than those offered by competitors. If you do not make the benefits of your product widely known, in most cases, it will not be successful. One reason that Apple is so successful is because of its stores. Apple's more than 400 national and international retail stores market computers and electronics in a way unlike any other computer manufacturer or retail establishment. The upscale stores, located in high-rent shopping districts, show off Apple's products in modern, spacious settings to encourage consumers to try new things—like making a movie on a computer. The stores also incorporate its products into the selling process. Not only are consumers allowed to try out or "test drive" Apple's tech products, but the company has also begun to install iPad stations in its stores equipped with a customer service app to answer customer questions.[7] So for some companies, like Apple Inc., you need to create stores to sell your product to consumers. You could also find stores that are willing to sell your product to consumers for you. In either situation, you must implement the marketing concept by making a product with satisfying benefits and making it available and visible.

Orville Wright said that an airplane is "a group of separate parts flying in close formation." This is what most companies are trying to accomplish: They are striving for a team effort to deliver the right good or service to customers. A breakdown at any point in the organization—whether it be in production, purchasing, sales, distribution, or advertising—can result in lost sales, lost revenue, and dissatisfied customers.

## Evolution of the Marketing Concept

The marketing concept may seem like the obvious approach to running a business and building relationships with customers. However, businesspeople are not always focused on customers when they create and operate businesses. Many companies fail to grasp the importance of customer relationships and fail to implement customer strategies. A firm's marketing department needs to share information about customers and their desires with the entire organization. Our society and economic system have changed over time, and marketing has become more important as markets have become more competitive.

**The Production Orientation.** During the second half of the 19th century, the Industrial Revolution was well under way in the United States. New technologies, such as electricity, railroads, internal combustion engines, and mass-production techniques, made it possible to manufacture goods with ever increasing efficiency. Together with new management ideas and ways of using labor, products poured into the marketplace, where demand for manufactured goods was strong.

### The Sales Orientation.

By the early part of the 20th century, supply caught up with and then exceeded demand, and businesspeople began to realize they would have to "sell" products to buyers. During the first half of the 20th century, businesspeople viewed sales as the primary means of increasing profits in what has become known as a sales orientation. Those who adopted the sales orientation perspective believed the most important marketing activities were personal selling and advertising. Today some people still inaccurately equate marketing with a sales orientation.

### The Market Orientation.

By the 1950s, some businesspeople began to recognize that even efficient production and extensive promotion did not guarantee sales. These businesses, and many others since, found that they must first determine what customers want and then produce it, rather than making the products first and then trying to persuade customers that they need them. Managers at General Electric first suggested that the marketing concept was a companywide philosophy of doing business. As more organizations realized the importance of satisfying customers' needs, U.S. businesses entered the marketing era, one of market orientation.

**market orientation**
an approach requiring organizations to gather information about customer needs, share that information throughout the firm, and use that information to help build long-term relationships with customers

A **market orientation** requires organizations to gather information about customer needs, share that information throughout the entire firm, and use it to help build long-term relationships with customers. Top executives, marketing managers, nonmarketing managers (those in production, finance, human resources, and so on), and customers all become mutually dependent and cooperate in developing and carrying out a market orientation. Nonmarketing managers must communicate with marketing managers to share information important to understanding the customer. Consider the 123-year history of Wrigley's gum. In 1891, the gum was given away to promote sales of baking powder (the company's original product). The gum was launched as its own product in 1893, and after four generations of Wrigley family CEOs, the company continues to reinvent itself and focus on consumers. Eventually, the family made the decision to sell the company to Mars. Wrigley now functions as a stand-alone subsidiary of Mars. The deal combined such popular brands as Wrigley's gums and Life Savers with Mars' M&M's, Snickers, and Skittles to form the world's largest confectionary company.

Trying to assess what customers want, which is difficult to begin with, is further complicated by the rate at which trends, fashions, and tastes can change. Businesses today want to satisfy customers and build meaningful long-term relationships with them. It is more efficient and less expensive for the company to retain existing customers and even increase the amount of business each customer provides the organization than to find new customers. Most companies' success depends on increasing the amount of repeat business; therefore, relationship building between company and customer is key. Many companies are turning to technologies associated with customer relationship management to help build relationships and boost business with existing customers.

The Nissan Leaf meets the needs of consumers who care about the environment and wish to improve their environmental footprint by driving an electric vehicle.

## Sheetz: The Starbucks of Convenience Stores

Imagine a convenience store that resembles and employs the same atmosphere as a Starbucks. This might seem unusual, but Sheetz is looking to change that. Sheetz is a family business and one of the largest and fastest-growing convenience store operators in the country. The company has annual revenues of $7 billion and has created its own category of stores. Sheetz opens stores that offer made-to-order foods, gasoline, and other food items, including private-label candy, nuts, and beef jerky. The company has more than 400 locations across the East Coast.

While sales at convenience stores have dwindled, Sheetz is trying an innovative approach it hopes will help change the view that convenience stores do not offer good food. The company has introduced "convenience restaurants" as a way to boost sales. Sheetz found that it is most profitable in an area dubbed as America's fourth meal—snacks. To take advantage of Americans' love of snacks, the company markets an array of food items, including deli sandwiches,

burgers and hot dogs, pizza, and burritos available at all hours, every day. Sheetz even lets users customize their food using a touchscreen ordering system. The company brands and delivers its own gas and encourages Millennials to hang out in the booths and tables provided for customers.

Sheetz has been recognized through multiple awards. *Forbes* ranked Sheetz as the 61st top privately held company in the United States. Although consumers usually spend very little time in a convenience store, Sheetz is aiming to reverse this trend and encourage customers to stay awhile.[8]

### Discussion Questions

1. How is Sheetz trying to change the image associated with convenience stores?
2. What demographics does Sheetz seem to be targeting with its convenience restaurants?
3. Why do you think Sheetz allows customers to customize their menus using a touch screen?

Although it might be easy to dismiss customer relationship management as time-consuming and expensive, this mistake could destroy a company. Customer relationship management (CRM) is important in a market orientation because it can result in loyal and profitable customers. Without loyal customers, businesses would not survive; therefore, achieving the full profit potential of each customer relationship should be the goal of every marketing strategy. At the most basic level, profits can be obtained through relationships by acquiring new customers, enhancing the profitability of existing customers, and extending the duration of customer relationships. The profitability of loyal customers throughout their relationship with the company (their lifetime customer value) should not be underestimated. For instance, Pizza Hut has a lifetime customer value of approximately $8,000, whereas Cadillac's lifetime customer value is approximately $332,000.[9]

Communication remains a major element of any strategy to develop and manage long-term customer relationships. By providing multiple points of interactions with customers—that is, websites, telephone, fax, e-mail, and personal contact—companies can personalize customer relationships.[10] Like many online retailers, Amazon.com stores and analyzes purchase data in an attempt to understand each customer's interests. This information helps the online retailer improve its ability to satisfy individual customers and thereby increase sales of books, music, movies, and other products to each customer. The ability to identify individual customers allows marketers to shift their focus from targeting groups of similar customers to increasing their share of an individual customer's purchases. Regardless of the medium through which communication occurs, customers should ultimately be the drivers of marketing strategy because they understand what they want. Customer relationship management systems should ensure that marketers listen to customers in order to respond to their needs and concerns and build long-term relationships.

LO 11-4

**marketing strategy**
a plan of action for
developing, pricing,
distributing, and promoting
products that meet the needs
of specific customers

**market**
a group of people who have
a need, purchasing power,
and the desire and authority
to spend money on goods,
services, and ideas

**target market**
a specific group of consumers
on whose needs and wants
a company focuses its
marketing efforts

**total-market approach**
an approach whereby a firm
tries to appeal to everyone
and assumes that all buyers
have similar needs

**market segmentation**
a strategy whereby a firm
divides the total market into
groups of people who have
relatively similar product needs

**market segment**
a collection of individuals,
groups, or organizations
who share one or more
characteristics and thus have
relatively similar product
needs and desires

Need help under-
standing Marketers
Segment Target
Market? Visit your
Connect ebook
video tab for a
brief animated
explanation.

# Developing a Marketing Strategy

To implement the marketing concept and customer relationship management, a business needs to develop and maintain a **marketing strategy,** a plan of action for developing, pricing, distributing, and promoting products that meet the needs of specific customers. This definition has two major components: selecting a target market and developing an appropriate marketing mix to satisfy that target market.

## Selecting a Target Market

A **market** is a group of people who have a need, purchasing power, and the desire and authority to spend money on goods, services, and ideas. A **target market** is a more specific group of consumers on whose needs and wants a company focuses its marketing efforts. For instance, Lego focused on young boys as the target market for its products. This narrower strategic focus allowed the company to tailor products to attract this demographic with much success: revenues increased 105 percent since 2006. In the past few years, the company has performed market studies on girls to reposition its brand to attract both genders.[11] It recently launched Lego Friends, a line launched specifically for girls.[12]

Marketing managers may define a target market as a relatively small number of people within a larger market, or they may define it as the total market (Figure 11.2). Rolls Royce, for example, targets its products at a very exclusive, high-income market—people who want the ultimate in prestige in an automobile. On the other hand, Ford Motor Company manufactures a variety of vehicles including Lincolns, Mercurys, and Ford Trucks in order to appeal to varied tastes, needs, and desires.

Some firms use a **total-market approach,** in which they try to appeal to everyone and assume that all buyers have similar needs and wants. Sellers of salt, sugar, and many agricultural products use a total-market approach because everyone is a potential consumer of these products. Most firms, though, use **market segmentation** and divide the total market into groups of people. A **market segment** is a collection of individuals, groups, or organizations who share one or more characteristics and thus have relatively similar product needs and desires. Women are the largest market segment, with 51 percent of the U.S. population. At the household level, segmentation can identify each woman's social attributes, culture, and stages in life to determine preferences and needs.

Another market segment on which many marketers are focusing is the growing Hispanic population. Dodge launched an advertising campaign for it 1500 Ram called "A Todo, Con Todo" and hired Columbian music artist Juanes to be spokesperson. Fast food chain Wendy's is also targeting the Hispanic market with its "Mucho Mejor" campaign, featuring the "Rojos family." The campaign's message is one of food, family, and working toward advancement.[13] The companies hope to create relationships with Hispanic consumers in order to gain their loyalty. One of the challenges for marketers in the future will be to effectively address an increasingly racially diverse United States. The minority population of the United States is about 116 million (37 percent of the total population).[14] In future decades, the purchasing power of minority market segments is set to grow by leaps and bounds. Table 11.1 shows the buying power of minority groups in the United States. Companies will have to learn how to most effectively reach these growing segments. Companies use market segmentation to focus their efforts and resources on specific target markets so that they can develop a productive marketing strategy. Two common approaches to segmenting markets are the concentration approach and the multisegment approach.

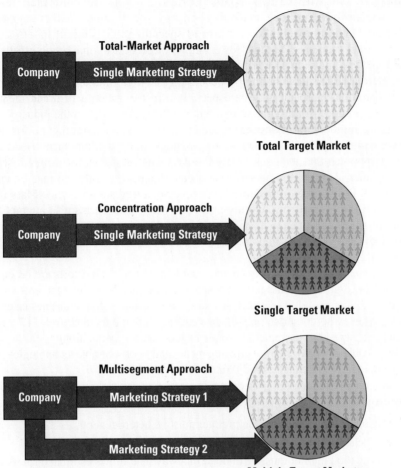

**FIGURE 11.2**
**Target Market Strategies**

| | 1990 | 2000 | 2010 | 2012 | 2015 |
|---|---|---|---|---|---|
| Total | $4,200 | $7,300 | $11,200 | $12,200 | $15,100 |
| Black | 316 | 600 | 947 | 1,000 | 1,300 |
| Native American | 20 | 40 | 87 | 103 | 148 |
| Asian | 115 | 272 | 609 | 718 | 1,000 |
| Hispanic* | 210 | 488 | 1,000 | 1,200 | 1,700 |

**TABLE 11.1**
**Buying Power of U.S. Minorities by Race (billions)**

*Because Hispanic is an ethnic group, they may belong to any of the other races.

Source: Jeffrey M. Humphreys, The Multicultural Economy 2012 *(Athens, GA: The University of Georgia Terry College of Business Selig Center for Economic Growth, 2013).*

**concentration approach**
a market segmentation
approach whereby a company
develops one marketing
strategy for a single market
segment

## Market Segmentation Approaches.

In the **concentration approach,** a company develops one marketing strategy for a single market segment. The concentration approach allows a firm to specialize, focusing all its efforts on the one market segment. Porsche, for example, directs all its marketing efforts toward high-income individuals who want to own high-performance vehicles. A firm can generate a large sales volume by penetrating a single market segment deeply. The concentration approach may be especially effective when a firm can identify and develop products for a segment ignored by other companies in the industry.

**multisegment approach**
a market segmentation
approach whereby the
marketer aims its efforts
at two or more segments,
developing a marketing
strategy for each

In the **multisegment approach,** the marketer aims its marketing efforts at two or more segments, developing a marketing strategy for each. Many firms use a multisegment approach that includes different advertising messages for different segments. Companies also develop product variations to appeal to different market segments. The U.S. Post Office, for example, offers personalized stamps, while Mars Inc. sells personalized M&M's through mymms.com. Many other firms also attempt to use a multisegment approach to market segmentation, such as the manufacturer of Raleigh bicycles, which has designed separate marketing strategies for racers, tourers, commuters, and children.

*Niche marketing* is a narrow market segment focus when efforts are on one small, well-defined group that has a unique, specific set of needs. Niche segments are usually very small compared to the total market for the products. Many airlines cater to first-class flyers, who comprise only 10 percent of international air travelers. To meet the needs of these elite customers, airlines include special perks along with the spacious seats. To take advantage of the growing niche market of wearable technologies, Apple is developing a smart watch called iWatch.[15]

For a firm to successfully use a concentration or multisegment approach to market segmentation, several requirements must be met:

1. Consumers' needs for the product must be heterogeneous.
2. The segments must be identifiable and divisible.
3. The total market must be divided in a way that allows estimated sales potential, cost, and profits of the segments to be compared.
4. At least one segment must have enough profit potential to justify developing and maintaining a special marketing strategy.
5. The firm must be able to reach the chosen market segment with a particular market strategy.

## Bases for Segmenting Markets.

Companies segment markets on the basis of several variables:

1. *Demographic*—age, sex, race, ethnicity, income, education, occupation, family size, religion, social class. These characteristics are often closely related to customers' product needs and purchasing behavior, and they can be readily measured. For example, deodorants are often segmented by sex: Secret and Soft n' Dri for women; Old Spice and Mennen for men.
2. *Geographic*—climate, terrain, natural resources, population density, subcultural values. These influence consumers' needs and product usage. Climate, for example, influences consumers' purchases of clothing, automobiles, heating and air conditioning equipment, and leisure activity equipment.
3. *Psychographic*—personality characteristics, motives, lifestyles. Soft-drink marketers provide their products in several types of packaging, including two-liter bottles and cases of cans, to satisfy different lifestyles and motives.

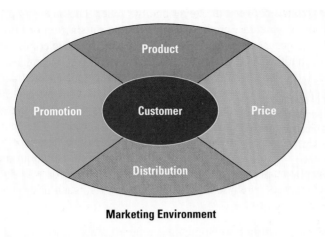

4. *Behavioristic*—some characteristic of the consumer's behavior toward the product. These characteristics commonly involve some aspect of product use.

## Developing a Marketing Mix

The second step in developing a marketing strategy is to create and maintain a satisfying marketing mix. The **marketing mix** refers to four marketing activities—product, price, distribution, and promotion—that the firm can control to achieve specific goals within a dynamic marketing environment (Figure 11.3). The buyer or the target market is the central focus of all marketing activities.

**Product.**   A product—whether a good, a service, an idea, or some combination— is a complex mix of tangible and intangible attributes that provide satisfaction and benefits. A *good* is a physical entity you can touch. A Porsche Cayenne, a Hewlett-Packard printer, and a kitten available for adoption at an animal shelter are examples of goods. A *service* is the application of human and mechanical efforts to people or objects to provide intangible benefits to customers. Air travel, dry cleaning, haircuts, banking, insurance, medical care, and day care are examples of services. *Ideas* include concepts, philosophies, images, and issues. For instance, an attorney, for a fee, may advise you about what rights you have in the event that the IRS decides to audit your tax return. Other marketers of ideas include political parties, churches, and schools.

A product has emotional and psychological, as well as physical characteristics, that include everything that the buyer receives from an exchange. This definition includes supporting services such as installation, guarantees, product information, and promises of repair. Products usually have both favorable and unfavorable attributes; therefore, almost every purchase or exchange involves trade-offs as consumers try to maximize their benefits and satisfaction and minimize unfavorable attributes.

Products are among a firm's most visible contacts with consumers. If they do not meet consumer needs and expectations, sales will be difficult, and product life spans will be brief. The product is an important variable—often the central focus—of the marketing mix; the other variables (price, promotion, and distribution) must be coordinated with product decisions.

**Price.**   Almost anything can be assessed by a **price,** a value placed on an object exchanged between a buyer and a seller. Although the seller usually establishes the price,

**marketing mix**
the four marketing activites— product, price, promotion, and distribution—that the firm can control to achieve specific goals within a dynamic marketing environment

**price**
a value placed on an object exchanged between a buyer and a seller

it may be negotiated between the buyer and the seller. The buyer usually exchanges purchasing power—income, credit, wealth—for the satisfaction or utility associated with a product. Because financial price is the measure of value commonly used in an exchange, it quantifies value and is the basis of most market exchanges.

Marketers view price as much more than a way of assessing value, however. It is a key element of the marketing mix because it relates directly to the generation of revenue and profits. Prices can also be changed quickly to stimulate demand or respond to competitors' actions. The sudden increase in the cost of commodities such as oil can create price increases or a drop in consumer demand for a product. When gas prices rise, consumers purchase more fuel-efficient cars; when prices fall, consumers return to larger vehicles.[17]

**distribution**
making products available to customers in the quantities desired

**Distribution.**   Distribution (sometimes referred to as "place" because it helps to remember the marketing mix as the "4 Ps") is making products available to customers in the quantities desired. For example, consumers can rent DVDs and videogames from a physical store, a vending machine, or an online service. Intermediaries, usually wholesalers and retailers, perform many of the activities required to move products efficiently from producers to consumers or industrial buyers. These activities involve transporting, warehousing, materials handling, and inventory control, as well as packaging and communication.

Critics who suggest that eliminating wholesalers and other middlemen would result in lower prices for consumers do not recognize that eliminating intermediaries would not do away with the need for their services. Other institutions would have to perform those services, and consumers would still have to pay for them. In addition, in the absence of wholesalers, all producers would have to deal directly with retailers or customers, keeping voluminous records and hiring extra people to deal with customers.

**promotion**
a persuasive form of communication that attempts to expedite a marketing exchange by influencing individuals, groups, and organizations to accept goods, services, and ideas

**Promotion.**   Promotion is a persuasive form of communication that attempts to expedite a marketing exchange by influencing individuals, groups, and organizations to accept goods, services, and ideas. Promotion includes advertising, personal selling, publicity, and sales promotion, all of which we will look at more closely in Chapter 12.

The aim of promotion is to communicate directly or indirectly with individuals, groups, and organizations to facilitate exchanges. When marketers use advertising and other forms of promotion, they must effectively manage their promotional resources and understand product and target-market characteristics to ensure that these promotional activities contribute to the firm's objectives.

Most major companies have set up websites on the Internet

Netflix uses both traditional mail and streaming to distribute its products.

to promote themselves and their products. While traditional advertising media such as television, radio, newspapers, and magazines remain important, digital advertising on websites and social media sites is growing. Not only can digital advertising be less expensive, but advertising offerings such as Google AdWords allow companies to only pay when users click on the link or advertisement.[18] Additionally, social media sites offer advertising opportunities for both large and small companies. Firms can create a Facebook page and post corporate updates for free. To appeal to smaller businesses, Facebook has begun offering deals such as a certain amount in free advertising credits.[19] Not to be outdone, Twitter also allows advertisers to purchase Promoted Tweets on the site. Promoted Tweets are just like regular tweets (except for the name), allowing users to respond or retweet them to their friends.[20]

Need help understanding the Marketing Mix? Visit your Connect ebook video tab for a brief animated explanation.

## Marketing Research and Information Systems

LO 11-5

Before marketers can develop a marketing mix, they must collect in-depth, up-to-date information about customer needs. **Marketing research** is a systematic, objective process of getting information about potential customers to guide marketing decisions. Such information might include data about the age, income, ethnicity, gender, and educational level of people in the target market, their preferences for product features, their attitudes toward competitors' products, and the frequency with which they use the product. For instance, marketing research has revealed that consumers often make in-store purchase decisions in three seconds or less.[21] Marketing research is vital because the marketing concept cannot be implemented without information about customers.

**marketing research** a systematic, objective process of getting information about potential customers to guide marketing decisions

A marketing information system is a framework for accessing information about customers from sources both inside and outside the organization. Inside the organization, there is a continuous flow of information about prices, sales, and expenses. Outside the organization, data are readily available through private or public reports and census statistics, as well as from many other sources. Computer networking technology provides a framework for companies to connect to useful databases and customers with instantaneous information about product acceptance, sales performance, and buying behavior. This information is important to planning and marketing strategy development.

Two types of data are usually available to decision makers. **Primary data** are observed, recorded, or collected directly from respondents. If you've ever participated in a telephone survey about a product, recorded your TV viewing habits for ACNielsen or Arbitron, or even responded to a political opinion poll, you provided the researcher with primary data. Primary data must be gathered by researchers who develop a method to observe phenomena or research respondents. Many companies use "mystery shoppers" to visit their retail establishments and report on whether the stores were adhering to the companies' standards of service. These undercover customers document their observations of store appearance, employee effectiveness, and customer treatment. Mystery shoppers provide valuable information that helps companies improve their organizations and refine their marketing strategies.[22] Companies also use surveys and focus groups to gauge customer opinion. Table 11.2 provides the results of a survey conducted by MSN Money on organizations with the best customer service. A weakness of surveys is that respondents are sometimes untruthful in order to avoid seeming foolish or ignorant. Although focus groups can be more expensive than surveys, they allow

**primary data** marketing information that is observed, recorded, or collected directly from respondents

**TABLE 11.2**
**Companies with the Best Customer Service**

| Rank | Companies | Excellence Rating (%) |
|:----:|:----------|:---------------------:|
| 1 | Amazon.com | 57.3 |
| 2 | Marriott | 42.6 |
| 3 | Hilton Hotels | 41.8 |
| 4 | UPS | 41.3 |
| 5 | FedEx | 40.6 |
| 6 | Google | 39.5 |
| 7 | State Farm | 37.9 |
| 8 | Samsung | 36.5 |
| 9 | Trader Joe's | 36.2 |
| 10 | Lowe's | 35.9 |

Source: Karen Aho, "2013 Customer Service Hall of Fame," MSN Money, http://money.msn.com/investing/2013-customer-service-hall-of-fame (accessed May 14, 2014).

marketers to understand how consumers express themselves as well as observe their behavior patterns.[23]

Some methods for marketing research use passive observation of consumer behavior and open-ended questioning techniques. Called ethnographic or observational research, the approach can help marketers determine what consumers really think about their products and how different ethnic or demographic groups react to them.

**secondary data**
information that is compiled inside or outside an organization for some purpose other than changing the current situation

**Secondary data** are compiled inside or outside the organization for some purpose other than changing the current situation. Marketers typically use information compiled by the U.S. census bureau and other government agencies, databases created by marketing research firms, as well as sales and other internal reports, to gain information about customers.

## Online Marketing Research

The marketing of products and collecting of data about buying behavior—information on what people actually buy and how they buy it—represents marketing research of the future. New information technologies are changing the way businesses learn about their customers and market their products. Interactive multimedia research, or *virtual testing,* combines sight, sound, and animation to facilitate the testing of concepts as well as packaging and design features for consumer products. The evolving development of telecommunications and computer technologies is allowing marketing researchers quick and easy access to a growing number of online services and a vast database of potential respondents.

Marketing research can use digital media and social networking sites to gather useful information for marketing decisions. Sites such as Twitter, Facebook, and LinkedIn can be good substitutes for focus groups. Online surveys can serve as an alternative to mail, telephone, or personal interviews.

Social networks are a great way to obtain information from consumers who are willing to share their experiences about products and companies. In a way, this process identifies those consumers who develop an identity or passion for certain products, as well as those consumers who have concerns about quality or performance. It is possible for firms to tap into existing online social networks and simply "listen" to what consumers have on their mind. Firms can also encourage consumers to join a community or group so that they can share their opinions with the business.

A good outcome from using social networks is the opportunity to reach new voices and gain varied perspectives on the creative process of developing new products and promotions. For instance, Kickstarter gives aspiring entrepreneurs the ability to market their ideas online. Funders can then choose whether to fund those ideas in return for a finished product or a steep discount.[24] To some extent, social networking is democratizing design by welcoming consumers to join in the development process for new products.[25]

Starbucks attempts to influence consumers' buying behavior by offering free Wi-Fi and a comfortable retail environment.

Online surveys are becoming an important part of marketing research. Traditionally, the process of conducting surveys online involved sending questionnaires to respondents either through email or through a website. However, digital communication has increased the ability of marketers to conduct polls on blogs and social networking sites. The benefits of online market research include lower costs and quicker feedback. For instance, when GNC launched its coconut-water beverage, it monitored online feedback to determine how customers viewed the product. The company found that feedback was negative, which convinced them to make product adjustments.[26] By monitoring consumers' feedback, companies can understand customer needs and adapt their goods or services.

## Buying Behavior

Carrying out the marketing concept is impossible unless marketers know what, where, when, and how consumers buy; conducting marketing research into the factors that influence buying behavior helps marketers develop effective marketing strategies. **Buying behavior** refers to the decision processes and actions of people who purchase and use products. It includes the behavior of both consumers purchasing products for personal or household use and organizations buying products for business use. Marketers analyze buying behavior because a firm's marketing strategy should be guided by an understanding of buyers. People view pets as part of their families, and they want their pets to have the best of everything. Iams, which markets the Iams and Eukanuba pet food brands, recognized this trend and shifted its focus. Today, it markets high-quality pet food, fancy pet treats, sauces, and other items. Both psychological and social variables are important to an understanding of buying behavior.

**buying behavior**
the decision processes and actions of people who purchase and use products

## Psychological Variables of Buying Behavior

Psychological factors include the following:

**perception**
the process by which a
person selects, organizes,
and interprets information
received from his or her
senses

**motivation**
inner drive that directs a
person's behavior toward
goals

**learning**
changes in a person's
behavior based on information
and experience

**attitude**
knowledge and positive
or negative feelings about
something

**personality**
the organization of an
individual's distinguishing
character traits, attitudes, or
habits

- **Perception** is the process by which a person selects, organizes, and interprets information received from his or her senses, as when experiencing an advertisement or touching a product to better understand it.
- **Motivation,** as we said in Chapter 9, is an inner drive that directs a person's behavior toward goals. A customer's behavior is influenced by a set of motives rather than by a single motive. A buyer of a tablet computer, for example, may be motivated by ease of use, ability to communicate with the office, and price.
- **Learning** brings about changes in a person's behavior based on information and experience. For instance, a smartphone app that provides digital news or magazine content could eliminate the need for print copies. If a person's actions result in a reward, he or she is likely to behave the same way in similar situations. If a person's actions bring about a negative result, however—such as feeling ill after eating at a certain restaurant—he or she will probably not repeat that action.
- **Attitude** is knowledge and positive or negative feelings about something. For example, a person who feels strongly about protecting the environment may refuse to buy products that harm the earth and its inhabitants.
- **Personality** refers to the organization of an individual's distinguishing character traits, attitudes, or habits. Although market research on the relationship between personality and buying behavior has been inconclusive, some marketers believe that the type of car or clothing a person buys reflects his or her personality.

## Social Variables of Buying Behavior

**social roles**
a set of expectations for
individuals based on some
position they occupy

Social factors include **social roles,** which are a set of expectations for individuals based on some position they occupy. A person may have many roles: mother, wife, student, executive. Each of these roles can influence buying behavior. Consider a woman choosing an automobile. Her father advises her to buy a safe, gasoline-efficient car, such as a Volvo. Her teenaged daughter wants her to buy a cool car, such as a Ford Mustang; her young son wants her to buy a Ford Explorer to take on camping trips. Some of her colleagues at work say she should buy a hybrid Prius to help the environment. Thus, in choosing which car to buy, the woman's buying behavior may be affected by the opinions and experiences of her family and friends and by her roles as mother, daughter, and employee.

Other social factors include reference groups, social classes, and culture.

**reference groups**
groups with whom buyers
identify and whose values or
attitudes they adopt

**social classes**
a ranking of people into higher
or lower positions of respect

**culture**
the integrated, accepted
pattern of human behavior,
including thought, speech,
beliefs, actions, and artifacts

- **Reference groups** include families, professional groups, civic organizations, and other groups with whom buyers identify and whose values or attitudes they adopt. A person may use a reference group as a point of comparison or a source of information. A person new to a community may ask other group members to recommend a family doctor, for example.
- **Social classes** are determined by ranking people into higher or lower positions of respect. Criteria vary from one society to another. People within a particular social class may develop common patterns of behavior. People in the upper-middle class, for example, might buy a Lexus or a BMW as a symbol of their social class.
- **Culture** is the integrated, accepted pattern of human behavior, including thought, speech, beliefs, actions, and artifacts. Culture determines what people

### Millennial Rejection of Car Culture Causes Automakers to Adapt

Millennials include consumers who were born between the early 1980s and the early 2000s. As Millennials grow to adulthood, they represent an important market for automakers. However, automakers are finding that Millennial car buying habits are differing from their predecessors. Namely, Millennials are beginning to reject the car culture in favor of public transportation, bicycling, and alternative services such as the car-sharing service Zipcar. Part of this may be attributed to lower incomes, as younger people often have less discretionary income to spend. Yet another concern is sustainability. Millennials are voicing their concerns for the environment and want more sustainable vehicles. As many customers find less need for vehicles in their everyday lives, the auto industry must adapt to the changing preferences of this demographic.

By 2025, automakers will be forced to implement fuel efficiency standards of 54.5 miles per gallon (MPG). However, automakers are finding that Millennials do not want to wait that long. They are holding automakers accountable, hoping to be provided with vehicles powered by alternative fuels to help diminish concerns over fuel emissions. With fewer Americans bothering to receive driver's licenses and even dubbing it "not cool" to purchase a car, automakers have to rethink their approach when developing vehicles. Time will tell whether they will be able to attract these reluctant car consumers with more sustainable, reasonably priced vehicles.[27]

#### Discussion Questions

1. Why do automakers have to adapt their strategies to attract the Millennial market?
2. Describe some of the differences between Millennials and previous generations regarding vehicle ownership.
3. What happens if automakers cannot sufficiently attract the Millennial market?

---

wear and eat and where they live and travel. Many Hispanic Texans and New Mexicans, for example, buy *masa trigo,* the dough used to prepare flour tortillas, which are basic to Southwestern and Mexican cuisine.

## Understanding Buying Behavior

Although marketers try to understand buying behavior, it is extremely difficult to explain exactly why a buyer purchases a particular product. The tools and techniques for analyzing consumers are not exact. Marketers may not be able to determine accurately what is highly satisfying to buyers, but they know that trying to understand consumer wants and needs is the best way to satisfy them. McDonald's, which has traditionally emphasized children, decided to focus more on Millennials because they are the most profitable. Millennials spend $247 billion annually on restaurants. To target Millennials, McDonald's has made changes to emphasize trends among Millennials. For example, it renovated its restaurants to look more modern, added more customized menu options, and improved the nutritional value of some of its products.[28]

## The Marketing Environment

A number of external forces directly or indirectly influence the development of marketing strategies; the following political, legal, regulatory, social, competitive, economic, and technological forces comprise the marketing environment.

- *Political, legal, and regulatory forces*—laws and regulators' interpretation of laws, law enforcement and regulatory activities, regulatory bodies, legislators and legislation, and political actions of interest groups. Specific laws, for example, require that advertisements be truthful and that all health claims be documented.

- *Social forces*—the public's opinions and attitudes toward issues such as living standards, ethics, the environment, lifestyles, and quality of life. For example, social concerns have led marketers to design and market safer toys for children.
- *Competitive and economic forces*—competitive relationships such as those in the technology industry, unemployment, purchasing power, and general economic conditions (prosperity, recession, depression, recovery, product shortages, and inflation).
- *Technological forces*—computers and other technological advances that improve distribution, promotion, and new-product development.

Marketing requires creativity and consumer focus because environmental forces can change quickly and dramatically. Changes can arise from social concerns and economic forces such as price increases, product shortages, and altering levels of demand for commodities. Recently, climate change, global warming, and the impact of carbon emissions on our environment have become social concerns and are causing businesses to rethink marketing strategies. These environmental issues have persuaded governments to institute stricter limits on greenhouse gas emissions. For instance, in the United States the government has mandated that by 2025 vehicles must be able to reach 54.5 miles per gallon.[29] This is causing automobile companies like General Motors to investigate ways to make their cars more fuel-efficient without significantly raising the price. At the same time, these laws are also introducing opportunities for new products. Concerns over the environment are encouraging automobile companies to begin releasing electric vehicles, such as the Chevrolet Volt and the Nissan Leaf.

Because such environmental forces are interconnected, changes in one may cause changes in others. Consider that because of evidence linking children's consumption of soft drinks and fast foods to health issues such as obesity, diabetes, and osteoporosis, marketers of such products have experienced negative publicity and calls for legislation regulating the sale of soft drinks in public schools.

Although the forces in the marketing environment are sometimes called uncontrollables, they are not totally so. A marketing manager can influence some environmental variables. For example, businesses can lobby legislators to dissuade them from passing unfavorable legislation. Figure 11.4 shows the variables in the marketing environment that affect the marketing mix and the buyer.

# Importance of Marketing to Business and Society

As this chapter has shown, marketing is a necessary function to reaching consumers, establishing relationships, and driving sales. While some critics might view marketing as a way to change what consumers want, marketing is essential in communicating the value of goods and services. For consumers, marketing is necessary to ensure that they get the products they desire at the right places in the right quantities at a reasonable price. From the perspective of businesses, marketing is necessary in order to form valuable relationships with customers to increase profitability and customer support.

It is not just for-profit businesses that engage in marketing activities. Nonprofit organizations, government institutions, and even people must market themselves to spread awareness and achieve desired outcomes. All organizations must reach their

FIGURE 11.4    **The Marketing Mix and the Marketing Environment**

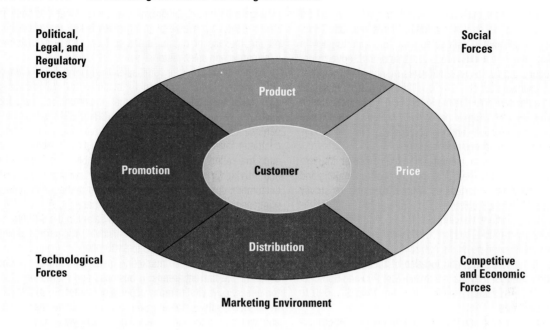

target markets, communicate their offerings, and establish high-quality services. For instance, nonprofit organization The Leukemia and Lymphoma Society uses print, radio, web, and other forms of media to market its Team in Training racing events to recruit participants and solicit support. Without marketing, it would be nearly impossible for organizations to connect with their target audiences. Marketing is therefore an important contributor to business and societal well-being.

You probably did not think as a child how great it would be to grow up and become a marketer. That's because often marketing is associated with sales jobs, but opportunities in marketing, public relations, product management, advertising, e-marketing, and customer relationship management and beyond represent almost one-third of all jobs in today's business world. To enter any job in the marketing field, you must balance an awareness of customer needs with business knowledge while mixing in creativity and the ability to obtain useful information to make smart business decisions.

Marketing starts with understanding the customer. Marketing research is a vital aspect in marketing decision making and presents many job opportunities. Market researchers survey customers to determine their habits, preferences, and aspirations. Activities include concept testing, product testing, package testing, test-market research, and new-product research. Salaries vary, depending on the nature and level of the position as well as the type, size, and location of the firm. An entry-level market analyst may make between $24,000 and $50,000, while a market research director may earn from $75,000 to $200,000 or more.

One of the most dynamic areas in marketing is direct marketing, where a seller solicits a response from a consumer using direct communications methods such as telephone, online communication, direct mail, or catalogs. Jobs in direct marketing include buyers, catalog managers, research/mail-list managers, or order fulfillment managers. Most positions in direct marketing involve planning and market analysis. Some require the use of databases to sort and analyze customer information and sales history.

Use of the Internet for retail sales is growing, and the Internet continues to be very useful for business-to-business sales, so e-marketing offers many career opportunities, including customer relationship management (CRM). CRM helps companies market to customers through relationships, maintaining customer loyalty. Information technology plays a huge role in such marketing jobs, as you need to combine technical skills and marketing knowledge to effectively communicate with customers. Job titles include e-marketing manager, customer relationship manager, and e-services manager. A CRM customer service manager may receive a salary in the $40,000 to $45,000 range, and experienced individuals in charge of online product offerings may earn up to $100,000.

A job in any of these marketing fields will require a strong sense of the current trends in business and marketing. Customer service is vital to many aspects of marketing, so the ability to work with customers and to communicate their needs and wants is important. Marketing is everywhere, from the corner grocery or local nonprofit organization to the largest multinational corporations, making it a shrewd choice for an ambitious and creative person. We will provide additional job opportunities in marketing in Chapter 12.

## Review Your Understanding

### Define *marketing,* and describe the exchange process.

Marketing is a group of activities designed to expedite transactions by creating, distributing, pricing, and promoting goods, services, and ideas. Marketing facilitates the exchange, the act of giving up one thing in return for something else. The central focus of marketing is to satisfy needs.

### Specify the functions of marketing.

Marketing includes many varied and interrelated activities: buying, selling, transporting, storing, grading, financing, marketing research, and risk taking.

### Explain the marketing concept and its implications for developing marketing strategies.

The marketing concept is the idea that an organization should try to satisfy customers' needs through coordinated activities that also allow it to achieve its goals. If a company does not implement the marketing concept by providing products that consumers need and want while achieving its own objectives, it will not survive.

### Examine the development of a marketing strategy, including market segmentation and marketing mix.

A marketing strategy is a plan of action for creating a marketing mix (product, price, distribution, promotion) for a specific target market (a specific group of consumers on whose needs and wants a company focuses its marketing efforts). Some firms use a total-market approach, designating everyone as the target market. Most firms divide the total market into segments of people who have relatively similar product needs. A company using a concentration approach develops one marketing strategy for a single market segment, whereas a multisegment approach aims marketing efforts at two or more segments, developing a different marketing strategy for each.

### Investigate how marketers conduct marketing research and study buying behavior.

Carrying out the marketing concept is impossible unless marketers know what, where, when, and how consumers buy; marketing research into the factors that influence buying behavior helps marketers develop effective marketing strategies. Marketing research is a systematic, objective process of getting information about potential customers to guide marketing decisions. Buying behavior is the decision processes and actions of people who purchase and use products.

### Summarize the environmental forces that influence marketing decisions.

There are several forces that influence marketing activities: political, legal, regulatory, social, competitive, economic, and technological.

### Assess a company's marketing plans, and propose a solution for resolving its problem.

Based on the material in this chapter, you should be able to answer the questions posed in "Solve the Dilemma" on page 353 and help the business understand what went wrong and how to correct it.

## Revisit the World of Business

1. How did marketing contribute toward creating the successful Banana Republic brand?

2. Why do you believe storytelling about the brand and themed stores attracted customers?

3. Despite the differences in Gap-owned Banana Republic stores today, what are similarities the modern retailer shares with its initial stores?

## Learn the Terms

| | | |
|---|---|---|
| attitude 346 | market segmentation 338 | price 341 |
| buying behavior 345 | marketing 330 | primary data 343 |
| concentration approach 340 | marketing concept 333 | promotion 342 |
| culture 346 | marketing mix 341 | reference groups 346 |
| distribution 342 | marketing research 343 | secondary data 344 |
| exchange 330 | marketing strategy 338 | social classes 346 |
| learning 346 | motivation 346 | social roles 346 |
| market 338 | multisegment approach 340 | target market 338 |
| market orientation 336 | perception 346 | total-market approach 338 |
| market segment 338 | personality 346 | value 333 |

## Check Your Progress

1. What is marketing? How does it facilitate exchanges?

2. Name the functions of marketing. How does an organization use marketing activities to achieve its objectives?

3. What is the marketing concept? Why is it so important?

4. What is a marketing strategy?

5. What is market segmentation? Describe three target market strategies.

6. List the variables in the marketing mix. How is each used in a marketing strategy?

7. Why are marketing research and information systems important to an organization's planning and development of strategy?

8. Briefly describe the factors that influence buying behavior. How does understanding buying behavior help marketers?

9. Discuss the impact of technological forces and political and legal forces on the market.

# Get Involved

1. With some or all of your classmates, watch several hours of television, paying close attention to the commercials. Pick three commercials for products with which you are somewhat familiar. Based on the commercials, determine who the target market is. Can you surmise the marketing strategy for each of the three?

2. Discuss the decision process and influences involved in purchasing a personal computer.

# Build Your Skills

## The Marketing Mix

### Background

You've learned the four variables—product, promotion, price, and distribution—that the marketer can select to achieve specific goals within a dynamic marketing environment. This exercise will give you an opportunity to analyze the marketing strategies of some well-known companies to determine which of the variables received the most emphasis to help the company achieve its goals.

### Task

In groups of three to five students, discuss the examples below and decide which variable received the most emphasis.

A. Product
B. Distribution
C. Promotion
D. Price

_____ 1. Starbucks Coffee began selling bagged premium specialty coffee through an agreement with Kraft Foods to gain access to more than 30,000 supermarkets.

_____ 2. Skype is a software application that allows consumers to make telephone calls over the web. Calls to Skype subscribers are free, while calls to land line and mobile phones cost around 2 cents per minute.

_____ 3. Amid great anticipation, Apple released its iPad, selling over 3 million within 3 months. The slim tablet computer is a major step forward in reading e-books, watching movies, and playing games.

_____ 4. After decades on the market, WD-40 is in about 80 percent of U.S. households—more than any other branded product. Although WD-40 is promoted as a product that can stop squeaks, protect metal, loosen rusted parts, and free sticky mechanisms, the WD-40 Company has received letters from customers who have sprayed the product on bait to attract fish, on pets to cure mange, and even on people to cure arthritis. Despite more than 200 proposals to expand the WD-40 product line and ideas to change the packaging and labeling, the company stands firmly behind its one highly successful and respected original product.

_____ 5. Southwest Airlines makes flying fun. Flight attendants try to entertain passengers, and the airline has an impeccable customer service record. Employees play a key role and take classes that emphasize that having fun translates into great customer service.

_____ 6. Hewlett-Packard offered a $100 rebate on a $799 HP LaserJet printer when purchased with an HP LaserJet toner cartridge. To receive the rebate, the buyer had to return a mail-in certificate to certify the purchase. A one-page ad with a coupon was used in *USA Today* stating, "We're taking $100 off the top."

_____ 7. Denny's, the largest full-service family restaurant chain in the United States, serves more than 1 million customers a day. The restaurants offer the Build Your Own Grand Slam Breakfast for about $7.15, lunch basket specials for $4–$6, and a value menu with prices ranging from $2 to $8.

# Solve the Dilemma LO 11-7

## Will It Go?

Ventura Motors makes midsized and luxury automobiles in the United States. Best selling models include its basic four-door sedans (priced from $20,000 to $25,000) and two-door and four-door luxury automobiles (priced from $40,000 to $55,000). The success of two-seat sports cars like the Mazda RX-8 started the company evaluating the market for a two-seat sports car priced midway between the moderate and luxury market. Research found that there was indeed significant demand and that Ventura needed to act quickly to take advantage of this market opportunity.

Ventura took the platform of the car from a popular model in its moderate line, borrowing the internal design from its luxury line. The car was designed, engineered, and produced in just over two years, but the coordination needed to bring the design together resulted in higher than anticipated costs. The price for this two-seat car, the Olympus, was set at $32,000. Dealers were anxious to take delivery on the car, and salespeople were well trained on techniques to sell this new model.

However, initial sales have been slow, and company executives are surprised and concerned. The Olympus was introduced relatively quickly, made available at all Ventura dealers, priced midway between luxury and moderate models, and advertised heavily since its introduction.

### Discussion Questions

1. What do you think were the main concerns with the Olympus two-door sports coupe? Is there a market for a two-seat, $32,000 sports car when the RX-8 sells for significantly less?

2. Evaluate the role of the marketing mix in the Olympus introduction.

3. What are some of the marketing strategies auto manufacturers use to stimulate sales of certain makes of automobiles?

# Build Your Business Plan

## Customer-Driven Marketing

The first step is to develop a marketing strategy for your good or service. Who will be the target market you will specifically try to reach? What group(s) of people has the need, ability, and willingness to purchase this product? How will you segment customers within your target market? Segmenting by demographic and geographic variables are often the easiest segmentation strategies to attempt. Remember that you would like to have the customers in your segment be as homogeneous and accessible as possible. You might target several segments if you feel your good or service has broad appeal.

The second step in your marketing strategy is to develop the marketing mix for your good or service. Whether you are dealing with an established product or you are creating your own good or service, you need to think about what is the differential advantage your product offers. What makes it unique? How should it be priced? Should the product be priced below, above, or at the market? How will you distribute the product? And last but certainly not least, you need to think about the promotional strategy for your product.

What about the uncontrollable variables you need to be aware of? Is your product something that can constantly be technologically advanced? Is your product a luxury that will not be considered by consumers when the economy is in a downturn?

# See for Yourself Videocase

## New Belgium Brews Customer Satisfaction

More and more people recognize the name New Belgium Brewing, and even more are familiar with the brewery's signature product, Fat Tire beer. New Belgium co-founder Jeff Lebesch first began brewing beer with a roommate in his basement. Although the first attempts failed, he and his then-wife Kim Jordon continued basement brewing, eventually creating the now famous Fat Tire—named after the tires Lebesch used to mountain bike through European villages famous for beer. The basement brewery officially went commercial in 1991, selling first to friends, family, and neighbors. A quality product, concern for employees, and commitment to environmental stewardship have led to fast sales growth, making New Belgium the third largest craft brewer in the United States behind Boston Beer and Sierra Nevada. It is also the seventh largest brewery in the nation.

For Lebesch and Jordon, the basement brewery turned out to be a blessing. Jordon became the brewery's first bottler, sales representative, distributor, marketer, and financial planner. (Today, she is the CEO.) Jordon would often deliver products in her Toyota to different stores until the company could afford a better mode of distribution. Her tireless efforts, combined with the low overhead, allowed Lebesch the freedom to experiment with creative beer formulas and innovative techniques without worry about investor expectations or paying off large bank loans. New Belgium's customers are drawn to the company's care over naming, labeling, and producing its beer as much as they are by all that the brewery represents. New Belgium is constantly coming up with new products and even forms partnerships with other craft breweries to help with idea generation. A collaboration with Cigar City Brewing resulted in the release of a new, special-edition ale for its Florida market brewed with Anaheim and Marash chiles.

From the beginning, NBB has been concerned with the brewery's impact on the environment and has made every effort to minimize that impact. When the firm grew beyond the basement and created what is today's New Belgium Brewing, the organization continued to put this concern at the forefront of all business operations. Today, the company is dedicated to balancing profitability with social and environmental responsibility—something its loyal consumers appreciate. The company has used 100 percent wind-powered electricity since 1999, using suntubes, light shelves, and evaporative coolers to reduce energy consumption. New Belgium is now using aluminum cans for some of its Fat Tire beer. Not only are aluminum cans more convenient for customers because they can be taken to places glass cannot, like baseball parks and other outdoor venues, they are more environmentally friendly as well.

Although many in the business world believe that to aid the environment is to destroy business and to earn a profit is to destroy the environment, New Belgium is an example of how a business can truly succeed financially while maintaining a dedication to the environment. The company's environmental practices have become synonymous with its brand, distinguishing it from other specialty beer on the market and creating customer loyalty through shared commitment.

NBB also connects with its fans through Facebook. By using social media, NBB can interact with its fans and understand their desires—an important component of the marketing process. Additionally, social media allows NBB to understand the value of their most loyal customers. In one study, NBB was able to determine that those who "liked" New Belgium on Facebook account for approximately half of the firm's annual sales. By understanding customer value, NBB can tailor marketing messages and create more customized products to attract a wider target market.

New Belgium began with innovation and a dedication to the environment and has stayed true to these elements throughout. The company has continued to grow, so much so that New Belgium has opened an East Coast brewery in Asheville, North Carolina. As the company grows, it focuses on the balance among producing a great product, profit, and environmental stewardship. Ever dedicated to bringing great, unique, and creative beer to its customers, today New Belgium is also striving to reduce its carbon footprint as well as connect with customers in new and innovative ways. Customers remain as loyal to New Belgium as it is to its roots.[30]

### Discussion Questions

1. Why is environmental stewardship so important at New Belgium Brewing?
2. How does a strong commitment to environmental and social responsibility help to attract new customers and maintain old ones?
3. Who do you think is New Belgium's target market?

You can find the related video in the Video Library in Connect. Ask your instructor how you can access Connect.

# Team Exercise

Form groups and assign the responsibility of finding examples of companies that excel in one dimension of the marketing mix (price, product, promotion, and distribution). Provide several company and product examples, and defend why this would be an exemplary case. Present your research to the class.

# 12

# Dimensions of Marketing Strategy

## Learning Objectives

**After reading this chapter, you will be able to:**

**LO 12-1** Describe the role of product in the marketing mix, including how products are developed, classified, and identified.

**LO 12-2** Define *price,* and discuss its importance in the marketing mix, including various pricing strategies a firm might employ.

**LO 12-3** Identify factors affecting distribution decisions, such as marketing channels and intensity of market coverage.

**LO 12-4** Specify the activities involved in promotion, as well as promotional strategies and promotional positioning.

**LO 12-5** Evaluate an organization's marketing strategy plans.

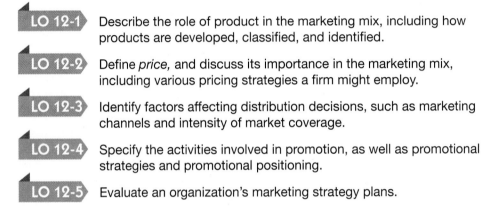

## Chapter Outline

## Corvette's New Look and Message

Chevrolet is revamping its sports car image with the seventh-generation Corvette Stingray to appeal to a younger, more affluent demographic and compete with the popularity of foreign sports cars. The Corvette has in recent years reached the maturity stage of the product life cycle, and many buyers are those in their 50s or older. Chevrolet wants to change this image with a hip new model. The new model of the Stingray is designed with leather, carbon-fiber, and aluminum as opposed to the plastic amenities of the older version. It is equipped with modern features such as a digital instrument panel that adjusts steering wheel resistance and timbre of exhaust. Drivers can also choose their mode of driving, whether it be for the racetrack, bad weather, economical driving, or sports driving. The base model starts at $52,000, and consumers who want the added luxuries can purchase them for an extra $8,000.

Due to the specific and unique nature of the new Stingray, the marketing communication for the product also has to be innovative. Chevy has been promoting the vehicle through more exclusive avenues such as auto shows, cover stories in major newspapers, and auto magazines, which leads to demand via word-of-mouth communication. The company also created a digitalized version of the car for the Sony PlayStation game *Gran Turismo* in order to create buzz among the younger demographic. Publicity, rather than advertising, is key for a product like this because it creates excitement and interest in the market rather than just giving information about the new features of the vehicle.[1]

# Introduction

The key to developing a marketing strategy is selecting a target market and maintaining a marketing mix that creates long-term relationships with customers. Getting just the right mix of product, price, promotion, and distribution is critical if a business is to satisfy its target customers and achieve its own objectives (implement the marketing concept).

In Chapter 11, we introduced the marketing concept and the various activities important in developing a marketing strategy. In this chapter, we'll take a closer look at the four dimensions of the marketing mix—product, price, distribution, and promotion—used to develop the marketing strategy. The focus of these marketing mix elements is a marketing strategy that builds customer relationships and satisfaction.

# The Marketing Mix

The marketing mix is the part of marketing strategy that involves decisions regarding controllable variables. After selecting a target market, marketers have to develop and manage the dimensions of the marketing mix to give their firm an advantage over competitors. Successful companies offer at least one dimension of value usually associated with a marketing mix element that surpasses all competitors in the marketplace in meeting customer expectations. However, this does not mean that a company can ignore the other dimensions of the marketing mix; it must maintain acceptable, and if possible distinguishable, differences in the other dimensions as well.

**DID YOU KNOW?**  Less than 10 percent of new products succeed in the marketplace, and 90 percent of successes come from a handful of companies.[2]

Walmart, for example, emphasizes price ("Save money, live better"). Procter & Gamble is well known for its promotion of top consumer brands such as Tide, Cheer, Crest, Ivory, and Head & Shoulders. Xiaomi, a three-year-old Chinese consumer electronics company, has achieved impressive scale by utilizing a low-cost, feature-rich strategy.[3]

# Product Strategy

As mentioned previously, the term *product* refers to goods, services, and ideas. Because the product is often the most visible of the marketing mix dimensions, managing product decisions is crucial. In this section, we'll consider product development, classification, mix, life cycle, and identification.

### Developing New Products

Each year, thousands of products are introduced, but few of them succeed. For example, Hewlett-Packard believed it could compete in the tablet computer industry with the TouchPad and its WebOS operating system. However, after six weeks of being on the market, HP dropped the TouchPad due to lackluster sales. Many companies have similar stories of product failure.[4] Figure 12.1 shows the different steps in the product development process. Before introducing a new product, a business must follow a multistep process: idea development, the screening of new ideas, business analysis, product development, test marketing, and commercialization. A firm can take considerable time to get a product ready for the market: It took more than 20 years for the first photocopier, for example. Additionally, sometimes an idea or product prototype might be shelved only to be returned to later. Former Apple CEO Steve Jobs admitted that the iPad actually came before the iPhone in the product development process. Once it was realized that the scrolling mechanism he was thinking of using could be used to develop a phone, the iPad idea was placed on a shelf for the time being. Apple later returned to develop the product and released the iPad in 2010.[5]

**Idea Development.**   New ideas can come from marketing research, engineers, and outside sources such as advertising agencies and management consultants. Nike has a separate division—Nike Sport Research Lab—where scientists, athletes, engineers, and designers work together to develop technology of the future. The teams research ideas in biomechanics, perception, athletic performance, and physiology to create unique, relevant, and innovative products. These final products are tested in environmental chambers with real athletes to ensure functionality and quality before being introduced into the market.[6] As we said in Chapter 11, ideas sometimes come from customers, too. Other sources are brainstorming and intracompany incentives or rewards for good ideas. New ideas

While attending Yale in 1966, FedEx founder Fred Smith studied a mathematical discipline called topology, which inspired his vision for creating the company. Realizing the potential efficiencies of connecting all points on a network through a central hub, Smith used what he learned to get FedEx off the ground.

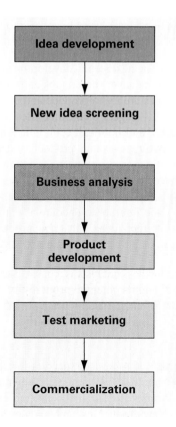

**FIGURE 12.1**
**Product Development Process**

## Plant-Based Food Products: The Future of Food?

John Tetrick has a vision to change the future of food. He founded Hampton Creek Foods in 2011. Hampton Creek offers plant-based replacements for foods that traditionally use animal-based products. Beyond Eggs, a plant-based egg replacement for baking purposes, was the catalyst for the business. Hampton Creek has also produced Just Mayo, a mayonnaise replacement, and is currently developing a scrambled egg version of the product. Tetrick hopes his creation will be the solution to the problems he sees in food: animal cruelty, health, cost, and sustainability.

The company makes sure to target every group through its integrated marketing communications. In addition to its 120,000 Facebook followers and 5,000 Twitter followers, Hampton Creek Foods sends out targeted e-mails to promote its brand with free sample offers. Sampling has proven effective because many people are skeptical that a plant-based egg product would taste good until they try

it. Another effective part of the marketing strategy is its press outreach program, as well as its endorsement by Bill Gates. The company relies heavily on storytelling to communicate its message, which is a promotional positioning strategy. Mothers whose children are allergic to eggs, people who are concerned about the environment and animal welfare, as well as those who want inexpensive but quality food tell their stories about how great the future of food can be.[7]

### Discussion Questions

1. Describe the different ways Hampton Creek markets its plant-based food products.
2. Why do sampling and storytelling appear to be effective techniques for promoting Hampton Creek products?
3. Why might an endorsement by Bill Gates add credibility to Hampton Creek products?

---

can even create a company. When Jeff Bezos came up with the idea to sell books over the Internet in 1992, he had no idea it would evolve into an $138 billion firm. After failing to convince his boss of the idea, Bezos left to start Amazon.com.[8]

**New Idea Screening.**  The next step in developing a new product is idea screening. In this phase, a marketing manager should look at the organization's resources and objectives and assess the firm's ability to produce and market the product. Important aspects to be considered at this stage are consumer desires, the competition, technological changes, social trends, and political, economic, and environmental considerations. Basically, there are two reasons new products succeed: They are able to meet a need or solve a problem better than products already available or they add variety to the product selection currently on the market. Bringing together a team of knowledgeable people including designers, engineers, marketers, and customers is a great way to screen ideas. Using the Internet to encourage collaboration represents a rich opportunity for marketers to screen ideas. Most new product ideas are rejected during screening because they seem inappropriate or impractical for the organization.

**Business Analysis.**  Business analysis is a basic assessment of a product's compatibility in the marketplace and its potential profitability. Both the size of the market and competing products are often studied at this point. The most important question relates to market demand: How will the product affect the firm's sales, costs, and profits?

**Product Development.**  If a product survives the first three steps, it is developed into a prototype that should reveal the intangible attributes it possesses as perceived by the consumer. Product development is often expensive, and few product ideas make it to this stage. New product research and development costs vary. Adding a new color to an existing item may cost $100,000 to $200,000, but launching a completely new product can cost millions of dollars. During product development, various elements of the marketing mix must be developed for testing. Copyrights, tentative advertising copy, packaging, labeling, and descriptions of a target market are integrated to develop an overall marketing strategy.

**Test Marketing.**   **Test marketing** is a trial minilaunch of a product in limited areas that represent the potential market. It allows a complete test of the marketing strategy in a natural environment, giving the organization an opportunity to discover weaknesses and eliminate them before the product is fully launched. SOHM Inc., a generic pharmaceutical manufacturing firm, began test marketing some of its over-the-counter and skin care products in U.S. retailers. Traditionally, SOHM has been more focused on emerging markets in Africa, Southeast Asia, and Latin America.[9] Because test marketing requires significant resources and expertise, market research companies like ACNielsen can assist firms in test marketing their products. Figure 12.2 shows the permanent sites as well as custom locations for test marketing.

**test marketing**
a trial minilaunch of a product in limited areas that represent the potential market

**Commercialization.**   **Commercialization** is the full introduction of a complete marketing strategy and the launch of the product for commercial success. During commercialization, the firm gears up for full-scale production, distribution, and promotion. Firms such as AquAdvantage Salmon are getting ready to release genetically modified salmon into the market. The Food and Drug Administration has announced a preliminary finding that engineered salmon would not significantly affect the U.S. environment, lending support to the idea that genetically modified salmon is safe to consume. Federal approval is one major step for AquAdvantage in its plans for large-scale commercialization. However, even with federal regulatory approval,

**commercialization**
the full introduction of a complete marketing strategy and the launch of the product for commercial success

**Market Decisions
Test Market Locations**

Portland
Boise
Peoria
Colorado Springs
Evansville
Lexington
Charleston
Tucson

◆ Permanent Test Markets
("Data Markets")

★ Additional "Custom" Test Markets

**FIGURE 12.2**
**Nielsen Market Decisions**

Source: Copyrighted information of The Nielsen Company, licensed for use herein.

Coca-Cola BlāK is a coffee-flavored soft drink that Coca-Cola introduced in 2006. It is an example of product that did not survive. Many consumers did not like the taste, and Coca-Cola discontinued the drink in 2008.

**consumer products**
products intended for household or family use

**business products**
products that are used directly or indirectly in the operation or manufacturing processes of businesses

AquAdvantage may face hurdles from state governments or rejection from consumers who are concerned about the health risks of engineered salmon.[10]

## Classifying Products

Products are usually classified as either consumer products or industrial products. **Consumer products** are for household or family use; they are not intended for any purpose other than daily living. They can be further classified as convenience products, shopping products, and specialty products on the basis of consumers' buying behavior and intentions.

- *Convenience products,* such as eggs, milk, bread, and newspapers, are bought frequently, without a lengthy search, and often for immediate consumption. Consumers spend virtually no time planning where to purchase these products and usually accept whatever brand is available.
- *Shopping products,* such as furniture, audio equipment, clothing, and sporting goods, are purchased after the consumer has compared competitive products and "shopped around." Price, product features, quality, style, service, and image all influence the decision to buy.
- *Specialty products,* such as ethnic foods, designer clothing and shoes, art, and antiques, require even greater research and shopping effort. Consumers know what they want and go out of their way to find it; they are not willing to accept a substitute.

**Business products** are used directly or indirectly in the operation or manufacturing processes of businesses. They are usually purchased for the operation of an organization or the production of other products; thus, their purchase is tied to specific goals and objectives. They too can be further classified:

- *Raw materials* are natural products taken from the earth, oceans, and recycled solid waste. Iron ore, bauxite, lumber, cotton, and fruits and vegetables are examples.
- *Major equipment* covers large, expensive items used in production. Examples include earth-moving equipment, stamping machines, and robotic equipment used on auto assembly lines.
- *Accessory equipment* includes items used for production, office, or management purposes, which usually do not become part of the final product. Computers, fax machines, calculators, and hand tools are examples.
- *Component parts* are finished items, ready to be assembled into the company's final products. Tires, window glass, batteries, and spark plugs are component parts of automobiles.
- *Processed materials* are things used directly in production or management operations but are not readily identifiable as component parts. Varnish, for example, is a processed material for a furniture manufacturer.
- *Supplies* include materials that make production, management, and other operations possible, such as paper, pencils, paint, cleaning supplies, and so on.
- *Industrial services* include financial, legal, marketing research, security, janitorial, and exterminating services. Purchasers decide whether to provide these services internally or to acquire them from an outside supplier.

**FIGURE 12.3 Colgate-Palmolive's Product Mix and Product Lines**

← Product Mix →

↕ Product Lines

| Oral Care | Personal Care | Home Care | Pet Nutrition |
|---|---|---|---|
| *Toothpaste*<br>Colgate Total Advanced<br>Colgate Optic White | *Deodorant*<br>Speed Stick<br>Lady Speed Stick | *Dishwashing*<br>Palmolive<br>AJAX<br>Dermassage | Hill's Prescription Diet<br>Hill's Science Diet<br>Hill's Ideal Balance |
| *Colgate Kids*<br>Colgate Dora the Explorer<br>Colgate SpongeBob SquarePants<br>Colgate 2in1 | *Body Wash*<br>Softsoap<br>Irish Spring<br><br>*Bar Soap*<br>Irish Spring Softsoap | *Fabric Conditioner*<br>Suavitel | |
| *Toothbrushes*<br>Colgate 360°<br>Colgate Max White<br>Colgate Total Professional | *Toiletries for Men*<br>Afta Skin Bracer | *Household cleaner*<br>Murphy Oil Soap<br>Fabuloso<br>AJAX | |

Source: Colgate Palmolive, "Colgate World of Care," www.colgatepalmolive.com/app/Colgate/US/CompanyHomePage.cvsp (accessed May 15, 2014).

## Product Line and Product Mix

Product relationships within an organization are of key importance. A **product line** is a group of closely related products that are treated as a unit because of a similar marketing strategy. At Colgate-Palmolive, for example, the oral-care product line includes Colgate toothpaste, toothbrushes, and dental floss. A **product mix** is all the products offered by an organization. Figure 12.3 displays a sampling of the product mix and product lines of the Colgate-Palmolive Company.

connect

Need help understanding Product Life Cycle? Visit your Connect ebook video tab for a brief animated explanation.

## Product Life Cycle

Like people, products are born, grow, mature, and eventually die. Some products have very long lives. Ivory Soap was introduced in 1879 and still exists (although competition leading to decreased sales may soon put the future of Ivory Soap in question). In contrast, a new computer chip is usually outdated within a year because of technological breakthroughs and rapid changes in the computer industry. There are four stages in the life cycle of a product: introduction, growth, maturity, and decline (Figure 12.4). The stage a product is in helps determine marketing strategy. In the personal computer industry, desktop computers are in the decline stage, laptop computers have reached the maturity stage, and tablet computers are currently in the growth stage of the product life cycle. Manufacturers of these products are adopting different advertising and pricing strategies to maintain or increase demand for these types of computers.

**product line** a group of closely related products that are treated as a unit because of similar marketing strategy, production, or end-use considerations

**product mix** all the products offered by an organization

In the *introductory stage,* consumer awareness and acceptance of the product are limited, sales are zero, and profits are negative. Profits are negative because the firm has spent money on research, development, and marketing to launch the product. During the introductory stage, marketers focus on making consumers aware of the product and its benefits. Google Glass is currently in the introductory stage of the product life cycle. Google Glass is a wearable technology that enables users to take pictures, make phone calls, and reply to e-mails through voice commands. Early adoption of

**FIGURE 12.4**
**The Life Cycle of a Product**

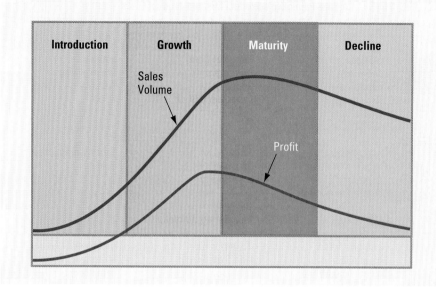

Glass seems promising, despite several potential barriers such as pricing, social and cultural factors, and the level of developer interest.[11] Table 12.1 shows some familiar products at different stages of the product life cycle. Sales accelerate as the product enters the growth stage of the life cycle.

In the *growth stage,* sales increase rapidly and profits peak, then start to decline. One reason profits start to decline during the growth stage is that new companies enter the market, driving prices down and increasing marketing expenses. Beats by Dre Studio headphones are currently in the growth stage. Launched in 2008, the premium headphone brand holds 27 percent of the $1.8 billion headphone market and 57 percent of the premium headphone market. Since the brand's debut, the company has increased products to include speakers, earphones, proprietary software technology, and a music streaming service.[12] During the growth stage, the firm tries to strengthen its position in the market by emphasizing the product's benefits and identifying market segments that want these benefits.

Sales continue to increase at the beginning of the *maturity stage,* but then the sales curve peaks and starts to decline while profits continue to decline. This stage is characterized by severe competition and heavy expenditures. In the United States, soft drinks have hit the maturity stage. Firms such as PepsiCo and Coca-Cola have taken many steps to try and revitalize sales, from introducing soda in smaller package sizes to adopting healthier product lines to expanding their reach internationally in places like Africa.[13]

**TABLE 12.1**
**Products at Different Stages of the Product Life Cycle**

| Introduction | Growth | Maturity | Decline |
|---|---|---|---|
| Google Glass | Tablet computer | Laptop computer | Desktop computer |
| Smartwatch | LEGO Friends | Print newspaper | CD player |
| Electric car | Ford Focus | Chevrolet Corvette | PT Cruiser |

During the *decline stage,* sales continue to fall rapidly. Profits also decline and may even become losses as prices are cut and necessary marketing expenditures are made. As profits drop, firms may eliminate certain models or items. To reduce expenses and squeeze out any remaining profits, marketing expenditures may be cut back, even though such cutbacks accelerate the sales decline. Finally, plans must be made for phasing out the product and introducing new ones to take its place. Apple iPods have been in decline in recent years as tablets and phones are being designed to serve as music listening devices. The iPod classic is rumored to be phased out of Apple's product line and has not been updated in a few years. Touchscreen iPods and the iPod shuffle, while also included in the decline stage of the product life cycle, are not yet being prepared for exit from the marketplace.[14]

At the same time, it should be noted that product stages do not always go one way. Some products that have moved to the maturity stage or to the decline stage can still rebound through redesign or new uses for the product. One prime example is baking soda. Originally, baking soda was only used for cooking, which meant it reached the maturity stage very quickly. However, once it was discovered that baking soda could be used as a deodorizer, sales shot up and bumped baking soda back into the growth stage.[15] Similarly, Acer is trying to make a comeback by releasing new lines of tablets and cell phones. The company focuses on value by offering quality products inexpensively. The Iconia One 7, for instance, is a 7-inch tablet that looks and functions just like the competition but costs significantly less. The company has also introduced a hybrid laptop/tablet combination product to appeal to more customers. Acer is aiming for the middle of the market positioning to achieve a successful comeback with these new products.[16]

## Identifying Products

Branding, packaging, and labeling can be used to identify or distinguish one product from others. As a result, they are key marketing activities that help position a product appropriately for its target market.

**Branding.**   **Branding** is the process of naming and identifying products. A *brand* is a name, term, symbol, design, or combination that identifies a product and distinguishes it from other products. Consider that Google, iPod, and TiVo are brand names that are used to identify entire product categories, much like Xerox has become synonymous with photocopying and Kleenex with tissues. Protecting a brand name is important in maintaining a brand identity. The world's 10 most valuable brands are shown in Table 12.2. The brand name is the part of the brand that can be spoken and consists of letters, words, and numbers—such as WD-40 lubricant. A *brand mark* is the part of the brand that is a distinctive design, such as the silver star on the hood of a Mercedes or McDonald's golden arches logo. A **trademark** is a brand that is registered with the U.S. Patent and Trademark Office and is thus legally protected from use by any other firm.

Two major categories of brands are manufacturer brands and private distributor brands. **Manufacturer brands** are brands initiated and owned by the manufacturer to identify products from the point of production to the point of purchase. Kellogg's, Sony, and Texaco are examples. **Private distributor brands,** which may be less expensive than manufacturer brands, are owned and controlled by a wholesaler or retailer, such as Pantry Essentials (Safeway), Great Value (Walmart), and Member's Mark (Sam's Wholesale Club). The names of private brands do not usually identify their manufacturer. While private-label brands were once considered cheaper and of poor

branding
the process of naming and identifying products

trademark
a brand that is registered with the U.S. Patent and Trademark Office and is thus legally protected from use by any other firm

manufacturer brands
brands initiated and owned by the manufacturer to identify products from the point of production to the point of purchase

private distributor brands
brands, which may cost less than manufacturer brands, that are owned and controlled by a wholesaler or retailer

**TABLE 12.2**
**The 10 Most Valuable Brands in the World**

| Rank | Brand | Brand Value ($ Millions) | Brand Value % Change |
|------|-------|--------------------------|----------------------|
| 1 | Google | 158,843 | 40 |
| 2 | Apple | 147,880 | −20 |
| 3 | IBM | 107,541 | −4 |
| 4 | Microsoft | 90,185 | 29 |
| 5 | McDonald's | 85,706 | −5 |
| 6 | Coca-Cola | 80,683 | 3 |
| 7 | Visa | 79,197 | 41 |
| 8 | AT&T | 77,883 | 3 |
| 9 | Marlboro | 67,341 | −3 |
| 10 | Amazon.com | 64,255 | 41 |

Source: Millward Brown Optimer, "Brandz™ Top 100 Most Valuable Global Brands 2014," www.millwardbrown.com/brandz/2014/Top100/Docs/2014_BrandZ_Top100_Chart.pdf (accessed May 27, 2014).

quality, such as Walmart's Ol'Roy dog food, many private-label brands are increasing in quality and image and are competing with national brands. For instance, a number of companies are hiring professional designers to design their private-label brands, replacing the traditional two-color packaging schemes often associated with private-label products. Target hired designer Jason Wu to design a limited-edition fashion collection, which sold out in a matter of hours.[17] The grocery retailer Tesco has several types of private-label brands, and its branding strategy has performed so effectively that consumers may end up paying more for Tesco's own products than for branded goods.[18] Manufacturer brands are fighting hard against private distributor brands to retain their market share.

**generic products**
products with no brand name that often come in simple packages and carry only their generic name

Another type of brand that has developed is **generic products**—products with no brand name at all. They often come in plain simple packages that carry only the generic name of the product—peanut butter, tomato juice, aspirin, dog food, and so on. They appeal to consumers who may be willing to sacrifice quality or product consistency to get a lower price. Generic brands increased more than 18 percent in the last several years as food prices have risen and economic conditions have declined.[19]

Companies use two basic approaches to branding multiple products. In one, a company gives each product within its complete product mix its own brand name. Warner-Lambert, which was acquired by Pfizer in 2000, sells many well-known consumer products—Dentyne, Chiclets, Listerine, Halls, Rolaids, and Trident—each individually branded. This branding policy ensures that the name of one product does not affect the names of others, and different brands can be targeted at different segments of the same market, increasing the company's market share (its percentage of the sales for the total market for a product). Another approach to branding is to develop a family of brands with each of the firm's products carrying the same name or at least part of the name. Gillette, Sara Lee, and IBM use this approach. Finally, consumers may react differently to domestic versus foreign brands. Table 12.3 provides a snapshot of the most popular car brands.

| Ranking | Vehicle Model | Country of Origin |
|---------|---------------|-------------------|
| 1 | Ford Focus | United States |
| 2 | Toyota Corolla | Japan |
| 3 | Volkswagen Jetta | Germany |
| 4 | Hyundai Elantra | South Korea |
| 5 | Chevrolet Cruze | United States |
| 6 | Toyota Camry | Japan |
| 7 | Volkswagen Golf | Germany |
| 8 | Ford Fiesta | United States |
| 9 | Honda CR-V | Japan |
| 10 | Volkswagen Polo | Germany |

**TABLE 12.3**
**Best-Selling Car Brands in the World**

Source: Joann Muller, "The World's Most Popular Cars: Ford Focus and Other Surprises," Forbes, December 23, 2013, www.forbes.com/sites/joannmuller/2013/12/23/the-worlds-most-popular-cars-ford-focus-and-other-surprises/ (accessed May 15, 2014).

**packaging**
the external container that holds and describes the product

**labeling**
the presentation of important information on a package

**Packaging.**   The **packaging,** or external container that holds and describes the product, influences consumers' attitudes and their buying decisions. Surveys have shown that consumers are willing to pay more for certain packaging attributes. One of the attributes includes clearly stated nutrition and ingredient labeling, especially those characteristics indicating whether a product is organic, gluten free, or environmentally friendly. Recyclable and biodegradable packaging is also popular.[20] It is estimated that consumers' eyes linger only 2.5 seconds on each product on an average shopping trip; therefore, product packaging should be designed to attract and hold consumers' attention.

A package can perform several functions, including protection, economy, convenience, and promotion. Packaging can also be used to appeal to emotions. For example, Chobani yogurt focuses on package design as a means of appealing to customers. Their design is meant to express that their product tastes as good as it looks.[21] On the other hand, organizations must also exert caution before changing the designs of highly popular products. Olive Garden received criticism after changing its logo design. Critics believe the new design relays a cheaper and carefree feeling that was not embodied by the traditional logo.[22]

**Labeling.**   **Labeling,** the presentation of important information on the package, is closely associated with packaging. The content of labeling, often required by law, may include ingredients or content, nutrition facts (calories, fat, etc.), care instructions, suggestions for use (such as recipes), the manufacturer's address and toll-free number, website, and other useful information. This information can have a strong impact on sales. The labels of many products, particularly food and drugs, must carry warnings, instructions, certifications, or manufacturers' identifications.

Clorox uses a family branding strategy so that consumers will recognize when a product is affiliated with the brand.

Google is the most valuable brand worldwide. It owns a variety of brands, including the search engine Google, the web browser Chrome, the video sharing site YouTube, and the social networking site Google+.

**Product Quality.**    **Quality** reflects the degree to which a good, service, or idea meets the demands and requirements of customers. Quality products are often referred to as reliable, durable, easily maintained, easily used, a good value, or a trusted brand name. The level of quality is the amount of quality that a product possesses, and the consistency of quality depends on the product maintaining the same level of quality over time.

Quality of service is difficult to gauge because it depends on customers' perceptions of how well the service meets or exceeds their expectations. In other words, service quality is judged by consumers, not the service providers. For this reason, it is quite common for perceptions of quality to fluctuate from year to year. For instance, General Motors recalled millions of vehicles due to quality control issues. Problems included faulty ignition switches that prompted General Motors to issue a recall on the Chevy Cobalt. These recalls are having a negative impact on  consumers' perceptions of GM's brands. A bank may define service quality as employing friendly and knowledgeable employees, but the bank's customers may be more concerned with waiting time, ATM access, security, and statement accuracy. Similarly, an airline traveler considers on-time arrival, on-board Internet or TV connections, and satisfaction with the ticketing and boarding process. The American Customer Satisfaction Index produces customer satisfaction scores for 10 economic sectors, 44 industries, and more than 200 companies. The latest results show that overall customer satisfaction was 76.8 (out of a possible 100) with increases in some industries balancing out drops in others.[23] Table 12.4 shows the customer satisfaction rankings of some of the most popular personal care and cleaning product companies.

The quality of services provided by businesses on the Internet can be gauged by consumers on such sites as ConsumerReports.org and BBBOnline. The subscription service offered by ConsumerReports.org provides consumers with a view of digital marketing sites' business, security, and privacy policies, while BBBOnline is dedicated to promoting responsibility online. As consumers join in by posting business

**quality**
the degree to which a good, service, or idea meets the demands and requirements of customers

**TABLE 12.4**
**Personal Care and Cleaning Products Customer Satisfaction Ratings**

| Company | Score |
|---|---|
| Clorox | 85 |
| Unilever | 85 |
| Colgate-Palmolive | 85 |
| Dial | 84 |
| Procter & Gamble | 84 |

Source: American Customer Satisfaction Index, "Consumers Less Satisfied with Food Manufacturers; Athletic Shoes Rebound," October 15, 2013, www.theacsi.org/news-and-resources/press-releases/acsi-press-releases-2013/press-release-october-2013 (accessed May 15, 2014).

and product reviews on the Internet on sites such as Yelp, the public can often get a much better idea of the quality of certain goods and services. Quality can also be associated with where the product is made. For example, "Made in U.S.A." labeling can be perceived as having a different value and quality. There are differences in the perception of quality and value between U.S. consumers and Europeans when comparing products made in the United States, Japan, Korea, and China.[24] Chinese brands are usually perceived as lower quality, while Japanese and Korean products are perceived as being of higher quality.

# Pricing Strategy

Previously, we defined price as the value placed on an object exchanged between a buyer and a seller. Buyers' interest in price stems from their expectations about the usefulness of a product or the satisfaction they may derive from it. Because buyers have limited resources, they must allocate those resources to obtain the products they most desire. They must decide whether the benefits gained in an exchange are worth the buying power sacrificed. Almost anything of value can be assessed by a price. Many factors may influence the evaluation of value, including time constraints, price levels, perceived quality, and motivations to use available information about prices.[25] Figure 12.5 illustrates a method for calculating the value of a product. Indeed, consumers vary in their response to price: Some focus solely on the lowest price, while others consider quality or the prestige associated with a product and its price. Some types of consumers are increasingly "trading up" to more status-conscious products, such as automobiles, home appliances, restaurants, and even pet food, yet remain price-conscious for other products such as cleaning and grocery goods. In setting prices, marketers must consider not just a company's cost to produce a good or service, but the perceived value of that item in the marketplace. Products' perceived value has benefited marketers at Starbucks, Sub-Zero, BMW, and Petco—which can charge premium prices for high-quality, prestige products—as well as Sam's Clubs and Costco—which offer basic household products at everyday low prices.

Price is a key element in the marketing mix because it relates directly to the generation of revenue and profits. In large part, the ability to set a price depends on the supply of and demand for a product. For most products, the quantity demanded goes up as the price goes down, and as the price goes up, the quantity demanded goes down. Changes in buyers' needs, variations in the effectiveness of other marketing mix variables, the

**FIGURE 12.5**    **Calculating the Value of a Product**

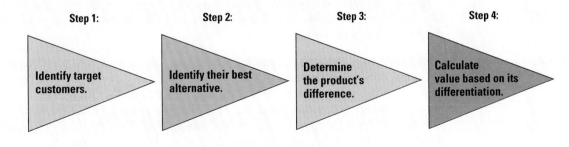

Source: Rafi Mohammed, "Use Price to Profit and Grow," *Forbes.com*, March 25, 2010, www.forbes.com/ 2010/03/25/profit-gain-value-mckinsey-sears-whirlpool-cmo-network-rafi-mohammed.html (accessed April 15, 2012).

presence of substitutes, and dynamic environmental factors can influence demand. The demand and price for coal has decreased as the price for natural gas has decreased due to an increase in supply.

Price is probably the most flexible variable in the marketing mix. Although it may take years to develop a product, establish channels of distribution, and design and implement promotion, a product's price may be set and changed in a few minutes. Under certain circumstances, of course, the price may not be so flexible, especially if government regulations prevent dealers from controlling prices. Of course, price also depends on the cost to manufacture a good or provide a service or idea. A firm may temporarily sell products below cost to match competition, to generate cash flow, or even to increase market share, but in the long run, it cannot survive by selling its products below cost.

## Pricing Objectives

Pricing objectives specify the role of price in an organization's marketing mix and strategy. They usually are influenced not only by marketing mix decisions but also by finance, accounting, and production factors. Maximizing profits and sales, boosting market share, maintaining the status quo, and survival are four common pricing objectives.

## Specific Pricing Strategies

Pricing strategies provide guidelines for achieving the company's pricing objectives and overall marketing strategy. They specify how price will be used as a variable in the marketing mix. Significant pricing strategies relate to the pricing of new products, psychological pricing, and price discounting.

**Pricing New Products.**    Setting the price for a new product is critical: The right price leads to profitability; the wrong price may kill the product. In general, there are two basic strategies to setting the base price for a new product. **Price skimming** is charging the highest possible price that buyers who want the product will pay. Price skimming is used with luxury goods items. Gucci bags, for example, often run into the thousands of dollars. Price skimming is often used to allow the company to generate much-needed revenue to help offset the costs of research and development. Conversely, a **penetration price** is a low price designed to help a product enter the market and gain market share rapidly. When Netflix entered the market, it offered its rentals at prices much lower than the average rental stores and did not charge late fees. Netflix quickly gained market share and eventually drove many rental stores out of business. Penetration pricing is less flexible than price skimming; it is more difficult to raise a penetration price than to lower a skimming price. Penetration pricing is used most often when marketers suspect that competitors will enter the market shortly after the product has been introduced.

**price skimming**
charging the highest possible price that buyers who want the product will pay

**penetration price**
a low price designed to help a product enter the market and gain market share rapidly

**psychological pricing**
encouraging purchases based on emotional rather than rational responses to the price

**Psychological Pricing.**    **Psychological pricing** encourages purchases based on emotional rather than rational responses to the price. For example, the assumption behind *even/odd pricing* is that people will buy more of a product for $9.99 than $10 because it seems to be a bargain at the odd price. The assumption behind *symbolic/ prestige pricing* is that high prices connote high quality. Thus the prices of certain fragrances and cosmetics are set artificially high to give the impression of superior quality. Some over-the-counter drugs are priced high because consumers associate a drug's price with potency.

## Moots Cycles

**Moots Cycles**
**Founder:** Kent Eriksen
**Founded:** 1981, in Steamboat, Colorado
**Success:** Moots is one of the few bicycle manufacturers that build only titanium bicycles, which has enabled it to charge a premium price and generate a loyal following.

Moots cycles is a bicycle manufacturer founded in 1981 by Kent Eriksen in Steamboat, Colorado. He started the company with the goal to provide a high-quality titanium bicycle. In so doing, Eriksen decided to adopt a premium pricing strategy. The average price of the company's bicycles is about $5,000. This reduces the market willing to purchase the bicycles to

the most avid bicyclists and individual riders. Yet, Moots is one of the few bicycle companies left that manufactures bicycles from titanium tubing, a stiff and strong alloy metal that is highly resilient. This fits with the company's goal of building the best-fitting, finest-riding bike its customers will ever own.

Moots pays special attention to the product component of the marketing mix. Moots is known for making its handlebars, stems, and frames by hand, which has grown them a strong customer base who desire the best in quality even if it means higher prices. The company has built one of the most expensive frames priced on the market, but its fans believe that the final product warrants every penny.[26]

**Reference Pricing.** **Reference pricing** is a type of psychological pricing in which a lower-priced item is compared to a more expensive brand in hopes that the consumer will use the higher price as a comparison price. The main idea is to make the item appear less expensive compared with other alternatives. For example, Walmart might place its Great Value brand next to a manufacturer's brand such as Bayer or Johnson & Johnson so that the Great Value brand will look like a better deal.

**reference pricing**
a type of psychological pricing in which a lower-priced item is compared to a more expensive brand in hopes that the consumer will use the higher price as a comparison price

**Price Discounting.** Temporary price reductions, or **discounts,** are often employed to boost sales. Although there are many types, quantity, seasonal, and promotional discounts are among the most widely used. Quantity discounts reflect the economies of purchasing in large volumes. Seasonal discounts to buyers who purchase goods or services out of season help even out production capacity. Promotional discounts attempt to improve sales by advertising price reductions on selected products to increase customer interest. Often promotional pricing is geared toward increased profits. Taco Bell, with its reputation for value, has been labeled the "best-positioned U.S. brand" to do well in a recession economy as consumers look for cheaper fast-food options. Taco Bell offers a Why Pay More? menu with selections priced at 89¢ and 99¢. KFC, Wendy's, and McDonald's all offer Value Menus as well, with items priced around $1.

**discounts**
temporary price reductions, often employed to boost sales

# Distribution Strategy

The best products in the world will not be successful unless companies make them available where and when customers want to buy them. In this section, we will explore dimensions of distribution strategy, including the channels through which products are distributed, the intensity of market coverage, and the physical handling of products during distribution.

LO 12-3

## Marketing Channels

A **marketing channel,** or channel of distribution, is a group of organizations that moves products from their producer to customers. Marketing channels make products available to buyers when and where they desire to purchase them. Organizations that

**marketing channel**
a group of organizations that moves products from their producer to customers; also called a channel of distribution

**TABLE 12.5**    **General Merchandise Retailers**

| Type of Retailer | Description | Examples |
|---|---|---|
| Department store | Large organization offering wide product mix and organized into separate departments | Macy's, JCPenney, Sears |
| Discount store | Self-service, general merchandise store offering brand name and private brand products at low prices | Walmart, Target, Kmart |
| Convenience store | Small self-service store offering narrow product assortment in convenient locations | 7-Eleven |
| Supermarket | Self-service store offering complete line of food products and some nonfood products | Kroger, Safeway, Publix |
| Superstore | Giant outlet offering all food and nonfood products found in supermarkets, as well as most routinely purchased products | Walmart Supercenters, SuperTarget |
| Hypermarket | Combination of supermarket and discount store, larger than a superstore | Carrefour |
| Warehouse club | Large-scale, members-only establishments combining cash-and-carry wholesaling with discount retailing | Sam's Club, Costco |
| Warehouse showroom | Facility in a large, low-cost building with large on-premises inventories and minimum service | Ikea |

Source: William M. Pride and O. C. Ferrell, Marketing Foundations, 2013, p. 431. Copyright South-Western, a part of Cengage Learning. Reprinted with permission.

bridge the gap between a product's manufacturer and the ultimate consumer are called *middlemen*, or intermediaries. They create time, place, and ownership utility. Two intermediary organizations are retailers and wholesalers.

**retailers**
intermediaries who buy products from manufacturers (or other intermediaries) and sell them to consumers for home and household use rather than for resale or for use in producing other products

**Retailers** buy products from manufacturers (or other intermediaries) and sell them to consumers for home and household use rather than for resale or for use in producing other products. Toys 'Я' Us, for example, buys products from Mattel and other manufacturers and resells them to consumers. By bringing together an assortment of products from competing producers, retailers create utility. Retailers arrange for products to be moved from producers to a convenient retail establishment (place utility). They maintain hours of operation for their retail stores to make merchandise available when consumers want it (time utility). They also assume the risk of ownership of inventories (ownership utility). Table 12.5 describes various types of general merchandise retailers.

Today, there are too many stores competing for too few customers, and, as a result, competition between similar retailers has never been more intense. In addition, retailers face challenges such as shoplifting. Further, competition between different types of stores is changing the nature of retailing. Supermarkets compete with specialty food stores, wholesale clubs, and discount stores. Department stores compete with nearly every other type of store, including specialty stores, off-price chains, category killers, discount stores, and online retailers. For this reason, many businesses have turned to nonstore retailing to sell their products. Some nonstore retailing is performed by traditional retailers to complement their in-store offerings. For instance, Walmart and Macy's have created online shopping sites to retain customers and compete against other businesses. Other companies retail outside of physical stores

**TABLE 12.6    Major Wholesaling Functions**

| | |
|---|---|
| Supply chain management | Creating long-term partnerships among channel members |
| Promotion | Providing a sales force, advertising, sales promotion, and publicity |
| Warehousing, shipping, and product handling | Receiving, storing, and stockkeeping<br>Packaging<br>Shipping outgoing orders<br>Materials handling<br>Arranging and making local and long-distance shipments |
| Inventory control and data processing | Processing orders<br>Controlling physical inventory<br>Recording transactions<br>Tracking sales data for financial analysis |
| Risk taking | Assuming responsibility for theft, product obsolescence, and excess inventories |
| Financing and budgeting | Extending credit<br>Making capital investments<br>Forecasting cash flow |
| Marketing research and information systems | Providing information about market<br>Conducting research studies<br>Managing computer networks to facilitate exchanges and relationships |

*Source: William M. Pride and O. C. Ferrell,* Marketing: Concepts and Strategies, *2008, p. 389. Copyright 2008 by Houghton Mifflin Company. Reprinted with permission.*

entirely. The Internet, vending machines, mail-order catalogs, and entertainment such as going to a Chicago Bulls basketball game all provide opportunities for retailing outside of a store environment. For instance, although traditional vending machines are decreasing, some businesses are achieving success by using vending machines in unusual ways. The bakery Sprinkle Cupcake has developed a pink Cupcake ATM machine outside some of its store locations that dispenses different flavored cupcakes with the swipe of a credit card. The machines are refilled several times each day. Cupcake ATMs are currently located in Beverly Hills, Las Vegas, Dallas, New York City, Chicago, and Atlanta, with plans to open four more in the future.[27]

**Wholesalers** are intermediaries who buy from producers or from other wholesalers and sell to retailers. They usually do not sell in significant quantities to ultimate consumers. Wholesalers perform the functions listed in Table 12.6.

Wholesalers are extremely important because of the marketing activities they perform, particularly for consumer products. Although it is true that wholesalers can be eliminated, their functions must be passed on to some other entity, such as the producer, another intermediary, or even the customer. Wholesalers help consumers and retailers by buying in large quantities, then selling to retailers in smaller quantities. By stocking an assortment of products, wholesalers match products to demand. Sysco is a food wholesaler for the food services industry. The company provides food, preparation, and serving products to restaurants, hospitals, and other institutions that provide meals outside of the home.[28]

**Supply Chain Management.**    In an effort to improve distribution channel relationships among manufacturers and other channel intermediaries, supply chain management creates alliances between channel members. In Chapter 8, we defined

**wholesalers** intermediaries who buy from producers or from other wholesalers and sell to retailers

supply chain management as connecting and integrating all parties or members of the distribution system in order to satisfy customers. It involves long-term partnerships among marketing channel members working together to reduce costs, waste, and unnecessary movement in the entire marketing channel in order to satisfy customers. It goes beyond traditional channel members (producers, wholesalers, retailers, customers) to include *all* organizations involved in moving products from the producer to the ultimate customer. In a survey of business managers, a disruption in the supply chain was viewed as the number-one crisis that could decrease revenue.[29]

The focus shifts from one of selling to the next level in the channel to one of selling products *through* the channel to a satisfied ultimate customer. Information, once provided on a guarded, "as needed" basis, is now open, honest, and ongoing. Perhaps most importantly, the points of contact in the relationship expand from one-on-one at the salesperson–buyer level to multiple interfaces at all levels and in all functional areas of the various organizations.

**Channels for Consumer Products.**   Typical marketing channels for consumer products are shown in Figure 12.6. In Channel A, the product moves from the producer directly to the consumer. Farmers who sell their fruit and vegetables to consumers at roadside stands or farmer's markets use a direct-from-producer-to-consumer marketing channel.

In Channel B, the product goes from producer to retailer to consumer. This type of channel is used for products such as college textbooks, automobiles, and appliances. In Channel C, the product is handled by a wholesaler and a retailer before it reaches the consumer. Producer-to-wholesaler-to-retailer-to-consumer marketing channels

**FIGURE 12.6**
**Marketing Channels for Consumer Products**

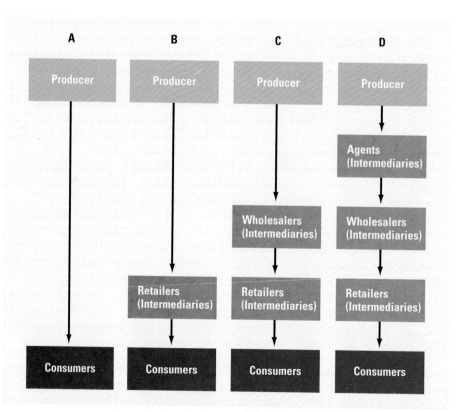

distribute a wide range of products including refrigerators, televisions, soft drinks, cigarettes, clocks, watches, and office products. In Channel D, the product goes to an agent, a wholesaler, and a retailer before going to the consumer. This long channel of distribution is especially useful for convenience products. Candy and some produce are often sold by agents who bring buyers and sellers together.

Services are usually distributed through direct marketing channels because they are generally produced *and* consumed simultaneously. For example, you cannot take a haircut home for later use. Many services require the customer's presence and participation: The sick patient must visit the physician to receive treatment; the child must be at the day care center to receive care; the tourist must be present to sightsee and consume tourism services.

**Channels for Business Products.**   In contrast to consumer goods, more than half of all business products, especially expensive equipment or technically complex products, are sold through direct marketing channels. Business customers like to communicate directly with producers of such products to gain the technical assistance and personal assurances that only the producer can offer. For this reason, business buyers prefer to purchase expensive and highly complex mainframe computers directly from IBM, Unisys, and other mainframe producers. Other business products may be distributed through channels employing wholesaling intermediaries such as industrial distributors and/or manufacturer's agents.

## Intensity of Market Coverage

A major distribution decision is how widely to distribute a product—that is, how many and what type of outlets should carry it. The intensity of market coverage depends on buyer behavior, as well as the nature of the target market and the competition. Wholesalers and retailers provide various intensities of market coverage and must be selected carefully to ensure success. Market coverage may be intensive, selective, or exclusive.

**Intensive distribution** makes a product available in as many outlets as possible. Because availability is important to purchasers of convenience products such as bread, milk, gasoline, soft drinks, and chewing gum, a nearby location with a minimum of time spent searching and waiting in line is most important to the consumer. To saturate markets intensively, wholesalers and many varied retailers try to make the product available at every location where a consumer might desire to purchase it. Zoom Systems provides robotic vending machines for products beyond candy and drinks. Zoom has 1,500 machines in airports and hotels across the United States, some selling items such as Apple iPods, Neutrogena hair and skin products, and Sony products. The vending machines accept credit cards and allow sales to occur in places where storefronts would be impossible.[30] Through

**intensive distribution**
a form of market coverage
whereby a product is made
available in as many outlets
as possible

The Jessica Simpson Collection is a line of fashion products for women. The collection is distributed through retailers including Macy's, Dillard's, Nordstrom, and Lord & Taylor.

partnering with different companies, today's ZoomShops sell a variety of brands, including products from Sephora, Best Buy, Macy's, and Rosetta Stone.[31]

**selective distribution**
a form of market coverage whereby only a small number of all available outlets are used to expose products

**Selective distribution** uses only a small number of all available outlets to expose products. It is used most often for products that consumers buy only after shopping and comparing price, quality, and style. Many products sold on a selective basis require salesperson assistance, technical advice, warranties, or repair service to maintain consumer satisfaction. Typical products include automobiles, major appliances, clothes, and furniture. Ralph Lauren is a brand that uses selective distribution.

**exclusive distribution**
the awarding by a manufacturer to an intermediary of the sole right to sell a product in a defined geographic territory

**Exclusive distribution** exists when a manufacturer gives an intermediary the sole right to sell a product in a defined geographic territory. Such exclusivity provides an incentive for a dealer to handle a product that has a limited market. Exclusive distribution is the opposite of intensive distribution in that products are purchased and consumed over a long period of time, and service or information is required to develop a satisfactory sales relationship. Products distributed on an exclusive basis include high-quality musical instruments, yachts, airplanes, and high-fashion leather goods. Aircraft manufacturer Piper Aircraft uses exclusive distribution by choosing only a few dealers in each region. The company has more than 30 locations in several countries, including the Americas and China.[32]

## Physical Distribution

**physical distribution**
all the activities necessary to move products from producers to customers— inventory control, transportation, warehousing, and materials handling

**Physical distribution** includes all the activities necessary to move products from producers to customers—inventory control, transportation, warehousing, and materials handling. Physical distribution creates time and place utility by making products available when they are wanted, with adequate service and at minimum cost. Both goods and services require physical distribution. Many physical distribution activities are part of supply chain management, which we discussed in Chapter 8; we'll take a brief look at a few more now.

**transportation**
the shipment of products to buyers

**Transportation.**    **Transportation,** the shipment of products to buyers, creates time and place utility for products, and thus is a key element in the flow of goods and services from producer to consumer. The five major modes of transportation used to move products between cities in the United States are railways, motor vehicles, inland waterways, pipelines, and airways.

Railroads are a cost-effective method of transportation for many products. Heavy commodities, foodstuffs, raw materials, and coal are examples of products carried by railroads. Trucks have greater flexibility than railroads because they can reach more locations. Trucks handle freight quickly and economically, offer door-to-door service, and are more flexible in their packaging requirements than are ships or airplanes. Air transport offers speed and a high degree of dependability but is the most expensive means of transportation; shipping is less expensive and is the slowest form. Pipelines are used to transport petroleum, natural gas, semiliquid coal, wood chips, and certain chemicals. Pipelines have the lowest costs for

The Burlington/Santa Fe Railroad is the second-largest freight railroad in North America. Although passenger trains have dwindled in favor of other forms of transportation, the railroad continues to be important for carrying freight to other parts of the country.

products that can be transported via this method. Many products can be moved most efficiently by using more than one mode of transportation.

Factors affecting the selection of a mode of transportation include cost, capability to handle the product, reliability, and availability, and, as suggested, selecting transportation modes requires trade-offs. Unique characteristics of the product and consumer desires often determine the mode selected.

**Warehousing.**    **Warehousing** is the design and operation of facilities to receive, store, and ship products. A warehouse facility receives, identifies, sorts, and dispatches goods to storage; stores them; recalls, selects, or picks goods; assembles the shipment; and finally, dispatches the shipment.

**warehousing**
the design and operation of facilities to receive, store, and ship products

Companies often own and operate their own private warehouses that store, handle, and move their own products. Firms might want to own or lease a private warehouse when their goods require special handling and storage or when it has large warehousing needs in a specific geographic area. Private warehouses are beneficial because they provide customers with more control over their goods. However, fixed costs for maintaining these warehouses can be quite high.[33] They can also rent storage and related physical distribution services from public warehouses. While public warehouses store goods for more than one company, providing firms with less control over distribution, they are often less expensive than private warehouses and are useful for seasonal production or low-volume storage.[34] Regardless of whether a private or a public warehouse is used, warehousing is important because it makes products available for shipment to match demand at different geographic locations.

**Materials Handling.**    **Materials handling** is the physical handling and movement of products in warehousing and transportation. Handling processes may vary significantly due to product characteristics. Efficient materials-handling procedures increase a warehouse's useful capacity and improve customer service. Well-coordinated loading and movement systems increase efficiency and reduce costs.

**materials handling**
the physical handling and movement of products in warehousing and transportation

## Importance of Distribution in a Marketing Strategy

Distribution decisions are among the least flexible marketing mix decisions. Products can be changed over time; prices can be changed quickly; and promotion is usually changed regularly. But distribution decisions often commit resources and establish contractual relationships that are difficult if not impossible to change. As a company attempts to expand into new markets, it may require a complete change in distribution. Moreover, if a firm does not manage its marketing channel in the most efficient manner and provide the best service, then a new competitor will evolve to create a more effective distribution system.

# Promotion Strategy

LO 12-4

The role of promotion is to communicate with individuals, groups, and organizations to facilitate an exchange directly or indirectly. It encourages marketing exchanges by attempting to persuade individuals, groups, and organizations to accept goods, services, and ideas. Promotion is used not only to sell products but also to influence opinions and attitudes toward an organization, person, or cause. The state of Texas, for example, has successfully used promotion to educate people about the costs of highway litter and thereby reduce littering. Most people probably equate promotion with advertising, but it also includes personal selling, publicity, and sales promotion. The role that these elements play in a marketing strategy is extremely important.

**integrated marketing communications**
coordinating the promotion mix elements and synchronizing promotion as a unified effort

**advertising**
a paid form of nonpersonal communication transmitted through a mass medium, such as television commercials or magazine advertisements

**advertising campaign**
designing a series of advertisements and placing them in various media to reach a particular target market

## The Promotion Mix

Advertising, personal selling, publicity, and sales promotion are collectively known as the promotion mix because a strong promotion program results from the careful selection and blending of these elements. The process of coordinating the promotion mix elements and synchronizing promotion as a unified effort is called **integrated marketing communications.** When planning promotional activities, an integrated marketing communications approach results in the desired message for customers. Different elements of the promotion mix are coordinated to play their appropriate roles in delivery of the message on a consistent basis.

**Advertising.**    Perhaps the best-known form of promotion, **advertising** is a paid form of nonpersonal communication transmitted through a mass medium, such as television commercials, magazine advertisements, or online ads. Even Google, one of the most powerful brands in the world, advertises. Google has turned to outdoor advertising on buses, trains, and ballparks in San Francisco and Chicago to promote its Google Maps feature.[35] Commercials featuring celebrities, customers, or unique creations serve to grab viewers' attention and pique their interest in a product.

An **advertising campaign** involves designing a series of advertisements and placing them in various media to reach a particular target audience. The basic content and form of an advertising campaign are a function of several factors. A product's features, uses, and benefits affect the content of the campaign message and individual ads. Characteristics of the people in the target audience—gender, age, education, race, income, occupation, lifestyle, and other attributes—influence both content and form. When Procter & Gamble promotes Crest toothpaste to children, the company emphasizes daily brushing and cavity control, whereas it promotes tartar control and whiter teeth when marketing to adults. To communicate effectively, advertisers use words, symbols, and illustrations that are meaningful, familiar, and attractive to people in the target audience.

An advertising campaign's objectives and platform also affect the content and form of its messages. If a firm's advertising objectives involve large sales increases, the message may include hard-hitting, high-impact language and symbols. When campaign objectives aim at increasing brand awareness, the message may use much repetition of the brand name and words and illustrations associated with it. Thus, the advertising platform is the foundation on which campaign messages are built.

Advertising media are the vehicles or forms of communication used to reach a desired audience. Print media include newspapers, magazines, direct mail, and billboards, while electronic media include television, radio, and Internet advertising. Choice of media obviously influences the content and form of the message. Effective outdoor displays and short broadcast spot announcements require concise, simple messages. Magazine and newspaper advertisements can include considerable detail

Hot Wheels uses celebrities, colorful packaging, and fun advertisements to appeal to children.

and long explanations. Because several kinds of media offer geographic selectivity, a precise message can be tailored to a particular geographic section of the target audience. For example, a company advertising in *Time* might decide to use one message in the New England region and another in the rest of the nation. A company may also choose to advertise in only one region. Such geographic selectivity lets a firm use the same message in different regions at different times. On the other hand, some companies are willing to pay extensive amounts of money to reach national audiences. Marketers spent approximately $4 million for one 30-second advertising slot during the 2014 Super Bowl due to its national reach and popularity.[36]

The use of online advertising is increasing. However, advertisers are demanding more for their ad dollars and proof that they are working, which is why Google AdWords only charges companies when users click on the ad. Certain types of ads are more popular than pop-up ads and banner ads that consumers find annoying. One technique is to blur the lines between television and online advertising. TV commercials may point viewers to a website for more information, where short "advertainment" films continue the marketing message. Marketers might also use the Internet to show advertisements or videos that were not accepted by mainstream television. SodaStream's original advertisement for the 2014 Super Bowl featured celebrity Scarlett Johansson criticizing rivals Coca-Cola and Pepsi by ending the ad with "Sorry, Coke and Pepsi." The last line was removed from the advertisement aired during the Super Bowl, but the original ad was featured online in its original uncensored format.[37]

Infomercials—typically 30-minute blocks of radio or television air time featuring a celebrity or upbeat host talking about and demonstrating a product—have evolved as an advertising method. Toll-free numbers and website addresses are usually provided so consumers can conveniently purchase the product or obtain additional information. Although many consumers and companies have negative feelings about infomercials, apparently they get results.

**Personal Selling.**    **Personal selling** is direct, two-way communication with buyers and potential buyers. For many products—especially large, expensive ones with specialized uses, such as cars, appliances, and houses—interaction between a salesperson and the customer is probably the most important promotional tool.

**personal selling**
direct, two-way communication with buyers and potential buyers

Personal selling is the most flexible of the promotional methods because it gives marketers the greatest opportunity to communicate specific information that might trigger a purchase. Only personal selling can zero in on a prospect and attempt to persuade that person to make a purchase. Although personal selling has a lot of advantages, it is one of the most costly forms of promotion. A sales call on an industrial customer can cost more than $400.

There are three distinct categories of salespersons: order takers (for example, retail sales clerks and route salespeople), creative salespersons (for example, automobile, furniture, and

Google used publicity to drive sales even before the its Google Glass product was officially launched to the public.

insurance salespeople), and support salespersons (for example, customer educators and goodwill builders who usually do not take orders). For most of these salespeople, personal selling is a six-step process:

1. *Prospecting:* Identifying potential buyers of the product.
2. *Approaching:* Using a referral or calling on a customer without prior notice to determine interest in the product.
3. *Presenting:* Getting the prospect's attention with a product demonstration.
4. *Handling objections:* Countering reasons for not buying the product.
5. *Closing:* Asking the prospect to buy the product.
6. *Following up:* Checking customer satisfaction with the purchased product.

**publicity**
nonpersonal communication transmitted through the mass media but not paid for directly by the firm

**Publicity.**    **Publicity** is nonpersonal communication transmitted through the mass media but not paid for directly by the firm. A firm does not pay the media cost for publicity and is not identified as the originator of the message; instead, the message is presented in news story form. Obviously, a company can benefit from publicity by releasing to news sources newsworthy messages about the firm and its involvement with the public. Many companies have *public relations* departments to try to gain favorable publicity and minimize negative publicity for the firm.

Although advertising and publicity are both carried by the mass media, they differ in several major ways. Advertising messages tend to be informative, persuasive, or both; publicity is mainly informative. Advertising is often designed to have an immediate impact or to provide specific information to persuade a person to act; publicity describes what a firm is doing, what products it is launching, or other newsworthy information, but seldom calls for action. When advertising is used, the organization must pay for media time and select the media that will best reach target audiences. The mass media willingly carry publicity because they believe it has general public interest. Advertising can be repeated a number of times; most publicity appears in the mass media once and is not repeated.

Advertising, personal selling, and sales promotion are especially useful for influencing an exchange directly. Publicity is extremely important when communication focuses on a company's activities and products and is directed at interest groups, current and potential investors, regulatory agencies, and society in general.

A variation of traditional advertising is buzz marketing, in which marketers attempt to create a trend or acceptance of a product. Companies seek out trendsetters in communities and get them to "talk up" a brand to their friends, family, co-workers, and others. Samsung displayed a piece of its marketing genius during the 2014 Oscars when they orchestrated a celebrity "selfie" with its new Galaxy Note III. They went so far as to teach the host of the awards show, Ellen Degeneres, exactly how to use the device and how to take the picture. The photo was quickly shared across various social media platforms, becoming one of the most widely shared images. The stunt caught Apple's attention to the extent that it created a "Buzz Marketing Manager" position in order to compete on this level.[38] Other marketers using the buzz technique include Hebrew National ("mom squads" grilled the company's hot dogs), and Red Bull (its sponsorship of the stratosphere space diving project). The idea behind buzz marketing is that an accepted member of a particular social group will be more credible than any form of paid communication.[39] The concept works best as part of an integrated marketing communication program that also includes traditional advertising, personal selling, sales promotion, and publicity.

A related concept is viral marketing, which describes the concept of getting Internet users to pass on ads and promotions to others. Dove's "Real Beauty Sketches" video compared sketches of women as they described themselves to sketches of themselves as others described them. The video was meant to show how women often do not recognize their outward beauty. The video went viral, reaching 114 million views just one month after its release. It became the most viral video of its time.[40]

**Sales Promotion.** **Sales promotion** involves direct inducements offering added value or some other incentive for buyers to enter into an exchange. Sales promotions are generally easier to measure and less expensive than advertising. The major tools of sales promotion are store displays, premiums, samples and demonstrations, coupons, contests and sweepstakes, refunds, and trade shows. Coupon-clipping in particular has become more common during

Companies use a pull strategy by offering coupons in the hopes of convincing customers to visit their stores.

the recent recession. While coupons in the past decade traditionally had a fairly low redemption rate, with about 2 percent being redeemed, the recent recession caused an upsurge in coupon usage. There has also been a major upsurge in the use of mobile coupons, or coupons sent to consumers over mobile devices. The redemption rate for mobile coupons is 10 times higher than that of traditional coupons, with a 10 percent rate versus a 1 percent redemption rate.[41] While coupons can be a valuable tool in sales promotion, they cannot be relied upon to stand by themselves, but should be part of an overall promotion mix. Sales promotion stimulates customer purchasing and increases dealer effectiveness in selling products. It is used to enhance and supplement other forms of promotion. Sampling a product may also encourage consumers to buy. This is why many grocery stores provide free samples in the hopes of influencing consumers' purchasing decisions. In a given year, almost three-fourths of consumer product companies may use sampling.

**sales promotion**
direct inducements offering added value or some other incentive for buyers to enter into an exchange

## Promotion Strategies: To Push or to Pull

In developing a promotion mix, organizations must decide whether to fashion a mix that pushes or pulls the product (Figure 12.7). A **push strategy** attempts to motivate intermediaries to push the product down to their customers. When a push strategy is used, the company attempts to motivate wholesalers and retailers to make the product available to their customers. Sales personnel may be used to persuade intermediaries to offer the product, distribute promotional materials, and offer special promotional incentives for those who agree to carry the product. For example, salespeople from pharmaceutical companies will often market new products to doctors in the hope that the doctors will recommend their products to their clients. A **pull strategy** uses promotion to create consumer demand for a product so that consumers exert pressure on marketing channel members to make it available. For a while, T-Mobile was the only major carrier that did not have the iPhone. The iPhone was not compatible with T-Mobile's 3G frequencies, so Apple largely sidestepped T-Mobile. However,

**push strategy**
an attempt to motivate intermediaries to push the product down to their customers

**pull strategy**
the use of promotion to create consumer demand for a product so that consumers exert pressure on marketing channel members to make it available

**FIGURE 12.7    Push and Pull Strategies**

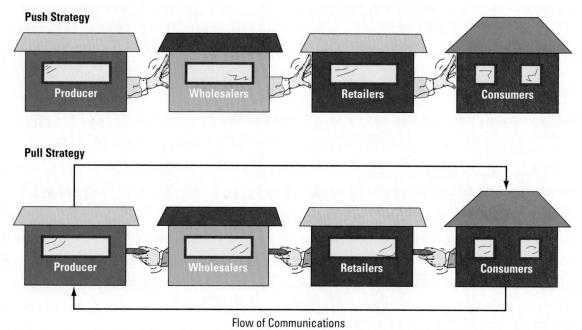

Flow of Communications

the popularity of the iPhone and decreasing market share caused T-Mobile to revamp its spectrum to run on the iPhone better. This is an example of how consumer pull caused a company to change its practices.[42] Additionally, offering free samples prior to a product rollout encourages consumers to request the product from their favorite retailer.

A company can use either strategy, or it can use a variation or combination of the two. The exclusive use of advertising indicates a pull strategy. Personal selling to marketing channel members indicates a push strategy. The allocation of promotional resources to various marketing mix elements probably determines which strategy a marketer uses.

## Objectives of Promotion

The marketing mix a company uses depends on its objectives. It is important to recognize that promotion is only one element of the marketing strategy and must be tied carefully to the goals of the firm, its overall marketing objectives, and the other elements of the marketing strategy. Firms use promotion for many reasons, but typical objectives are to stimulate demand, to stabilize sales, and to inform, remind, and reinforce customers.

Increasing demand for a product is probably the most typical promotional objective. Stimulating demand, often through advertising and sales promotion, is particularly important when a firm is using a pull strategy.

Another goal of promotion is to stabilize sales by maintaining the status quo—that is, the current sales level of the product. During periods of slack or decreasing sales, contests, prizes, vacations, and other sales promotions are sometimes offered to customers to maintain sales goals. Advertising is often used to stabilize sales by making

## Flying at a Higher Altitude: JetBlue Introduces Luxury Seating

JetBlue, the well-known discount airline, is changing its marketing mix to compete with other airlines. Historically, the airline offered only coach seating and, like Southwest Airlines, allowed bags to be checked for free. However, as the dynamics of the airline market have evolved, JetBlue has not been adaptable. As a result, it has lost market share. While the low-cost model appeals to many flyers, those who have to travel long distances will pay higher prices for more comfortable seats.

In order to cater to a wider range of consumers, JetBlue is introducing premium seating on some of its cross-country flights. Flyers will have the option of simply more leg room at the front of the plane or, if they rather, they can opt for suites. Suites are seats equipped with a massager and density adjuster that converts into a bed. The passenger can also have more privacy at these seats with a moving partition serving as a closed door. Hot meals, free alcoholic beverages, and a larger screen on which to watch DirectTV are also offered for these luxury seats. JetBlue is trying to keep up with the competition by optimizing its product offerings and varying its price points.[43]

### Discussion Questions

1. How has JetBlue positioned its brand in the past?
2. What is JetBlue doing to become more adaptable and gain more market share?
3. Do you think JetBlue can successfully transition from a low-cost carrier into a more high-end airline?

---

customers aware of slack use periods. For example, auto manufacturers often provide rebates, free options, or lower-than-market interest rates to stabilize sales and thereby keep production lines moving during temporary slowdowns. A stable sales pattern allows the firm to run efficiently by maintaining a consistent level of production and storage and utilizing all its functions so that it is ready when sales increase.

An important role of any promotional program is to inform potential buyers about the organization and its products. A major portion of advertising in the United States, particularly in daily newspapers, is informational. Providing information about the availability, price, technology, and features of a product is very important in encouraging a buyer to move toward a purchase decision. Nearly all forms of promotion involve an attempt to help consumers learn more about a product and a company.

Promotion is also used to remind consumers that an established organization is still around and sells certain products that have uses and benefits. Often advertising reminds customers that they may need to use a product more frequently or in certain situations. Pennzoil, for example, has run television commercials reminding car owners that they need to change their oil every 3,000 miles to ensure proper performance of their cars.

Reinforcement promotion attempts to assure current users of the product that they have made the right choice and tells them how to get the most satisfaction from the product. Also, a company could release publicity statements through the news media about a new use for a product. Additionally, firms can have salespeople communicate with current and potential customers about the proper use and maintenance of a product—all in the hope of developing a repeat customer.

## Promotional Positioning

**Promotional positioning** uses promotion to create and maintain an image of a product in buyers' minds. It is a natural result of market segmentation. In both promotional positioning and market segmentation, the firm targets a given product or brand at a portion of the total market. A promotional strategy helps differentiate the product

**promotional positioning**
the use of promotion to create and maintain an image of a product in buyers' minds

and makes it appeal to a particular market segment. For example, to appeal to safety-conscious consumers, Volvo heavily promotes the safety and crashworthiness of Volvo automobiles in its advertising. Volkswagen has done the same thing with its edgy ads showing car crashes. Promotion can be used to change or reinforce an image. Effective promotion influences customers and persuades them to buy.

## Importance of Marketing Strategy

Marketing creates value through the marketing mix. For customers, value means receiving a product in which the benefit of the product outweighs the cost, or price paid for it. For marketers, value means that the benefits (usually monetary) received from selling the product outweigh the costs it takes to develop and sell it. This requires carefully integrating the marketing mix into an effective marketing strategy. One misstep could mean a loss in profits, whether it be from a failed product idea, shortages or oversupply of a product, a failure to effectively promote the product, or prices that are too high or too low. And while some of these marketing mix elements can be easily fixed, other marketing mix elements such as distribution can be harder to adapt.

On the other hand, firms that develop an effective marketing mix to meet customer needs will gain competitive advantages over those that do not. Often, these advantages occur when the firm excels at one or more elements of the marketing mix. Walmart has a reputation for its everyday low prices, while Tiffany's is known for its high-quality jewelry. However, excelling at one element of the marketing mix does not mean that a company can neglect the others. The best product cannot succeed if consumers do not know about it or if they cannot find it in stores. Additionally, firms must constantly monitor the market environment to understand how demand is changing and whether adaptations in the marketing mix are needed. It is therefore essential that every element of the marketing mix be carefully evaluated and synchronized with the marketing strategy. Only then will firms be able to achieve the marketing concept of providing products that satisfy customers' needs while allowing the organization to achieve its goals.

Many jobs in marketing are closely tied to the marketing mix functions: distribution, product, promotion, and price. Often the job titles could be sales manager, distribution or supply chain manager, advertising account executive, or store manager.

A distribution manager arranges for transportation of goods within firms and through marketing channels. Transportation can be costly, and time is always an important factor, so minimizing their effects is vital to the success of a firm. Distribution managers must choose one or a combination of transportation modes from a vast array of options, taking into account local, federal, and international regulations for different freight classifications; the weight, size, and fragility of products to be shipped; time schedules; and loss and damage ratios. Manufacturing firms are the largest employers of distribution managers.

A product manager is responsible for the success or failure of a product line. This requires a general knowledge of advertising, transportation modes, inventory control, selling and sales management, promotion, marketing research, packaging, and pricing. Frequently, several years of selling and sales management experience are prerequisites for such a position as well as college training in business administration. Being a product manager can be rewarding both financially and psychologically.

Some of the most creative roles in the business world are in the area of advertising. Advertising pervades our daily lives, as businesses and other organizations try to grab our attention and tell us about what they have to offer. Copywriters, artists, and account executives in advertising must have creativity, imagination, artistic talent, and expertise in expression and persuasion. Advertising is an area of business in which a wide variety of educational backgrounds may be useful, from degrees in advertising itself, to journalism or liberal arts degrees. Common entry-level positions in an advertising agency are found in the traffic department, account service (account coordinator), or the media department (media assistant). Advertising jobs are also available in many manufacturing or retail firms, nonprofit organizations, banks, professional associations, utility companies, and other arenas outside of an advertising agency.

Although a career in retailing may begin in sales, there is much more to retailing than simply selling. Many retail personnel occupy management positions, focusing on selecting and ordering merchandise, promotional activities, inventory control, customer credit operations, accounting, personnel, and store security. Many specific examples of retailing jobs can be found in large department stores. A section manager coordinates inventory and promotions and interacts with buyers, salespeople, and consumers. The buyer's job is fast-paced, often involving much travel and pressure. Buyers must be open-minded and foresighted in their hunt for new, potentially successful items. Regional managers coordinate the activities of several retail stores within a specific geographic area, usually monitoring and supporting sales, promotions, and general procedures. Retail management can be exciting and challenging. Growth in retailing is expected to accompany the growth in population and is likely to create substantial opportunities in the coming years.

While a career in marketing can be very rewarding, marketers today agree that the job is getting tougher. Many advertising and marketing executives say the job has gotten much more demanding in the past 10 years, viewing their number-one challenge as balancing work and personal obligations. Other challenges include staying current on industry trends or technologies, keeping motivated/inspired on the job, and measuring success. If you are up to the challenge, you may find that a career in marketing is just right for you to utilize your business knowledge while exercising your creative side as well.

## Review Your Understanding

**Describe the role of product in the marketing mix, including how products are developed, classified, and identified.**

Products (goods, services, ideas) are among a firm's most visible contacts with consumers and must meet consumers' needs and expectations to ensure success. New-product development is a multistep process: idea development, the screening of new ideas, business analysis, product development, test marketing, and commercialization. Products are usually classified as either consumer or business products. Consumer products can be further classified as convenience, shopping, or specialty products. The business product classifications are raw materials, major equipment, accessory equipment, component parts, processed materials, supplies, and industrial services. Products also can be classified by the stage of the product life cycle (introduction, growth, maturity, and decline). Identifying products includes branding (the process of naming and identifying products); packaging (the product's container); and labeling (information, such as content and warnings, on the package).

**Define price, and discuss its importance in the marketing mix, including various pricing strategies a firm might employ.**

Price is the value placed on an object exchanged between a buyer and a seller. It is probably the most flexible variable of the marketing mix. Pricing objectives include survival, maximization of profits and sales volume, and maintaining the status quo. When a firm introduces a new product, it may use price skimming or penetration pricing. Psychological pricing and price discounting are other strategies.

### Identify factors affecting distribution decisions, such as marketing channels and intensity of market coverage.

Making products available to customers is facilitated by middlemen, or intermediaries, who bridge the gap between the producer of the product and its ultimate user. A marketing channel is a group of marketing organizations that directs the flow of products from producers to consumers. Market coverage relates to the number and variety of outlets that make products available to customers; it may be intensive, selective, or exclusive. Physical distribution is all the activities necessary to move products from producers to consumers, including inventory planning and control, transportation, warehousing, and materials handling.

### Specify the activities involved in promotion, as well as promotional strategies and promotional positioning.

Promotion encourages marketing exchanges by persuading individuals, groups, and organizations to accept goods, services,

and ideas. The promotion mix includes advertising (a paid form of nonpersonal communication transmitted through a mass medium), personal selling (direct, two-way communication with buyers and potential buyers), publicity (nonpersonal communication transmitted through the mass media but not paid for directly by the firm), and sales promotion (direct inducements offering added value or some other incentive for buyers to enter into an exchange). A push strategy attempts to motivate intermediaries to push the product down to their customers, whereas a pull strategy tries to create consumer demand for a product so that consumers exert pressure on marketing channel members to make the product available. Typical promotion objectives are to stimulate demand; stabilize sales; and inform, remind, and reinforce customers. Promotional positioning is the use of promotion to create and maintain in the buyer's mind an image of a product.

### Evaluate an organization's marketing strategy plans.

Based on the material in this chapter, you should be able to answer the questions posed in "Solve the Dilemma" on page 388 and evaluate the company's marketing strategy plans, including its target market and marketing mix.

## Revisit the World of Business

1. How is Chevrolet attempting to bring new life to the Corvette Stingray?

2. Is the Corvette Stingray using a price skimming or penetration pricing strategy? Explain your answer.

3. Describe the different ways Chevrolet is using promotion to market the Chevy Stingray.

## Learn the Terms

advertising   378
advertising campaign   378
branding   365
business products   362
commercialization   361
consumer products   362
discounts   371
exclusive distribution   376
generic products   366
integrated marketing
  communications   378
intensive distribution   375
labeling   367

manufacturer brands   365
marketing channel   371
materials handling   377
packaging   367
penetration price   370
personal selling   379
physical distribution   376
price skimming   370
private distributor brands   365
product line   363
product mix   363
promotional positioning   383
psychological pricing   370

publicity   380
pull strategy   381
push strategy   381
quality   368
reference pricing   371
retailers   372
sales promotion   381
selective distribution   376
test marketing   361
trademark   365
transportation   376
warehousing   377
wholesalers   373

## Check Your Progress

1. What steps do companies generally take to develop and introduce a new product?

2. What is the product life cycle? How does a product's life cycle stage affect its marketing strategy?

3. Which marketing mix variable is probably the most flexible? Why?

4. Distinguish between the two ways to set the base price for a new product.

5. What is probably the least flexible marketing mix variable? Why?

6. Describe the typical marketing channels for consumer products.

7. What activities are involved in physical distribution? What functions does a warehouse perform?

8. How do publicity and advertising differ? How are they related?

9. What does the personal selling process involve? Briefly discuss the process.

10. List the circumstances in which the push and pull promotional strategies are used.

## Get Involved

1. Pick three products you use every day (in school, at work, or for pleasure—perhaps one of each). Determine what phase of the product life cycle each is in. Evaluate the marketer's strategy (product, price, promotion, and distribution) for the product and whether it is appropriate for the life-cycle stage.

2. Design a distribution channel for a manufacturer of stuffed toys.

3. Pick a nearby store, and briefly describe the kinds of sales promotion used and their effectiveness.

## Build Your Skills

### Analyzing Motel 6's Marketing Strategy

#### Background

Made famous through the well-known radio and TV commercials spoken in the distinctive "down-home" voice of Tom Bodett, the Dallas-based Motel 6 chain of budget motels is probably familiar to you. Based on the information provided here and any personal knowledge you may have about the company, you will analyze the marketing strategy of Motel 6.

#### Task

Read the following paragraphs; then complete the questions that follow.

Motel 6 was established in 1962 with the original name emphasizing its low-cost, no-frills approach. Rooms at that time were $6 per night. Today, Motel 6 has more than 760 units, and the average nightly cost is $49.99. Motel 6 is the largest company-owned and operated lodging chain in the United States. Customers receive HBO, ESPN, free morning coffee, and free local phone calls, and most units have pools and some business services. Motel 6 has made a name for itself by offering clean, comfortable rooms at the lowest prices of any national motel chain and by standardizing both its product offering and its operating policies and procedures. The company's national spokesperson, Tom Bodett, is featured in radio and television commercials that use humorous stories to show why it makes sense to stay at Motel 6 rather than a pricey hotel.

In appealing to pleasure travelers on a budget as well as business travelers looking to get the most for their dollar, one commercial makes the point that all hotel and motel rooms look the same at night when the lights are out—when customers are getting what they came for, a good night's sleep. Motel 6 location sites are selected based on whether they provide convenient access to the highway system and whether they are close to areas such as shopping centers, tourist attractions, or business districts.

1. In SELECTING A TARGET MARKET, which approach is Motel 6 using to segment markets?

   a. concentration approach

   b. multisegment approach

2. In DEVELOPING A MARKETING MIX, identify in the second column of the table what the current strategy is and then identify any changes you think Motel 6 should consider for carrying it successfully through the next five years.

| Marketing Mix Variable | Current Strategy | 5-Year Strategy |
|---|---|---|
| a. Product | | |
| b. Price | | |
| c. Distribution | | |
| d. Promotion | | |

## Solve the Dilemma — LO 12-5

### Better Health with Snacks

 Deluxe Chips is one of the leading companies in the salty-snack industry, with almost one-fourth of the $10 billion market. Its Deluxos tortilla chips are the number-one selling brand in North America, and its Ridgerunner potato chip is also a market share leader. Deluxe Chips wants to stay on top of the market by changing marketing strategies to match changing consumer needs and preferences. Promoting specific brands to market segments with the appropriate price and distribution channel is helping Deluxe Chips succeed.

As many middle-aged consumers modify their snacking habits, Deluxe Chips is considering a new product line of light snack foods with less fat and cholesterol and targeted at the 35- to 50-year-old consumer who enjoys snacking but wants to be more health conscious. Marketing research suggests that the product will succeed as long as it tastes good and that consumers may be willing to pay more for it. Large expenditures on advertising may be necessary to overcome the competition. However, it may be possible to analyze customer profiles and retail store characteristics and then match the right product with the right neighborhood. Store-specific micromarketing would allow Deluxe Chips to spend its promotional dollars more efficiently.

### Discussion Questions

1. Design a marketing strategy for the new product line.

2. Critique your marketing strategy in terms of its strengths and weaknesses.

3. What are your suggestions for implementation of the marketing strategy?

## Build Your Business Plan

### Dimensions of Marketing Strategy

 If you think your product/business is truly new to or unique to the market, you need to substantiate your claim. After a thorough exploration on the web, you want to make sure there has not been a similar business/product recently launched in your community. Check with your Chamber of Commerce or Economic Development Office that might be able to provide you with a history of recent business failures. If you are not confident about the ability or willingness of customers to try your new good or service, collecting your own primary data to ascertain demand is highly advisable.

The decision of where to initially set your prices is a critical one. If there are currently similar products in the market, you need to be aware of the competitors' prices before you determine yours. If your product is new to the market, you can price it high (market skimming strategy) as long as you realize that the high price will probably attract competitors to the market more quickly (they will think they can make the same product for less), which will force you to drop your prices sooner than you would like. Another strategy to consider is market penetration pricing, a strategy that sets price lower and discourages competition from entering the market as quickly. Whatever strategy you decide to use, don't forget to examine your product elasticity.

At this time, you need to start thinking about how to promote your product. Why do you feel your product is different or new to the market? How do you want to position your product so customers view it favorably? Remember this is all occurring *within the consumer's mind.*

## See for Yourself Videocase

### Groupon Masters Promotion to Become a Popular Daily Deal Site

 In 2008, a startup company called Groupon launched an innovative business model. The model works in the following way: Groupon partners with businesses to offer subscribers daily deals. These deals are provided through the Groupon website, e-mail, and mobile devices. Groupon deals are similar to coupons, but with one major catch. A certain number of people (a group) must agree to purchase the deal. If enough people purchase, then the deal becomes available to everyone. If not enough people purchase, then no one receives that particular deal. In this way, Groupon has made the idea of coupons or deals into a social process.

The model quickly caught on with consumers. In many ways, Groupon lowers the risk for consumers when purchasing a new product because the product or activity costs less than its regular price. This encourages consumers to try out new activities such as skydiving or dining at a certain restaurant. Groupon also alerts consumers about deals that they were not aware of beforehand. Making consumers aware of products is one of the major purposes of promotion.

When it first started promoting Groupon deals, the company used social media sites such as Twitter and Facebook. One of the advantages of this type of advertising is the chance for an Internet ad or posting to go viral. With just a simple click of a button, an Internet user can inform his or her friends about the deal, spreading awareness of the company or product. This word-of-mouth marketing has been proven to be one of the most effective and trusted forms of promotion.

The benefit for businesses is the possibility of attracting repeat customers. By offering deals through the Groupon site, businesses are able to get consumers into the store. If consumers have a good experience, then they might return or tell their friends about the business. Groupon, therefore, acts as a type of conduit that brings consumers and businesses together. Bo Hurd, national sales manager/business development, describes how this works for businesses. "We're going to get the word out there, and then we're actually going have these people decide that they want to come in and try your services. And then it's up to you to actually convert them into long-term, full-paying customers."

Because Groupon depends on businesses as much as consumers, it must get businesses to agree to offer deals through its site. Groupon engages heavily in public relations to make its name known among companies. Personal selling is also very important to Groupon's promotion mix. Groupon's sales force uses phone calls and e-mails to contact businesses in the major cities in which it does business. Because it wants to offer the best deals, Groupon will generate leads by looking at review websites such as Yelp and Citysearch. By looking at how consumers rate certain businesses, Groupon can get a better idea of which businesses to target.

The introduction of rival deal sites such as Google Offers and Living Social is requiring Groupon to continue innovating. The firm has begun to invest in new product offerings, such as Groupon Now! Groupon Now! is a mobile app that provides time-specific deals to consumers based on their location at a particular moment. Each new product that Groupon introduces requires adaptations to the promotion mix. For instance, promoting Groupon Now! to businesses resulted in some challenges. At first there were two separate sales teams, one for Groupon's daily deal service and another for Groupon Now! The problem was that both sales teams would call up the same business, essentially duplicating the sales calls and making the business feel overwhelmed. As a result, Groupon changed its structure so that now one sales representative will offer both products during the sales call. Because promotion is an easier variable to modify than distribution or product, Groupon was able to adapt part of its promotion mix to increase its effectiveness.

Groupon's ability to master different forms of promotion has contributed to its success as a company. However, recently the company has faced some challenges. After becoming a publicly traded company in 2011, Groupon's net earnings were on the decline, and its executives have a reputation for buying back large amounts of stock. In 2013, CEO and co-founder Andrew Mason was forced out of his position by the board of directors. Furthermore, the previously successful business model is being called into question as the high customer acquisition costs are depleting profits. In order to address this issue, the company launched a service called Deal Builder that allows businesses to create their own deals on the company's site, eliminating the need for salespeople for this service. Going forward, it will need to continue to communicate its value, particularly of new products, to both businesses and consumers.[44]

### Discussion Questions

1. How has Groupon effectively used personal selling, advertising, and public relations to market its products?

2. Is there a difference in how Groupon markets itself to consumers versus how it markets itself to businesses? If so, describe these differences.

3. Groupon had to adapt the personal selling component of the promotion mix. Why is it sometimes necessary for businesses to adapt the promotion mix?

**You can find the related video in the Video Library in Connect. Ask your instructor how you can access Connect.**

## Team Exercise

Form groups and search for examples of convenience products, shopping products, specialty products, and business products. How are these products marketed? Provide examples of any ads that you can find to show examples of the promotional strategies for these products. Report your findings to the class.

# 13

# Digital Marketing and Social Networking

## Learning Objectives

**After reading this chapter, you will be able to:**

**LO 13-1** Define *digital media* and *digital marketing*, and recognize their increasing value in strategic planning.

**LO 13-2** Demonstrate the role of digital marketing and social networking in today's business environment.

**LO 13-3** Show how digital media affect the marketing mix.

**LO 13-4** Define *social networking*, and illustrate how businesses can use different types of social networking media.

**LO 13-5** Identify legal and ethical considerations in digital media.

**LO 13-6** Evaluate a marketer's dilemma and propose recommendations.

## Chapter Outline

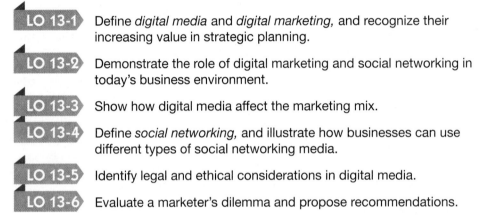

## Microblog Marketing: Reaching Millions of Consumers with One Click

Companies such as Starbucks and Mercedes Benz are using microblog sites like Sina Weibo as a way to reach consumers in China. Sina Weibo, the Chinese version of Twitter but with more social networking features, has approximately 309 million active users, of which 70 percent check their pages every day. Users can post up to 140 characters on the site. More than 1,000 multinational businesses—including IKEA, Royal Caribbean International, and Nokia—use this platform for marketing, brand building, and gathering customer feedback. Because of the large user base, marketing over this channel is not only useful but also cost-effective. For example, Mercedes Benz launched a digital marketing campaign to sell more than 600 of its smart cars over Weibo. These cars sold in about eight hours.

Starbucks also received significant returns by marketing and communicating with customers on Sina Weibo. With more than 700,000 followers, the company launched an $80,000 campaign to promote Frappuccino sales. Over a two-month period, Starbucks made 60 Weibo posts, which were reposted and commented on approximately 200,000 times. As a result, more than 95 million friend-to-friend recommendations were made, and the company saw a 14 percent growth in sales.

The quick comments and responses allow companies to immediately address customer feedback, whether it is positive or negative. This has helped companies reduce the impact of bad public relations and successfully market to the largest population in the world.[1]

## Introduction[2]

The Internet and information technology have dramatically changed the environment for business. Marketers' new ability to convert all types of communications into digital media has created efficient, inexpensive ways of connecting businesses and consumers and has improved the flow and the usefulness of information. Businesses have the information they need to make more informed decisions, and consumers have access to a greater variety of products and more information about choices and quality.

The defining characteristic of information technology in the 21st century is accelerating change. New systems and applications advance so rapidly that it is almost impossible to keep up with the latest developments. Startup companies emerge that quickly overtake existing approaches to digital media. When Google first arrived on the scene, a number of search engines were fighting for dominance. With its fast, easy-to-use search engine, Google became number one and is now challenging many industries, including advertising, newspapers, mobile phones, and book publishing. Despite its victory, Google is constantly being challenged itself by competitors like Yahoo! and Baidu. Baidu is gaining ground with 77 percent of the Chinese search engine market. Baidu has aggressively entered the mobile technology market and has successfully overtaken Google's market share. It is estimated that Baidu's market share of total mobile search queries in China is 57 percent.[3] Social networking continues to advance as the channel most observers believe will dominate digital communication in the near future. Today, people spend more time on social networking sites, such as Facebook, than they spend on e-mail.

In this chapter, we first provide some key definitions related to digital marketing and social networking. Next, we discuss using digital media in business and digital marketing. We look at marketing mix considerations when using digital media and pay special attention to social networking. Then we focus on digital marketing strategies—particularly new communication channels like social networks—and consider how consumers are changing their information searches and consumption behavior to fit emerging technologies and trends. Finally, we examine the legal and social issues associated with information technology, digital media, and e-business.

## Growth and Benefits of Digital Communication

Let's start with a clear understanding of our focus in this chapter. First, we can distinguish **e-business** from traditional business by noting that conducting e-business means carrying out the goals of business

**e-business**
carrying out the goals of business through utilization of the Internet

Amazon's mobile applications make it easier for users to shop and purchase items on the go.

**TABLE 13.1**    **Characteristics of Digital Marketing**

| Characteristic | Definition | Example |
|---|---|---|
| Addressability | The ability of the marketer to identify customers before they make a purchase | Amazon installs cookies on a user's computer that allows it to identify the owner when he or she returns to the website. |
| Interactivity | The ability of customers to express their needs and wants directly to the firm in response to its marketing communications | Texas Instruments interacts with its customers on its Facebook page by answering concerns and posting updates. |
| Accessibility | The ability for marketers to obtain digital information | Google can use web searches done through its search engine to learn about customer interests. |
| Connectivity | The ability for consumers to be connected with marketers along with other consumers | The Avon Voices website encouraged singers to upload their singing videos, which can then be voted on by other users for the chance to be discovered. |
| Control | The customer's ability to regulate the information they view as well as the rate and exposure to that information | Consumers use Kayak to discover the best travel deals. |

through the use of the Internet. **Digital media** are electronic media that function using digital codes—when we refer to digital media, we mean media available via computers and other digital devices, including mobile and wireless ones like smartphones.

**Digital marketing** uses all digital media, including the Internet and mobile and interactive channels, to develop communication and exchanges with customers. Digital marketing is a term we will use often, because we are interested in all types of digital communications, regardless of the electronic channel that transmits the data. Digital marketing goes beyond the Internet and includes mobile phones, banner ads, digital outdoor marketing, and social networks.

The Internet has created tremendous opportunities for businesses to forge relationships with consumers and business customers, target markets more precisely, and even reach previously inaccessible markets at home and around the world. The Internet also facilitates business transactions, allowing companies to network with manufacturers, wholesalers, retailers, suppliers, and outsource firms to serve customers more quickly and more efficiently. The telecommunication opportunities created by the Internet have set the stage for digital marketing's development and growth.

Digital communication offers a completely new dimension in connecting with others. Some of the characteristics that distinguish digital from traditional communication are addressability, interactivity, accessibility, connectivity, and control. These terms are discussed in Table 13.1.

**digital media**
electronic media that function using digital codes via computers, cellular phones, smartphones, and other digital devices that have been released in recent years

**digital marketing**
uses all digital media, including the Internet and mobile and interactive channels, to develop communication and exchanges with customers

## Using Digital Media in Business

The phenomenal growth of digital media has provided new ways of conducting business. Given almost instant communication with precisely defined consumer groups, firms can use real-time exchanges to create and stimulate interactive communication, forge closer relationships, and learn more accurately about consumer and supplier needs. Consider that Amazon.com, one of the most successful electronic businesses, ranked number 49 on the *Fortune* 500 list of America's largest corporations. Amazon is a true digital marketer, getting 40 percent of its revenue from international sales.[4] Many of you may not remember a world before Amazon because it has completely transformed how many people shop.

Because it is fast and inexpensive, digital communication is making it easier for businesses to conduct marketing research, provide and obtain price and product information, and advertise, as well as to fulfill their business goals by selling goods and services online. Even the U.S. government engages in digital marketing activities—marketing everything from Treasury bonds and other financial instruments to oil-drilling leases and wild horses. Procter & Gamble uses the Internet as a fast, cost-effective means for marketing research, judging consumer demand for potential new products by inviting online consumers to sample new-product prototypes and provide feedback. If a product gets rave reviews from the samplers, the company might decide to introduce it. By testing concepts online, companies can save significant time and money in getting new products to market.

New businesses and even industries are evolving that would not exist without digital media. Vimeo is a video website founded by filmmakers to share creative videos. The site lets users post or view videos from around the world. It has become the third most popular video website after YouTube and Netflix.[5]

The reality, however, is that Internet markets are more similar to traditional markets than they are different. Thus, successful digital marketing strategies, like traditional business strategies, focus on creating products that customers need or want, not merely developing a brand name or reducing the costs associated with online transactions. Instead of changing all industries, digital technology has had much more impact in certain industries where the cost of business and customer transactions has been very high. For example, investment trading is less expensive online because customers can buy and sell investments, such as stocks and mutual funds, on their own. Firms such as Charles Schwab Corp., the biggest online brokerage firm, have been innovators in promoting online trading. Traditional brokers such as Merrill Lynch have had to follow with online trading for their customers.

Home Depot has an application that connects mobile users to its website to search and shop for products.

Because the Internet lowers the cost of communication, it can contribute significantly to any industry or activity that depends on the flow of digital information such as entertainment, health care, government services, education, and computer services like software development. The publishing industry is transitioning away from print newspapers, magazines, and books as more consumers purchase e-readers, like the Kindle Fire or iPad, or read the news online. Even your textbook is available electronically. Because publishers save money on paper, ink, and shipping, many times electronic versions of books are cheaper than their paper counterparts.

Digital media can also improve communication within and between businesses. In the future, most significant gains will come from productivity improvements within businesses. Communication is a key business function, and improving the speed and clarity of communication can help businesses save time and improve employee problem-solving abilities. Digital media can be a communications backbone that helps to store knowledge, information, and records in management information systems so co-workers can access it when faced with a problem to solve. A well-designed management information system that utilizes digital technology can, therefore, help reduce confusion, improve organization and efficiency, and facilitate clear communications. Given the crucial role of communication and information in business, the long-term impact of digital media on economic growth is substantial, and it will inevitably grow over time.

Firms also need to control access to their digital communication systems to ensure worker productivity. This can be a challenge. For example, in companies across the United States, employees are surfing the Internet for as much as an hour during each workday. Many firms are trying to curb this practice by limiting employees' access to instant messaging services, streaming music, and websites with adult content.[6]

# Digital Media and the Marketing Mix

While digital marketing shares some similarities with conventional marketing techniques, a few valuable differences stand out. First, digital media make customer communications faster and interactive. Second, digital media help companies reach new target markets more easily, affordably, and quickly than ever before. Finally, digital media help marketers utilize new resources in seeking out and communicating with customers. One of the most important benefits of digital marketing is the ability of marketers and customers to easily share information. Through websites, social networks, and other digital media, consumers can learn about everything they consume and use in their lives, ask questions, voice complaints, indicate preferences, and otherwise communicate about their needs and desires. Many marketers use e-mail, mobile phones, social networking, wikis, media sharing, blogs, videoconferencing, and other technologies to coordinate activities and communicate with employees, customers, and suppliers. Twitter, considered both a social network and a micro-blog, illustrates how these digital technologies can combine to create new communication opportunities.

Nielsen Marketing Research revealed that consumers now spend more time on social networking sites than they do on e-mail, and social network use is still growing. Figure 13.1 shows the use of social media among Internet users in select countries. With digital media, even small businesses can reach new markets through these

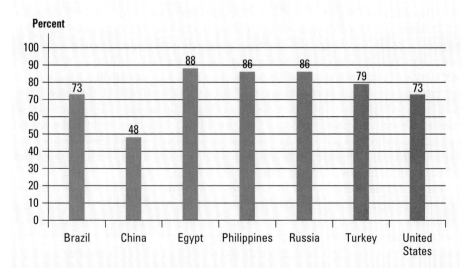

**FIGURE 13.1**

**Social Networking Use in Select Countries**

Note: Internet users in the United States represent adults who said they use the Internet or e-mail or connect via a mobile device "at least occasionally." International Internet users represent adults who use the Internet at least occasionally or own a smartphone.

Source: Lee Rainie and Jacob Poushter, "Emerging Nations Catching Up to U.S. on Technology Adoption, Especially Mobile and Social Media Use," Pew Research Center, www.pewresearch.org/fact-tank/2014/02/13/emerging-nations-catching-up-to-u-s-on-technology-adoption-especially-mobile-and-social-media-use/ (accessed May 19, 2014).

inexpensive communication channels. Brick-and-mortar companies like Walmart utilize online catalogs and company websites and blogs to supplement their retail stores. Internet companies like Amazon and Zappos that lack physical stores let customers post reviews of their purchases on their websites, creating company-sponsored communities.

One aspect of marketing that has not changed with digital media is the importance of achieving the right marketing mix. Product, distribution, promotion, and pricing are as important as ever for successful online marketing strategies. More than 40 percent of the world's population now uses the Internet.[7] That means it is essential for businesses large and small to use digital media effectively, not only to grab or maintain market share but also to streamline their organizations and offer customers entirely new benefits and convenience. Let's look at how businesses are using digital media to create effective marketing strategies on the web.

**Product Considerations.**    Like traditional marketers, digital marketers must anticipate consumer needs and preferences, tailor their goods and services to meet these needs, and continually upgrade them to remain competitive. The connectivity created by digital media provides the opportunity for adding services and can enhance product benefits. Some products, such as online games, applications, and virtual worlds, are only available via digital media. The more than 800,000 applications available on the iPad, for instance, provide examples of products that are only available in the digital world.[8] Businesses can often offer more items online than they could in a retail store. Additionally, Netflix offers a much wider array of movies and games than the average movie rental stores and original content, along with a one-month free trial, quick delivery and easy returns, online video streaming of some movies, and no late fees. Netflix also prides itself on its recommendation engine, which recommends movies for users based on their previous rental history and how they rate movies they have seen. As Netflix demonstrates, the Internet can make it much easier to anticipate consumer needs. However, fierce competition makes quality product offerings more important than ever.[9]

**Distribution Considerations.**    The Internet is a new distribution channel for making products available at the right time, at the right place, and in the right quantities. Marketers' ability to process orders electronically and increase the speed of communications via the Internet reduces inefficiencies, costs, and redundancies while increasing speed throughout the marketing channel. Shipping times and costs have become an important consideration in attracting customers, prompting many companies to offer consumers low shipping costs or next-day delivery. For example, Walmart is attempting to take market share away from e-marketers like Amazon.com by reducing delivery time and creating a "site to store" system that eliminates shipping costs for consumers who pick up their deliveries in the store. This offer has the increased benefit of getting customers into the store, where they might make add-on purchases. Walmart is also testing the concept of delivering groceries to individual homes. Through even more sophisticated distribution systems, Walmart hopes to overtake online retailers to become the biggest online merchant.[10]

These changes in distribution are not limited to the Western world. In a revolutionary shift in China, where online shopping had not been widely adopted by consumers, businesses are now realizing the benefits of marketing online. One of the first adopters of Internet selling was the Chinese company Taobao, a consumer auction site that also features sections for Chinese brands and retailers. Taobao has been enormously successful; the company is estimated to be worth $650 billion in the next few years.[11]

Consumer trends like these demonstrate that the shift of distributing through digital networks is well under way worldwide.

**Promotion Considerations.**  Perhaps one of the best ways businesses can utilize digital media is for promotion purposes—whether they are increasing brand awareness, connecting with consumers, or taking advantage of social networks or virtual worlds (discussed later) to form relationships and generate positive publicity or "buzz" about their products. Thanks to online promotion, consumers can be more informed than ever, including reading customer-generated content before making purchasing decisions. Consumer consumption patterns are radically changing, and marketers must adapt their promotional efforts to meet them.

If marketers find it difficult to adapt their promotional strategies to online marketing, many social networks offer tools to help. For instance, Facebook has its "Facebook Exchange" and "Facebook Offers" to help businesses target their promotions to the right audiences. "Facebook Exchange" is a tool that provides marketers with the ability to target their advertisements to people based upon other activities they have done on the Internet. "Facebook Offers" is a tool allowing businesses to provide customers with discounts on their Facebook pages. MGM Resorts International used both these tools in a campaign to acquire new customers, promote loyalty, and increase current customer activity. It is estimated that MGM received a fivefold return on its advertising investment using "Facebook Offers" and a 15-fold return using "Facebook Exchange."[12] Marketers that choose to capitalize on these opportunities have the chance to significantly boost their firms' brand exposure.

**Pricing Considerations.**  Price is the most flexible element of the marketing mix. Digital marketing can enhance the value of products by providing extra benefits such as service, information, and convenience. Through digital media, discounts and other promotions can be quickly communicated. As consumers have become better informed about their options, the demand for low-priced products has grown, leading to the creation of deal sites where consumers can directly compare prices. Expedia.com, for instance, provides consumers with a wealth of travel information about everything from flights to hotels that lets them compare benefits and prices. Many marketers offer buying incentives like online coupons or free samples to generate consumer demand for their products. For the business that wants to compete on price, digital marketing provides unlimited opportunities.

## Social Networking

A **social network** is a website where users can create a profile and interact with other users, post information, and engage in other forms of web-based communication. Social networks are a valued part of marketing because they are changing the way consumers communicate with each other and with firms. Sites such as Facebook and Twitter have emerged as opportunities for marketers to build communities, provide product information, and learn about consumer needs. By the time you read this, it is possible there will be new social network sites that continue to advance digital communication and opportunities for marketers.

You might be surprised to know that social networks have existed in some form or other for 40 years. The precursors of today's social networks began in the 1970s as online bulletin boards that allowed users with common interests to interact with one another. The first modern social network was Six Degrees.com, launched in 1997. This system permitted users to create a profile and connect with friends—the core

**social network**
a website where users can create a profile and interact with other users, post information, and engage in other forms of web-based communication

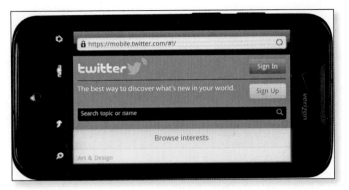

Marketers can use the popular micro blogging site Twitter to connect with customers and answer questions.

attributes of today's networks.[13] Although Six Degrees eventually shut down for lack of interest, the seed of networking had been planted.[14] Other social networks followed, with each new generation becoming increasingly sophisticated. Today's sites offer a multitude of consumer benefits, including the ability to download music, games, and applications; upload photos and videos; join groups; find and chat with friends; comment on friends' posts; and post and update status messages.

As the number of social network users increases, interactive marketers are finding opportunities to reach out to consumers in new target markets. CafeMom is a family of branded social communities that offer mothers a forum in which to connect and write about parenting and other topics important to them. At more than 20 million users, this particular site is an opportunity to reach out to mothers, a demographic that has a significant influence on family purchasing behavior. Walmart, Playskool, General Mills, and Johnson & Johnson have all advertised through this site.[15] We'll have more to say about how marketers utilize social networks later in this chapter.

An important question relates to how social media sites are adding value to the economy. Marketers at companies like Ford and Zappos, for instance, are using social media to promote products and build consumer relationships. Most corporations are supporting Facebook pages and Yammer accounts for employees to communicate across departments and divisions. Professionals such as professors, doctors, and engineers also share ideas on a regular basis. Even staffing organizations use social media, bypassing traditional e-mail and telephone channels. While billions of dollars in investments are being funneled into social media, it may be too early to assess the exact economic contribution of social media to the entire economy.[16]

## Types of Consumer-Generated Marketing and Digital Media

While digital marketing has generated exciting opportunities for companies to interact with their customers, digital media are also more consumer-driven than traditional media. Internet users are creating and reading consumer-generated content as never before and are having a profound effect on marketing in the process.

Two factors have sparked the rise of consumer-generated information:

1. The increased tendency of consumers to publish their own thoughts, opinions, reviews, and product discussions through blogs or digital media.

2. Consumers' tendencies to trust other consumers over corporations. Consumers often rely on the recommendations of friends, family, and fellow consumers when making purchasing decisions.

Marketers who know where online users are likely to express their thoughts and opinions can use these forums to interact with them, address problems, and promote their companies. Types of digital media in which Internet users are likely to participate include social networks, blogs, wikis, video sharing sites, podcasts, virtual reality sites, and mobile applications. Let's look a little more closely at each.

## Facebook Praised for Tackling Carbon Emissions

It's no secret that Facebook and Google are competitors, particularly when it comes to advertising. Both companies have a wide global reach and the ability to segment the market. However, there is one area in which Facebook performs better than Google: its carbon footprint. Facebook's yearly carbon emissions amount to approximately 285,000 metric tons per year compared to Google's 1.5 million.

As concern for the planet increases, consumers are demanding that companies become more sustainable. Therefore, the fact that Facebook is more carbon-efficient than competitors places it at an advantage. Greenpeace has praised the company for its transparency after Facebook released a detailed report describing its carbon footprint. In the report, Facebook announced its goals of getting 25 percent of its energy from renewable sources by 2015. This report provided information about Facebook's goals and data centers as well as the carbon footprint from the company's more than 90 million Facebook users.

So how much energy does each user's Facebook use emit? Facebook has calculated that each user's annual use is equivalent to the carbon footprint of a medium latte. Unfortunately, with more than 900 million users, this adds up significantly. And while the firm plans to create a hydro-powered data center in Sweden, other expansions will likely increase its carbon emissions in the short term. Despite these downsides, Facebook's transparency has earned it accolades from stakeholders—including environmental groups.[17]

### Discussion Questions

1. How is Facebook trying to increase its sustainability?
2. Why do you think Facebook released a report on its sustainability accomplishments?
3. Do you feel that Facebook's sustainability initiatives will give it an edge over Google?

## Social Networks

The increase in social networking across the world is exponential. It is estimated that today's adults spend approximately 37 minutes per day on social networking sites.[18] As social networks evolve, both marketers and the owners of social networking sites are realizing the opportunities such networks offer—an influx of advertising dollars for site owners and a large reach for the advertiser. As a result, marketers have begun investigating and experimenting with promotion on social networks. Three popular sites are Facebook, Twitter, and Google+.

**Facebook.** In April 2008, the social networking site Facebook surpassed Myspace in its number of members, becoming the most popular social networking site in the world.[19] Facebook users create profiles, which they can make public or private, and then search the network for people with whom to connect. Many believe Facebook appeals to a broader demographic than does Myspace, attracting parents and grandparents as well as teens and college students.[20] In fact, the fastest-growing group on Facebook is consumers 55 and over.[21]

Many companies have Facebook pages to promote products and stay connected to consumers.

For this reason, many marketers are turning to Facebook to market products, interact with consumers, and gain free publicity. It is possible for a consumer to become a "fan" of a major company like Starbucks by clicking on the "Like" icon on the coffee retailer's Facebook page. Facebook is also partnering with businesses to offer unique incentives to businesses. American Express offers customers special discounts if they link their cards to Facebook, Twitter, and/or Foursquare accounts. This incentive allows the firm to build loyalty and gain more information about customers.[22] Advertising on Facebook has also been increasing. The firm generated $1.8 billion from advertising during a four-month period, with 49 percent coming from mobile advertising.[23] Promoted posts, one of the features Facebook has to offer businesses, allows companies to develop advertisements that show up in the News Feeds of those who have "liked" the organization and in the News Feeds of their friends.[24]

Additionally, social networking sites are useful for relationship marketing, or the creation of relationships that mutually benefit the marketing business and the customer. Companies are utilizing relationship marketing through Facebook to help consumers feel more connected to their products. For instance, New Belgium Brewing has more than 35 local Facebook pages and uses the website to target advertisements toward its fan base. After conducting a study on its Facebook fans, the company determined that its fans generate half of the company's annual sales.[25] Thanks to Facebook, companies like New Belgium are able to understand who their customers are and how they can meet their needs.

**Twitter.**    Twitter is a hybrid of a social networking site and a micro-blogging site that asks users one simple question: "What's happening?" Members can post answers of up to 140 characters, which are then available for their registered "followers" to read. It sounds simple enough, but Twitter's effect on digital media has been immense. The site quickly progressed from a novelty to a social networking staple, attracting millions of viewers each month.[26] The site quickly progressed from a novelty to a social networking staple, attracting more than 215 million active users each month. Nearly half of these users visit the site on a daily basis, while approximately 30 percent visit the site multiple times per day.[27]

Although 140 characters may not seem like enough for companies to send an effective message, some have become experts at using Twitter in their marketing strategies. Southwest Airlines has an entire team to monitor its account during its business operations to answer questions on Twitter ranging from refunds to lost baggage. These efforts are having an impact; more than half of Twitter's active and monthly users follow companies or brands. This indicates three times more the exposure for businesses on Twitter than on Facebook.[28]

Like other social networking tools, Twitter is also being used to build, or in some cases rebuild, customer relationships. For example, Zappos posts on Twitter to update followers on company activities and address customer complaints.[29] Other companies are using Twitter in conjunction with other social media sites to create unique viral marketing campaigns. For example, Royal Dutch Airlines implemented a campaign called KLM Surprise in which employees looked for waiting passengers on Twitter and Foursquare. Once discovered, they learned a little more about them and surprised them with gifts before they left the terminal.[30]

Finally, companies are using Twitter to gain a competitive advantage. Sports organizations and media companies are using Twitter to rebroadcast game highlights with short advertisements on their site. These postings have received several thousand comments and retweets as a result.[31] Twitter is also expanding into video with its acquisition of the mobile application Vine. In keeping with Twitter's reputation for short, concise postings, Vine allows users to display up to 6 seconds of video and share them with other users. Vine has become highly popular among celebrities and teenagers, with more than 13 million users. Marketers are taking notice. Burberry, for instance, developed a video on Vine that featured its London menswear fashion show.[32] The race is on among companies that want to use Twitter to gain a competitive edge.

**Google+.**    In 2011, Google launched its Google+ network, a social media site intended to rival Facebook and identify users across Google's various services.[33] The initial launch was invitation-only as a field test. Eventually, Google abandoned the invite-only feature and opened the site to all users over the age of 13.

CEO Larry Page initiated a move to get more people to use Google+ by requiring those that use Google services, such as Gmail and YouTube, to have a Google+ account. This requirement has many implications for Google. For instance, integration between the social network and its other services means that users who post reviews on different Google platforms can no longer do so anonymously—they are now tied to a person's Google+ account.[34] In another controversial move, Google began requiring users who wanted to leave comments on YouTube to do so using Google+.[35] The move has led to a 58 percent jump in users on the site.[36]

Google+ gives digital marketers an opportunity to capitalize on its growing user base. Because Google+ is linked with search results on Google, sharing a firm's information on Google+ could push the firm up through the ranks of Google search results. Google+ postings with links to a company's website encourage more traffic on the corporate website. Google+ also has tools that allow companies to see how often their posts are shared. Additionally, because Google+ is integrated with other Google services, a search for an organization such as Ford will not only bring up information on Ford, but will also display recent posts about Ford that have been placed on Google+.[37] Although Google+ does not yet have the same influence as Facebook, marketers are discovering a number of possibilities to engage users with Google+.

## Blogs and Wikis

Today's marketers must recognize that the impact of consumer-generated material like blogs and wikis and their significance to online consumers have increased a great deal. **Blogs** (short for web logs) are web-based journals in which writers can editorialize and interact with other Internet users. More than three-fourths of Internet users read blogs.[38] In fact, the blogging site Tumblr, which allows anyone to post text, hyperlinks, pictures, and other media for free, became one of the top 10 online destinations. The site has 187 million blogs, and more than 98 million posts are posted on the site daily. In 2013, Yahoo! purchased Tumblr for $1.1 billion.[39]

**blog**
a web-based journal in which a writer can editorialize and interact with other Internet users

Blogs give consumers power, sometimes more than companies would like. Bloggers can post whatever they like about a company or its products, whether their opinions are positive or negative, true or false. For instance, although companies sometimes force bloggers to remove blogs, readers often create copies of the blog post and spread it across the Internet after the original's removal. In other cases, a positive review of a good or service posted on a popular blog can result in large increases in sales. Thus, blogs can represent a potent threat or opportunity to marketers.

**DID YOU KNOW?** Searching is the most popular online activity, while social networking and blogging are fourth.[40]

Rather than trying to eliminate blogs that cast their companies in a negative light, some firms are using their own blogs, or employee blogs, to answer consumer concerns or defend their corporate reputations. Boeing operates a corporate blog to highlight company news and to post correspondence from Boeing enthusiasts from all over the world.[41] As blogging changes the face of media, smart companies are using it to build enthusiasm for their products and create relationships with consumers.

**wiki**
software that creates an interface that enables users to add or edit the content of some types of websites

**Wikis** are websites where users can add to or edit the content of posted articles. One of the best known is Wikipedia, an online encyclopedia with more than 30 million entries in more than 285 languages on nearly every subject imaginable. (Encyclopedia Britannica only has 120,000 entries.)[42] Wikipedia is one of the 10 most popular sites on the web, and because much of its content can be edited by anyone, it is easy for online consumers to add detail and supporting evidence and to correct inaccuracies in content. Wikipedia used to be completely open to editing, but in order to stop vandalism, the site had to make some topics off-limits that are now editable only by a small group of experts.

Like all digital media, wikis have advantages and disadvantages for companies. Wikis about controversial companies like Walmart and Nike often contain negative publicity, such as about workers' rights violations. However, monitoring relevant wikis can provide companies with a better idea of how consumers feel about the company or brand. Some companies have also begun to use wikis as internal tools for teams working on projects that require a great deal of documentation.[43]

There is too much at stake financially for marketers to ignore wikis and blogs. Despite this fact, statistics show that only 34 percent of *Fortune* 500 companies have a corporate blog.[44] Marketers who want to form better customer relationships and promote their company's products must not underestimate the power of these two media outlets.

## Media Sharing

Businesses can also share their corporate messages in more visual ways through media sharing sites. Media sharing sites allow marketers to share photos, videos, and podcasts. Media sharing sites are more limited in scope in how companies interact with consumers. They tend to be more promotional than reactive. This means that while firms can promote their products through videos or photos, they usually do not interact with consumers through personal messages or responses. At the same time, the popularity of these sites provides the potential to reach a global audience of consumers.

**viral marketing**
a marketing tool that uses the Internet, particularly social networking and video sharing sites, to spread a message and create brand awareness

Video sharing sites allow virtually anybody to upload videos, from professional marketers at *Fortune* 500 corporations to the average Internet user. Some of the most popular video sharing sites include YouTube, Vimeo, and Daily*motion*. Video sharing sites give companies the opportunity to upload ads and informational videos about their products. A few videos become viral at any given time, and although many of these gain popularity because they embarrass the subject in some way, others reach viral status because people find them entertaining. **Viral marketing** occurs when a message gets sent from person to person to person. It can be an extremely effective tool for marketers—particularly on the Internet, where one click can send a message to dozens or hundreds of people simultaneously. Marketers are taking advantage of the viral nature of video sharing sites like YouTube, either by creating their own unique videos or advertising on videos that have already reached viral status. For instance, Disney bought Maker Studios, one of the most successful online video companies, in order to target the Millennial generation, a prime group for viral marketing. With more than

Flickr is a popular photo sharing site. Marketers can use Flickr to post photos of products or company activities.

5.5 million views on YouTube, Maker Studios seems a promising acquisition to put Disney at a significant competitive advantage in this arena.[45]

Businesses have also begun to utilize consumer-generated video content, saving money they would have spent on hiring advertising firms to develop professional advertising campaigns. GoPro was transformed from a small camera firm into a successful company due to the videos consumers took of themselves using GoPro cameras. The company is partnering with YouTube to create its own network for consumer-generated GoPro videos.[46] Marketers believe consumer videos appear more authentic and create enthusiasm for the product among consumer participants.

Photo sharing sites allow users to upload and share their photos and short videos with the world. Well-known photo sharing sites include Instagram, Imgur, Shutterfly, Photobucket, and Flickr. Flickr is owned by Yahoo! and is one of the most popular photo sharing sites on the Internet. A Flickr user can upload images, edit them, classify the images, create photo albums, and share photos with friends without having to e-mail bulky image files or send photos through the mail. However, Instagram has surpassed Flickr as the most popular photo sharing site. Instagram is a mobile application that allows users to make their photos look dreamy or retrospective with different tints and then share them with their friends.[47] The Eddie Bauer website has an icon on its main website that will take users to its Instagram stream.[48] To compete against Twitter's short-form video service Vine, Facebook has added 13 filters for video to the Instagram app.[49] With more and more people using mobile apps or accessing the Internet through their smartphones, the use of photo sharing through mobile devices is likely to increase.

Other sites are emerging that take photo sharing to a new level. Pinterest is a photo sharing bulletin board site that combines photo sharing with elements of bookmarking and social networking. Users can share photos and images among other Internet users, communicating mostly through images that they "pin" to their boards. Other users can "repin" these images to their boards, follow each other, "like" images, and make comments. Marketers have found that an effective way of marketing through Pinterest is to post images conveying a certain emotion that represents their brand.[50]

Photo sharing represents an opportunity for companies to market themselves visually by displaying snapshots of company events, company staff, and/or company products. Nike, Audi, and MTV have all used Instagram in digital marketing campaigns. Whole Foods has topic boards on Pinterest featuring recipes, farm scenes, and more to reinforce its brand image.[51] Zales Jewelers has topic boards on Pinterest featuring rings as well as other themes of love, including songs, wedding cake, and wedding dresses.[52] Virgin Mobile has a Flickr photostream that features photos of company events such as product launches.[53] Many businesses with pictures on Flickr have a link connecting their Flickr photostreams to their corporate websites.[54]

**Podcasts** are audio or video files that can be downloaded from the Internet via a subscription that automatically delivers new content to listening devices or personal computers. Podcasting offers the benefit of convenience, giving users the ability to listen to or view content when and where they choose. It is estimated that approximately 39 million U.S. consumers download podcasts every month. The markets podcasts reach are ideal for marketers, especially the 18–34 demographic, which includes the young and the affluent.[55] For instance, the podcast *Mad Money,* hosted by Jim Cramer, gives investment advice and teaches listeners how to analyze stocks and other financial instruments. These are important topics for young adults who do not have much investment experience.[56]

**podcast**
an audio or video file that can be downloaded from the Internet with a subscription that automatically delivers new content to listening devices or personal computers

### Smirnoff's Mixhibit: An Example of Ethical Digital Marketing

Smirnoff Vodka is taking digital marketing to a new level. The company has developed Mixhibit, a mobile application allowing users to create short videos made up of snapshots from various social networking platforms. Users can scour their Facebook, Twitter, Instagram, and Foursquare profiles for photos and posts they want to include in their video. Then they can set the motion picture to music with any one of the 10,000 tracks available on the app. The goal of Mixhibit is to generate global consumer participation with the brand that extends beyond liking, following, and sharing—such activities are passive and do not optimize consumer participation. Mixhibit brings the physical world in closer contact with the digital world, which is a more realistic form of consumer participation.

Smirnoff is the top global seller of vodka in value and volume. As a major player in 133 countries, it is gaining traction in developing economies. The use of social networking is a way to include participants on a global scale and get them involved together in the physical world. The influence Smirnoff holds comes with two major responsibilities in marketing, however. First, it has an economic responsibility not to become complacent in its success. Despite its number-one status around the world, Smirnoff must be sensitive to environmental changes. Mixhibit achieves this goal by keeping the brand fresh and interesting to customers. Second, Smirnoff has a sociocultural and legal responsibility to market only to those who are of legal drinking age.[57]

#### Discussion Questions

1. How is Smirnoff Vodka using digital marketing to encourage consumer participation?
2. How do you think the Mixhibit app helps to keep the firm from becoming complacent in its success?
3. Are there any risks associated with promoting the Mixhibit app? If so, how can Smirnoff Vodka overcome them?

As podcasting continues to catch on, radio stations and television networks like CBC Radio, NPR, MSNBC, and PBS are creating podcasts of their shows to profit from this growing trend. Many companies hope to use podcasts to create brand awareness, promote their products, and encourage customer loyalty.

### Virtual Worlds

Games and programs allowing viewers to develop avatars that exist in an online virtual world have exploded in popularity in the 21st century. Virtual worlds include Second Life, Everquest, Sim City, and the role-playing game World of Warcraft. These sites can be described as social networks with a twist. Virtual realities are three-dimensional, user-created worlds that have their own currencies, lands, and residents that come in every shape and size. Internet users who participate in virtual realities such as Second Life choose a fictional persona, called an *avatar*. Residents of Second Life connect with other users, purchase goods with virtual Linden dollars (convertible to real dollars), and even own virtual businesses. For entertainment purposes, residents can shop, attend concerts, or travel to virtual environments—all while spending real money. Farmville provides a similar virtual world experience, except it is limited to life on a farm.

Real-world marketers and organizations have been eager to capitalize on the popularity of virtual gaming sites. MediaSpike specializes in placing brands into mobile games. Geico Powersports and Mountain Dew are two brands that have worked with MediaSpike to appear in mobile games.[58] Other businesses are looking toward virtual worlds to familiarize consumers with their goods and services. For instance, McDonald's partnered with the virtual gaming site Zynga to bring its virtual store and brand to Zynga's popular virtual gaming site Cityville.[59]

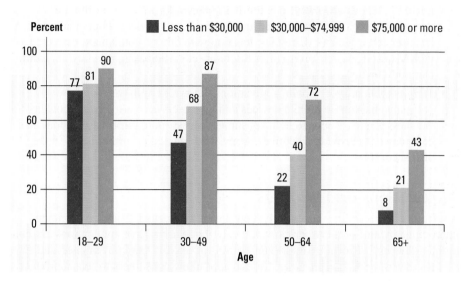

**Percent**

Legend: ■ Less than $30,000  ■ $30,000–$74,999  ■ $75,000 or more

18–29: 77, 81, 90
30–49: 47, 68, 87
50–64: 22, 40, 72
65+: 8, 21, 43

**Age**

**FIGURE 13.2**

**Smartphone Ownership by Age and Income**

Based on percentage within each age/income group who own a smartphone.

Source: Pew Research Center's Internet & American Life Project, April 17–May 19, 2013, Tracking Survey. Interviews were conducted in English and Spanish and on land-line and cell phones. Margin of error is +/–2.3 percentage points based on adults ($n = 2,252$).

## Mobile Marketing

As digital marketing becomes increasingly sophisticated, consumers are beginning to utilize mobile devices like smartphones as a highly functional communication method. The iPhone and iPad have changed the way consumers communicate, and a growing number of travelers are using their smartphones to find online maps, travel guides, and taxis. In industries such as hotels, airlines, and car rental agencies, mobile phones have become a primary method for booking reservations and communicating about services. They can act as airline boarding passes, GPS devices, and even hotel room keys. Other marketing uses of mobile phones include sending shoppers timely messages related to discounts and shopping opportunities.[60] Figure 13.2 breaks down smartphone usage by age and income. Mobile marketing is exploding—marketers are estimated to spend $31.45 billion on mobile marketing in 2014.[61] To avoid being left behind, brands must recognize the importance of mobile marketing.

E-commerce sales on smartphones is also rapidly growing. Sales are estimated to reach $638 billion by 2018.[62] This makes it essential for companies to understand how to use mobile tools to create effective campaigns. Some of the more common mobile marketing tools include the following:

- *SMS messages:* SMS messages are text messages of 160 words or less. SMS messages have been an effective way to send coupons to prospective customers.[63]
- *Multimedia messages:* Multimedia messaging takes SMS messaging a step further by allowing companies to send video, audio, photos, and other types of media over mobile devices. Gap used Instagram Direct as the outlet for their "What I Wore Today (#WIWT)" campaign, allowing users to win a Gap denim tablet case.[64]
- *Mobile advertisements:* Mobile advertisements are visual advertisements that appear on mobile devices. Companies might choose to advertise through search engines, websites, or even games accessed on mobile devices. Marketers spent approximately $3 billion within a six-month period on mobile advertising.[65]
- *Mobile websites:* Mobile websites are websites designed for mobile devices. Mobile devices constitute one-third of web traffic.[66]

- *Location-based networks:* Location-based networks are built for mobile devices. One of the most popular location-based networks is Foursquare, which lets users check in and share their location with others. Foursquare partnered with Visa and MasterCard to offer discounts at participating retailers, including Dunkin' Donuts and Burger King.[67]
- *Mobile applications:* Mobile applications (known as *apps*) are software programs that run on mobile devices and give users access to certain content.[68] Businesses release apps to help consumers access more information about their company or to provide incentives. Apps are discussed in further detail in the next section.

## Applications and Widgets

Applications are adding an entirely new layer to the marketing environment, as approximately half of all American adult cell phone users have applications on their mobile devices.[69] The most important feature of apps is the convenience and cost savings they offer to the consumer. Certain apps allow consumers to scan a product's barcode and then compare it with the prices of identical products in other stores. Mobile apps also enable customers to download in-store discounts. As of 2014, an estimated 58 percent of American adults have smartphones, so businesses cannot afford to miss out on the chance to profit from these new trends.[70]

To remain competitive, companies are beginning to use mobile marketing to offer additional incentives to consumers. Starwood Hotels & Resorts Worldwide developed an app customers can use to research their travel location straight from their smartphones and receive discounts and personalized incentives. Starwood Hotels believes the app will enhance customer relationships, thereby increasing customer loyalty.[71] Another application that marketers are finding useful is the QR scanning app. QR codes are black-and-white squares that sometimes appear in magazines, posters, and storefront displays. Smartphone users who have downloaded the QR scanning application can open their smartphones and scan the code, which contains a hidden message accessible with the app. The QR scanning app recognizes the code and opens the link, video, or image on the phone's screen. Marketers are using QR codes to promote their companies and offer consumer discounts.[72]

Mobile payments are also gaining traction, and companies like Google are working to capitalize on this opportunity.[73] Google Wallet is a mobile app that stores credit card information on the smartphone. When the shopper is ready to check out, he or she can tap the phone at the point of sale for the transaction to be registered.[74] Square is a company launched by Twitter co-founder Jack Dorsey. The company provides organizations with smartphone swiping devices for credit cards as well as tablets that can be used to tally purchases. A newer service called Square Cash is enabling users to send up to $2,500 digitally through e-mail.[75] Bitcoin is a virtual peer-to-peer currency that can be used to make a payment via smartphone. Smaller organizations have begun to accept Bitcoin at some of their stores. Virtual currency exchanges have run into legal issues, however, due to state money-transmission laws. Bitcoin also fluctuates in value, making it risky for companies to hold onto the virtual currency for long periods.[76] It is not backed by a central bank and its software is run on a network of volunteers' computers. Bitcoin is being increasingly accepted among officials, and Germany has recognized it as a unit of account.[77] However, a recent scandal has caused some to question Bitcoin's use. Mt. Gox, a Bitcoin exchange, reportedly lost hundreds of thousands of Bitcoins amounting to $620 million in value. A lawsuit has been filed, and Mt. Gox declared bankruptcy.[78] The success of mobile payments in revolutionizing the shopping experience will largely depend upon retailers to adopt this payment system, but companies such as Starbucks are already jumping at the opportunity.

Widgets are small bits of software on a website, desktop, or mobile device that perform a simple purpose, such as providing stock quotes or blog updates. Marketers might use widgets to display news headlines, clocks, or games on their web pages.[79] Widgets have been used by companies such as A&E Television Network as a form of viral marketing—users can download the widget and send it to their friends with a click of a button.[80] Widgets downloaded to a user's desktop can update the user on the latest company or product information, enhancing relationship marketing between companies and their fans. Hotels, restaurants, and other tourist locations can download TripAdvisor widgets to their websites. These widgets display the latest company reviews, rewards, and other TripAdvisor content directly to the company's website.[81] Widgets are an innovative digital marketing tool to personalize web pages, alert users to the latest company information, and spread awareness of the company's products.

## Using Digital Media to Reach Consumers

We've seen that customer-generated communications and digital media connect consumers as never before. These connections let consumers share information and experiences without company interference so they get more of the "real story" on a product or company feature. In many ways, these media take some of the professional marketer's power to control and dispense information and place it in the hands of the consumer.

However, this shift does not have to spell doom for marketers, who can choose to utilize the power of the consumer and Internet technology to their advantage. While consumers use digital media to access more product information, marketers can use the same sites to get better and more targeted information about the consumer—often more than they could gather through traditional marketing venues. Marketers increasingly use consumer-generated content to aid their own marketing efforts, even going so far as to incorporate Internet bloggers in their publicity campaigns. Finally, marketers are also beginning to use the Internet to track the success of their online marketing campaigns, creating an entirely new way of gathering marketing research.

The challenge for digital media marketers is to constantly adapt to new technologies and changing consumer patterns. Unfortunately, the attrition rate for digital media channels is very high, with some dying off each year as new ones emerge. As time passes, digital media are becoming more sophisticated so as to reach consumers in more effective ways. Those that are not able to adapt and change eventually fail.

Charlene Li and Josh Bernoff of Forrester Research, a technology and market research company, emphasize the need for marketers to understand these changing relationships in the online media world. By grouping consumers into different segments based on how they utilize digital media, marketers can gain a better understanding of the online market and how best to proceed.[82]

The use of mobile coupons is increasing. Consumers appreciate these types of coupons for their convenience. Retailers like mobile coupons because they save money from having to print and distribute them.

**TABLE 13.2**
**Social Technographics**

| | |
|---|---|
| Creators | Publish a blog |
| | Publish personal web pages |
| | Upload original video |
| | Upload original audio/music |
| | Write articles or stories and post them |
| Conversationalists | Update status on social networking sites |
| | Post updates on Twitter |
| Critics | Post ratings/reviews of products or services |
| | Comment on someone else's blog |
| | Contribute to online forums |
| | Contribute to/edit articles in a wiki |
| Collectors | Use RSS feeds |
| | Add tags to web pages or photos |
| | "Vote" for websites online |
| Joiners | Maintain profile on a social networking site |
| | Visit social networking sites |
| Spectators | Read blogs |
| | Watch video from other users |
| | Listen to podcasts |
| | Read online forums |
| | Read customer ratings/reviews |
| Inactives | None of the activities |

*Source: Charlene Li and Josh Bernoff,* Groundswell *(Boston: Harvard Business Press, 2008), p. 43. "Forrester Unveils New Segment of Social Technographics—The Conversationalists," 360 Digital Connections, January 21, 2010, http://blog.360i.com/social-media/forrester-new-segment-social-technographics-conversationalists (accessed May 19, 2014).*

Table 13.2 shows seven ways that Forrester Research groups consumers based on their Internet activity (or lack thereof). The categories are not mutually exclusive; online consumers can participate in more than one at a time.

*Creators* are consumers who create their own media outlets, such as blogs, podcasts, consumer-generated videos, and wikis.[83] Consumer-generated media are increasingly important to online marketers as a conduit for addressing consumers directly. The second group of Internet users is *conversationalists.* Conversationalists regularly update their Twitter feeds or status updates on social networking sites. Although they are less involved than creators, conversationalists spend time at least once a week (and often more) on digital media sites posting updates.[84] The third category, *critics,* consists of people who comment on blogs or post ratings and reviews on review websites such as Yelp. Because many online shoppers read ratings and reviews to aid their purchasing decisions, critics should be a primary component in a company's digital marketing strategy. The next category is *collectors.* They collect information and organize content generated by critics and creators.[85] Because collectors are active members of the online community, a company story or site that catches the eye of a collector is likely

### Fab.com: How an e-Business Generated Growth through Digital Marketing

**Fab.com**
**Founders:** Bradford Shelhammer and Jason Goldberg
**Founded:** 2011, in Manhattan
**Success:** This online retailer has 20,000 designers selling through its site and a valuation of $1 billion after only two years in business.

Fab.com understands the value of digital marketing. When founders Bradford Shellhammer and Jason Goldberg launched Fab.com, an e-business retailer selling designer-made products, they saw an opportunity to inspire word-of-mouth promotion. In order to build their user base, Shelhammer and Goldberg used sites such as Facebook, Twitter, and Pinterest to encourage people to post designs they liked on Fab.com. They also bought advertisements on Facebook for flash sales, where items are offered at a discount price for the first week they are sold on Fab.com. These tactics generated buzz and worked as a word-of-mouth marketing tool in the social media realm. By the time Fab.com launched, it had 175,000 members, and each of those members had invited approximately three friends to view the site. The company estimates that 30,000 of the 175,000 members joined as a result of its social media ads. Goldberg continues to measure social media marketing and constantly blogs about the company.[86]

to be posted, discussed on collector sites, and made available to other online users looking for information.

*Joiners* include all who become users of Twitter, Facebook, or other social networking sites. It is not unusual for consumers to be members of several social networking sites at once. Joiners use these sites to connect and network with other users, but as we've seen, marketers too can take significant advantage of these sites to connect with consumers and form customer relationships.[87] The last two segments are Spectators and Inactives. *Spectators,* who read online information but do not join groups or post anywhere, are the largest group in most countries. *Inactives* are online users who do not participate in any digital online media, but their numbers are dwindling.

Marketers need to consider what proportion of online consumers are creating, conversing, rating, collecting, joining, or simply reading online materials. As in traditional marketing efforts, they need to know their target market. For instance, where spectators make up the majority of the online population, companies should post their own corporate messages through blogs and websites promoting their organizations.

## Using Digital Media to Learn about Consumers

Marketing research and information systems can use digital media and social networking sites to gather useful information about consumers and their preferences. Sites such as Twitter and Facebook can be good substitutes for focus groups. Online surveys can serve as an alternative to mail, telephone, or personal interviews.

*Crowdsourcing* describes how marketers use digital media to find out the opinions or needs of the crowd (or potential markets). Communities of interested consumers join sites like threadless.com, which designs T-shirts, or crowdspring.com, which creates logos and print and web designs. These companies give interested consumers opportunities to contribute and give feedback on product ideas. Crowdsourcing lets companies gather and utilize consumers' ideas in an interactive way when creating new products.

About three-quarters of online shoppers read ratings and reviews before making a decision.

Consumer feedback is an important part of the digital media equation. Ratings and reviews have become exceptionally popular. Online reviews are estimated to influence the buying decisions of approximately 90 percent of U.S. consumers.[88] Retailers such as Amazon, Netflix, and Priceline allow consumers to post comments on their sites about the books, movies, and travel arrangements they sell. Today, most online shoppers search the Internet for ratings and reviews before making major purchase decisions.

While consumer-generated content about a firm can be either positive or negative, digital media forums do allow businesses to closely monitor what their customers are saying. In the case of negative feedback, businesses can communicate with consumers to address problems or complaints much more easily than through traditional communication channels. Yet despite the ease and obvious importance of online feedback, many companies do not yet take full advantage of the digital tools at their disposal.

# Legal and Social Issues in Internet Marketing

The extraordinary growth of information technology, the Internet, and social networks has generated many legal and social issues for consumers and businesses. These issues include privacy concerns, the risk of identity theft and online fraud, and the need to protect intellectual property. The U.S. Federal Trade Commission (FTC) compiles an annual list of consumer complaints related to the Internet and digital media. We discuss these in this section, as well as steps that individuals, companies, and the government have taken to address them.

## Privacy

Businesses have long tracked consumers' shopping habits with little controversy. However, observing the contents of a consumer's shopping cart or the process a consumer goes through when choosing a box of cereal generally does not result in the collection of specific, personally identifying data. Although using credit cards, shopping cards, and coupons forces consumers to give up a certain degree of anonymity in the traditional shopping process, they can still choose to remain anonymous by paying cash. Shopping on the Internet, however, allows businesses to track them on a far more personal level, from the contents of their online purchases to the websites they favor. Current technology has made it possible for marketers to amass vast quantities of personal information, often without consumers' knowledge, and to share and sell this information to interested third parties.

How is personal information collected on the web? Many sites follow users online by storing a "cookie," or an identifying string of text, on users' computers. Cookies permit website operators to track how often a user visits the site, what he or she looks at while there, and in what sequence. They also allow website visitors to customize services, such as virtual shopping carts, as well as the particular content they see when they log onto a web page. Users have the option of turning off cookies on their machines, but nevertheless the potential for misuse has left many consumers uncomfortable with this technology.

Google, Facebook, and other Internet firms have also come under fire for privacy issues. For instance, when Facebook announced it would give teenagers between the ages of 13 and 17 the ability to make their posts public, privacy advocates quickly protested the move.[89] Google has been a particular target of privacy advocates. Google has the ability to collect a trove of data on consumers who use its various services. Although Google has attempted to develop a "slider" tool that would provide users with a greater ability to control the data collected about them, the tool was abandoned after it was deemed too difficult to implement. However, past privacy snafus have caused Google to make Internet privacy a major priority. For instance, its Google Now product—a new tool that provides information to people before they search for it—underwent many legal and privacy hurdles before its final development. The European Union has been particularly cautious regarding the collection of user data and has instituted more restrictive regulations to control how much data these Internet firms can gather.[90]

Due to consumer concerns over privacy, the Federal Trade Commission (FTC) is considering developing regulations that would better protect consumer privacy by limiting the amount of consumer information that businesses can gather online. Other countries are pursuing similar actions. The European Union passed a law requiring companies to get users' consent before using cookies to track their information. In the United States, one proposed solution for consumer Internet privacy is a "do not track" bill, similar to the "do not call" bill for telephones, to allow users to opt out of having their information tracked.[91] While consumers may welcome such added protections, web advertisers, who use consumer information to better target advertisements to online consumers, see it as a threat. In response to impending legislation, many web advertisers are attempting self-regulation in order to stay ahead of the game. For instance, the Interactive Advertising Board is encouraging its members to adopt a do-not-track icon that users can click on to avoid having their online activity tracked. However, it is debatable whether members will choose to participate or honor users' do-not-track requests.[92]

## Identity Theft

**Identity theft** occurs when criminals obtain personal information that allows them to impersonate someone else in order to use the person's credit to access financial accounts and make purchases. This requires organizations to implement increased security measures to prevent database theft. As you can see in Figure 13.3, the most common complaints relate to government documents/benefits fraud, followed by credit card fraud, utility fraud, bank fraud, employment fraud, and loan fraud.

The Internet's relative anonymity and speed make possible both legal and illegal access to databases storing Social Security numbers, drivers' license numbers, dates of birth, mothers' maiden names, and other information that can be used to establish a credit card or bank account in another person's name in order to make fraudulent transactions. One growing scam used to initiate identity theft fraud is the practice of *phishing,* whereby con artists counterfeit a well-known website and send out e-mails directing victims to it. There visitors find instructions to reveal sensitive information such as their credit card numbers. Phishing scams have faked websites for PayPal, AOL, and the Federal Deposit Insurance Corporation.

Some identity theft problems are resolved quickly, while other cases take weeks and hundreds of dollars before a victim's bank balances and credit standings are restored. To deter identity theft, the National Fraud Center wants financial institutions

**identity theft**
when criminals obtain personal information that allows them to impersonate someone else in order to use their credit to access financial accounts and make purchases

**FIGURE 13.3**

**Main Sources of Identity Theft**

Source: Federal Trade Commission, "Consumer Sentinel Network Data Book: January–December 2013," February 2014, www.ftc.gov/system/files/documents/reports/consumer-sentinel-network-data-book-january-december-2013/sentinel-cy2013.pdf (accessed May 19, 2014).

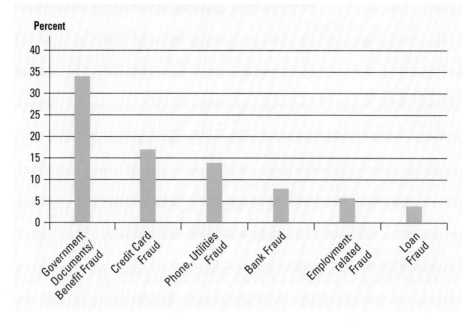

online fraud
any attempt to conduct fraudulent activities online

to implement new technologies such as digital certificates, digital signatures, and biometrics—the use of fingerprinting or retina scanning.

## Online Fraud

**Online fraud** includes any attempt to conduct fraudulent activities online, such as by deceiving consumers into releasing personal information. It is becoming a major source of frustration among users of social networking sites, because cybercriminals are finding new ways to use sites like Facebook and Twitter to commit fraudulent activities. Twitter has experienced an influx of fake Twitter accounts to try to boost publicity. A celebrity, for instance, might pay somebody to rebroadcast their tweets on a number of fake Twitter accounts. It is estimated that between 5 and 9 percent of Twitter accounts could be fake. While these accounts might not be used to solicit money or harm users directly, they are used for the express purpose of deceiving users.[93] Mobile payments are another concern. Perhaps the most disturbing is the practice of using social networking sites to pose as charitable institutions or victims of natural disasters. A good method for people to avoid getting scammed through social media sites is to research charities before giving.

In another case, 1.5 million Europeans who had enrolled in customer-loyalty programs found that their personal data had been stolen. Although these consumers dealt with a number of different websites, these websites were all linked by a loyalty program management firm in Ireland.[94] Privacy advocates advise that the best way to stay out of trouble is to avoid giving out personal information, such as Social Security numbers or credit card information, unless the site is definitely legitimate.

## Intellectual Property

In addition to protecting personal privacy, Internet users and others want to protect their rights to property they may create, including songs, movies, books, and software. Such intellectual property consists of the ideas and creative materials developed to solve problems, carry out applications, and educate and entertain others.

Although intellectual property is generally protected by patents and copyrights, each year losses from the illegal copying of computer programs, music, movies, compact discs, and books reach billions of dollars in the United States alone. This has become a particular problem with digital media sites. YouTube has often faced lawsuits on intellectual property infringement. With millions of users uploading content to YouTube, it can be hard for Google to monitor and remove all the videos that may contain copyrighted materials.

Illegal sharing of content is another major intellectual property problem. Consumers rationalize the pirating of software, videogames, movies, and music for a number of reasons. First, many feel they just don't have the money to pay for what they want. Second, because their friends engage in piracy and swap digital content, some users feel influenced to engage in this activity. Others enjoy the thrill of getting away with something with a low risk of consequences. And finally, some people feel being tech-savvy allows them to take advantage of the opportunity to pirate content.[95]

The file-sharing protocol BitTorrent allows users to share and download files. The U.S. Copyright Group obtained the IP addresses of users who downloaded specific movies using BitTorrent technology and are taking action against thousands of BitTorrent users for illegally downloading protected content.

The software industry loses more than $63 billion globally each year due to theft and illegal use of software products, according to the Business Software Alliance.[96] About 90 percent of illegal software copying is actually done by businesses. For example, a firm may obtain a license to install a specific application on 100 of its computers but actually installs it on 300. In some cases, software is illegally made available through the Internet by companies that have taken the software from the producer and set up their own distribution system.

## Digital Media's Impact on Marketing

To be successful in business, you need to know much more than how to use a social networking site to communicate with friends. Developing a strategic understanding of how digital marketing can make business more efficient and productive is increasingly necessary. If you are thinking of becoming an entrepreneur, then the digital world can open doors to new resources and customers. Smartphones, mobile broadband, and webcams are among the tools that can make the most of an online business world, creating greater efficiency at less cost. For example, rather than using traditional phone lines, Skype helps people make and receive calls via the Internet and provides free video calling and text messaging for about 10 percent of the cost of a land line.[97] It is up to businesses and entrepreneurs to develop strategies that achieve business success using existing and future technology, software, and networking opportunities.

Traditional businesses accustomed to using print media can find the transition to digital challenging. New media may require employees with new skills or additional training for current employees. There is often a gap between technical knowledge of how to develop sites and how to develop effective digital marketing strategies to enhance business success. Determining the correct blend of traditional and new media requires careful consideration; the mix will vary depending on the business, its size, and its target market. Future career opportunities will require skills in both traditional and digital media areas so that marketers properly understand and implement marketing strategies that help businesses achieve a competitive advantage.

The business world has grown increasingly dependent on digital marketing to maintain communication with stakeholders. Reaching customers is often a major concern, but digital marketing can also be used to communicate with suppliers, concerned community members, and special interest groups about issues related to sustainability, safety practices, and philanthropic activities. Many types of jobs exist: account executive directors of social media and director of marketing for digital products, as well as digital advertisers, online marketers, global digital marketers, and brand managers are prominently listed on career opportunity websites.

Entrepreneurs are taking advantage of the low cost of digital marketing, building social networking sites to help market their products. In fact, some small businesses such as specialty publishing, personal health and beauty, and other specialty products can use digital marketing as the primary channel for reaching consumers. Many small businesses are posting signs outside their stores with statements such as "Follow us on Twitter" or "Check out our Facebook page."

To utilize digital marketing, especially social networking, requires more than information technology skills related to constructing websites, graphics, videos, podcasts, etc. Most importantly, one must be able to determine how digital media can be used in implementing a marketing strategy. All marketing starts with identifying a target market and developing a marketing mix to satisfy customers. Digital marketing is just another way to reach customers, provide information, and develop relationships. Therefore, your opportunity for a career in this field is greatly based on understanding the messages, desired level of interactivity, and connectivity that helps achieve marketing objectives.

As social media use skyrockets, digital marketing professionals will be in demand. The experience of many businesses and research indicate digital marketing is a powerful way to increase brand exposure and generate traffic. In fact, a study conducted on Social Media Examiner found that 85 percent of marketers surveyed believe generating exposure for their business is their number-one advantage in Internet marketing. As consumers use social networking for their personal communication, they will be more open to obtaining information about products through this channel. Digital marketing could be the fastest-growing opportunity in business.

To prepare yourself for a digital marketing career, learn not only the technical aspects, but also how social media can be used to maximize marketing performance. A glance at careerbuilder.com indicates that management positions such as account manager, digital marketing manager, and digital product manager can pay from $60,000 to $170,000 or more per year.

## Review Your Understanding

### Define *digital media* and *digital marketing,* and recognize their increasing value in strategic planning.

Digital media are electronic media that function using digital codes and are available via computers, cellular phones, smartphones, and other digital devices. Digital marketing refers to the strategic process of distributing, promoting, pricing products, and discovering the desires of customers in the virtual environment of the Internet. Because they can enhance the exchange of information between the marketer and the customer, digital media have become an important component of firms' marketing strategies.

### Demonstrate the role of digital marketing and social networking in today's business environment.

Digital communication facilitates marketing research and lowers the cost of communication and consumer service and support. Through websites, social networks, and other digital media, consumers can learn about everything they purchase and use in life and businesses can reach new markets through inexpensive and interactive communication channels. Social networking is expanding so fast that no business can ignore its impact on customer relationships.

### Show how digital media affect the marketing mix.

The ability to process orders electronically and increase the speed of communications via the Internet has reduced many distribution inefficiencies, costs, and redundancies while increasing speed throughout the marketing channel. Digital media help firms increase brand awareness, connect with consumers, form relationships, and spread positive publicity about their products. Because consumers are more informed than ever and consumer consumption patterns are changing, marketers must adapt their promotional efforts. The Internet gives consumers access to more information about costs and prices.

### Define *social networking,* and illustrate how businesses can use different types of social networking media.

Social networking occurs when online consumers interact with other users on a web-based platform to discuss or view topics of interest. Types of social networking media include social networking sites, blogs, wikis, media sharing sites, virtual reality sites, mobile marketing, mobile applications, and widgets.

Blogs not only give consumers power but also allow companies to answer consumer concerns and obtain free publicity.

Wikis give marketers a better understanding of how consumers feel about their companies. Photo sharing sites enable companies to share images of their businesses or products with consumers and often have links that connect users to company-sponsored blogs. Video sharing is allowing many businesses to engage in viral marketing. Amateur filmmakers are also becoming a potential low-cost, effective marketing venue for companies. Podcasts are audio or video files that can be downloaded from the Internet with a subscription that automatically delivers new content to listening devices or personal computers.

Marketers have begun joining and advertising on social networking sites like Facebook and Twitter due to their global reach. Virtual realities can be fun and creative ways to reach consumers, create brand loyalty, and use consumer knowledge to benefit companies. Mobile marketing includes advertising, text messages, and other types of digital marketing through mobile devices. Mobile apps can be anything from games, to news updates, to shopping assistance. They provide a way for marketers to reach consumers via their cell phones. Apps can help consumers to perform services and make purchases more easily, such as checking in at a hotel or comparing and contrasting the price of appliances or a new dress. Widgets are small bits of software on a website, desktop, or mobile device. They can be used to inform consumers about company updates and can easily go viral.

### Identify legal and ethical considerations in digital media.

Increasing consumer concerns about privacy are prompting the FTC to look into regulating the types of information marketers can gather from Internet users, while many web advertisers and trade groups try to engage in self-regulation to prevent the passage of new Internet privacy laws. Online fraud includes any attempt to conduct fraudulent activities online. Intellectual property losses cost the United States billions of dollars and have become a particular problem for sites such as YouTube, which often finds it hard to monitor the millions of videos uploaded to its site for copyright infringement.

Based on the material in this chapter, you should be able to answer the questions posed in "Solve the Dilemma" on page 416 and evaluate where the company's marketing strategy has failed. How could Paul utilize new digital media to help promote his product and gather data on how to improve it?

## Revisit the World of Business

1. How are multinational companies using Chinese microblogging sites to reach consumers?

2. Why do you think Sina Weibo is a good platform for digital marketing in China?

3. Twitter is currently blocked in China. How do you think the success of Sina Weibo may affect Twitter if it is eventually able to enter the country?

## Learn the Terms

blog 401
digital marketing 393
digital media 393
e-business 392

identity theft 411
online fraud 412
podcast 403
social network 397

viral marketing 402
wiki 402

## Check Your Progress

1. What is digital marketing?

2. How can marketers utilize digital media to improve business?

3. Define *accessibility, addressability, connectivity, interactivity,* and *control*. What do these terms have to do with digital marketing?

4. What is e-business?

5. How is the Internet changing the practice of marketing?

6. What impact do digital media have on the marketing mix?

7. How can businesses utilize new digital and social networking channels in their marketing campaigns?

8. What are some of the privacy concerns associated with the Internet and e-business? How are these concerns being addressed in the United States?

9. What is identity theft? How can consumers protect themselves from this crime?

10. Why do creators want to protect their intellectual property? Provide an example on the Internet where intellectual property may not be protected or where a copyright has been infringed.

# Get Involved

1. Amazon.com is one of the most recognized e-businesses. Visit the site (**www.amazon.com**) and identify the types of products the company sells. Explain its privacy policy.

2. Visit some of the social networking sites identified in this chapter. How do they differ in design, audience, and features? Why do you think some social networking sites like Facebook are more popular than others?

3. It has been stated that digital technology and the Internet are to business today what manufacturing was to business during the Industrial Revolution. The technology revolution requires a strategic understanding greater than learning the latest software and programs or determining which computer is the fastest. Leaders in business can no longer delegate digital media to specialists and must be the connectors and the strategists of how digital media will be used in the company. Outline a plan for how you will prepare yourself to function in a business world where digital marketing knowledge will be important to your success.

# Build Your Skills

## Planning a Digital Marketing and Social Networking Site

### Background

Many companies today utilize digital media in a way that reflects their images and goals. They can also help to improve customer service, loyalty, and satisfaction while reaching out to new target markets. Companies use these sites in a variety of ways, sometimes setting up Facebook pages or Twitter accounts to gather customer feedback, to promote new products, or even to hold competitions.

The U.S. economy has experienced many ups and downs in recent decades, but e-commerce has been an area that has continued to grow throughout economic ups and downs. Many dot-com companies and social networking sites have risen and collapsed. Others such as Amazon.com, eBay, Facebook, and Twitter have not only survived, but thrived. Many that succeed are "niche players"; that is, they cater to a very specific market that a brick-and-mortar business (existing only in a physical marketplace) would find hard to reach. Others are able to compete with brick-and-mortar stores because they offer a wider variety of products, lower prices, or better customer service. Many new digital media outlets help companies compete on these fronts.

As a manager of Biodegradable Packaging Products Inc., a small business that produces packaging foam from recycled agricultural waste (mostly corn), you want to expand into e-business by using digital media to help market your product. Your major customers are other businesses and could include environmentally friendly companies like Tom's of Maine (natural toothpaste) and Celestial Seasonings (herbal tea). Your first need is to develop a social networking site or blog that will help you reach your potential customers. You must decide who your target market is and which medium will attract it the best.

### Task

Plan a digital media marketing campaign using online social networking sites, blogs, or another digital media outlet using the template below.

Social networking/blog/other site: _____

Overall image and design of your site: _____

Strategy for attracting followers to your site: _____

Potential advertising partners to draw in more customers: _____

## Solve the Dilemma  LO 13-6

### Developing Successful Freeware

Paul Easterwood, a recent graduate of Colorado State University with a degree in computer science, entered the job market during a slow point in the economy. Tech sector positions were hard to come by, and Paul felt he wouldn't be making anywhere near what he was worth. The only offer he received was from an entrepreneurial firm, Pentaverate Inc., that produced freeware. Freeware, or public domain software, is offered to consumers free of charge in exchange for revenues generated later. Makers of freeware (such as Adobe and Netscape)

can earn high profits through advertisements their sites carry, from purchases made on the freeware site, or, for more specialized software, through fee-based tutorials and workshops offered to help end users. Paul did some research and found an article in *Worth* magazine documenting the enormous success of freeware.

Pentaverate Inc. offered compensation mainly in the form of stock options, which had the potential to be highly profitable if the company did well. Paul's job would be to develop freeware that people could download from the Internet and that would generate significant income for Pentaverate. With this in mind, he decided to accept the position, but he quickly realized he knew very little about business. With no real experience in marketing, Paul was at a loss to know what software he should produce that would make the company money. His first project, IOWatch, was designed to take users on virtual tours of outer space, especially the moons of Jupiter (Paul's favorite subject), by continually searching the Internet for images and video clips associated with the cosmos and downloading them directly to a PC. The images would then appear as soon as the person

logged on. Advertisements would accompany each download, generating income for Pentaverate.

However, IOWatch experienced low end-user interest and drew little advertising income as a result. Historically at Pentaverate, employees were fired after two failed projects. Desperate to save his job, Paul decided to hire a consultant. He needed to figure out what customers might want so he could design some useful freeware for his second project. He also needed to know what went wrong with IOWatch, because he loved the software and couldn't figure out why it had failed to find an audience. The job market has not improved, so Paul realizes how important it is for his second project to succeed.

### Discussion Questions

1. As a consultant, what would you do to help Paul figure out what went wrong with IOWatch?

2. What ideas for new freeware can you give Paul? What potential uses will the new software have?

3. How will it make money?

## Build Your Business Plan

### Digital Marketing and Social Networking

If you are considering developing a business plan for an established good or service, find out whether it is currently marketed digitally. If it is not, think about why that is the case. Can you think of how you might overcome any obstacles and engage in digital marketing on the Internet?

If you are thinking about introducing a new good or service, now is the time to think about whether you might want to market this product on the Internet. Remember, you do not have to have a brick-and-mortar store to open your own business anymore. Perhaps you might want to consider click instead of brick!

## See for Yourself Videocase

### Should Employees Use Social Media Sites at Work?

As Facebook and other social media sites have gained popularity and expanded, managing their use at work has become an increasingly hot topic. Studies on the use of social media in the workplace conflict over how much it inhibits productivity. Should employees be allowed to access social media at work? Many offices have banned access to the Facebook site. The results are as mixed as the research. A National Business Ethics Survey (NBES) revealed that 11 percent of employees who engage in social networking are "active" social networkers who spend 30 percent or more of the workday on social networking sites. Many managers are conflicted as to whether this constitutes enough of a problem to be banned outright.

Another study conducted by Nucleus Research (an IT research company) revealed a 1.5 percent loss of productivity for businesses allowing social media access. It found that 77 percent of Facebook users used the site during work for as

much as two hours a day; 87 percent of those surveyed admitted they were using social media sites to waste time. NBES also found that active social networkers were more likely to find certain questionable behaviors to be acceptable, such as criticizing the company or its managers on social networking sites. Procter & Gamble realized that many of its employees were using social networking sites for nonwork purposes. Its investigations revealed that employees across the company were watching an average of 50,000 five-minute YouTube videos and listening to 4,000 hours of music on Pandora daily.

However, an outright ban could cause problems. Some younger employees have expressed that they do not want to work for companies without social media access; they view restricting or eliminating access like removing a benefit. Employees at companies with an outright ban often resent the lack of trust associated with such a move and feel that management is censuring their activities. Other employees who use Facebook during their lunch hours or break times may feel that they are being punished because of others' actions. Additionally, Procter & Gamble uses YouTube and Facebook extensively for marketing purposes. Banning these sites would disrupt the firm's marketing efforts.

An Australian study indicates that employees taking time out to pursue Facebook and other social media were actually 9 percent more productive than those who did not. Brent Coker, the study's author and University of Melbourne faculty member, says people are more productive when they take time to "zone out" throughout the workday. Doing so can improve concentration. Coker's study focused on those using less than 20 percent of the workday on such breaks, which is less than the amount of time "active" social networkers spend on these sites.

Some companies actually encourage employees to use social networking as part of their integrated marketing strategy. In fact, not having a social media page such as Facebook or LinkedIn might be seen as a missed opportunity for marketing the firm. Even the law industry is starting to use social media on a more daily basis. One study of the top 50 highest ranked law firms in the country determined that 64 percent use Facebook and 90 percent are on Twitter. Approximately 80 percent post something every day or once a week. Although larger law firms tend not to use social media as effectively as smaller law firms, the use of social media to interact with clients is clearly gaining throughout the industry.

Despite the benefits that companies have received from allowing their employees to use social media, many companies have gone ahead with social media bans. Procter & Gamble has restricted the use of Netflix and Pandora, but not Facebook or YouTube. Companies all need to ask, "Can management use social media to benefit the company?" If so, it may be more advantageous to take the risks of employees using social media for personal use if they can also be encouraged to use social networks to publicize their organizations, connect with customers, and view consumer comments or complaints. By restricting social media use, companies may be forfeiting an effective marketing tool.[98]

### Discussion Questions

1. Why do you think results are so mixed on the use of social networking in the workplace?

2. What are some possible upsides to utilizing social media as part of an integrated marketing strategy, especially in digital marketing?

3. What are the downsides to restricting employee access to social networking sites?

**You can find the related video in the Video Library in Connect. Ask your instructor how you can access Connect.**

## Team Exercise

Develop a digital marketing promotion for a local sports team. Use Twitter, Facebook, and other social networking media to promote ticket sales for next season's schedule. In your plan, provide specific details and ideas for the content you would use on the sites. Also, describe how you would encourage fans and potential fans to go to your site. How would you use digital media to motivate sports fans to purchase tickets and merchandise and attend games?

# PART 6

# Financing the Enterprise

# 14

# Accounting and Financial Statements

## Learning Objectives

**After reading this chapter, you will be able to:**

**LO 14-1** Define accounting, and describe the different uses of accounting information.

**LO 14-2** Demonstrate the accounting process.

**LO 14-3** Examine the various components of an income statement in order to evaluate a firm's "bottom line."

**LO 14-4** Interpret a company's balance sheet to determine its current financial position.

**LO 14-5** Analyze the statement of cash flows to evaluate the increase and decrease in a company's cash balance.

**LO 14-6** Assess a company's financial position using its accounting statements and ratio analysis.

## Chapter Outline

## Former Enron CFO Talks about Accounting Fraud

One of the major players in the Enron fraud is now lecturing on business ethics. Andrew Fastow was the CFO of Enron responsible for hiding debt using financial structures he designed, including off-balance sheet partnerships. These structures misled investors about Enron's true financial situation. The result was one of the biggest business ethics scandals, leading to the demise of a firm that had been nominated by *Fortune* as "the most innovative company in corporate America" six times.

Fastow spent five years in prison for his role in the fraud. While he currently works at a law firm as a document review clerk, Fastow often gives free lectures to business schools such as the Leeds School of Business at the University of Colorado–Boulder. More recently, he spoke at the Certified Fraud Examiner's annual convention, which invites a criminal speaker to its convention each year.

Fastow maintains that while he did not embezzle or engage in insider trading, he did commit fraud by making Enron's financials look better than they really were—despite approval from company lawyers, accountants, and directors. According to Fastow, rather than obeying accounting and securities rules, the chief players at Enron looked for ways to interpret the rules to the company's advantage. In his presentations, Fastow takes care to warn audiences that while he did not think what he was doing was illegal, he knew it was wrong and misleading—a strong signal that accounting fraud is occurring. He believes that adhering to principles is more important to preventing misconduct than just trying to follow rules and regulations. Fastow also believes companies today are engaging in activities "10 times worse" than what Enron did, pointing out the continued use of off-balance sheet entities and unrealistically high estimates for future cash flows.[1]

# Introduction

Accounting, the financial "language" that organizations use to record, measure, and interpret all of their financial transactions and records, is very important in business. All businesses—from a small family farm to a giant corporation—use the language of accounting to make sure they use their money wisely and to plan for the future. Nonbusiness organizations such as charities and governments also use accounting to demonstrate to donors and taxpayers how well they are using their funds and meeting their stated objectives.

This chapter explores the role of accounting in business and its importance in making business decisions. First, we discuss the uses of accounting information and the accounting process. Then, we briefly look at some simple financial statements and accounting tools that are useful in analyzing organizations worldwide.

# The Nature of Accounting

**LO 14-1**

**accounting**
the recording, measurement, and interpretation of financial information

Simply stated, **accounting** is the recording, measurement, and interpretation of financial information. Large numbers of people and institutions, both within and outside businesses, use accounting tools to evaluate organizational operations. The Financial Accounting Standards Board has been setting the principles and standards of financial accounting and reporting in the private sector since 1973. Its mission is to establish and improve standards of financial accounting and reporting for the guidance and education of the public, including issuers, auditors, and users of financial information. However, the accounting scandals at the turn of the last century resulted when many accounting firms and businesses failed to abide by generally accepted accounting principles, or GAAP. Consequently, the federal government has taken a greater role in making rules, requirements, and policies for accounting firms and businesses through the Securities and Exchange Commission's (SEC) Public Company Accounting Oversight Board. For example, the Public Company Accounting Oversight Board filed a disciplinary order against Deloitte & Touche for permitting a suspended auditor to participate in auditing activities. This violated the Sarbanes-Oxley Act (SOX). The Public Company Accounting Oversight Board imposed a $2 million fine against Deloitte for the violation.[2]

To better understand the importance of accounting, we must first understand who prepares accounting information and how it is used.

## Accountants

Many of the functions of accounting are carried out by public or private accountants.

**certified public accountant (CPA)**
an individual who has been state certified to provide accounting services ranging from the preparation of financial records and the filing of tax returns to complex audits of corporate financial records

**Public Accountants.**   Individuals and businesses can hire a **certified public accountant (CPA),** an individual who has been certified by the state in which he or she practices to provide accounting services ranging from the preparation of financial records and the filing of tax returns to complex audits of corporate financial records. Certification gives a public accountant the right to express, officially, an unbiased opinion regarding the accuracy of the client's financial statements. Most public accountants are either self-employed or members of large public accounting firms such as Ernst & Young, KPMG, Deloitte, and PricewaterhouseCoopers, together referred to as "the Big Four." In addition, many CPAs work for one of the second-tier accounting firms that are much smaller than the Big Four firms, as illustrated in Table 14.1.

| 2015 Rank | 2014 Rank | Company | Revenues* (in millions) | Score | Location |
|---|---|---|---|---|---|
| 1 | 1 | (PricewaterhouseCoopers) LLP | $11,041.00 | 8.717 | New York, NY |
| 2 | 2 | Ernst & Young LLP | $ 9,100.00 | 8.451 | New York, NY |
| 3 | 3 | Deloitte LLP | $13,894.00 | 8.433 | New York, NY |
| 4 | 4 | KPMG LLP | $ 6,140.00 | 7.520 | New York, NY |
| 5 | 5 | Grant Thornton LLP | $ 1,302.83 | 6.677 | Chicago, IL |
| 6 | 6 | McGladrey LLP | $ 1,366.59 | 6.054 | Chicago, IL |
| 7 | 7 | BDO USA LLP | $ 683.00 | 5.725 | Chicago, IL |
| 8 | 8 | Crowe Horwath LLP | $ 664.62 | 4.517 | Chicago, IL |
| 9 | 9 | Moss Adams LLP | $ 403.00 | 4.299 | Seattle, WA |
| 10 | 10 | Baker Tilly Virchow Krause, LLP | $ 301.30 | 4.220 | Chicago, IL |

**TABLE 14.1**
**Prestige Rankings of Accounting Firms**

*Revenues taken from Accounting Today, "The 2014 Accounting Today Top 100 Firms," March 2014, Supplement P, 15–18.

Source: www.vault.com/company-rankings/accounting/.

While there will always be companies and individual money managers who can successfully hide illegal or misleading accounting practices for a while, eventually they are exposed. After the accounting scandals of Enron and Worldcom in the early 2000s, Congress passed the Sarbanes-Oxley Act, which required firms to be more rigorous in their accounting and reporting practices. Sarbanes-Oxley made accounting firms separate their consulting and auditing businesses and punished corporate executives with potential jail sentences for inaccurate, misleading, or illegal accounting statements. This seemed to reduce the accounting errors among nonfinancial companies, but declining housing prices exposed some of the questionable practices by banks and mortgage companies. Only five years after the passage of the Sarbanes-Oxley Act, the world experienced a financial crisis starting in 2008—part of which was due to excessive risk taking and inappropriate accounting practices. Many banks failed to understand the true state of their financial health. Banks also developed questionable lending practices and investments based on subprime mortgages made to individuals who had poor credit. When housing prices declined and people suddenly found that they owed more on their mortgages than their homes were worth, they began to default. To prevent a depression, the government intervened and bailed out some of the United States' largest banks. Congress passed the Dodd-Frank Act in 2010 to strengthen the oversight of financial institutions. This act gave the Federal Reserve Board the task of implementing the legislation. It is expected that financial institutions will have at least one year to implement the requirements. This legislation limits the types of assets commercial banks can buy; the amount of capital they must maintain; and the use of derivative instruments such as options, futures, and structured investment products.

A growing area for public accountants is *forensic accounting,* which is accounting that is fit for legal review. It involves analyzing financial documents in search of fraudulent entries or financial misconduct. Functioning

**DID YOU KNOW?** Corporate fraud costs are estimated at $3.7 trillion annually.[3]

Ernst & Young is a part of the "Big Four," or the four largest international accounting firms. The other three are PricewaterhouseCoopers, KPMG, and Deloitte Touche Tohmatsu.

**private accountants**
accountants employed by large corporations, government agencies, and other organizations to prepare and analyze their financial statements

as much like detectives as accountants, forensic accountants have been used since the 1930s. In the wake of the accounting scandals of the early 2000s, many auditing firms are rapidly adding or expanding forensic or fraud-detection services. Additionally, many forensic accountants root out evidence of "cooked books" for federal agencies like the Federal Bureau of Investigation or the Internal Revenue Service. The Association of Certified Fraud Examiners, which certifies accounting professionals as *certified fraud examiners (CFEs),* has grown to more than 70,000 members.[4]

**certified management accountants (CMAs)**
private accountants who, after rigorous examination, are certified by the National Association of Accountants and who have some managerial responsibility

**Private Accountants.**   Large corporations, government agencies, and other organizations may employ their own **private accountants** to prepare and analyze their financial statements. With titles such as controller, tax accountant, or internal auditor, private accountants are deeply involved in many of the most important financial decisions of the organizations for which they work. Private accountants can be CPAs and may become **certified management accountants (CMAs)** by passing a rigorous examination by the Institute of Management Accountants.

## Accounting or Bookkeeping?

The terms *accounting* and *bookkeeping* are often mistakenly used interchangeably. Much narrower and far more mechanical than accounting, bookkeeping is typically limited to the routine, day-to-day recording of business transactions. Bookkeepers are responsible for obtaining and recording the information that accountants require to analyze a firm's financial position. They generally require less training than accountants. Accountants, on the other hand, usually complete course work beyond their basic four- or five-year college accounting degrees. This additional training allows accountants not only to record financial information, but to understand, interpret, and even develop the sophisticated accounting systems necessary to classify and analyze complex financial information.

## The Uses of Accounting Information

Accountants summarize the information from a firm's business transactions in various financial statements (which we'll look at in a later section of this chapter) for a variety of stakeholders, including managers, investors, creditors, and government agencies. Many business failures may be directly linked to ignorance of the information "hidden" inside these financial statements. Likewise, most business successes can be traced to informed managers who understand the consequences of their decisions. While maintaining and even increasing short-run profits is desirable, the failure to plan sufficiently for the future can easily lead an otherwise successful company to insolvency and bankruptcy court.

Basically, managers and owners use financial statements (1) to aid in internal planning and control and (2) for external purposes such as reporting to the Internal Revenue Service, stockholders, creditors, customers, employees, and other interested parties. Figure 14.1 shows some of the users of the accounting information generated by organizations and other stakeholders.

**Internal Uses.**    **Managerial accounting** refers to the internal use of accounting statements by managers in planning and directing the organization's activities. Perhaps management's greatest single concern is **cash flow,** the movement of money through an organization over a daily, weekly, monthly, or yearly basis. Obviously, for any business to succeed, it needs to generate enough cash to pay its bills as they fall

**managerial accounting**
the internal use of accounting statements by managers in planning and directing the organization's activities

**cash flow**
the movement of money through an organization over a daily, weekly, monthly, or yearly basis

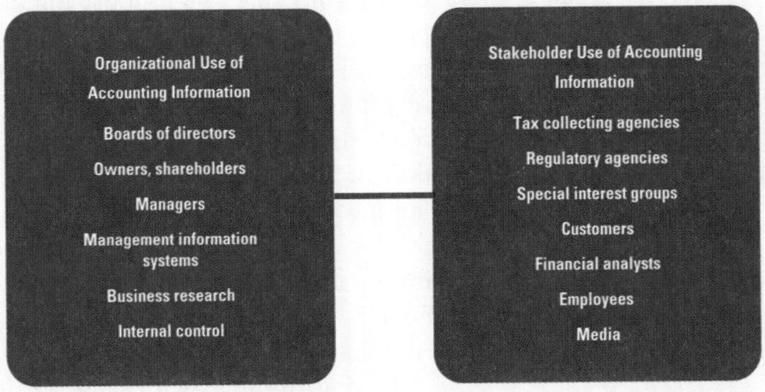

**FIGURE 14.1**
**The Users of Accounting Information**

Source: Adapted from *Principles of Accounting,* 4th edition. Houghton Mifflin Company, 1990. Authors: Belverd E. Needles, Henry R. Anderson, and James C. Caldwell.

| Organizational Use of Accounting Information | Stakeholder Use of Accounting Information |
| --- | --- |
| Boards of directors | Tax collecting agencies |
| Owners, shareholders | Regulatory agencies |
| Managers | Special interest groups |
| Management information systems | Customers |
| Business research | Financial analysts |
| Internal control | Employees |
|  | Media |

due. However, it is not at all unusual for highly successful and rapidly growing companies to struggle to make payments to employees, suppliers, and lenders because of an inadequate cash flow. One common reason for a so-called cash crunch, or shortfall, is poor managerial planning.

**budget**
an internal financial plan that forecasts expenses and income over a set period of time

Managerial accountants also help prepare an organization's **budget,** an internal financial plan that forecasts expenses and income over a set period of time. It is not unusual for an organization to prepare separate daily, weekly, monthly, and yearly budgets. Think of a budget as a financial map, showing how the company expects to move from Point A to Point B over a specific period of time. While most companies prepare *master budgets* for the entire firm, many also prepare budgets for smaller segments of the organization such as divisions, departments, product lines, or projects. "Top-down" master budgets begin at the upper management level and filter down to the individual department level, while "bottom-up" budgets start at the department or project level and are combined at the chief executive's office. Generally, the larger and more rapidly growing an organization, the greater will be the likelihood that it will build its master budget from the ground up.

**annual report**
summary of a firm's financial information, products, and growth plans for owners and potential investors

Regardless of focus, the principal value of a budget lies in its breakdown of cash inflows and outflows. Expected operating expenses (cash outflows such as wages, materials costs, and taxes) and operating revenues (cash inflows in the form of payments from customers) over a set period of time are carefully forecast and subsequently compared with actual results. Deviations between the two serve as a "trip wire" or "feedback loop" to launch more detailed financial analyses in an effort to pinpoint trouble spots and opportunities.

The annual report is a summary of the firm's financial information, products, and growth plans for owners and potential investors. Many investors look at a firm's annual report to determine how well the company is doing financially.

**External Uses.** Managers also use accounting statements to report the business's financial performance to outsiders. Such statements are used for filing income taxes, obtaining credit from lenders, and reporting results to the firm's stockholders. They become the basis for the information provided in the official corporate **annual report,** a summary of the firm's financial information, products, and growth plans for owners and potential investors. While frequently presented between slick, glossy covers prepared by major advertising firms, the single most important component of an annual report is the signature of a certified public accountant attesting that the required financial statements are an accurate reflection of the underlying financial condition of the firm. Financial statements meeting these conditions are termed *audited*. The primary external users of audited accounting information are government agencies, stockholders and potential investors, and lenders, suppliers, and employees.

During the global financial crisis, it turns out that Greece had been engaging in deceptive accounting practices, with the help of U.S.

## Going Green

### Companies Investigate Ways to Integrate Financial Information and Sustainability Costs

Most people believe that financial statements such as income statements and balance sheets provide the entire picture of a firm's financial standing. In reality, however, this is not the case. It has been estimated that about 80 percent of a firm's value is not found on the balance sheet. One of the least understood areas involves sustainability. For instance, how much does violating an environmental law truly cost a firm, not only monetarily but also regarding its reputation? Some socially responsible businesses have adopted a triple bottom line approach in which the organization reports its financial results, its impact on society, and its impact on the planet. Yet, even these companies find it difficult to take three different dimensions and add them up to provide an overall report.

A pilot program consisting of 75 global companies is investigating ways to overcome these challenges. This program, monitored by the International Integrated Reporting Council, seeks to create an integrated reporting model giving investors the opportunity to receive a holistic view of the company's operations and business strategies. Integrated reporting combines both financial and nonfinancial information. Companies testing this program include Microsoft, Unilever, Clorox, and Coca-Cola. Although most of these firms already develop sustainability or social responsibility reports, these reports are separate from the company's financial information. Such an endeavor requires the active participation of both company financial officers and accountants. Integrated reporting may become the new norm for investor reports—stock exchanges such as NASDAQ are beginning to require more information on a firm's corporate governance and environmental activities.[5]

### Discussion Questions

1. Why might it be important to include sustainability and other factors in a firm's financial reports?
2. What is the purpose of the Integrated Reporting Council?
3. Why do you think NASDAQ is beginning to require more information on a firm's corporate governance and environmental activities?

investment banks. Greece used financial techniques to hide massive amounts of debt from its public balance sheets. Eventually, the markets figured out the country might not be able to pay off its creditors. The European Union and the International Monetary Fund came up with a plan to give Greece some credit relief, but tied to this was the message to "get your financial house in order." The European problem was often referred to as the PIGS. This referred to Portugal, Italy, Ireland, Greece, and Spain—all of which were having debt problems. The PIGS caused cracks in the European Monetary Union. While Germany demanded austerity, others wanted more growth-oriented strategies. By the middle of 2014, Europe was pursuing more growth strategies but the PIGS were still stuck in the mud, except for Ireland, which was making better progress than the others.

To top this off, *The New York Times* reported that many states, such as Illinois and California, have the same problems as the PIGS—debt overload. These states have "budgets that will not balance, accounting that masks debt, the use of derivatives to plug holes, and armies of retired public workers who are counting on

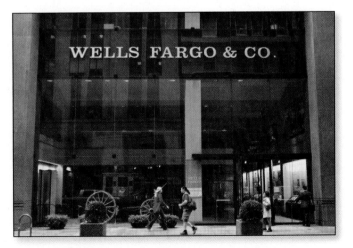

As one of the biggest banks in the United States, Wells Fargo specializes in banking, mortgage, and financial services. The data it provides can be used in financial statements.

pension benefits that are proving harder and harder to pay." Fortunately for California, by the middle of 2014, it was making better progress than Illinois. Clearly, the financial crisis will have some lasting effects that need clear accounting solutions.[6]

Financial statements evaluate the return on stockholders' investment and the overall quality of the firm's management team. As a result, poor performance, as documented in the financial statements, often results in changes in top management. Potential investors study the financial statements in a firm's annual report to determine whether the company meets their investment requirements and whether the returns from a given firm are likely to compare favorably with other similar companies.

Banks and other lenders look at financial statements to determine a company's ability to meet current and future debt obligations if a loan or credit is granted. To determine this ability, a short-term lender examines a firm's cash flow to assess its ability to repay a loan quickly with cash generated from sales. A long-term lender is more interested in the company's profitability and indebtedness to other lenders.

Labor unions and employees use financial statements to establish reasonable expectations for salary and other benefit requests. Just as firms experiencing record profits are likely to face added pressure to increase employee wages, so too are employees unlikely to grant employers wage and benefit concessions without considerable evidence of financial distress.

**assets**
a firm's economic resources, or items of value that it owns, such as cash, inventory, land, equipment, buildings, and other tangible and intangible things

## The Accounting Process

Many view accounting as a primary business language. It is of little use, however, unless you know how to "speak" it. Fortunately, the fundamentals—the accounting equation and the double-entry bookkeeping system—are not difficult to learn. These two concepts serve as the starting point for all currently accepted accounting principles.

**liabilities**
debts that a firm owes to others

**owners' equity**
equals assets minus liabilities and reflects historical values

### The Accounting Equation

Accountants are concerned with reporting an organization's assets, liabilities, and owners' equity. To help illustrate these concepts, consider a hypothetical floral shop called Anna's Flowers, owned by Anna Rodriguez. A firm's economic resources, or items of value that it owns, represent its **assets**—cash, inventory, land, equipment, buildings, and other tangible and intangible things. The assets of Anna's Flowers include counters, refrigerated display cases, flowers, decorations, vases, cards, and other gifts, as well as something known as "goodwill," which in this case is Anna's reputation for preparing and delivering beautiful floral arrangements on a timely basis. **Liabilities,** on the other hand, are debts the firm owes to others. Among the liabilities of Anna's Flowers are a loan from the Small Business Administration and money owed to flower suppliers and other creditors for items purchased. The **owners' equity** category contains all of the money that has ever been contributed to

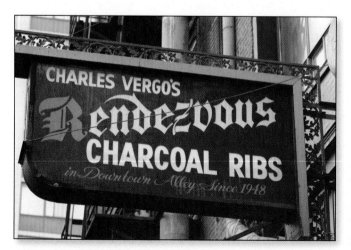

The owners' equity portion of a company's balance sheet, such as that of Rendezvous Barbecue in Memphis, Tennessee, includes the money the company's owners have put into the firm.

the company that never has to be paid back. The funds can come from investors who have given money or assets to the company, or it can come from past profitable operations. In the case of Anna's Flowers, if Anna were to sell off, or liquidate, her business, any money left over after selling all the shop's assets and paying off its liabilities would comprise her owners' equity. The relationship among assets, liabilities, and owners' equity is a fundamental concept in accounting and is known as the **accounting equation:**

accounting equation
assets equal liabilities plus
owners' equity

$$\textbf{Assets = Liabilities + Owners' equity}$$

## Double-Entry Bookkeeping

**Double-entry bookkeeping** is a system of recording and classifying business transactions in separate accounts in order to maintain the balance of the accounting equation. Returning to Anna's Flowers, suppose Anna buys $325 worth of roses on credit from the Antique Rose Emporium to fill a wedding order. When she records this transaction, she will list the $325 as a liability or a debt to a supplier. At the same time, however, she will also record $325 worth of roses as an asset in an account known as "inventory." Because the assets and liabilities are on different sides of the accounting equation, Anna's accounts increase in total size (by $325) but remain in balance:

double-entry
bookkeeping
a system of recording
and classifying business
transactions that maintains
the balance of the accounting
equation

$$\textbf{Assets = Liabilities + Owners' equity}$$
$$\textbf{\$325 = \$325}$$

Thus, to keep the accounting equation in balance, each business transaction must be recorded in two separate accounts.

In the final analysis, all business transactions are classified as assets, liabilities, or owners' equity. However, most organizations further break down these three accounts to provide more specific information about a transaction. For example, assets may be broken down into specific categories such as cash, inventory, and equipment, while liabilities may include bank loans, supplier credit, and other debts.

Figure 14.2 shows how Anna used the double-entry bookkeeping system to account for all of the transactions that took place in her first month of business. These transactions include her initial investment of $2,500, the loan from the Small Business Administration, purchases of equipment and inventory, and the purchase of roses on credit. In her first month of business, Anna generated revenues of $2,000 by selling $1,500 worth of inventory. Thus, she deducts, or (in accounting notation that is appropriate for assets) *credits,* $1,500 from inventory and adds, or *debits,* $2,000 to the cash account. The difference between Anna's $2,000 cash inflow and her $1,500 outflow is represented by a credit to owners' equity, because it is money that belongs to her as the owner of the flower shop.

## The Accounting Cycle

In any accounting system, financial data typically pass through a four-step procedure sometimes called the **accounting cycle.** The steps include examining source documents, recording transactions in an accounting journal, posting recorded transactions, and preparing financial statements. Figure 14.3 shows how Anna works through them. Traditionally, all of these steps were performed using paper, pencils, and erasers (lots of erasers!), but today the process is often fully computerized.

accounting cycle
the four-step procedure of an
accounting system: examining
source documents, recording
transactions in an accounting
journal, posting recorded
transactions, and preparing
financial statements

**FIGURE 14.2**    The Accounting Equation and Double-Entry Bookkeeping for Anna's Flowers

| | Assets | | | = Liabilities | + | Owners' Equity |
|---|---|---|---|---|---|---|
| | Cash | Equipment | Inventory | Debts to suppliers | Loans | Equity |
| Cash invested by Anna | $2,500.00 | | | | | $2,500.00 |
| Loan from SBA | $5,000.00 | | | | $5,000.00 | |
| Purchase of furnishings | −$3,000.00 | $3,000.00 | | | | |
| Purchase of inventory | −$2,000.00 | | $2,000.00 | | | |
| Purchase of roses | | | $325.00 | $325.00 | | |
| First month sales | $2,000.00 | | −$1,500.00 | | | $500.00 |
| Totals | $4,500.00 | $3,000.00 | $825.00 | $325.00 | $5,000.00 | $3,000.00 |

$8,325    =    $5,325    +    $3,000

$8,325 Assets    =    $8,325 (Liabilities + Owners' Equity)

**Step One: Examine Source Documents.**    Like all good managers, Anna Rodriguez begins the accounting cycle by gathering and examining source documents—checks, credit card receipts, sales slips, and other related evidence concerning specific transactions.

**Step Two: Record Transactions.**    Next, Anna records each financial transaction in a **journal,** which is basically just a time-ordered list of account transactions. While most businesses keep a general journal in which all transactions are recorded, some classify transactions into specialized journals for specific types of transaction accounts.

**journal**
a time-ordered list of account transactions

**Step Three: Post Transactions.**    Anna next transfers the information from her journal into a **ledger,** a book or computer program with separate files for each account. This process is known as *posting.* At the end of the accounting period (usually yearly, but occasionally quarterly or monthly), Anna prepares a *trial balance,* a summary of the balances of all the accounts in the general ledger. If, upon totaling, the trial balance doesn't balance (that is, the accounting equation is not in balance), Anna or her accountant must look for mistakes (typically an error in one or more of the ledger entries) and correct them. If the trial balance is correct, the accountant can then begin to prepare the financial statements.

**ledger**
a book or computer file with separate sections for each account

**Step Four: Prepare Financial Statements.**    The information from the trial balance is also used to prepare the company's financial statements. In the case of public corporations and certain other organizations, a CPA must *attest,* or certify, that the organization followed generally accepted accounting principles in preparing the financial statements. When these statements have been completed, the organization's books are "closed," and the accounting cycle begins anew for the next accounting period.

**connect**

▶ Need help understanding the Accounting Cycle? Visit your Connect ebook video tab for a brief animated explanation.

**FIGURE 14.3**   The Accounting Process for Anna's Flowers

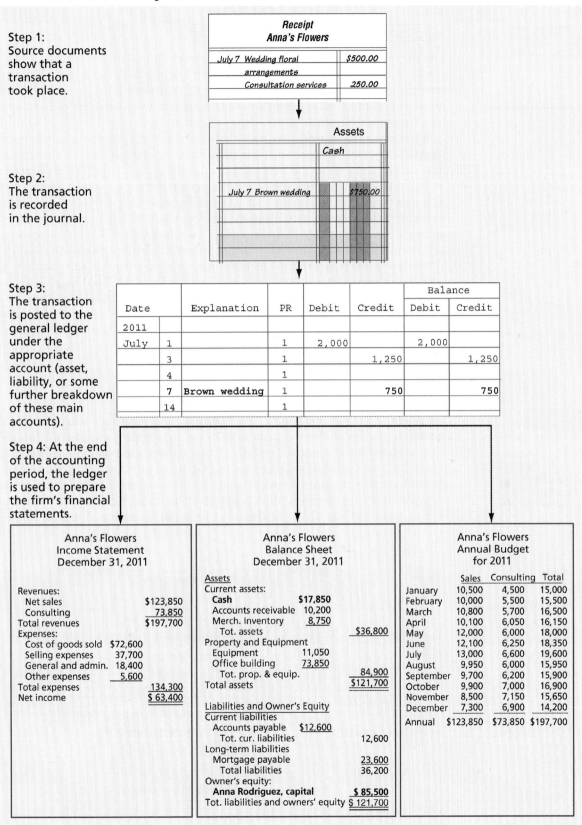

Step 1:
Source documents show that a transaction took place.

**Receipt**
**Anna's Flowers**

| | |
|---|---|
| July 7 Wedding floral arrangements | $500.00 |
| Consultation services | 250.00 |

Step 2:
The transaction is recorded in the journal.

**Assets**

Cash

July 7 Brown wedding   $750.00

Step 3:
The transaction is posted to the general ledger under the appropriate account (asset, liability, or some further breakdown of these main accounts).

| | Date | | Explanation | PR | Debit | Credit | Balance Debit | Balance Credit |
|---|---|---|---|---|---|---|---|---|
| 2011 | | | | | | | | |
| July | 1 | | | 1 | 2,000 | | 2,000 | |
| | 3 | | | 1 | | 1,250 | | 1,250 |
| | 4 | | | 1 | | | | |
| | 7 | | Brown wedding | 1 | | 750 | | 750 |
| | 14 | | | 1 | | | | |

Step 4: At the end of the accounting period, the ledger is used to prepare the firm's financial statements.

**Anna's Flowers**
**Income Statement**
**December 31, 2011**

| | | |
|---|---|---|
| Revenues: | | |
| Net sales | | $123,850 |
| Consulting | | 73,850 |
| Total revenues | | $197,700 |
| Expenses: | | |
| Cost of goods sold | $72,600 | |
| Selling expenses | 37,700 | |
| General and admin. | 18,400 | |
| Other expenses | 5,600 | |
| Total expenses | | 134,300 |
| Net income | | $ 63,400 |

**Anna's Flowers**
**Balance Sheet**
**December 31, 2011**

Assets
Current assets:
| | | |
|---|---|---|
| **Cash** | **$17,850** | |
| Accounts receivable | 10,200 | |
| Merch. Inventory | 8,750 | |
| Tot. assets | | $36,800 |
| Property and Equipment | | |
| Equipment | 11,050 | |
| Office building | 73,850 | |
| Tot. prop. & equip. | | 84,900 |
| Total assets | | $121,700 |

Liabilities and Owner's Equity
Current liabilities
| | | |
|---|---|---|
| Accounts payable | $12,600 | |
| Tot. cur. liabilities | | 12,600 |
| Long-term liabilities | | |
| Mortgage payable | | 23,600 |
| Total liabilities | | 36,200 |
| Owner's equity: | | |
| **Anna Rodriguez, capital** | | **$ 85,500** |
| Tot. liabilities and owners' equity | | $ 121,700 |

**Anna's Flowers**
**Annual Budget**
**for 2011**

| | Sales | Consulting | Total |
|---|---|---|---|
| January | 10,500 | 4,500 | 15,000 |
| February | 10,000 | 5,500 | 15,500 |
| March | 10,800 | 5,700 | 16,500 |
| April | 10,100 | 6,050 | 16,150 |
| May | 12,000 | 6,000 | 18,000 |
| June | 12,100 | 6,250 | 18,350 |
| July | 13,000 | 6,600 | 19,600 |
| August | 9,950 | 6,000 | 15,950 |
| September | 9,700 | 6,200 | 15,900 |
| October | 9,900 | 7,000 | 16,900 |
| November | 8,500 | 7,150 | 15,650 |
| December | 7,300 | 6,900 | 14,200 |
| Annual | $123,850 | $73,850 | $197,700 |

# Financial Statements

The end result of the accounting process is a series of financial statements. The income statement, the balance sheet, and the statement of cash flows are the best-known examples of financial statements. They are provided to stockholders and potential investors in a firm's annual report as well as to other relevant outsiders such as creditors, government agencies, and the Internal Revenue Service.

It is important to recognize that not all financial statements follow precisely the same format. The fact that different organizations generate income in different ways suggests that when it comes to financial statements, one size definitely does not fit all. Manufacturing firms, service providers, and nonprofit organizations each use a different set of accounting principles or rules upon which the public accounting profession has agreed. As we have already mentioned, these are sometimes referred to as *generally accepted accounting principles (GAAP)*. Each country has a different set of rules that the businesses within that country are required to use for their accounting process and financial statements. However, a number of countries have adopted a standard set of accounting principles known as International Financial Reporting Standards. The United States has discussed adopting these standards to create a more standardized system of reporting for global investors. Moreover, as is the case in many other disciplines, certain concepts have more than one name. For example, *sales* and *revenues* are often interchanged, as are *profits, income,* and *earnings.* Table 14.2 lists a few common equivalent terms that should help you decipher their meaning in accounting statements.

## The Income Statement

**income statement**
a financial report that shows an organization's profitability over a period of time—month, quarter, or year

The question, "What's the bottom line?" derives from the income statement, where the bottom line shows the overall profit or loss of the company after taxes. Thus, the **income statement** is a financial report that shows an organization's profitability over a period of time, be that a month, quarter, or year. By its very design, the income statement offers one of the clearest possible pictures of the company's overall revenues and the costs incurred in generating those revenues. Other names for the income statement include profit and loss (P&L) statement or operating statement. A sample income

**TABLE 14.2**
**Equivalent Terms in Accounting**

| Term | Equivalent Term |
|---|---|
| Revenues | Sales |
|  | Goods or services sold |
| Gross profit | Gross income |
|  | Gross earnings |
| Operating income | Operating profit |
|  | Earnings before interest and taxes (EBIT) |
|  | Income before interest and taxes (IBIT) |
| Income before taxes (IBT) | Earnings before taxes (EBT) |
|  | Profit before taxes (PBT) |
| Net income (NI) | Earnings after taxes (EAT) |
|  | Profit after taxes (PAT) |
| Income available to common stockholders | Earnings available to common stockholders |

## TABLE 14.3   Sample Income Statement

The following exhibit presents a sample income statement with all the terms defined and explained.

| Company Name for the Year Ended December 31 | |
| --- | --- |
| Revenues (sales) | Total dollar amount of products sold (includes income from other business services such as rental-lease income and interest income). |
| Less: Cost of goods sold | The cost of producing the goods and services, including the cost of labor and raw materials as well as other expenses associated with production. |
| Gross profit | The income available after paying all expenses of production. |
| Less: Selling and administrative expense | The cost of promoting, advertising, and selling products as well as the overhead costs of managing the company. This includes the cost of management and corporate staff. One non-cash expense included in this category is depreciation, which approximates the decline in the value of plant and equipment assets due to use over time. In most accounting statements, depreciation is not separated from selling and administrative expenses. However, financial analysts usually create statements that include this expense. |
| Income before interest and taxes (operating income or EBIT) | This line represents all income left over after operating expenses have been deducted. This is sometimes referred to as operating income since it represents all income after the expenses of operations have been accounted for. Occasionally, this is referred to as EBIT, or earnings before interest and taxes. |
| Less: Interest expense | Interest expense arises as a cost of borrowing money. This is a financial expense rather than an operating expense and is listed separately. As the amount of debt and the cost of debt increase, so will the interest expense. This covers the cost of both short-term and long-term borrowing. |
| Income before taxes (earnings before taxes—EBT) | The firm will pay a tax on this amount. This is what is left of revenues after subtracting all operating costs, depreciation costs, and interest costs. |
| Less: Taxes | The tax rate is specified in the federal tax code. |
| Net income | This is the amount of income left after taxes. The firm may decide to retain all or a portion of the income for reinvestment in new assets. Whatever it decides not to keep it will usually pay out in dividends to its stockholders. |
| Less: Preferred dividends | If the company has preferred stockholders, they are first in line for dividends. That is one reason why their stock is called "preferred." |
| Income to common stockholders | This is the income left for the common stockholders. If the company has a good year, there may be a lot of income available for dividends. If the company has a bad year, income could be negative. The common stockholders are the ultimate owners and risk takers. They have the potential for very high or very poor returns since they get whatever is left after all other expenses. |
| Earnings per share | Earnings per share is found by taking the income available to the common stockholders and dividing by the number of shares of common stock outstanding. This is income generated by the company for each share of common stock. |

statement with line-by-line explanations is presented in Table 14.3, while Table 14.4 presents the income statement of Microsoft. The income statement indicates the firm's profitability or income (the bottom line), which is derived by subtracting the firm's expenses from its revenues.

**TABLE 14.4**
Microsoft Corporation Consolidated Statement of Earnings (in millions, except share per data)

| Year Ended June 30, | 2013 | 2012 | 2011 |
|---|---|---|---|
| Revenue | $77,849 | $73,723 | $69,943 |
| Cost of revenue | 20,249 | 17,530 | 15,577 |
| Gross profit | 57,600 | 56,193 | 54,366 |
| Operating expenses: | | | |
| Research and development | 10,411 | 9,811 | 9,043 |
| Sales and marketing | 15,276 | 13,857 | 13,940 |
| General and administrative | 5,149 | 4,569 | 4,222 |
| Goodwill impairment | 0 | 6,193 | 0 |
| Total operating expenses | 30,836 | 34,430 | 27,205 |
| Operating income | 26,764 | 21,763 | 27,161 |
| Other income | 288 | 504 | 910 |
| Income before income taxes | 27,052 | 22,267 | 28,071 |
| Provision for income taxes | 5,189 | 5,289 | 4,921 |
| Net income | $21,863 | $16,978 | $23,150 |
| Earnings per share: | | | |
| Basic | $ 2.61 | $ 2.02 | $ 2.73 |
| Diluted | $ 2.58 | $ 2.00 | $ 2.69 |
| Weighted average shares outstanding: | | | |
| Basic | 8,375 | 8,396 | 8,490 |
| Diluted | 8,470 | 8,506 | 8,593 |
| Cash dividents declared per common share | $ 0.92 | $ 0.80 | $ 0.64 |

Source: Microsoft Corporation 2013 Annual Report.

revenue
the total amount of money received from the sale of goods or services, as well as from related business activities

**Revenue.**    **Revenue** is the total amount of money received (or promised) from the sale of goods or services, as well as from other business activities such as the rental of property and investments. Nonbusiness entities typically obtain revenues through donations from individuals and/or grants from governments and private foundations. One of the controversies in accounting has been when a business should recognize revenue. For instance, should an organization book revenue during a project or after the project is completed? Differences in revenue recognition have caused similar organizations to book different accounting results. A proposed rule states that firms should book revenue when "it satisfie[s] a performance obligation by transferring a promised good or service to a customer."[7]

For most manufacturing and retail concerns, the next major item included in the income statement is the **cost of goods sold,** the amount of money the firm spent (or promised to spend) to buy and/or produce the products it sold during the accounting period. This figure may be calculated as follows:

**Cost of goods sold = Beginning inventory + Interim purchases − Ending inventory**

Let's say that Anna's Flowers began an accounting period with an inventory of goods for which it paid $5,000. During the period, Anna bought another $4,000 worth of goods, giving the shop a total inventory available for sale of $9,000. If, at the end of the accounting period, Anna's inventory was worth $5,500, the cost of goods sold during the period would have been $3,500 ($5,000 + $4,000 − $5,500 = $3,500). If Anna had total revenues of $10,000 over the same period of time, subtracting the cost of goods sold ($3,500) from the total revenues of $10,000 yields the store's **gross income** or **profit** (revenues minus the cost of goods sold required to generate the revenues): $6,500. The same process occurs at Microsoft. As indicated in Table 14.4, the cost of goods sold was more than $20.249 billion in 2013. Notice that Microsoft calls it cost of revenues, rather than cost of goods sold.

**Expenses.**   **Expenses** are the costs incurred in the day-to-day operations of an organization. Three common expense accounts shown on income statements are (1) selling, general, and administrative expenses; (2) research, development, and engineering expenses; and (3) interest expenses (remember that the costs directly attributable to selling goods or services are included in the cost of goods sold). Selling expenses include advertising and sales salaries. General and administrative expenses include salaries of executives and their staff and the costs of owning and maintaining the general office. Research and development costs include scientific, engineering, and marketing personnel and the equipment and information used to design and build prototypes and samples. Interest expenses include the direct costs of borrowing money.

The number and type of expense accounts vary from organization to organization. Included in the general and administrative category is a special type of expense known as **depreciation,** the process of spreading the costs of long-lived assets such as buildings and equipment over the total number of accounting periods in which they are expected to be used. Consider a manufacturer that purchases a $100,000 machine expected to last about 10 years. Rather than showing an expense of $100,000 in the first year and no expense for that equipment over the next nine years, the manufacturer is allowed to report depreciation expenses of $10,000 per year in each of the next 10 years because that better matches the cost of the machine to the years the machine is used. Each time this depreciation is "written off" as an expense, the book value of the machine is also reduced by $10,000. The fact that the equipment has a zero value on the firm's balance sheet when it is fully depreciated (in this case, after 10 years) does not necessarily mean that it can no longer be used or is economically worthless. Indeed, in some industries, machines used every day have been reported as having no book value whatsoever for more than 30 years.

**Net Income.**   **Net income** (or net earnings) is the total profit (or loss) after all expenses including taxes have been deducted from revenue. Generally, accountants divide profits into individual sections such as operating income and earnings before interest and taxes. Microsoft, for example, lists earnings before income taxes, net

---

**cost of goods sold**
the amount of money a firm spent to buy or produce the products it sold during the period to which the income statement applies

**gross income (profit)**
revenues minus the cost of goods sold required to generate the revenues

**expenses**
the costs incurred in the day-to-day operations of an organization

**depreciation**
the process of spreading the costs of long-lived assets such as buildings and equipment over the total number of accounting periods in which they are expected to be used

**net income**
the total profit (or loss) after all expenses, including taxes, have been deducted from revenue; also called net earnings

earnings, and earnings per share of outstanding stock (see Table 14.4). Like most companies, Microsoft presents not only the current year's results but also the previous two years' income statements to permit comparison of performance from one period to another.

**Temporary Nature of the Income Statement Accounts.**   Companies record their operational activities in the revenue and expense accounts during an accounting period. Gross profit, earnings before interest and taxes, and net income are the results of calculations made from the revenues and expenses accounts; they are not actual accounts. At the end of each accounting period, the dollar amounts in all the revenue and expense accounts are moved into an account called "Retained Earnings," one of the owners' equity accounts. Revenues increase owners' equity, while expenses decrease it. The resulting change in the owners' equity account is exactly equal to the net income. This shifting of dollar values from the revenue and expense accounts allows the firm to begin the next accounting period with zero balances in those accounts. Zeroing out the balances enables a company to count how much it has sold and how many expenses have been incurred during a period of time. The basic accounting equation (Assets = Liabilities + Owners' equity) will not balance until the revenue and expense account balances have been moved or "closed out" to the owners' equity account.

One final note about income statements: You may remember that corporations may choose to make cash payments called dividends to shareholders out of their net earnings. When a corporation elects to pay dividends, it decreases the cash account (in the assets category of the balance sheet) as well as a capital account (in the owners' equity category of the balance sheet). During any period of time, the owners' equity account may change because of the sale of stock (or contributions/withdrawals by owners), the net income or loss, or the dividends paid.

ExxonMobil is the world's fifth largest company with approximately $408 billion in annual revenue.

### Al Dente Pasta Serves Up Perfect Pasta to Customers Nationwide

**Al Dente® Pasta Company**
**Founder:** Monique Deschaine
**Founded:** 1981, in Whitmore Lake, Michiga
**Success:** The company's Al Dente Perfect Pasta™ and Monique's Sumptuous Sauces™ are now sold nationwide.

Monique Deschaine dreamed of making the perfect pasta. She turned that dream into a reality in 1981 by launching the Al Dente® Pasta Company. Deschaine befriended celebrated Italian chef and cookbook author Marcella Hazan, using Hazan's restaurant kitchen after-hours as her pasta-making location. Dedication to the recipe and technique taught to her by Hazan convinced Deschaine to market to niche consumers looking for perfect al dente pasta rather than competing with large pasta companies.

In the beginning, Deschaine assumed the firm's accounting responsibilities. She was responsible for monitoring and responding to growth by keeping the company's financial statements up-to-date according to the generally accepted accounting principles (GAAP).

As the pasta's popularity has grown, so has the company—expanding from Deschaine and her husband to more than 20 employees. Al Dente now sells products nationwide and has been featured on The Food Network. Financial information is distributed throughout the company, allowing managers to examine strengths and weaknesses. Through Deschaine's institution of good accounting systems and proper management, Al Dente Pasta Company is achieving sustainable profits and growth.[8]

### The Balance Sheet

The second basic financial statement is the **balance sheet,** which presents a "snapshot" of an organization's financial position at a given moment. As such, the balance sheet indicates what the organization owns or controls and the various sources of the funds used to pay for these assets, such as bank debt or owners' equity.

**balance sheet**
a "snapshot" of an organization's financial position at a given moment

The balance sheet takes its name from its reliance on the accounting equation: Assets *must* equal liabilities plus owners' equity. Table 14.5 provides a sample balance sheet with line-by-line explanations. Unlike the income statement, the balance sheet does not represent the result of transactions completed over a specified accounting period. Instead, the balance sheet is, by definition, an accumulation of all financial transactions conducted by an organization since its founding. Following long-established traditions, items on the balance sheet are listed on the basis of their original cost less accumulated depreciation, rather than their present values.

Balance sheets are often presented in two different formats. The traditional balance sheet format placed the organization's assets on the left side and its liabilities and owners' equity on the right. More recently, a vertical format, with assets on top followed by liabilities and owners' equity, has gained wide acceptance. Microsoft's balance sheet for 2012 and 2013 is presented in Table 14.6. In the sections that follow, we'll briefly describe the basic items found on the balance sheet; we'll take a closer look at a number of these in Chapter 16.

**Assets.** All asset accounts are listed in descending order of *liquidity*—that is, how quickly each could be turned into cash. **Current assets,** also called short-term assets, are those that are used or converted into cash within the course of a calendar year. Cash is followed by temporary investments, accounts receivable, and inventory, in that order. **Accounts receivable** refers to money owed the company by its clients or customers who have promised to pay for the products at a later date. Accounts receivable usually includes an allowance for bad debts that management does not expect to collect. The bad-debts adjustment is normally based on historical collections

**current assets**
assets that are used or converted into cash within the course of a calendar year

**accounts receivable**
money owed a company by its clients or customers who have promised to pay for the products at a later date

**TABLE 14.5   Sample Balance Sheet**

The following exhibit presents a balance sheet in word form with each item defined or explained.

| Typical Company | December 31 |
|---|---|
| Assets | This is the major category for all physical, monetary, or intangible goods that have some dollar value. |
| Current assets | Assets that are either cash or are expected to be turned into cash within the next 12 months. |
| Cash | Cash or checking accounts. |
| Marketable securities | Short-term investments in securities that can be converted to cash quickly (liquid assets). |
| Accounts receivable | Cash due from customers in payment for goods received. These arise from sales made on credit. |
| Inventory | Finished goods ready for sale, goods in the process of being finished, or raw materials used in the production of goods. |
| Prepaid expense | A future expense item that has already been paid, such as insurance premiums or rent. |
| Total current assets | The sum of the above accounts. |
| Fixed assets | Assets that are long term in nature and have a minimum life expectancy that exceeds one year. |
| Investments | Assets held as investments rather than assets owned for the production process. Most often the assets include small ownership interests in other companies. |
| Gross property, plant, and equipment | Land, buildings, and other fixed assets listed at original cost. |
| Less: Accumulated depreciation | The accumulated expense deductions applied to all plant and equipment over their life. Land may not be depreciated. The total amount represents in general the decline in value as equipment gets older and wears out. The maximum amount that can be deducted is set by the U.S. Federal Tax Code and varies by type of asset. |
| Net property, plant, and equipment | Gross property, plant, and equipment minus the accumulated depreciation. This amount reflects the book value of the fixed assets and not their value if sold. |
| Other assets | Any other asset that is long term and does not fit into the above categories. It could be patents or trademarks. |
| Total assets | The sum of all the asset values. |
| Liabilities and Stockholders' Equity | This is the major category. Liabilities refer to all indebtedness and loans of both a long-term and short-term nature. Stockholders' equity refers to all money that has been contributed to the company over the life of the firm by the owners. |
| Current liabilities | Short-term debt expected to be paid off within the next 12 months. |
| Accounts payable | Money owed to suppliers for goods ordered. Firms usually have between 30 and 90 days to pay this account, depending on industry norms. |
| Wages payable | Money owned to employees for hours worked or salary. If workers receive checks every two weeks, the amount owed should be no more than two weeks' pay. |
| Taxes payable | Firms are required to pay corporate taxes quarterly. This refers to taxes owed based on earnings estimates for the quarter. |

*(continued)*

**TABLE 14.5**   **Sample Balance Sheet** *(continued)*

| | |
|---|---|
| Notes payable | Short-term loans from banks or other lenders. |
| Other current liabilities | The other short-term debts that do not fit into the above categories. |
| Total current liabilities | The sum of the above accounts. |
| Long-term liabilities | All long-term debt that will not be paid off in the next 12 months. |
| Long-term debt | Loans of more than one year from banks, pension funds, insurance companies, or other lenders. These loans often take the form of bonds, which are securities that may be bought and sold in bond markets. |
| Deferred income taxes | This is a liability owed to the government but not due within one year. |
| Other liabilities | Any other long-term debt that does not fit the above two categories. |
| Stockholders' equity | The following three categories are the owners' investment in the company. |
| Common stock | The tangible evidence of ownership is a security called common stock. The par value is stated value and does not indicate the company's worth. |
| Capital in excess of par (a.k.a. contributed capital) | When shares of stock were sold to the owners, they were recorded at the price at the time of the original sale. If the price paid was $10 per share, the extra $9 per share would show up in this account at 100,000 shares times $9 per share, or $900,000. |
| Retained earnings | The total amount of earnings the company has made during its life and not paid out to its stockholders as dividends. This account represents the owners' reinvestment of earnings into company assets rather than payments of cash dividends. This account does not represent cash. |
| Total stockholders' equity | This is the sum of the above equity accounts representing the owner's total investment in the company. |
| Total liabilities and stockholders' equity | The total short-term and long-term debt of the company plus the owner's total investment. This combined amount *must* equal total assets. |

experience and is deducted from the accounts receivable balance to present a more realistic view of the payments likely to be received in the future, called net receivables. Inventory may be held in the form of raw materials, work-in-progress, or finished goods ready for delivery.

Long-term or fixed assets represent a commitment of organizational funds of at least one year. Items classified as fixed include long-term investments, plant and equipment, and intangible assets, such as corporate "goodwill," or reputation, as well as patents and trademarks.

**Liabilities.**   As seen in the accounting equation, total assets must be financed either through borrowing (liabilities) or through owner investments (owners' equity). **Current liabilities** include a firm's financial obligations to short-term creditors, which must be repaid within one year, while long-term liabilities have longer repayment terms. **Accounts payable** represents amounts owed to suppliers for goods and services purchased with credit. For example, if you buy gas with a BP credit card, the purchase represents an account payable for you (and an account receivable for BP). Other liabilities include wages earned by employees but not yet paid and taxes owed to the government. Occasionally, these accounts are consolidated into an **accrued expenses** account, representing all unpaid financial obligations incurred by the organization.

**current liabilities**
a firm's financial obligations to short-term creditors, which must be repaid within one year

**accounts payable**
the amount a company owes to suppliers for goods and services purchased with credit

**accrued expenses**
is an account representing all unpaid financial obligations incurred by the organization

**TABLE 14.6**   Microsoft Corporation Consolidated Balance Sheets (in millions, except per share data)

| June 30, | 2013 | 2012 |
|---|---|---|
| **Assets** | | |
| Current assets: | | |
| Cash and cash equivalents | $ 3,804 | $ 6,938 |
| Short-term investments (including securities loaned of $579 and $785) | 73,218 | 56,102 |
| Total cash, cash equivalents, and short-term investments | 77,022 | 63,040 |
| Accounts receivable, net of allowance for doubtful accounts of $336 and $389 | 17,486 | 15,780 |
| Inventories | 1,938 | 1,137 |
| Deferred income taxes | 1,632 | 2,035 |
| Other | 3,388 | 3,092 |
| Total current assets | 101,466 | 85,084 |
| Property and equipment, net of accumulated depreciation of $12,513 and $10,962 | 9,991 | 8,269 |
| Equity and other investments | 10,844 | 9,776 |
| Goodwill | 14,655 | 13,452 |
| Intangible assets, net | 3,083 | 3,170 |
| Other long-term assets | 2,392 | 1,520 |
| Total assets | $142,431 | $ 121,271 |
| **Liabilities and stockholders' equity** | | |
| Current liabilities: | | |
| Accounts payable | $ 4,828 | $ 4,175 |
| Current portion of long-term debt | 2,999 | 1,231 |
| Accrued compensation | 4,117 | 3,875 |
| Income taxes | 592 | 789 |
| Short-term unearned revenue | 20,639 | 18,653 |
| Securities lending payable | 645 | 814 |
| Other | 3,597 | 3,151 |
| Total current liabilities | 37,417 | 32,688 |
| Long-term debt | 12,601 | 10,713 |
| Long-term unearned revenue | 1,760 | 1,406 |
| Deferred income taxes | 1,709 | 1,893 |
| Other long-term liabilities | 10,000 | 8,208 |
| Total liabilities | 63,487 | 54,908 |

*(continued)*

**TABLE 14.6**    Microsoft Corporation Consolidated Balance Sheets (in millions, except per share data) (*continued*)

| | | |
|---|---:|---:|
| Commitments and contingencies | | |
| Stockholders' equity: | | |
| Common stock and paid-in capital–shares authorized 24,000; outstanding 8,328 and 8,381 | 67,306 | 65,797 |
| Retained earnings (deficit) | 9,895 | (856) |
| Accumulated other comprehensive Income | 1,743 | 1,422 |
| Total stockholders' equity | 78,944 | 66,363 |
| Total liabilities and stockholders' equity | $ 142,431 | $ 121,271 |

**Owners' Equity.**    Owners' equity includes the owners' contributions to the organization along with income earned by the organization and retained to finance continued growth and development. If the organization were to sell off all of its assets and pay off all of its liabilities, any remaining funds would belong to the owners. Not surprisingly, the accounts listed as owners' equity on a balance sheet may differ dramatically from company to company. Corporations sell stock to investors, who then become the owners of the firm. Many corporations issue two, three, or even more different classes of common and preferred stock, each with different dividend payments and/or voting rights. Google has three classes of stock, with the class B stock having more voting rights than class A shares. These are sometimes called founder's shares and allow the founders to maintain control over the company even though they do not own the majority of the shares. Ford Motor has the same type of voting structure. Because each type of stock issued represents a different claim on the organization, each must be represented by a separate owners' equity account, called contributed capital.

## The Statement of Cash Flows

The third primary financial statement is called the **statement of cash flows,** which explains how the company's cash changed from the beginning of the accounting period to the end. Cash, of course, is an asset shown on the balance sheet, which provides a snapshot of the firm's financial position at one point in time. However, many investors and other users of financial statements want more information about the cash flowing into and out of the firm than is provided on the balance sheet in order to better understand the company's financial health. The statement of cash flows takes the cash balance from one year's balance sheet and compares it with the next while providing detail about how the firm used the cash. Table 14.7 presents Microsoft's statement of cash flows.

**statement of cash flows** explains how the company's cash changed from the beginning of the accounting period to the end

The change in cash is explained through details in three categories: cash from (used for) operating activities, cash from (used for) investing activities, and cash from (used for) financing activities. *Cash from operating activities* is calculated by combining the changes in the revenue accounts, expense accounts, current asset accounts, and current liability accounts. This category of cash flows includes all the accounts on the balance sheet that relate to computing revenues and expenses for the accounting period. If this amount is a positive number, as it is for Microsoft, then the business is making extra cash that it can use to invest in increased long-term capacity or to pay off debts such as loans or bonds. A negative number may indicate a business that is in a declining position with regards to operations. Negative cash flow is not always a bad thing, however. Negative cash flow might indicate a company is in the rapid growth phase but not yet making a profit. This is often true of small growth companies in technology and biotech.

**TABLE 14.7    Consolidated Statements of Cash Flows (in millions)**

| Year Ended June 30, | 2013 | 2012 | 2011 |
|---|---|---|---|
| **Operations** | | | |
| Net income | $ 21,863 | $ 16,978 | $ 23,150 |
| Adjustments to reconcile net income to net cash from operations: | | | |
| Goodwill impairment | 0 | 6,193 | 0 |
| Depreciation, amortization, and other | 3,755 | 2,967 | 2,766 |
| Stock-based compensation expense | 2,406 | 2,244 | 2,166 |
| Net recognized losses (gains) on investments and derivatives | 80 | (200) | (362) |
| Excess tax benefits from stock-based compensation | (209) | (93) | (17) |
| Deferred income taxes | (19) | 954 | 2 |
| Deferral of unearned revenue | 44,253 | 36,104 | 31,227 |
| Recognition of unearned revenue | (41,921) | (33,347) | (28,935) |
| Changes in operating assets and liabilities: | | | |
| Accounts receivable | (1,807) | (1,156) | (1,451) |
| Inventories | (802) | 184 | (561) |
| Other current assets | (129) | 493 | (1,259) |
| Other long-term assets | (478) | (248) | 62 |
| Accounts payable | 537 | (31) | 58 |
| Other current liabilities | 146 | 410 | (1,146) |
| Other long-term liabilities | 1,158 | 174 | 1,294 |
| Net cash from operations | 28,833 | 31,626 | 26,994 |
| **Financing** | | | |
| Short-term debt repayments, maturities of 90 days or less, net | 0 | 0 | (186) |
| Proceeds from issuance of debt | 4,883 | 0 | 6,960 |
| Repayments of debt | (1,346) | 0 | (814) |
| Common stock issued | 931 | 1,913 | 2,422 |
| Common stock repurchased | (5,360) | (5,029) | (11,555) |
| Common stock cash dividends paid | (7,455) | (6,385) | (5,180) |
| Excess tax benefits from stock-based compensation | 209 | 93 | 17 |
| Other | (10) | 0 | (40) |
| Net cash used in financing | (8,148) | (9,408) | (8,376) |

*(continued)*

**TABLE 14.7    Consolidated Statements of Cash Flows (in millions) *(continued)***

| Investing | | | |
|---|---:|---:|---:|
| Additions to property and equipment | (4,257) | (2,305) | (2,355) |
| Acquisition of companies, net of cash acquired, and purchases of intangible and other assets | (1,584) | (10,112) | (71) |
| Purchases of investments | (75,396) | (57,250) | (35,993) |
| Maturities of investments | 5,130 | 15,575 | 6,897 |
| Sales of investments | 52,464 | 29,700 | 15,880 |
| Securities lending payable | (168) | (394) | 1,026 |
| Net cash used in investing | (23,811) | (24,786) | (14,616) |
| Effect of exchange rates on cash and cash equivalents | (8) | (104) | 103 |
| Net change in cash and cash equivalents | (3,134) | (2,672) | 4,105 |
| Cash and cash equivalents, beginning of period | 6,938 | 9,610 | 5,505 |
| Cash and cash equivalents, end of period | $ 3,804 | $ 6,938 | $ 9,610 |

*Cash from investing activities* is calculated from changes in the long-term or fixed asset accounts. If this amount is negative, as is the case with Microsoft, we can see that the company bought $4.2 billion of property and equipment. It also purchased $75 billion of investments and sold $52 billion of investments for a total negative cash flow of $23.8 billion. A positive figure usually indicates a business that is selling off existing long-term assets and reducing its capacity for the future.

Finally, *cash from financing activities* is calculated from changes in the long-term liability accounts and the contributed capital accounts in owners' equity. If this amount is negative, the company is likely paying off long-term debt or returning contributed capital to investors. In the case of Microsoft, it sold some debt for an increase in cash of $4.88 billion, but repurchased stock and paid a dividend, which resulted in negative cash flow from financing.

## Ratio Analysis: Analyzing Financial Statements

The income statement shows a company's profit or loss, while the balance sheet item-izes the value of its assets, liabilities, and owners' equity. Together, the two statements provide the means to answer two critical questions: (1) How much did the firm make or lose? and (2) How much is the firm presently worth based on historical values found on the balance sheet? **Ratio analysis,** calculations that measure an organiza-tion's financial health, brings the complex information from the income statement and balance sheet into sharper focus so that managers, lenders, owners, and other inter-ested parties can measure and compare the organization's productivity, profitability, and financing mix with other similar entities.

**ratio analysis**
calculations that measure an organization's financial health

As you know, a ratio is simply one number divided by another, with the result showing the relationship between the two numbers. For example, we measure fuel efficiency with miles per gallon. This is how we know that 55 mpg in a Toyota Prius is much better than the average car. Financial ratios are used to weigh and evaluate a firm's performance. An absolute value such as earnings of $70,000 or accounts receivable of $200,000 almost never provides as much useful information as a well-constructed ratio. Whether those numbers are good or bad depends on their relation to other numbers. If a company earned $70,000 on $700,000 in sales (a 10 percent return), such an earnings level might be quite satisfactory. The president of a company earning this same $70,000 on sales of $7 million (a 1 percent return), however, should probably start looking for another job!

Ratios by themselves are not very useful. It is the relationship of the calculated ratios to both prior organizational performance and the performance of the organization's "peers," as well as its stated goals, that really matters. Remember, while the profitability, asset utilization, liquidity, debt ratios, and per share data we'll look at here can be very useful, you will never see the forest by looking only at the trees.

## Profitability Ratios

**profitability ratios**
ratios that measure the amount of operating income or net income an organization is able to generate relative to its assets, owners' equity, and sales

**Profitability ratios** measure how much operating income or net income an organization is able to generate relative to its assets, owners' equity, and sales. The numerator (top number) used in these examples is always the net income after taxes. Common profitability ratios include profit margin, return on assets, and return on equity. The following examples are based on the 2013 income statement and balance sheet for Microsoft, as shown in Tables 14.4 and 14.6. Except where specified, all data are expressed in millions of dollars.

**profit margin**
net income divided by sales

The **profit margin,** computed by dividing net income by sales, shows the overall percentage of profits earned by the company. It is based solely upon data obtained from the income statement. The higher the profit margin, the better the cost controls within the company and the higher the return on every dollar of revenue. Microsoft's profit margin is calculated as follows:

$$\text{Profit margin} = \frac{\text{Net income (Net earnings)}}{\text{Sales (Total net revenues)}} = \frac{\$21,863}{\$77,849} = 28.08\%$$

Thus, for every $1 in sales, Microsoft generated profits after taxes of 28 cents.

**return on assets**
net income divided by assets

**Return on assets,** net income divided by assets, shows how much income the firm produces for every dollar invested in assets. A company with a low return on assets is probably not using its assets very productively—a key managerial failing. For its construction, the return on assets calculation requires data from both the income statement and the balance sheet.

$$\text{Return on assets} = \frac{\text{Net income (Net earnings)}}{\text{Total assets}} = \frac{\$21,863}{\$142,431} = 15.35\%$$

In the case of Microsoft, every $1 of assets generated a return of close to 15 percent, or profits of 15.35 cents per dollar.

Stockholders are always concerned with how much money they will make on their investment, and they frequently use the return on equity ratio as one of their key performance yardsticks. **Return on equity** (also called return on investment [ROI]), calculated by dividing net income by owners' equity, shows how much income is generated by each $1 the owners have invested in the firm. Obviously, a low return on equity means low stockholder returns and may indicate a need for immediate managerial attention. Because some assets may have been financed with debt not contributed by the owners, the value of the owners' equity is usually

**return on equity**
net income divided by owners' equity; also called return on investment (ROI)

### Deloitte Partners with New Profit Inc. to Drive Social Innovation

Deloitte LLP is one of the largest consulting firms in the world, specializing in financial advisory, risk management, and audit and tax services. The organization has a far-reaching reputation for being one of the most philanthropic firms in the world. It is therefore no surprise that it has established a multi-million-dollar partnership with New Profit Inc. to promote and support social innovation initiatives.

New Profit Inc. is a social innovation nonprofit and venture philanthropy fund, investing in social entrepreneurs whose ideas promise to contribute to a greater social good. Areas of interest include education, workforce development, public health, and community development because they facilitate social mobility and enact powerful systemic change by providing better opportunities for children, families, and communities. Deloitte shares these values and has committed to providing pro bono consulting services to New Profit as well

as to those in New Profit's portfolio. As one of the largest employers with top talent, Deloitte recognizes that human and intellectual capital is its most valuable asset, and it has based its corporate citizenship strategy—Impact Imperative—around this.

This collaboration between a large public financial firm and a small private organization is a profound example of social responsibility that has the potential to affect many people for the better.[9]

#### Discussion Questions

1. Do you believe Deloitte should be investing so many resources in philanthropy? Why or why not?
2. How is Deloitte contributing to New Profit Inc.'s mission?
3. What benefits do both organizations receive through this partnership?

---

considerably lower than the total value of the firm's assets. Microsoft's return on equity is calculated as follows:

$$\text{Return on equity} = \frac{\text{Net income}}{\text{Stockholders' equity}} = \frac{\$21,863}{\$78,944} = 27.69\%$$

For every dollar invested by Microsoft stockholders, the company earned a 27.69 percent return, or 27.69 cents per dollar invested.

### Asset Utilization Ratios

**Asset utilization ratios** measure how well a firm uses its assets to generate each $1 of sales. Obviously, companies using their assets more productively will have higher returns on assets than their less efficient competitors. Similarly, managers can use asset utilization ratios to pinpoint areas of inefficiency in their operations. These ratios (receivables turnover, inventory turnover, and total asset turnover) relate balance sheet assets to sales, which are found on the income statement.

**asset utilization ratios** ratios that measure how well a firm uses its assets to generate each $1 of sales

The **receivables turnover,** sales divided by accounts receivable, indicates how many times a firm collects its accounts receivable in one year. It also demonstrates how quickly a firm is able to collect payments on its credit sales. Obviously, no payments means no profits. Microsoft collected its receivables 4.45 times per year, which translates to about 80 days that receivables are outstanding. This is most likely due to the trade terms they give their corporate customers.

**receivables turnover** sales divided by accounts receivable

$$\text{Receivables turnover} = \frac{\text{Sales (Total net revenues)}}{\text{Receivables}} = \frac{\$77,849}{\$17,486} = 4.45\times$$

**Inventory turnover,** sales divided by total inventory, indicates how many times a firm sells and replaces its inventory over the course of a year. A high inventory

**inventory turnover** sales divided by total inventory

turnover ratio may indicate great efficiency but may also suggest the possibility of lost sales due to insufficient stock levels. Microsoft's inventory turnover indicates that it replaced its inventory 40.17 times last year, or about every 9 days. This high inventory turnover is a reflection that Microsoft has very little physical inventory and instead downloads its Windows programs over the Internet.

$$\text{Inventory turnover} = \frac{\text{Sales (Total net revenues)}}{\text{Inventory}} = \frac{\$77,849}{\$1,938} = 40.17\times$$

**total asset turnover**
sales divided by total assets

**Total asset turnover,** sales divided by total assets, measures how well an organization uses all of its assets in creating sales. It indicates whether a company is using its assets productively. Microsoft generated $0.55 in sales for every $1 in total corporate assets. The cause of this low total asset turnover is the $77 billion of cash that Micosoft has on its balance sheet. Cash does not produce sales dollars.

$$\text{Total asset turnover} = \frac{\text{Sales (Total net revenues)}}{\text{Total assets}} = \frac{\$77,849}{\$142,431} = 0.55\times$$

## Liquidity Ratios

**liquidity ratios**
ratios that measure the speed with which a company can turn its assets into cash to meet short-term debt

**Liquidity ratios** compare current (short-term) assets to current liabilities to indicate the speed with which a company can turn its assets into cash to meet debts as they fall due. High liquidity ratios may satisfy a creditor's need for safety, but ratios that are too high may indicate that the organization is not using its current assets efficiently. Liquidity ratios are generally best examined in conjunction with asset utilization ratios because high turnover ratios imply that cash is flowing through an organization very quickly—a situation that dramatically reduces the need for the type of reserves measured by liquidity ratios.

**current ratio**
current assets divided by current liabilities

The **current ratio** is calculated by dividing current assets by current liabilities. Microsoft's current ratio indicates that for every $1 of current liabilities, the firm had $2.71 of current assets on hand. The relatively high current ratio is also due to the $77 billion of cash on hand, which is part of the current asset total. If we take cash out of current assets, the numerator drops to $24,444, and the current ratio drops to 0.65.

$$\text{Current ratio} = \frac{\text{Current assets}}{\text{Current liabilities}} = \frac{\$101,466}{\$37,417} = 2.71\times$$

**quick ratio (acid test)**
a stringent measure of liquidity that eliminates inventory

The **quick ratio** (also known as the **acid test**) is a far more stringent measure of liquidity because it eliminates inventory, the least liquid current asset. It measures how well an organization can meet its current obligations without resorting to the sale of its inventory. Because Microsoft has so little inventory ($1.9 billion out of $101.4 billion of current assets), the quick ratio is almost exactly the same as the current ratio.

$$\text{Quick ratio} = \frac{\text{Current assets} - \text{Inventory}}{\text{Current liabilities}} = \frac{\$99,528}{\$37,417} = 2.66\times$$

## Debt Utilization Ratios

**debt utilization ratios**
ratios that measure how much debt an organization is using relative to other sources of capital, such as owners' equity

**Debt utilization ratios** provide information about how much debt an organization is using relative to other sources of capital, such as owners' equity. Because the use of debt carries an interest charge that must be paid regularly regardless of profitability, debt financing is much riskier than equity. Unforeseen negative events such as recessions affect heavily indebted firms to a far greater extent than those financed exclusively with owners' equity. Because of this and other factors, the managers of most firms tend to keep debt-to-asset levels below 50 percent. However, firms in very stable and/or regulated industries, such as electric utilities, often are able to carry debt ratios well in excess of 50 percent with no ill effects.

The **debt to total assets ratio** indicates how much of the firm is financed by debt and how much by owners' equity. To find the value of Microsoft's total debt, you must add current liabilities to long-term debt and other liabilities.

**debt to total assets ratio**
a ratio indicating how much of the firm is financed by debt and how much by owners' equity

$$\text{Debt to total assets} = \frac{\text{Debt (Total liabilities)}}{\text{Total assets}} = \frac{\$63,487}{\$142,431} = 45\%$$

Thus, for every $1 of Microsoft's total assets, 45 percent is financed with debt. The remaining 65 percent is provided by owners' equity.

The **times interest earned ratio,** operating income divided by interest expense, is a measure of the safety margin a company has with respect to the interest payments it must make to its creditors. A low times interest earned ratio indicates that even a small decrease in earnings may lead the company into financial straits. Microsoft had so little interest expense that it did not list it as a separate item on the income statement. In this case, the analyst has to go searching through the footnotes to the financial statements. In note 3, we find that interest expense was $429 million. Putting this into the calculation, we find that interest expense is covered 62.39 times by operating income. A lender would have no worries about receiving interest payments from Microsoft.

**times interest earned ratio**
operating income divided by interest expense

$$\text{Times interest earned} = \frac{\text{EBIT (Operating income)}}{\text{Interest (from note 3)}} = \frac{\$26,863}{\$429} = 62.39\times$$

## Per Share Data

Investors may use **per share data** to compare the performance of one company with another on an equal, or per share, basis. Generally, the more shares of stock a company issues, the less income is available for each share.

**Earnings per share** is calculated by dividing net income or profit by the number of shares of stock outstanding. This ratio is important because yearly changes in earnings per share, in combination with other economywide factors, determine a company's overall stock price. When earnings go up, so does a company's stock price—and so does the wealth of its stockholders.

**per share data**
data used by investors to compare the performance of one company with another on an equal, per share basis

**earnings per share**
net income or profit divided by the number of stock shares outstanding

$$\text{Diluted earnings per share} = \frac{\text{Net income}}{\text{Number of shares outstanding (diluted)}}$$

$$= \frac{\$21,863}{8,470} = \$2.58$$

We can see from the income statement that Microsoft's basic earnings per share declined from $2.73 per share to $2.61, and this decline also shows up in diluted earnings per share. This drop in earnings can be attributed to Microsoft's new Windows software, which the market did not embrace. You can see from the income statement that diluted earnings per share include more shares than the basic calculation; this is because diluted shares include potential shares that could be issued due to the exercise of stock options or the conversion of certain types of debt into common stock. Investors generally pay more attention to diluted earnings per share than basic earnings per share.

**Dividends per share** are paid by the corporation to the stockholders for each share owned. The payment is made from earnings after taxes by the corporation but is taxable income to the stockholder. Thus, dividends result in double taxation: The corporation pays tax once on its earnings, and the stockholder pays tax a second time on his or her dividend income. Since 2004, Microsoft has raised its dividend every

**dividends per share**
the actual cash received for each share owned

year, from $0.16 per share to $0.92 per share. A note of clarification on the number of shares outstanding of 8,375 million versus the 8,103 million listed in the denominator. Share count for earnings per share are weighted average shares over the year. However, as the share count goes up, the weighted average can be higher than the actual shares on which dividends were paid. The 8,103 shares were found by dividing $0.92 into the dividends paid on the statement of cash flow.

$$\text{Dividends per share} = \frac{\text{Dividends paid}}{\text{Number of shares outstanding}} = \frac{\$7,456}{8,103} = \$0.92$$

## Industry Analysis

We have used Microsoft as a comparison to Google because they are competitive in many technology areas, including software and the Internet. They both have a lot of intellectual property and cash balances, and they do not produce hardware like Apple and Hewlett-Packard do. Google has revenues of $59.8 billion. Many investors view Microsoft as an old technology company and Google as a new technology company with more growth opportunities. In fact, between 2011 and 2013, Microsoft's revenues grew only 11 percent while Google's revenues grew almost 58 percent. Reflecting this growth is that investors are willing to pay more for one dollar of Google's earnings per share than one dollar of Microsoft's EPS. In fact, in June of 2014, Google had a price to earnings per share ratio (PE) of 30.7 times and Microsoft had a PE of 15.5 times.

Microsoft dominates Google on the profitability ratios generating a higher profit margin, return on assets, and return on equity ratios. Both companies have very little accounts receivable or inventory, so they show very high receivables and inventory turnover ratios. However, because they each have large cash balances, their total asset turnover ratios are very low, which is not what you would expect with low receivables and inventory investment. At the end of 2013, Microsoft had $77 billion and Google had $58.7 billion of cash, cash equivalents, and short-term investments on their balance sheets. Because of their high cash balances, both companies show high current and quick ratios and, because of very little inventory, their quick ratios are almost equal to their current ratios.

Increased profit margins allow companies such as New Belgium to invest in new production facilities in Asheville, North Carolina.

Microsoft has more debt than Google, which is indicated by the debt to total assets ratio. While Microsoft has more debt than Google, the times interest earned ratio indicates that Microsoft's earnings before interest and taxes cover its interest expense at a higher level than does Google.

Table 14.8 doesn't show earnings per share growth, but it is important in forecasting dividend growth. As you can see from the table, Google does not pay a dividend even though it has cash and its earnings per share grew 28 percent between 2011 and 2013. Microsoft pays $0.92 per share even though its earnings per share had negative growth of 4 percent. Despite the negative earnings per share growth, Microsoft raised its dividends 43 percent over the same time period. That is easy to do when you

|  | Google | Microsoft |
|---|---|---|
| Profit margin | 21.60% | 28.08% |
| Return on assets | 11.65% | 15.35% |
| Return on equity | 14.80% | 27.69% |
| Receivables turnover | 6.74× | 4.45× |
| Inventory turnover | 140.43× | 40.17× |
| Total asset turnover | 0.54× | 0.55× |
| Current ratio | 4.58× | 2.71× |
| Quick ratio | 4.55× | 2.66× |
| Debt to total assets | 21.00% | 45.00% |
| Times interest earned | 26.35× | 62.31× |
| Diluted earnings per share | $38.13 | $2.58 |
| Dividends per share | $0.00 | $0.92 |

**TABLE 14.8**
**Industry Analysis Year Ending 2013**

Source: Data calculated from 2013 annual reports.

have $77 billion of cash on hand and dividends only cost $7.5 billion. The moral of the story is that the faster a company grows, the more funds the company retains for future growth or, in the case of both companies, acquisitions of new technology created by smaller companies.

## Importance of Integrity in Accounting

The financial crisis and the recession that followed provided another example of a failure in accounting reporting. Many firms attempted to exploit loopholes and manipulate accounting processes and statements. Banks and other financial institutions often held assets off their books by manipulating their accounts. In 2010, the examiner for the Lehman Brothers' bankruptcy found that the most common example of removing assets or liabilities from the books was entering into what is called a "repurchase agreement." In a repurchase agreement, assets are transferred to another entity with the contractual promise of buying them back at a set price. In the case of Lehman Brothers and other companies, repurchase agreements were used as a method of "cooking the books" that allowed them to manipulate accounting statements so that their ratios looked better than they actually were. If the accountants, the SEC, and the bank regulators had been more careful, these types of transactions would have been discovered and corrected.

As another member of the "Big Four" accounting firms, Deloitte must maintain high standards of accounting ethics to secure its reputation for integrity.

On the other hand, strong compliance to accounting principles creates trust among stakeholders. Accounting and financial planning is important for all organizational entities, even cities. The City of Maricopa in Arizona received the Government Finance Officers Association of the United States and Canada (GFOA) Distinguished Budget Presentation Award for its governmental budgeting. The city scored proficient in its policy, financial plan, operations guide, and communications device. Integrity in accounting is crucial to creating trust, understanding the financial position of an organization or entity, and making financial decisions that will benefit the organization.[10]

It is most important to remember that integrity in accounting processes requires ethical principles and compliance with both the spirit of the law and professional standards in the accounting profession. Most states require accountants preparing to take the CPA exam to take accounting ethics courses. Transparency and accuracy in reporting revenue, income, and assets develops trust from investors and other stakeholders.

## So You Want to Be an Accountant

Do you like numbers and finances? Are you detail oriented, a perfectionist, and highly accountable for your decisions? If so, accounting may be a good field for you. If you are interested in accounting, there are always job opportunities available no matter the state of the economy. Accounting is one of the most secure job options in business. Of course, becoming an accountant is not easy. You will need at least a bachelor's degree in accounting to get a job, and many positions require additional training. Many states demand coursework beyond the 120 to 150 credit hours collegiate programs require for an accounting degree. If you are really serious about getting into the accounting field, you will probably want to consider getting your master's in accounting and taking the CPA exam. The field of accounting can be complicated, and the extra training provided through a master's in accounting program will prove invaluable when you go out looking for a good job. Accounting is a volatile discipline affected by changes in legislative initiatives.

With corporate accounting policies changing constantly and becoming more complex, accountants are needed to help keep a business running smoothly and within the bounds of the law. In fact, the number of jobs in the accounting and auditing field are expected to increase 16 percent between 2010 and 2020, with more than 1.4 million jobs in the United States alone by 2020. Jobs in accounting tend to pay quite well, with the median salary standing at $61,690. If you go on to get your master's degree in accounting, expect to see an even higher starting wage. Of course, your earnings could be higher or lower than these averages, depending on where you work, your level of experience, the firm, and your particular position.

Accountants are needed in the public and the private sectors, in large and small firms, in for-profit and not-for-profit organizations. Accountants in firms are generally in charge of preparing and filing tax forms and financial reports. Public-sector accountants are responsible for checking the veracity of corporate and personal records in order to prepare tax filings. Basically, any organization that has to deal with money and/or taxes in some way or another will be in need of an accountant, either for in-house service or occasional contract work. Requirements for audits under the Sarbanes-Oxley Act and rules from the Public Company Accounting Oversight Board are creating more jobs and increased responsibility to maintain internal controls and accounting ethics. The fact that accounting rules and tax filings tend to be complex virtually ensures that the demand for accountants will never decrease.[11]

# Review Your Understanding

### Define accounting, and describe the different uses of accounting information.

Accounting is the language businesses and other organizations use to record, measure, and interpret financial transactions. Financial statements are used internally to judge and control an organization's performance and to plan and direct its future activities and measure goal attainment. External organizations such as lenders, governments, customers, suppliers, and the Internal Revenue Service are major consumers of the information generated by the accounting process.

### Demonstrate the accounting process.

Assets are an organization's economic resources; liabilities, debts the organization owes to others; and owners' equity, the difference between the value of an organization's assets and liabilities. This principle can be expressed as the accounting equation: Assets = Liabilities + Owners' equity. The double-entry bookkeeping system is a system of recording and classifying business transactions in accounts that maintain the balance of the accounting equation. The accounting cycle involves examining source documents, recording transactions in a journal, posting transactions, and preparing financial statements on a continuous basis throughout the life of the organization.

### Decipher the various components of an income statement in order to evaluate a firm's "bottom line."

The income statement indicates a company's profitability over a specific period of time. It shows the "bottom line," the total profit (or loss) after all expenses (the costs incurred in the day-to-day operations of the organization) have been deducted from revenue (the total amount of money received from the sale of goods or services and other business activities). The cash flow statement details how much cash is moving through the firm and thus adds insight to a firm's "bottom line."

### Interpret a company's balance sheet to determine its current financial position.

The balance sheet, which summarizes the firm's assets, liabilities, and owners' equity since its inception, portrays its financial position as of a particular point in time. Major classifications included in the balance sheet are current assets (assets that can be converted to cash within one calendar year), fixed assets (assets of greater than one year's duration), current liabilities (bills owed by the organization within one calendar year), long-term liabilities (bills due more than one year hence), and owners' equity (the net value of the owners' investment).

### Analyze financial statements, using ratio analysis, to evaluate a company's performance.

Ratio analysis is a series of calculations that brings the complex information from the income statement and balance sheet into sharper focus so that managers, lenders, owners, and other interested parties can measure and compare the organization's productivity, profitability, and financing mix with similar entities. Ratios may be classified in terms of profitability (measure dollars of return for each dollar of employed assets), asset utilization (measure how well the organization uses its assets to generate $1 in sales), liquidity (assess organizational risk by comparing current assets to current liabilities), debt utilization (measure how much debt the organization is using relative to other sources of capital), and per share data (compare the performance of one company with another on an equal basis).

### Assess a company's financial position using its accounting statements and ratio analysis.

Based on the information presented in the chapter, you should be able to answer the questions posed in "Solve the Dilemma" on page 453. Formulate a plan for determining BrainDrain's bottom line, current worth, and productivity.

# Revisit the World of Business

1. Even if Fastow did not believe what he was doing was illegal, how did his activities qualify as accounting fraud?

2. If Fastow's claim that he received approval from accountants, lawyers, and directors for his financial structures is true, does this make him less liable for the fraud? Why or why not?

3. Why do you think Fastow believes companies today are engaging in accounting and financial manipulation that is worse than Enron's?

## Learn the Terms

## Check Your Progress

1. Why are accountants so important to a corporation? What function do they perform?

2. Discuss the internal uses of accounting statements.

3. What is a budget?

4. Discuss the external uses of financial statements.

5. Describe the accounting process and cycle.

6. The income statements of all corporations are in the same format. True or false? Discuss.

7. Which accounts appear under "current liabilities"?

8. Together, the income statement and the balance sheet answer two basic questions. What are they?

9. What are the five basic ratio classifications? What ratios are found in each category?

10. Why are debt ratios important in assessing the risk of a firm?

## Get Involved

1. Go to the library or the Internet and get the annual report of a company with which you are familiar. Read through the financial statements, then write up an analysis of the firm's performance using ratio analysis. Look at data over several years and analyze whether the firm's performance is changing through time.

2. Form a group of three or four students to perform an industry analysis. Each student should analyze a company in the same industry, and then all of you should compare your results. The following companies would make good group projects:

Automobiles: Fiat Chryslesr, Ford, General Motors

Computers: Apple, Hewlett-Packard, Dell

Brewing: MillerCoors, Molson Coors, The Boston Beer Company

Chemicals: DuPont, Dow Chemical, Monsanto

Petroleum: Chevron, ExxonMobil, BP

Pharmaceuticals: Merck, Lilly, Amgen

Retail: Sears, JCPenney, Macy's, The Limited

# Build Your Skills

## Financial Analysis

### Background

The income statement for Western Grain Company, a producer of agricultural products for industrial as well as consumer markets, is shown below. Western Grain's total assets are $4,237.1 million, and its equity is $1,713.4 million.

*Consolidated Earnings and Retained Earnings Year Ended December 31*

| (Millions) | 2010 |
| --- | --- |
| *Net sales* | $6,295.4 |
| Cost of goods sold | 2,989.0 |
| Selling and administrative expense | 2,237.5 |
| *Operating profit* | 1,068.9 |
| Interest expense | 33.3 |
| Other income (expense), net | (1.5) |

| | |
| --- | --- |
| *Earnings before income taxes* | 1,034.1 |
| Income taxes | 353.4 |
| *Net earnings* | 680.7 |
| (Net earnings per share) | $2.94 |
| Retained earnings, beginning of year | 3,033.9 |
| *Dividends paid* | (305.2) |
| Retained earnings, end of year | $3,409.4 |

### Task

Calculate the following profitability ratios: profit margin, return on assets, and return on equity. Assume that the industry averages for these ratios are as follows: profit margin, 12 percent; return on assets, 18 percent; and return on equity, 25 percent. Evaluate Western Grain's profitability relative to the industry averages. Why is this information useful?

# Solve the Dilemma  `LO 14-6`

## Exploring the Secrets of Accounting

You have just been promoted from vice president of marketing of BrainDrain Corporation to president and CEO! That's the good news. Unfortunately, while you know marketing like the back of your hand, you know next to nothing about finance. Worse still, the "word on the street" is that BrainDrain is in danger of failure if steps to correct large and continuing financial losses are not taken immediately. Accordingly, you have asked the vice president of finance and accounting for a complete set of accounting statements detailing the financial operations of the company over the past several years.

Recovering from the dual shocks of your promotion and feeling the weight of the firm's complete accounting report for the very first time, you decide to attack the problem systematically and learn the "hidden secrets" of the company, statement by statement. With Mary Pruitt, the firm's trusted senior financial analyst, by your side, you delve into the accounting statements as never before. You resolve to "get to the bottom" of the firm's financial problems and set a new course for the future—a course that will take the firm from insolvency and failure to financial recovery and perpetual prosperity.

### Discussion Questions

1.  Describe the three basic accounting statements. What types of information does each provide that can help you evaluate the situation?

2.  Which of the financial ratios are likely to prove to be of greatest value in identifying problem areas in the company? Why? Which of your company's financial ratios might you expect to be especially poor?

3.  Discuss the limitations of ratio analysis.

# Build Your Business Plan

## Accounting and Financial Statements

After you determine your initial *reasonable selling price,* you need to estimate your sales forecasts (in terms of units and dollars of sales) for the first year of operation. Remember to be conservative and set forecasts that are more modest.

While customers may initially try your business, many businesses have seasonal patterns. A good budgeting/planning system allows managers to anticipate problems, coordinate activities of the business (so that subunits within the organization are all working toward the common goal of the organization), and control operations (how we know whether spending is "in line").

The first financial statement you need to prepare is the income statement. Beginning with your estimated sales revenue, determine what expenses will be necessary to generate that level of sales revenue.

The second financial statement you need to create is your balance sheet. Your balance sheet is a snapshot of your financial position in a moment in time. Refer to Table 14.6 to assist you in listing your assets, liabilities, and owner's equity.

The last financial statement, the cash flow statement, is the most important one to a bank. It is a measure of your ability to get and repay the loan from the bank. Referring to Table 14.7, be as realistic as possible as you are completing it. Allow yourself enough cash on hand until the point in which the business starts to support itself.

# See for Yourself Videocase

## The Accounting Function at Goodwill Industries International Inc.

Goodwill Industries International Inc. consists of a network of 165 independent, community-based organizations located throughout the United States and Canada. The mission of this nonprofit is to enhance the lives of individuals, families, and communities "through learning and the power of work." Local Goodwill stores sell donated goods and then donate the proceeds to fund job training programs, placement services, education, and more. Despite its nonprofit status, Goodwill establishments are in many ways run similar to for-profit businesses. One of these similarities involves the accounting function.

Like for-profit firms, nonprofit organizations like Goodwill must provide detailed information about how they are using the donations that are provided to them. Indeed, fraud can occur just as easily at a nonprofit organization as for a for-profit company, making it necessary for nonprofits to reassure stakeholders that they are using their funds legitimately. Additionally, donors want to know how much of their donations is going toward activities such as job creation and how much is going toward operational and administrative expenses. It sometimes surprises people that nonprofits use part of the funds they receive for operational costs. Yet such a perspective fails to see that nonprofits must also pay for electricity, rent, wages, and other services.

"We have revenue and support for the revenue pieces, and then we have direct and indirect expenses for our program services, and then we have G and A, general administrative services. And we have what's called the bottom line, or other people call net profit. We have what's called net change in assets. The concept is pretty much the same as far as accounting," says Jeff McGraw, CFO of Goodwill.

Goodwill creates the equivalent of a balance sheet and income statement. Yet because Goodwill is a nonprofit entity, its financials are known by the names *statement of financial position and statement of activities*. These financials have some differences compared to financial statements of for-profit companies. For instance, Goodwill's statement of financial position does not have shareholder's equity but instead has net assets.

The organization's financials are audited, and stakeholders can find the firm's information in form 990 through Goodwill's public website (form 990 is the IRS form for nonprofits).

Because Goodwill sells goods at its stores, the company must also figure in costs of goods sold. In fact, most of the organization's revenue comes from its store activities. In the most recent year, the retail division or sale of donated goods and contributed goods generated $3.53 billion. The contracts division generated $636 million, which provides custodial, janitorial, and lawn maintenance service contracts to government agencies. Grants from foundations, corporations, individuals, and government account for $148 million. The fact that Goodwill is able to generate much of its own funding through store activities and contracts is important. Many nonprofits that rely solely on donated funds find it hard to be sustainable in the long run, particularly during economic downturns.

Remember that even though nonprofits are different from for-profit companies, they must still make certain that their financial information is accurate. This requires nonprofit accountants to be meticulous and thorough in gathering and analyzing information. Like all accountants, accountants at Goodwill record transactions in journals and then carefully review the information before it is recorded in the general ledger. The organization uses trial balances to ensure that everything balances out, as well as advanced software to record transactions, reconcile any discrepancies, and provide an idea of how much cash the organization has on hand.

Finally, Goodwill uses ratio analysis to determine the financial health of the company. For instance, the common ratio allows Goodwill to determine how much revenue it brings in for every dollar it spends on costs. The organization also uses ratio analysis to compare its results to similar organizations. It is important for Goodwill to identify the best performers in its field so that it can generate ideas and even form partnerships with other organizations. By using accounting to identify how best to use its resources, Goodwill is advancing its mission of helping others.[12]

## Discussion Questions

1. What are some similarities between the type of accounting performed at Goodwill compared to accounting at for-profit companies?

2. What are some differences between the type of accounting performed at Goodwill compared to accounting at for-profit companies?

3. How can Goodwill use ratio analysis to improve its operations?

**You can find the related video in the Video Library in Connect. Ask your instructor how you can access Connect.**

# Team Exercise

You can look at websites such as Yahoo! Finance (http://finance.yahoo.com/), under the company's "key statistics" link, to find many of its financial ratios, such as return on assets and return on equity. Have each member of your team look up a different company, and explain why you think there are differences in the ratio analysis for these two ratios among the selected companies.

# 15

# Money and the Financial System

## Learning Objectives

**After reading this chapter, you will be able to:**

**LO 15-1** Define *money*, its functions, and its characteristics.

**LO 15-2** Describe various types of money.

**LO 15-3** Specify how the Federal Reserve Board manages the money supply and regulates the American banking system.

**LO 15-4** Compare and contrast commercial banks, savings and loan associations, credit unions, and mutual savings banks.

**LO 15-5** Distinguish among nonbanking institutions such as insurance companies, pension funds, mutual funds, and finance companies.

**LO 15-6** Investigate the challenges ahead for the banking industry.

**LO 15-7** Recommend the most appropriate financial institution for a hypothetical small business.

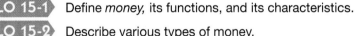

## The Good and the Bad of a Cashless Society

The rise of alternative payment methods is making people wonder whether our future is headed toward a cashless society. Such a society would involve further development and integration of technology, big data, and cashless payment methods. However, we see evidence of this occurring with the use of virtual money and payment methods such as Bitcoin, PayPal, and Mastercard's Paypass. More than 80 percent of consumer transactions in the United States are electronic, and Sweden estimates that only 3 percent of its transactions are made with actual currency.

Critics feel that a cashless society could be used to control consumer purchasing. For instance, algorithms are currently used to alert debit and credit card users of fraud. While these technologies protect customers, Visa and MasterCard are also using them to prohibit credit and debit transactions in online gambling, even if it is not illegal. Could this type of consumer regulation be applied to all purchases? For example, if an overweight person tries to purchase a sugary drink, could data about the person be used to deny the purchase? While this might seem to be a way to protect consumers from bad decision making, it also limits consumer choice.

On the other hand, there are many advantages. Governments support the idea of a cashless society because it eliminates the cost of printing money and makes monetary policy easier. It can save consumers in costs as well. People lose approximately $200 billion through various ATM fees, theft, and taxes. Controls can be used to protect electronic currency and guard against theft, perhaps leading to less crime. There is still one major benefit for using cash, however. Psychological research has shown that people tend to make wiser purchasing decisions when they use cash over any other payment method.[1]

# Introduction

From Wall Street to Main Street, both overseas and at home, money is the one tool used to measure personal and business income and wealth. **Finance** is the study of money: how it's made, how it's lost, and how it's managed. This chapter introduces you to the role of money and the financial system in the economy. Of course, if you have a checking account, automobile insurance, a college loan, or a credit card, you already have personal experience with some key players in the financial world.

We begin our discussion with a definition of money and then explore some of the many forms money may take. Next, we examine the roles of the Federal Reserve Board and other major institutions in the financial system. Finally, we explore the future of the finance industry and some of the changes likely to occur over the course of the next several years.

# Money in the Financial System

Strictly defined, **money,** or *currency,* is anything generally accepted in exchange for goods and services. Materials as diverse as salt, cattle, fish, rocks, shells, cloth, as well as precious metals such as gold, silver, and copper have long been used by various cultures as money. Most of these materials were limited-supply commodities that had their own value to society (for example, salt can be used as a preservative and shells and metals as jewelry). The supply of these commodities therefore determined the supply of "money" in that society. The next step was the development of "IOUs," or slips of paper that could be exchanged for a specified supply of the underlying commodity. "Gold" notes, for instance, could be exchanged for gold, and the money supply was tied to the amount of gold available. While paper money was first used in North America in 1685 (and even earlier in Europe), the concept of *fiat money*—a paper money not readily convertible to a precious metal such as gold—did not gain full acceptance until the Great Depression in the 1930s. The United States abandoned its gold-backed currency standard largely in response to the Great Depression and converted to a fiduciary, or fiat, monetary system. In the United States, paper money is really a government "note" or promise, worth the value specified on the note.

## Functions of Money

No matter what a particular society uses for money, its primary purpose is to enable a person or organization to transform a desire into an action. These desires may be for entertainment actions, such as party expenses; operating actions, such as paying for rent, utilities, or employees; investing actions, such as buying property or equipment; or financing actions, such as for starting or growing a business. Money serves three important functions: as a medium of exchange, a measure of value, and a store of value.

**Medium of Exchange.**   Before fiat money, the trade of goods and services was accomplished through *bartering*—trading one good or service for another of similar value. As any school-age child knows, bartering can become quite inefficient— particularly in the case of complex, three-party transactions involving peanut butter sandwiches, baseball cards, and hair barrettes. There had to be a simpler way, and that was to decide on a single item—money—that can be freely converted to any other good upon agreement between parties.

**Measure of Value.**    As a measure of value, money serves as a common standard or yardstick of the value of goods and services. For example, $2 will buy a dozen large eggs and $25,000 will buy a nice car in the United States. In Japan, where the currency is known as the yen, these same transactions would cost about 185 yen and 2.3 million yen, respectively. Money, then, is a common denominator that allows people to compare the different goods and services that can be consumed on a particular income level. While a star athlete and a "burger-flipper" are paid vastly different wages, each uses money as a measure of the value of their yearly earnings and purchases.

**Store of Value.**    As a store of value, money serves as a way to accumulate wealth (buying power) until it is needed. For example, a person making $1,000 per week who wants to buy a $500 computer could save $50 per week for each of the next 10 weeks. Unfortunately, the value of stored money is directly dependent on the health of the economy. If, due to rapid inflation, all prices double in one year, then the purchasing power value of the money "stuffed in the mattress" would fall by half. On the other hand, deflation occurs when prices of goods fall. Deflation might seem like a good thing for consumers, but in many ways it can be just as problematic as inflation. Periods of major deflation often lead to decreases in wages and increases in debt burdens.[2] Deflation also tends to be an indicator of problems in the economy. Deflation use indicates a very slow growth or shrinking economy with high unemployment and falling prices. Over the past 25 years, we have seen deflation in Japan and more recently Ireland in 2009.

For centures, people on the Micronesian island of Yap have used giant round stones, like the ones shown here, for money. The stones aren't moved, but their ownership can change.

## Characteristics of Money

To be used as a medium of exchange, money must be acceptable, divisible, portable, stable in value, durable, and difficult to counterfeit.

**Acceptability.**    To be effective, money must be readily acceptable for the purchase of goods and services and for the settlement of debts. Acceptability is probably the most important characteristic of money: If people do not trust the value of money, businesses will not accept it as a payment for goods and services, and consumers will have to find some other means of paying for their purchases.

**Divisibility.**    Given the widespread use of quarters, dimes, nickels, and pennies in the United States, it is no surprise that the principle of divisibility is an important one. With barter, the lack of divisibility often makes otherwise preferable trades impossible, as would be an attempt to trade a steer for a loaf of bread. For money to serve effectively as a measure of value, all items must be valued in terms of comparable units—dimes for a piece of bubble gum, quarters for laundry machines, and dollars (or dollars and coins) for everything else.

**Portability.**    Clearly, for money to function as a medium of exchange, it must be easily moved from one location to the next. Large colored rocks could be used as money, but you couldn't carry them around in your wallet. Paper currency and metal coins, on the other hand, are capable of transferring vast purchasing power into small, easily carried (and hidden!) bundles. Few Americans realize it, but more U.S. currency is in circulation outside the United States than within. Currently, about $1.280 trillion of U.S. currency is in circulation, and the majority is held outside the United States.[3] Some countries, such as Panama, even use the U.S. dollar as their currency. Retailers in other countries often state prices in dollars and in their local currency.

**Stability.**    Money must be stable and maintain its declared face value. A $10 bill should purchase the same amount of goods or services from one day to the next. The principle of stability allows people who wish to postpone purchases and save their money to do so without fear that it will decline in value. As mentioned earlier, money declines in value during periods of inflation, when economic conditions cause prices to rise. Thus, the same amount of money buys fewer and fewer goods and services. In some countries, people spend their money as fast as they can in order to keep it from losing any more of its value. Instability destroys confidence in a nation's money and its ability to store value and serve as an effective medium of exchange. Ultimately, people faced with spiraling price increases avoid the increasingly worthless paper money at all costs, storing all of their savings in the form of real assets such as gold and land.

**Durability.**    Money must be durable. The crisp new dollar bills you trade at the music store for the hottest new Blu-ray movie will make their way all around town for about six years before being replaced (see Table 15.1). Were the value of an old, faded bill to fall in line with the deterioration of its appearance, the principles of stability and universal acceptability would fail (but, no doubt, fewer bills would pass through the washer!). Although metal coins, due to their much longer useful life, would appear to be an ideal form of money, paper currency is far more portable than metal because of its light weight. Today, coins are used primarily to provide divisibility.

### TABLE 15.1    Life Expectancy of Money
**How long is the life span of U.S. paper money?**

When currency is deposited with a Federal Reserve Bank, the quality of each note is evaluated by sophisticated processing equipment. Notes that meet our strict quality criteria—that is, they are still in good condition—continue to circulate, while those that do not are taken out of circulation and destroyed. This process determines the life span of a Federal Reserve note.

Life span varies by denomination. One factor that influences the life span of each denomination is how the denomination is used by the public. For example, $100 notes are often used as a store of value. This means that they pass between users less frequently than lower denominations that are more often used for transactions, such as $5 notes. Thus, $100 notes typically last longer than $5 notes.

| Denomination | Estimated Life Span* |
|---|---|
| $ 1 | 5.9 years |
| $ 5 | 4.9 years |
| $ 10 | 4.2 years |
| $ 20 | 7.7 years |
| $ 50 | 3.7 years |
| $100 | 15.0 years |

*Estimated life spans as of December 2012. Because the $2 note does not widely circulate, we do not publish its estimated life span.

Source: Board of Governors of the Federal Reserve System, "How Long Is the Life Span of U.S. Paper Money?" www.federalreserve.gov/faqs/how-long-is-the-life-span-of-us-paper-money.htm (accessed June 12, 2014).

The U.S. government redesigns currency to stay ahead of counterfeiters and protect the public.

**Difficulty to Counterfeit.**    Finally, to remain stable and enjoy universal acceptance, it almost goes without saying that money must be very difficult to counterfeit—that is, to duplicate illegally. Every country takes steps to make counterfeiting difficult. Most use multicolored money, and many use specially watermarked papers that are virtually impossible to duplicate. Counterfeit bills represent less than 0.03 percent of the currency in circulation in the United States,[5] but it is becoming increasingly easy for counterfeiters to print money. This illegal printing of money is fueled by hundreds of people who often circulate only small amounts of counterfeit bills. To thwart the problem of counterfeiting, the U.S. Treasury Department redesigned the U.S. currency, starting with the $20 bill in 2003, the $50 bill in 2004, the $10 bill in 2006, the $5 bill in 2008, and the $100 bill in 2010. For the first time, U.S. money includes subtle colors in addition to the traditional green, as well as enhanced security features, such as a watermark, security thread, and color-shifting ink.[6] Although counterfeiting is not as much of an issue with coins, U.S. metal coins are usually worth more for the metal than their face value. It has begun to cost more to manufacture coins than what they are worth monetarily.

> **DID YOU KNOW?** Around 75 percent of counterfeit currency is found and destroyed before it ever reaches the public.[4]

As Table 15.2 indicates, it costs more than a penny to manufacture a penny, resulting in a call to discontinue it. Because it costs more to produce pennies and nickels than what they are worth, these coins have generated losses of $573.5 million in a seven-year period.[7] The redeeming feature of printing money is that the U.S. mint makes money on dimes, quarters, and dollars. Also, it only costs 5.4 cents to make a $1 bill and 10.2 cents to make a $20 or $50 bill. So what the U.S. Mint loses on pennies and nickels, the Treasury makes up on paper money.

## Types of Money

While paper money and coins are the most visible types of money, the combined value of all of the printed bills and all of the minted coins is actually rather insignificant when compared with the value of money kept in checking accounts, savings accounts, and other monetary forms.

**TABLE 15.2**
**Costs to Produce Pennies and Nickels**

| Fiscal Year | Cent Unit Cost (¢) | Nickel Unit Cost (¢) | Revenue from Coins (millions) |
|---|---|---|---|
| 2013 | 1.83 | 9.40 | ($104.5) |
| 2012 | 1.99 | 10.1 | ($109.2) |
| 2011 | 2.41 | 11.18 | ($116.70) |
| 2010 | 1.79 | 9.22 | ($42.60) |
| 2009 | 1.62 | 6.03 | ($22.00) |
| 2008 | 1.42 | 8.83 | ($47.00) |
| 2007 | 1.67 | 9.53 | ($98.60) |
| 2006 | 1.21 | 5.97 | ($32.90) |
| Total | | | ($573.5) |

Source: Various annual reports of the U.S. Mint.

**checking account**
money stored in an account at a bank or other financial institution that can be withdrawn without advance notice; also called a demand deposit

　　You probably have a **checking account** (also called a *demand deposit*), money stored in an account at a bank or other financial institution that can be withdrawn without advance notice. One way to withdraw funds from your account is by writing a *check,* a written order to a bank to pay the indicated individual or business the amount specified on the check from money already on deposit. Figure 15.1 explains the significance of the numbers found on a typical U.S. check. As legal instruments, checks serve as a substitute for currency and coins and are preferred for many transactions

**FIGURE 15.1　A Check**

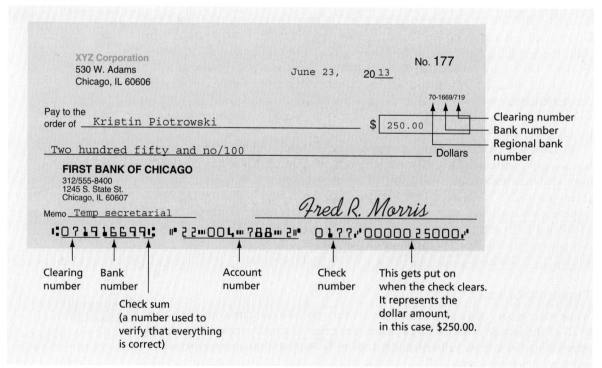

due to their lower risk of loss. If you lose a $100 bill, anyone who finds or steals it can spend it. If you lose a blank check, however, the risk of catastrophic loss is quite low. Not only does your bank have a sample of your signature on file to compare with a suspected forged signature, but you can render the check immediately worthless by means of a stop-payment order at your bank.

There are several types of checking accounts, with different features available for different monthly fee levels or specific minimum account balances. Some checking accounts earn interest (a small percentage of the amount deposited in the account that the bank pays to the depositor). One such interest-bearing checking account is the *NOW (Negotiable Order of Withdrawal) account* offered by most financial institutions. The interest rate paid on such accounts varies with the interest rates available in the economy but is typically quite low (more recently less than 1 percent but in the past between 2 and 5 percent).

**Savings accounts** (also known as *time deposits*) are accounts with funds that usually cannot be withdrawn without advance notice and/or have limits on the number of withdrawals per period. While seldom enforced, the "fine print" governing most savings accounts prohibits withdrawals without two or three days' notice. Savings accounts are not generally used for transactions or as a medium of exchange, but their funds can be moved to a checking account or turned into cash.

**Money market accounts** are similar to interest-bearing checking accounts, but with more restrictions. Generally, in exchange for slightly higher interest rates, the owner of a money market account can write only a limited number of checks each month, and there may be a restriction on the minimum amount of each check.

**Certificates of deposit (CDs)** are savings accounts that guarantee a depositor a set interest rate over a specified interval of time as long as the funds are not withdrawn before the end of the interval—six months, one year, or seven years, for example. Money may be withdrawn from these accounts prematurely only after paying a substantial penalty. In general, the longer the term of the CD, the higher is the interest rate it earns. As with all interest rates, the rate offered and fixed at the time the account is opened fluctuates according to economic conditions.

**Credit cards** allow you to promise to pay at a later date by using preapproved lines of credit granted by a bank or finance company. They are a popular substitute for cash payments because of their convenience, easy access to credit, and acceptance by merchants around the world. The institution that issues the credit card guarantees payment of a credit charge to merchants and assumes responsibility for collecting the money from the cardholders. Card issuers charge a transaction fee to the merchants for performing the credit check, guaranteeing the payment, and collecting the payment. The fee is typically between 2 and 5 percent, depending on the type of card. American Express fees are usually higher than Visa and MasterCard.

The original American Express cards require full payment at the end of each month, but American Express now offers credit cards similar

**savings accounts** accounts with funds that usually cannot be withdrawn without advance notice; also known as time deposits

**money market accounts** accounts that offer higher interest rates than standard bank rates but with greater restrictions

**certificates of deposit (CDs)** savings accounts that guarantee a depositor a set interest rate over a specified interval as long as the funds are not withdrawn before the end of the period—six months or one year, for example

**credit cards** means of access to preapproved lines of credit granted by a bank or finance company

Credit cards have many advantages, including being able to buy expensive items and pay them off a little at a time. However, this can easily lead an individual to incur spiraling credit card debt that is hard to pay off.

to Visa, MasterCard, and Discover that allow cardholders to make installment payments and carry a maximum balance. There is a minimum monthly payment with interest charged on the remaining balance. Some people pay off their credit cards monthly, while other make monthly payments. Charges for unpaid balances can run 18 percent or higher at an annual rate, making credit card debt one of the most expensive ways to borrow money.

Besides the major credit card companies, many stores—Target, Saks Fifth Avenue, Macy's, Bloomingdales, Sears, and others—have their own branded credit cards. They use credit rating agencies to check the credit of the cardholders and they generally make money on the finance charges.

The Credit CARD (Card Accountability Responsibility and Disclosure) Act of 2009 was passed to regulate the practices of credit card companies. Without going into the details, the law limited the ability of card issuers to raise interest rates, limited credit to young adults, gave people more time to pay bills, required that if there were various levels of interest rates that the balances with the highest rate would be paid off first, and made clearer due dates on billing cycles, along with several other provisions. For college students, the most important part of the law is that young adults under the age of 21 will have to have an adult co-signer or show proof that they have enough income to handle the debt limit on the card.

This act is important to all companies and cardholders. Research indicates that approximately 40 percent of lower- and middle-income households use credit cards to pay for basic necessities. Yet there is also good news. The average credit card debt for lower- and middle-income households has decreased in recent years. On the other hand, studies also show that college students tend to lack the financial literacy needed to understand credit cards and their requirements. Approximately 90 percent of college students with credit cards have credit card debt. Therefore, vulnerable segments of the population such as college students should be careful about which credit cards to choose and how often they use them.[8]

**debit card**
a card that looks like a credit card but works like a check; using it results in a direct, immediate, electronic payment from the cardholder's checking account to a merchant or third party

A **debit card** looks like a credit card but works like a check. The use of a debit card results in a direct, immediate, electronic payment from the cardholder's checking account to a merchant or other party. While they are convenient to carry and profitable for banks, they lack credit features, offer no purchase "grace period," and provide no hard "paper trail." Debit cards are gaining more acceptance with merchants, and consumers like debit cards because of the ease of getting cash from an increasing number of ATM machines. Financial institutions also want consumers to use debit cards because they reduce the number of teller transactions and check processing costs. Some cash management accounts at retail brokers like Merrill Lynch offer deferred debit cards. These act like a credit card but debit to the cash management account once a month. During that time, the cash earns a money market return.

Traveler's checks, money orders, and cashier's checks are other common forms of "near money." Although each is slightly different from the others, they all share a common characteristic: A financial institution, bank, credit company, or neighborhood currency exchange issues them in exchange for cash and guarantees that the purchased note will be honored and exchanged for cash when it is presented to the institution making the guarantee.

**Credit Card Fraud.** More and more computer hackers have managed to steal credit card information and either use the information for Internet purchases or actually make a card exactly the same as the stolen card. The most significant breach was at Target, where the retail giant lost the information for more than 40 million credit cards to hackers. Losses on credit card theft run into the billions, but consumers are usually not liable for the losses. However, consumers should be careful with debit cards because once the money is out of the account, the bank and credit card companies cannot get it back. Debit cards do not have the same level of protection as credit cards.

# The American Financial System

The U.S. financial system fuels our economy by storing money, fostering investment opportunities, and making loans for new businesses and business expansion as well as for homes, cars, and college educations. This amazingly complex system includes banking institutions, nonbanking financial institutions such as finance companies, and systems that provide for the electronic transfer of funds throughout the world. Over the past 20 years, the rate at which money turns over, or changes hands, has increased exponentially. Different cultures place unique values on saving, spending, borrowing, and investing. The combination of this increased turnover rate and increasing interactions with people and organizations from other countries has created a complex money system. First, we need to meet the guardian of this complex system.

## The Federal Reserve System

The guardian of the American financial system is the **Federal Reserve Board,** or "the Fed," as it is commonly called, an independent agency of the federal government established in 1913 to regulate the nation's banking and financial industry. The Federal Reserve System is organized into 12 regions, each with a Federal Reserve Bank that serves its defined area (Figure 15.2). All the Federal Reserve banks except those in Boston and Philadelphia have regional branches. The Cleveland Federal Reserve Bank, for example, is responsible for branch offices in Pittsburgh and Cincinnati.

**Federal Reserve Board**
an independent agency of the federal government established in 1913 to regulate the nation's banking and financial industry

The Federal Reserve Board is the chief economic policy arm of the United States. Working with Congress and the president, the Fed tries to create a positive economic environment capable of sustaining low inflation, high levels of employment, a balance in international payments, and long-term economic growth. To this end, the Federal Reserve Board has four major responsibilities: (1) to control the supply of money, or monetary policy; (2) to regulate banks and other financial institutions; (3) to manage regional and national checking account procedures, or check clearing; and (4) to supervise the federal deposit insurance programs of banks belonging to the Federal Reserve System.

**Monetary Policy.**    The Fed controls the amount of money available in the economy through **monetary policy.** Without this intervention, the supply of and demand for money might not balance. This could result in either rapid price increases (inflation) because of too little money or economic recession and a slowdown of price increases (disinflation) because of too little growth in the money supply. In very rare cases (the depression of the 1930s) the United States has suffered from deflation, when the actual purchasing power of the dollar has increased as prices declined. To effectively control the supply of money in the economy, the Fed must have a good idea of how much money is in circulation at any given time. This has become increasingly challenging because the global nature of our economy means that more and more U.S. dollars are circulating overseas. Using several different measures of the money supply, the Fed establishes specific growth targets which, presumably, ensure a close balance between money supply and money demand. The

**monetary policy**
means by which the Fed controls the amount of money available in the economy

**FIGURE 15.2    Federal Reserve System**

| | |
|---|---|
| ▬▬▬ Boundaries of Federal Reserve Districts | ○ Federal Reserve Bank Cities |
| —— Boundaries of Federal Reserve Branch Territories | ● Federal Reserve Branch Cities |
| ● Board of Governors of the Federal Reserve System | ■ Federal Reserve Bank Facility |

Fed fine-tunes money growth by using four basic tools: open market operations, reserve requirements, the discount rate, and credit controls (see Table 15.3). There is generally a lag of 6 to 18 months before the effect of these charges shows up in economic activity.

**open market operations**
decisions to buy or sell U.S. Treasury bills (short-term debt issued by the U.S. government) and other investments in the open market

**Open market operations** refer to decisions to buy or sell U.S. Treasury bills (short-term debt issued by the U.S. government; also called T-bills) and other investments in the open market. The actual purchase or sale of the investments is performed by the New York Federal Reserve Bank. This monetary tool, the most commonly employed of all Fed operations, is performed almost daily in an effort to control the money supply.

When the Fed buys securities, it writes a check on its own account to the seller of the investments. When the seller of the investments (usually a large bank) deposits the check, the Fed transfers the balance from the Federal Reserve account into the seller's account, thus increasing the supply of money in the economy and, hopefully, fueling economic growth. The opposite occurs when the Fed sells investments. The buyer writes a check to the Federal Reserve, and when the funds are transferred out of the purchaser's account, the amount of money in circulation falls, slowing economic growth to a desired level.

**TABLE 15.3**
**Fed Tools for Regulating the Money Supply**

| Activity | Effect on the Money Supply and the Economy |
|---|---|
| Buy government securities | The money supply increases; economic activity increases. |
| Sell government securities | The money supply decreases; economic activity slows down. |
| Raise discount rate | Interest rates increase; the money supply decreases; economic activity slows down. |
| Lower discount rate | Interest rates decrease; the money supply increases; economic activity increases. |
| Increase reserve requirements | Banks make fewer loans; the money supply declines; economic activity slows down. |
| Decrease reserve requirements | Banks make more loans; the money supply increases; economic activity increases. |
| Relax credit controls | More people are encouraged to make major purchases, increasing economic activity. |
| Restrict credit controls | People are discouraged from making major purchases, decreasing economic activity. |

The second major monetary policy tool is the **reserve requirement,** the percentage of deposits that banking institutions must hold in reserve ("in the vault," as it were). Funds so held are not available for lending to businesses and consumers. For example, a bank holding $10 million in deposits, with a 10 percent reserve requirement, must have reserves of $1 million. If the Fed were to reduce the reserve requirement to, say, 5 percent, the bank would need to keep only $500,000 in reserves. The bank could then lend to customers the $500,000 difference between the old reserve level and the new lower reserve level, thus increasing the supply of money. Because the reserve requirement has such a powerful effect on the money supply, the Fed does not change it very often, relying instead on open market operations most of the time.

The third monetary policy tool, the **discount rate,** is the rate of interest the Fed charges to loan money to any banking institution to meet reserve requirements. The Fed is the lender of last resort for these banks. When a bank borrows from the Fed, it is said to have borrowed at the "discount window," and the interest rates charged there are often higher than those charged on loans of comparable risk elsewhere in the economy. This added interest expense, when it exists, serves to discourage banks from borrowing from the Fed.

When the Fed wants to expand the money supply, it lowers the discount rate to encourage borrowing. Conversely, when the Fed wants to decrease the money supply, it raises the discount rate. The increases in interest rates that occurred in the United States from 2003 through 2006 were the result of more than 16 quarter-point (0.25 percent) increases in the Fed discount rate. The purpose was to keep inflation under control and to raise rates to a more normal level as the economy recovered from the recession of 2001. During the most recent recession, which started in 2007, the Fed lowered interest rates to nearly zero in order to encourage borrowing. In an environment where credit markets were nearly frozen, the Fed utilized monetary policy to stimulate spending. Not surprisingly, economists watch changes in this sensitive interest rate as an indicator of the Fed's monetary policy.

**reserve requirement**
the percentage of deposits that banking institutions must hold in reserve

**discount rate**
the rate of interest the Fed charges to loan money to any banking institution to meet reserve requirements

**connect**

Need help understanding how the Federal Reserve Tries to Stablize the Economy? Visit your Connect ebook video tab for a brief animated explanation.

**credit controls**
the authority to establish and enforce credit rules for financial institutions and some private investors

The final tool in the Fed's arsenal of weapons is **credit controls**—the authority to establish and enforce credit rules for financial institutions and some private investors. For example, the Fed can determine how large a down payment individuals and businesses must make on credit purchases of expensive items such as automobiles, and how much time they have to finish paying for the purchases. By raising and lowering minimum down payment amounts and payment periods, the Fed can stimulate or discourage credit purchases of "big ticket" items. The Fed also has the authority to set the minimum down payment investors must use for the credit purchases of stock. Buying stock with credit—"buying on margin"—is a popular investment strategy among individual speculators. By altering the margin requirement (currently set at 50 percent of the price of the purchased stocks), the Fed can effectively control the total amount of credit borrowing in the stock market.

**Regulatory Functions.**   The second major responsibility of the Fed is to regulate banking institutions that are members of the Federal Reserve System. Accordingly, the Fed establishes and enforces banking rules that affect monetary policy and the overall level of the competition between different banks. It determines which non-banking activities, such as brokerage services, leasing, and insurance, are appropriate for banks and which should be prohibited. The Fed also has the authority to approve or disapprove mergers between banks and the formation of bank holding companies. In an effort to ensure that all rules are enforced and that correct accounting procedures are being followed at member banks, surprise bank examinations are conducted by bank examiners each year.

**Check Clearing.**   The Federal Reserve provides national check processing on a huge scale. Divisions of the Fed known as check clearinghouses handle almost all the checks written against a bank in one city and presented for deposit to a bank in a second city. Any banking institution can present the checks it has received from others around the country to its regional Federal Reserve Bank. The Fed passes the checks to the appropriate regional Federal Reserve Bank, which then sends the checks to the issuing bank for payment. With the advance of electronic payment systems and the passage of the Check Clearing for the 21st Century Act (Check 21 Act), checks can now be processed in a day. The Check 21 Act allows banks to clear checks electronically by presenting an electronic image of the check. This eliminates mail delays and time-consuming paper processing.

**Depository Insurance.**   The Fed is also responsible for supervising the federal insurance funds that protect the deposits of member institutions. These insurance funds will be discussed in greater detail in the following section.

## Banking Institutions

Banking institutions accept money deposits from and make loans to individual consumers and businesses. Some of the most important banking institutions include commercial banks, savings and loan associations, credit unions, and mutual savings banks. Historically, these have all been separate institutions. However, new hybrid forms of banking institutions that perform two or more of these functions have emerged over the past two decades. The following all have one thing in common: They are businesses whose objective is to earn money by managing, safeguarding, and lending money to others. Their sales revenues come from the fees and interest that they charge for providing these financial services.

**Commercial Banks.** The largest and oldest of all financial institutions are **commercial banks,** which perform a variety of financial services. They rely mainly on checking and savings accounts as their major source of funds and use only a portion of these deposits to make loans to businesses and individuals. Because it is unlikely that all the depositors of any one bank will want to withdraw all of their funds at the same time, a bank can safely loan out a large percentage of its deposits.

JPMorgan Chase is the second-largest commercial bank in the United States behind Bank of America.

**commercial banks**
the largest and oldest of all financial institutions, relying mainly on checking and savings accounts as sources of funds for loans to businesses and individuals

Today, banks are quite diversified and offer a number of services. Commercial banks make loans for virtually any conceivable legal purpose, from vacations to cars, from homes to college educations. Banks in many states offer *home equity loans,* by which home owners can borrow against the appraised value of their already purchased homes. Banks also issue Visa and MasterCard credit cards and offer CDs and trusts (legal entities set up to hold and manage assets for a beneficiary). Many banks rent safe deposit boxes in bank vaults to customers who want to store jewelry, legal documents, artwork, and other valuables. In 1999, Congress passed the Financial Services Modernization Act, also known as the Gramm-Leach-Bliley Bill. This act repealed the Glass Steagall Act, which was enacted in 1929 after the stock market crash and prohibited commercial banks from being in the insurance and investment banking business. This puts U.S. commercial banks on the same competitive footing as European banks and provides a more level playing field for global banking competition. As commercial banks and investment banks have merged, the financial landscape has changed. Consolidation remains the norm in the U.S. banking industry. The financial crisis and the economic recession that began in 2007 and lasted into 2012 only accelerated the consolidation as large, healthy banks ended up buying weak banks that were in trouble. JPMorgan Chase bought Wachovia and the investment bank Bear Stearns; Wells Fargo bought Washington Mutual; PNC bought National City Bank; and Bank of America bought Countrywide Credit and Merrill Lynch. Most of these purchases were made with financial help from the U.S. Treasury and Federal Reserve. By 2012, the banks had paid back their loans, but the financial meltdown exposed some high-risk activities in the banking industry that Congress wanted to curtail. The result was the passage of the Dodd-Frank Act. This act added many new regulations, but the two most important changes raised the required capital banks had to hold on their balance sheet and limited certain types of high-risk trading activities.

**Savings and Loan Associations.** Savings and loan associations (S&Ls), often called "thrifts," are financial institutions that primarily offer savings accounts and make long-term loans for residential mortgages. A mortgage is a loan made so that a business or individual can purchase real estate, typically a home; the real estate itself is pledged as a guarantee (called *collateral*) that the buyer will repay the loan. If the loan is not repaid, the savings and loan has the right to repossess the property. Prior to the 1970s, S&Ls focused almost exclusively on real estate lending and accepted only savings accounts. Today, following years of regulatory changes, S&Ls compete directly with commercial banks by offering many types of services.

**savings and loan associations (S&Ls)**
financial institutions that primarily offer savings accounts and make long-term loans for residential mortgages; also called "thrifts"

## Banks Increase Investment in Sustainability

What does banking have to do with green technology? If companies such as Bank of America, Goldman Sachs, and Wells Fargo have their way, banks will be seen as major supporters of sustainability. Banks not only want to incorporate greener processes into their operations, but they are also investing in green technology initiatives. For instance, in addition to reducing its paper and energy consumption, Bank of America is investing in projects that focus on areas such as water reduction and energy conservation. Goldman Sachs has pledged $40 billion toward solar, wind, energy storage, and transportation initiatives.

Wells Fargo has set lofty goals for the year 2020. The company announced that it was pledging $30 billion toward green technologies, increasing its own operational sustainability, and pledging $100 million in grants for grassroots environmental projects. In reducing its own environmental footprint, Wells Fargo plans to decrease its greenhouse gas emissions by 35 percent over 2008

levels. Although these initiatives will cost Wells Fargo in the short term, the company believes that sustainability is the future of business. In interacting with customers in an online forum, Wells Fargo found that 80 percent valued environmental commitment on the part of businesses. By investing in greener initiatives, banks such as Wells Fargo and Bank of America could create competitive advantages through better customer relationships and a more positive reputation.[9]

### Discussion Questions

1. Discuss some of the ways in which banks are investing in sustainability.
2. What are the advantages of investing in sustainability? The disadvantages?
3. Do you think Wells Fargo's sustainability goals represent a genuine commitment, or are they more window-dressing to make the company look good?

---

Savings and loans have gone through a metamorphosis since the early 1990s, after having almost collapsed in the 1980s. Today, many of the largest savings and loans have merged with commercial banks. This segment of the financial services industry plays a diminished role in the mortgage lending market.

**credit union**
a financial institution owned and controlled by its depositors, who usually have a common employer, profession, trade group, or religion

**Credit Unions.**    A **credit union** is a financial institution owned and controlled by its depositors, who usually have a common employer, profession, trade group, or religion. The Aggieland Credit Union in College Station, Texas, for example, provides banking services for faculty, employees, and current and former students of Texas A&M University. A savings account at a credit union is commonly referred to as a share account, while a checking account is termed a share draft account. Because the credit union is tied to a common organization, the members (depositors) are allowed to vote for directors and share in the credit union's profits in the form of higher interest rates on accounts and/or lower loan rates.

While credit unions were originally created to provide depositors with a short-term source of funds for low-interest consumer loans for items such as cars, home appliances, vacations, and college, today they offer a wide range of financial services. Generally, the larger the credit union, the more sophisticated its financial service offerings will be.

**mutual savings banks**
financial institutions that are similar to savings and loan associations but, like credit unions, are owned by their depositors

**Mutual Savings Banks.**    **Mutual savings banks** are similar to savings and loan associations, but, like credit unions, they are owned by their depositors. Among the oldest financial institutions in the United States, they were originally established to provide a safe place for savings of particular groups of people, such as fishermen. Found mostly in New England, they are becoming more popular in the rest of the country as some S&Ls have converted to mutual savings banks to escape the stigma created by the widespread S&L failures in the 1980s.

## Insurance for Banking Institutions.

The **Federal Deposit Insurance Corporation (FDIC),** which insures individual bank accounts, was established in 1933 to help stop bank failures throughout the country during the Great Depression. Today, the FDIC insures personal accounts up to a maximum of $250,000 at nearly 8,000 FDIC member institutions.[10] While most major banks are insured by the FDIC, small institutions in some states may be insured by state insurance funds or private insurance companies. Should a member bank fail, its depositors can recover all of their funds, up to $250,000. Amounts over $250,000, while not legally covered by the insurance, are in fact usually covered because the Fed understands very well the enormous damage that would result to the financial system should these large depositors withdraw their money. When the financial crisis occurred, the FDIC increased the deposit insurance amount from $100,000 to $250,000 on a temporary basis to increase consumer confidence in the banking system. The Wall Street Reform and Consumer Protection Act passed on July 21, 2010, made the $250,000 insurance per account permanent. The *Federal Savings and Loan Insurance Corporation (FSLIC)* insured thrift deposits prior to its insolvency and failure during the S&L crisis of the 1980s. Now, the insurance functions once overseen by the FSLIC are handled directly by the FDIC through its Savings Association Insurance Fund. The **National Credit Union Administration (NCUA)** regulates and charters credit unions and insures their deposits through its National Credit Union Insurance Fund.

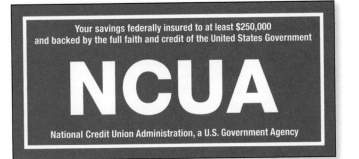

The National Credit Union Administration has the important job of regulating and chartering credit unions and insuring their deposits through its National Credit Union Insurance Fund.

**Federal Deposit Insurance Corporation (FDIC)**
an insurance fund established in 1933 that insures individual bank accounts

**National Credit Union Administration (NCUA)**
an agency that regulates and charters credit unions and insures their deposits through its National Credit Union Insurance Fund

When they were originally established, Congress hoped that these insurance funds would make people feel secure about their savings so that they would not panic and withdraw their money when news of a bank failure was announced. The "bank run" scene in the perennial Christmas movie *It's a Wonderful Life,* when dozens of Bailey Building and Loan depositors attempted to withdraw their money (only to have the reassuring figure of Jimmy Stewart calm their fears), was not based on mere fiction. During the Great Depression, hundreds of banks failed and their depositors lost everything. The fact that large numbers of major financial institutions failed in the 1980s and 1990s—without a single major banking panic—underscores the effectiveness of the current insurance system. Large bank failures occurred once again during the most recent recession. According to the FDIC, 474 banks failed between January 2009 and May 31, 2014. Compare this to 52 failures between January 2000 and December 31, 2008, and you can grasp the impact of the financial crisis and long-lasting recession. For the March 2014 ending quarter, the FDIC reported that the number of problem banks had declined for 12 quarters in a row. This reflects an improving economy and a healthier financial system. It is safe to say that most depositors go to sleep every night without worrying about the safety of their savings.

## Nonbanking Institutions

Nonbank financial institutions offer some financial services, such as short-term loans or investment products, but do not accept deposits. These include insurance companies, pension funds, mutual funds, brokerage firms, nonfinancial firms, and finance companies. Table 15.4 lists some other diversified financial services firms.

**TABLE 15.4**
**Leading Diversified Financial Services Firms**

| | 2013 Assets (in millions) |
|---|---|
| JPMorgan Chase | $2,415,666 |
| Citigroup Inc. | 1,880,382 |
| Ameriprise | 144,576 |
| American Express | 71,601 |
| Visa | 35,956 |
| AON | 30,251 |
| Invesco | 19,271 |
| Marsh & McLennan | 16,980 |
| Apollo Investment Corp. | 3,642 |

Source: S&P Capital IQ reports.

**Diversified Firms.**   There are many nonfinancial firms that help finance their customers' purchases of expensive equipment. For example, Caterpillar (construction equipment), Boeing (airplanes), and General Electric (jet engines and locomotives) help their customers finance these large-scale expensive purchases through their finance subsidiaries. At one time, General Electric's credit subsidiary accounted for 40 percent of the company's revenues, but this is slowly falling as the company divests itself of consumer credit operations. Automobile companies such as Ford and General Motors have also traditionally had credit subsidiaries to help customers finance their cars.

**insurance companies**
businesses that protect their clients against financial losses from certain specified risks (death, accident, and theft, for example)

**Insurance Companies.**   **Insurance companies** are businesses that protect their clients against financial losses from certain specified risks (death, injury, disability, accident, fire, theft, and natural disasters, for example) in exchange for a fee, called a premium. Because insurance premiums flow into the companies regularly, but major insurance losses cannot be timed with great accuracy (though expected risks can be assessed with considerable precision), insurance companies generally have large amounts of excess funds. They typically invest these or make long-term loans, particularly to businesses in the form of commercial real estate loans.

**pension funds**
managed investment pools set aside by individuals, corporations, unions, and some nonprofit organizations to provide retirement income for members

**Pension Funds.**   **Pension funds** are managed investment pools set aside by individuals, corporations, unions, and some nonprofit organizations to provide retirement income for members. One type of pension fund is the *individual retirement account (IRA),* which is established by individuals to provide for their personal retirement needs. IRAs can be invested in a variety of financial assets, from risky commodities such as oil or cocoa to low-risk financial "staples" such as U.S. Treasury securities. The choice is up to each person and is dictated solely by individual objectives and tolerance for risk. The interest earned by all of these investments may be deferred tax-free until retirement.

In 1997, Congress revised the IRA laws and created a Roth IRA. Although similar to a traditional IRA in that investors may contribute $5,500 per year, the money in a Roth IRA is considered an after-tax contribution. Workers over 50 can add an extra $1,000, but in all cases, if you make too much money, you cannot fund a Roth. When the money is withdrawn at retirement, no tax is paid on the distribution. The Roth

IRA is beneficial to young people who can allow a long time for their money to compound and who may be able to have their parents or grandparents fund the Roth IRA with gift money.

Most major corporations provide some kind of pension plan for their employees. Many of these are established with bank trust departments or life insurance companies. Money is deposited in a separate account in the name of each individual employee, and when the employee retires, the total amount in the account can be either withdrawn in one lump sum or taken as monthly cash payments over some defined time period (usually for the remaining life of the retiree).

Social Security, the largest pension fund, is publicly financed. The federal government collects Social Security funds from payroll taxes paid by both employers and employees. The Social Security Administration then takes these monies and makes payments to those eligible to receive Social Security benefits—the retired, the disabled, and the young children of deceased parents.

State Farm Insurance allows users to input their information on its website to receive an auto insurance quote quickly and conveniently.

**Mutual Funds.**   A **mutual fund** pools individual investor dollars and invests them in large numbers of well-diversified securities. Individual investors buy shares in a mutual fund in the hope of earning a high rate of return and in much the same way as people buy shares of stock. Because of the large numbers of people investing in any one mutual fund, the funds can afford to invest in hundreds (if not thousands) of securities at any one time, minimizing the risks of any single security that does not do well. Mutual funds provide professional financial management for people who lack the time and/or expertise to invest in particular securities, such as government bonds. While there are no hard-and-fast rules, investments in one or more mutual funds are one way for people to plan for financial independence at the time of retirement.

**mutual fund**
an investment company that pools individual investor dollars and invests them in large numbers of well-diversified securities

A special type of mutual fund called a *money market fund* invests specifically in short-term debt securities issued by governments and large corporations. Although they offer services such as check-writing privileges and reinvestment of interest income, money market funds differ from the money market accounts offered by banks primarily in that the former represent a pool of funds, while the latter are basically specialized, individual checking accounts. Money market funds usually offer slightly higher rates of interest than bank money market accounts.

**Brokerage Firms and Investment Banks.**   **Brokerage firms** buy and sell stocks, bonds, and other securities for their customers and provide other financial services. Larger brokerage firms like Merrill Lynch, Charles Schwab, and Edward Jones offer financial services unavailable at their smaller competitors. Merrill Lynch, for example, offers the Merrill Lynch Cash Management Account (CMA), which pays interest on deposits and allows clients to write checks, borrow money, and withdraw cash much like a commercial bank. The largest of the brokerage firms (including Merrill Lynch) have developed so many specialized services that they may be considered financial networks—organizations capable of offering virtually all of the services

**brokerage firms**
firms that buy and sell stocks, bonds, and other securities for their customers and provide other financial services

### Unregulated Bitcoin Industry Has Regulators Worried

Bitcoin is a digital currency that can be used to make purchases without the use of cash, credit, or debit cards. Bitcoins are not backed by the government, not circulated by banks or other intermediaries, and not currently taxed. Bitcoin transactions are public, but users often use pseudonyms that are difficult to track to the real person. The increasing use of Bitcoin has generated ethical concerns, especially because it is an unregulated industry. This can lead to issues such as the ability to purchase illegal substances and firearms as well as being susceptible to fraud and theft. Users place their trust in other users when making purchases via Bitcoin, which increases the risk of using it. Additionally, because it is not backed by anything of credibility, its value is much more volatile.

While the use of Bitcoin is generally online, there are some brick-and-mortar locations that have set up a system to receive payments with Bitcoin. Authorities are investigating ways to regulate digital currencies to guard against money laundering and to protect investors and consumers who use it. Interestingly, Bitcoin sparked enough interest in investors to be traded on Mt Gox, a Tokyo-based exchange. However, Bitcoin was dealt a blow after Mt Gox lost 850,000 Bitcoins to a hacking attack (although it says it recovered 200,000), resulting in bankruptcy for the firm and numerous lawsuits. The threat of hacking is obviously an underappreciated risk for Bitcoin as a digital currency. Also, regulators worry that without boundaries, the nascent digital currency industry may lose viability.[11]

#### Discussion Questions

1. How does Bitcoin differ from other forms of currency?
2. What are some of the ethical concerns involved with Bitcoin?
3. Why do you think investors are interested in Bitcoin?

---

traditionally associated with commercial banks. The rise of online brokerage firms has helped investors who want to do it themselves at low costs. Firms like E-Trade, TDAmeritrade, and Scottrade offer investors the ability to buy and sell securities for $7 to $10 per trade, while the same trade at Morgan Stanley might cost $125. E-Trade offers banking services, debit cards, wire transfers, and many of the same services that the traditional brokerage firms offer.

Most brokerage firms are really part financial conglomerates that provide many different kinds of services besides buying and selling securities for clients. For example, Merrill Lynch also is an investment banker, as are Morgan Stanley and Goldman Sachs. The **investment banker** underwrites new issues of securities for corporations, states, and municipalities needed to raise money in the capital markets. The new issue market is called a *primary market* because the sale of the securities is for the first time. After the first sale, the securities trade in the *secondary markets* by brokers. The investment banker advises on the price of the new securities and generally guarantees the sale while overseeing the distribution of the securities through the selling brokerage houses. Investment bankers also act as dealers who make markets in securities. They do this by offering to sell the securities at an asked price (which is a higher rate) and buy the securities at a bid price (which is a lower rate)—the difference in the two prices represents the profit for the dealer.

**investment banker**
underwrites new issues of securities for corporations, states, and municipalities

**Finance Companies.** **Finance companies** are businesses that offer short-term loans at substantially higher rates of interest than banks. Commercial finance companies make loans to businesses, requiring their borrowers to pledge assets such as equipment, inventories, or unpaid accounts as collateral for the loans. Consumer finance companies make loans to individuals. Like commercial finance companies, these firms require some sort of personal collateral as security against the borrower's possible inability to repay their loans. Because of the high interest rates they charge and other factors, finance

**finance companies**
businesses that offer short-term loans at substantially higher rates of interest than banks

companies typically are the lender of last resort for individuals and businesses whose credit limits have been exhausted and/or those with poor credit ratings.

## Electronic Banking

Since the advent of the computer age, a wide range of technological innovations has made it possible to move money all across the world electronically. Such "paperless" transactions have allowed financial institutions to reduce costs in what has been, and continues to be, a virtual competitive battlefield. **Electronic funds transfer (EFT)** is any movement of funds by means of an electronic terminal, telephone, computer, or magnetic tape. Such transactions order a particular financial institution to subtract money from one account and add it to another. The most commonly used forms of EFT are automated teller machines, automated clearinghouses, and home banking systems.

**electronic funds transfer (EFT)**
any movement of funds by means of an electronic terminal, telephone, computer, or magnetic tape

**Automated Teller Machines.**    Probably the most familiar form of electronic banking is the **automated teller machine (ATM),** which dispenses cash, accepts deposits, and allows balance inquiries and cash transfers from one account to another. ATMs provide 24-hour banking services—both at home (through a local bank) and far away (via worldwide ATM networks such as Cirrus and Plus). Rapid growth, driven by both strong consumer acceptance and lower transaction costs for banks (about half the cost of teller transactions), has led to the installation of hundreds of thousands of ATMs worldwide. Table 15.5 presents some interesting statistics about ATMs.

**automated teller machine (ATM)**
the most familiar form of electronic banking, which dispenses cash, accepts deposits, and allows balance inquiries and cash transfers from one account to another

**Automated Clearinghouses.**    **Automated clearinghouses (ACHs)** permit payments such as deposits or withdrawals to be made to and from a bank account by magnetic computer tape. Most large U.S. employers, and many others worldwide, use ACHs to deposit their employees' paychecks directly to the employees' bank accounts. While direct deposit is used by only 50 percent of U.S. workers, nearly 100 percent of Japanese workers and more than 90 percent of European workers utilize it. The largest user of automated clearinghouses in the United States is the federal government, with 99 percent of federal government employees and 65 percent of the private workforce receiving their pay via direct deposit. More than 82 percent of all Social Security payments are made through an ACH system. The Social Security Administration is trying to reduce costs and reduce theft and fraud, so if you apply for Social Security benefits on or after May 1, 2011, you must receive your payments electronically.

**automated clearinghouses (ACHs)**
a system that permits payments such as deposits or withdrawals to be made to and from a bank account by magnetic computer tape

**TABLE 15.5**
**Facts about ATM Use**

| |
|---|
| There are 2.2 million ATM machines currently in use. |
| The average cash withdrawal from ATMs is $60. |
| The typical ATM consumer will visit an ATM 7.4 times per month. |
| The total ratio of people per ATM machine is 3,000:1. |
| ATM users spend approximately 23 percent more than non-ATM users. |
| The top ATM owners are Cardtronics, Payment Alliance, Bank of America, JPMorgan Chase, and Wells Fargo. |

*Source: Lenpenzo, Trends Today, "ATM Machines Statistics," March 2, 2012, www.statisticbrain.com/atm-machine-statistics/ (accessed June 12, 2014).*

The advantages of direct deposits to consumers include convenience, safety, and potential interest earnings. It is estimated that more than 4 million paychecks are lost or stolen annually, and FBI studies show that 2,000 fraudulent checks are cashed every day in the United States. Checks can never be lost or stolen with direct deposit. The benefits to businesses include decreased check-processing expenses and increased employee productivity. Research shows that businesses that use direct deposit can save more than $1.25 on each payroll check processed. Productivity could increase by $3 to $5 billion annually if all employees were to use direct deposit rather than taking time away from work to deposit their payroll checks.

Some companies also use ACHs for dividend and interest payments. Consumers can also use ACHs to make periodic (usually monthly) fixed payments to specific creditors without ever having to write a check or buy stamps. The estimated number of bills paid annually by consumers is 20 billion, and the total number paid through ACHs is estimated at only 8.5 billion. The average consumer who writes 10 to 15 checks each month would save $41 to $62 annually in postage alone.[12]

Computers and handheld devices have made online banking extremely convenient. However, hackers have stolen millions from banking customers by tricking them into visiting websites and downloading malicious software that gives hackers access to their passwords.

**Online Banking.**   Many banking activities are now conducted on a computer at home or at work, or through wireless devices such as cell phones and PDAs anywhere there is a wireless "hot point." Consumers and small businesses can now make a bewildering array of financial transactions at home or on the go 24 hours a day. Functioning much like a vast network of personal ATMs, companies like Google and Apple provide online banking services through mobile phones, allowing subscribers to make sophisticated banking transactions, buy and sell stocks and bonds, and purchase products and airline tickets without ever leaving home or speaking to another human being. Many banks allow customers to log directly into their accounts to check balances, transfer money between accounts, view their account statements, and pay bills via home computer or other Internet-enabled devices. Computer and advanced telecommunications technology have revolutionized world commerce; 62 percent of adults list Internet banking as their preferred banking method, making it the most popular banking method in the United States.[13]

## Future of Banking

Rapid advances and innovations in technology are challenging the banking industry and requiring it to change. As we said earlier, more and more banks, both large and small, are offering electronic access to their financial services. ATM technology is rapidly changing, with machines now dispensing more than just cash. Online financial services, ATM technology, and bill presentation are just a few of the areas where rapidly changing technology is causing the banking industry to change as well.

## Square Inc. Introduces the Square Stand

**Business:** Square Inc.

**Founder:** Jack Dorsey

**Founded:** 2009, in San Francisco, California

**Success:** Square, *Fast Company's* fifth most innovative company of 2012, has released a new product to complement the iPad and its Square Register point-of-sale app.

In an effort to change the way customers pay for goods, Twitter founder Jack Dorsey has delivered a digital cash register. The Square Stand, paired with the Square Register app, is a piece of hardware that allows Google Android and Apple IOS operating systems to become a point-of-sale system for many businesses. With technology moving at a rapid pace,

it was only a matter of time before an iPad became a cash register.

The Square Stand enables the built-in card reader to connect with other accessories that allow businesses to print receipts and scan bar codes. With the advertised quick setup, Square claims that you can get your hardware up and running in just minutes. The swiveling stand is priced at $299. The Square Stand will allow businesses an easy and affordable way to grow and manage their business. With this innovative device, Square Stand is aiming to change the payment industry for good.[14]

---

**Impact of Financial Crisis.**   The premise that banks will get bigger over the next 10 years is uncertain. During 2007–2008, the financial markets collapsed under the weight of declining housing prices, subprime mortgages (mortgages with low-qualifying borrowers), and risky securities backed by these subprime mortgages. Because the value of bank assets declined dramatically, most large banks like CitiBank, Bank of America, and Wachovia had a shrinking capital base. That is, the amount of debt in relation to their equity was so high that they were below the minimum required capital requirements.

During this period, the Federal Reserve took unprecedented actions that included buying up troubled assets from the banks and lending money at the discount window to nonbanks such as investment banks and brokers. The Fed also entered into the financial markets by making markets in commercial paper and other securities where the markets had ceased to function in an orderly fashion. Additionally, the Fed began to pay interest on reserves banks kept at the Fed and finally, it kept interest rates low to stimulate the economy and to help the banks regain their health. Because banks make money by the spread between their borrowing and lending rates, the Fed managed the spread between long- and short-term rates to generate a fairly large spread for the banks.

Additionally, to keep interest rates low and stimulate the economy, the Fed bought $85 billion of mortgages and other financial assets on a monthly basis. By mid-2014, it had accumulated close to $4 trillion of securities on its balance sheet and was beginning to taper off its asset purchases as the economy improved. A major issue involves the impact this will have on the economy once the Fed begins to sell these securities.

Lastly, the future of the structure of the banking system is in the hands of the U.S. Congress. In reaction to the financial meltdown and severe recession, Congress passed the Dodd-Frank Wall Street Reform and Consumer Protection Act. The full name implies that the intent of the act is to eliminate the ability of banks to create this type of problem in the future.

**Shadow Banking.**   In broad general terms, shadow banking refers to companies performing banking functions of some sort that are not regulated by banking regulators. All the types of financial institutions listed on pages 471 through 474 can be considered shadow banks under this definition. Shadow banking activities are increasing. In a letter to shareholders in the 2013 annual report, Jamie Dimon, CEO and chairman of JPMorgan Chase, was quoted as saying to his shareholders that the bank will face tough competitors, including shadow banking. He may have said it best in the following quote.

> Many of these institutions are smart and sophisticated and will benefit as banks move out of certain products and services. Non-bank financial competitors will look at every product we price, and if they can do it cheaper with their set of capital providers, they will. There is nothing inherently wrong with this—it is a natural state of affairs and, in some cases, may benefit the clients who get the better price. But regulators should—and will—be looking at how all financial companies (including non-bank competitors) need to be regulated and will be evaluating what is better to be done by banks vs. non-banks and vice versa.[15]

In addition to shadow banks mentioned by Mr. Dimon, there are the peer-to-peer lenders like Prosper, a company that matches investors and borrowers with loans of between $2,000 and $35,000. There are other sources of funding by Internet websites such as GoFundMe, which helps people enhance their life skills, raise money for health care issues, and more. Another similar website is Kickstarter, which funds creative projects in the worlds of art, film, games, music, publishing, and so on. In many cases, funds provided for these projects replace loans that might have been used to develop the project. These forms of funding are growing rapidly. Kickstarter was formed in October 2009 and has already received a total of $1.15 billion to fund more than 63,000 projects. There is also the budding use of virtual money and other futuristic ideas, so only time will tell how the world of banking changes over time and how bank regulators will deal with these nonbank institutions.

# So You're Interested in Financial Systems or Banking

You think you might be interested in going into finance or banking, but it is so hard to tell when you are a full-time student. Classes that seem interesting when you take them might not translate in an interesting work experience after you graduate. A great way to see if you would excel at a career in finance is to get some experience in the industry. Internships, whether they are paid or unpaid, not only help you figure out what you might really want to do after you graduate but they are also a great way to build up your résumé, put your learning to use, and start generating connections within the field.

For example, Pennsylvania's Delaware County District Attorney's Office has been accepting business students from Villanova University for a six-month internship. The student works in the economic-crime division, analyzing documents of people under investigation for financial crimes ranging from fraud to money laundering. The students get actual experience in forensic accounting and have the chance to see whether this is the right career path. On top of that, the program has saved the county an average of $20,000 annually on consulting and accounting fees, not to mention that detectives now have more time to take on larger caseloads. One student who completed the program spent his six months investigating a case in which the owner of a sewage treatment company had embezzled a total of $1 million over the course of nine years. The student noted that the experience helped him gain an understanding about how different companies handle their financial statements, as well as how accounting can be applied in forensics and law enforcement.

Internship opportunities are plentiful all over the country, although you may need to do some research to find them. To start, talk to your program advisor and your professors about opportunities. Also, you can check company websites where you think you might like to work to see if they have any opportunities available. City, state, or federal government offices often provide student internships as well. No matter where you end up interning, the real-life skills you pick up, as well as the résumé boost you get, will be helpful in finding a job after you graduate. When you graduate, commercial banks and other financial institutions offer major employment opportunities. In 2008–2009, a major downturn in the financial industry resulted in mergers, acquisitions, and financial restructuring for many companies. While the immediate result was a decrease in job opportunities, as the industry recovers, there will be many challenging job opportunities available.[16]

# Review Your Understanding

### Define *money,* its functions, and its characteristics.

Money is anything generally accepted as a means of payment for goods and services. Money serves as a medium of exchange, a measure of value, and a store of wealth. To serve effectively in these functions, money must be acceptable, divisible, portable, durable, stable in value, and difficult to counterfeit.

### Describe various types of money.

Money may take the form of currency, checking accounts, or other accounts. Checking accounts are funds left in an account in a financial institution that can be withdrawn (usually by writing a check) without advance notice. Other types of accounts include savings accounts (funds left in an interest-earning account that usually cannot be withdrawn without advance notice), money market accounts (an interest-bearing checking account that is invested in short-term debt instruments), certificates of deposit (deposits left in an institution for a specified period of time at a specified interest rate), credit cards (access to a preapproved line of credit granted by a bank or company), and debit cards (means of instant cash transfers between customer and merchant accounts), as well as traveler's checks, money orders, and cashier's checks.

### Specify how the Federal Reserve Board manages the money supply and regulates the American banking system.

The Federal Reserve Board regulates the U.S. financial system. The Fed manages the money supply by buying and selling government securities, raising or lowering the discount rate (the rate of interest at which banks may borrow cash reserves from the Fed), raising or lowering bank reserve requirements (the percentage of funds on deposit at a bank that must be held to cover expected depositor withdrawals), and adjusting down payment and repayment terms for credit purchases. It also regulates banking practices, processes checks, and oversees federal depository insurance for institutions.

### Compare and contrast commercial banks, savings and loan associations, credit unions, and mutual savings banks.

Commercial banks are financial institutions that take and hold deposits in accounts for and make loans to individuals and businesses. Savings and loan associations are financial institutions that primarily specialize in offering savings accounts and mortgage loans. Credit unions are financial institutions

479

owned and controlled by their depositors. Mutual savings banks are similar to S&Ls except that they are owned by their depositors.

### Distinguish among nonbanking institutions such as insurance companies, pension funds, mutual funds, and finance companies.

Insurance companies are businesses that protect their clients against financial losses due to certain circumstances, in exchange for a fee. Pension funds are investments set aside by organizations or individuals to meet retirement needs. Mutual funds pool investors' money and invest in large numbers of different types of securities. Brokerage firms buy and sell stocks and bonds for investors. Finance companies make short-term loans at higher interest rates than do banks.

### Investigate the challenges ahead for the banking industry.

Future changes in financial regulations are likely to result in fewer but larger banks and other financial institutions.

### Recommend the most appropriate financial institution for a hypothetical small business.

Using the information presented in this chapter, you should be able to answer the questions in "Solve the Dilemma" on page 481 and find the best institution for Hill Optometrics.

## Revisit the World of Business

1. What are some positive implications of a cashless society?

2. What could be some disadvantages to a cashless society?

3. Why do you think using cash is more effective for making wiser purchasing decisions?

## Learn the Terms

automated clearinghouses (ACHs)  475
automated teller machine (ATM)  475
brokerage firms  473
certificates of deposit (CDs)  463
checking account  462
commercial banks  469
credit cards  463
credit controls  468
credit union  470
debit card  464
discount rate  467

electronic funds transfer (EFT)  475
Federal Deposit Insurance
  Corporation (FDIC)  471
Federal Reserve Board  465
finance  458
finance companies  474
insurance companies  472
investment banker  474
monetary policy  465
money  458
money market accounts  463

mutual fund  473
mutual savings banks  470
National Credit Union
  Association (NCUA)  471
open market operations  466
pension funds  472
reserve requirement  467
savings accounts  463
savings and loan
  associations (S&Ls)  469

## Check Your Progress

1. What are the six characteristics of money? Explain how the U.S. dollar has those six characteristics.

2. What is the difference between a credit card and a debit card? Why are credit cards considerably more popular with U.S. consumers?

3. Discuss the four economic goals the Federal Reserve must try to achieve with its monetary policy.

4. Explain how the Federal Reserve uses open market operations to expand and contract the money supply.

5. What are the basic differences between commercial banks and savings and loans?

6. Why do credit unions charge lower rates than commercial banks?

7. Why do finance companies charge higher interest rates than commercial banks?

8. How are mutual funds, money market funds, and pension funds similar? How are they different?

9. What are some of the advantages of electronic funds transfer systems?

# Get Involved

1. Survey the banks, savings and loans, and credit unions in your area, and put together a list of interest rates paid on the various types of checking accounts. Find out what, if any, restrictions are in effect for NOW accounts and regular checking accounts. In which type of account and in what institution would you deposit your money? Why?

2. Survey the same institutions as in question one, this time inquiring as to the rates asked for each of their various loans. Where would you prefer to obtain a car loan? A home loan? Why?

# Build Your Skills

## Managing Money

### Background

You have just graduated from college and have received an offer for your dream job (annual salary: $35,000). This premium salary is a reward for your hard work, perseverance, and good grades. It is also a reward for the social skills you developed in college doing service work as a tutor for high school students and interacting with the business community as the program chairman of the college business fraternity, Delta Sigma Pi. You are engaged and plan to be married this summer. You and your spouse will have a joint income of $60,000, and the two of you are trying to decide the best way to manage your money.

### Task

Research available financial service institutions in your area, and answer the following questions.

1. What kinds of institutions and services can you use to help manage your money?

2. Do you want a full service financial organization that can take care of your banking, insurance, and investing needs or do you want to spread your business among individual specialists? Why have you made this choice?

3. What retirement alternatives do you have?

# Solve the Dilemma      `LO 15-7`

## Seeing the Financial Side of Business

Dr. Stephen Hill, a successful optometrist in Indianapolis, Indiana, has tinkered with various inventions for years. Having finally developed what he believes is his first saleable product (a truly scratch-resistant and lightweight lens), Hill has decided to invest his life savings and open Hill Optometrics to manufacture and market his invention.

Unfortunately, despite possessing true genius in many areas, Hill is uncertain about the "finance side" of business and the various functions of different types of financial institutions in the economy. He is, however, fully aware that he will need financial services such as checking and savings accounts, various short-term investments that can easily and quickly be converted to cash as needs dictate, and sources of borrowing capacity—should the need for either short- or long-term loans arise.

Despite having read mounds of brochures from various local and national financial institutions, Hill is still somewhat unclear about the merits and capabilities of each type of financial institution. He has turned to you, his 11th patient of the day, for help.

### Discussion Questions

1. List the various types of U.S. financial institutions and the primary function of each.

2. What services of each financial institution is Hill's new company likely to need?

3. Which single financial institution is likely to be best able to meet Hill's small company's needs now? Why?

# Build Your Business Plan

## Money and the Financial System

This chapter provides you with the opportunity to think about money and the financial system and just how many new businesses fail every year. In some industries, the failure rate is as high as 80 percent. One reason for such a high failure rate is the inability to manage the finances of the organization. From the start of the business, financial planning plays a key role. Try getting a loan without an accompanying budget/forecast of earnings and cash flow.

While obtaining a loan from a family member may be the easiest way to fund your business, it may cause more problems for you later on if you are unable to pay the money back as scheduled. Before heading to a lending officer at a bank, contact your local SBA center to see what assistance it might provide.

# See for Yourself Videocase

## Controversy over Bank Lending Policies

The last financial crisis affected people and businesses in different ways, including the temporary restriction of credit both for businesses and individuals. As the recent recession worsened, banks turned inward and significantly reduced or stopped lending money, and businesses began having difficulty accessing credit. Bank credit usually falls under a business's notes payable or long-term debt. This increases liabilities on the balance sheet because businesses must pay off this debt over a certain time period. A company that depends too much on credit might incur long-term debt that it will be unable to pay off, resulting in bankruptcy. However, during the recession, the opposite problem occurred: a severe reduction in credit and loans.

While credit does result in debt, it is usually necessary in order for small business owners to have the necessary funds available to start a business. Indeed, small business owners were among those most affected by the loss of credit, which in turn harmed the economy. It is estimated that the United States alone supports 23 million small businesses, making up roughly 54 percent of all U.S. sales. Many small businesses that rely on credit to survive were forced to lay off employees or shut down altogether, resulting in the loss of hundreds of thousands of jobs.

The main roadblock that faced people seeking these types of loans was their credit score. Banks hesitated to lend to anyone with a credit score of less than 700 out of 850, while the average credit score hovers around 680. Financial experts advise individuals to focus on improving their credit scores as a critical component of financial security. Additionally, a healthy amount of current assets that are liquid—easily converted to cash—is advisable for businesses, which can then use this cash to pay for inventory, equipment, or debt in case credit becomes unavailable.

Now that the United States appears to be in a recovery, one would think that bank lending would increase. However, this is not necessarily the case. Bank loans and leases are lower than they were in 2008. This decrease in lending is occurring for several reasons. At the four largest banks—Wells Fargo, Bank of America, JPMorgan Chase, and Citigroup—lending has fallen significantly. Interestingly, regulation might be one of the reasons for the decrease. Due to increased regulation, large banks feel pressured to get rid of their risky loans. This bodes ill for large banks but is good for smaller regional banks that are not subject to these regulatory requirements. The extension of credit at smaller banks has gone up. Small banks may be closer to their customers and can better assess risk, especially in areas such as small business loans and real estate. Many large banks have to manage risks on a global basis.

Another potential theory for why banks are not lending is that they are provided with an incentive not to lend. Some economists believe that because the Fed is paying banks interest on their reserves, these interest payments are convincing banks to hold more money in reserve. Every bank is required to hold a certain amount of money in reserve as a form of protection. Traditionally, banks want to hold as little in reserve as necessary because money that is in reserve cannot earn income. However, in 2008 the Fed began to pay interest on reserves. Could this be one reason why banks are not extending as much credit?

Banks themselves claim otherwise. They state that the reason that they are not extending as much credit is due to lack of demand. Nonbanking financial institutions such as insurance companies, finance companies, and venture capital firms are extending loans to businesses globally. These financial institutions are called shadow banks and now represent an estimated 25 percent of all business loans. Therefore, perhaps banks should share some of the blame for not being more aggressive in making loans to businesses that have had to go to other financial institutions to acquire the credit they need to operate. Of course, as recovery gains strength, it is possible that by the time you read this, banks may be lending more but facing increasing competition from shadow banks[17].

**Discussion Questions**

1. While it does involve taking on debt, why is credit so important for businesses to function?

2. How do you think people can improve their credit scores in order to look more attractive for loans?

3. How might a lack of demand for business credit affect the economy?

You can find the related video in the Video Library in Connect. Ask your instructor how you can access Connect.

# Team Exercise

Mutual funds pool individual investor dollars and invest them in a number of different securities. Go to **http://finance.yahoo.com/** and select some top-performing funds using criteria such as sector, style, or strategy. Assume that your group has $100,000 to invest in mutual funds. Select five funds in which to invest, representing a balanced (varied industries, risk, etc.) portfolio, and defend your selections.

# 16

# Financial Management and Securities Markets

## Learning Objectives

**After reading this chapter, you will be able to:**

**LO 16-1** Describe some common methods of managing current assets.

**LO 16-2** Identify some sources of short-term financing (current liabilities).

**LO 16-3** Summarize the importance of long-term assets and capital budgeting.

**LO 16-4** Specify how companies finance their operations and manage fixed assets with long-term liabilities, particularly bonds.

**LO 16-5** Discuss how corporations can use equity financing by issuing stock through an investment banker.

**LO 16-6** Describe the various securities markets in the United States.

**LO 16-7** Critique the position of short-term assets and liabilities of a small manufacturer, and recommend corrective action.

## Chapter Outline

## Standard & Poor's Defends Ratings

Credit rating agencies are facing regulatory scrutiny for actions leading up to the 2008–2009 financial crisis. The fallout was partially due to the buying and selling of complex, high-risk financial instruments such as mortgage-backed collateralized debt obligations (CDOs). When the housing boom collapsed, firms were unable to pay their debt obligations. Standard & Poor's, Moody's Investors Services, and Fitch Ratings are three major credit rating agencies, holding approximately 95 percent of the market share. Credit rating agencies provide investors with a credible and accurate evaluation of the risk of debt securities. These agencies use a letter system to denote the riskiness of the financial instrument, and investors depend upon these ratings to make investment decisions.

The U.S. government has sued Standard & Poor's for $5 billion, alleging that it rated CDOs higher than they should have been. According to allegations, the credit rating agencies were paid by the debt issuers for their ratings, creating an incentive for the agencies to give these securities high ratings. Of the approximately 75 percent of the debt securities rated at AAA (the highest rating), more than 70 percent of them defaulted. Some argue that investors need to conduct their own due diligence rather than relying on ratings. However, because these financial instruments are so complex, investors depend on credit rating agencies to know the specifics of each individual loan in the portfolio.

In defense, the agencies argue that committees determine ratings rather than individual analysts and compensation is not dependent upon ratings. They claim that being paid by the banks is not a conflict of interest and the credibility of ratings lies in the transparency of the models used by raters.[1]

# Introduction

While it's certainly true that money makes the world go around, financial management is the discipline that makes the world turn more smoothly. Indeed, without effective management of assets, liabilities, and owners' equity, all business organizations are doomed to fail—regardless of the quality and innovativeness of their products. Financial management is the field that addresses the issues of obtaining and managing the funds and resources necessary to run a business successfully. It is not limited to business organizations: All organizations, from the corner store to the local nonprofit art museum, from giant corporations to county governments, must manage their resources effectively and efficiently if they are to achieve their objectives.

In this chapter, we look at both short- and long-term financial management. First, we discuss the management of short-term assets, which companies use to generate sales and conduct ordinary day-to-day business operations. Next we turn our attention to the management of short-term liabilities, the sources of short-term funds used to finance the business. Then, we discuss the management of long-term assets such as plants, equipment, and the use of common stock (equity) and bonds (long-term liability) to finance these long-term corporate assets. Finally, we look at the securities markets, where stocks and bonds are traded.

# Managing Current Assets and Liabilities

**working capital management**
the managing of short-term assets and liabilities

Managing short-term assets and liabilities involves managing the current assets and liabilities on the balance sheet (discussed in Chapter 14). Current assets are short-term resources such as cash, investments, accounts receivable, and inventory. Current liabilities are short-term debts such as accounts payable, accrued salaries, accrued taxes, and short-term bank loans. We use the terms *current* and *short term* interchangeably because short-term assets and liabilities are usually replaced by new assets and liabilities within three or four months, and always within a year. Managing short-term assets and liabilities is sometimes called **working capital management** because short-term assets and liabilities continually flow through an organization and are thus said to be "working."

## Managing Current Assets

The chief goal of financial managers who focus on current assets and liabilities is to maximize the return to the business on cash, temporary investments of idle cash, accounts receivable, and inventory.

**Managing Cash.**   A crucial element facing any financial manager is effectively managing the firm's cash flow. Remember that cash flow is the movement of money through an organization on a daily, weekly, monthly, or yearly basis. Ensuring that sufficient (but not excessive) funds are on hand to meet the company's obligations is one of the single most important facets of financial management.

**transaction balances**
cash kept on hand by a firm to pay normal daily expenses, such as employee wages and bills for supplies and utilities

Idle cash does not make money, and corporate checking accounts typically do not earn interest. As a result, astute money managers try to keep just enough cash on hand, called **transaction balances,** to pay bills—such as employee wages, supplies, and utilities—as they fall due. To manage the firm's cash and ensure that enough cash flows through the organization quickly and efficiently, companies try to speed up cash collections from customers.

## Going Green

### Finance Executives Recognize the Benefits of Method's Green Efficiencies

Method is a green company in more ways than one. Not only does it sell eco-friendly household supplies, but it also generates more than $100 million in annual revenues. Thanks to companies like Method, finance executives are beginning to realize the financial benefits of going green. At a time when the prices of commodities are rapidly fluctuating, finance executives are looking for ways to cut costs. Eco-friendly options such as decreasing energy use, using recycled materials, and reducing packaging are becoming viable methods for saving money and improving efficiency. A recent poll found that 40 percent of finance executives are increasing their facilities' efficiency through better energy management, while one-third are undertaking initiatives to increase the efficiency of their shipping, including the adoption of more fuel-efficient vehicles. Method, for instance, has significantly increased its use of biodiesel trucks, which emit 20 percent less carbon and air pollutants than traditional trucks.

Method aligns its environmental objectives with its cost-saving goals. The operations and finance departments routinely work together to look at what ingredients and processes would save money while also reducing Method's environmental impact. Sometimes, this requires the company to adopt additional costs in the short run in order to save money over the long term. Method's long-term perspective, efficient operations, and popularity with customers are catching on with competitors. It is estimated that eco-friendly household supplies consist of 30 percent of household cleaning products. And as green products and operational processes increase, Method already has a head start.[2]

#### Discussion Questions

1. If greener operations cut company costs, how will this affect a company's current assets and liabilities?
2. Why might Method decide to pursue greener business activities that are costly in the short run?
3. Do you think other household supply companies are beginning to realize how green products can improve their financial conditions?

To facilitate collection, some companies have customers send their payments to a **lockbox,** which is simply an address for receiving payments, instead of directly to the company's main address. The manager of the lockbox, usually a commercial bank, collects payments directly from the lockbox several times a day and deposits them into the company's bank account. The bank can then start clearing the checks and get the money into the company's checking account much more quickly than if the payments had been submitted directly to the company. However, there is no free lunch: The costs associated with lockbox systems make them worthwhile only for those companies that receive thousands of checks from customers each business day.

> **lockbox**
> an address, usually a commercial bank, at which a company receives payments in order to speed collections from customers

Large firms with many stores or offices around the country, such as HSBC Finance Corporation, frequently use electronic funds transfer to speed up collections. HSBC Finance Corporation's local offices deposit checks received each business day into their local banks and, at the end of the day, HSBC Finance Corporation's corporate office initiates the transfer of all collected funds to its central bank for overnight investment. This technique is especially attractive for major international companies, which face slow and sometimes uncertain physical delivery of payments and/or less-than-efficient check-clearing procedures.

More and more companies are now using electronic funds transfer systems to pay and collect bills online. Companies generally want to collect cash quickly but pay out cash slowly. When companies use electronic funds transfers between buyers and suppliers, the speed of collections and disbursements increases to one day. Only with the use of checks can companies delay the payment of cash by three or four days until the check is presented to their bank and the cash leaves their account.

**TABLE 16.1**    Short-Term Investment Possibilities for Idle Cash

| Type of Security | Maturity | Seller of Security | Interest Rate 6/23/2006 | Interest Rate 6/10/2014 | Safety Level |
|---|---|---|---|---|---|
| U.S. Treasury bills | 90 days | U.S. government | 4.80% | 0.04% | Excellent |
| U.S. Treasury bills | 180 days | U.S. government | 5.05 | 0.06 | Excellent |
| Commercial paper | 30 days | Major corporations | 5.14 | 0.09 | Very good |
| Certificates of deposit | 90 days | U.S. commercial banks | 5.40 | 0.30 | Very good |
| Certificates of deposit | 180 days | U.S. commercial banks | 5.43 | 0.35 | Very good |
| Eurodollars | 90 days | European commercial banks | 5.48 | 0.25 | Very good |

Sources: Board of Governors of the Federal Reserve System, "Selected Interest Rates (Weekly)—H.15," June 9, 2014, www.federalreserve.gov/releases/H15/current/default. htm (accessed June 10, 2014); Fidelity, "Certificates of Deposit," www.fidelity.com/fixed-income-bonds/cds (accessed June 10, 2014).

**Investing Idle Cash.**    As companies sell products, they generate cash on a daily basis, and sometimes cash comes in faster than it is needed to pay bills. Organizations often invest this "extra" cash, for periods as short as one day (overnight) or for as long as one year, until it is needed. Such temporary investments of cash are known as **marketable securities.** Examples include U.S. Treasury bills, certificates of deposit, commercial paper, and eurodollar deposits. Table 16.1 summarizes a number of different marketable securities used by businesses and some sample interest rates on these investments as of June 23, 2006, and June 10, 2014. The safety rankings are relative. While all of the listed securities are very low risk, the U.S. government securities are the safest. You can see from the table that interest rates have declined during the two periods presented.

> **marketable securities**
> temporary investment of "extra" cash by organizations for up to one year in U.S. Treasury bills, certificates of deposit, commercial paper, or eurodollar loans

You may never see interest rates this low in your lifetime. The Fed used monetary policy to lower interest rates to stimulate borrowing and investment during the severe recession of 2007–2009 and continued to maintain low rates into 2014 in order to stimulate employment and economic growth. The Fed has stated that it expects to continue with low interest rates into 2015 or even 2016, which would be unprecedented.

Many large companies invest idle cash in U.S. **Treasury bills (T-bills),** which are short-term debt obligations the U.S. government sells to raise money. Issued weekly by the U.S. Treasury, T-bills carry maturities of between one week and one year. U.S. T-bills are generally considered to be the safest of all investments and are called risk free because the U.S. government will not default on its debt.

> **Treasury bills (T-bills)**
> short-term debt obligations the U.S. government sells to raise money

**Commercial certificates of deposit (CDs)** are issued by commercial banks and brokerage companies. They are available in minimum amounts of $100,000 but are typically in units of $1 million for large corporations investing excess cash. Unlike consumer CDs (discussed in Chapter 15), which must be held until maturity, commercial CDs may be traded prior to maturity. Should a cash shortage occur, the organization can simply sell the CD on the open market and obtain needed funds.

> **commercial certificates of deposit (CDs)**
> certificates of deposit issued by commercial banks and brokerage companies, available in minimum amounts of $100,000, which may be traded prior to maturity

One of the most popular short-term investments for the largest business organizations is **commercial paper**—a written promise from one company to another to pay a specific amount of money. Because commercial paper is backed only by the name and reputation of the issuing company, sales of commercial paper are restricted to only the largest and most financially stable companies. As commercial paper is frequently

> **commercial paper**
> a written promise from one company to another to pay a specific amount of money

bought and sold for durations of as short as one business day, many "players" in the market find themselves buying commercial paper with excess cash on one day and selling it to gain extra money the following day.

During 2007 and 2008, the commercial paper market simply stopped functioning. Investors no longer trusted the IOUs of even the best companies. Companies that had relied on commercial paper to fund short-term cash needs had to turn to the banks for borrowing. Those companies who had existing lines of credit at their bank were able to draw on their line of credit. Others were in a tight spot. Eventually, the Federal Reserve entered the market to buy and sell commercial paper for its own portfolio. This is something the Fed was not in the habit of doing. But it rescued the market, and the market functioned well in the past few years.

Some companies invest idle cash in international markets such as the **eurodollar market,** a market for trading U.S. dollars in foreign countries. Because the eurodollar market was originally developed by London banks, any dollar-denominated deposit in a non-U.S. bank is called a eurodollar deposit, regardless of whether the issuing bank is actually located in Europe, South America, or anyplace else. For example, if you travel overseas and deposit $1,000 in a German bank, you will have "created" a eurodollar deposit in the amount of $1,000. Because the U.S. dollar is accepted by most countries for international trade, these dollar deposits can be used by international companies to settle their accounts. The market created for trading such investments offers firms with extra dollars a chance to earn a slightly higher rate of return with just a little more risk than they would face by investing in U.S. Treasury bills.

Individuals and companies can invest their idle cash in marketable securities such as U.S. Treasury bills, commercial paper, and eurodollar deposits.

**eurodollar market**
a market centered in London for trading U.S. dollars in foreign countries

## Maximizing Accounts Receivable.

After cash and marketable securities, the balance sheet lists accounts receivable and inventory. Remember that accounts receivable is money owed to a business by credit customers. For example, if you charge your Shell gasoline purchases, until you actually pay for them with cash or a check, they represent an account receivable to Shell. Many businesses make the vast majority of their sales on credit, so managing accounts receivable is an important task.

Each credit sale represents an account receivable for the company, the terms of which typically require customers to pay the full amount due within 30, 60, or even 90 days from the date of the sale. To encourage quick payment, some businesses offer some of their customers discounts of between 1 and 2 percent if they pay off their balance within a specified period of time (usually between 10 and 30 days). On the other hand, late payment charges of between 1 and 1.5 percent serve to discourage

Loans are important for most consumers purchasing a home or business. Interest rates have been at historic lows over the past few years but are expected to increase in the long run.

slow payers from sitting on their bills forever. The larger the early payment discount offered, the faster customers will tend to pay their accounts. Unfortunately, while discounts increase cash flow, they also reduce profitability. Finding the right balance between the added advantages of early cash receipt and the disadvantages of reduced profits is no simple matter. Similarly, determining the optimal balance between the higher sales likely to result from extending credit to customers with less than sterling credit ratings and the higher bad-debt losses likely to result from a more lenient credit policy is also challenging. Information on company credit ratings is provided by local credit bureaus, national credit-rating agencies such as Dun and Bradstreet, and industry trade groups.

**Optimizing Inventory.**    While the inventory that a firm holds is controlled by both production needs and marketing considerations, the financial manager has to coordinate inventory purchases to manage cash flows. The object is to minimize the firm's investment in inventory without experiencing production cutbacks as a result of critical materials shortfalls or lost sales due to insufficient finished goods inventories. Every dollar invested in inventory is a dollar unavailable for investment in some other area of the organization. Optimal inventory levels are determined in large part by the method of production. If a firm attempts to produce its goods just in time to meet sales demand, the level of inventory will be relatively low. If, on the other hand, the firm produces materials in a constant, level pattern, inventory increases when sales decrease and decreases when sales increase. One way that companies are optimizing inventory is through the use of radio frequency identification (RFID) technology. Companies such as Walmart better manage their inventories by using RFID tags. An RFID tag, which contains a silicon chip and an antenna, allows a company to use radio waves to track and identify the products to which the tags are attached. These tags are primarily used to track inventory shipments from the manufacturer to the buyer's warehouses and then to the individual stores and also cut down on trucking theft because the delivery truck and its contents can be tracked.

The automobile industry is an excellent example of an industry driven almost solely by inventory levels. Because it is inefficient to continually lay off workers in slow times and call them back in better times, Ford, General Motors, and Toyota try to set and stick to quarterly production quotas. Automakers typically try to keep a 60-day supply of unsold cars. During particularly slow periods, however, it is not unusual for inventories to exceed 100 days of sales.

Although less publicized, inventory shortages can be as much of a drag on potential profits as too much inventory. Not having an item on hand may send the customer to a competitor—forever. Complex computer inventory models are frequently employed to determine the optimum level of inventory a firm should hold to support a given level of sales. Such models can indicate how and when parts inventories should be ordered so that they are available exactly when required—and not a day before. Developing and maintaining such an intricate production and inventory system is difficult, but it can often prove to be the difference between experiencing average profits and spectacular ones.

## Managing Current Liabilities

While having extra cash on hand is a delightful surprise, the opposite situation—a temporary cash shortfall—can be a crisis. The good news is that there are several potential sources of short-term funds. Suppliers often serve as an important source through credit sales practices. Also, banks, finance companies, and other organizations offer short-term funds through loans and other business operations.

 LO 16-2

**Accounts Payable.**    Remember from Chapter 14 that accounts payable is money an organization owes to suppliers for goods and services. Just as accounts receivable must be actively managed to ensure proper cash collections, so too must accounts payable be managed to make the best use of this important liability.

The most widely used source of short-term financing, and therefore the most important account payable, is **trade credit**—credit extended by suppliers for the purchase of their goods and services. While varying in formality, depending on both the organizations involved and the value of the items purchased, most trade credit agreements offer discounts to organizations that pay their bills early. A supplier, for example, may offer trade terms of "1/10 net 30," meaning that the purchasing organization may take a 1 percent discount from the invoice amount if it makes payment by the 10th day after receiving the bill. Otherwise, the entire amount is due within 30 days. For example, pretend that you are the financial manager in charge of payables. You owe Ajax Company $10,000, and it offers trade terms of 2/10 net 30. By paying the amount due within 10 days, you can save 2 percent of $10,000, or $200.

**trade credit**
credit extended by suppliers for the purchase of their goods and services

Assume you place orders with Ajax once per month and have 12 bills of $10,000 each per year. By taking the discount every time, you will save 12 times $200, or $2,400, per year. Now assume you are the financial manager of Gigantic Corp., and it has monthly payables of $100 million per month. Two percent of $100 million is $2 million per month. Failure to take advantage of such trade discounts can add up to large opportunity losses over the span of a year.

**Bank Loans.**     Virtually all organizations—large and small—obtain short-term funds for operations from banks. In most instances, the credit services granted these firms take the form of a line of credit or fixed dollar loan. A **line of credit** is an ar-rangement by which a bank agrees to lend a specified amount of money to the organi-zation upon request—provided that the bank has the required funds to make the loan. In general, a business line of credit is very similar to a consumer credit card, with the exception that the preset credit limit can amount to millions of dollars.

In addition to credit lines, banks also make **secured loans**—loans backed by collateral that the bank can claim if the borrowers do not repay the loans—and **unsecured loans**—loans backed only by the borrowers' good reputation and previous credit rating. Both individuals and businesses build their credit rating from their his-tory of borrowing and repaying borrowed funds on time and in full. The three national credit-rating services are Equifax, TransUnion, and Experian. A lack of credit history or a poor credit history can make it difficult to get loans from financial institutions. The *principal* is the amount of money borrowed; *interest* is a percentage of the princi-pal that the bank charges for use of its money. As we mentioned in Chapter 15, banks also pay depositors interest on savings accounts and some checking accounts. Thus, banks charge borrowers interest for loans and pay interest to depositors for the use of their money. In addition, these loans may include origination fees.

One of the complaints from borrowers during the financial meltdown and recession was that banks weren't willing to lend. There were several causes. Banks were trying to rebuild their capital, and they didn't want to take the extra risk that lending offers in an economic recession. They were drowning in bad debts and were not sure how future loan losses would affect their capital. The banks' lack of lending caused problems for small businesses. Smaller regional banks did a better job of maintaining small business loans than the major money center banks who suffered most in the recession.

The **prime rate** is the interest rate commercial banks charge their best customers (usually large corporations) for short-term loans. While for many years, loans at the prime rate represented funds at the lowest possible cost, the rapid development of the market for commercial paper has dramatically reduced the importance of commercial banks as a source of short-term loans. Today, most "prime" borrowers are actually small- and medium-sized businesses.

The interest rates on commercial loans may be either fixed or variable. A variable or floating-rate loan offers an advantage when interest rates are falling but represents a distinct disadvantage when interest rates are rising. Between 1999 and 2004, interest rates plummeted, and borrowers refinanced their loans with low-cost fixed-rate loans. Nowhere was this more visible than in the U.S. mortgage markets, where homeown-ers lined up to refinance their high-percentage home mortgages with lower-cost loans, in some cases as low as 5 percent on a 30-year loan. These mortgage interest rates had returned to 6.5 percent by mid-2006, but between 2012 and 2014 had declined to less than 4.0 percent. Individuals and corporations have the same motivation: to minimize their borrowing costs. During this period of historically low interest rates, companies ramped up their borrowing, bought back stock, and locked in large amounts of debt at

**line of credit**
an arrangement by which a bank agrees to lend a specified amount of money to an organization upon request

**secured loans**
loans backed by collateral that the bank can claim if the borrowers do not repay them

**unsecured loans**
loans backed only by the borrowers' good reputation and previous credit rating

**prime rate**
the interest rate that commercial banks charge their best customers (usually large corporations) for short-term loans

low rates. Think back to Chapter 14 and imagine what impact this behavior will have on the interest coverage ratio.

**Nonbank Liabilities.**   Banks are not the only source of short-term funds for businesses. Indeed, virtually all financial institutions, from insurance companies to pension funds, from money market funds to finance companies, make short-term loans to many organizations. The largest U.S. companies also actively engage in borrowing money from the eurodollar and commercial paper markets. As noted earlier, both of these funds' sources are typically slightly less expensive than bank loans.

In some instances, businesses actually sell their accounts receivable to a finance company known as a **factor,** which gives the selling organizations cash and assumes responsibility for collecting the accounts. For example, a factor might pay $60,000 for receivables with a total face value of $100,000 (60 percent of the total). The factor profits if it can collect more than what it paid for the accounts. Because the selling organization's customers send their payments to a lockbox, they may have no idea that a factor has bought their receivables.

**factor**
a finance company to which businesses sell their accounts receivable—usually for a percentage of the total face value

Additional nonbank liabilities that must be efficiently managed to ensure maximum profitability are taxes owed to the government and wages owed to employees. Clearly, businesses are responsible for many different types of taxes, including federal, state, and local income taxes, property taxes, mineral rights taxes, unemployment taxes, Social Security taxes, workers' compensation taxes, excise taxes, and more. While the public tends to think that the only relevant taxes are on income and sales, many industries must pay other taxes that far exceed those levied against their income. Taxes and employees' wages represent debt obligations of the firm, which the financial manager must plan to meet as they fall due.

## Managing Fixed Assets

Up to this point, we have focused on the short-term aspects of financial management. While most business failures are the result of poor short-term planning, successful ventures must also consider the long-term financial consequences of their actions. Managing the long-term assets and liabilities and the owners' equity portion of the balance sheet is important for the long-term health of the business.

 LO 16-3

**Long-term (fixed) assets** are expected to last for many years—production facilities (plants), offices, equipment, heavy machinery, furniture, automobiles, and so on. In today's fast-paced world, companies need the most technologically advanced, modern facilities and equipment they can afford. Automobile, oil refining, and transportation companies are dependent on fixed assets.

**long-term (fixed) assets**
production facilities (plants), offices, and equipment—all of which are expected to last for many years

Modern and high-tech equipment carry high price tags, and the financial arrangements required to support these investments are by no means trivial. Leasing is just one approach to financing. Obtaining major long-term financing can be challenging for even the most profitable organizations. For less successful firms, such challenges can prove nearly impossible. One approach is leasing assets such as equipment, machines, and buildings. Leasing involves paying a fee for usage rather than owning the asset. There are two kinds of leases: capital leases and operating leases. A capital lease is a long-term contract and shows up on the balance sheet as an asset and liability. The operating lease is a short-term cancelable lease and does not show up on the balance sheet. We'll take a closer look at long-term financing in a moment, but first let's address some issues associated with fixed assets, including capital budgeting, risk assessment, and the costs of financing fixed assets.

## Capital Budgeting and Project Selection

**capital budgeting**
the process of analyzing the needs of the business and selecting the assets that will maximize its value

One of the most important jobs performed by the financial manager is to decide what fixed assets, projects, and investments will earn profits for the firm beyond the costs necessary to fund them. The process of analyzing the needs of the business and selecting the assets that will maximize its value is called **capital budgeting,** and the capital budget is the amount of money budgeted for investment in such long-term assets. But capital budgeting does not end with the selection and purchase of a particular piece of land, equipment, or major investment. All assets and projects must be continually reevaluated to ensure their compatibility with the organization's needs. Financial executives believe most budgeting activities are occasionally or frequently unrealistic or irrelevant. If a particular asset does not live up to expectations, then management must determine why and take necessary corrective action. Budgeting is not an exact process, and managers must be flexible when new information is available.

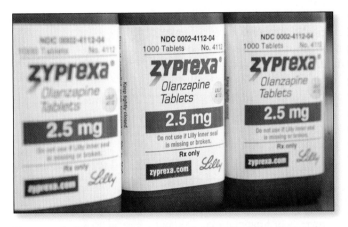

Pharmaceutical companies spend millions of dollars developing drugs such as Zyprexa without knowing if the drug will pass FDA approval and have a significant profit margin.

## Assessing Risk

Every investment carries some risk. Figure 16.1 ranks potential investment projects according to estimated risk. When considering investments overseas, risk assessments must include the political climate and economic stability of a region. The decision to introduce a product or build a manufacturing facility in England would be much less risky than a decision to build one in the Middle East, for example.

The longer a project or asset is expected to last, the greater its potential risk because it is hard to predict whether a piece of equipment will wear out or become obsolete in 5 or 10 years. Predicting cash flows one year down the road is difficult, but projecting them over the span of a 10-year project is a gamble.

The level of a project's risk is also affected by the stability and competitive nature of the marketplace and the world economy as a whole. IBM's latest high-technology computer product is far more likely to become obsolete overnight than is a similar $10 million investment in a manufacturing plant. Dramatic changes in the marketplace are not uncommon. Indeed, uncertainty created by the rapid devaluation of Asian currencies in the late 1990s wrecked a host of assumptions in literally hundreds of projects worldwide. Financial managers must constantly consider such issues when making long-term decisions about the purchase of fixed assets.

## Pricing Long-Term Money

The ultimate profitability of any project depends not only on accurate assumptions of how much cash it will generate, but also on its financing costs. Because a business must pay interest on money it borrows, the returns from any project must cover not only the costs of operating the project but also the interest expenses for the debt used to finance its construction. Unless an organization can effectively cover all of its costs—both financial and operating—it will eventually fail.

Clearly, only a limited supply of funds is available for investment in any given enterprise. The most efficient and profitable companies can attract the lowest-cost

**Highest Risk**

Introduce a New Product in Foreign Markets (risk depends on stability of country)

Expand into a New Market

Introduce a New Product in a Familiar Area

Add to a Product Line

Buy New Equipment for an Established Market

Repair Old Machinery

**Lowest Risk**

**FIGURE 16.1**

**Qualitative Assessment of Capital Budgeting Risk**

funds because they typically offer reasonable financial returns at very low relative risks. Newer and less prosperous firms must pay higher costs to attract capital because these companies tend to be quite risky. One of the strongest motivations for companies to manage their financial resources wisely is that they will, over time, be able to reduce the costs of their funds and in so doing increase their overall profitability.

In our free-enterprise economy, new firms tend to enter industries that offer the greatest potential rewards for success. However, as more and more companies enter an industry, competition intensifies, eventually driving profits down to average levels. The digital music player market of the early 2000s provides an excellent example of the changes in profitability that typically accompany increasing competition. The sign of a successful capital budgeting program is that the new products create higher than normal profits and drive sales and the stock price up. This has certainly been true for Apple when it made the decision to enter the consumer electronics industry. In 2001, Apple introduced the first iPod. Since then, the iPod has undergone many enhancements in size, style, and different versions such as the small Nano. Sales of iPods have declined over time as iPhones took their place as music players. It was the iPod that

Apple stock trades at approximately 100 times what it did nearly ten years ago.

made the iTunes Store possible, which has continued to grow at rates of 38 percent from 2011 to 2012 and 25 percent from 2012 to 2013. It now accounts for $16 billion in revenues. The iPhone, introduced in 2007, has now gone through many annual updates with the latest being the iPhone 6. During 2013, the iPhone sold 150 million units accounting for $91 billion in sales, up 100 percent since 2011. Finally, the iPad tablet was introduced in 2010 and is now the second best product after the iPhone, selling 71 million units and generating almost $32 billion in sales. Interestingly, Apple did not appear to be negatively affected by the recession. In fact, its sales grew from $42.9 billion in 2009 to $170.9 billion in 2013. It is on track to keep up its growth as it expands into China, India, and other emerging markets. An interesting development was that the ease of synchronization with all Apple computers caused an increase in the sale of iMacs and MacBooks.

Even with a well-planned capital budgeting program, it may be difficult for Apple to stay ahead of the competition because the Google Android platform is being used by Apple's competitors. This intense competition may make it difficult to continue market dominance for any extended period. However, Apple is now the most valuable company in the world, valued at $568 billion on June 10, 2014. On June 9, 2014, Apple split its stock seven for one, meaning that for every share you owned, you would get six more for a total of seven shares. There is no real gain involved because the stock price is divided by 7, so stockholders still have the same value, just more shares at a lower price. An investor who bought $1,000 of Apple stock in 2003 for $0.91 would have had Apple stock worth $103,700 on June 10, 2014. The problem is having the patience to continue to hold such a winner without taking some profits along the way.[3]

Maintaining market dominance is also difficult in the personal computer industry, particularly because tablet computers are taking away market share. With increasing competition, prices have fallen dramatically since the 1990s. Weaker companies have failed, leaving the most efficient producers/marketers scrambling for market share. The expanded market for personal computers dramatically reduced the financial returns generated by each dollar invested in productive assets. The "glory days" of the personal computer industry—the time in which fortunes could be won and lost in the space of an average-sized garage—have long since passed into history. Personal computers have essentially become commodity items, and profit margins for companies in this industry have shrunk as the market matures.

## Financing with Long-Term Liabilities

**LO 16-4**

As we said earlier, long-term assets do not come cheaply, and few companies have the cash on hand to open a new store across town, build a new manufacturing facility, research and develop a new life-saving drug, or launch a new product worldwide. To develop such fixed assets, companies need to raise low-cost long-term funds to finance them. Two common choices for raising these funds are attracting new owners *(equity financing),* which we'll look at in a moment, and taking on long-term liabilities *(debt financing),* which we'll look at now.

**Long-term liabilities** are debts that will be repaid over a number of years, such as long-term bank loans and bond issues. These take many different forms, but in the end, the key word is *debt.* Companies may raise money by borrowing it from commercial banks or other financial institutions in the form of lines of credit, short-term loans, or long-term loans. Many corporations acquire debt by borrowing money from pension funds, mutual funds, or life-insurance funds.

Companies that rely too heavily on debt can get into serious trouble should the economy falter; during these times, they may not earn enough operating income to make the required interest payments (remember the times interest earned ratio in Chapter 14). In severe cases when the problem persists too long, creditors will not restructure loans but will instead sue for the interest and principal owed and force the company into bankruptcy.

## Bonds: Corporate IOUs

Much long-term debt takes the form of **bonds,** which are debt instruments that larger companies sell to raise long-term funds. In essence, the buyers of bonds (bondholders) loan the issuer of the bonds cash in exchange for regular interest payments until the loan is repaid on or before the specified maturity date. The bond itself is a certificate, much like an IOU, that represents the company's debt to the bondholder. Bonds are issued by a wide variety of entities, including corporations; national, state, and local governments; public utilities; and nonprofit corporations. Most bondholders need not hold their bonds until maturity; rather, the existence of active secondary markets of brokers and dealers allows for the quick and efficient transfer of bonds from owner to owner.

The bond contract, or *indenture,* specifies all of the terms of the agreement between the bondholders and the issuing organization. The indenture, which can run more than 100 pages, specifies the basic terms of the bond, such as its face value, maturity date, and the annual interest rate. Table 16.2 briefly explains how to determine these and more things about a bond from a bond quote, as it might appear in *Barron's* magazine. The face value of the bond, its initial sales price, is typically $1,000. After this, however, the price of the bond on the open market will fluctuate along with changes in the economy (particularly, changes in interest rates) and in the creditworthiness of the issuer. Bondholders receive the face value of the bond along with the final interest payment on the maturity date. The annual interest rate (often called the *coupon rate*) is the guaranteed percentage of face value that the company will pay to the bond owner every year. For example, a $1,000 bond with a coupon rate of 7 percent would pay $70 per year in interest. In most cases, bond indentures specify that interest payments be made every six months. In the example above, the $70 annual payment would be divided into two semiannual payments of $35.

In addition to the terms of interest payments and maturity date, the bond indenture typically covers other important topics, such as repayment methods, interest payment dates, procedures to be followed in case the organization fails to make the interest payments, conditions for the early repayment of the bonds, and any conditions requiring the pledging of assets as collateral.

## Types of Bonds

Not surprisingly, there are a great many different types of bonds. Most are **unsecured bonds,** meaning that they are not backed by collateral; such bonds are termed *debentures.* **Secured bonds,** on the other hand, are backed by specific collateral that must be forfeited

**long-term liabilities** debts that will be repaid over a number of years, such as long-term loans and bond issues

**bonds** debt instruments that larger companies sell to raise long-term funds

**unsecured bonds** debentures, or bonds that are not backed by specific collateral

**secured bonds** bonds that are backed by specific collateral that must be forfeited in the event that the issuing firm defaults

**TABLE 16.2**
**Bonds—Global Investment Grade Quoted in U.S. Dollars**

| 13-June-14 | Coupon | Maturity | Last Price | Last Yield | Est. Spread** | UST*** | Est $ Vol (000s) |
|---|---|---|---|---|---|---|---|
| GE Capital | 3.450 | May 15, 2024 | 100.172 | 3.429 | 83 | 10 | 147,634 |
| AT&T | 4.800 | June 15, 2044 | 100.787 | 4.750 | 135 | 30 | 260,529 |
| Goldman Sachs | 6.750 | October 1, 2037 | 120.425 | 5.223 | 182 | 30 | 173,795 |

*\*Estimated spreads, in basis points (100 basis points is one percentage point), over the 2-, 5-, 10-, or 30-year hot run Treasury note/bond.*

*\*\*\*Comparable U.S. Treasury issue.*

*Coupon—the percentage in interest payment that the bond pays based on a $1,000 bond*

*Maturity—the day on which the issuer will reissue the principal*

*Last Price—last price at which the security is traded*

*Last Yield—yield-to-maturity for the investor that buys the bond today and holds it until it matures*

*Est. Spread—amount of additional yield the investor will earn each year compared to a U.S. Treasury bond or note of the same maturity*

*UST—U.S. Treasury bond*

*Est $ Vol (000s)—number of individual bonds that were bought and sold on the date indicated*

*Sources: MarketAxess Corporate BondTicker, www.bondticker.com; Barron's, "Corporate Bonds," June 16, 2014, http://online.barrons.com/public/page/9_0210-corpbonds.html (accessed June 16, 2014).*

in the event that the issuing firm defaults. Whether secured or unsecured, bonds may be repaid in one lump sum or with many payments spread out over a period of time. **Serial bonds,** which are different from secured bonds, are actually a sequence of small bond issues of progressively longer maturity. The firm pays off each of the serial bonds as they mature. **Floating-rate bonds** do not have fixed interest payments; instead, the interest rate changes with current interest rates otherwise available in the economy.

**serial bonds**
a sequence of small bond issues of progressively longer maturity

In recent years, a special type of high-interest-rate bond has attracted considerable attention (usually negative) in the financial press. High-interest bonds, or **junk bonds** as they are popularly known, offer relatively high rates of interest because they have higher inherent risks. Historically, junk bonds have been associated with companies in poor financial health and/or startup firms with limited track records. In the mid-1980s, however, junk bonds became a very attractive method of financing corporate mergers; they remain popular today with many investors as a result of their very high relative interest rates. But higher risks are associated with those higher returns (upward of 12 percent per year in some cases) and the average investor would be well-advised to heed those famous words: Look before you leap!

**floating-rate bonds**
bonds with interest rates that change with current interest rates otherwise available in the economy

**junk bonds**
a special type of high interest-rate bond that carries higher inherent risks

## Financing with Owners' Equity

**LO 16-5**

Need help understanding Equity Financing and Debt Financing? Visit your Connect ebook video tab for a brief animated explanation.

A second means of long-term financing is through equity. Remember from Chapter 14 that owners' equity refers to the owners' investment in an organization. Sole proprietors and partners own all or a part of their businesses outright, and their equity includes the money and assets they have brought into their ventures. Corporate owners, on the other hand, own stock or shares of their companies, which they hope will provide them with a return on their investment. Stockholders' equity includes common stock, preferred stock, and retained earnings.

Common stock (introduced in Chapter 4) is the single most important source of capital for most new companies. On the balance sheet, the common stock account

**TABLE 16.3    A Basic Stock Quote**

**Nike, Inc. (NKE)** - NYSE ★ Follow

**76.31** ⬇ 0.36(0.47%) Jun 10, 4:00PM EDT

After Hours: **76.39** ⬆ 0.08 (0.10%) Jun 10, 7:16PM EDT

| | | | |
|---|---|---|---|
| Prev Close: | **76.67** | Day's Range: | **76.24 - 76.92** |
| Open: | **76.34** | 52wk Range: | **59.11 - 80.26** |
| Bid: | **75.88 x 100** | Volume: | **2,576,422** |
| Ask: | **77.00 x 300** | Avg Vol (3m): | **3,608,820** |
| 1y Target Est: | **82.54** | Market Cap: | **67.01B** |
| Beta: | **0.67** | P/E (ttm): | **26.05** |
| Next Earnings Date: | **26-Jun-14** 📅 | EPS (ttm): | **2.93** |
| | | Div & Yield: | **0.96 (1.30%)** |

1. The **52-week high and low**—the highest and lowest prices, respectively, paid for the stock in the last year; for Nike stock, the highest was $80.26 and the lowest price, $59.11.
2. **Stock**—the name of the issuing company. When followed by the letters "pf," the stock is a preferred stock.
3. **Symbol**—the ticker tape symbol for the stock; NKE.
4. **Dividend**—the annual cash dividend paid to stockholders; Nike paid a dividend of $0.96 per share of stock outstanding.
5. **Dividend yield**—the dividend return on one share of common stock; 1.30 percent.
6. **Volume**—the number of shares traded on this day; Nike, 2,576,422.
7. **Close**—Nike's last sale of the day was for $76.31.
8. **Net change**—the difference between the previous day's close and the close on the day being reported; Nike was down $0.36.

*Source: Yahoo! Finance, http://finance.yahoo.com/q?s (accessed June 16, 2014).*

is separated into two basic parts—common stock at par and capital in excess of par. The *par value* of a stock is simply the dollar amount printed on the stock certificate and has no relation to actual *market value*—the price at which the common stock is currently trading. The difference between a stock's par value and its offering price is called *capital in excess of par.* Except in the case of some very low-priced stocks, the capital in excess of par account is significantly larger than the par value account. Table 16.3 briefly explains how to gather important information from a stock quote, as it appears on Yahoo!'s website. You should be familiar with EPS from Chapter 14. However, *beta* is a new term, and Nike's beta of 0.67 indicates that its stock price is 67 percent as volatile as the Standard & Poor's 500 Index. The market cap represents the total value of Nike's common stock, or the value of the company. The target price is the analysts' consensus of the potential stock price.

Preferred stock was defined in Chapter 14 as corporate ownership that gives the stockholder preference in the distribution of the company's profits but not the voting and control rights accorded to common stockholders. Thus, the primary advantage of owning preferred stock is that it is a safer investment than common stock.

All businesses exist to earn profits for their owners. Without the possibility of profit, there can be no incentive to risk investors' capital and succeed. When a

## Venture Capital Firm Y Combinator Riding on Startup Success

Y Combinator
**Founder:** Paul Graham
**Founded:** 2005, in Mountain View, California
**Success:** Y Combinator has been ranked as the top startup incubator by *Forbes,* with a portolio approaching $10 billion.

Y Combinator and the companies it assists are among those thriving in an uncertain economic environment. Founder Paul Graham (famous in tech circles for creating Viaweb—sold to Yahoo! in 1998 for $49 million) launched the venture capital firm Y Combinator in 2005. His method is somewhat like a school for startups, and his funding is similar to financial aid. Graham gathers entrepreneurs for three-month periods, during which time he provides them with small loans (typically under $20,000) to meet basic needs, allowing them to focus on developing their fledgling companies. He also offers them access to his experienced eye, solid advice, and a positive and creative environment. In exchange, Y Combinator receives a 2 to 10 percent company stake. While not all of the companies that Y Combinator has funded have become successful, three well-known firms that received funding from Y Combinator include Dropbox, Reddit, and Airbnb.[4]

---

**retained earnings**
earnings after expenses and taxes that are reinvested in the assets of the firm and belong to the owners in the form of equity

corporation has profits left over after paying all of its expenses and taxes, it has the choice of retaining all or a portion of its earnings and/or paying them out to its shareholders in the form of dividends. **Retained earnings** are reinvested in the assets of the firm and belong to the owners in the form of equity. Retained earnings are an important source of funds and are, in fact, the only long-term funds that the company can generate internally.

When the board of directors distributes some of a corporation's profits to the owners, it issues them as cash dividend payments. But not all firms pay dividends. Many fast-growing firms like Google retain all of their earnings because they can earn high rates of return on the earnings they reinvest. Companies with fewer growth opportunities like Campbell Soup or Verizon typically pay out large proportions of their earnings in the form of dividends, thereby allowing their stockholders to reinvest their dividend payments in higher-growth companies. Table 16.4 presents a sample of companies and the dividend each paid on a single share of stock. As shown in the table, when the dividend is divided by the price the result is the **dividend yield.** The dividend yield is the cash return as a percentage of the price but does not reflect the total return an investor earns on the individual stock. If the dividend yield is 2.76 percent on Campbell Soup and the stock price increases by 10 percent from $45.26 to $49.79 then the total return would be 12.76 percent. It is not clear that stocks with high dividend yields will be preferred by investors to those with little or no dividends. Most large companies pay their stockholders dividends on a quarterly basis.

**dividend yield**
the dividend per share divided by the stock price

## Investment Banking

A company that needs more money to expand or take advantage of opportunities may be able to obtain financing by issuing stock. The first-time sale of stocks and bonds directly to the public is called a *new issue.* Companies that already have stocks or bonds outstanding may offer a new issue of stock to raise additional funds for specific projects. When a company offers its stock to the public for the very first time, it is said to be "going public," and the sale is called an *initial public offering* (IPO).

---

**DID YOU KNOW?**  A single share of Coca-Cola stock purchased during its original 1919 IPO would be worth more than $5 million today.[5]

| Ticker Symbol | Company Name | Price per Share | Dividend per Share | Dividend Yield | Earnings per Share (*) | Price Earnings Ratio |
|---|---|---|---|---|---|---|
| AEO | American Eagle | $11.06 | $0.50 | 4.52% | $0.31 | 35.68 |
| AXP | American Express | 94.76 | 1.04 | 1.10% | 5.06 | 18.73 |
| AAPL | Apple | 92.29 | 1.88 | 2.04% | 5.96 | 15.48 |
| CPB | Campbell Soup | 45.26 | 1.25 | 2.76% | 1.66 | 27.27 |
| DIS | Disney | 84.31 | 0.86 | 1.02% | 3.89 | 21.67 |
| F | Ford | 16.52 | 0.50 | 3.03% | 1.61 | 10.26 |
| GOOG | Google | 551.35 | 0.00 | 0.00% | 19.09 | 28.88 |
| HOG | Harley Davidson | 69.79 | 1.10 | 1.58% | 3.49 | 20.00 |
| HD | Home Depot | 78.43 | 1.88 | 2.40% | 3.93 | 19.96 |
| MCD | McDonald's | 99.76 | 3.24 | 3.25% | 5.50 | 18.14 |
| MSFT | Microsoft | 40.58 | 1.12 | 2.76% | 2.67 | 15.20 |
| PG | Procter & Gamble | 79.76 | 2.57 | 3.22% | 3.75 | 21.27 |
| LUV | Southwest Airlines | 25.72 | 0.24 | 0.93% | 1.20 | 21.43 |
| VZ | Verizon | 49.04 | 2.12 | 4.32% | 4.48 | 10.95 |

**TABLE 16.4**
**Estimated Common Stock Price-Earnings Ratios and Dividends for Selected Companies**

*Earnings per share are for the latest 12-month period and do not necessarily match year-end numbers.

Source: Yahoo! Finance, http://finance.yahoo.com/ (June 12, 2014).

New issues of stocks and bonds are sold directly to the public and to institutions in what is known as the **primary market**—the market where firms raise financial capital. The primary market differs from **secondary markets,** which are stock exchanges and over-the-counter markets where investors can trade their securities with other investors rather than the company that issued the stock or bonds. Primary market transactions actually raise cash for the issuing corporations, while secondary market transactions do not. For example, when Facebook went public on May 18, 2012, its IPO raised $16 billion for the company and stockholders, who were cashing in on their success. Once the investment bankers distributed the stock to retail brokers, the brokers sold it to clients in the secondary market for $38 per share. The stock got off to a rocky start and hit a low of $17.73 in September 2012. However, by March 2014, it was at $71.97. You might want to check out its current price for fun.

**Investment banking,** the sale of stocks and bonds for corporations, helps such companies raise funds by matching people and institutions who have money to invest with corporations in need of resources to exploit new opportunities. Corporations usually employ an investment banking firm to help sell their securities in the primary market. An investment banker helps firms establish appropriate offering prices for their securities. In addition, the investment banker takes care of the myriad details and securities regulations involved in any sale of securities to the public.

Just as large corporations such as IBM and Microsoft have a client relationship with a law firm and an accounting firm, they also have a client relationship with an

**primary market**
the market where firms raise financial capital

**secondary markets**
stock exchanges and over-the-counter markets where investors can trade their securities with others

**investment banking**
the sale of stocks and bonds for corporations

investment banking firm. An investment banking firm such as Merrill Lynch, Goldman Sachs, or Morgan Stanley can provide advice about financing plans, dividend policy, or stock repurchases, as well as advice on mergers and acquisitions. Many now offer additional banking services, making them "one-stop shopping" banking centers. When Pixar merged with Disney, both companies used investment bankers to help them value the transaction. Each firm wanted an outside opinion about what it was worth to the other. Sometimes mergers fall apart because the companies cannot agree on the price each company is worth or the structure of management after the merger. The advising investment banker, working with management, often irons out these details. Of course, investment bankers do not provide these services for free. They usually charge a fee of between 1 and 1.5 percent of the transaction. A $20 billion merger can generate between $200 and $300 million in investment banking fees. The merger mania of the late 1990s allowed top investment bankers to earn huge sums. Unfortunately, this type of fee income is dependent on healthy stock markets, which seem to stimulate the merger fever among corporate executives.

## The Securities Markets

**securities markets**
the mechanism for buying and selling securities

**Securities markets** provide a mechanism for buying and selling securities. They make it possible for owners to sell their stocks and bonds to other investors. Thus, in the broadest sense, stocks and bonds markets may be thought of as providers of liquidity—the ability to turn security holdings into cash quickly and at minimal expense and effort. Without liquid securities markets, many potential investors would sit on the sidelines rather than invest their hard-earned savings in securities. Indeed, the ability to sell securities at well-established market prices is one of the very pillars of the capitalistic society that has developed over the years in the United States.

Unlike the primary market, in which corporations sell stocks directly to the public, secondary markets permit the trading of previously issued securities. There are many different secondary markets for both stocks and bonds. If you want to purchase 100 shares of Google common stock, for example, you must purchase this stock from another investor or institution. It is the active buying and selling by many thousands of investors that establishes the prices of all financial securities. Secondary market trades may take place on organized exchanges or in what is known as the over-the-counter market. Many brokerage houses exist to help investors with financial decisions, and many offer their services through the Internet. One such broker is Charles Schwab. Its site offers a wealth of information and provides educational material to individual investors.

The New York Stock Exchange is the world's largest stock exchange in terms of market capitalization.

## Stock Markets

Stock markets exist around the world in New York, Tokyo, London, Frankfort, Paris, and other world locations. The two biggest stock markets in the United States are the New York Stock Exchange (NYSE) and the NASDAQ market.

Exchanges used to be divided into organized exchanges and over-the-counter markets, but during the past several years, dramatic changes have occurred in the markets. Both the NYSE and NASDAQ became publicly traded companies. They were previously not-for-profit organizations but are now for-profit companies. Additionally, both exchanges bought or merged with electronic exchanges. In an attempt to expand their markets, NASDAQ acquired the OMX, a Nordic stock exchange headquartered in Sweden, and the New York Stock Exchange merged with Euronext, a large European electronic exchange that trades options and futures contracts as well as common stock.

Traditionally, the NASDAQ market has been an electronic market, and many of the large technology companies such as Microsoft, Google, Apple, and Facebook trade on the NASDAQ market. The NASDAQ operates through dealers who buy and sell common stock (inventory) for their own accounts. The NYSE used to be primarily a floor-traded market, where brokers meet at trading posts on the floor of the New York Stock Exchange to buy and sell common stock. The brokers act as agents for their clients and do not own their own inventory. Today, more than 50 percent of NYSE trading is electronic. This traditional division between the two markets is becoming less significant as the exchanges become electronic.

Electronic markets have grown quickly because of the speed, low cost, and efficiency of trading that they offer over floor trading. One of the fastest-growing electronic markets has been the Intercontinental Exchange (referred to as ICE). ICE, based in Atlanta, Georgia, primarily trades financial and commodity futures products. It started out as an energy futures exchange, and in its 14 years of existence, it has broadened its futures contracts into an array of commodities and derivative products. In December 2012, ICE made an offer to buy the New York Stock Exchange. When the NYSE became a public company and had common stock trading in the secondary market, rather than the hunter, it became the prey. On November 13, 2013, ICE completed its takeover of the NYSE. One condition of the takeover was that ICE had to divest itself of Euronext because international regulators thought the company would have a monopoly on European derivative markets. Also acquired as part of the NYSE family of exchanges was LIFFE, the London International Financial Futures Exchange. Many analysts thought that LIFFE was the major reason ICE bought the NYSE—not for its equity markets trading common stocks. So sometime in 2014, ICE will sell Euronext to a group of European investors, many of whom will be institutional investors such as bank, mutual funds, and investment banks. What we are seeing is the globalization of securities markets and the increasing reliance on electronic trading.

## The Over-the-Counter Market

Unlike the organized exchanges, the **over-the-counter (OTC) market** is a network of dealers all over the country linked by computers, telephones, and Teletype machines. It has no central location. Today, the OTC market consists of small stocks, illiquid bank stocks, penny stocks, and companies whose stocks trade on the "pink sheets." Once NASDAQ was classified as an exchange by the SEC, it was no longer part of the OTC market. Further, because most corporate bonds and all U.S. securities are traded over the counter, the OTC market regularly accounts for the largest total dollar value of all of the secondary markets.

**over-the-counter (OTC) market**
a network of dealers all over the country linked by computers, telephones, and Teletype machines

## Measuring Market Performance

Investors, especially professional money managers, want to know how well their investments are performing relative to the market as a whole. Financial managers also need to know how their companies' securities are performing when compared with their competitors'. Thus, performance measures—averages and indexes—are very important to many different people. They not only indicate the performance of a particular securities market but also provide a measure of the overall health of the economy.

Indexes and averages are used to measure stock prices. An *index* compares current stock prices with those in a specified base period, such as 1944, 1967, or 1977. An *average* is the average of certain stock prices. The averages used are usually not simple calculations, however. Some stock market averages (such as the Standard & Poor's Composite Index) are weighted averages, where the weights employed are the total market values of each stock in the index (in this case 500). The Dow Jones Industrial Average (DJIA) is a price-weighted average. Regardless of how they are constructed, all market averages of stocks move together closely over time. See Figure 16.2, which graphs the Dow Jones Industrial Average. Notice the sharp downturn in the market during the 2008–2009 time period and the recovery that started in 2010. Investors perform better by keeping an eye on the long-term trend line and not the short-term fluctuations. Contrarian investors buy when everyone else is panicked and prices are low because they play the long-term trends. However, for many, this is psychologically a tough way to play the market.

Many investors follow the activity of the Dow Jones Industrial Average to see whether the stock market has gone up or down. Table 16.5 lists the 30 companies that currently make up the Dow. Although these companies are only a small fraction of the total number of companies listed on the New York Stock Exchange, because of their size they account for about 25 percent of the total value of the NYSE.

The numbers listed in an index or average that tracks the performance of a stock market are expressed not as dollars but as a number on a fixed scale. If you know, for example, that the Dow Jones Industrial Average climbed from 860 in August 1982 to a high of 11,497 at the beginning of 2000, you can see clearly that the value of the Dow Jones Average increased more than 10 times in this 19-year period, making it one of the highest rate of return periods in the history of the stock market.

**FIGURE 16.2**    **Recent Performance of Stock Market and Dow Jones Industrial Average (DJIA)**

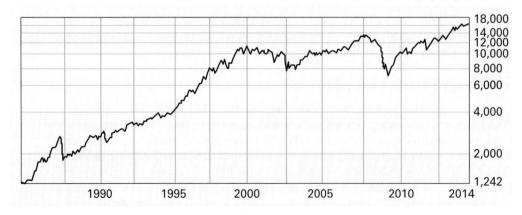

Source: "Dow Jones Industrial Average," Yahoo! Finance, http://finance.yahoo.com/q/bc?s=%5EDJI+Basic+Chart&t=my (accessed June 12, 2014).

## JPMorgan Struggles to Repair Reputation

The London Whale scandal is making waves for JPMorgan. A trader known as the London Whale (because of his large portfolio and extensive trading) became the center of a trading loss that cost the bank more than $6 billion. Two traders in JPMorgan's London offices face charges from the U.S. and U.K. governments for allegedly trying to cover up the losses. While investigations have shown that top executives were not involved in a cover-up and were unaware of the bad trades, JPMorgan could face civil charges for lacking the oversight needed to prevent this kind of misconduct in its organization. Reports have indicated that one employee was in charge of ensuring proper conduct over these trades, but that the standards for oversight were so broad that they were ineffective.

As a result, the bank has paid more than $920 million in fines to several U.S. and U.K. regulators plus an additional $100 million to the Commodity Futures Trading Commission (CFTC). In addition, JPMorgan is battling this scandal while trying to come to terms with regulators on faulty mortgage securities that contributed to the 2008 financial crisis. JPMorgan paid record fines of about $13 billion, in addition to the $1 billion it paid to resolve U.K. and U.S. investigations into the Whale scandal.[6]

### Discussion Questions

1. What are some of the ethical issues involved with the JPMorgan trading scandal?
2. Why is JPMorgan facing a civil suit if executives did not have knowledge of the wrongdoing?
3. Describe some of the lapses in JPMorgan's oversight of its trades.

---

Unfortunately, prosperity did not last long once the Internet bubble burst. Technology stocks and new Internet companies were responsible for the huge increase in stock prices. Even companies with few sales and no earnings were selling at prices that were totally unreasonable. It is always easier to realize that a bubble existed after it has popped. By September 2002, the Dow Jones Industrial Average hit 7,461. The markets stabilized and the economy kept growing; investors were euphoric when the Dow Jones Industrial Average hit an all-time high of 14,198 in October 2007. However, once the housing bubble burst, the economy and the stock market went into a free fall. The Dow Jones Industrial Average bottomed out at 6,470 in March 2009. The market entered a period of recovery, and by April 2010, it hit a new high for the

**TABLE 16.5**
**The 30 Stocks in the Dow Jones Industrial Average**

| | | |
|---|---|---|
| 3M Co | General Electric | Nike |
| American Express Co | Goldman Sachs | Pfizer |
| AT&T Inc. | Home Depot | Procter & Gamble |
| Boeing | Intel | Travelers Companies |
| Caterpiller | IBM | United Health Group |
| Chevron | Johnson & Johnson | United Technologies |
| Cisco Systems | JPMorgan Chase | Verizon |
| Coca-Cola | McDonald's | Visa |
| Du Pont | Merck | Walmart |
| ExxonMobil | Microsoft | Walt Disney |

Source: "Dow Jones Industrial Average," http://finance.yahoo.com/q/cp?s=%5EDJI (accessed June 16, 2014).

During the housing bubble, banks provided loans to riskier subprime borrowers. Although these loans were highly profitable, it was only a matter of time before the bubble burst.

year of 10,975. By June 2014, the Dow Jones Industrial Average hit an all-time record high of 16,970. The good news is that even when the market has been rather flat, an investor would have collected dividends, which are not reflected in the index. Perhaps this roller coaster ride indicates why some people are afraid to enter the market and buy common stocks. If you look at the long-term trend and long-term returns in common stocks, they far outdistance bonds and government securities.

Recognizing financial bubbles can be difficult. It is too easy to get caught up in the enthusiasm that accompanies rising markets. Knowing what something is worth in economic terms is the test of true value. During the housing bubble, banks made loans to subprime borrowers to buy houses. (Remember that the prime rate is the rate for the highest quality borrowers and subprime loans are generally made to those who do not qualify for regular ones.) As more money poured into the housing market, the obvious supply and demand relationship from economics would indicate that housing prices would rise. As prices rose, speculators entered the real estate market trying to make a fast buck. States such as Florida, Arizona, Nevada, and California were the favorite speculative spots and the states with the largest decline in house prices. To make matters worse, banks had created the home equity loan years ago so that borrowers could take out a second mortgage against their house and deduct the interest payment for tax purposes. Many homeowners no longer thought about paying off their mortgages but instead used the increase in the price of their houses to borrow more money. This behavior was unsustainable.

The bankers engaged in risky financial behavior packaged up billions of dollars of mortgages into securitized assets. In other words, an investor could buy a pool of assets and collect the interest income and eventually get a payment at the end of the life of the product. This technique allowed banks to make a mortgage, collect a fee, package the mortgage, and collect another fee. These securitized mortgages were sold to the market as asset-backed securities with a AAA credit rating off their books and replaced with cash to make more loans. In this case, when the bubble burst, it had extremely severe consequences for the economy, workers, and investors.

People defaulted on loans when they could no longer afford to pay the mortgage. Many of these people shouldn't have been able to borrow in the first place. The defaults caused housing prices to fall, and some people who had home equity loans no longer had any equity left in their house. Some homeowners owed the bank more than the house was worth, and they started walking away from their mortgage. At the same time, investors realized that the mortgage-backed securities they owned were probably not worth what they thought they were worth, and prices of these assets plummeted. Banks and other financial service firms that had these assets on their books suffered a double whammy. They had loan losses and losses on mortgage-backed securities that another division of the bank had bought for investment purposes. Soon, many banks were close to violating their capital requirement, and the U.S. Treasury and Federal Reserve stepped in—with the help of funding from Congress—to make bank loans, buy securities that were illiquid, and invest in the capital of the banks by buying preferred stocks.

The consensus of most economists is that through the actions of the U.S. Treasury and the Federal Reserve, the U.S. economy escaped what might have been another depression equal to or worse than the depression of the 1930s. The recession of 2007–2009 lasted 18 months and was the longest recession since the 1930s. Some worry that as the Federal Reserve becomes less accommodating and lets interest rates rise, the rising interest rates will have a negative effect on stock prices. This is always possible if corporate earnings do not increase enough to outweigh the impact of higher required returns motivated by higher rates and higher inflation.

For investors to make sound financial decisions, it is important that they stay in touch with business news, markets, and indexes. Of course, business and investment magazines, such as *Bloomberg Businessweek, Fortune,* and *Money,* offer this type of information. Many Internet sites, including the CNN/*Money, Business Wire, USA Today,* other online newspapers, and *PR Newswire,* offer this information, as well. Many sites offer searchable databases of information by topic, company, or keyword. However investors choose to receive and review business news, doing so is a necessity in today's market.

## Review Your Understanding

### Describe some common methods of managing current assets.

Current assets are short-term resources such as cash, investments, accounts receivable, and inventory, which can be converted to cash within a year. Financial managers focus on minimizing the amount of cash kept on hand and increasing the speed of collections through lockboxes and electronic funds transfer and investing in marketable securities. Marketable securities include U.S. Treasury bills, certificates of deposit, commercial paper, and money market funds. Managing accounts receivable requires judging customer creditworthiness and creating credit terms that encourage prompt payment. Inventory management focuses on determining optimum inventory levels that minimize the cost of storing and ordering inventory without sacrificing too many lost sales due to stockouts.

### Identify some sources of short-term financing (current liabilities).

Current liabilities are short-term debt obligations that must be repaid within one year, such as accounts payable, taxes payable, and notes (loans) payable. Trade credit is extended by suppliers for the purchase of their goods and services. A line of credit is an arrangement by which a bank agrees to lend a specified amount of money to a business whenever the business needs it. Secured loans are backed by collateral; unsecured loans are backed only by the borrower's good reputation.

### Summarize the importance of long-term assets and capital budgeting.

Long-term, or fixed, assets are expected to last for many years, such as production facilities (plants), offices, and equipment. Businesses need modern, up-to-date equipment to succeed in today's competitive environment. Capital budgeting is the process of analyzing company needs and selecting the assets that will maximize its value; a capital budget is the amount of money budgeted for the purchase of fixed assets. Every investment in fixed assets carries some risk.

### Specify how companies finance their operations and manage fixed assets with long-term liabilities, particularly bonds.

Two common choices for financing are equity financing (attracting new owners) and debt financing (taking on long-term liabilities). Long-term liabilities are debts that will be repaid over a number of years, such as long-term bank loans and bond issues. A bond is a long-term debt security that an organization sells to raise money. The bond indenture specifies the provisions of the bond contract—maturity date, coupon rate, repayment methods, and others.

### Discuss how corporations can use equity financing by issuing stock through an investment banker.

Owners' equity represents what owners have contributed to the company and includes common stock, preferred stock, and retained earnings (profits that have been reinvested in the assets of the firm). To finance operations, companies can issue new common and preferred stock through an investment banker that sells stocks and bonds for corporations.

### Describe the various securities markets in the United States.

Securities markets provide the mechanism for buying and selling stocks and bonds. Primary markets allow companies to raise capital by selling new stock directly to investors through investment bankers. Secondary markets allow the buyers of previously issued shares of stock to sell them to other owners. The major secondary markets are the New York Stock Exchange, the American Stock Exchange, and the over-the-counter market. Investors measure stock market performance by watching stock market averages and indexes such as the Dow Jones Industrial Average and the Standard & Poor's (S&P) Composite Index.

### Critique the position of short-term assets and liabilities of a small manufacturer, and recommend corrective action.

Using the information presented in this chapter, you should be able to "Solve the Dilemma" on page 511 presented by the current bleak working capital situation of Glasspray Corporation.

## Revisit the World of Business

1. Do you think that credit rating agencies had the incentive to rate securities highly even if they were risky?

2. Should credit rating agencies such as Standard & Poor's be forced to pay for their erroneous ratings?

3. What can credit rating agencies do to ensure that their ratings remain objective?

## Learn the Terms

bonds  497

capital budgeting  494

commercial certificates of deposit (CDs)  488

commercial paper  488

dividend yield  500

eurodollar market  489

factor  493

floating-rate bonds  498

investment banking  501

junk bonds  498

line of credit  492

lockbox  487

long-term (fixed) assets  493

long-term liabilities  497

marketable securities  488

over-the-counter (OTC) market  503

primary market  501

prime rate  492

retained earnings  500

secondary markets  501

secured bonds  497

secured loans  492

securities markets  502

serial bonds  498

trade credit  491

transaction balances  486

Treasury bills (T-bills)  488

unsecured bonds  497

unsecured loans  492

working capital management  486

## Check Your Progress

1. Define working capital management.
2. How can a company speed up cash flow? Why should it?
3. Describe the various types of marketable securities.
4. What does it mean to have a line of credit at a bank?
5. What are fixed assets? Why is assessing risk important in capital budgeting?
6. How can a company finance fixed assets?
7. What are bonds and what do companies do with them?
8. How can companies use equity to finance their operations and long-term growth?
9. What are the functions of securities markets?
10. What were some of the principal causes of the most recent recession?

## Get Involved

1. Using your local newspaper or *The Wall Street Journal,* find the current rates of interest on the following marketable securities. If you were a financial manager for a large corporation, which would you invest extra cash in? Which would you invest in if you worked for a small business?
   a. Three-month T-bills
   b. Six-month T-bills
   c. Commercial certificates of deposit
   d. Commercial paper
   e. Eurodollar deposits
   f. Money market deposits

2. Select five of the Dow Jones Industrials from Table 16.5. Look up their earnings, dividends, and prices for the past five years. What kind of picture is presented by this information? Which stocks would you like to have owned over this past period? Do you think the next five years will present a similar picture?

## Build Your Skills

### Choosing among Projects

**Background**

As the senior executive in charge of exploration for High Octane Oil Co., you are constantly looking for projects that will add to the company's profitability—without increasing the company's risk. High Octane Oil is an international oil company with operations in Latin America, the Middle East, Africa, the United States, and Mexico. The company is one of the world's leading experts in deep-water exploration and drilling. High Octane currently produces 50 percent of its oil in the United States, 25 percent in the Middle East, 5 percent in Africa, 10 percent in Latin America, and 10 percent in Mexico. You are considering six projects from around the world.

**Project 1**—Your deep-water drilling platform in the Gulf of Mexico is producing at maximum capacity from the Valdez oil field, and High Octane's geological engineers think there is a high probability that there is oil in the Sanchez field, which is adjacent to Valdez. They recommend drilling a new series of wells. Once commercial quantities of oil have been discovered, it will take two more years to build the collection platform and pipelines. It will be four years before the discovered oil gets to the refineries.

**Project 2**—The Brazilian government has invited you to drill on some unexplored tracts in the middle of the central jungle region. There are roads to within 50 miles of the tract and British Petroleum has found oil 500 miles away from this tract. It would take about three years to develop this property and several more years to build pipelines and pumping stations to carry the oil to the refineries. The Brazilian government wants 20 percent of all production as its fee for giving High Octane Oil Co. the drilling rights or a $500 million up-front fee and 5 percent of the output.

**Project 3**—Your fields in Saudi Arabia have been producing oil for 50 years. Several wells are old, and the pressure has diminished. Your engineers are sure that if you were to initiate high-pressure secondary recovery procedures, you would increase the output of these existing wells by 20 percent. High-pressure recovery methods pump water at high pressure into the underground limestone formations to enhance the movement of petroleum toward the surface.

**Project 4**—Your largest oil fields in Alaska have been producing from only 50 percent of the known deposits. Your geological engineers estimate that you could open up 10 percent of the remaining fields every two years and offset your current declining production from existing wells. The pipeline capacity is available and, while you can only drill during six months of the year, the fields could be producing oil in three years.

**Project 5**—Some of High Octane's west Texas oil fields produce in shallow stripper wells of 2,000- to 4,000-foot depths. Stripper wells produce anywhere from 10 to 2,000 barrels per day and can last for six months or 40 years. Generally, once you find a shallow deposit, there is an 80 percent chance that offset wells will find more oil. Because these wells are shallow, they can be drilled quickly at a low cost. High Octane's engineers estimate that in your largest tract, which is closest to the company's Houston refinery, you could increase production by 30 percent for the next 10 years by increasing the density of the wells per square mile.

**Project 6**—The government of a republic in Russia has invited you to drill for oil in Siberia. Russian geologists think that this oil field might be the largest in the world, but there have been no wells drilled and no infrastructure exists to carry oil if it should be found. The republic has no money to help you build the infrastructure but if you find oil, it will let you keep the first five years' production before taking its 25 percent share. Knowing that oil fields do not start producing at full capacity for many years after initial production, your engineers are not sure that your portion of the first five years of production will pay for

the infrastructure they must build to get the oil to market. The republic also has been known to have a rather unstable government, and the last international oil company that began this project left the country when a new government demanded a higher than originally agreed-upon percentage of the expected output. If this field is in fact the largest in the world, High Octane's supply of oil would be ensured well into the 21st century.

## Task

1. Working in groups, rank the six projects from lowest risk to highest risk.

2. Given the information provided, do the best you can to rank the projects from lowest cost to highest cost.

3. What political considerations might affect your project choice?

4. If you could choose one project, which would it be and why?

5. If you could choose three projects, which ones would you choose? In making this decision, consider which projects might be highly correlated to High Octane Oil's existing production and which ones might diversify the company's production on a geographical basis.

## Solve the Dilemma — LO 16-7

### Surviving Rapid Growth

Glasspray Corporation is a small firm that makes industrial fiberglass spray equipment. Despite its size, the company supplies a range of firms from small mom-and-pop boatmakers to major industrial giants, both overseas and here at home. Indeed, just about every molded fiberglass resin product, from bathroom sinks and counters to portable spas and racing yachts, is constructed with the help of one or more of the company's machines.

Despite global acceptance of its products, Glasspray has repeatedly run into trouble with regard to the management of its current assets and liabilities as a result of extremely rapid and consistent increases in year-to-year sales. The firm's president and founder, Stephen T. Rose, recently lamented the sad

state of his firm's working capital position: "Our current assets aren't, and our current liabilities are!" Rose shouted in a recent meeting of the firm's top officers. "We can't afford any more increases in sales! We're selling our way into bankruptcy! Frankly, our *working* capital doesn't!"

### Discussion Questions

1. Normally, rapidly increasing sales are a good thing. What seems to be the problem here?

2. List the important components of a firm's working capital. Include both current assets and current liabilities.

3. What are some management techniques applied to current liabilities that Glasspray might use to improve its working capital position?

## Build Your Business Plan

### Financial Management and Securities Market

This chapter helps you realize that once you are making money, you need to be careful in determining how to invest it. Meanwhile, your team should consider the pros and cons of establishing a line of credit at the bank.

Remember the key to building your business plan is to be realistic!!

# See for Yourself Videocase

## Morningstar Inc. Makes Investing Easier

Many individuals find stocks and bonds to be confusing, but Joe Mansueto has begun to change that by making investing easier to understand. In 1984, Mansueto founded Morningstar Inc., which provides independent investment research to individuals, financial advisors, and institutional advisors. The company's top asset is that it is independent and its assessments are based on impartial research. Although it works with advisors, its main focus is on individuals. From the beginning, Mansueto, a former stock analyst, aimed to take the chaos of the investment world and create tools that would help individuals make sense of it. With so much investment information and opportunities available, it is easy for the average person to feel lost.

The idea for Morningstar began when Mansueto realized that in order to compare funds and get enough information to begin investing effectively he would have to order prospectuses from each individual fund. The amount of information needed was overwhelming. Mansueto thought that if he could create a compendium of information for the different funds out there, it would make it much easier for the average person to invest intelligently. In 1984, Mansueto founded Morningstar Inc. and began by focusing on mutual funds. He created the Mutual Fund Sourcebook, a compilation of information on roughly 400 different mutual funds. More than two decades later, Morningstar assists more than 8.9 million individual investors with mutual funds, stocks, bonds, and more. The company employs more than 3,600 global employees, who research, write up, and rate investments along with guiding individuals toward making wise business decisions. Morningstar is dedicated to serving investors. It does not charge the companies that it rates and prides itself on maintaining an independent view. Analysts regularly compile data on more than 456,000 global investment offerings.

Morningstar uses a five star rating system to inform investors about the financial strength of investment choices. High stars, such as 4 and 5, mean that the investment choices have the highest value and are expected to have a high level of return. Lower stars, such as 1 and 2, have lower perceived value compared to their cost and are perceived to be riskier investments.

The company focuses on offering information for three different types of investment choices: mutual funds, stocks, and bonds. Mutual funds are pools of investments (often called portfolios) selected by fund managers. A mutual fund can be good for someone wanting less risk. The idea is to offset the high-risk investments by investing in multiple securities. Mutual funds are also well suited for investors who do not want to take the time or who lack the expertise to invest in individual securities. Morningstar also works with stocks and bonds. Stocks are ownerships, or stakes, in a particular company, whereas a bond is like a company IOU. A bond investor basically loans a company money with the understanding that the company will pay back the money with interest. Bonds generally carry less risk than stocks do.

Multiply all this information by the thousands of mutual funds, stocks, and bonds out there, and it is easy to see why someone might become confused when deciding where to invest. Morningstar has even geared its website toward new investors, with features such as the investing classroom, analyst picks, data tools, and articles. In a post-Enron, post-recession world, it is more critical than ever that people understand how to manage their finances and keep their debt in check. Mansueto believes firmly that investing is a key component to financial solvency. He recommends investing early, even suggesting that high school students take the plunge. According to him, it is not the amount of money a person invests that matters; it is getting started early, being consistent, and patiently waiting for initial investments to grow.[8]

### Discussion Questions

1. What is it about investing that Mansueto discovered is so confusing for the average investor?

2. How does Morningstar Inc. make investing easier for individuals?

3. Why does Mansueto recommend investing early in life, even in high school?

You can find the related video in the Video Library in Connect. Ask your instructor how you can access Connect.

# Team Exercise

Compare and contrast financing with long-term liabilities, such as bonds versus financing with owner's equity, typically retained earnings, common stock, and preferred stock. Form groups and suggest a good mix of long-term liabilities and owner's equity for a new firm that makes wind turbines for generating alternative energy and would like to grow quickly.

# Appendix D

## Personal Financial Planning*

## The Financial Planning Process

**Personal financial planning** is the process of managing your finances so that you can achieve your financial goals. By anticipating future needs and wants, you can take appropriate steps to prepare for them. Your needs and wants will undoubtedly change over time as you enter into various life circumstances. Although financial planning is not entirely about money management, a large part of this process is concerned with decisions related to expenditures, investments, and credit.

Although every person has unique needs, everyone can benefit from financial planning. Even if the entire financial plan is not implemented at once, the process itself will help you focus on what is important. With a little forethought and action, you may be able to achieve goals that you previously thought were unattainable. Table D.1 shows how teens handle finances.

### TABLE D.1   Teens and Money

| | |
|---|---|
| Learned about money from their parents | 82% |
| Know how to balance a checkbook or check the accuracy of a bank statement | 35% |
| Consider themselves to be "super savers" | 77% |
| Know how to manage a credit card | 35% |
| Get money from a job | 67% |
| Get money from borrowing | 28% |
| Have an ATM/debit card | 42% |
| Would like to know more about money management | 80% |

*Source: "2011 Teens & Money Survey Findings: Insights into Money Attitudes, Behaviors and Expectations of 16- to 18-Year-Olds," Charles Schwab Foundation, www.aboutschwab.com/images/press/teensmoneyfactsheet.pdf (accessed June 16, 2014).*

*This appendix was contributed by Dr. Vickie Bajtelsmit.

The steps in development and implementation of an effective financial plan are:

- Evaluate your financial health.
- Set short-term and long-term financial goals.
- Create and adhere to a budget.
- Manage credit wisely.
- Develop a savings and investment plan.
- Evaluate and purchase insurance.
- Develop an estate plan.
- Adjust your financial plan to new circumstances.

## Evaluate Your Financial Health

Just as businesses make use of financial reports to track their performance, good personal financial planning requires that individuals keep track of their income and expenses and their overall financial condition. Several software packages are readily available to help track personal finances (for example, Quicken and Microsoft Money), but all that is really needed is a simple spreadsheet program. This appendix includes some simple worksheets that can be reproduced to provide a starting point for personal financial planning. Comprehensive financial planning sites are also available on the Internet. For example, **http://money.msn.com/** and **www.smartmoney.com** both provide information and tools to simplify this process.

While it is possible to track all kinds of information over time, the two most critical elements of your finances are your personal net worth and your personal cash flow. The information necessary for these two measures is often required by lending institutions on loan applications, so keeping it up to date can save you time and effort later.

### The Personal Balance Sheet

For businesses, net worth is usually defined as *assets minus liabilities,* and this is no different for individuals. **Personal net worth** is simply the total value of all personal assets less the total value of unpaid debts or liabilities. Although a business could not survive with a negative net worth since it would be technically insolvent, many students have negative net worth. As a student, you probably are not yet earning enough to have accumulated significant assets, such as a house or stock portfolio, but you are likely to have incurred various forms of debt, including student loans, car loans, and credit card debt.

At this stage in your life, negative net worth is not necessarily an indication of poor future financial prospects. Current investment in your "human capital" (education) is usually considered to have a resulting payoff in the form of better job opportunities and higher potential lifetime income, so this "upside-down" balance sheet should not stay that way forever. Unfortunately, there are many people in the United States who have negative net worth much later in their lives. This can

result from unforeseen circumstances, like divorce, illness, or disability, but the easy availability of credit in the last couple of decades has also been blamed for the heavy debt loads of many American families. The most recent recession, caused partially by excessive risk-taking, has resulted in many bankruptcies and housing foreclosures. No matter the immediate trigger, it is usually poor financial planning—the failure to prepare in advance for those unforeseen circumstances—that makes the difference between those who fail and those who survive. It is interesting to note that we could say the exact same thing about business failures. Most are attributable to poor financial planning. If your net worth is negative, you should definitely include debt reduction on your list of short-and/or long-term goals.

You can use Table D.2 to estimate your net worth. On the left-hand side of the balance sheet, you should record the value of *assets,* all the things you own that

### TABLE D.2    Personal Net Worth

| Assets | $ | Liabilities | $ |
|---|---|---|---|
| Checking accounts | ___ | Credit cards balances (list) | ___ |
| Savings accounts | ___ | 1 _____ | ___ |
| Money market accounts | ___ | 2 _____ | ___ |
| Other short-term investment | ___ | 3 _____ | ___ |
|  | ___ | Personal loans | ___ |
| Market value of investments (stocks, bonds, mutual funds) | ___ | Student loans | ___ |
|  | ___ | Car loans | ___ |
| Value of retirement funds | ___ | Home mortgage balance | ___ |
| College savings plan | ___ | Home equity loans | ___ |
| Other savings plans | ___ | Other real estate loans | ___ |
| Market value of real estate | ___ | Alimony/child support owed | ___ |
| Cars | ___ | Taxes owed (above withholding) | ___ |
| Home furnishings | ___ | Other investment loans | ___ |
| Jewelry/art/collectibles | ___ | Other liabilities/debts | ___ |
| Clothing/personal assets | ___ |  | ___ |
| Other assets | ___ |  | ___ |
| TOTAL ASSETS | ___ | TOTAL LIABILITIES | ___ |
| PERSONAL NET WORTH = TOTAL ASSETS − TOTAL LIABILITIES = $ ___ | | | |

have value. These include checking and savings account balances, investments, furniture, books, clothing, vehicles, houses, and the like. As with business balance sheets, assets are usually arranged from most liquid (easily convertible to cash) to least liquid. If you are a young student, it should not be surprising to find that you have little, if anything, to put on this side of your balance sheet. You should note that balance sheets are sensitive to the point in time chosen for evaluation. For example, if you always get paid on the first day of the month, your checking balance will be greatest at that point but will quickly be depleted as you pay for rent, food, and other needs. You may want to use your average daily balance in checking and savings accounts as a more accurate reflection of your financial condition. The right-hand side of the balance sheet is for recording *liabilities,* amounts of money that you owe to others. These include bank loans, mortgages, credit card debt, and other personal loans and are usually listed in order of how soon they must be paid back to the lender.

## The Cash Flow Statement

Businesses forecast and track their regular inflows and outflows of cash with a cash budget and summarize annual cash flows on the statement of cash flows. Similarly, individuals should have a clear understanding of their flow of cash as they budget their expenditures and regularly check to be sure that they are sticking to their budget.

What is cash flow? Anytime you receive cash or pay cash (including payments with checks), the dollar amount that is moving from one person to another is a **cash flow.** For students, the most likely cash inflows will be student loans, grants, and income from part-time jobs. Cash outflows will include rent, food, gas, car payments, books, tuition, and personal care expenses. Although it may seem obvious that you need to have enough inflows to cover the outflows, it is very common for people to estimate incorrectly and overspend. This may result in hefty bank overdraft charges or increasing debt as credit lines are used to make up the difference. Accurate forecasting of cash inflows and outflows allows you to make arrangements to cover estimated shortfalls before they occur. For students, this can be particularly valuable when cash inflows primarily occur at the beginning of the semester (for example, student loans) but outflows are spread over the semester.

How should you treat credit card purchases on your cash flow worksheet? Because credit purchases do not require payment of cash *now,* your cash flow statement should not reflect the value of the purchase as an outflow until you pay the bill. Take for example the purchase of a television set on credit. The $500 purchase will increase your assets and your liabilities by $500 but will only result in a negative cash flow of a few dollars per month, since payments on credit cards are cash outflows when they are made. If you always pay your credit card balances in full each month, the purchases are really the same thing as cash, and your balance sheet will never reflect the debt. But if you purchase on credit and only pay minimum balances, you will be living beyond your means, and your balance sheet will get more and more "upside down." A further problem with using credit to purchase assets that decline in value is that the liability may still be there long after the asset you purchased has no value.

Table D.3 can be used to estimate your cash flow. The purpose of a cash flow worksheet for your financial plan is to heighten your awareness of where the cash is going. Many people are surprised to find that they are spending more than they make (by using too much credit) or that they have significant "cash leakage"—those little expenditures that add up to a lot without their even noticing. Examples include afternoon lattes or snacks, too many nights out at the local pub, eating lunch at the Student Center instead of packing a bag, and regularly paying for parking (or parking tickets) instead of biking or riding the bus to school. In many cases, plugging the little leaks can free up enough cash to make a significant contribution toward achieving long-term savings goals.

# Set Short-Term and Long-Term Financial Goals

Just as a business develops its vision and strategic plan, individuals should have a clear set of financial goals. This component of your financial plan is the road map that will lead you to achieving your short-term and long-term financial goals.

**Short-term goals** are those that can be achieved in two years or less. They may include saving for particular short-term objectives, such as a new car, a down payment for a home, a vacation, or other major consumer purchases. For many people, short-term financial goals should include tightening up on household spending patterns and reducing outstanding credit.

**TABLE D.3**   **Personal Cash Flow**

| Cash Inflows | Monthly | Annual |
|---|---|---|
| Salary/wage income (gross) | $ _____ | $ _____ |
| Interest/dividend income | _____ | _____ |
| Other income (self-employment) | _____ | _____ |
| Rental income (after expenses) | _____ | _____ |
| Capital gains | _____ | _____ |
| Other income | _____ | _____ |
| Total income | _____ | _____ |
| **Cash Outflows** | **Monthly** | **Annual** |
| Groceries | $ _____ | $ _____ |
| Housing | _____ | _____ |
|   Mortgage or rent | _____ | _____ |
|   House repairs/expenses | _____ | _____ |
|   Property taxes | _____ | _____ |
| Utilities | _____ | _____ |
|   Heating | _____ | _____ |
|   Electric | _____ | _____ |
|   Water and sewer | _____ | _____ |
|   Cable/phone/satellite/Internet | _____ | _____ |
| Car loan payments | _____ | _____ |
| Car maintenance/gas | _____ | _____ |
| Credit card payments | _____ | _____ |
| Other loan payments | _____ | _____ |
| Income and payroll taxes | _____ | _____ |
| Other taxes | _____ | _____ |
| Insurance | _____ | _____ |
|   Life | _____ | _____ |
|   Health | _____ | _____ |
|   Auto | _____ | _____ |
|   Disability | _____ | _____ |
|   Other insurance | _____ | _____ |
| Clothing | _____ | _____ |
| Gifts | _____ | _____ |

*(continued)*

**TABLE D.3    Personal Cash Flow (*continued*)**

| | | |
|---|---|---|
| Other consumables (TVs, etc.) | —— | —— |
| Child care expenses | —— | —— |
| Sports-related expenses | —— | —— |
| Health club dues | —— | —— |
| Uninsured medical expenses | —— | —— |
| Education | —— | —— |
| Vacations | —— | —— |
| Entertainment | —— | —— |
| Alimony/child support | —— | —— |
| Charitable contributions | —— | —— |
| Required pension contributions | —— | —— |
| Magazine subscriptions/books | —— | —— |
| Other payments/expenses | —— | —— |
| Total Expenses | $ —— | $ —— |

NET PERSONAL CASH FLOW = TOTAL INCOME − TOTAL EXPENSES = $ ——

**Long-term goals** are those that require substantial time to achieve. Nearly everyone should include retirement planning as a long-term objective. Those who have or anticipate having children will probably consider college savings a priority. Protection of loved ones from the financial hazards of your unexpected death, illness, or disability is also a long-term objective for many individuals. If you have a spouse or other dependents, having adequate insurance and an estate plan in place should be part of your long-term goals.

## Create and Adhere to a Budget

Whereas the cash flow table you completed in the previous section tells you what you are doing with your money currently, a **budget** shows what you plan to do with it in the future. A budget can be for any period of time, but it is common to budget in monthly and/or annual intervals.

### Developing a Budget

You can use the cash flow worksheet completed earlier to create a budget. Begin with the amount of income you have for the month. Enter your nondiscretionary

Do you know whether your expenses are going up or going down? Use a budget to track them.

expenditures (that is, bills you *must* pay, such as tuition, rent, and utilities) on the worksheet and determine the leftover amount. Next list your discretionary expenditures, such as entertainment and cable TV, in order of importance. You can then work down your discretionary list until your remaining available cash flow is zero.

An important component of your budget is the amount that you allocate to savings. If you put a high priority on saving and you do not use credit to spend beyond your income each month, you will be able to accumulate wealth that can be used to meet your short-term and long-term financial goals. In the bestseller *The Millionaire Next Door,* authors Thomas J. Stanley and William D. Danko point out that most millionaires have achieved financial success through hard work and thriftiness as opposed to luck or inheritance. You cannot achieve your financial goals unless your budget process places a high priority on saving and investing.

## Tracking Your Budgeting Success

Businesses regularly identify budget items and track their variance from budget forecasts. People who follow a similar strategy in their personal finances are better able to meet their financial goals as well. If certain budgeted expenses routinely turn out to be under or over your previous estimates, then it is important to either revise the budget estimate or develop a strategy for reducing that expense.

College students commonly have trouble adhering to their budget for food and entertainment expenses. A strategy that works fairly well is to limit yourself to cash payments. At the beginning of the week, withdraw an amount from checking that will cover your weekly budgeted expenses. For the rest of the week, leave your checkbook, ATM card, and debit and credit cards at home. When the cash is gone, don't spend any more. While this is easier said than done, after a couple of weeks, you will learn to cut down on the cash leakage that inevitably occurs without careful cash management.

A debit card looks like a credit card but works like a check. For example, in the Netherlands almost no one writes a check, and everything is paid by debit card, which drafts directly from a checking account. You do not build up your credit rating when using a debit card. Figure D.1 indicates that the use of debit cards is growing rapidly in the United States. On the other hand, credit cards allow you to promise to pay for something at a later date by using preapproved lines of credit granted by a bank or finance company. Credit cards are easy to use and are accepted by most retailers today.

**FIGURE D.1    Number of Debit Card Transactions**

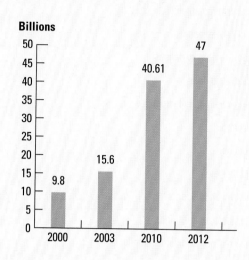

Sources: David Stuckey and Adrienne Lewis, "Swiping," *USA Today Snapshots,* March 20, 2008, A1, from The Nilson Report; "General Purpose Cards—U.S. 2011," *The Nilson Report,* Issue 988, February 2012; Creditcard.com, "Credit Card Statistics, Industry Facts, Debt Statistics," 2014, www.creditcards.com/credit-card-news/credit-card-industry-facts-personal-debt-statistics-1276.php (accessed June 16, 2014).

## Manage Credit Wisely

One of the cornerstones of your financial plan should be to keep credit usage to a minimum and to work at reducing outstanding debt. The use of credit for consumer and home purchases is well entrenched in our culture and has arguably fueled our economy and enabled Americans to better their standard of living as compared to earlier generations. Nevertheless, credit abuse is a serious problem in this country, and the most recent economic downturn undoubtedly pushed many households over the edge into bankruptcy as a result.

To consider the pros and cons of credit usage, compare the following two scenarios. In the first case, Joel takes an 8 percent fixed-rate mortgage to purchase a house to live in while he is a college student. The mortgage payment is comparable to alternative monthly rental costs, and his house appreciates 20 percent in value over the four years he is in college. At the end of college, Joel will be able to sell his house and reap the return, having invested only a small amount of his own cash. For example, if he made an initial 5 percent down payment on a $100,000 home that is now worth $120,000 four years later, he has earned $12,800 (after a 6 percent commission to the real estate agent) on an investment of $5,000. This amounts to a sizable return on investment of more than 250 percent over four years. This example is oversimplified in that we did not take into account the principal that has been repaid over the four years, and we did not consider the mortgage payment costs or the tax deductibility of interest paid during that time. However, the point is still clear; borrowing money to buy an asset that appreciates in value by more than the cost of the debt is a terrific way to invest.

In the second case, Nicole uses her credit card to pay for some of her college expenses. Instead of paying off the balance each month, Nicole makes only the minimum payment and incurs 16 percent interest costs. Over the course of several years of college, Nicole's credit card debt is likely to amount to several thousand dollars, typical of college graduates in the United States. The beer and pizza Nicole purchased have long ago been digested, yet the debt remains, and the payments continue. If Nicole continues making minimum payments, it will take many years to pay back that original debt, and in the meantime the interest paid will far exceed the original amount borrowed. Credit card debt in the amount of $1,000 will usually require a minimum payment of at least $15 per month. At this payment level, it will take 166 months (almost 14 years) to pay the debt in full, and the total interest paid will be more than $1,400!

So when is borrowing a good financial strategy? A rule of thumb is that you should borrow only to buy assets that will appreciate in value or when your financing charges are less than what you are earning on the cash that you would otherwise use to make the purchase. This rule generally will limit your borrowing to home purchases and investments.

## Use and Abuse of Credit Cards

Credit cards should be used only as a cash flow management tool. If you pay off your balance every month, you avoid financing charges (assuming no annual fee), you have proof of expenditures, which may be necessary for tax or business reasons, and you may be able to better match your cash inflows and outflows over the course of the month. There are several aspects of credit cards that you should be familiar with.

- *Finance charges.* Credit card companies make money by lending to you at a higher rate than it costs them to obtain financing. Since many of their customers don't pay back their debts in a timely fashion (default), they must charge enough to cover the risk of default as well. Interest is usually calculated on the average daily balance over the month, and payments are applied to old debts first. Although there are "teaser" rates that may be less than 5 percent, most credit cards regularly charge 13 to 24 percent annual interest. The low introductory rates are subject to time limitations (often six months or less), and they revert to the higher rates if you don't pay on time.

- *Annual fee.* Many credit cards assess an annual fee that may be as low as $15 or as much as $100 per year. If you regularly carry a very low balance, this amounts to the equivalent of a very high additional interest charge. For example, a $50 annual fee is the equivalent of an additional 5 percent on your annual interest rate if your balance is $1,000. Because the cards with fees do not generally provide you with different services, it is best to choose no-annual-fee credit cards.

- *Credit line.* The credit line is the maximum you are allowed to borrow. This may begin with a small amount for a new customer, perhaps as low as $300. As the customer shows the ability and intent to repay (by doing so in a timely fashion), the limit can increase to many thousands of dollars.

- *Grace period.* The grace period for most credit cards is 25 days. This may amount to twice as long a period of free credit depending on when your purchase date falls in the billing cycle. For example, if you used your card on January 1 and your billing cycle goes from the 1st to the 31st, then the bill for January purchases will arrive the first week in February and will be due on February 25. If you pay it in full on the last possible day, you will have had 55 days of free credit. Keep in mind that the lender considers the bill paid when the check is *received,* not when it is mailed.

- *Fees and penalties.* In addition to charging interest and annual fees, credit card companies charge extra for late payments and for going over the stated limit on the card. These fees have been on the rise in the past decade, and $25 or higher penalties are now fairly common.

- *ATM withdrawals.* Most credit cards can be used to obtain cash from ATMs. Although this may be convenient, it contributes to your increasing credit card balance and may result in extra expenditures that you would otherwise have avoided. In addition, these withdrawals may have hidden costs. Withdrawing cash from a machine that is not owned by your credit card lender will usually cause you to incur a fee of $1 or $1.50. The effective interest that this represents can be substantial if you are withdrawing small amounts of cash. A $1 charge on a withdrawal of $50 is the equivalent of 2 percent interest in addition to any interest you might pay to the credit card lender.

- *Perks.* Most credit cards provide a number of additional services. These may include a limitation on your potential liability in the event your card is lost or stolen or trip insurance. Some cards promise "cash back" in the form of a small rebate based on dollar volume of credit purchases. Many credit card companies offer the opportunity to participate in airline mileage programs. The general rule of thumb is that none of these perks is worth the credit card interest that is charged. If, however, you use your credit card as a cash management tool only, paying off your balance every month, then these perks are truly free to you.

## Student Loans

Student loans are fairly common in today's environment of rising college tuition and costs. These loans can be a great deal, offering lower interest rates than other loans and terms that allow deferral of repayment until graduation. Furthermore, the money is being borrowed to pay for an asset that is expected to increase in value—your human capital. Don't underestimate, however, the monthly payments that will be required upon graduation. Students today graduate with average student loan debt of approximately $33,000. This is the most debt to date that graduates are carrying after graduation, and it is double the amount graduates carried 20 years ago. It is likely that next year's graduating class will have a higher average debt burden as the rate increases every year. The rate of student debt is increasing at a rate higher than inflation.[9] Table D.4 shows the monthly payments required to repay the debt under various term

### TABLE D.4   How Much Will It Take to Pay That Debt?

| Months to Pay | Interest Rate | Amount of Debt | | | |
| --- | --- | --- | --- | --- | --- |
| | | $1,000 | $2,500 | $5,000 | $10,000 |
| 12 | 15% | $90.26 | $225.65 | $451.29 | $902.58 |
| | 18% | $91.68 | $229.20 | $458.40 | $916.80 |
| | 21% | $93.11 | $232.78 | $465.57 | $931.14 |
| 24 | 15% | $48.49 | $121.22 | $242.43 | $484.87 |
| | 18% | $49.92 | $124.81 | $249.62 | $499.24 |
| | 21% | $51.39 | $128.46 | $256.93 | $513.86 |
| 36 | 15% | $34.67 | $ 86.66 | $173.33 | $346.65 |
| | 18% | $36.15 | $ 90.38 | $180.76 | $361.52 |
| | 21% | $37.68 | $ 94.19 | $188.38 | $376.75 |
| 48 | 15% | $27.83 | $ 69.58 | $139.15 | $278.31 |
| | 18% | $29.37 | $ 73.44 | $146.87 | $293.75 |
| | 21% | $30.97 | $ 77.41 | $154.83 | $309.66 |
| 60 | 15% | $23.79 | $ 59.47 | $118.95 | $237.90 |
| | 18% | $25.39 | $ 63.48 | $126.97 | $253.93 |
| | 21% | $27.05 | $ 67.63 | $135.27 | $270.53 |
| 72 | 15% | $21.15 | $ 52.86 | $105.73 | $211.45 |
| | 18% | $22.81 | $ 57.02 | $114.04 | $228.08 |
| | 21% | $24.54 | $ 61.34 | $122.68 | $245.36 |

and interest scenarios. For larger outstanding debt amounts, new college graduates in entry-level positions find that it is difficult to make the necessary payments without help.

Although the average student loan debt is $33,000, many students end up owing much more than that. In 2014, the amount of student loan debt among Americans reached $1.08 trillion, exceeding the amount of credit card debt they owe. Figure D.2 shows how much the average debt per borrower has increased over the past 20 years.[10] Both political parties agree that something must be done to curb this debt, although they appear split on how to do so. In 2013, Congress passed the Bipartisan Student Loan Certainty Act, which bases the interest rate on federal student loans according to market rate fluctuations. The year in which the loan is borrowed will determine the interest rate for the life of the loan. For example, the rate for the 2014–2015 school year is set at 4.66 percent. This will be the rate at which the loan generates interest until it is repaid.[11] Also in 2014, President Obama signed an executive order mandating that repayments not exceed 10 percent of the borrower's monthly income.[12]

Before borrowing for your education, check into federal student loans because they are less risky and less expensive than private loans. In order to see what kind of federal loans for which you qualify, fill out the Free Application for Federal Student Aid (FAFSA). It is important to keep track of the details of your loans, and keep your loan servicer updated on any changes in your information to avoid expensive late fees. For a list of all your federal student loans, frequently visit the National Student Loan Data System at www. nslds.ed.gov. Private loans can be accessed from your credit report, of which you can request a copy at www.annualcreditreport.com.

It is also helpful to understand your repayment plan options. The most common are standard repayment and income-driven repayment. Standard repayment is when the same sum is paid every month, and while the payment may be high, you will pay off your loans more quickly and pay fewer interest payments. Income-driven repayment bases your monthly payments on a percentage of income. They require annual income verification and other paperwork, and interest charges are high. Visit the Department of Education at www. studentaid.ed.gov/repay-loans for information and calculators regarding the different repayment options. Those who work in government, nonprofit, and other public service jobs may be eligible for student loan forgiveness after 10 years of faithful repayments. Other programs offer forgiveness of debt for teachers, military service members, or medical practitioners. More information can be found at www.studentloanborrowerassistance.org.[13]

**FIGURE D.2    Average Debt per Student**

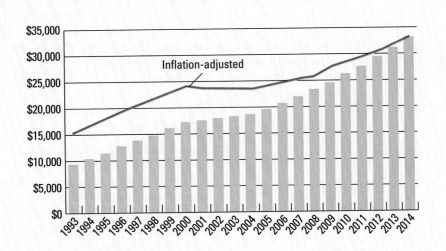

Source: Mark Kantrowitz analysis of National Center for Education Statistics data, wsj.com

# Develop a Savings and Investment Plan

The next step to achieving your financial goals is to decide on a savings plan. A common recommendation of financial planners is to "pay yourself first." What this means is that you begin the month by setting aside an amount of money for your savings and investments, as compared to waiting until the end of the month and seeing what's left to save or invest. The budget is extremely important for deciding on a reasonable dollar amount to apply to this component of your financial plan.

As students, you might think that you cannot possibly find any extra dollars in your budget for saving, but, in fact, nearly everyone can stretch their budget a little. Some strategies for students might include taking public transportation several times a week and setting aside the gas or parking dollars you would have spent, buying regular coffees instead of Starbucks lattes, or eating at home one more night per week.

## Understanding the Power of Compounded Returns

Even better, if you are a college student living on a typically small budget, you should be able to use this experience to help jump-start a viable savings program after graduation. If you currently live on $10,000 per year and your first job pays $30,000, it should be easy to "pay yourself" $2,000 or more per year. Putting the current maximum of $3,000 in an individual retirement account (IRA) will give you some tax advantages and can result in substantial wealth accumulation over time. An investment of only $2,000 per year from age 22 to retirement at 67 at 6 percent return per year will result in $425,487 at the retirement date. An annual contribution of $5,000 for 45 years will result in retirement wealth of about $1 million, not considering any additional tax benefits you might qualify for. If you invest that $5,000 per year for only 10 years and discontinue your contributions, you will still have about half a million dollars at age 67. And that assumes only a 6 percent return on investment!

What happens if you wait 10 years to start, beginning your $5,000 annual savings at age 32? By age 67, you will have only about a half million. Thirty-five years of investing instead of 45 doesn't sound like a big difference, but it cuts your retirement wealth in half. These examples illustrate an important point

about long-term savings and wealth accumulation— the earlier you start, the better off you will be.

## The Link between Investment Choice and Savings Goals

Once you have decided how much you can save, your choice of investment should be guided by your financial goals and the investment's risk and return and whether it will be long term or short term.

In general, investments differ in risk and return. The types of risk that you should be aware of are:

- Liquidity risk—How easy/costly is it to convert the investment to cash without loss of value?
- Default risk—How likely are you to receive the promised cash flows?
- Inflation risk—Will changes in purchasing power of the dollar over time erode the value of future cash flows your investment will generate?
- Price risk—How much might your investment fluctuate in value in the short run and the long run?

In general, the riskier an investment, the higher the return it will generate to you. Therefore, even though individuals differ in their willingness to take risk, it is important to invest in assets that expose you to at least moderate risk so that you can accumulate sufficient wealth to fund your long-term goals. To illustrate this more clearly, consider a $1 investment made in 1926. If this dollar had been invested in short-term Treasury bills, at the end of 2000 it would have grown to only $16.57. If the dollar had been invested in the S&P 500 index, which includes a diversified mix of stocks, the investment would be worth $2,586 in 2000 and about the same value in 2008, almost 200 times more than an investment in Treasury bills. But this gain was not without risk. In some of those 70 years, the stock market lost money and your investment would have actually declined in value.

## Short-Term versus Long-Term Investment

Given the differences in risk exposure across investments, your investment time horizon plays an important role in choice of investment vehicle. For example, suppose you borrow $5,000 on a student loan today but the money will be needed to pay tuition six months from now. Because you cannot afford to lose *any* of this principal in the short run, your investment should be in a low-risk security such as a bank certificate of deposit. These types of accounts promise that the original

$5,000 principal plus promised interest will be available to you when your tuition is due. During the bull market of the 1990s, many students were tempted to take student loans and invest in the stock market in the hopes of doubling their money (although this undoubtedly violated their lender's rules). However, in the recent bear market, this strategy might have reduced the tuition funds by 20 percent or more.

In contrast to money that you are saving for near-term goals, your retirement is likely to be many decades away, so you can afford to take more risk for greater return. The average return on stocks over the past 25 years has been around 17 percent. In contrast, the average return on long-term corporate bonds, which offer regular payments of interest to investors, has been around 10 percent. Short-term, low-risk debt securities have averaged 7 percent but were lower in 2010. The differences in investment returns between these three categories is explainable based on the difference in risk imposed on the owners. Stock is the most risky. Corporate bonds with their regular payments of interest are less risky to you since you do not have to wait until you sell your investment to get some of your return on the investment. Because they are less risky, investors expect a lower percentage return.

## Investment Choices

There are numerous possible investments, both domestic and international. The difficulty lies in deciding which ones are most appropriate for your needs and risk tolerance.

**Savings Accounts and Certificates of Deposit.**   The easiest parking spot for your cash is in a savings account. Unfortunately, investments in these low-risk (FDIC-insured), low-return accounts will barely keep up with inflation. If you have a need for liquidity but not necessarily immediate access to cash, a certificate of deposit wherein you promise to leave the money in the bank for six months or more will give you a slightly higher rate of return.

**Bonds.**   Corporations regularly borrow money from investors and issue bonds, which are securities that contain the firm's promise to pay regular interest and to repay principal at the end of the loan period, often 20 or more years in the future. These investments provide higher return to investors than short-term, interest-bearing accounts, but they also expose investors to price volatility, liquidity, and default risk.

Want to buy a home someday? Lenders will look at how you have handled your past debts before loaning you money.

A second group of bonds are those offered by government entities, commonly referred to as municipal bonds. These are typically issued to finance government projects, such as roads, airports, and bridges. Like corporate bonds, municipal bonds will pay interest on a regular basis, and the principal amount will be paid back to the investor at the end of a stated period of time, often 20 or more years. This type of bond has fewer interested investors and therefore has more liquidity risk.

**Stocks.**   A share of stock represents proportionate ownership interest in a business. Stockholders are thus exposed to all the risks that impact the business environment—interest rates, competition from other firms, input and output price risk, and others. In return for being willing to bear this risk, shareholders may receive dividends and/or capital appreciation in the value of their share(s). In any given year, stocks may fare better or worse than other investments, but there is substantial evidence that for long holding periods (20-plus years) stocks tend to outperform other investment choices.

**Mutual Funds.**   For the novice investor with a small amount of money to invest, the best choice is mutual funds. A mutual fund is a pool of funds from many investors that is managed by professionals who allocate the pooled dollars among various investments that meet the requirements of the mutual fund investors. There are literally thousands of these funds from which to choose, and they differ in type of investment (bonds, stocks, real estate, etc.), management style (active versus passive), and fee structure. Although even small investors have access to the market for individual securities, professional investors spend 100 percent of their time following the market and are likely to have more information at their disposal to aid in making buy and sell decisions.

### Purchase of a Home.

For many people, one of the best investments is the purchase of a home. With a small up-front investment (your down payment) and relatively low borrowing costs, modest appreciation in the home's value can generate a large return on investment. This return benefits from the tax deductibility of home mortgage interest and capital gains tax relief at the point of sale. And to top it off, you have a place to live and thus save any additional rental costs you would incur if you invested your money elsewhere. There are many sources of information about home ownership for investors on the Internet. What type of home can you afford? What mortgage can you qualify for? How much difference does investment choice make?

Everyone needs to have a place to live, and two-thirds of Americans own their own homes. Nevertheless, owning a home is not necessarily the best choice for everyone. The decision on when and how to buy a house and how much to spend must be made based on a careful examination of your ability to pay the mortgage and to cover the time and expense of maintenance and repair. A home is probably the largest purchase you will ever make in your life. It is also one of the best investments you can make. As in the example given earlier, the ability to buy with a small down payment and to deduct the cost of interest paid from your taxable income provides financial benefits that are not available with any other investment type.

Few people could afford to buy homes at young ages if they were required to pay the full purchase price on their own. Instead, it is common for people to borrow most of the money from a financial institution and pay it back over time. The process of buying a home can begin with your search for the perfect home or it can begin with a visit to your local lender, who can give you an estimate of the amount of mortgage for which

you can qualify. Mortgage companies and banks have specific guidelines that help them determine your creditworthiness. These include consideration of your ability and willingness to repay the loan in a timely fashion, as well as an estimate of the value of the house that will be the basis for the loan.

A **mortgage** is a special type of loan that commonly requires that you make a constant payment over time to repay the lender the original money you borrowed (**principal**) together with **interest,** the amount that the lender charges for your use of its money. In the event that you do not make timely payments, the lender has the right to sell your property to get its money back (a process called **foreclosure**).

Mortgage interest rates in the past decade have ranged from 5 to 10 percent per year, depending on the terms and creditworthiness of the borrower. There are many variations on mortgages, some that lock in an interest rate for the full term of the loan, often 30 years, and others that allow the rate to vary with market rates of interest. In low-interest-rate economic circumstances, it makes sense to lock in the mortgage at favorable low rates.

Several measures are commonly applied to assess your *ability to repay* the loan. In addition to requiring some work history, most lenders will apply two ratio tests. First, the ratio of your total mortgage payment (including principal, interest, property taxes, and home-owners insurance) to your gross monthly income can be no more than a prespecified percentage that varies from lender to lender but is rarely greater than 28 percent. Second, the ratio of your credit payments (including credit cards, car loan or lease payments, and mortgage payment) to your gross monthly income is limited to no more than 36 percent. More restrictive lenders will have lower limits on both of these ratios.

Lenders also consider your *willingness to repay* the loan by looking at how you have managed debt obligations in the past. The primary source of information will be a credit report provided by one of the large credit reporting agencies. Late payments and defaulted loans will appear on that report and may result in denial of the mortgage loan. Most lenders, however, will overlook previously poor credit if more recent credit management shows a change in behavior. This can be helpful to college students who had trouble paying bills before they were gainfully employed.

The value of the home is important to the lender since it is the **collateral** for the loan; that is, in the event that you default on the loan (don't pay), the lender has the right to take the home in payment of the loan. To ensure that they are adequately covered, lenders will rarely lend more than 95 percent of the appraised value of the home. If you borrow more than 80 percent of the value, you will usually be required to pay a mortgage insurance premium with your regular payments. This will effectively increase the financing costs by ½ percent per year.

To illustrate the process of buying a home and qualifying for a mortgage, consider the following example. Jennifer graduated from college two years ago and has saved $7,000. She intends to use some of her savings as a down payment on a home. Her current salary is $36,000. She has a car payment of $250 per month and credit card debt that requires a minimum monthly payment of $100 per month. Suppose that Jennifer has found her dream home, which has a price of $105,000. She intends to make a down payment of $5,000 and borrow the rest. Can she qualify for the $100,000 loan at a rate of 7 percent?

Using Table D.5, her payment of principal and interest on a loan of $100,000 at 7 percent annual interest will be $665. With an additional $150 per month for property taxes and insurance (which may vary substantially in different areas of the country), her total payment will be $815. Since her gross monthly income is $3,000, the ratio of her payment to her income is 27 percent. Unless her lender has fairly strict rules, this should be acceptable. Her ratio of total payments

to income will be ($815 + $250 + $150)/$3,000 = 40.5 percent. Unfortunately, Jennifer will not be able to qualify for this loan in her current financial circumstances.

So what can she do? The simplest solution is to use some of her remaining savings to pay off her credit card debt. By doing this, her debt ratio will drop to 35.5 percent and she will be accomplishing another element of good financial planning—reducing credit card debt and investing in assets that increase in value.

## Planning for a Comfortable Retirement

Although it may seem like it's too early to start thinking about retirement when you are still in college, this is actually the best time to do so. In the investment section of this Appendix, you learned about the power of compound interest over long periods of time. The earlier you start saving for long-term goals, the easier it will be to achieve them.

**How Much to Save.**    There is no "magic number" that will tell you how much to save. You must determine, based on budgeted income and expenses, what amount is realistic to set aside for this important goal. Several factors should help to guide this decision:

- Contributions to qualified retirement plans can be made before tax. This allows you to defer the payment of taxes until you retire many years from now.
- Earnings on retirement plan assets are tax deferred. If you have money in nonretirement vehicles, you will have to pay state and federal taxes on your earnings, which will significantly reduce your ending accumulation.
- If you need the money at some time before you reach age 59½, you will be subject to a withdrawal penalty of 10 percent, and the distribution will also be subject to taxes at the time of withdrawal.

In planning for your retirement needs, keep in mind that inflation will erode the purchasing power of your money. You should consider your ability to replace preretirement income as a measure of your success in retirement preparation. You can use the Social Security Administration website (**www.ssa .gov**) to estimate your future benefits from that program. In addition, most financial websites provide calculators to aid you in forecasting the future accumulations of your savings.

**TABLE D.5**    **Calculating Monthly Mortgage Payments** (30 year loan, principal and interest only)

| Annual Interest % | Amount Borrowed | | | |
|---|---|---|---|---|
| | $75,000 | $100,000 | $125,000 | $150,000 |
| 6.0 | $450 | $600 | $ 749 | $ 899 |
| 6.5 | $474 | $632 | $ 790 | $ 948 |
| 7.0 | $499 | $665 | $ 832 | $ 998 |
| 7.5 | $524 | $699 | $ 874 | $1,049 |
| 8.0 | $550 | $734 | $ 917 | $1,101 |
| 8.5 | $577 | $769 | $ 961 | $1,153 |
| 9.0 | $603 | $805 | $1,006 | $1,207 |
| 9.5 | $631 | $841 | $1,051 | $1,261 |
| 10.0 | $658 | $878 | $1,097 | $1,316 |

**Employer Retirement Plans.** Many employers offer retirement plans as part of their employee benefits package. **Defined benefit plans** promise a specific benefit at retirement (for example, 60 percent of final salary). More commonly, firms offer **defined contribution plans,** where they promise to put a certain amount of money into the plan in your name every pay period. The plan may also allow you to make additional contributions or the employer may base its contribution on your contribution (for example, by matching the first 3 percent of salary that you put in). Employers also may make it possible for their employees to contribute additional amounts toward retirement on a tax-deferred basis. Many plans now allow employees to specify the investment allocation of their plan contributions and to shift account balances between different investment choices.

Some simple rules to follow with respect to employer plans include the following:

- If your employer offers you the opportunity to participate in a retirement plan, you should do so.
- If your employer offers to match your contributions, you should contribute as much as is necessary to get the maximum match, if you can afford to. Every dollar that the employer matches is like getting a 100 percent return on your investment in the first year.
- If your plan allows you to select your investment allocation, do not be too conservative in your choices if you still have many years until retirement.

## Individual Retirement Accounts (IRAs).

Even if you do not have an employer-sponsored plan, you can contribute to retirement through an individual retirement account (IRA). There are two types of IRAs with distinctively different characteristics (which are summarized in Table D.6). Although previously subject to a $2,000 maximum annual contribution limit, tax reform in 2001 increased that limit gradually to $5,000 by 2008. The critical difference between Roth IRAs and traditional IRAs is the taxation of contributions and withdrawals. Roth IRA contributions are taxable, but the withdrawals are tax-free. Traditional IRAs are deductible, but the withdrawals are taxable. Both types impose a penalty of 10 percent for withdrawal before the qualified retirement age of 59½, subject to a few exceptions.

**TABLE D.6**   **Comparing Individual Retirement Account Options**

|  | Roth IRA | Traditional IRA |
|---|---|---|
| 2008–2010 allowable contribution | $5,000 | $5,000 |
| Contributions deductible from current taxable income | No | Yes |
| Current tax on annual investment earnings | No | No |
| Tax due on withdrawal in retirement | No | Yes |
| 10% penalty for withdrawal before age 59½ | Yes | Yes |
| Mandatory distribution before age 70½ | No | Yes |
| Tax-free withdrawals allowed for first-time homebuyers | Yes | No |

**Social Security.** Social Security is a public pension plan sponsored by the federal government and paid for by payroll taxes equally split between employers and employees. In addition to funding the retirement portion of the plan, Social Security payroll taxes pay for Medicare insurance (an old-age health program), disability insurance, and survivors benefits for the families of those who die prematurely.

The aging of the U.S. population has created a problem for funding the current Social Security system. Whereas it has traditionally been a pay-as-you-go program, with current payroll taxes going out to pay current retiree benefits, the impending retirement of baby boomers is forecast to bankrupt the system early in this century if changes are not made in a timely fashion. To understand the problem, consider that when Social Security began, there were 17 workers for each retiree receiving benefits. There are currently fewer than four workers per beneficiary. After the baby boom retirement, there will be only two workers to pay for each retiree. Obviously, that equation cannot work.

Does that mean that Social Security will not be around when you retire? Contrary to popular belief, it is unlikely that this will happen. There are simply too many voters relying on the future of Social Security for Congress to ever take such a drastic action. Instead, it is likely that the current system will be revised to help

**FIGURE D.3**    **Confidence in Social Security for Those with Retirement Plans**

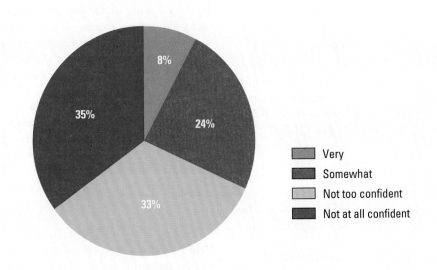

Source: Ruth Helman, Nevin Adams, and Jack VanDerhei, "The 2014 Retirement Confidence Survey: Confidence Rebounds—for Those with Retirement Plans," March 2014, No. 397 (Washington, D.C.: Employee Benefit Research Institute, 2014).

it balance. Prior to the heavy declines in the stock market in 2008–2009 there was some general support for a plan that would divert some of the current payroll taxes to fund individual retirement accounts that could be invested in market assets. In addition, it seems likely that the retirement age will increase gradually to age 67. Other possible changes are to increase payroll taxes or to limit benefits payable to wealthier individuals. The proposed solutions are all complicated by the necessity of providing a transition program for those who are too old to save significant additional amounts toward their retirement. Figure D.3 indicates that most people are concerned about receiving fewer Social Security benefits when they retire.

## Evaluate and Purchase Insurance

The next step in personal financial planning is the evaluation and purchase of insurance. Insurance policies are contracts between you and an insurance company wherein the insurer promises to pay you money in the event that a particular event occurs. Insurance is important, not only to protect your own assets from claims but also to protect your loved ones and dependents. The most common types of insurance for individuals are identified and briefly described below.

## Automobile Insurance

In most states, drivers are required by law to carry a minimum amount of **auto liability insurance.** In the event that you are in a car accident, this coverage promises to pay claims against you for injuries to persons or property, up to a maximum per person and per accident. The basic liability policy will also cover your own medical costs. If you want to insure against damage to your own vehicle, you must purchase an additional type of coverage called **auto physical damage insurance.** If you have a car loan, the lender will require that you carry this type of insurance, since the value of the car is the collateral for that loan and the lender wants to be sure that you can afford to fix any damage to the vehicle following an accident. The minimum limits in most states are too low to cover typical claim levels. Good financial planning requires that you pay for insurance coverage with much higher limits.

Auto physical damage insurance coverage is always subject to a **deductible.** A deductible is an amount that you must pay before the insurance company will pay. To illustrate this, suppose your policy has a $250 deductible. You back into your garage door and damage your bumper, which will cost $750 to fix. The insurer will only pay $500, because you are responsible for the first $250. Once you receive the check from the insurer, you are free to try to get it fixed for less than the full $750.

## Homeowners/Renters Insurance

**Homeowners insurance** provides coverage for liability and property damage in your home. For example, if someone slips and falls on your front steps and sues you for medical expenses, this insurance policy will pay the claim (or defend you against the claim if the insurer thinks it is not justified). If your house and/or property are damaged in a fire, the insurance will pay for lost property and the costs of repair. It is a good idea to pay extra for replacement cost insurance, since otherwise the insurance company is only obligated to pay you the depreciated value, which won't be enough to replace your belongings.

    **Renters insurance** is similar to homeowners in that it covers you for liability on your premises (for example, if your dog bites someone) and for damage to your personal property. Because you do not own the house, your landlord needs to carry separate insurance for his building. This insurance is very cheap and is well worth the cost, since your landlord's insurance will not pay anything to you in the event that the house burns down and you lose all your belongings.

## Life Insurance

As compared to other types of insurance, the primary purpose of life insurance is to provide protection for others. **Life insurance** pays a benefit to your designated beneficiary (usually your spouse or other family members) in the event that you die during the coverage period. Life insurance premiums will depend on the face amount of the policy, your age and health, your habits (smoker versus nonsmoker), and the type of policy (whether it includes an investment component in addition to the death benefit).

    The simplest type of life insurance is **term insurance.** This policy is usually for one year and the insurer promises to pay your designated beneficiary only the face amount of the policy in the event that you die during the year of coverage. Because the probability of dying at a young age is very small, the cost of providing this promise to people in their 20s and 30s is very inexpensive, and premiums are fairly low. Term insurance becomes more expensive at older ages, since the probability of dying is much higher and insurers must charge more.

Other types of life insurance usually fall into a category often called **permanent insurance,** because they are designed to provide you with insurance protection over your lifetime. To provide lifetime coverage at a reasonable cost, premiums will include an investment component. While there are many variations, typically in the early years of the policy you are paying a lot more than the actual cost of providing the death protection. The insurer takes that extra cost and invests it so that when you are older, the company has sufficient funds to cover your death risk. The primary difference between different types of permanent insurance is the way that they treat the investment component. Some policies allow the buyer to direct the investment choice and others do not.

## Health Insurance

**Health insurance** pays the cost of covered medical expenses during the policy period, which is usually six months or one year. Most health insurance is provided under group policies through employers, but it is possible to purchase an individual policy. Because those who want to buy individual insurance are likely to be people who anticipate medical expenses, individual policies can be very expensive and are usually subject to exclusions, high coinsurance (the percentage of each dollar of expenses that you must pay out of pocket), and deductibles (the amount you must pay in full before the insurance pays).

    From a financial-planning perspective, the type of health coverage that is most important is that which will protect you and your family from unexpected large medical costs. The usual checkups, shots, and prescription drugs are all budgetable expenses and need not be insured. At a minimum, you should have a policy that covers hospitalization and care for major disease or injury. This can be accomplished at relatively low cost by contracting for a large deductible (e.g., you pay the first $1,000 of costs per year).

    The two main types of health insurance plans are *fee-for-service* and *managed care.* In a fee-for-service arrangement, the insurer simply pays for whatever covered medical costs you incur, subject to the deductible and coinsurance. Blue Cross and Blue Shield plans are the best known of this type. Managed care includes health maintenance organizations (HMOs) and preferred provider organizations (PPOs). In these health insurance arrangements, your health insurer pays all your costs (subject sometimes to small co-pays for office visits), but the care you receive is determined by

Medical costs can be astronomical. Part of keeping your finances in order is making sure you have health insurance.

your physician, who has contracted with the health insurer and has incentives to control overall costs. You are often limited in your choice of physician and your ability to seek specialist care under these plans.

Major changes in health insurance began to occur after the 2010 passage of the Patient Protection and Affordable Care Act. According to the law, individuals who are self-employed or who do not receive health insurance through their businesses can pay for insurance through state-based exchanges. Exchanges will also be created for small businesses to purchase health coverage, along with tax breaks for this purpose. All individuals who do not have insurance from their employers must pay for their own insurance or face penalties, but low-income people who cannot afford to pay can receive government subsidies. Employers with more than 50 employees must also pay for health care coverage. The purpose of this legislation is to provide health insurance for the more than 32 million Americans who were uninsured. The act also puts limits on insurers. For instance, insurers can no longer deny coverage or benefits based on a preexisting condition. The Patient Protection and Affordable Care Act will have a wide-ranging impact on the health care industry, including how much you will pay for future health care insurance.[14]

## Disability Insurance

One of the most overlooked types of insurance is **disability insurance,** which pays replacement income to you in the event you are disabled under the definition in your policy. One in three people will be disabled for a period of three months or more during their lifetime, so disability insurance should be a component of the financial plan for anyone without sufficient financial resources to weather a period of loss of income.

## Develop an Estate Plan

As with retirement planning, it is difficult to think about estate planning when you are young. In fact, you probably don't need to think much about it yet. If you have no dependents, there is little point in doing so. However, if you are married or have other dependents, you should include this as a necessary part of your financial plan. The essential components of an **estate plan** are

- Your will, including a plan for guardianship of your children.
- Minimization of taxes on your estate.
- Protection of estate assets.

Estate planning is a complicated subject that is mired in legal issues. As such, appropriate design and implementation of an estate plan requires the assistance of a qualified professional.

## The Importance of Having a Will

There are several circumstances that necessitate having a will. If you have a spouse and/or dependent children, if you have substantial assets, or if you have specific assets that you would like to give to certain individuals in the event of your death, you *should* have a will. On the other hand, if you are single with no assets or obligations (like many students), a will is probably not necessary—yet.

Having a valid will makes the estate settlement simpler for your spouse. If your children are left parentless, will provisions specify who will take guardianship of the children and direct funds for their support. You might also like to include a *living will,* which gives your family directions for whether to keep you on life support in the event that an illness or injury makes it unlikely for you to survive without extraordinary interventions. Lastly, you may want to make a will so that you can give your iPad to your college roommate or Grandma's china to your daughter. Absent such

## Gender Differences Create Special Financial Planning Concerns

Although most people would agree that there are some essential differences between men and women, it is not as clear why their financial planning needs should be different. After all, people of both sexes need to invest for future financial goals like college educations for their children and retirement income for themselves. In the past few years, professionals have written articles considering this subject. The results are both controversial and eye-opening.

- Even though 75 percent of women in the United States are working, they still have greater responsibility for household chores, child care, and care of aging parents than their husbands. This leaves less time for household finances.

- Women still earn much less than men, on average.

- Women are much less likely to have a pension sponsored through their employer. Only one-third of all working women have one at their current employer.

- Women are more conservative investors than men. Although there is evidence that women are gradually getting smart about taking a little more risk in their portfolios, on average they allocate half as much as men do to stocks.

- Most women will someday be on their own, either divorced or widowed.

Because women live an average of five years longer than men, they actually need to have saved more to provide a comparable retirement income. The combined impact of these research findings makes it difficult but not impossible for women to save adequately for retirement. Much of the problem lies in education. Women need to be better informed about investing in order to make choices early in life that will pay off in the end. If they don't take the time to become informed about their finances or can't due to other obligations, in the end they will join the ranks of many women over age 65 who are living in poverty. But when women earn less, they don't have access to an employer pension, and they invest too conservatively, it is no surprise that women have so little wealth accumulation.

In her book, *The Busy Woman's Guide to Financial Freedom,* Dr. Vickie Bajtelsmit, an associate professor at Colorado State University, provides a road map for women who are interested in taking charge of their financial future. With simple-to-follow instructions for all aspects of financial planning, from investing to insurance to home buying, the book provides information for women to get on the right financial track.

**FIGURE D.4**   **How Do You Prepare Your Taxes?**

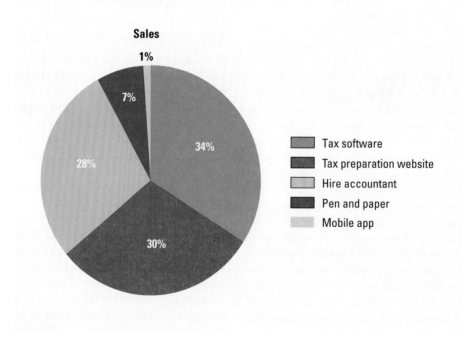

n=912 respondents, conducted in Mach 2013

provisions, relatives and friends have been known to take whatever they want without regard to your specific desires.

### Avoiding Estate Taxes

As students, it will likely be many years before you will have accumulated a large enough estate (all your "worldly possessions") to have to worry about estate taxes. Although federal tax law changes eliminated the estate tax in 2010, the tax was reinstated and raised to 35 percent in 2011. Today, the estate tax is at a maximum of 40 percent of assets upon death, with talks to raise it as high as 45 percent.[15] This is an area of law that frequently changes. Because no one can predict the date of his or her death, this implies that estate tax planning should be done assuming the worst-case scenario. Current estate taxes can take a big bite out of your family's inheritance for wealthy taxpayers. Thus, much of estate planning is actually tax-avoidance planning. Professionals can help set up trust arrangements that allow all or part of your estate to pass to your heirs without incurring taxes.

## Adjust Your Financial Plan to New Circumstances

Finally, to ensure the success of your overall financial plan, it is vital that you evaluate it on a periodic basis and adjust it to accommodate changes in your life, such as marriage, children, or the addition or deletion of a second income from your spouse. You may be preparing income tax returns now, but as your income increases, you may have to make a decision about professional assistance. Figure D.4 indicates that most people prepare their own taxes, but many taxpayers use a professional service. Your plan also must be adjusted as your financial goals change (for example, desires to own a home, make a large purchase, or retire at an early age). Whatever your goals may be, the information and worksheets provided here will help with your personal financial planning.

# Notes

## Chapter 1

1. Travis Hoium, "Coke and Pepsi Up Against a Young Monster, and Losing," *Daily Finance,* March 26, 2013, www.dailyfinance.com/on/coke-pepsi-monster-beverage-energy-drinks/ (accessed July 26, 2013); Geoff Colvin, "The 50 Greatest Business Rivalries of All Time—A Little Competition," *Fortune,* March 21, 2013, http://money.cnn.com/gallery/news/companies/2013/03/21/greatest-business-rivalries.fortune/index.html (accessed July 26, 2013); Kim Bhasin, "Coke vs. Pepsi: The Amazing Story Behind the Cola Wars," *Business Insider,* November 2, 2011, www.businessinsider.com/soda-wars-coca-cola-pepsi-history-infographic-2011-11?op=1 (accessed July 26, 2013); Anastasia Kourovskaia, "Soft Drink Top 2013," *Kantar UK Insights,* June 28, 2013, www.kantar.com/business/brands/brandz-top-10-most-valuable-soft-drinks-brands-2013/ (accessed July 26, 2013).

2. "Diversity Resources," The Graduate Management Admissions Council, www.gmac.com/reach-and-recruit-students/recruit-students-for-your-program/diversify-your-candidate-pool/diversity-resources-2.aspx (accessed April 2, 2014).

3. Philip Fava, "Recycling E-Waste: How One Company Gets It Right," *Forbes,* November 13, 2012, www.forbes.com/sites/philfava/2012/11/13/recycling-e-waste-how-one-company-gets-it-right/ (accessed February 19, 2014).

4. Loretta Chao, "As Rivals Outsource, Lenovo Keeps Production In-House," *The Wall Street Journal,* July 9, 2012, http://online.wsj.com/news/articles/SB10001424052702303302504577325522699291362 (accessed February 19, 2014).

5. Serena Ng, "Soap Opera: Amazon Moves In With P&G," *The Wall Street Journal,* October 15, 2013, pp. A1 and A2.

6. Caleb Melby, "Hershey Invests $300 Million in Future of American Manufacturing . . . and Consumption," *Forbes,* September 25, 2012, www.forbes.com/sites/calebmelby/2012/09/25/hershey-invests-300-million-in-future-of-american-manufacturing-and-consumption/ (accessed February 19, 2014).

7. Michael McCutcheon, "How Millennials Are Responding to Coca Cola's New Anti-Obesity Campaign," *Policy Mic,* January 16, 2013, www.policymic.com/articles/23432/how-millennials-are-responding-to-coca-cola-s-new-anti-obesity-campaign (accessed February 19, 2014); Steven Reinberg, "Food Companies Cut 6.4 Trillion Calories from Supermarket Shelves: Report," *Health Day,* January 9, 2014, http://consumer.healthday.com/vitamins-and-nutrition-information-27/food-and-nutrition-news-316/food-companies-cut-6-4-trillion-calories-from-supermarket-shelves-report-683691.html (accessed February 19, 2014).

8. "Got Milk?" www.gotmilk.com/ (accessed April 2, 2014).

9. "About Bill Daniels," www.danielsfund.org/About-Us/About-Bill-Daniels.asp (accessed April 2, 2014).

10. "Reforms Please Cubans, But Is It Communism?" *Associated Press,* April 2, 2008, www.msnbc.msn.com/id/23925259 (accessed April 2, 2014).

11. "Special Report: The Visible Hand," *The Economist,* January 21, 2012, pp. 3–5.

12. James T. Areddy and Craig Karmin, "China Stocks Once Frothy, Fall by Half in Six Months," *The Wall Street Journal,* April 16, 2008, pp. 1, 7.

13. "Special Report: The Visible Hand."

14. "Special Report: The World in Their Hands," *The Economist,* January 21, 2012, pp. 15–17.

15. "The Shark Tank," *ABC,* http://abc.go.com/shows/shark-tank/bios (accessed April 2, 2014).

16. "World Ranking 2013 of Hotel Groups and Brands," Hospitality.net, April 3, 2013, www.hospitalitynet.org/news/4060119.html (accessed February 20, 2014); Dan Schawbel, "J.W. Marriott Jr: From Root Beer Stand to Global Hotel Company," *Forbes,* February 4, 2013, www.forbes.com/sites/danschawbel/2013/02/04/j-w-marriott-jr-from-root-beer-stand-to-global-hotel-company/ (accessed February 20, 2014); "Marriott Gets Small to Go Big," *Fortune*, February 24, 2014, p. 14.

17. The Economist, "Swiss Watchmakers: Time Is Money," *The Economist,* February 16, 2013, www.economist.com/news/business/21571943-industry-ripe-shake-up-time-money (accessed July 16, 2013); James Shotter, "Swiss Regulator Winds Back on Swatch Deal," *Financial Times,* July 12, 2013, www.ft.com/intl/cms/s/0/88f23d20-eacb-11e2-bfdb-00144feabdc0.html#axzz2ZF7Aa99D (accessed July 16, 2013); Thomas Mulier, "Swatch Allowed to Cut Only Movement Sales, Regulator Says," *Bloomberg,* July 12, 2013, www.bloomberg.com/news/2013-07-12/swatch-allowed-to-cut-only-movement-sales-regulator-says.html (accessed July 16, 2013).

18. World International Property Organization, "International Patent Filings Set New Record in 2011," March 5, 2012, www.wipo.int/pressroom/en/articles/2012/article_0001.html (accessed February 20, 2014).

19. Paul Toscano, "The Worst Hyperinflation Situations of All Time," *CNBC,* February 14, 2011, http://www.cnbc.com/id/41532451 (accessed February 20, 2014).

20. "Zimbabwe," *CIA—The World Factbook,* www.cia.gov/library/publications/the-world-factbook/

geos/zi.html# (accessed April 2, 2014).

21. Stephan Dinan, "U.S. Debt Jumps a Record $328 Billion—Tops $17 Trillion for the First Time," *Washington Times,* October 18, 2013, www.washingtontimes.com/news/2013/oct/18/us-debt-jumps-400-billion-tops-17-trillion-first-t/ (accessed February 20, 2014).

22. Chris Woodyard, "If a Tree Falls in the Forest, Does It End Up in a Car?" *USA Today,* June 28, 2013, p. 3B; Bill Esler, "Real Wood Preferred in Eco Car Interiors," Wood Working Network, July 8, 2013, www.woodworkingnetwork.com/wood/component-sourcing/Reclaimed-Wood-Dresses-Car-Interiors-214604411.html#sthash.cuo9IOEi.dpbs (accessed July 26, 2013); Ford, "Ford Uses Kenaf Plant Inside Doors in the All-New Escape, Saving Weight and Energy," http://media.ford.com/article_display.cfm?article_id=35895 (accessed July 26, 2013).

23. U.S. Census Bureau, "State & County Quick Facts," http://quickfacts.census.gov/qfd/states/00000.html (accessed February 20, 2014); Haya El Nasser, Gregory Korte, and Paul Overberg, "308.7 Million," *USA Today,* December 22, 2010, p. 1A.

24. Liz Peek, "Why Women Are Leaving the Workforce in Record Numbers," *The Fiscal Times,* April 17, 2013, www.thefiscaltimes.com/Columns/2013/04/17/Why-Women-Are-Leaving-the-Workforce-in-Record-Numbers (accessed April 2, 2014).

25. Telis Demos and Ian Sherr, "IPO Action for GoPro Camera Maker," *The Wall Street Journal*, February 8–9, 2014, p. B3.

26. Eli Lilly, "Heritage," www.lilly.com/about/heritage/Pages/heritage.aspx (accessed February 20, 2014).

27. Emeco, "About Emeco," Emeco website, www.emeco.net/about-emeco/1944 (accessed January 6, 2014); CBS News, "Exploring the History of An Iconic Chair," *CBS,* January 6, 2014, www.cbsnews.com/videos/exploring-the-history-of-an-

iconic-chair/ (accessed January 6, 2014); Christopher Jon Sprigman and Kal Raustiala, "Can Restoration Hardware Legally Knockoff the Navy Chair?" *Slate*, November 26, 2012, www.slate.com/articles/news_and_politics/jurisprudence/2012/11/the_navy_chair_restoration_hardware_s_imitation_of_emeco_s_original_design.html (accessed January 6, 2014).

28. Walmart, "Corporate and Financial Facts," February 2014, http://news.walmart.com/walmart-facts/corporate-financial-fact-sheet (accessed April 2, 2014); Anthony Bianco and Wendy Zellner, "Is Wal-Mart Too Powerful?" *BusinessWeek,* October 6, 2003, pp. 100–10.

29. "Stopping SOPA," *The Economist,* January 21, 2012, p. 33.

30. "The 2011 World's Most Ethical Companies," *Ethisphere,* 2011, Q1, pp. 37–43.

31. Isabelle Maignon, Tracy L. Gonzalez-Padron, G. Tomas M. Hult, and O. C. Ferrell, "Stakeholder Orientation: Development and Testing of a Framework for Socially Responsible Marketing," *Journal of Strategic Marketing,* 19, no. 4 (July 2011), pp. 313–338.

32. Small Business Administration Office of Advocacy, *Frequently Asked Questions,* 2012, www.sba.gov/sites/default/files/FAQ_Sept_2012.pdf (accessed February 20, 2014); Joel Holland, "Save the World, Make a Million," *Entrepreneur,* April 2010, www.entrepreneur.com/magazine/entrepreneur/2010/april/205556.html (accessed April 20, 2010); iContact, www.icontact.com (accessed April 2, 2014).

33. Kevin Kelleher, "The Rise of Redbox Should Spook Netflix," *CNNMoney,* February 10, 2012, http://tech.fortune.cnn.com/2012/02/10/the-rise-of-redbox-should-spook-netflix/ (accessed May 14, 2014); Marc Graser, "Redbox Now Controls More than 50% of Home Video Disc Rental Biz," *Variety,* July 25, 2013, http://variety.com/2013/biz/news/redbox-now-controls-more-than-50-of-home-video-disc-rental-biz-1200568295/

(accessed May 14, 2014); Joan E. Solsman, "Verizon-Redbox Venture Advances," *The Wall Street Journal*, December 12, 2012, http://online.wsj.com/news/articles/SB10001424127887324296604578175653423616518 (accessed May 14, 2014); Kyle Stock, "Redbox Sacrifices Margins to Drive DVD Rentals," *Bloomberg Businessweek*, September 17, 2013, www.businessweek.com/articles/2013-09-17/redbox-sacrifices-margins-to-drive-dvd-rentals (accessed May 14, 2014).

## Chapter 2

1. Thomas M. Burton and Serena Ng, "FDA Seeks Stricter Rules on Antibacterial Soaps," *The Wall Street Journal*, December 16, 2013, http://online.wsj.com/news/articles/SB10001424052702304403804579262131820434674 (accessed March 28, 2014); Brian Clark Howard, "Avoid Antibacterial Soaps, Say Consumer Advocates," *National Geographic,* http://news.nationalgeographic.com/news/2013/12/131217-antibacterial-soaps-triclosan-fda-hygiene-safety-health/?rptregcta=reg_free_np&rptregcampaign=20131016_rw_membership_r1p_us_se_w# (accessed March 28, 2014); Allison E. Aiello, Bonnie Marshall, Stuart B. Levy, Phyllis Della-Latta, and Elaine Larson, "Relationship between Triclosan and Susceptibilities of Bacteria Isolated from Hands in Community," *Antimicrob Agents Chemother,* 48, no. 8 (2004), pp. 2973–79; Elizabeth Weise, "FDA: Antibacterial Soaps Could Pose Health Risks," *USA Today*, December 16, 2013, www.usatoday.com/story/news/nation/2013/12/16/fda-antibacterial-soap/4038907/ (accessed March 28, 2014); Andrew Martin, "Antibacterial Chemical Raises Safety Issues," *The New York Times,* August 19, 2011, www.nytimes.com/2011/08/20/business/triclosan-an-antibacterial-chemical-in-consumer-products-raises-safety-issues.html?pagewanted=all&_r=0 (accessed March 28, 2014).

2. Kimberly Blanton, "Creating a Culture of Compliance," *CFO,* July/August 2011, pp. 19–21.

3. Better Business Bureau, "Origaudio," www.bbb.org/chicago/business-reviews/speakers-rebuild-and-repair/origaudio-in-chicago-il-88480280 (accessed October 10, 2013); Jenna Schnuer, "Emerging Entrepreneur of 2012: Jason Lucash," *Entrepreneur,* December 18, 2012, www.entrepreneur.com/article/225215 (accessed October 9, 2013); Jan Norman, "Fold Up Speakers Launch O.C. Company," *OC Register,* August 21, 2013, www.ocregister.com/articles/lucash-327250-origaudio-company.html (accessed October 9, 2013); "The Foldable Speaker: The 50 Best Inventions of 2009," *Time,* http://content.time.com/time/specials/packages/article/0,28804,1934027_1934003_1933984,00.html (accessed October 10, 2013); OrigAudio website, www.origaudio.com/shop/index.php?dispatch=categories.view&category_id=176 (accessed April 1, 2014).

4. Kate Pickert, "Medicare Fraud Horror: Cancer Doctor Indicted for Billing Unnecessary Chemo," *Time,* August 15, 2013, http://nation.time.com/2013/08/15/medicare-fraud-horror-cancer-doctor-indicted-for-billing-unnecessary-chemo/ (accessed February 24, 2014).

5. Ronald Alsop, "Corporate Scandals Hit Home," *The Wall Street Journal,* February 19, 2004, http://online.wsj.com/news/articles/SB107715182807433462 (accessed April 4, 2014).

6. Serena Ng and Joann S. Lublin, "Avon Raises Estimate of Bribery-Probe's Cost," *The Wall Street Journal,* February 14, 2014, p. B3.

7. O. C. Ferrell, John Fraedrich, and Linda Ferrell, *Business Ethics: Ethical Decision Making and Cases,* 8th ed. (Mason, OH: South-Western Cengage Learning, 2011), p. 7.

8. David Callahan, as quoted in Archie Carroll, "Carroll: Do We Live in a Cheating Culture?" *Athens Banner-Herald,* February 21, 2004, http://onlineathens.com/stories/022204/bus_20040222028.shtml (accessed April 4, 2014).

9. Elliot Blair Smith and Phil Kuntz, "CEO Pay 1,795-to-1 Multiple of Wages Skirts the Law," *Bloomberg,* April 29, 2013, www.bloomberg.com/news/2013-04-30/ceo-pay-1-795-to-1-multiple-of-workers-skirts-law-as-sec-delays.html (accessed February 24, 2014).

10. Christopher Palmeri, "Disney's CEO Iger Sees Fiscal 2013 Compensation Slide 15%," *Bloomberg,* December 24, 2013, www.bloomberg.com/news/2013-12-23/disney-s-iger-sees-pay-drop-15-to-34-3-million-last-year-1-.html (accessed February 24, 2014).

11. Rick Jervis, "Guilty Verdict for Ex-Mayor Nagin Adds to Rubble of Katrina," *USA Today*, February 13, 2014, p. 2A.

12. The Editorial Board, "A-Rod's Drug Testing," *The New York Times*, January 19, 2014, www.nytimes.com/2014/01/20/opinion/a-rods-drug-testing.html?_r=0 (accessed February 24, 2014).

13. Ferrell, Fraedrich, and Ferrell, *Business Ethics.*

14. Ethics Resource Center, *2011 National Business Ethics Survey®: Ethics in Transition* (Arlington, VA: Ethics Resource Center, 2012).

15. Bobby White, "The New Workplace Rules: No Video Watching," *The New York Times,* March 3, 2008, p. B1.

16. Shana Lebowitz, "What's Behind a Rise in Workplace Bullying?" *USA Today,* October 8, 2013, www.usatoday.com/story/news/health/2013/10/08/hostile-workplace-less-productive/2945833/ (accessed February 25, 2014).

17. Theodore V. Wells Jr., Brad S. Karp, Bruce Birenboim, and David W. Brown, *Report to the National Football League Concerning Issues of Workplace Conduct at the Miami Dolphins,* February 14, 2014, http://63bba9dfdf9675bf3f10-68be460ce43dd2a60dd64ca5eca4ae1d.r37.cf1.rackcdn.com/PaulWeissReport.pdf (accessed February 25, 2014).

18. Robert Ottinger, "No Such Thing as a Free Minute: City Employee Fired for Misusing Work Cellphone and What That Means for New York Workers," *NY Employment Lawyer,* June 30, 2013, http://newyorkemploymentlawyerblog.com/no-such-thing-as-a-free-minute-city-employee-fired-for-misusing-work-cellphone-and-what-that-means-for-new-york-workers/ (accessed February 25, 2014).

19. April Warren, "Man Who Misused Company Credit Card Sentenced to 240 Days in Jail," *Ocala Star Banner,* July 31, 2013, www.ocala.com/article/20130731/ARTICLES/130739945 (accessed February 25, 2014).

20. "Proper Use of Company, Customer, and Supplier Resources," Boeing, November 19, 2001, www.hcca-info.org/Portals/0/PDFs/Resources/Conference_Handouts/Compliance_Institute/2004/LS1handout12.pdf (accessed April 7, 2014).

21. Barbara Kiviat, "A Bolder Approach to Credit-Agency Rating Reform," *Time,* September 18, 2009, http://business.time.com/2009/09/18/a-bolder-approach-to-credit-rating-agency-reform/ (accessed April 7, 2014).

22. Christopher M. Matthews and John Carreyrou, "Ex-SAC Trader Found Guilty," *The Wall Street Journal*, February 7, 2014, A1–A2.

23. *Corruption Perceptions Index 2013.* Copyright Transparency International 2013. For more information, visit http://cpi.transparency.org/cpi2013/results/ (accessed February 21, 2014).

24. Matthew Garrett, "Your Best Employee Stinks and May Be Stealing From You," *Forbes,* October 1, 2013, www.forbes.com/sites/matthewgarrett/2013/10/01/your-best-employee-sucks-and-may-be-stealing-from-you/ (accessed February 27, 2014).

25. Associated Press, "EU Suspects 13 Banks of Collusion in Swaps Trading," *USA Today,* July 1, 2013, www.usatoday.com/story/money/business/2013/07/01/eu-banks-collusion-derivatives/2479393/ (accessed February 25, 2014).

26. Federal Trade Commission, "Nation's Largest Pool Products Distributor Settles FTC Charges of Anticompetitive Tactics," November 21, 2011, www.ftc.gov/news-events/

press-releases/2011/11/nations-largest-pool-products-distributor-settles-ftc-charges (accessed April 7, 2014).

27. Brady Dennis, "Trans Fats to Be Phased Out, FDA Says," *Washington Post,* November 7, 2013, www.washingtonpost.com/national/health-science/trans-fats-to-be-phased-out-fda-says/2013/11/07/80cfc8be-47c4-11e3-a196-3544a03c2351_story.html (accessed February 25, 2014).

28. Josephson Institute, "The Ethics of American Youth: 2012," November 20, 2012, http://charactercounts.org/programs/reportcard/2012/installment_report-card_honesty-integrity.html (accessed February 24, 2014).

29. Tom Vanden Hook, "Kickback Scandal Rocks Army," *USA Today,* February 4, 2014, p. 1A; Helene Cooper, "92 Air Force Officers Suspended for Cheating on Their Missile Exam," *The New York Times,* January 30, 2014, www.nytimes.com/2014/01/31/us/politics/92-air-force-officers-suspended-for-cheating-on-their-missile-exam.html?_r=0 (accessed January 31, 2014); Kevin Liptak, "U.S. Navy Discloses Nuclear Exam Cheating," *CNN,* February 4, 2014, www.cnn.com/2014/02/04/us/navy-cheating-investigation/ (accessed February 24, 2014); Julian E. Barnes, "Military Makes Ethics a Priority," *The Wall Street Journal,* February 3, 2014, p. A4.

30. James R. Healey and Fred Meier, "GM Knew about Cobalt Ignition Fault, Suit Says," *USA Today,* February 19, 2014, p. 1A; Alex Rogers, "GM Announces Another Major Recall Before Testimony," *Time,* March 31, 2013, http://time.com/44412/general-motors-recall-testimony/ (accessed April 1, 2014).

31. "Campaign Warns about Drugs from Canada," *CNN,* February 5, 2004, www.cnn.com; Gardiner Harris and Monica Davey, "FDA Begins Push to End Drug Imports," *The New York Times,* January 23, 2004, p. C1.

32. Lara Salahi, "FDA Appeals Block on Cigarette Warning Label," *ABC News,* November 30, 2011, http://abcnews.go.com/Health/Wellness/fda-appealsblock-cigarette-warning-labels/story?id=15059707 (accessed April 7, 2014).

33. Ethics Resource Center, *2005 National Business Ethics Survey* (Washington, DC: Ethics Resource Center, 2005), p. 43.

34. Thomas M. Jones, "Ethical Decision Making by Individuals in Organizations: An Issue-Contingent Model," *Academy of Management Review* 2 (April 1991), pp. 371–73.

35. Sir Adrian Cadbury, "Ethical Managers Make Their Own Rules," *Harvard Business Review* 65 (September–October 1987), p. 72.

36. Chad Bray, "Perfume, Dresses and Cash in Ralph Lauren Bribe Scheme," *The Wall Street Journal,* April 22, 2013, http://online.wsj.com/article/SB10001424127887324235304578438704093187288.html (accessed July 22, 2013); Foreign Corrupt Practices Act, www.foreign-corrupt-practices-act.org/fcpa-guide.html (accessed July 22, 2013); Peter Lattman, "Ralph Lauren Corp Agrees to Pay Fine in Bribery Case," *The New York Times,* April 22, 2013, http://dealbook.nytimes.com/2013/04/22/ralph-lauren-pays-1-6-million-to-resolve-bribery-case/ (accessed July 22, 2013).

37. Ferrell, Fraedrich, and Ferrell, *Business Ethics,* pp. 174–75.

38. Ethics Resource Center, *2009 National Business Ethics Survey* (Washington, DC: Ethics Resource Center, 2009), p. 41.

39. Texas Instruments, "Texas Instruments Rated One of the 'World's Most Ethical Companies' by Ethisphere Institute," March 6, 2013, http://newscenter.ti.com/2013-03-06-Texas-Instruments-rated-one-of-the-Worlds-Most-Ethical-Companies-by-Ethisphere-Institute (accessed February 25, 2014).

40. Ethics Resource Center, *2013 National Business Ethics Survey® of the U.S. Workforce* (Arlington, VA: Ethics Resource Center, 2014).

41. Ferrell, Fraedrich, and Ferrell, *Business Ethics,* p. 13.

42. "Trust in the Workplace: 2010 Ethics & Workplace Survey," Deloitte LLP (n.d.), www.deloitte.com/assets/Dcom-UnitedStates/Local%20Assets/Documents/us_2010_Ethics_and_Workplace_Survey_report_071910.pdf (accessed April 7, 2014).

43. Archie B. Carroll, "The Pyramid of Corporate Social Responsibility: Toward the Moral Management of Organizational Stakeholders," *Business Horizons* 34 (July/August 1991), p. 42.

44. Kelly Kennedy, "Pharmacies Look to Snuff Tobacco Sales," *USA Today,* February 6, 2014, p. 1A.

45. Bryan Walsh, "Why Green Is the New Red, White and Blue," *Time,* April 28, 2008, p. 46.

46. Adam Shriver, "Not Grass-Fed, But at Least Pain-Free," *The New York Times,* February 18, 2010, www.nytimes.com/2010/02/19/opinion/19shriver.html (accessed February 25, 2010)

47. Alan Beattie, "Countries Rush to Restrict Trade in Basic Foods," *Financial Times,* April 2, 2008, p. 1.

48. PR Newswire, "Next Generation Philips 75 & 100 Watt LED Equivalents Achieve ENERGY STAR Certification and Could Sell for $10–15 After Rebates," February 18, 2014, www.prnewswire.com/news-releases/next-generation-philips-75--100-watt-led-equivalents-achieve-energy-star-certification-and-could-sell-for-10-15-after-rebates-245968901.html (accessed February 25, 2014).

49. Cone Communications, "Cone Releases 2013 Cone Communications Green Gap Trend Tracker," April 2, 2013, www.conecomm.com/2013-green-gap-trend-tracker-1 (accessed February 24, 2014).

50. "2014 World's Most Ethical Companies—Honorees," *Ethisphere,* http://ethisphere.com/worlds-most-ethical/wme-honorees/ (accessed April 7, 2014).

51. Indra Nooyi, "The Responsible Company," *The Economist, The*

*World in 2008 Special Edition,* March 2008, p. 132.

52. Ferrell, Fraedrich, and Ferrell, *Business Ethics,* pp. 13–19.

53. Abha Bhattarai, "Union Approves Contract with Safeway, Giant," *Washington Post,* December 22, 2013, www.washingtonpost. com/business/capitalbusiness/ union-approves-contract-with- safeway-giant/2013/12/20/ ef553a64-68d3-11e3-a0b9- 249bbb34602c_story.html (accessed February 25, 2014).

54. U.S. Equal Employment Opportunity Commission, "Ruby Tuesday Will Pay $575,000 to Resolve EEOC Class Age Discrimination Lawsuit," December 9, 2013, www1.eeoc.gov/eeoc/ newsroom/release/12-9-13.cfm (accessed February 25, 2014).

55. Alan Zibel and Robin Sidel, "AmEx to Pay $76 Million in Car 'Add-On' Settlement," *The Wall Street Journal,* December 26, 2013, p. C3.

56. Todd Littman, "Win-Win Emissions Reductions Strategies," Victoria Transport Policy Institute, www.vtpi. org/wwclimate.pdf (accessed April 7, 2014).

57. Cornelia Dean, "Drugs Are in the Water, Does It Matter?" *The New York Times,* April 3, 2007, www. nytimes.com/2007/04/03/science/ earth/03water.html?_r=1&scp=55& sq=%22cornelia+dean%22&st=nyt &oref=slogin (accessed February 25, 2010).

58. Chris Woodyard, "Lighter Cars Add Weight to Repair," *USA Today,* September 16, 2013, 1B; Automotive News, "Adhesives Tapped to Make Cars Lighter," *Europe Auto News,* June 8, 2013, http://europe.autonews.com/ article/20130608/ANE/130609897/ adhesives-tapped-to-make-cars- lighter-tougher#axzz2hogv25cv (accessed October 15, 2013); Brad Plumer, "Why Cars Will Keep Getting Lighter," *Washington Post,* January 12, 2012, www. washingtonpost.com/blogs/ wonkblog/post/why-cars-will- keep-getting-lighter/2012/01/12/ gIQARefVtP_blog.html (accessed October 15, 2013).

59. "Amazon Rainforest Deforestation at Lowest in 23 Years, Brazil Government Says," *Reuters,* December 5, 2011, www.reuters. com/article/2011/12/06/us-brazil- amazon-idUSTRE7B42OE20111206 (accessed August 11, 2014).

60. "Few State Laws Restrict Plastic Bags," *International New York Times,* May 18, 2013, www.nytimes. com/interactive/2013/05/19/sunday- review/few-state-laws-restrict- plastic-bags.html?ref=sunday-review (accessed February 25, 2014).

61. Josie Huang, "LA to Become Biggest City to Ban Plastic Bags on Jan. 1," *Southern California Public Radio,* December 24, 2013, www. scpr.org/news/2013/12/24/41147/ plastic-bag-ban-los-angeles-la/ (accessed February 25, 2014).

62. Brian Dumaine, "Brighter Days for First Solar," *CNN Money,* May 6, 2013, http://money.cnn. com/2013/05/06/technology/first- solar.pr.fortune/ (accessed February 25, 2014).

63. "San Diego Hotel Makes Smart Sustainable Changes to Save Energy & Money," SDGE, September 5, 2013, www.sdge.com/ newsroom/2013-09-05/san-diego- hotel-makes-smart-sustainable- changes-save-energy-money (accessed February 25, 2014).

64. Adam Minter, "U.S. Isn't Flooding the Third World With E-Waste," *Bloomberg View,* May 26, 2013, www.bloombergview.com/ articles/2013-05-26/stop-the- baseless-panicking-over-u-s-e-waste (accessed February 25, 2014).

65. "GreenChoice Program Details," Austin Energy (n.d.), http:// austinenergy.com/wps/wcm/ connect/d6b29f5f-052c- 4aeb-b52d-73e4dd0265b7/ updatedProgramDetails. pdf?MOD=AJPERES (accessed April 7, 2014).

66. "Certification," Home Depot, https://corporate.homedepot. com/CorporateResponsibility/ Environment/WoodPurchasing/ Pages/Certification.aspx (accessed February 25, 2010).

67. Chiquita, Bananalink, www. bananalink.org.uk/ (accessed April 7, 2014).

68. GE Foundation, "United Way," www.gefoundation.com/employee- programs/united-way/ (accessed February 25, 2014).

69. Blue Smoke Coffee website, www. bluesmokecoffee.com/Soul.html (accessed February 25, 2014).

70. Bureau of Labor Statistics, "Labor Force Statistics from the Current Population Survey, http://data. bls.gov/timeseries/LNS14000000 (accessed February 20, 2014).

71. Clare Kane, "Spain PM Sees Hope for Unemployment on Day of Protests," *Reuters,* June 1, 2013, www.reuters.com/ article/2013/06/01/us-spain- jobless-idUSBRE9500DJ20130601 (accessed February 26, 2014).

72. Andrea Hsu, "Iowa Town Braces for New Reality in Factory Closure's Wake," *NPR,* April 8, 2013, www. npr.org/2013/04/08/176596732/ iowa-town-braces-for-new-reality- in-factory-closures-wake (accessed February 25, 2014).

73. Peter Cappelli, "Why Companies Aren't Getting the Employees They Need," *The Wall Street Journal,* October 24, 2011, pp. R1, R6.

74. "Create Jobs for USA Supporters," http://createjobsforusa.org/ supporters (accessed February 25, 2014); "Starbucks and Opportunity Finance Network: Taking Action to Reduce Unemployment in America," *Huffington Post,* February 5, 2013, www.huffingtonpost. com/create-jobs-for-usa/starbucks- and-opportunity_b_2622773.html (accessed February 25, 2014).

75. "The Boston Consulting Group," *CNN Money,* February 4, 2013, http://money.cnn.com/magazines/ fortune/best-companies/2013/ snapshots/4.html (accessed February 26, 2014); "100 Best Companies to Work For," *CNNMoney,* http:// money.cnn.com/magazines/fortune/ bestcompanies/2011/snapshots/2. html (accessed April 7, 2014).

76. "Who Really Pays for CSR Initiatives," *Environmental Leader,* February 15, 2008,

www.environmentalleader. com/2008/02/15/who-really-pays-for-csr-initiatives/ (accessed April 7, 2014); "Global Fund," www.joinred. com/globalfund (accessed April 7, 2014); Reena Jana, "The Business of Going Green," *BusinessWeek Online,* June 22, 2007, www.businessweek. com/stories/2007-06-22/the-business-benefits-of-going-greenbusinessweek-business-news-stock-market-and-financial-advice (accessed April 7, 2014).

77. Permission granted by the author of *Gray Matters,* George Sammet Jr., Vice President, Office of Corporate Ethics, Lockheed Martin Corporation, Orlando, Florida, to use these portions of *Gray Matters: The Ethics Game* © 1992.

78. Edelman, *Edelman Trust Barometer,* 2012, http://trust.edelman.com/ trustdownload/global-results/ (accessed July 26, 2012); "Occupying the Future: Benefit Corporations Now Opening Shop in NY, Six Other States," *Daily Kos,* December 14, 2011, www.dailykos. com/story/2011/12/14/1043152/-Occupyingthe-Future-Benefit-Corporations-nowopening-shop-in-NY-six-other-states (accessed July 26, 2012); Jessica Silver-Greenberg, Tara Kalwarski, and Alexis Leondis, "CEO Pay Drops, But . . . Cash Is King," *Bloomberg Businessweek,* April 5, 2010, pp. 50–56; "The Dynamics of Public Trust in Business—Emerging Opportunities for Leaders," Business Roundtable Institute for Corporate Ethics, www. corporate-ethics.org/pdf/public_ trust_in_business.pdf/ (accessed July 26, 2012).

79. M. P. McQueen, "Agency Misses Chance to Curb Lead in Jewelry," *The Wall Street Journal,* February 12, 2008, p. D1.

80. Bart Jansen, "Justice Settles Merger Lawsuit with AA, US Airways," *USA Today,* November 12, 2013, www.usatoday.com/story/travel/ flights/2013/11/12/justice-merger-american-us-airways/3506367/ (accessed February 26, 2014).

81. Chad Bray, "Marvel Wins in Dispute Over Characters," *The Wall Street Journal,* August 8, 2013, http:// blogs.wsj.com/law/2013/08/08/ nuff-said-marvel-wins-in-dispute-over-characters/ (accessed December 10, 2013); U.S. Copyright Office, "Definitions," www.copyright. gov/help/faq/faq-definitions.html (accessed December 10, 2013); Michael Cieply, "Disney Wins Marvel Copyright Case," *The New York Times,* July 28, 2011, www. nytimes.com/2011/07/29/business/ media/disney-wins-marvel-comics-copyright-case.html?_r=0 (accessed December 10, 2013).

82. Maureen Dorney, "Congress Passes Federal Anti-Spam Law: Preempts Most State Anti-Spam Laws," *DLA Piper,* December 3, 2003, http:// franchiseagreements.com/global/ publications/detail.aspx?pub=622 (accessed April 7, 2014),

83. Elizabeth Alterman, "As Kids Go Online, Identity Theft Claims More Victims," *CNBC,* October 10, 2011, www.cnbc.com/id/44583556/As_ Kids_Go_Online_Identity_Theft_ Claims_More_Victims (accessed April 7, 2014).

84. Federal Trade Commission, "Path Social Networking App Settles FTC Charges It Deceived Consumers and Improperly Collected Personal Information from Users' Mobile Address Books," February 1, 2013, http://ftc.gov/opa/2013/02/path.shtm (accessed November 4, 2013).

85. Jean Eaglesham and Ashby Jones, "Whistle-blower Bounties Pose Challenges," *The Wall Street Journal,* December 13, 2010, pp. C1, C3.

86. "Office of Financial Research," U.S. Department of Treasury, www.treasury.gov/initiatives/ Pages/ofr.aspx (accessed February 22, 2011); "Initiatives: Financial Stability Oversight Council," U.S. Department of Treasury, www. treasury.gov/initiatives/Pages/FSOC-index.aspx (accessed April 7, 2014).

## Chapter 3

1. Simon Montlake and Ryan Ma, "China's Steve Jobs," *Forbes,* July 18, 2012, www.forbes. com/global/2012/0806/feature-technology-lei-jun-smartphones-china-steve-jobs.html (accessed August 31, 2012); Laura He, "Chinese Billionaire Lei Jun and His iPhone Challenger Jump Into Fierce Smartphone Price War," *Forbes,* August 15, 2012, www.forbes.com/ sites/laurahe/2012/08/15/lei-jun-and-apples-chinese-challenger-jump-into-fierce-smartphone-price-war/ (accessed August 31, 2012); Hannah Beech/Chengdu, "The Cult of Apple in China," *Time,* July 2, 2012, www.time.com/time/magazine/ article/0,9171,2117765,00.html (accessed August 31, 2012); Matt Schiavenza, "How Xiaomi's Hip, Inexpensive Smart Phones Conquered China," *The Atlantic,* October 24, 2013, www.theatlantic. com/china/archive/2013/10/how-xiaomis-hip-inexpensive-smart-phones-conquered-china/280803/ (accessed January 8, 2014); Mark Milian, "China Loves Xiaomi Phones. Will Anyone Else?" *Bloomberg Technology,* January 5, 2014, www.bloomberg.com/ news/2014-01-03/china-loves-xiaomi-phones-will-anyone-else-. html (accessed January 8, 2014).

2. Tim Kelly, "Squash the Caterpillar," *Forbes,* April 21, 2008, p. 136.

3. Subway, "Explore Our World," www.subway.com/subwayroot/ exploreourworld.aspx (accessed February 27, 2014).

4. Deloitte, "2013 Global Manufacturing Competitiveness Index," 2013, www.deloitte. com/assets/Dcom-UnitedStates/ Local%20Assets/Documents/us_ pip_GMCI_11292012.pdf (accessed February 24, 2014).

5. Seeking Alpha, "Starbucks' CEO Discusses F4Q 2013 Results—Earnings Call Transcript," *Yahoo! Finance,* October 30, 2013, http:// finance.yahoo.com/news/starbucks-ceo-discusses-f4q-2013-030232109. html (accessed February 24, 2014).

6. Elisabeth Sullivan, "Choose Your Words Wisely," *Marketing News,* February 15, 2008, p. 22.

7. UPI, "Apple Store in 2013 Hit $10 Billion Mark in App

Sales," January 7, 2014, www.upi.com/Science_News/Technology/2014/01/07/Apple-Store-in-2013-hit-10-billion-mark-in-app-sales/UPI-89931389121203/ (accessed February 24, 2014); Alex Williams, "Apple Reports Q4 Retail Sales of $4.5 Billion with $50 Million in Sales per Apple Store," *Tech Crunch,* October 28, 2013, http://techcrunch.com/2013/10/28/apple-reports-q4-retail-sales-of-4-5-billion-with-50-million-in-sales-per-apple-store/ (accessed February 24, 2014).

8. Statista, "Total Population in the United States from 2003 to 2013 (in millions)," 2013, www.statista.com/statistics/263762/total-population-of-the-united-states/ (accessed February 24, 2014).

9. Sullivan, "Choose Your Words Wisely."

10. Stephan Faris, "How Poland Became Europe's Most Dynamic Economy," *Bloomberg Businessweek,* November 27, 2013, www.businessweek.com/articles/2013-11-27/how-poland-became-europes-most-dynamic-economy (accessed February 24, 2014).

11. Tim Worstall, "Which Should We Have: Public Utilities or Regulated Private Monopolies?" *Forbes,* March 24, 2013, www.forbes.com/sites/timworstall/2013/03/24/which-should-we-have-public-utilities-or-regulated-private-monopolies/ (accessed February 24, 2014).

12. Danielz Pylypczak, "Mexico Takes Steps to End Oil Monopoly," *Commodity HQ,* August 15, 2013, www.minyanville.com/trading-and-investing/commodities/articles/Mexico-Takes-Steps-to-End-Oil/8/15/2013/id/51313?refresh=1 (accessed February 24, 2014).

13. T. S., "Why Does Kenya Lead the World in Mobile Money?" *The Economist,* May 27, 2013, www.economist.com/blogs/economist-explains/2013/05/economist-explains-18 (accessed February 24, 2014).

14. Paul Davidson, "We Produce More at Home with New Drilling Methods," *USA Today,* February 11, 2014, p. 1B.

15. Rosalie C. Periabras, "Philippines: The New Call Center Capital of the World," *The Manila Times,* October 26, 2013, http://manilatimes.net/philippines-the-new-call-center-capital-of-the-world/47984/ (accessed March 3, 2014).

16. U.S. Bureau of the Census, Foreign Trade Division, *U.S. Trade in Goods and Services—Balance of Payments (BOP) Basis,* February 6, 2014, www.census.gov/foreign-trade/statistics/historical/gands.pdf (accessed February 27, 2014).

17. Colum Murphy and Mike Ramsey, "Tesla Plans to Add Charging Network in China," *The Wall Street Journal*, January 15, 2014, p. B6; Daisuke Wakabayashi, Lorraine Luk, Ian Sherr, and Paul Mozur, "Apple Nears Major Expansion," *The Wall Street Journal*, September 7–8, 2014, p. B1.

18. U.S. Bureau of the Census, Foreign Trade Division, *U.S. Trade in Goods and Services—Balance of Payments (BOP) Basis,* February 6, 2014, www.census.gov/foreign-trade/statistics/historical/gands.pdf (accessed February 27, 2014).

19. Ibid.

20. Keith Bradsher, "G.M. Plans to Develop Electric Cars With China," *The New York Times,* September 20, 2011, www.nytimes.com/2011/09/21/business/global/gm-plans-to-develop-electric-cars-with-chinese-automaker.html (accessed April 9, 2014).

21. Fortune Industry Perspectives and Dupont, "Sustainable Energy for Growing China," May 2013, www.dupont.com/content/dam/assets/corporate-functions/our-approach/global-challenges/documents/DuPont_SustainableEnergyforGrowingChina_052013.pdf (accessed January 21, 2014); Josh Bateman, "The New Global Leader in Renewable Energy," *RenewableEnergyWorld. Com,* January 13, 2014, www.renewableenergyworld.com/rea/news/article/2014/01/the-new-global-leader-in-renewable-energy (accessed January 21, 2014); Wayne Ma, "China Boosts Renewable-Energy Surcharge," *The Wall Street Journal,* August 30, 2013, http://online.wsj.com/news/articles/SB10001424127887324324404579044592532822898 (accessed January 21, 2014).

22. Richard Silk, "Yuan's Climb Adds to Chinese Export Woes," *The Wall Street Journal*, January 11–12, 2014, p. A7.

23. Shelly Banjo and R. Jai Krishna, "Wal-Mart Curbs Ambitions in India," *The Wall Street Journal*, October 10, 2013, pp. B1–B2; Loretta Chao and Paulo Trevisani, "Brazil Presses on Internet Bill," *The Wall Street Journal*, November 19, 2013, p. B4; Brazilia, "Brazil Delays Vote on Anti-Spying Internet Bill-Lawmaker," *Reuters*, December 4, 2013, www.reuters.com/article/2013/12/04/us-brazil-internet-bill-idUSBRE9B30UD20131204 (accessed February 26, 2014).

24. Kurt Badenhausen, "Ireland Heads Forbes' List of the Best Countries for Business," *Forbes,* December 4, 2013, www.forbes.com/sites/kurtbadenhausen/2013/12/04/ireland-heads-forbes-list-of-the-best-countries-for-business/ (accessed February 26, 2014).

25. "The Restricted Zone in Mexico," Penner & Associates—Mexico Law Firm and Business Consulting for Mexico, www.mexicolaw.com/LawInfo17.htm (accessed April 9, 2014).

26. "Sixth Annual BSA and IDC Global Software Piracy Study," Business Software Alliance, May 2009, http://global.bsa.org/globalpiracy2008/index.html (accessed April 9, 2014).

27. "USA: President Obama Should Take the Lead on Lifting Embargo against Cuba," Amnesty International, September 2, 2009, www.amnesty.org/en/for-media/press-releases/usa-president-obama-should-take-lead-lifting-embargo-against-cuba-200909 (accessed March 15, 2010); Kitty Bean Yancey, "Back to Cuba: 'People-to-People Trips' Get the Green Light," *USA Today,* August 4, 2011, p. 4A.

28. Kitty Bean Yancey and Laura Bly, "Door May Be Inching Open for Tourism," *USA Today,* February 20, 2008, p. A5; Sue Kirchhoff and Chris Woodyard, "Cuba Trade Gets 'New Opportunity,'" *USA Today,* February 20, 2008, p. B1.

29. Daniel Trotta, "U.S. Charges Five in 'Honeygate' Anti-Dumping Probe," *Reuters*, February 20, 2013, www.reuters.com/ article/2013/02/20/usa-china-honey-idUSL1N0BKCRX20130220 (accessed February 26, 2014).

30. Ibid.

31. Chris Huber, "Five of the Worst Natural Disasters in 2013," *World Vision*, December 19, 2013, www. worldvision.org/news-stories-videos/2013-top-natural-disasters (accessed February 26, 2014).

32. Julie Jargon, "Burger King Heads to India—Finally," *The Wall Street Journal*, November 20, 2013, p. B9.

33. Laurie Burkitt, "Tiffany Finds Sparkle in Overseas Markets," *The Wall Street Journal*, December 26, 2013, p. B4.

34. Julie Jargon, "Starbucks Shifts in Europe," *The Wall Street Journal*, November 30–December 1, 2013, p. B3.

35. "Slogans Gone Bad," Joe-ks, www. joe-ks.com/archives_apr2004/ slogans_gone_bad.htm (accessed April 9, 2014).

36. Preetika Rana, "Ad Confronts Taboos for Women in India," *The Wall Street Journal*, November 20, 2013, p. A8.

37. J. Bonasia, "For Web, Global Reach Is Beauty—and Challenge," *Investor's Business Daily,* June 13, 2001, p. A6.

38. Chuck Jones, "PC Market Consolidating Around Top 3 Vendors," *Forbes*, October 10, 2013, www.forbes.com/sites/ chuckjones/2013/10/10/pc-market-consolidating-around-top-3-vendors/ (accessed March 3, 2014); Jason Evangelho, "2013 Represented Worst Decline in PC Market's History," *Forbes,* January 9, 2014, www.forbes.com/sites/ jasonevangelho/2014/01/09/2013-represented-worst-decline-in-pc-markets-history/ (accessed March 3, 2014).

39. Heidi Vogt, "Startup Keeps Africa's Jet Set Aloft," *The Wall Street Journal,* August 16, 2013, http:// online.wsj.com/article/SB1000142 4127887323838204579001043808 796128.html (accessed September 9, 2013); Travel Pulse, "World Economic Forum Honors TanJet Founder Mashibe," Travel Pulse, Marche 21, 2011, www.travelpulse. com/world-economic-forum-honors-tanjet-founder-mashibe.html (accessed September 9, 2013); Jacey Fortin, "African Air Travel: Why Are Airlines in Africa So Expensive, Unsafe and Impossible to Navigate," *IBT Media*, May 4, 2013, www. ibtimes.com/african-air-travel-why-are-airlines-africa-so-expensive-unsafe-impossible-navigate-1234609 (accessed September 10, 2013).

40. "What Is the WTO," World Trade Organization (n.d.), www.wto.org/ english/thewto_e/whatis_e/whatis_e. htm (accessed April 9, 2014).

41. World Trade Organization, "Argentina Files Dispute against the European Union over Biodiesel," December 20, 2013, www.wto. org/english/news_e/news13_e/ ds473rfc_20dec13_e.htm (accessed March 3, 2014).

42. "North American Free Trade Agreement," NAFTANOW.ORG, April 4, 2012, www.naftanow.org/ facts/ (accessed March 3, 2014).

43. Central Intelligence Agency, "Country Comparison: GDP—Per Capital (PPP)," *The CIA World Factory,* www.cia.gov/library/ publications/the-world-factbook/ rankorder/2004rank.html (accessed March 3, 2014).

44. Executive Office of the President of the United States, "U.S.–Canada Trade Facts," www.ustr.gov/ countries-regions/americas/canada (accessed March 3, 2014).

45. Trading Economics, "Canada Exports," www.tradingeconomics. com/canada/exports (accessed March 3, 2013); Executive Office of the President of the United States, "U.S.–Canada Trade Facts."

46. "America's Biggest Partners," *CNBC.com,* www.cnbc.com/ id/31064179?slide=11 (accessed April 10, 2014).

47. Central Intelligence Agency, "Country Comparison: GDP—Per Capital (PPP)."

48. Executive Office of the President of the United States, "U.S.–Mexico Trade Facts," www.ustr.gov/ countries-regions/americas/mexico (accessed March 3, 2014).

49. Jen Wieczner, "Why 2014 Could Be Mexico's Year," *Fortune,* January 13, 2014, pp. 37–38.

50. "A Tale of Two Mexicos: North and South," *The Economist,* April 26, 2008, pp. 53–54.

51. United States Census Bureau, "Top Trading Partners—December 2013: Year-to-Date Total Trade," www. census.gov/foreign-trade/statistics/ highlights/top/top1312yr.html (accessed March 3, 2014).

52. Pete Engardio and Geri Smith, "Business Is Standing Its Ground," *BusinessWeek,* April 20, 2009, pp. 34–39.

53. "Europe in 12 Lessons," http:// europa.eu/abc/12lessons/lesson_2/ index_en.htm (accessed March 3, 2010).

54. Central Intelligence Agency, "Country Comparison: GDP (Official Exchange Rate)," *The CIA World Factbook,* www.cia. gov/library/publications/the-world-factbook/fields/2195.html (accessed March 3, 2014).

55. Stanley Reed, with Ariane Sains, David Fairlamb, and Carol Matlack, "The Euro: How Damaging a Hit?" *BusinessWeek,* September 29, 2003, p. 63; "The Single Currency," *CNN* (n.d.), www.cnn.com/ SPECIALS/2000/eurounion/story/ currency/ (accessed July 3, 2001).

56. Claire Cain Miller, "Google Settles Its European Antitrust Case; Critics Remain," *International New York Times,* February 5, 2014, www.nytimes.com/2014/02/06/ technology/google-reaches-tentative-antitrust-settlement-with-european-union.html?_r=0 (accessed March 4, 2014).

57. Abigail Moses, "Greek Contagion Concern Spurs European Sovereign Default Risk to Record," *Bloomberg,* April 26, 2010, www.bloomberg. com/news/2010-04-26/greek-contagion-concern-spurs-european-sovereign-default-risk-to-record. html (accessed March 18, 2011).

58. James G. Neuger and Joe Brennan, "Ireland Weighs Aid as EU Spars over Debt-Crisis Remedy," *Bloomberg,* www.bloomberg.com/ news/2010-11-16/ireland-discusses-financial-bailout-as-eu-struggles-to-defuse-debt-crisis.html (accessed March 18, 2011).

59. Charles Forelle and Marcus Walker, "Dithering at the Top Turned EU Crisis to Global Threat," *The Wall Street Journal,* December 29, 2011, p. A1; Jeff Cox, "US, Europe Face More Ratings Cuts in Coming Years," *CNBC,* January 20, 2012, www.cnbc.com/id/46072354?__ source=google%7Ceditorspicks% 7C&par=google (accessed January 20, 2012); Charles Forelle, "Greece Defaults and Tries to Move On," *The Wall Street Journal,* March 10, 2012, http://online.wsj.com/article/ SB10 0014240529702046030045772705 42625035960.html (accessed July 19, 2012).

60. Kiran Moodley, "S&P Cuts Netherlands Rating; Cyprus and Spain Seen More Positive," *CNBC,* November 29, 2013, www.cnbc. com/id/101234699 (accessed March 4, 2014).

61. "Powerhouse Deutschland," *Bloomberg Businessweek,* January 3, 2011, p. 93; Alan S. Blinder, "The Euro Zone's German Crisis," *The Wall Street Journal,* http://online. wsj.com/article/SB1000142405297 02034304045770943137071907 08. html (accessed April 10, 2014).

62. "About APEC," www.apec.org/ about-us/about-apec.aspx (accessed March 4, 2014).

63. "China Economic Growth Rate Stabilises at 7.7%," *BBC News,* January 20, 2014, www.bbc.com/ news/business-25805227 (accessed March 4, 2014).

64. Charles Riley and Feng Ke, "China to Overtake U.S. as World's Top Trader," *CNN,* January 10, 2014, http://money.cnn.com/2014/01/10/ news/economy/china-us-trade/ (accessed March 4, 2014).

65. U.S. Environmental Protection Agency, "Global Greenhouse Gas Emissions Data," www.epa.gov/ climatechange/ghgemissions/global. html (accessed March 4, 2014); Joshua Keating, "China Passes U.S. as World's Largest Oil Importer," *Slate,* October 11, 2013, www.slate. com/blogs/the_world_/2013/10/11/ china_now_world_s_largest_net_ oil_importer_surpassing_united_ states.html (accessed March 4, 2014).

66. Jayne O'Donnell and Calum Macleod, "Bangladesh Fire Ads Pressure on Retailers," *USA Today*, May 10, 2013, p. 1B; Anne D'Innocenzio, "Companies Adopt Safety Plan for Bangladesh Factories," *Boston Globe,* July 9, 2013, www.bostonglobe. com/business/2013/07/08/ companies-move-ahead-with-bangladesh-safety-accord/ qm8qAjOF5auROxKOt7po5M/ story.html (accessed July 15, 2013); Steven Greenhouse, "As Firms Line Up on Factories, Wal-Mart Plans Solo Effort," *The New York Times,* May 14, 2013, www.nytimes.com/2013/05/15/ business/six-retailers-join-bangladesh-factory-pact. html?pagewanted=all&_r=1&#h[] (accessed July 15, 2013).

67. "The Rise of Capitalism," *The Economist,* January 21, 2012, p. 11.

68. Dexter Roberts, "Corporate China's Black Hole of Debt," *Bloomberg Businessweek,* November 19–22, 2012, pp. 15–16.

69. Charles Riley, "Starbucks to Open First Store in Vietnam," *CNN,* January 3, 2013, http://money.cnn. com/2013/01/03/news/starbucks-vietnam/ (accessed March 4, 2014).

70. "Overview," Association of Southeast Asian Nations, www. aseansec.org/64.htm (accessed April 10, 2014).

71. Wang Yan, "ASEAN Works to 'Act as Unison' on Global Stage," *China Daily,* November 19, 2011, www. chinadaily.com.cn/cndy/2011-11/19/ content_14122972.htm (accessed April 10, 2014).

72. ASEAN website, www.aseansec.org/ (accessed April 10, 2014).

73. "Agreement on the Common Effective Preferential Tariff (CEPT) Scheme for the ASEAN Free Trade Area (AFTA)," Association of Southeast Asian Nations, www.asean.org/communities/ asean-economic-community/ item/agreement-on-the-common-effective-preferential-tariff-cept-scheme-for-the-asean-free-trade-area-afta (accessed April 10, 2014).

74. R.C., "No Brussels Sprouts in Bali," *The Economist,* November 18, 2011, www.economist.com/blogs/ banyan/2011/11/asean-summits (accessed April 10, 2014).

75. Eric Bellman, "Asia Seeks Integration Despite EU's Woes," *The Wall Street Journal,* July 22, 2011, p. A9.

76. David J. Lynch, "The IMF is . . . Tired Fund Struggles to Reinvent Itself," *USA Today,* April 19, 2006. p. B1.

77. Walter B. Wriston, "Ever Heard of Insourcing?" Commentary, *The Wall Street Journal,* March 24, 2004, p. A20.

78. "Here, There and Everywhere," A Special Report, *The Economist,* January 19, 2013, pp. 1–20.

79. Nick Heath, "Banks: Offshoring, Not Outsourcing," *BusinessWeek,* March 10, 2009, www.businessweek.com/ globalbiz/content/mar2009/ gb20090310_619247.htm (accessed April 10, 2014).

80. Panos Mourdoukoutas, "How GM Wins in China," *Forbes,* February 19, 2013, www.forbes.com/sites/ panosmourdoukoutas/2013/02/19/ how-gm-wins-in-china/ (accessed March 4, 2014).

81. PR Newswire, "PKO Bank Polski and EVO Payments International Finalize Sale of 66 Percent of eService Shares and Creation of a 20 Year Strategic Alliance," January 8, 2014, www.prnewswire.com/ news-releases/pko-bank-polski-and-

evo-payments-international-finalize-sale-of-66-percent-of-eservice-shares-and-creation-of-a-20-year-strategic-alliance-239245501.html (accessed March 4, 2014).

82. Nokia Corporation, "Nokia to Fully Acquire Siemens' Stake in Nokia Siemens Network," July 1, 2013, http://press.nokia.com/2013/07/01/nokia-to-fully-acquire-siemens-stake-in-nokia-siemens-networks/ (accessed March 4, 2014).

83. Guo Changdong and Ren Ruqin, "Nestle CEO visits Tianjin," *China Daily,* August 12, 2010, www.chinadaily.com.cn/m/tianjin/e/2010-08/12/content_11146560.htm (accessed April 10, 2014); "Employee Profiles," Nestlé, www.nestle-ea.com/en/jobssite/beingatnestleear/Pages/EmployessProfiles.aspx (accessed April 10, 2014).

84. O. C. Ferrell, John Fraedrich, and Linda Ferrell, *Business Ethics,* 6th ed. (Boston: Houghton Mifflin, 2005), pp. 227–30.

85. Vu Trong Khanh, "Vietnam Gets Its First McDonald's," *The Wall Street Journal,* February 11, 2014, p. B4.

86. Export.gov, www.export.gov/about/index.asp (accessed April 10, 2014); CIBER Web, http://CIBERWEB.msu.edu (accessed April 10, 2014).

87. Zachary-Cy Vanasse, "Rendez Vous En France Brings the World Travel Industry to Paris," *Travel Hot News,* April 5, 2012, www.travelhotnews.com/reportages.php?sequence_no=38537 (accessed July 26, 2012); Malcolm Moore, "Disney Breaks Ground on Shanghai Theme Park," *The Telegraph,* April 8, 2011, www.telegraph.co.uk/news/worldnews/asia/china/8437153/Disney-breaks-groundon-Shanghai-theme-park.html (accessed July 26, 2012); Jeff Chu, "Happily Ever After?" *Time,* March 18, 2002, www.time.com/time/magazine/article/0,9171,901020325-218398,00.html (accessed May 6, 2010); Wendy Leung, "Disney Set to Miss Mark on Visitors," *The Standard,* September 5, 2006, www.thestandard.com.hk/news_detail.asp?we_cat=4&art_id=26614&sid=9732977&con_type=1&d_str=20060905 (accessed July 26, 2012); Robert Mendick, "Race Against Time to Make That Disney Magic Work," *The London Independent,* February 6, 2000, www.independent.co.uk/news/uk/thisbritain/race-againsttime-to-make-thatnew-disney-magicwork-726623.html (accessed May 6, 2010); "The Narrative of Numbers," Disneyland Paris, http://corporate.disneylandparis.com/aboutourcompany/the-narrative-of-numbers/index.xhtml (accessed April 20, 2010).

## Chapter 4

1. Emily Chasan and Maxwell Murphy, "Activist Investors Go Big," *The Wall Street Journal*, October 1, 2013, p. B6; Michael J. De La Merced, "How Elliot and Hess Settled a Bitter Proxy Battle," *The New York Times,* May 16, 2013, http://dealbook.nytimes.com/2013/05/16/hess-and-elliott-settle-fight-over-companys-board/ (accessed October 16, 2013); Heidi Moore, "Activist Investor David Einhorn Drops 'iPref' Lawsuit against Apple," *The Guardian,* March 1, 2013, http://www.theguardian.com/technology/2013/mar/01/david-einhorn-apple-iprefs-lawsuit (accessed October 16, 2013).

2. The Entrepreneurs' Help Page, www.tannedfeet.com/sole_proprietorship.htm (accessed April 10, 2014); Kent Hoover, "Startups Down for Women Entrepreneurs, Up for Men," *SanFrancisco Business Times,* May 2, 2008, http://sanfrancisco.bizjournals.com/sanfrancisco/stories/2008/05/05/smallb2.html (accessed April 10, 2014).

3. Maggie Overfelt, "Start-Me-Up: How the Garage Became a Legendary Place to Rev Up Ideas," *Fortune Small Business,* September 1, 2003, http://money.cnn.com/magazines/fsb/fsb_archive/2003/09/01/350784/index.htm (accessed April 10, 2014).

4. Forbes, "Barrett Business Services," October 2013, www.forbes.com/companies/barrett-business-services/ (accessed March 4, 2014). BBSI, "Our Solutions," www.barrettbusiness.com/our-solutions (accessed March 4, 2014).

5. Bruce Horovitz, "Smashburger Thinks Outside Box to Compete," *USA Today,* August 19, 2013, p. 3B; Michael Thrasher, "Smashburger Founder Attributes Success to Unorthodox Marketing Strategy," *Business Insider,* August 8, 2013, www.businessinsider.com/smashburger-reveals-reason-for-success-2013-8 (accessed October 1, 2013); "Smashburger Lands on the Inc. 500," Smashburger, 2011, http://smashburger.com/2011/12/smashburger-lands-on-the-inc-500/ (accessed October 7, 2013).

6. Webco, "Webco's General Partnership," ww2.webcogp.com/webcos-approach.html (accessed March 4, 2014).

7. Crimson Renewable website, www.crimsonrenewable.com/ (accessed August 5, 2013); Stephanie Paul, "LLC or LP: What's Best for Your Business?" Legal Zoom, February 2011, www.legalzoom.com/business-management/starting-your-business/llc-or-lp-whats-best (accessed August 14, 2013); Celia Lamb, "Biodiesel Company Eyes Port of Sacramento for Manufacturing, Storage Facility," *Sacramento Business Journal,* July 13, 2008, www.bizjournals.com/sacramento/stories/2008/07/14/story10.html (accessed August 23, 2013).

8. Julie Triedman, "The Am Law 100, the Early Numbers: Profits Spike at Davis Polk," *American Lawyer,* February 28, 2014, www.americanlawyer.com/id=1202645063552/The-Am-Law-100,-the-Early-Numbers%3A-Profits-Spike-at-Davis-Polk%0D%0A (accessed March 11, 2014).

9. Bill Orben, "uBreakiFix Launches Franchise Unit, Sets Sights on 125 Stores This Year," *Orlando Business Journal,* February 20, 2013, www.bizjournals.com/orlando/blog/2013/02/ubreakifix-launches-franchise-unit.html (accessed March 4, 2014).

10. PwC, "Facts and Figures," 2013, www.pwc.com/gx/en/about-pwc/

facts-and-figures.jhtml (accessed March 4, 2014).

11. Henry Blodget, "Come On, Snapchat, Here's What Your Ousted Co-Founder Deserves—Settle This Lawsuit and Move On," *Business Insider*, November 22, 2013, www.businessinsider.com/ snapchat-lawsuit-settlement-2013-11 (accessed March 4, 2014); Alyson Shantell, "Snapchat Has Tried Twice to Settle Its Lawsuit with Ousted Co-Founder Reggie Brown," *Business Insider*, December 18, 2013, www.businessinsider.com/ snapchat-lawsuit-settlement-talks-2013-12 (accessed March 4, 2014).

12. Warren Buffett's Berkshire Hathaway Letter to Shareholders, www.berkshirehathaway.com/ letters/2010ltr.pdf (accessed April 10, 2014).

13. "America's Largest Private Companies," *Forbes*, December 31, 2013, www.forbes.com/largest-private-companies/list/ (accessed March 5, 2014).

14. "America's Largest Private Companies," *Forbes*, December 31, 2013, www.mars.com/global/ about.aspx (accessed March 5, 2014); Carla Zanetos Scully, "2014 Global Top 100: Candy Industry's Exclusive List of the Top 100 Confectionery Companies in the World!" *Candy Industry*, January 31, 2014, www.candyindustry. com/articles/86039-global-top-100-candy-industrys-exclusive-list-of-the-top-100-confectionery-companies-in-the-world?page=5 (accessed March 5, 2014).

15. Deborah Orr, "The Secret World of Mars," *Forbes,* April 28, 2008, www.forbes.com/2008/04/28/ billionaires-mars-wrigley-biz-billies-cz_do_0428marsfamily.html (accessed April 10, 2014).

16. "America's Largest Private Companies."

17. David Streitfeld, "Amazon's Revenue Soars, but No Profit Is in Sight," *New York Times*, October 24, 2013, www.nytimes. com/2013/10/25/technology/ amazons-revenue-soars-but-no-

profit-in-sight.html?_r=0 (accessed March 5, 2014).

18. Liz Hoffman, "Moelis Founder to Keep Control after IPO," *Money Beat*, March 4, 2014, http://blogs. wsj.com/moneybeat/2014/03/04/ moelis-founder-to-keep-control-after-ipo/ (accessed March 5, 2014).

19. Forbes Corporate Communications, "Forbes 2013 10th Annual Global 2000: The World's Biggest Public Companies," *Forbes*, April 17, 2013, www.forbes.com/sites/ forbespr/2013/04/17/forbes-2013-10th-annual-global-2000-the-worlds-biggest-public-companies/ (accessed March 5, 2014).

20. Ibid.; Scott DeCarlo, "The World's Biggest Companies," *Forbes*, April 17, 2013, www.forbes.com/sites/ scottdecarlo/2013/04/17/the-worlds-biggest-companies-2/ (accessed March 5, 2014).

21. Ingrid Lunden, "Big Data Analytics Specialist Tableau Software Raises $254M in IPO, Shares Close 64% Up; Marketo's First Day Up 78% to $23.10," *Tech Crunch*, May 17, 2013, http://techcrunch. com/2013/05/17/big-data-visualization-goes-public-tableau-software-raises-254m-as-shares-pop-58-while-marketo-raises-85m/ (accessed March 5, 2014); Chris Preston, "Rocket Fuel Headlines Huge Week for IPOs," *Yahoo! Finance*, September 25, 2013, http:// finance.yahoo.com/news/rocket-fuel-headlines-huge-week-183020256. html (accessed March 5, 2014); Josh Costine, "Veeva Systems' Life Science Cloud IPO Is a Hit, Raising $217M and Closing up 85%," *Tech Crunch*, October 16, 2013, http:// techcrunch.com/2013/10/16/veeva-ipo/ (accessed March 5, 2014).

22. Brendan Marasco, "3 Reasons Dell Went Private," *The Motley Fool*, November 1, 2013, www.fool.com/ investing/general/2013/11/01/3-reasons-dell-went-private.aspx (accessed March 5, 2014).

23. O. C. Ferrell, John Fraedrich, and Linda Ferrell, *Business Ethics: Ethical Decision Making and Cases,* 8th ed. (Mason, OH: South-Western Cengage Learning, 2011), p. 109.

24. Chris Burritt and Jeffrey McCracken, "Best Buy Says It Got No Offer from Founder Schulze," *Bloomberg,* March 1, 2013, www. bloomberg.com/news/2013-03-01/ best-buy-talks-with-founder-richard-schulze-said-to-have-ended. html (accessed March 11, 2014); Abram Brown, "Best Buy Founder Schulze Returns as Chairman Emeritus after Failed LBO," *Forbes,* March 25, 2013, www.forbes.com/ sites/abrambrown/2013/03/25/ best-buy-billionaire-founder-schulze-to-return-as-chairman-emeritus-after-failed-lbo/ (accessed March 11, 2014)

25. Diane Brady, "Cozy Corporate Directors Raise Their Pay to $1,000 an Hour," *Bloomberg Businessweek*, May 30, 2013, www.businessweek. com/articles/2013-05-30/cozy-corporate-boards-vote-to-pay-themselves-1-000-an-hour (accessed March 10, 2014).

26. P&G, "Board Composition," 2013, www.pg.com/en_US/company/ global_structure_operations/ governance/board_composition. shtml (accessed March 10, 2014).

27. Joseph Nathan Kane, *Famous First Facts,* 4th ed. (New York: The H.W. Wilson Company, 1981), p. 202.

28. Reuters, "Venezuela Launches Joint Venture with Samsung Electronics," November 20, 2013, www. reuters.com/article/2013/11/20/ us-venezuela-samsung-idUSBRE9AJ14A20131120 (accessed March 10, 2014).

29. Robert D. Hisrich and Michael P. Peters, *Entrepreneurship,* 5th ed. (Boston: McGraw-Hill, 2002), pp. 315–16.

30. SEC, "List of Companies," www. sec.gov/rules/other/4-460list.htm (accessed March 10, 2014).

31. Coop Directory, "Coop Directory Service Listing," www. coopdirectory.org/directory. htm#Massachusetts (accessed March 10, 2014).

32. David Gelles, "For Once-Mighty Sears, Pictures of Decay," *The New York Times,* October 13, 2013, pp. B1, B5; Sears, "Sears History," www.searsarchives.

com/history/index.htm (accessed January 13, 2014); Brigid Sweeney, "Sears—Where America Shopped," Crane's Chicago Business, April 23, 2012, www.chicagobusiness. com/article/20120421/ ISSUE01/304219970/sears-where-america-shopped (accessed January 13, 2014); Associated Press, "Kmart to Acquire Sears in $11 Billion Deal," *NBC News,* November 17, 2004, www.nbcnews.com/ id/6509683/ns/business-stocks_ and_economy/t/kmart-acquire-sears-billion-deal/#.UtW3VfXLQ4k (accessed January 14, 2014).

33. Aaron Tilley, "Google Acquires Smart Thermostat Maker Nest for $3.2 Billion," *Forbes*, January 13, 2014, www.forbes.com/sites/ aarontilley/2014/01/13/google-acquires-nest-for-3-2-billion/ (accessed March 10, 2014).

34. Eric Savitz, "Did Google Buy a Lemon? Motorola Mobility Whiffs Q4," *Forbes,* January 8, 2012, www.forbes.com/sites/ ericsavitz/2012/01/08/did-google-buy-a-lemon-motorola-mobility-whiffs-q4/ (accessed February2, 2012); Brian Womack, "Google Discloses $151 Million Price Tag for Zagat Service," *Bloomberg Businessweek,* October 26, 2011, www.businessweek.com/news/2011-10-26/google-discloses-151-million-price-tag-for-zagat-service.html (accessed April 10, 2014).

35. Andrew Edgecliffe-Johnson, "News Corp Adopts 'Poison Pill' Share Plan to Protect Divisions," *Financial Times,* May 24, 2013, www.ft.com/ cms/s/0/b4f00712-c475-11e2-bc94-00144feab7de.html#axzz2vghF7500 (accessed March 11, 2014).

36. "Company Overview of PODS Enterprises, Inc.," *Bloomberg Businessweek,* http://investing. businessweek.com/research/ stocks/private/snapshot. asp?privcapId=1833278 (accessed July 26, 2012); "PODS Taking a Chunk Out of Moving and Storage Market," *USA Today,* August 4, 2006, www.usatoday.com/money/ smallbusiness/2006-08-04-pods_x. htm (accessed July 26, 2012); Consortium Media Services,

"PODS Recognized as One of the Nation's Best Service Providers by Professional Organizing Association," *Yahoo!® Voices,* February 28, 2011, http://voices. yahoo.com/pods-recognized-as-one-nationsbest-service-7701664.html (accessed July 26, 2012).

## Chapter 5

1. Megan Durisin, "Chobani CEO: Our Success Has Nothing to Do With Yogurt," *Business Insider*, May 3, 2013, www.businessinsider. com/the-success-story-of-chobani-yogurt-2013-5; Deveon Pendleton, "Hidden Chobani Billionaire Emerges as Greek Yogurt Soars," *Bloomberg*, September 14, 2012 www.bloomberg.com/news/2012-09-14/hidden-chobani-billionaire-emerges-as-greek-yogurt-soars.html; Maria Bartiromo, "A Conversation with the 'Steve Jobs of Yogurt,' " *USA Today*, June 17, 2013, p. 3B; Kimberly Weisul, "Even Chobani Can't Stay Independent Forever: Yogurtmaker Looks to Raise $500 Million," *Inc.,* March 11, 2014, www.inc.com/kimberly-weisul/ even-chobani-cant-be-independent-forever.html (accessed April 10, 2014).

2. Small Business Administration Department of Advocacy, "Frequently Asked Questions," March 2014, www.sba.gov/sites/ default/files/FAQ_March_2014_0. pdf (accessed April 10, 2014).

3. Joshua Yaffa, "Signs of a Russian Thaw (Toward Business)," *The New York Times,* December 28, 2013, www.nytimes.com/2013/12/29/ business/international/signs-of-a-russian-thaw-toward-business. html?pagewanted=1&_r=0 (accessed April 10, 2014).

4. Dinah Eng and Dal LaMagna, "The Rise of the Tweezerman," *Fortune,* January 13, 2014, pp. 23–26.

5. Small Business Administration Department of Advocacy, "Frequently Asked Questions."

6. National Association of Women Business Owners Indianapolis, "Women-Owned Businesses Key Facts," www.

nawboindy.org/pagesroot/Pages/ AboutWBOKeyFacts.aspx (accessed April 10, 2014).

7. U.S. Census Bureau, "2007 Survey of Business Owners Summaries of Findings," www.census.gov/ econ/sbo/getsof.html?07hispanic (accessed April 10, 2014).

8. Marie Gray, "From the Frontier to Fashion's Peak," *Fortune,* November 18, 2013, pp. 29–32.

9. Small Business Administration Department of Advocacy, "Frequently Asked Questions."

10. "Statistics of U.S. Businesses (SUSB)," *Statistics of U.S. Businesses,* www.census.gov/econ/susb/index. html (accessed April 10, 2014).

11. "Bittersweet Synergy: Domestic Outsourcing in India," *The Economist,* October 22, 2009, p. 74.

12. John Tozzi, "Innovation: Tap to Unlock," *Bloomberg Businessweek*, June 13, 2013, p. 42.

13. "Small Biz Stats & Trends," SCORE®, www.score.org/small_ biz_stats.html (accessed April 22, 2014).

14. Business Insurance Quotes, "10 Mom-and-Pop Businesses That Turned Into Empires," Business Insurance, www.businessinsurance. org/10-mom-and-pop-businesses-that-turned-into-empires/ (accessed November 12, 2013).

15. Michael Wolff, "Uber: Tech Company of the Year," *USA Today*, December 23, 2013, pp. 1B, 3B.

16. Dinah Eng and Patrick Leon Esquerré, "Even Texans Can Love Quiche," *Fortune,* September 2, 2013, pp. 27–30.

17. Dinah Eng, "Soft Pretzels Out of Hard Times," *Fortune*, July 22, 2013, pp. 23–26; Auntie Anne's, "National News," Auntie Anne's website, www.auntieannes.com/ aboutus/newsroom/headlines.aspx (accessed August 12, 2013); Auntie Anne's, "About Us," Auntie Anne's website, www.auntieannes.com/ AboutUs/AboutUs.aspx (accessed August 12, 2013).

18. Christine Birkner, "Southern Sweet Spot," *Marketing News,* January 2014, pp. 16–17.

19. Small Business Administration Department of Advocacy, "Frequently Asked Questions."

20. Lev Grossman, "Head Trip," *Time*, April 7, 2014, pp. 36–41.

21. Jefferson Graham, "Start-Up Cooks Up a Future for Food," *USA Today*, December 23, 2013, p. 4B.

22. Small Business Administration Department of Advocacy, "Frequently Asked Questions."

23. Jeff Bercovici, "Why (Some) Psychopaths Make Great CEOs," *Forbes*, June 14, 2011, www.forbes.com/sites/jeffbercovici/2011/06/14/why-some-psychopaths-make-great-ceos/# (accessed July 22, 2013); Sebastian Bailey, "What Do Entrepreneurs, U.S. Presidents and Psychopaths Have in Common?" *Forbes*, August 29, 2012, www.forbes.com/sites/sebastianbailey/2012/08/29/what-do-entrepreneurs-us-presidents-and-psychopaths-have-in-common/ (accessed July 22, 2013); Alexander Stein, "What Entrepreneurs and Con Men Have in Common," *Inc.*, June 2013, p. 58.

24. Eric Butterman, "Shark Tank-Like Business Plan Competition Helps Launch Rutgers Business Ideas," Rutgers Business School, http://business.rutgers.edu/news/shark-tank-business-plan-competition-helps-launch-rutgers-business-ideas (accessed April 10, 2014).

25. Danielle Kucera, "Stitch Fix Nabs $12 Million From Benchmark to Customize Commerce," *Bloomberg*, October 17, 2013, www.bloomberg.com/news/2013-10-17/stitch-fix-nabs-12-million-from-benchmark-to-customize-commerce.html (accessed April 10, 2014); Nicole Laporte, "Getting Their Fix," *Fast Company*, March 2014, pp. 44–46.

26. Josh Hyatt, "An Idea Up His Sleeve," *Fortune*, January/February 2013, pp. 41–42; Kelly Kearsley, "What I Gave Up to Start My Business," *CNN Money*, June 12, 2013, http://money.cnn.com/gallery/smallbusiness/2013/06/12/entrepreneur-sacrifice/3.html (accessed July 17, 2013); ReFleece website, www.refleece.com/ (accessed July 26, 2013).

27. Thomas W. Zimmerer and Norman M. Scarborough, *Essentials of Entrepreneurship and Small Business Management*, 6th ed. (Upper Saddle River, NJ: Pearson Prentice Hall, 2005), pp. 118–24.

28. Ibid.

29. "The SCORE Association Media Fact Sheet," *SCORE*, www.score.org/system/files/u209922/SCORE_media_fact_sheet_2011_0.pdf (accessed April 22, 2014).

30. Adapted from "Tomorrow's Entrepreneur," *Inc. State of Small Business*, 23, no. 7 (2001), pp. 80–104.

31. Dan Barry, "Boomers Hit New Self-Absorption Milestone: Age 65," *International New York Times*, December 21, 2010, www.nytimes.com/2011/01/01/us/01boomers.html?pagewanted=all&_r=0 (accessed April 22, 2014).

32. Molly Smith, "Managing Generation Y as They Change the Workforce," *Reuters*, January 8, 2008, www.reuters.com/article/2008/01/08/idUS129795+08-Jan-2008+BW20080108 (accessed April 22, 2014).

33. Jeffrey Passal and D'Vera Cohn, "Immigration to Play Lead Role in Future U.S. Growth," Pew Research, February 11, 2008, http://pewresearch.org/pubs/729/united-states-population-projections (accessed April 22, 2014); U.S. Bureau of the Census, *Statistical Abstract of the United States, 2011*.

34. "How Imgur Became a Photo-Sharing Hit," *Bloomberg Businessweek*, January 23, 2013, pp. 31–32.

35. Gifford Pinchott III, *Intrapreneuring* (New York: Harper & Row, 1985), p. 34.

36. Paul Brown, "How to Cope with Hard Times," *The New York Times*, June 10, 2008, www.nytimes.com/2008/06/10/business/smallbusiness/10toolkit.html?_r%205%201&ref%205%20smallbusiness&orefs login&gwh=A256B42494736F9E2C604851BF6451DC&gwt=regi (accessed April 22, 2014).

37. Adapted from Carol Kinsey Gorman, *Creativity in Business:*

*A Practical Guide for Creative Thinking*, Crisp Publications Inc., 1989, pp. 5–6. © Crisp Publications Inc., 1200 Hamilton Court, Menlo Park, CA 94025.

38. Sam Oches, "Top 50 Unit Breakdown Sorted by 2010 Total Units," *QSR*, August 2011, www.qsrmagazine.com/reports/top-50-unit-breakdownsorted-2010-total-units (accessed July 27, 2012); "About Sonic Beach," *Sonic Beach*, www.sonicbeach.com/sonicbeach-restaurant (accessed July 27, 2012); Sonic website, www.sonicdrivein.com (accessed July 27, 2012); "Strictly Speaking," Sonic website, www.sonicdrivein.com/business/franchise/faq.jsp (accessed July 27, 2012).

## Chapter 6

1. Rachel Feintzeig, "Building Middle-Manager Morale," *The Wall Street Journal*, April 7, 2013, http://online.wsj.com/article/SB10001424127887323838204578654233406634610.html (accessed August 29, 2013); Melissa Korn and Anita Hofschneider, "How to Get Ahead as a Middle Manager: Try These Tips," *The Wall Street Journal*, August 7, 2013, http://online.wsj.com/article/SB10001424127887323838204578654404251084008.html (accessed August 29, 2013); "Managers by the Numbers," *The Wall Street Journal*, August 6, 2013, http://online.wsj.com/public/resources/documents/st_MIDMANSALARY.html (accessed August 29, 2013); Melissa Korn, "How I Survived Life as a Middle Manager," *The Wall Street Journal*, August 5, 2013, http://online.wsj.com/article/SB100014241278873239970045786442810459666670.html (accessed August 29, 2013); Melissa Korn, "What It's Like Being a Middle Manager Today," *The Wall Street Journal*, August 5, 2013, http://online.wsj.com/article/SB10001424127887323420604578650074170664066.html (accessed August 29, 2013); "Using Their Own Words, Middle Managers Describe the Nature of Their Jobs," *The Wall Street Journal*, http://online.wsj.com/article/SB10001424127887323420604578652110485

397972.html (accessed August 29, 2013).

2. Pete Pachal, "Samsung Bets Big on Curved TVs," *Mashable*, March 20, 2014, http://mashable.com/2014/03/20/samsung-curved-tvs/ (accessed March 28, 2014); Brian X. Chen, "Television Sales Look Grim Again This Year," *The New York Times*, November 6, 2013, http://bits.blogs.nytimes.com/2013/11/06/television-sales-look-grim-again-this-year/?_php=true&_type=blogs&_r=0 (accessed March 28, 2014).

3. Barbara Thau, "New Toys "R" Us CEO Reveals 'Diagnosis,' Treatment Plan for Ailing Chain," *Forbes*, March 27, 2014, www.forbes.com/sites/barbarathau/2014/03/27/new-toys-r-us-ceo-reveals-diagnosis-treatment-plan-for-ailing-chain/ (accessed March 29, 2014); Suzanne Kapner, "Toys 'R' Us CEO Sets Revamp Plan to Return to Profitability," *The Wall Street Journal*, March 26, 2014, http://online.wsj.com/news/articles/SB10001424052702303779504579463062400027516?KEYWORDS=toys+r+us&mg=reno64-wsj (accessed March 29, 2014).

4. "Seventh Generation: Ethosolution Go Green Products and All Natural Cleaners," EthoSolutions, www.ethosolutions.org/seventh-generation-ethosolution-go-green/ (accessed April 30, 2014).

5. Stephanie Strom, "CVS Vows to Quit Selling Tobacco Products," *The New York Times*, February 5, 2014, www.nytimes.com/2014/02/06/business/cvs-plans-to-end-sales-of-tobacco-products-by-october.html?_r=0 (accessed March 29, 2014); Kyle Stock, "The Strategy Behind CVS's No-Smoking Campaign," *Bloomberg Businessweek*, February 5, 2014, www.businessweek.com/articles/2014-02-05/the-strategy-behind-cvss-no-smoking-campaign (accessed March 29, 2014).

6. Jayson Derrick, "Nike's 2017 Objective: $36 Billion Revenue," *The Motley Fool*, October 20, 2014, www.fool.com/investing/general/2013/10/20/nikes-2017-objectives-36-billion-in-revenue.aspx (accessed March 29, 2014).

7. Eric Pfanner, "After Losses, Yet Another Overhaul for Sony," *The New York Times*, February 6, 2014, www.nytimes.com/2014/02/07/technology/sony-to-sell-pc-unit-amid-dwindling-sales.html (accessed March 29, 2014); Jackie Northam, "As Overseas Costs Rise, More U.S. Companies Are 'Reshoring,'" *NPR*, January 27, 2014, www.npr.org/blogs/parallels/2014/01/22/265080779/as-overseas-costs-rise-more-u-s-companies-are-reshoring (accessed March 29, 2014).

8. G. Tomas, M. Hult, David W. Cravens, and Jagdish Sheth, "Competitive Advantage in the Global Marketplace: A Focus on Marketing Strategy," *Journal of Business Research* 51 (January 2001), p. 1.

9. Michigan Department of Natural Resources Fisheries Division, "Tactical Plan," October 24, 2013, www.michigan.gov/documents/dnr/FD-TacticalPlan-Oct2013-FINAL_438248_7.pdf (accessed April 16, 2014).

10. Dennis McCafferty, "The Ten Commandments of Disaster Recovery," May 13, 2013, www.cioinsight.com/it-strategy/infrastructure/slideshows/the-ten-commandments-of-disaster-recovery-10/ (accessed April 16, 2014).

11. Tamara Lytle, "Rising for the Rubble," *Society for Human Resource Management*, 56, no. 9 (September 1, 2011), www.shrm.org/publications/hrmagazine/editorialcontent/2011/0911/pages/0911lytle.aspx (accessed April 30, 2014).

12. Mariko Yasu, "Panasonic Plans to Eliminate 17,000 Jobs in Reorganization," *Bloomberg Businessweek*, April 28, 2011, www.bloomberg.com/news/2011-04-28/panasonic-plans-to-reduce-its-workforce-by-17-000-to-350-000-by-march-2013.html (accessed March 5, 2012).

13. PRWeb, "Collabera Named 2014 'Best Staffing Firm to Work For' by Staffing Industry Analysts for Record Third Consecutive Year," *PRWeb*, March 25, 2014, www.prweb.com/releases/2014/03/prweb11698621.htm (accessed March 29, 2014); Collabera, "Home," www.collabera.com (accessed March 29, 2014).

14. "Labor Force Statistics from the Current Population Survey," Bureau of Labor Statistics, www.bls.gov/cps/ (accessed April 30, 2014).

15. C. O. Trevor, and A. J. Nyberg, "Keeping Your Headcount When All About You Are Losing Theirs: Downsizing, Voluntary Turnover Rates, and the Moderating Role of HR Practices," *Academy of Management Journal,* 51 (2008), pp. 259–76.

16. Jon Kaufman and Rob Markey, "Who Keeps You Jazzed About Your Job?" *Forbes*, February 11, 2014, www.forbes.com/sites/baininsights/2014/02/11/who-keeps-you-jazzed-about-your-job/ (accessed March 29, 2014).

17. Liz Welch, "The Way I Work: Ken Grossman, Sierra Nevada," *Inc.,* April 24, 2013, www.inc.com/magazine/201304/liz-welch/the-way-i-work-ken-grossman-sierra-nevada.html (accessed January 23, 2014); Bryan Carey, "Sierra Nevada Brewery Tops $200 Million Mark," *The Examiner,* September 11, 2013, www.examiner.com/article/sierra-nevada-brewing-tops-200-million-mark (accessed January 23, 2014); Tip Top, "Beyond the Pale: The Story of Sierra Nevada Brewing Co.," *Beer Spot,* August 27, 2013, www.thebeerspot.com/news/article/2013/08/beyond-the-pale-the-story-of-sierra-nevada-brewing-co (accessed January 23, 2014).

18. International Association of Privacy Professionals, "About IAPP," www.privacyassociation.org/about_iapp (accessed March 29, 2014).

19. Catalyst, "Women CEOs of the Fortune 1000," Catalyst, January 15, 2014, www.catalyst.org/knowledge/women-ceos-fortune-1000 (accessed March 29, 2014).

20. Ross Kerber, "Growth in Compensation for U.S. CEOs May HaveSslowed," *Reuters*, March 17, 2014, www.reuters.com/article/2014/03/17/

us-compensation-ceos-2013-insight-idUSBREA2G05520140317 (accessed March 29, 2014).

21. DiversityInc, "The DiversityInc Top 50 Companies for Diversity," *DiversityInc*, 2014, www.diversityinc.com/the-diversityinc-top-50-companies-for-diversity-2014/ (accessed March 29, 2014); Diversity Best Practices Staff, "Inside Diversity Structure at Sodexo, Johnson & Johnson, and Rockwell Automation," *Diversity Best Practices*, January 29, 2013, www.diversitybestpractices.com/news-articles/inside-diversity-structure-sodexo-johnson-johnson-and-rockwell-automation (accessed March 29, 2014).

22. Laura Nichols, "Agencies Called to Step Up the Pace on Diversity Efforts," *PRWeek*, February 7, 2014, www.prweekus.com/article/agencies-called-step-pace-diversity-efforts/1283550 (accessed March 29, 2014).

23. Clay Latimer, "Philip Pillsbury's Treats Turned Into Tasty Sales," *Investor's Business Daily*, August 1, 2013, p. A3; Funding Universe, "The Pillsbury Company History," *International Directory of Company Histories*, Vol. 62, St. James Press, 2004, www.fundinguniverse.com/company-histories/the-pillsbury-company-history/ (accessed December 9, 2013); Walter Waggoner, "Philip Pillsbury of Minnesota; Led Food Products Concern," *The New York Times*, June 16, 1984, www.nytimes.com/1984/06/16/obituaries/philip-pillsbury-of-minnesota-led-food-products-concern.html (accessed December 9, 2013); Constance L. Hays and Andrew Ross Sorkin, "General Mills Is Seen in a $10.5 Billion Deal for Pillsbury," *The New York Times*, July 17, 2000, www.nytimes.com/2000/07/17/business/general-mills-is-seen-in-a-10.5-billion-deal-for-pillsbury.html (accessed December 10, 2013).

24. Del Jones, "Autocratic Leadership Works—Until It Fails," *USA Today*, June 5, 2003, www.usatoday.com/news/nation/2003-06-05-raines-usat_x.htm (accessed April 16, 2014).

25. George Manning and Kent Curtis, *The Art of Leadership* (New York: McGraw-Hill, 2003), p. 125.

26. Joann S. Lublin and Dana Mattioli, "Penney CEO Out, Old Boss Back In," *The Wall Street Journal*, April 8, 2013, http://online.wsj.com/news/articles/SB10001424127887324504704578411031708241800 (accessed March 29, 2014).

27. Bruce J. Avolio and William L. Gardner, "Authentic Leadership Development: Getting to the Root of Positive Forms of Leadership," *The Leadership Quarterly*, 2005, pp. 315–38.

28. John P. Kotter, "What Leaders Really Do," *Harvard Business Review*, December 2001, http://fs.ncaa.org/Docs/DIII/What%20Leaders%20Really%20Do.pdf (accessed April 30, 2014).

29. Lisa Baertlein, "McDonald's CEO Jim Skinner to Retire," *Reuters*, March 22, 2012, www.reuters.com/article/2012/03/22/us-mcdonalds-idUSTRE8170YW20120322 (accessed April 30, 2014).

30. C. L. Pearce and C. C. Manz, "The New Silver Bullets of Leadership: The Importance of Self- and Shared Leadership in Knowledge Work," *Organizational Dynamics*, 34, no. 2 (2005), pp. 130–40.

31. Deborah Harrington-Mackin, *The Team Building Tool Kit* (New York: New Directions Management, 1994); Joseph P. Folger, Marshall Scott Poole, and Randall K. Stutman, *Working through Conflict: Strategies for Relationships, Groups, and Organizations*, 6th ed. (Upper Saddle River, NJ: Pearson Education, 2009).

32. Leigh Buchanan, "Between Venus and Mars," *Inc.*, June 2013, pp. 64–74; Leigh Buchanan, "What a Leader Needs Now: 7 'Feminine' Qualities," *Inc.*, June 2013, www.inc.com/magazine/201306/leigh-buchanan/what-leaders-need-to-know.html (accessed July 15, 2013).

33. Kerrie Unsworth, "Unpacking Creativity," *Academy of Management Review*, 26 (April 2001), pp. 289–97.

34. Pallavi Gogoi, "A Bittersweet Deal or Wrigley," *BusinessWeek*, May 12, 2008, p. 34l "About Us," Wrigley, www.wrigley.com/global/about-us.aspx (accessed April 30, 2014).

35. *Harvard Business Review* 60 (November–December 1982), p. 160.

36. Dan Schwabel, "5 Reasons Why Your Online Presence Will Replace Your Resume in 10 Years," *Forbes*, February 21, 2012, www.forbes.com/sites/danschawbel/2011/02/21/5-reasons-why-your-online-presence-will-replace-your-resume-in-10-years/ (accessed April 30, 2014).

37. "Salary After Taxes," *Employment Spot*, www.employmentspot.com/employment-articles/salary-after-taxes (accessed September 4, 2014).

38. Bureau of Labor Statistics, "May 2013 National Occupational Employment and Wage Estimates United States," www.bls.gov/oes/current/oes_nat.htm#11-0000 (accessed April 30, 2014).

39. Ford, "Our Strategy," 2011–2012, http://corporate.ford.com/microsites/sustainability-report-2011-12/blueprint-strategy (accessed May 15, 2014); Mark Vaughn, "2013 Ford Fusion Drive Review," *Autoweek*, September 21, 2012, www.autoweek.com/article/20120921/CARREVIEWS/120929976 (accessed May 15, 2014); Lawrence Ulrich, "A Hybrid Done Right, but Not Without Glitches," *The New York Times*, November 2, 2012, www.nytimes.com/2012/11/04/automobiles/autoreviews/a-hybrid-done-right-but-not-without-glitches.html?_r=0 (accessed May 23, 2014).

## Chapter 7

1. Erika Fry, "How CarMax Cares," *Fortune*, April 8, 2013, p. 21; CarMax website, "CarMax Culture and Values," www.carmax.com/enUS/company-info/culture.html (accessed July 19, 2013); Michael Myser, "The Wal-Mart of Used Cars," *CNN Money*, October

2, 2006, http://money.cnn.com/magazines/business2/business2_archive/2006/09/01/8384327/ (accessed July 19, 2013).

2. Horace Dediu, "Understanding Apple's Organizational Structure," *Asymco*, July 3, 2013, www.asymco.com/2013/07/03/understanding-apples-organizational-structure/ (accessed March 31, 2014); Sam Grobart, "How Samsung Became the World's No. 1 Smartphone Maker," *Bloomberg Businessweek*, March 28, 2013, www.businessweek.com/articles/2013-03-28/how-samsung-became-the-worlds-no-dot-1-smartphone-maker#p1 (accessed March 31, 2014); Jay Yarow, "Apple's New Organizational Structure Could Help It Move Faster," *Business Insider*, May 1, 2013, www.businessinsider.com/apples-new-organizational-structure-could-help-it-move-faster-2013-5 (accessed March 31, 2014).

3. Reed Hastings, "How to Set Your Employees Free: Reed Hastings," *Bloomberg Businessweek*, April 12, 2012, www.businessweek.com/articles/2012-04-12/how-to-set-your-employees-free-reed-hastings (accessed March 31, 2014); Dan Lyons, "Advice on Corporate Culture From Netflix's Former Chief Talent Officer," *HubSpot*, May 7, 2013, http://blog.hubspot.com/marketing/netflix-hubspot-corporate-culture-advice (accessed March 31, 2014).

4. "A New Future for Toms Shoes, Tweed Shire and Room to Read," *Reputation Report*, August 7, 2009, www.reputationreport.com.au/2009/08/a-new-future-by-toms-shoes-tweed-shire-and-room-to-read/ (accessed April 30, 2014); "Our Movement," TOMS Shoes, www.toms.com/our-movement/l (accessed April 30, 2014).

5. "Best Companies to Work For: Happy Campers," *CNNMoney,* http://money.cnn.com/galleries/2011/news/companies/1104/gallery.best_companies_happy_campers.fortune/2.html (accessed April 30, 2014); Christopher Palmeri, "Zappos Retails Its Culture," *Bloomberg*

*Businessweek,* December 30, 2009, www.businessweek.com/magazine/content/10_02/b4162057120453.htm (accessed April 30, 2014).

6. Rachel Emma Sullivan, "When Water-Cooler Chats Aren't Enough," *The Wall Street Journal*, May 1, 2013, p. B6; Max Nisen, "Zappos to Build Intentionally Inconvenient Office in Las Vegas, Arch Daily, March 28, 2013, www.archdaily.com/351790/zappos-to-build-intentionally-inconvenient-office-in-las-vegas/ (accessed August 2, 2013); Ben Kesling and James R. Hagerty, "Say Goodbye to the Office Cubicle," *The Wall Street Journal*, April 2, 2013, http://online.wsj.com/article/SB100014241278873234662045783830224346801196.html (accessed August 2, 2013).

7. Joe Light, "Finance and Tech Signal Bold Attitudes on Ethics," *The Wall Street Journal,* March 7, 2011, http://online.wsj.com/article/SB10001424052748704728004576176711042012064.html (accessed April 30, 2014).

8. Lisa Magloff, "Examples of Transformational Change," *Chron*, http://smallbusiness.chron.com/examples-transformational-change-18261.html (accessed March 31, 2014); Nokia, "The Nokia Story," www.nokia.com/global/about-nokia/about-us/the-nokia-story/ (accessed March 31, 2014).

9. Adam Smith, *Wealth of Nations* (New York: Modern Library, 1937; originally published in 1776).

10. Malcolm Moore, "What Has Triggered the Suicide Cluster at Foxconn?" *The Telegraph,* May 16, 2010, http://blogs.telegraph.co.uk/news/malcolmmoore/100039883/ (accessed April 30, 2014).

11. Unilever, "Annual Report and Accounts 2013," www.unilever.com/images/Unilever_AR13_tcm13-383757.pdf (accessed March 31, 2014).

12. PepsiCo Inc., *The New York Times,* March 31, 2014, http://topics.nytimes.com/top/news/business/companies/pepsico_inc/index.html (accessed March 31, 2014). PepsiCo

Inc., "Global Business Units," www.pepsico.com/Company/Global-Business-Units (accessed March 31, 2014).

13. Diageo, "Regions," www.diageo.com/en-row/ourbusiness/ourregions/Pages/default.aspx (accessed March 31, 2014).

14. Procter & Gamble, "P&G Organizes Global Business Units into Industry-Based Sectors," *P&G Corporate Newsroom*, June 5, 2013, http://news.pg.com/press-release/pg-corporate-announcements/procter-gamble-announces-organization-changes (accessed March 31, 2014).

15. Micah Solomon, "Take These Two Steps to Rival Nordstrom's Customer Service Experience," *Forbes*, March 15, 2014, www.forbes.com/sites/micahsolomon/2014/03/15/the-nordstrom-two-part-customer-experience-formula-lessons-for-your-business/ (accessed March 31, 2014).

16. Kerry Hannon, "The Write Stuff," *Money*, October 2013, pp. 29–30; Nota Bene, "About Us," http://notabenepaper.com/about/ (accessed September 23, 2013); "Nota Bene," *Whirl Magazine,* June 9, 2010, http://whirlmagazine.com/nota-bene/ (accessed September 30, 2013); "Shopping Guide," *Pittsburgh Magazine,* www.pittsburghmagazine.com/Pittsburgh-Magazine/Shopping/Shopping-Guide/index.php/name/NOTA-BENE/listing/31677/ (accessed September 30, 2013).

17. Julie Jargon, "Burger King Joins Crowd in India," *The Wall Street Journal*, November 19, 2014, http://online.wsj.com/news/articles/SB10001424052702303531204579207792423911748 (accessed April 1, 2014); Lily Kuo, "Why Burger King Should Sell Pizza at Its New Restaurants in India," *Quartz*, November 21, 2013, http://qz.com/149434/why-burger-king-should-sell-pizza-at-its-new-restaurants-in-india/ (accessed April 1, 2014).

18. "Why Work Here?" www.wholefoodsmarket.com/careers/workhere.php (accessed April 30, 2014).

19. PR Newswire, "PepsiCo Unveils New Organizational Structure, Names CEOs of Three Principle Operating Units," November 5, 2007, www.prnewswire.com/news-releases/pepsico-unveils-new-organizational-structure-names-ceos-of-three-principal-operating-units-58668152.html (accessed April 30, 2014); "The PepsiCo Family," PepsiCo, www.pepsico.com/Company/The-Pepsico-Family/PepsiCo-Americas-Beverages.html (accessed April 30, 2014).

20. Jon R. Katzenbach and Douglas K. Smith, "The Discipline of Teams," *Harvard Business Review,* 71 (March– April 1993), p. 19.

21. Ibid.

22. John Baldoni, "The Secret to Team Collaboration: Individuality," *Inc.,* January 18, 2012, www.inc.com/john-baldoni/the-secret-to-team-collaboration-is-individuality.html (accessed February 17, 2012).

23. Gregory Ciotti, "Why Remote Teams Are the Future (and How to Make Them Work)," *Help Scout,* October 23, 2013, www.helpscout.net/blog/virtual-teams/ (accessed April 1, 2014).

24. Esther Shein, "Making the Virtual Team Real," *The Network,* April 2, 2008, http://newsroom.cisco.com/dlls/2008/ts_040208.html (accessed April 30, 2014).

25. Patrick Kiger, "Task Force Training Develops New Leaders, Solves Real Business Issues and Helps Cut Costs," *Workforce,* September 7, 2011, www.workforce.com/article/20070521/NEWS02/305219996/task-force-training-develops-new-leaders-solves-real-business-issues-and-helps-cut-costs (accessed March 4, 2013); Duane D. Stanford, "Coca-Cola Woman Board Nominee Bucks Slowing Diversity Trend," *Bloomberg,* February 22, 2013, www.bloomberg.com/news/2013-02-22/coca-cola-s-woman-director-nominee-bucks-slowing-diversity-trend.html (accessed March 4, 2013).

26. Jerry Useem, "What's That Spell? TEAMWORK," *Fortune,* June 12, 2006, p. 66.

27. Jia Lynnyang, "The Power of Number 4.6," *Fortune,* June 12, 2006, p. 122.

28. Natasha Singer, "Intel's Sharp-Eyed Social Scientist," *The New York Times,* February 15, 2014, www.nytimes.com/2014/02/16/technology/intels-sharp-eyed-social-scientist.html?_r=0 (accessed April 1, 2014).

29. Catherine Dunn, "Brother-and-Sister Brewer," *Fortune,* November 18, 2013, http://money.cnn.com/2013/10/31/news/numi-tea-rahim.pr.fortune/ (accessed January 13, 2014); Esha Chhabra, "Fair Trade Crucial Ingredient in Numi Organic Teas," *SF Gate,* December 30, 2011, www.sfgate.com/business/article/Fair-trade-crucial-ingredient-in-Numi-Organic-Teas-2431049.php (accessed January 13, 2014); Certified B Corporation, "Numi Organic Tea," www.bcorporation.net/community/numi-organic-tea (accessed January 13, 2014); Kristen, "Numi Organic Tea Brews 'Pure Tea' Precedent with Non-GMO Verification," *The Shelby Report,* August 27, 2012, www.theshelbyreport.com/2012/08/27/numi-organic-tea-brews-pure-tea-precedent-with-non-gmo-verification/#.UtQjjNJDtc8 (accessed January 13, 2014).

30. Richard S. Wellins, William C. Byham, and Jeanne M. Wilson, *Empowered Teams: Creating Self-Directed Work Groups That Improve Quality, Productivity, and Participation* (San Francisco: Jossey-Bass Publishers, 1991), p. 5.

31. Matt Krumrie, "Are Meetings a Waste of Time? Survey Says Yes," *Minneapolis Workplace Examiner,* May 12, 2009, www.examiner.com/article/are-meetings-a-waste-of-time-survey-says-yes (accessed March 11, 2010).

32. Peter Mell and Timothy Grance, "The NIST Definition of Cloud Computing," National Institute of Standards and Technology, Special Publication 800-145, September 2011, http://csrc.nist.gov/publications/nistpubs/800-145/SP800-145.pdf (accessed April 30, 2014).

33. Michael Christian, "Top 10 Ideas: Making the Most of Your Corporate Intranet," April 2, 2009, www.claromentis.com/blog/top-10-ideas-making-the-most-of-your-corporate-intranet/ (accessed February 12, 2010).

34. Kim Komando, "Why You Need a Company Policy on Internet Use," www.microsoft.com/business/en-us/resources/management/employee-relations/why-you-need-a-company-policy-on-internet-use.aspx?fbid=HEChiHWK7CU (accessed April 30, 2014).

35. PBSNewsHour, "Apple Supplier Foxconn Pledges Better Working Conditions, but Will It Deliver?" *YouTube,* www.youtube.com/watch?v=ZduorbCkSBQ (accessed April 30, 2014).

36. Michael D. Maginn, *Effective Teamwork,* 1994, p. 10. © 1994 Richard D. Irwin, a Times Mirror Higher Education Group Inc. Company.

37. Tony Hsieh, "Zappos CEO: Training, Mentorship at the Core of Our Employee 'Pipeline Strategy,'" *The Huffington Post,* January 21, 2011, www.huffingtonpost.com/tony-hsieh/zappos-ceo-how-weve-built_b_812187.html (accessed May 27, 2014); Eleanor Bloxham, "Zappos and the Search for a Better Way to Run a Business," *CNN Money,* January 29, 2014, http://management.fortune.cnn.com/2014/01/29/zappos-holacracy/ (accessed May 27, 2014).

## Chapter 8

1. James R. Hagerty, "Keeping Plants Running from Afar," *The Wall Street Journal,* September 5, 2013, p. B8; ABB Communications Services, "ABB Integrates Plant, Stops Batch Rejects," 2004, http://search-ext.abb.com/library/Download.aspx?DocumentID=3BUS390002R0001&LanguageCode=en&DocumentPartID=&Action=Launch (accessed October 15, 2013); "Turbine Remote Monitoring Service Allows for Scalability," *Automation World,* September 17, 2012, www.automationworld.com/asset-management/turbine-remote-monitoring-service-allows-

scalability (accessed October 15, 2013); Eaton, "eNotify Remote Monitoring," http://powerquality. eaton.com/products-services/ Services/remote-monitoring. asp?id=&key=&Quest_user_ id=&leadg_Q_QRequired=&site =&menu=&cx=179&x=11&y=10 (accessed October 15, 2013).

2. Reshma Memon Yaqub, "Matching Stars to Their Dream Cars," *Inc.*, September 2013. www.inc.com/ magazine/201309/reshma-memon-yaqub/celebrity-auto-group-matches-celebrities-to-cars.html (accessed September 16, 2013); Celebrity Auto Group, www. celebrityautogroup.com/luxury-car-dealer-sarasota/ (accessed September 16, 2013); "Celebrity Auto Group Rolls-Royce Phantom with Build-in iPads," GTSpirit.com, November 14, 2012, www.gtspirit. com/2012/11/14/celebrity-auto-group-rolls-royce-phantom-with-build-in-ipads/ (accessed September 16, 2013).

3. Rina Rapuano, "Check Please!" *The Washingtonian Blog,* February 18, 2010, www.washingtonian. com/blogarticles/restaurants/ bestbites/15008.html (accessed May 12, 2014).

4. Leonard L. Berry, *Discovering the Soul of Service* (New York: The Free Press, 1999), pp. 86–96.

5. Valerie A. Zeithaml and Mary Jo Bitner, *Services Marketing*, 3rd ed. (Boston: McGraw-Hill Irwin, 2003), pp. 3, 22.

6. Chris Mock, "Quality Control in 2014," *Freddie Mac*, February 10, 2014, www.freddiemac.com/news/ blog/chris_mock/20140210_quality_ control.html (accessed April 1, 2014).

7. Bernard Wysocki Jr., "To Fix Health Care, Hospitals Take Tips from the Factory Floor," *The Wall Street Journal,* April 9, 2004, via www.chcanys.org/clientuploads/ downloads/Clinical_resources/ Leadership%20Articles/ LeanThinking_ACF28EB.pdf (accessed May 12, 2014).

8. Tim Mullaney, "Social Media Is Reinventing How Business Is Done," *USA Today*, May 16, 2012, http://usatoday30.usatoday. com/money/economy/story/2012-05-14/social-media-economy-companies/55029088/1 (accessed April 24, 2014); David Lavenda, "How Red Robin Transformed Its Business with Yammer," *Fast Company,* February 6, 2014, www. fastcompany.com/3025396/work-smart/how-red-robin-burgers-got-yummier-with-yammer (accessed April 24, 2014).

9. Matthew Peach, "UK's First Laser Vibrometry Test Facility Opening in Early 2014," Optics.org, October 29, 2013, http://optics.org/news/4/10/52 (accessed April 1, 2014).

10. Christina Cooke, "America's Rebel Band of Custom-Bike Builders," *The Atlantic*, April 3, 2014, www.theatlantic.com/ business/archive/2014/04/americas-rebel-band-of-custom-bike-builders/360058/ (accessed April 22, 2014).

11. Marie Singer, "The Hershey Company—Company Information," Market Business News, April 14, 2014, www.marketbusinessnews. com/hershey-company-company-information/18006 (accessed May 12, 2014).

12. Honda, "Honda to Build New Automobile Plant in Mexico for Production of Subcompact Vehicles, Starting in 2014," *Business Wire,* August 12, 2011, www.businesswire. com/news/home/20110812005178/ en/Honda-Build-Automobile-Plant-Mexico-Production-Subcompact#. U3FFpvXLQ4k (accessed May 12, 2014).

13. "Top 10 Solar Friendly States," *Cooler Planet*, http://solar. coolerplanet.com/Articles/top-10-solar-friendly-states.aspx (accessed May 12, 2014).

14. Ross Toro, "How 3D Printers Work (Infographic)," *Live Science,* June 18, 2013, www.livescience. com/37513-how-3d-printers-work-infographic.html (accessed November 18, 2013).

15. Robotic Industries Association, "North American Robotics Shipments Grow in 2013 While New Orders Contract," Robotics Online, February 4, 2014, www. robotics.org/content-detail.cfm/ Industrial-Robotics-News/North-American-Robotics-Shipments-Grow-in-2013-While-New-Orders-Contract/content_id/4648 (accessed April 2, 2014); Sian Harris, "Will Robots Be the Answer to Our Next Manufacturing Revolution?" *E&T*, January 20, 2014, http://eandt.theiet. org/magazine/2014/01/robots-are-coming.cfm?origin=EtOtherStories (accessed April 2, 2014). Elisabeth Eitel, "Technology forecast 2014: Robots Priced for the Masses," *Machine Design*, January 8, 2014, http://machinedesign.com/robotics/ technology-forecast-2014-robots-priced-masses (accessed April 2, 2014).

16. Tiffany Kaiser, "Lenovo Launches Its First U.S. PC Manufacturing Line in North Carolina," *Daily Tech,* June 6, 2013. www.dailytech.com/ Lenovo+Launches+Its+First+US+PC+ Manufacturing+Line+in+North+ Carolina/article31705.htm (accessed January 23, 2014); Shane McGlaun, "Lenovo Eyes Smartphone Push in the U.S.," *Daily Tech,* May 27, 2013, www.dailytech.com/Lenovo+Eyes+ Smartphone+Push+in+the+US/ article31631.htm (accessed January 23, 2014); Loretta Chao, "As Rivals Outsource, Lenovo Keeps Production In-House," *The Wall Street Journal,* July 9, 2012, http:// online.wsj.com/news/articles/SB10 0014240527023033025045773255 22699291362 (accessed January 23, 2014); Simon Montlake, The Middle Way: Inside Lenovo's Bid to Build a Better Tablet," *Forbes*, November 18, 2013, www.forbes.com/sites/ simonmontlake/2013/10/30/the-middle-way-inside-lenovos-bid-to-build-a-better-tablet/ (accessed January 23, 2014).

17. Biogen Idec, "Corporate Citizenship Report," 2012, www. biogenidec.com/Files/Filer/USA/ CC_2013/2012_Biogen_Idec_ Corporate_Citizenship_Report.pdf (accessed April 22, 2014); Business Wire via The Motley Fool, "Biogen Idec Becomes First U.S.-Based Biotech Named to Dow Jones Sustainability World Index," *Daily*

*Finance,* September 24, 2013, www. dailyfinance.com/2013/09/24/biogen-idec-becomes-first-us-based-biotech-named-t/ (accessed April 22, 2014).

18. Bryan Walsh, "Why Green Is the New Red, White and Blue," *Time,* April 28, 2008, p. 53.

19. Megan Kamerick, "How To Go Green," *New Mexico Business Weekly,* May 23–29, 2008, p. 3.

20. O. C. Ferrell and Michael D. Hartline, *Marketing Strategy* (Mason, OH: South Western, 2011), p. 215.

21. Keisha A. Simmons, "UPS Introduces New Cloud-Based Technology Platform to Improve International Supply Chain Management," *UPS,* November 13, 2012, www.pressroom.ups.com/Press+Releases/Archive/2012/Q4/UPS+Introduces+New+Cloud-Based+Technology+Platform+to+Improve+International+Supply+Chain+Management (accessed April 23, 2014).

22. Ferrell and Hartline, *Marketing Strategy,* p. 215.

23. Susan Berfield and Manuel Baigorri, "Zara's Fast-Fashion Edge," *Bloomberg Businessweek*, November 14, 2013, www.businessweek.com/articles/2013-11-14/2014-outlook-zaras-fashion-supply-chain-edge (accessed April 23, 2014).

24. Investment Mine, "Historical Copper Prices and Price Chart," April 8, 2014, www.infomine.com/investment/metal-prices/copper/all/ (accessed April 9, 2014).

25. "Broken Links," *The Economist,* March 31, 2011, www.economist.com/node/18486015 (accessed May 12, 2014).

26. Jez Fredenburgh, "Horsemeat: Tesco's Pledges, One Year On," *Farmer's Weekly*, February 21, 2014, www.fwi.co.uk/articles/21/02/2014/143348/horsemeat-tesco39s-pledges-one-year-on.htm (accessed April 23, 2014).

27. Brian Dumaine, "Fill 'Er Up with Hydrogen?" *Fortune,* September 2, 2013, p. 23; Sarah Zielinski, "George W. Bush vs. Elon Musk: Who Was Right about the Future of Hydrogen Cars?" *Slate,* August 27, 2013, www.slate.com/articles/health_and_science/transportation/2013/08/hydrogen_fuel_cell_cars_honda_s_clarity_and_toyota_models_use_zero_emission.html (accessed October 1, 2013); "Hobbled by High Cost, Hydrogen Fuel Cells Will Be a Modest $3 Billion Market in 2020," Lux Research, January 8, 2013, www.luxresearchinc.com/news-and-events/press-releases/143.html (accessed October 3, 2013); Alissa Priddle, "Toyota to Start Selling Hydrogen Fuel-Cell Car in 2015," *USA Today,* August 8, 2012, http://content.usatoday.com/communities/driveon/post/2012/08/toyota-to-start-selling-hydrogen-fuel-cell-car-in-2015/1 (accessed October 3, 2013).

28. Susan Carey, "Airlines Play Up Improvements in On-Time Performance," *The Wall Street Journal,* February 10, 2010, p. B6; U.S. Department of Transportation, "Air Travel Consumer Report," March 2014, www.dot.gov/sites/dot.gov/files/docs/2014_March_ATCR.pdf (accessed April 23, 20014).

29. Michael E. Newman, "Three U.S. Organizations Honored with the 2013 Baldrige National Quality Award," Baldridge Performance Excellence Program, November 13, 2013, www.nist.gov/baldrige/baldrige_recipients2013.cfm (accessed April 23, 2014).

30. Roger Yu, "Kia Looks to Buff Image with Value, New Designs," *USA Today,* June 29, 2011, http://usatoday30.usatoday.com/money/autos/2011-06-27-kia-rising_n.htm (accessed May 12, 2014); Jonathon Ramsey, "Kia Using Quality and Technology to Increase Sales and Brand Prestige," *AutoBlog,* April 11, 2013, www.autoblog.com/2013/04/11/kia-using-quality-and-technology-to-increase-sales-and-brand-pre/ (accessed April 24, 2014).

31. Philip B. Crosby, *Quality Is Free: The Art of Making Quality Certain* (New York: McGraw-Hill, 1979), pp. 9–10.

32. Nigel F. Piercy, *Market-Led Strategic Change* (Newton, MA: Butterworth-Heinemann, 1992), pp. 374–85.

33. Bloomberg LLP, "Compuware Gomez Introduces Free Web Performance Benchmarking Tool," *Bloomberg,* February 16, 2010, www.bloomberg.com/apps/news?pid=newsarchive&sid=a3bTx6JLlx7I (accessed May 12, 2014).

34. "ISO 9001 Certification," GE Power & Water, www.geinstruments.com/company/iso-9001-certification.html (accessed May 12, 2014).

35. Charles Duhigg and David Barboza, "In China, Human Costs Are Built into an iPad," *The New York Times,* January 25, 2012, www.nytimes.com/2012/01/26/business/ieconomy-apples-ipad-and-the-human-costs-for-workers-in-china.html?pagewanted=all (accessed February 8, 2012).

36. "Monitoring and Auditing Global Supply Chains Is a Must," *Ethisphere,* 2011, Q3, pp. 38–45.

37. "Employment Opportunities," Careers in Supply Chain Management, www.careersinsupplychain.org/career-outlook/empopp.asp (accessed May 12, 2014).

38. "Best Jobs in America," *CNN Money,* http://money.cnn.com/magazines/moneymag/bestjobs/2009/snapshots/48.html (accessed April 24, 2014).

39. James Wetherbe, "Principles of Cycle Time Reduction," *Cycle Time Research,* 1995, p. iv.

40. Stan Davis and Christopher Meyer, *Blur: The Speed of Change in the Connected Economy* (Reading, MA: Addison-Wesley, 1998), p. 5.

41. "Home Run Inn," *CBS Chicago,* January 4, 2012, http://chicago.cbslocal.com/2012/01/04/home-run-inn/ (accessed May 21, 2014); Home Run Inn, *Home Run Inn All-Star Catering*, www.orderstart.com/choose/homeruninn/catering_sales_kit.pdf (accessed May 21, 2014); "Consumer Reports Names Home Run Inn Best Frozen Pizza," August 20, 2013, www.nbcchicago.com/news/local/Home-Run-Inn-Named-Best-Frozen-Pizza-220344721.html (accessed May 21, 2014); Home Run Inn, "Frozen Pizza," www.homeruninnpizza.com/frozen-pizza (accessed May 21, 2014).

## Chapter 9

1. David A. Kaplan, "Inside Mars," *Fortune,* 73–82; "Mars," *Forbes,* www.forbes.com/companies/mars/ (accessed July 22, 2013); "100 Best Companies to Work For: Mars," *CNN Money,* 2013, http://money. cnn.com/magazines/fortune/best-companies/2013/snapshots/95.html (accessed July 22, 2013); "Brands," Mars website, www.mars.com/ global/brands.aspx (accessed July 22, 2013).

2. Dan Heath and Chip Heath, "Business Advice from Van Halen," *Fast Company,* March 1, 2010, www.fastcompany.com/1550881/ business-advice-van-halen (accessed May 12, 2014).

3. Google, "Benefits," www.google. com/about/careers/lifeatgoogle/ benefits/ (accessed April 23, 2014).

4. "How Much Does Absenteeism Cost Your Business," The Perfect Labor Storm 2.0, December 10, 2008, http://hrblog.typepad.com/ perfect_labor_storm/2008/12/how-much-does-absenteeism-cost-your-business.html#axzz31XnQY6D2 (accessed March 11, 2010).

5. Brad Stone, "Costco CEO Craig Jelinek Leads the Cheapest, Happiest Company in the World," *Bloomberg Businessweek,* June 6, 2013, www.businessweek.com/ articles/2013-06-06/costco-ceo-craig-jelinek-leads-the-cheapest-happiest-company-in-the-world#p1 (accessed April 24, 2014).

6. Equilar Inc., "20 Top Paid CEOs," *CNN Money,* April 8, 2013, http:// money.cnn.com/gallery/news/ companies/2013/04/08/executive-pay/ (accessed April 23, 2014).

7. Jillian Berman, "Wegmans Improves Its Bottom Line by Helping Employees Shrink Their Waistlines," *The Huffington Post,* August 5, 2013, www.huffingtonpost. com/2013/08/05/wegmans-wellness_n_3696411.html (accessed January 28, 2014); "100 Best Companies to Work For: Wegmans Food Markets," *CNN Money,* 2014, http://money.cnn.com/magazines/ fortune/best-companies/2014/ snapshots/12.html (accessed January 29, 2014); Ariel Schwartz, "Greenpeace Ranks Sustainable Seafood in Grocery Stores, Wegmans Tops List," *Fast Company,* June 30, 2009, www.fastcompany. com/1302498/greenpeace-ranks-sustainable-seafood-grocery-stores-wegmans-tops-list (accessed January 29, 2014); David Rohde, "The Anti-Walmart: The Secret Sauce of Wegmans Is People," *The Atlantic,* March 23, 2012, www.theatlantic. com/business/archive/2012/03/ the-anti-walmart-the-secret-sauce-of-wegmans-is-people/254994/ (accessed January 29, 2014); John Failla, "An Inside Look at Wegmans' Sustainability Efforts," *Green Retail Decisions,* April 14, 2011, www.greenretaildecisions.com/ news/2011/04/14/an-inside-look-at-wegmans-sustainability-efforts (accessed January 29, 2014).

8. Fortune, "100 Best Companies to Work For—USAA," *CNN Money,* 2014, http://money.cnn. com/magazines/fortune/best-companies/2014/snapshots/17. html?iid=BC14_fl_list (accessed April 24, 2014); Fortune, "100 Best Companies to Work For—Genentech," *CNN Money,* 2014, http://money.cnn.com/magazines/ fortune/best-companies/2014/ snapshots/6.html?iid=BC14_fl_list (accessed April 24, 2014).

9. "25 Well-Paying Jobs That Most People Overlook (and Why)," *Business Pundit,* www. businesspundit.com/25-well-paying-jobs-that-most-people-overlook-and-why/ (accessed May 12, 2014).

10. Christina Couch, "10 Companies with Excellent Customer Service," *The Huffington Post,* August 15, 2013, www.huffingtonpost.com/2013/08/15/ best-customer-service_n_3720052. html (accessed April 24, 2014).

11. Douglas McGregor, *The Human Side of Enterprise* (New York: McGraw-Hill, 1960), pp. 33–34.

12. Hadley Malcolm, "CEO Close Up: Jay Stein's Personal Stein Mart Touch," *USA Today,* October 23, 2013, www.usatoday.com/story/ money/business/2013/10/23/ceo-profile-jay-stein/3010021/ (accessed January 28, 2014); Press Release, "Stein Mart Launches Online Store," *The Wall Street Journal,* September 6, 2013, http://online. wsj.com/article/PR-CO-20130906-904963.html (accessed January 28, 2014); Stein Mart, "About Us," Stein Mart website, www.steinmart. com/helpdeskarticle/-/-helpdesk_ category_cmp_20121219_173037-cmp_20130729_114711-SMTUS-WFS-en_US---USD;pgid=RPJ MGQZ2lSmRp0l8Whh.58Jj00 00pJKmU0oi;sid=I7zUvT3V-ejXvW89Oom1uaXfkXbaLiloJpuQ P0Ov (accessed January 28, 2014); "Stein Mart Inc (SMRT:NASDAQ GS)," *Bloomberg Businessweek,* http://investing.businessweek.com/ research/stocks/financials/financials. asp?ticker=SMRT (accessed January 29, 2014).

13. Douglas McGregor, *The Human Side of Enterprise* (New York: McGraw-Hill, 1960), pp. 33–34.

14. Richard Branson, "Richard Branson on Giving Your Employees Freedom," *Entrepreneur,* December 31, 2012, www.entrepreneur.com/article/225272 (accessed April 24, 2014).

15. Jon L. Pierce, Tatiana Kostova, and Kurt T. Kirks, "Toward a Theory of Psychological Ownership in Organizations, *Academy of Management Review,* 26, no. 2 (2001), p. 298.

16. Liz Rappaport, "Goldman Cuts Blankfein's Bonus," *The Wall Street Journal,* February 4, 2012, http:// online.wsj.com/article/SB10001424 05297020466220457720148334778 7346.html (accessed May 12, 2014).

17. Ethics Resource Center, *2011 National Business Ethics Survey: Ethics in Transition* (Arlington, VA: Ethics Resource Center, 2012), p. 16.

18. Archie Carroll, "Carroll: Do We Live in a Cheating Culture?" *Athens Banner-Herald,* February 21, 2004, www.onlineathens.com/ stories/022204/bus_20040222028. shtml (accessed May 12, 2014).

19. Geoff Colvin, "How Top Companies Breed Stars," September 20, 2007, http://money.cnn.com/ magazines/fortune/fortune_ archive/2007/10/01/100351829/ index.htm (accessed May 12, 2014).

20. Donald Liebenson, "Home Is Where the Work Is (Mostly for Men)," *Millionaire Corner*, March 5, 2014, http://millionairecorner.com/Content_Free/Home-is-where-the-work-is-mostly-for-men.aspx (accessed April 24, 2014).

21. Robert Preidt, "Workplace Flexibility Can Boost Healthy Behaviors," *ABC News*, March 23, 2008, http://abcnews.go.com/Health/Healthday/story?id=4509753 (accessed May 12, 2014).

22. My Guides USA.com, "Which Jobs Offer Flexible Work Schedules?" http://jobs.myguidesusa.com/answers-to-myquestions/which-jobs-offer-flexible-workschedules?/ (accessed May 12, 2014).

23. Randy Mayers, "The Great Debate: Should You Let Employees Work from Home?" *Entrepreneur*, June 3, 2013, www.entrepreneur.com/article/226888 (accessed July 15, 2013); Rick Hampson, "Boss vs. You," *USA Today*, March 12, 2013, pp. 1A–2A; Anita Bruzzese, "On the Job: Act Like an Entrepreneur Even If You're Not," *USA Today*, June 30, 2012, www.usatoday.com/story/money/columnist/bruzzese/2013/06/30/on-the-job-big-company-entrepreneurs/2466611/ (accessed July 15, 2013).

24. Global Workplace Analytics, "Latest Telecommuting Statistics," www.globalworkplaceanalytics.com/telecommuting-statistics (accessed May 12, 2014).

25. PGi, "Telecommuting Reduces Stress and Increases Productivity According to PGi Survey," *PR Newswire*, March 3, 2014, www.prnewswire.com/news-releases/telecommuting-reduces-stress-and-increases-productivity-according-to-pgi-survey-248244671.html (accessed April 24, 2014); PR Web, "Fortune 500 Companies Are Looking for People to Work Remotely (Work From Home)," January 26, 2014, www.prweb.com/releases/2014/01/prweb11520034.htm (accessed April 24, 2014).

26. Dori Meinert, "Make Telecommuting Pay Off," *Society for Human Resource Management*, June 1, 2011, www.shrm.org/Publications/hrmagazine/EditorialContent/2011/0611/Pages/0611meinert.aspx (accessed May 12, 2014).

27. "Best Places For Business and Careers," *Forbes*, March 25, 2009, www.forbes.com/lists/2009/1/bizplaces09_Best-Places-For-Business-And-Careers_Rank.html (accessed May 12, 2014).

28. "Best Places for Businesses and Careers 2013," *Forbes*, 2014, www.forbes.com/pictures/mli45eegfe/1-des-moines-iowa/ (accessed April 25, 2014).

29. "100 Best Companies to Work for 2009," *Fortune*, http://money.cnn.com/magazines/fortune/bestcompanies/2009/snapshots/32.html (accessed March 15, 2014; "The Container Store: An Employee-Centric Retailer," UNM Daniels Fund Business Ethics Initiative, http://danielsethics.mgt.unm.edu/pdf/Container%20Store%20Case.pdf (accessed May 15, 2014); Fortune 100 Best Companies to Work For, "The Container Store," *CNN Money*, 2013, http://money.cnn.com/magazines/fortune/best-companies/2013/snapshots/16.html (accessed May 14, 2014); The Container Store, "Employee-First Culture," http://standfor.containerstore.com/putting-our-employees-first/ (accessed May 14, 2014); Bureau of Labor Statistics, "How to Become a Retail Sales Worker," January 8, 2014, www.bls.gov/ooh/sales/retail-sales-workers.htm#tab-4 (accessed May 14, 2014); The Container Store, "Communication IS Leadership," http://standfor.containerstore.com/our-foundation-principles/communication-is-leadership/ (accessed May 14, 2014); The Container Store, "Happy National We Love Our Employees Day," February 13, 2014, http://standfor.containerstore.com/happy-national-we-love-our-employees-day/ (accessed May 14, 2014); The Container Store, "Great Benefits," www.containerstore.com/careers/index.html?state=UT (accessed May 14, 2014); Maria Halkias, "The Container Store Set Up an Emergency Fund for Its Employee," *Dallas News*, February 14, 2014, http://bizbeatblog.dallasnews.com/2014/02/the-container-store-set-up-an-emergency-fund-for-its-employees.html/ (accessed May 14, 2014).

## Chapter 10

1. Kristie Lu Stout, "How Cirque de Soleil Scouts Clowns, Trapeze Artists and Gymnasts," CNN, September 12, 2012, http://edition.cnn.com/2012/09/12/business/leading-women-krista-monson/index.html (accessed September 17, 2012); Mehrdad Baghai and James Quigley, "Cirque de Soleil: A Very Different Vision of Teamwork," book excerpt from *As One: Individual Action, Collective Power*, reprinted in *Fast Company*, February 4, 2011, www.fastcompany.com/1724123/cirque-du-soleil-very-different-vision-teamwork (accessed on September 17, 2012); Cirque du Soleil Jobs website, www.cirquedusoleil.com/en/jobs/recruitment/home.aspx (accessed September 21, 2012).

2. "About O*NET," O*NET Resource Center, www.onetcenter.org/overview.html (accessed May 27, 2014).

3. "P&G Careers," www.pg.com/en_US/careers/career_main.shtml (accessed May 27, 2014).

4. U.S. Department of Health and Human Services, "Results from the 2010 National Survey on Drug Use and Health: Summary of National Findings," September 2011, www.samhsa.gov/data/NSDUH/2k10NSDUH/2k10Results.htm#3.1.7 (accessed April 5, 2012).

5. "Substance Abuse Costs Employers Billions," *The National Registry of Workers' Compensation Specialists*, www.nrwcs.com/substance-abuse-costs-billions (accessed May 27, 2014).

6. Manuel Valdes and Shannon McFarland, "Job Seekers' Facebook Password Asked for During U.S. Interviews," *Huffington Post*, March 20, 2012, www.huffingtonpost.com/2012/03/20/facebook-passwordsjob-seekers_n_1366577.html? (accessed May 27, 2014).

7. Jonathan Dame, "Will Employers Still Ask for Facebook Passwords in 2014?" *USA Today*, January 10, 2014, www.usatoday.com/

story/money/business/2014/01/10/facebook-passwords-employers/4327739/ (accessed April 28, 2014).

8. Allison Linn, "Desperate Measures: Why Some People Fake Their Resumes," *CNBC,* February 7, 2014, www.cnbc.com/id/101397212 (accessed April 28, 2014); "Martoma Trial: Ex-SAC Trader Was Expelled by Harvard," *CNBC,* January 10, 2014, www.cnbc.com/id/101324969 (accessed April 28, 2014).

9. Christopher T. Marquet and Lisa J. B. Peterson, "Résumé Fraud: The Top Ten Lies," Marquet International, Ltd., www.marquetinternational.com/pdf/Resume%20Fraud-Top%20Ten%20Lies.pdf (accessed May 27, 2014).

10. U.S. Equal Employment Opportunity Commission, "Charge Statistics FY 1997 Through FY 2013," http://eeoc.gov/eeoc/statistics/enforcement/charges.cfm (accessed April 28, 2014); U.S. Equal Employment Opportunity Commission, "Sexual Harassment Charges FY 2010–FY 2013," www.eeoc.gov/eeoc/statistics/enforcement/sexual_harassment_new.cfm (accessed May 2, 2014).

11. Bryce Covert, "Only White, Male CEOs Make the Big Bucks," *Think Progress,* October 22, 2013, http://thinkprogress.org/economy/2013/10/22/2816041/white-men-ceos/ (accessed April 28, 2014); Alliance for Board Diversity Census, "Missing Pieces: Women and Minorities on Fortune 500 Boards," 2012, http://theabd.org/2012_ABD%20Missing_Pieces_Final_8_15_13.pdf (accessed April 28, 2014).

12. "Compulsory Retirement Age at 65 Fully Abolished," *BBC News,* October 1, 2011, www.bbc.co.uk/news/business-15127835 (accessed April 4, 2012); "Can You Legally Force Someone to Retire or Is It Age Discrimination?" *LawInfo blog,* http://blog.lawinfo.com/2011/04/10/can-you-legally-force-someone-to-retire-or-is-it-age-discrimination/ (accessed May 27, 2014).

13. Stephen Bastien, "12 Benefits of Hiring Older Workers," *Entrepreneur.com,* September 20, 2006, www.entrepreneur.com/

article/167500 (accessed May 29, 2014).

14. Bureau of Labor Statistics, "Usual Weekly Earnings of Wage and Salary Workers First Quarter 2014," April 17, 2014, www.bls.gov/news.release/pdf/wkyeng.pdf (accessed April 28, 2014).

15. "Gender and Pay at Work," PayScale, www.payscale.com/data-packages/gender-wage-gap/job-distribution-by-gender (accessed April 28, 2014).

16. Catherine Rampell, "The Gender Wage Gap, Around the World," March 9, 2010, http://economix.blogs.nytimes.com/2010/03/09/the-gender-wage-gap-around-the-world/?_php=true&_type=blogs&_r=0 (accessed May 29, 2014).

17. "Our Curriculum," Hamburger University, www.aboutmcdonalds.com/mcd/careers/hamburger_university/our_curriculum.html (accessed May 29, 2014).

18. "100 Best Companies to Work for 2011," *Fortune,* February 7, 2011, http://money.cnn.com/magazines/fortune/bestcompanies/2011/snapshots/21.html (accessed May 29, 2014).

19. Doug Stewart, "Employee-Appraisal Software," *Inc.,* www.inc.com/magazine/19940615/3288_pagen_2.html (accessed May 29, 2014).

20. Maury A. Peiperl, "Getting 360-Degree Feedback Right," *Harvard Business Review,* January 2001, pp. 142–48.

21. Chris Musselwhite, "Self Awareness and the Effective Leader," Inc.com, www.inc.com/resources/leadership/articles/20071001/musselwhite.html (accessed May 29, 2014).

22. Rebecca Vesely, "Companies Aim to Improve Wellness of Telecommuting, Traveling Employees, Too," *Workforce,* October 30, 2012, www.workforce.com/articles/companies-aim-to-improve-wellness-of-telecommuting-traveling-employees-too (accessed May 2, 2014).

23. Marcia Zidle, "Employee Turnover: Seven Reasons Why People Quit Their Jobs," Alrakoba, www.alrakoba.net/articles2/showarticle.

php?article=23459 (accessed March 16, 2010).

24. Scott Neuman, "RadioShack to Close 1,000 Stores Nationwide Amid Big Losses," *NPR,* March 4, 2014, www.npr.org/blogs/thetwo-way/2014/03/04/285896344/radioshack-to-close-1-000-stores-nationwide-amid-big-losses (accessed April 28, 2014).

25. Kevin Doyle, "Job Market Sees Growing Demand for Sustainability Managers," *Experience,* 2008, www.experience.com/alumnus/article?channel_id=green&source_page=home&article_id=article_1208550373072 (accessed January 21, 2014); Oliver Balch, "How to Get a Career in Sustainability: Hard Work, Talent, and Perseverance," *The Guardian,* October 9, 2013, www.theguardian.com/sustainable-business/how-to-career-sustainability-work (accessed January 21, 2014); Andrew Martin, "In Eco-Friendly Factory, Low-Guilt Potato Chips," *The New York Times,* November 15, 2007, www.nytimes.com/2007/11/15/business/15plant.html?_r=1&ex=1352782800&en=3a3e8aea2280595d&ei=5090&partner=rssuserland&emc=rss&oref=login (accessed January 21, 2014).

26. "Wage and Hour Division (WHD)," U.S. Department of Labor, www.dol.gov/whd/flsa/index.htm (accessed May 29, 2014).

27. Lauren Fox, "Democrats Push to Pass Minimum Wage Hike Ahead of 2014 Elections," *U.S. News,* April 28, 2014, www.usnews.com/news/articles/2014/04/28/democrats-push-to-pass-minimum-wage-hike-ahead-of-2014-elections (accessed May 2, 2014).

28. "Fair Labor Standards Act Advisor," U.S. Department of Labor, www.dol.gov/elaws/faq/esa/flsa/002.htm (accessed May 29, 2014).

29. City of Santa Fe, "Santa Fe's Living Wage Rises to $10.66 an Hour on March 1, 2014," January 22, 2014, www.santafenm.gov/news/detail/santa_fes_living_wage_rises_to_1066_an_hour_on_march_1_2014 (accessed April 28, 2014); New Mexico Department of Workforce Solutions, "Minimum Wage Information," www.dws.state.

nm.us/LaborRelations/Resources/
MinimumWageInformation
(accessed April 28, 2014); Daniel J.
Chacón, "Minimum-Wage Workers
in City to See Pay Rise to $10.66,"
*Santa Fe New Mexican*, January 22,
2014, www.santafenewmexican.
com/news/local_news/minimum-
wage-workers-in-city-to-see-pay-
rise-to/article_6ec202d2-862c-50f3-
a4eb-5b8587e102b4.html (accessed
April 28, 2014).

30. "Kele & Co: First Innovative Jewelry
Company in Direct Sales," May 5,
2008, www.pressreleasepoint.com/
kele-ampco-first-innovative-jewelry-
companydirect-sales (accessed
March 16, 2010); Kele & Co.,
"About Kele & Co," 2010, www.
keleonline.com/pages/about.html
(accessed May 29, 2014).

31. Sarah Anderson, "Wall Street's
2013 Bonuses Were More Than
All Workers Earned Making the
Federal Minimum," *Moyers &
Company*, March 12, 2014, http://
billmoyers.com/2014/03/12/
wall-streets-2013-bonuses-were-
more-than-all-workers-earned-
making-the-federal-minimum/
(accessed April 29, 2014).

32. The National Center for Employee
Ownership, "ESOP (Employee
Stock Ownership Plan) Facts," 2014,
www.esop.org (accessed April 29,
2014).

33. Bureau of Labor Statistics,
"Employer Costs for Employee
Compensation," March 12, 2014,
www.bls.gov/news.release/ecec.nr0.
htm (accessed April 29, 2014).

34. Stephan Miller, "Employee Loyalty
Hits 7-Year Low; Benefits Promote
Retention," *Society for Human
Resource Management,* March 22,
2012, www.shrm.org/hrdisciplines/
benefits/Articles/Pages/LoyaltyLow.
aspx (accessed May 29, 2014).

35. "Work/Life," Lowe's, https://careers.
lowes.com/benefits_work.aspx
(accessed May 29, 2014).

36. Elaine Pofeldt, "Having Trouble
Finding Talent? Look Beyond
Resumes," *Inc.,* November 2013,
www.inc.com/magazine/201311/
elaine-pofeldt/hire-power-awards-
urban-lending-solutions.html

(accessed January 21, 2014);
Urban Lending Solutions, "About
Us," www.urban-ls.com/about-us
(accessed January 21, 2014); Paul J.
Gough, "*Inc.* Honors Urban Lending
Solutions as Top Job-Creator,"
*Pittsburg Business Times*, December
6, 2012, www.bizjournals.com/
pittsburgh/news/2012/12/06/inc-
honors-urban-lending-solutions-as.
html (accessed January 21, 2014).

37. Bureau of Labor Statistics, "Union
Members Summary," January 24,
2014, www.bls.gov/news.release/
union2.nr0.htm (accessed April 29,
2014).

38. Josh Eidelson, "Walmart Fires
Eleven Strikers in Alleged
Retaliation," *The Nation*, June
22, 2013, www.thenation.com/
blog/174937/walmart-fires-eleven-
strikers-alleged-retaliation#
(accessed April 29, 2014); Carlyn
Kolker, "U.S. Labor Board
May Issue Complaint Against
Wal-Mart on Strikes," *Reuters*,
November 18, 2013, www.
reuters.com/article/2013/11/19/
us-usa-employment-walmart-
idUSBRE9AI00S20131119
(accessed April 29, 2014); Dave
Jamieson, "Feds Charge Walmart
with Breaking Labor Law in
Black Friday Strikes," *Huffington
Post*, January 25, 2014, www.
huffingtonpost.com/2014/01/15/
walmart-complaint_n_4604069.html
(accessed April 29, 2014).

39. Steven Greenhouse, "Labor Battle
at Kellogg Plant in Memphis
Drags On," *The New York Times*,
February 10, 2014, www.nytimes.
com/2014/02/11/business/kellogg-
workers-in-4th-month-of-lockout-in-
memphis.html (accessed April 29,
2014).

40. Ed Stoddard and Zandi Shabalala,
"Producers, Union to Meet
Mediator Separately in Platinum
Strike," *Reuters*, February
10, 2014, www.reuters.com/
article/2014/02/10/us-safrica-strikes-
idUSBREA190BW20140210
(accessed April 29, 2014).

41. Paul M. Barrett, "Chevron Inches
Closer to Legal Victory over
Ecuador Pollution," *Bloomberg
Businessweek*, September 19,

2013, www.businessweek.com/
articles/2013-09-19/chevron-inches-
closer-to-legal-victory-over-ecuador-
pollution (accessed April 29, 2014).

42. Eric Kayne, "Census: White
Majority in U.S. Gone by
2043," *NBC News*, June 13,
2013, http://usnews.nbcnews.
com/_news/2013/06/13/18934111-
census-white-majority-in-us-gone-
by-2043?lite (accessed April 29,
2014).

43. Press Release, "Kaiser Permanente
Named No. 4 on DiversityInc's
Top 50 Companies for Diversity
List for 2014," Kaiser Permanente,
April 24, 2014, http://share.
kaiserpermanente.org/article/
kaiser-permanente-named-no-4-on-
diversityincs-top-50-companies-for-
diversity-list-for-2014/ (accessed
April 29, 2014).

44. Melanie Tervalon, "At a Decade:
Centers of Excellence in Culturally
Competent Care," *The Permanente
Journal,* 13, no. 1 (2009), pp. 87–91.

45. Taylor H. Cox, Jr., "The
Multicultural Organization,"
*Academy of Management Executives*
5 (May 1991), pp. 34–47; Marilyn
Loden and Judy B. Rosener,
*Workforce America! Managing
Employee Diversity as a Vital
Resource* (Homewood, IL: Business
One Irwin, 1991).

46. Jean Eaglesham and Michael
Rothfeld, "Wall Street vs. Its
Employees' Privacy," *The Wall
Street Journal*, April 22, 2013, p.
A1; Jennifer Van Grove, "Securities
Regulators Balk at Employee
Social Media Privacy," *CNet*,
April 22, 2013; http://news.cnet.
com/8301-1023_3-57580814-93/
securities-regulators-balk-at-
employee-social-media-privacy/
(accessed July 23, 2013); Rachel
Emma Silverman, "Facebook and
Twitter Postings Cost CFO His Job,"
*The Wall Street Journal,* May 14,
2012, http://online.wsj.com/article/
SB1000142405270230350550457
7404542168061590.html (accessed
August 2, 2013).

47. Kathryn Brenzel, "Taco Hell:
Lawsuit against Food Truck Claims
Employee Was Overworked
without Pay," *NJ.com,* December 9,

2013, www.nj.com/hudson/index.ssf/2013/12/taco_hell_employee_files_lawsuit_against_food_truck_owners_claiming_he_was_overworked_without_pay.html (accessed April 29, 2014); Dave Jamieson, "More Amazon Warehouse Workers Sue Retailer over Unpaid Security Waits," *The Huffington Post,* September 19, 2013, www.huffingtonpost.com/2013/09/19/more-amazon-warehouse-workers-sue_n_3950295.html (accessed April 29, 2014); Dave Jamieson, "Join the Booming Dollar Store Economy! Low Pay, Long Hours, May Work While Injured," *Huffington Post*, August 29, 2013, www.huffingtonpost.com/2013/08/29/dollar-stores-work_n_3786781.html (accessed April 29, 2014).

48. Paul Davidson, "Overworked and Underpaid?" *USA Today,* April 16, 2012, pp. 1A–2A.

49. Ibid.

50. Melanie Trottman, "For Angry Employees, Legal Cover for Rants," *The Wall Street Journal,* December 2, 2011, http://online.wsj.com/article/SB10001424052970203710704577049822809710332.html (accessed May 29, 2014).

51. Martin Crutsinger, "Hiring Grows as Companies Hit Limits with Workers," *MPR News,* March 7, 2012, http://minnesota.publicradio.org/display/web/2012/03/07/hiring-grows-as-companies-hit-limit/ (accessed May 29, 2014).

52. Actors Equity Association, "Equity Timeline," Actors Equity, 2006, www.actorsequity.org/aboutequity/timeline/timeline_1919.html (accessed May 15, 2014); Writers Guild of America, West, Inc., "History," Writers Guild of America, West, 2012, www.wga.org/history/timeline.html (accessed May 15, 2014); Jonathon Mandell, "Recalling 1988 Strike," *CBS News,* February 11, 2009, www.cbsnews.com/2100-207_162-3447509.html (accessed July 30, 2012); Screen Actors Guild, "History," SAG-AFTRA One Union, 2012, www.sag.org/history (accessed May 15, 2014); Richard Verrier, "SAG and AFTRA Members Give Thumbs Up to Merger," *Los Angeles Times,* March 30, 2012, http://latimesblogs.latimes.com/entertainmentnewsbuzz/2012/03/sag-and-aftra-members-give-thumbs-up-to-merger.html (accessed May 15, 2014).

## Chapter 11

1. Dinah King, Mel Ziegler, and Patricia Ziegler, "Turning Khaki Into Gold," *Fortune*, March 18, 2013, pp. 53–56; Peter Hartlaub, "Banana Republic Rising: Remembering the Store's Safari Years," *SF Gate*, http://blog.sfgate.com/thebigevent/2013/05/10/banana-republic-rising-remembering-the-stores-safari-years/ (accessed May 13, 2014); "Banana Republic's New 'Mad Men' Collection," *USA Today,* February 26, 2013, www.usatoday.com/story/life/style/2013/02/25/banana-republic-mad-men-collection/1946703 (accessed May 13, 2014).

2. Adapted from Wiliam M. Pride and O. C. Ferrell, "Value-Driven Marketing," *Foundations of Marketing,* 4th ed. (Mason, OH: South-Western Cengage Learning), pp. 13–14.

3. Ryan Bradley, "A Candy Chain's Sweet Success," *Fortune,* July 1, 2013, pp. 18–19; Jaime Winston, "Sugar Rush: IT'SUGAR opens in Farmington," *Salt Lake,* June 30, 2013, http://saltlakemagazine.com/blog/2013/06/30/sugar-rush-itsugar-opens-in-farmington/ (accessed August 2, 2013); Glenwood, "It'Sugar: An Ornate Candy Store in NYC's Upper West Side," *Glenwood,* September 7, 2012, www.glenwoodnyc.com/manhattan-living/itsugar-candy-store-nyc/ (accessed August 2, 2013); Lori Wilk, "IT'S SUGAR celebrates Retail Candy Sales Success," *Examiner,* October 16, 2012, www.examiner.com/article/it-s-sugar-celebrates-retail-candy-sales-success (accessed August 2, 2013); Richard Lane, "Inside the Biggest Candy Store (Yet) in Vegas," *Vegas Chatter*, April 23, 2012, www.vegaschatter.com/story/2012/4/23/142230/927/vegas-travel/Inside+The+Biggest +Candy+Store+%28Yet%29+in+Vegas (accessed August 2, 2013); It'Sugar website, www.itsugar.com/ (accessed August 2, 2013).

4. Bruce Horovitz, "Domino's Offers Gluten-Free Pizza Crust," *USA Today,* May 7, 2012, p. B1.

5. "Beauty Queen," *People,* May 10, 2004, p. 187.

6. Michael Treacy and Fred Wiersema, *The Discipline of Market Leaders* (Reading, MA: Addison Wesley, 1995), p. 176.

7. Jefferson Graham, "At Apple Stores, iPads at Your Service," *USA Today*, May 23, 2011, p. 1B; Apple Inc., "Apple Retail Store," www.apple.com/retail/storelist/ (accessed May 14, 2014).

8. "America's Largest Private Companies List," *Forbes*, www.forbes.com/companies/sheetz/ (accessed July 25, 2013); Sheetz, "Our Menu," www.sheetz.com/subpages/menu.jsp (accessed July 26, 2013); Ken Otterbourg, "Sheetz Puts the Gas in Gastronomy," *Fortune,* May 20, 2013, pp. 142–48.

9. Customer Insight Group Inc. "Program Design: Loyalty and Retention," www.customerinsightgroup.com/loyalty_retention.php (accessed January 4, 2011).

10. Venky Shankar, "Multiple Touch Point Marketing," American Marketing Association, Faculty Consortium on Electronic Commerce, Texas A&M University, July 14–17, 2001.

11. Brad Wieners, "Lego Is for Girls," *Bloomberg Businessweek,* December 19–25, 2011, pp. 68–73.

12. "January 2014 Princess and Friends LEGO Sets," Toys N Bricks, January 2014, http://toysnbricks.com/january-2014-girls-lego-sets/ (accessed April 29, 2014).

13. Eric Kanye, "Census: White Majority in U.S. Gone by 2043," *NBC News,* June 13, 2013, http://usnews.nbcnews.com/_news/2013/06/13/18934111-census-white-majority-in-us-gone-by-2043?lite (accessed May 14, 2014).

14. "Minority Report," *The Economist,* March 31, 2011, www.economist.com/node/18488452 (accessed May 29, 2014).

15. Richard Goodwin, "Apple iWatch Release Date, Specs, Features & Design: WWDC Sneak Peek?" *Know Your Mobile,* April 28, 2014, www.knowyourmobile.com/apple/apple-iwatch/19775/apple-iwatch-release-date-specs-features-design-wwdc-sneak-peek (accessed April 29, 2014).

16. "The Coca-Cola Company Fact Sheet," http://assets.coca-colacompany.com/90/11/5f21b88444bab46d430b4c578e80/Company_Fact_Sheet.pdf (accessed May 29, 2014); "Growth, Leadership, and Sustainability," The Coca-Cola Company, www.thecocacolacompany.com/ourcompany (accessed August 16, 2012).

17. Hannah Elliott, "Most Fuel-Efficient Cars For The Buck," *Forbes,* March 30, 2009, www.forbes.com/2009/03/30/fuel-efficient-cars-lifestyle-vehicles-efficient-cars.html (accessed May 29, 2014).

18. "AdWords," Google, https://adwords.google.com/um/gaiaauth?apt%3DNone%26ltmpl%3Djfk%26ltmpl%3Djfk&error=newacct&sacu=1&sarp=1 (accessed May 29, 2014).

19. Sarah E. Needleman, "Facebook 'Likes' Small Business," *The Wall Street Journal,* September 26, 2011, p. B11.

20. Twitter, "What Are Promoted Tweets?" Twitter Help Center, https://support.twitter.com/articles/142101-what-are-promoted-tweets# (accessed May 14, 2014).

21. Christine Birkner, "10 Minutes with . . . Raul Murguia Villegas," *Marketing News,* July 30, 2011, pp. 26–27.

22. "MSPA North America," Mystery Shopping Providers Association, http://mysteryshop.org/ (accessed May 29, 2014).

23. Piet Levy, "10 Minutes with . . . Robert J. Morais," *Marketing News,* May 30, 2011, pp. 22–23.

24. Steven Kurutz, "On Kickstarter, Designers' Dream Materialize," *The New York Times,* September 21, 2011, www.nytimes.com/2011/09/22/garden/on-kickstarter-designers-dreams-materialize.html (accessed May 29, 2014).

25. Mya Frazier, "CrowdSourcing," *Delta Sky Mag,* February 2010, p. 73.

26. David Rosenbaum, "Who's Out There?" *CFO,* January/February 2012, pp. 44–49.

27. Office of the Press Secretary, "Obama Administration Finalizes Historic 54.5 MPG Fuel Efficiency Standards," *The White House,* August 28, 2012, www.whitehouse.gov/the-press-office/2012/08/28/obama-administration-finalizes-historic-545-mpg-fuel-efficiency-standard (accessed August 2, 2013); Dan Becker, "Millennials Reject Our Doddering Car Culture," *USA Today,* June 20, 2013, p. 14A; Brad Tuttle, "Gen Y's Take on Car Ownership? 'Not Cool'," *Time,* May 2, 2012, http://business.time.com/2012/05/02/gen-ys-take-on-car-ownership-not-cool/ (accessed August 2, 2013).

28. Alex, "McDonald's Premium McWrap Nutrition vs Subway," *Fast Food Nutrition,* May 21, 2013, www.fastfoodnutrition.org/blog/30_b-mcdonalds-premium-mcwrap-nutrition-vs-subway.html (accessed May 14, 2014); Maureen Morrison, "McDonald's Has a Millennial Problem," *Advertising Age,* March 25, 2013, http://adage.com/article/news/mcdonald-s-1-rank-millennials/240497/ (accessed May 14, 2014).

29. Bruce Horovitz, "Gum Goes from Humdrum to Teen Fashion Statement," *USA Today,* May 8, 2012, p. B1.

30. "Brewers Association Release 2010 Top 50 Breweries List," Brewers Association, 2012, www.brewersassociation.org/pages/media/press-releases/show?title=brewers-association-releases-2010-top-50-breweries-lists (accessed July 30, 2012); Cotton Delo, "New Belgium Toasts to Its Facebook Fans," *Advertising Age,* February 13, 2012, http://adage.com/article/news/belgium-toasts-facebook-fans/232681/ (accessed July 30, 2012); New Belgium Brewing, www.newbelgium.com (accessed June 18, 2014); New Belgium Brewing: Ethical and Environmental Responsibility," In O. C. Ferrell, John Fraedrich, and Linda Ferrell, *Business Ethics: Ethical Decision Making and Cases,* 9th ed. (Mason, OH: South-Western Cengage Learning, 2013), pp. 355–63; Devin Leonard, "New Belgium and the Battle of the Microbrews," *Bloomberg Businessweek,* December 1, 2011, www.businessweek.com/magazine/new-belgium-and-the-battle-of-the-microbrews-12012011.html (accessed June 18, 2014); New Belgium Brewing, "Cigar City Collaboration," www.newbelgium.com/beer/detail.aspx?id=10ea9a69-b6d0-43f0-aa74-0bb307e1b366 (accessed June 18, 2014).

**Chapter 12**

1. Chris Woodyard, "Corvette Revs Its Image to Attract Younger Buyers," *USA Today,* August 20, 2013, pp. 1B–2B; David Undercuffler, "Car Review: 2014 Corvette Stingray Shifts Away from Tradition," *LA Times,* August 17, 2013, http://articles.latimes.com/2013/aug/17/business/la-fi-autos-chevrolet-corvette-stingray-review-20130817 (accessed August 27, 2013); Paul A. Elsenstein, "Chevy Steers 2014 Corvette Stingray Into Luxury Market," *NBC News,* August 16, 2013, www.nbcnews.com/business/chevy-steers-2014-corvette-stingray-luxury-market-6C10930051 (accessed August 27, 2013).

2. Narendra Rao, "The Keys to New Product Success (Part 1)—Collecting Unarticulated & Invisible Customer Needs," *Product Management & Strategy,* June 19, 2007, http://productstrategy.wordpress.com/2007/06/19/the-keys-to-new-product-succeess-part-1-collecting-unarticulated-invisible-customer-needs/ (accessed May 29, 2014).

3. Christina Larson, "Xiaomi," *Fast Company*, 2014, www.fastcompany.com/most-innovative-companies/2014/xiaomi (accessed April 30, 2014).

4. Nicholas Kolakowski, "HP's Touch Pad Proves a Bestseller in Its Dying Moments," eWeek.com, August 22, 2011, www.eweek.com/c/a/Mobile-and-Wireless/HPs-TouchPad-Proves-a-Bestseller-In-its-Dying-Moments-373816/ (accessed May 29, 2014).

5. Associated Press, "Jobs Says iPad Idea Came Before iPhone," June 2, 2010, www.foxnews.com/tech/2010/06/02/jobs-says-ipad-idea-came-iphone/ (accessed May 29, 2014).

6. Nike, "Nike Sport Research Lab Incubates Innovation," July 16, 2013, http://nikeinc.com/news/nike-sport-research-lab-incubates-innovation (accessed April 30, 2014).

7. Christine Birkner, "The Good Egg," *Marketing News,* September 2013, pp. 22–29; Anthony Ha, "Khosla-Backed Hampton Creek Foods Launches Beyond Eggs, A Genuinely Convincing Egg Replacer," *TechCrunch*, February 13, 2013, http://techcrunch.com/2013/02/13/hampton-creek-foods/ (accessed September 23, 2013); Anthony Ha, "Hampton Creek Foods Shows Off Its Egg-Less Scrambled Eggs," June 15, 2013. *TechCrunch,* http://techcrunch.com/2013/06/15/hampton-creek-foods-shows-off-its-egg-less-scrambled-eggs/ (accessed September 23, 2013).

8. John A. Byrne, "Greatest Entrepreneurs of Our Time," *Fortune,* April 9, 2012, pp. 68–86; Google Finance, "Amazon.com, Inc.," April 30, 2014, www.google.com/finance?cid=660463 (accessed April 30, 2014).

9. "SHMN:US," *Bloomberg,* May 14, 2014, www.bloomberg.com/quote/SHMN:US/profile (accessed May 14, 2014); "SOHM, Inc. Receives Confirmation for Test Marketing of Its OTC Products from a Retail Chain Store," *The Wall Street Journal*, April 22, 2014, http://online.wsj.com/article/PR-CO-20140422-908133.html (accessed May 14, 2014).

10. Maxx Chatsko, "Politicians Jeopardize Commercialization of Engineered Salmon," *The Motley Fool,* May 4, 2014, www.fool.com/investing/general/2014/05/04/politicians-jeopardize-commercialization-of-engine.aspx (accessed May 15, 2014); Hannah Sentenac, "GMO Salmon May Soon Hit Food Stores, But Will Anyone Buy It?" *Fox News,* March 11, 2014, www.foxnews.com/leisure/2014/03/11/gmo-salmon-may-soon-hit-food-stores-but-will-anyone-buy-it/ (accessed May 15, 2014).

11. Tony Danova, "BI INTELLIGENCE FORECAST: Google Glass Will Become a Mainstream Product and Sell Millions by 2016," *Business Insider*, December 31, 2013, www.businessinsider.com/google-glass-sales-projections-2013-11#!IVtvA (accessed May 5, 2014).

12. Todd Leopold, "How Beats Headphones Changed the Audio World," *CNN*, January 12, 2014, www.cnn.com/2014/01/13/tech/beats-headphones-audio-market/ (accessed May 5, 2014); Beats by Dre, "About Us," www.beatsbydre.com/aboutus (accessed May 5, 2014).

13. Duane Stanford, "Africa: Coke's Last Frontier," *Bloomberg Businessweek,* October 28, 2010, www.businessweek.com/magazine/content/10_45/b4202054144294.htm (accessed May 29, 2014); Kim Peterson, "Coke Debuts Smaller Bottles," *MSN Money,* September 19, 2011, http://money.msn.com/top-stocks/post.aspx?post=2e4eaa5c-2162-4135-81c6-6d41a02d91b9 (accessed May 29, 2014); Meghra Bahree and Mike Esterl, "PepsiCo's Health Push," *The Wall Street Journal,* July 7, 2011, p. B8.

14. Tom White, "iPod in the Decline Phase of the Product Life Cycle," *tutor2u*, January 29, 2014, http://www.tutor2u.net/blog/index.php/business-studies/comments/ipod-in-the-decline-phase-of-the-product-life-cycle (accessed May 5, 2014); Christina Bonnington, "Say Goodbye to the iPod Classic," *Wired*, September 6, 2013, www.wired.com/2013/09/goodbye-ipod-classic/ (accessed May 5, 2014).

15. "Product Life Cycle," Answers.com, www.answers.com/topic/product-lifecycle (accessed May 29, 2014).

16. Christina Warren, "Can Acer's New Strategy Help It Make a Comeback?" *Mashable*, April 30, 2014, http://mashable.com/2014/04/30/acer-comeback-strategy/ (accessed May 5, 2014).

17. "Jason Wu for Target Apparel Sells Out in Hours," *ABC News,* February 6, 2011, http://abcnewsradioonline.com/business-news/jason-wu-for-target-apparel-sells-out-in-hours.html (accessed May 14, 2012).

18. "Private Label Gets Personal," *Shopper Culture,* October 1, 2009, http://shopperculture.integer.com/2009/10/private-label-gets-personal.html (accessed May 29, 2014).

19. James Haggerty, "Shoppers Not Shy on Store Brand Labels," *The Times Tribune*, January 5, 2014, http://thetimes-tribune.com/news/business/shoppers-not-shy-on-store-brand-labels-1.1611508 (accessed May 5, 2014).

20. Mintel, "Beverage Packaging Trends—US—February 2014," February 2014, http://oxygen.mintel.com/sinatra/oxygen/list/id=680559&type=RCItem#0_1___page_RCItem=0 (accessed May 5, 2014).

21. Denise Lee Yohn, "Let Design Do the Talking for Brands," *Forbes*, January 27, 2014, www.forbes.com/sites/onmarketing/2014/01/27/let-design-do-the-talking-for-brands/ (accessed May 5, 2014).

22. Lisa Whetstone, "Why Olive Garden Needed Consumer Feedback," *Gutcheckit*, March 20, 2014, http://gutcheckit.com/2014/03/did-olive-garden-do-consumer-research/ (accessed May 5, 2014).

23. American Customer Satisfaction Index, "Press Release National Customer Satisfaction Index Q4 2013," April 4, 2014, www.theacsi.org/news-and-resources/

press-releases/press-2014/ press-release-national-customer-satisfaction-index-q4-2013 (accessed May 5, 2014).

24. "American Demographics 2006 Consumer Perception Survey," *Advertising Age,* January 2, 2006, p. 9. Data by Synovate.

25. Rajneesh Suri and Kent B. Monroe, "The Effects of Time Constraints on Consumers' Judgments of Prices and Products," *Journal of Consumer Research,* 30 (June 2003), p. 92.

26. Lisa Ryckman, "First Four Reflections," *Colorado Business Magazine,* June 2013, pp. 25–27; Jim Merithew, "Moots' Point: For Premium Biker Maker, It's Titanium or Bust," *Wired,* November 7, 2012, www.wired.com/playbook/2012/11/ moots/ (accessed May 13, 2014); Moots, "Our Craft," http://moots. com/our-craft/ (accessed July 25, 2013).

27. Genevieve Shaw Brown, "Cupcake ATM Pops Out Treats in 10 Seconds," *ABC News,* March 26, 2014, http://abcnews.go.com/ Lifestyle/cupcake-atm-pops-treats-10-seconds/story?id=23065509 (accessed May 15, 2014); "Sprinkles Cupcake ATM," www.sprinkles. com/cupcake-atm (accessed May 15, 2014); Jennifer Weiss, "Video: Sweet! Cupcake ATM Opens in Manhattan," *The Wall Street Journal,* March 28, 2014, http://blogs.wsj. com/metropolis/2014/03/28/ video-sweet-cupcake-atm-opens-in-manhattan/ (accessed May 15, 2014).

28. Sysco, "The Sysco Story," www. sysco.com/about-sysco.html# (accessed May 29, 2014).

29. "Top Threats to Revenue," *USA Today,* February 1, 2006, p. A1.

30. Zoom Systems, "Company Overview," www.zoomsystems. com/about-us (accessed May 15, 2014); Brad Howarth, "Hear This, iPods from a Vending Machine," *The Sydney Morning Herald,* November 14, 2006, www.smh.com.au/news/ biztech/hearthis-ipods-from-a-vending-machine/2006/11/13/ 1163266481869.html (accessed May 29, 2014).

31. "Welcome to the Future of Shopping," Zoom Systems, www. zoomsystems.com/zoomshops/zs_ index.html (accessed April 5, 2010).

32. Piper, "Piper Expands Its Global Sales Network," March 19, 2013, www.piper.com/piper-expands-global-sales-network-2/ (accessed May 5, 2014); Rick Durden, "Piper Names Dealer for China," *AV Web,* January 10, 2014, www.avweb.com/ avwebflash/news/Piper-Names-Dealer-for-China221250-1.html (accessed May 5, 2014).

33. William Pride and O. C. Ferrell, *Marketing Foundations,* 5th ed. (Mason, OH: Cengage South-Western Learning, 2013), pp. 415–416.

34. Ibid.

35. Abbey Klaassen, "Even Google Has to Advertise," *Advertising Age,* June 2, 2008, p. 4.

36. On Marketing, "Yes, A Super Bowl Ad Really Is Worth $4 Million," *Forbes,* January 29, 2014, www.forbes.com/sites/ onmarketing/2014/01/29/yes-a-super-bowl-ad-really-is-worth-4-million/ (accessed May 5, 2014).

37. Zayda Rivera, "Scarlett Johansson's Uncensored SodaStream Super Bowl Ad Banned by Fox," *NY Daily News,* www.nydailynews. com/entertainment/tv-movies/ scarlett-johansson-uncensored-sodastream-super-bowl-ad-banned-article-1.1595712 (accessed May 15, 2014).

38. Don Reisinger, "Apple Follows Samsung in Search for 'Buzz Marketing Manager,'" *CNET,* May 2, 2014, www.cnet.com/news/apple-to-follow-samsungs-lead-with-search-for-buzz-marketing-manager/ (accessed May 5, 2014); Jay Yarrow, "Apple Is Hiring a 'Buzz Marketing Manager' to Get iPhones in the Hands of More Famous People," *Business Insider,* May 2, 2014, www.businessinsider.com/apple-is-hiring-a-buzz-marketing-manager-2014-5#!JheGI (accessed May 5, 2014).

39. Gerry Khermouch and Jeff Green, "Buzz Marketing," *BusinessWeek,* July 30, 2001, pp. 50–56.

40. Laura Stampler, "How Dove's 'Real Beauty Sketches' Became the Most Viral Video of All Time," *Business Insider,* May 22, 2013, www. businessinsider.com/how-doves-real-beauty-sketches-became-the-most-viral-ad-video-of-all-time-2013-5 (accessed May 15, 2014).

41. Ajmal Kohgadai, "Why Mobile Coupons Have 10x Higher Redemption Rate Than Traditional Coupons," *Fun Mobility,* October 11, 2013, http://blog. funmobility.com/2013/10/11/ why-mobile-coupons-have-10x-higher-redemption-rate-than-traditional-coupons/ (accessed May 5, 2014); Chuck Martin, "Coupons & the Gradual Migration to Mobile," *Media Post,* May 2, 2014, www. mediapost.com/publications/ article/199496/coupons-the-gradual-migration-to-mobile.html (accessed May 5, 2014).

42. Evan Niu, "At Long Last, T-Mobile Is Getting the iPhone," *Daily Finance,* December 7, 2012, www. dailyfinance.com/2012/12/07/ at-long-last-t-mobile-is-getting-the-iphone/ (accessed May 15, 2014).

43. Susan Carey, "Discount Carrier JetBlue Goes Upmarket," *The Wall Street Journal,* August 4, 2013, http://online.wsj.com/article/SB100 01424127887323997004578644448 1433619930.html (accessed August 12, 2013); Jon Hemmerdinger, "JetBlue Unveils Premium Seats, Reveals New Economy Seating," Flight Global, August 5, 2013, www.flightglobal.com/news/ articles/jetblue-unveils-premium-seats-reveals-new-economy-seating-389131/ (accessed August 12, 2013); Mary Schlangenstein, "JetBlue Seeks First-Class Boost to Trim Gap on Rivals," *Bloomberg,* August 6, 2013, www.bloomberg. com/news/2013-08-05/jetblue-seeks-cross-country-revenue-boost-to-close-gap-on-rivals.html (accessed August 12, 2013).

44. Lauren Etter and Douglas MacMillan, "The Education of Groupon CEO Andrew Mason," *Bloomberg Businessweek,* July 12, 2012, www.businessweek.com/ articles/2012-07-12/the-education-

of-groupon-ceo-andrew-mason#p1 (accessed May 15, 2014); Joan Lappin, "Groupon Still Groping for a Viable Business Plan as Stock Crashes," *Forbes*, February 23, 2014, www.forbes.com/sites/joanlappin/2014/02/23/groupon-still-groping-for-a-viable-business-plan-as-stock-crashes/ (accessed May 15, 2014).

## Chapter 13

1. Lin Jing and Chen Yingqun, "Taking It Up Online," *The Wall Street Journal,* April 22, 2013, p. A10; Tania Branigan, "China Tries to Reign in Microbloggers," *The Guardian,* May 14, 2013, www.guardian.co.uk/world/2013/may/15/china-microblogging-accounts-closed (accessed July 29, 2013); Fan Wenxin, "A Twitter Knockoff Has China Talking," *Bloomberg Businessweek,* February 17, 2011, www.businessweek.com/magazine/content/11_09/b4217039139980.htm (accessed August 2, 2013).

2. This material in this chapter is reserved for use in the authors' other textbooks and teaching materials.

3. The Oxen Group, "Baidu: Google of China Has 25% Upside, at Least," *Seeking Alpha*, March 5, 2014, http://seekingalpha.com/article/2068143-baidu-google-of-china-has-25-percent-upside-at-least (accessed May 6, 2014); Sabrina, "China Search Engine Market Reached 11.16 Bn Yuan in Q1 2014," China Internet Watch, April 30, 2014, www.chinainternetwatch.com/7375/china-search-engine-market-q1-2014/ (accessed May 6, 2014); Ye Xie, "Baidu Gain Lifts ADRs from Two-Month Low: China Overnight," *Bloomberg,* January 10, 2014, www.bloomberg.com/news/2014-01-10/baidu-gain-lifts-adrs-from-two-month-low-china-overnight.html (accessed May 19, 2014).

4. Fortune, "Fortune 500," *CNN Money*, 2013, http://money.cnn.com/magazines/fortune/fortune500/2013/full_list/ (accessed May 6, 2014); Deepa Seetharaman, "Amazon's Revenue Increases Even as Spending Rises," *Reuters*,

April 24, 2014, www.reuters.com/article/2014/04/24/us-amazoncom-results-idUSBREA3N20J20140424 (accessed May 6, 2014).

5. "Top 15 Most Popular Video Websites," eBiz MBA, May 2014, www.ebizmba.com/articles/video-websites (accessed May 19, 2014); Vimeo, "About Vimeo," http://vimeo.com/about (accessed May 19, 2014).

6. Bobby White, "The New Workplace Rules: No Video-Watching," *The Wall Street Journal,* March 4, 2008, p. B1; Ben Bryant, "Workers Waste an Hour a Day on Facebook, Shopping and Browsing Holidays, Study Finds," *The Telegraph,* July 22, 2013, www.telegraph.co.uk/news/uknews/10194322/Workers-waste-an-hour-a-day-on-Facebook-shopping-and-browsing-holidays-study-finds.html (accessed May 19, 2014).

7. Voice of Russia, "World to Have 3 Billion Internet Users by the End of 2014—UN Report," May 6, 2014, http://voiceofrussia.com/news/2014_05_06/World-to-have-3-billion-users-by-end-of-2014-UN-report-1710/ (accessed May 6, 2014).

8. MobiThinking, "Global Mobile Statistics 2013 Section E: Mobile Apps, App Stores, Pricing, and Failure Rates," May 2013, http://mobithinking.com/mobile-marketing-tools/latest-mobile-stats/e#lotsofapps (accessed May 6, 2014).

9. Michael V. Copeland, "Tapping Tech's Beautiful Mind," *Fortune,* October 12, 2009, pp. 35–36.

10. Matthew Boyle and Douglas MacMillan, "Wal-Mart's Rocky Path from Bricks to Clicks," *Bloomberg Businessweek,* July 25–31, 2011, pp. 31–33; "Free Shipping With Site to Store®," Walmart, www.walmart.com/cp/Siteto-Store/538452 (accessed May 29, 2014).

11. Christina Larson, "The Secret of Taobao's Success," *Bloomberg Businessweek,* February 18, 2014, www.businessweek.com/articles/2014-02-18/the-secret-of-taobaos-success (accessed May 6, 2014).

12. Facebook, "MGM Resources International," www.facebook.com/business/success/mgm-resorts-international (accessed May 19, 2014); Facebook, "Offers," www.facebook.com/help/410451192330456 (accessed May 19, 2014); Facebook, "Facebook Exchange," www.facebook.com/business/a/online-sales/facebook-exchange (accessed May 19, 2014).

13. Cameron Chapman, "The History and Evolution of Social Media," *WebDesigner Depot,* October 7, 2009, www.webdesignerdepot.com/2009/10/the-history-and-evolution-of-social-media/ (accessed May 29, 2014).

14. "The history of social media in a blink," Windows Live, November 22, 2007, http://mbresseel.spaces.live.com/Blog/cns%2133234018BF280C82%21345.entry (accessed February 18, 2010).

15. "CafeMom," Highland Capital Partners, www.hcp.com/cafemom (accessed May 29, 2014); CafeMom, "What We're About," www.cafemom.com/about/ (accessed May 19, 2014).

16. Zachary Karabell, "To Tweet or Not to Tweet," *Time,* April 12, 2011, p. 24.

17. Klint Finley, "Facebook Praised by Greenpeace Despite Expanding Footprint," *Wired,* August 1, 2012, www.wired.com/wiredenterprise/2012/08/greenpeace-facebook-carbon/ (accessed August 31, 2012); Adam Vaughn, "Facebook Reveals Its Carbon Footprint," *The Guardian,* August 1, 2012, www.guardian.co.uk/environment/2012/aug/01/facebook-google-carbon-footprint (accessed August 31, 2012); Benedict Buckley, "Behind the Numbers: Inside Facebook's Carbon Footprint," *GreenBiz.com,* August 15, 2012, www.greenbiz.com/news/2012/08/15/look-inside-facebook-footprint (accessed August 31, 2012).

18. Emily Adler, "Social Media Engagement: The Surprising Facts about How Much Time People Spend on Major Social Networks,"

*Business Insider,* January 5, 2014, www.businessinsider.com/social-media-engagement-statistics-2013-12#!JLyDq (accessed May 6, 2014).

19. "Facebook: Largest, Fastest Growing Social Network," *Tech Tree,* August 13, 2008, www.techtree.com/India/News/Facebook_Largest_Fastest_Growing_Social_Network/551-92134-643.html (accessed January 12, 2010).

20. Nick Summers. "Heated Rivalries:#9 Facebook vs. MySpace," *Newsweek,* www.2010.newsweek.com/top-10/heated-rivalries/facebook-vs-myspace.html (accessed May 29, 2014).

21. Courtney Rubin, "Internet Users Over Age 50 Flocking to Social Media," *Inc.,* August 30, 2010, www.inc.com/news/articles/2010/08/users-over-50-are-fastest-growing-social-media-demographic.html (accessed May 29, 2014).

22. "Best in Marketing," *Fortune,* September 16, 2013, p. 138.

23. Scott Martin, "Facebook Posts Profit; Mobile Advertising Up," *USA Today,* October 31, 2013, p. 1B.

24. Jefferson Graham, "How to Ride Facebook's Giant Wave," *USA Today,* May 30, 2013, p. 5B.

25. Cotton Delo, "New Belgium Toasts to Its Facebook Fans," *Advertising Age,* February 13, 2012, http://adage.com/article/news/belgium-toasts-facebookfans/232681/ (accessed May 29, 2014).

26. Jefferson Graham, "Cake Decorator Finds Twitter a Tweet Recipe for Success," *USA Today,* April 1, 2009, p. 5B.

27. Jeff Bullas, "22 Social Media Facts and Statistics You Should Know in 2014," Jeffbullas.com, 2014, www.jeffbullas.com/2014/01/17/20-social-media-facts-and-statistics-you-should-know-in-2014/ (accessed May 6, 2014); Pew Research Internet Project, "Social Media Update 2013," December 30, 2013, www.pewinternet.org/2013/12/30/social-media-update-2013/ (accessed May 6, 2014).

28. Stephanie Frasco, "100 Facts and Figures about Twitter, and Why They Matter for Your Business," *Social Media Today*, September 26, 2013, http://socialmediatoday.com/stephaniefrasco/1770161/100-facts-figures-about-twitter-business (accessed May 6, 2014).

29. Zachary Karabell, "To Tweet or Not to Tweet," *Time,* April 11, 2011, p. 24.

30. Craig Carter, "15 Viral Marketing Examples Over the Past 5 Years," *Ignite Social Media,* September 18, 2013, www.ignitesocialmedia.com/social-media-examples/15-viral-marketing-examples-campaigns-past-5-years/ (accessed May 6, 2014).

31. Brad Stone, "Twitter Wants to Be Your TV," *Bloomberg Businessweek*, April 24, 2014, www.businessweek.com/articles/2014-04-24/twitter-ad-strategy-team-up-with-tv-content-creators (accessed May 6, 2014).

32. Evelyn M. Rusli and Shira Ovide, "Facebook Plays Catch-Up on Video," *The Wall Street Journal*, June 20, 2013, p. B12.

33. Alistair Barr, "Google+ Sees a Measurable Plus: 58 Percent More Users," *USA Today*, October 30, 2013, p. 1B.

34. Amir Efrati, "There's No Avoiding Google+," *The Wall Street Journal,* http://online.wsj.com/news/articles/SB10001424127887324731304578193781852024980 (accessed December 16, 2013).

35. Paul Tassi, "Google Plus Creates Uproar over Forced YouTube Integration," *Forbes,* November 9, 2013, www.forbes.com/sites/insertcoin/2013/11/09/google-plus-creates-uproar-over-forced-youtube-integration (accessed December 16, 2013).

36. Barr, "Google+ Sees a Measurable Plus: 58 Percent More Users."

37. Allison Rice, "5 Big Reasons Why You Should Consider Google Plus Marketing," *Yahoo! Small Business Advisor,* http://smallbusiness.yahoo.com/advisor/5-big-reasons-why-consider-google-plus-marketing-235637145.html (accessed December 16, 2013).

38. "Social Media Summit," Harrisburg University, 2012, www.harrisburgu.edu/academics/professional/socialmedia/index-2012.php (accessed February 16, 2012).

39. Jeff Bercovici, "Tumblr: David Karp's $800 Million Art Project," *Forbes,* January 2, 2013, www.forbes.com/sites/jeffbercovici/2013/01/02/tumblr-david-karps-800-million-art-project/ (accessed May 6, 2014); Tumblr, "About Tumblr," www.tumblr.com/about (accessed May 6, 2014).

40. A.C. Neilson, "Global Faces and Networked Places: A Neilson Report on Social Networking's New Global Foot print," March 2009, http://www.nielsen.com/content/dam/corporate/us/en/newswire/uploads/2009/03/nielsen_globalfaces_mar09.pdf (accessed May 29, 2014).

41. Randy Tinseth, "Randy's Journal," Boeing, http://boeingblogs.com/randy/ (accessed May 29, 2014).

42. Drake Bennett, "Ten Years of Inaccuracy and Remarkable Detail: Wikipedia," *Bloomberg Businessweek,* January 10–16, 2011, pp. 57–61; "Wikipedia: About," *Wikipedia*, http://en.wikipedia.org/wiki/Wikipedia:About (accessed May 7, 2014).

43. Charlene Li and Josh Bernoff, *Groundswell* (Boston: Harvard Business Press, 2008), pp. 25–26.

44. Susan Gunelius, "Fortune 500 Companies Are Getting More Social in 2013 with Twitter on Top," *Newstex,* August 8, 2013, http://newstex.com/2013/08/08/fortune-500-companies-are-getting-more-social-in-2013-with-twitter-on-top/ (accessed May 7, 2014).

45. Brian Stelter, "Disney to Pay at Least $500 Million for YouTube Video Maker," *CNN Money*, March 24, 2014, http://money.cnn.com/2014/03/24/news/companies/disney-maker-studios-acquisition/ (accessed May 7, 2014).

46. Tom Foster, "The GoPro Army," *Inc.,* February 2012, pp. 52–59.

47. Steven Bertoni, "How Stanford Made Instagram an Instant Success," *Forbes,* August 20, 2012, pp. 56–63; Jefferson Graham, "Instagram Is a Start-Up Magnet," *USA Today,*

August 9, 2012, www.usatoday.com/tech/news/story/2012-08-07/instagram-economy/56883474/1 (accessed May 7, 2014); Karen Rosenberg, "Everyone's Lives, in Pictures," *The New York Times,* April 12, 2012, www.nytimes.com/2012/04/22/sunday-review/everyones-lives-in-pictures-from-instagram.html (accessed May 7, 2014); K. Ian Crouch, "Instagram's Instant Nostalgia," *The New Yorker,* April 10, 2012, www.newyorker.com/online/blogs/culture/2012/04/instagrams-instant-nostalgia.html#slide_ss_0=1 (accessed May 7, 2014); "Top 15 Most Popular Photo Sharing Websites," May 2014, www.ebizmba.com/articles/photo-sharing-sites (accessed May 19, 2014).

48. Eddie Bauer website, www.eddiebauer.com/home.jsp (accessed December 12, 2013).

49. Scott Martin, "Action! Facebook Rolls Out Video Features," *USA Today*, June 21, 2013, p. B1; Victor Luckerson, "A Year Later, Instagram Hasn't Made a Dime. Was It Worth $1 Billion?" *Time,* April 9, 2013, http://business.time.com/2013/04/09/a-year-later-instagram-hasnt-made-a-dime-was-it-worth-1-billion (accessed December 17, 2013).

50. Laura Schlereth, "Marketers' Interest in Pinterest," *Marketing News,* April 30, 2012, pp. 8–9; The Creative Group, "PINTEREST INTEREST: Survey: 17 Percent of Marketers Currently Using or Planning to Join Pinterest," August 22, 2012, www.sacbee.com/2012/08/22/4747399/pinterest-interest-survey-17-percent.html; www.entrepreneur.com/article/222740 (accessed May 7, 2014); Pinterest website, http://pinterest.com/ (accessed May 7, 2014); http://pinterest.com/wholefoods/whole-planet-foundation/ (accessed May 7, 2014).

51. Kelly Clay, "3 Things You Can Learn about Your Business with Instagram," *Forbes,* August 9, 2012, www.forbes.com/sites/kellyclay/2012/08/09/3-things-you-can-learn-about-your-business-with-instagram/ (accessed May 7, 2014).

52. Zale Jewelers Pinterest page, www.pinterest.com/zalesjewelers (accessed December 12, 2013).

53. Virgin Mobile USA, www.flickr.com/photos/37089719@N08 (accessed December 12, 2013).

54. "How to Market on Flickr," Small Business Search Marketing, http://www.smallbusinesssem.com/how-to-market-on-flickr/6031/ (accessed May 29, 2014).

55. Natalie Wires, "The Rising Popularity of Podcasts: Why Listeners Are Rediscovering Podcasts," *Perspective*, March 26, 2014, http://blog.tunheim.com/2014/03/26/rising-popularity-podcasts-listeners-rediscovering-podcasts/1438#.U2pMWYFdVc8 (accessed May 7, 2014).

56. "About Made Money," *CNBC,* www.cnbc.com/id/17283246/ (accessed May 29, 2014).

57. E.J. Shultz, "Video: Smirnoff App Lets Consumers Make Videos from Their Tweets and Photos," *Advertising Age*, October 9, 2013, http://adage.com/article/special-report-ana-annual-meeting-2013/video-smirnoff-pushes-mixhibit-app/244637/ (accessed December 26, 2013); Lydia Bishman, "Smirnoff's 'Mixhibit' App Is a Heady Cocktail That Mixes Social Utility with Branding," *Fast Company,* www.fastcocreate.com/1682594/smirnoffs-mixhibit-app-is-a-heady-cocktail-that-mixes-social-utility-with-branding (accessed December 26, 2013); "Relive Good Times with Mixhibit, the First Collaborative Video Storytelling App," *PR Newswire,* November 14, 2013, www.prnewswire.com/news-releases/relive-good-times-with-mixhibit-the-first-collaborative-video-storytelling-app-231873491.html (accessed December 26, 2013); E.J. Schultz, "Madonna Signs with Smirnoff," *Advertising Age,* August 17, 2011, http://adage.com/article/news/madonna-signs-smirnoff/229343/ (accessed December 26, 2013); "Smirnoff's 'Midnight Circus' Celebrates Nightlife with Interactive Installations," *Branding Magazine,* August 30, 2012, www.

brandingmagazine.com/2012/08/30/smirnoff-midnight-circus/ (accessed December 26, 2013).

58. Dean Takahashi, "MediaSpike Reaches 20M Monthly Users with Product Placement in Social–Mobile Games," *Venture Beat,* October 24, 2013, http://venturebeat.com/2013/10/24/mediaspike-reaches-20m-monthly-users-with-product-placement-in-socialmobile-games (accessed December 18, 2013).

59. Brandy Shaul, "CityVille Celebrates the Golden Arches with Branded McDonald's Restaurant," Games.com, October 19, 2011, http://blog.games.com/2011/10/19/cityville-mcdonalds-restaurant (accessed December 18, 2013).

60. Roger Yu, "Smartphones Help Make Bon Voyages," *USA Today,* March 5, 2010, p. B1.

61. Brian Hongiman, "10 Mobile Marketing Statistics to Help Justify Your Budget," *Digital Lab,* May 5, 2014, http://digitallabblog.com/post/84827360253/10-mobile-marketing-statistics-to-help-justify-your (accessed May 7, 2014).

62. Cooper Smith, "US E-Commerce Growth Is Now Far Outpacing Overall Retail Sales," *Business Insider*, April 2, 2014, www.businessinsider.com/us-e-commerce-growth-is-now-far-outpacing-overall-retail-sales-2014-4#!Kk54l (accessed May 7, 2014).

63. Mark Milian, "Why Text Messages Are Limited to 160 Characters," *Los Angeles Times,* May 3, 2009, http://latimesblogs.latimes.com/technology/2009/05/invented-text-messaging.html (accessed May 29, 2014); "Eight Reasons Why Your Business Should Use SMS Marketing," *Mobile Marketing Ratings,* www.mobilemarketingratings.com/eight-reasons-sms-marketing.html (accessed May 29, 2014).

64. Sheldon Ferraro, "Gap the First to Use New Instagram Direct for Their WIWT Campaign," HashSlush, December 14, 2013, www.hashslush.com/gap-instagram-direct-wwit-campaign/ (accessed May 7, 2014).

65. Amy Dusto, "Mobile Devices Account for Nearly a Third of Web Traffic," *Internet Retailer*, February 6, 2014, www.internetretailer.com/2014/02/06/mobile-devices-account-nearly-third-web-traffic (accessed May 7, 2014).

66. Amy Dusto, "Mobile Devices Account For Nearly A Third of Web Traffic," Internet Retailer, February 6, 2014, http://www.internetretailer.com/2014/02/06/mobile-devices-account-nearly-third-web-traffic (accessed May 7, 2014).

67. Cotton Delo, "Foursquare Partners with Visa and MasterCard to Give Discounts When Users Shop," *Advertising Age*, February 25, 2013, http://adage.com/article/digital/foursquare-partners-visa-mastercard-discounts/240020 (accessed May 19, 2014).

68. Anita Campbell, "What the Heck Is an App?" *Small Business Trends*, March 7, 2011, http://smallbiztrends.com/2011/03/what-is-an-app.html (accessed March 29, 2014).

69. "Half of All Adult Cell Phone Owners Have Apps on Their Phones," Pew Internet and American Life Project, November 2, 2011, http://pewinternet.org/~/media/Files/Reports/2011/PIP_Apps-Update-2011.pdf (accessed May 29, 2014).

70. Pew Internet Research, "Mobile Technology Fact Sheet," January 2014, www.pewinternet.org/fact-sheets/mobile-technology-fact-sheet/ (accessed May 7, 2014).

71. Catherine Dunn, "Making Room for Technology," *Fortune*, October 7, 2013, p. 49.

72. Umika Pidaparthy, "Marketers Embracing QR Codes, for Better or Worse," *CNN Tech*, March 28, 2011, http://articles.cnn.com/2011-03-28/tech/qr.codes.marketing_1_qr-smartphone-users-symbian?_s=PM:TECH (accessed May 29, 2014).

73. Brad Stone and Olga Kharif, "Pay As You Go," *Bloomberg Businessweek*, July 18–24, 2011, pp. 66–71.

74. "Google Wallet," www.google.com/wallet/what-is-google-wallet.html (accessed May 29, 2014).

75. Walter S. Mossberg, "Square Cash Lets You Say the Money Is in the Email," *The Wall Street Journal*, October 16, 2013, pp. D1, D3.

76. Sarah E. Needleman, "Banking on Bitcoin's Novelty," *The Wall Street Journal*, June 27, 2013, p. B4; Robin Sidel and Andrew R. Johnson, "States Put Heat on Bitcoin," *The Wall Street Journal*, June 26, 2013, pp. C1–C2.

77. "The Bitcoin Bubble," *The Economist*, November 30, 2013, p. 13.

78. "MtGox Bitcoin Exchange Reopens So Users Can Stare Listlessly at Their Loss," *The Guardian*, March 18, 2014, www.theguardian.com/technology/2014/mar/18/mtgox-bitcoin-exchange-reopens-so-users-can-stare-listlessly-at-their-loss (accessed May 27, 2014).

79. "All About Widgets," *Webopedia*™, September 14, 2007, www.webopedia.com/DidYouKnow/Hardware_Software/widgets.asp (accessed May 29, 2014).

80. Rachael King, "Building a Brand with Widgets," *Bloomberg Businessweek*, March 3, 2008, www.businessweek.com/technology/content/feb2008/tc20080303_000743.htm (accessed May 29, 2014).

81. TripAdvisor, "Welcome to TripAdvisor's Widget Center," www.tripadvisor.com/Widgets (accessed December 16, 2013).

82. Li and Bernoff, *Groundswell*, p. 41.

83. Li and Bernoff, *Groundswell*, pp. 41–42.

84. "Forrester Unveils New Segment of Social Technographics— The Conversationalists," *360 Digital Connections*, January 21, 2010, http://blog.360i.com/social-marketing/forrester-new-segment-social-technographics-conversationalists (accessed May 29, 2014).

85. Li and Bernoff, *Groundswell*, p. 44.

86. Danielle Sacks, "How High Can Fab Climb?" *Fast Company*, October 2013, pp. 122–33, 156–58; Natasha Singer, "Learning to Chase Online Word of Mouth," *The New York Times*, May 26, 2013, www.nytimes.com/2012/05/27/business/fabcom-and-the-value-of-online-word-of-mouth.html?_r=0 (accessed September 23, 2013); Fab website, http://fab.com/ (accessed September 23, 2013).

87. Li and Bernoff, *Groundswell*, pp. 44–45.

88. Ryan Pinkham, "90% of Consumers Say Online Reviews Impact Buying Decisions . . . And Other Hot Topics," YAHOO! Small Business Advisor, April 12, 2013, https://smallbusiness.yahoo.com/advisor/90-consumers-online-reviews-impact-buying-decisions-other-211526956.html (accessed May 19, 2014).

89. Reed Albergotti, "Facebook Draws Fires on Teems," *The Wall Street Journal*, October 18, 2013, p. B5.

90. Amir Efrati, "Google's Data Trove Dance," *The Wall Street Journal*, July 31, 2013, pp. B1, B4.

91. Jon Swartz, "Facebook Changes Its Status in Washington," *USA Today*, January 13, 2011, pp. 1B–2B; John W. Miller, "Yahoo Cookie Plan in Place," *The Wall Street Journal*, March 19, 2011, http://online.wsj.com/news/articles/SB10001424052748703512404576208700813815570 (accessed May 29, 2014).

92. Byron Acohido, "Net Do-Not-Track Option Kicks off to Criticism," *USA Today*, August 30, 2011, p. 2B.

93. Jeff Elder, "Bogus Accounts Dog Twitter," *The Wall Street Journal*, November 25, 2013, pp. B1, B6.

94. Carol Matlack, "Now, Your Reward for Being a Loyal Customer: Identity Theft," *Bloomberg Businessweek*, November 13, 2013, www.businessweek.com/articles/2013-11-13/now-your-reward-for-being-a-loyal-customer-identity-theft (accessed December 19, 2013).

95. Kevin Shanahan and Mike Hyman "Motivators and Enablers of SCOURing," *Journal of Business Research*, 63 (September–October 2010), pp. 1095–1102.

96. Business Software Alliance, "Global Software Piracy," *BSA*, 2011, http://globalstudy.bsa.org/2011 (accessed December 19, 2013).

97. Max Chafkin, "The Case, and the Plan, for the Virtual Company," *Inc.,* April 2010, p. 68.

98. "Social Media at Work–Bane or Boon?" *CNN,* March 8, 2010, www.cnn.com/2010/LIVING/worklife/03/08/cb.social.media.banned/index.html (accessed June 18, 2014); Emily Glazer, "P&G Curbs Employees' Internet Use," *The Wall Street Journal,* April 4, 2012, http://online.wsj.com/article/SB10001424052702304072004577324142847006340.html (June 18, 2014); Ethics Resource Center, *2011 National Business Ethics Survey®: Ethics in Transition* (Arlington, VA: Ethics Resource Center, 2012); Miral Fahmy, "Facebook, YouTube at Work Make Better Employees: Study," *San Francisco Chronicle,* April 2, 2009, www.sanfranciscosentinel.com/?p=21639 (accessed June 18, 2014); Sharon Gaudin, "Study: Facebook Use Cuts Productivity at Work," *Computer World,* July 22, 2009, www.computerworld.com/s/article/9135795/Study_Facebook_use_cuts_productivity_at_work (accessed June 18, 2014); Sharon Gaudin, "Study: 54% of Companies Ban Facebook, Twitter at Work," *Computer World,* October 6, 2009, www.computerworld.com/s/article/9139020/Study_54_of_companies_ban_Facebook_Twitter_at_work (accessed June 18, 2014); Guy Alvarez, Brian Dalton, Joe Lamport, and Kristina Tsamis, "The Social Law Firm," *Above the Law,* http://good2bsocial.com/wp-content/uploads/2013/12/THE-SOCIAL-LAW-FIRM.pdf (accessed June 18, 2014).

## Chapter 14

1. Walter Pavlo, "Fmr Enron CFO Andrew Fastow Speaks at ACFE Annual Conference," *Forbes,* June 26, 2013, www.forbes.com/sites/walterpavlo/2013/06/26/fmr-enron-cfo-andrew-fastow-speaks-at-acfe-annual-conference/ (accessed August 29, 2013); Bethany McLean and Peter Elkind, "The Guiltiest Men in the Room," *CNN Money,* July 5, 2006, http://money.cnn.com/2006/05/29/news/enron_guiltyest/ (accessed August 29, 2013); Peter Elkind, "The Confessions of Andy Fastow," *CNN Money,* July 1, 2013, http://features.blogs.fortune.cnn.com/2013/07/01/the-confessions-of-andy-fastow/ (accessed August 29, 2013); Francesca Di Meglio, "Enron's Andrew Fastow: The Mistakes I Made," March 22, 2012, www.businessweek.com/articles/2012-03-22/enrons-andrew-fastow-the-mistakes-i-made (accessed August 29, 2013).

2. Public Company Accounting Oversight Board, "PCAOB Announces Settled Disciplinary Order against Deloitte & Touche for Permitting Suspended Auditor to Participate in Firm's Public Company Audit Practice," October 22, 2013, http://pcaobus.org/News/Releases/Pages/10222013_Deloitte.aspx (accessed June 11, 2014).

3. Walter Pavlo, "Association of Certified Fraud Examiners Release 2014 Report on Fraud," *Forbes,* May 21, 2014, www.forbes.com/sites/walterpavlo/2014/05/21/association-of-certified-fraud-examiners-release-2014-report-on-fraud/ (accessed June 11, 2014).

4. Association of Certified Fraud Examiners, "About the ACFE," www.acfe.com/about-the-acfe.aspx (accessed June 11, 2014).

5. "Integrated Reporting," www.theiirc.org/ (accessed September 7, 2012); Kathleen Hoffelder, "What Does Sustainability *Really* Cost?" *CFO,* August 28, 2012, www3.cfo.com/article/2012/8/cash-flow_integrated-reporting-edelman-sustainability-vancity-cash-flow-iirc?currpage=0 (accessed September 7, 2012); "Triple Bottom Line," *The Economist,* November 17, 2009, www.economist.com/node/14301663 (accessed September 7, 2012).

6. Mary Williams Walsh, "State Woes Grow Too Big to Camouflage," *CNBC,* March 30, 2010, www.cnbc.com/id/36096491/ (accessed March 31, 2010).

7. Sarah Johnson, "Averting Revenue-Recognition Angst," *CFO,* April 2012, p. 21.

8. "Al Dente Pasta Co.," www.goodlifer.com/2009/09/al-dente-pasta-co/ (accessed January 6, 2014); Al Dente Pasta website, www.aldentepasta.com (accessed January 6, 2014); "Marcella Hazan," HarperCollins, www.harpercollins.com/authors/4331/Marcella_Hazan/index.aspx (accessed January 6, 2014).

9. Danielle Lee, "Deloitte, New Profit Strategically Align to Drive Social Innovation," *Accounting Today,* June 19, 2013, www.accountingtoday.com/acto_blog/deloitte-new-profit-strategically-align-social-innovation-67158-1.html (accessed January 6, 2014); "New Profit and Deloitte Announce a New Strategic Collaboration to Drive Social Innovation," *Yahoo! Finance,* June 19, 2013, http://finance.yahoo.com/news/profit-deloitte-announce-strategic-collaboration-120600190.html (accessed January 6, 2014); Deloitte, "About Deloitte," www.deloitte.com/view/en_US/us/About/index.htm (accessed January 6, 2014); New Profit Inc., "What We Do," http://newprofit.com/cgi-bin/iowa/do/index.html (accessed January 6, 2014); Deloitte, "Corporate Citizenship," www.deloitte.com/view/en_US/us/About/Community-Involvement/index.htm (accessed January 8, 2014).

10. Source: City of Maricopa, "City Finance Department Receives Distinguished Presentation Award for Its Budget," March 25, 2014, www.maricopa-az.gov/web/finance-administrativeservice-home/1029-city-s-finance-department-recieves-distinguished-budget-presentation-award-for-its-budget (accessed June 11, 2014).

11. "Accountants and Auditors: Occupational Outlook Handbook," *Bureau of Labor Statistics,* April 6, 2012, www.bls.gov/ooh/Business-and-Financial/Accountants-and-auditors.htm (accessed June 16, 2014).

12. Goodwill website, www.goodwill.org/ (accessed May 15, 2014); Goodwill Industries International Inc., "About Us—Revenue Sources," www.goodwill.org/about-us/ (accessed May 14, 2014).

## Chapter 15

1. Scott A. Shay, "Cashless Society: A Huge Threat to Our Freedom," *CNBC,* December 12, 2013, www. cnbc.com/id/101266173 (accessed January 15, 2014); Oliver Burkeman, "The Cashless Society Is Coming. More Reason Than Ever to Use Cash," *The Guardian,* September 27, 2013, www.theguardian.com/ news/oliver-burkeman-s-blog/2013/ sep/27/cashless-society-spend-money-clinkle (accessed January 15, 2014); Jason Del Rey, "Here's the Bizarre Commercial from Clinkle, the Stealth Payments Startup That Richard Branson Just Backed," *All Things D,* September 26, 2013, http://allthingsd.com/20130926/ heres-the-bizarre-commercial-from-the-stealth-payments-startup-that-richard-branson-just-backed/ (accessed January 15, 2014); Patrick Henningsen, "The Cashless Society Is Almost Here—And with Some Very Sinister Implications," *Global Research,* November 29, 2012, www.globalresearch.ca/ the-cashless-society-is-almost-here-and-with-some-very-sinister-implications/5313515 (accessed January 21, 2014).

2. Paul Krugman, "Why Is Deflation Bad?" *The New York Times,* August 2, 2010, http://krugman.blogs. nytimes.com/2010/08/02/why-is-deflation-bad/ (accessed June 16, 2014).

3. Economic Research Federal Reserve Bank of St. Louis, "Currency in Circulation," June 4, 2014, http:// research.stlouisfed.org/fred2/series/ WCURCIR (accessed June 12, 2014).

4. "Weird and Wonderful Money Facts and Trivia," *Happy Worker,* www. happyworker.com/magazine/facts/ weird-and-wonderful-money-facts (accessed June 16, 2014).

5. Ibid.

6. "About the Redesigned Currency," The Department of the Treasury Bureau of Engraving and Printing, www.newmoney.gov/newmoney/ currency/aboutnotes.htm (accessed April 2, 2010).

7. Various annual reports of the U.S. Mint.

8. Jessica Dickler, "Americans Still Relying on Credit Cards to Get By," *CNN Money,* May 23, 2012, http:// money.cnn.com/2012/05/22/pf/ credit-card/index.htm (accessed June 16, 2014); Martin Merzer, "Survey: Students Fail the Credit Card Test," *Fox Business,* April 16, 2012, www. creditcards.com/credit-card-news/ survey-students-fail-credit-card-test-1279.php (accessed June 16, 2014).

9. Joel Makower, "Why Wells Fargo Is Banking on Sustainability," *GreenBiz.com*, April 23, 2012, www. greenbiz.com/blog/2012/04/23/why-wells-fargo-banking-sustainability (accessed November 15, 2012); Wells Fargo, "Wells Fargo: $30+ Billion in Environmental Investments by 2020," April 23, 2012, www.wellsfargo. com/press/2012/20120423_ WellsFargo30Billion (accessed November 15, 2012); Nelson D. Schwartz, "Banks Look to Burnish Their Images by Backing Green Technology Firms," *The New York Times,* June 10, 2012, www.nytimes. com/2012/06/11/business/banks-look-to-burnish-their-images-by-backing-green-technology-firms. html?_r=0 (accessed June 12, 2014).

10. "Deposit Insurance Simplification Fact Sheet," FDIC website, www. unitedamericanbank.com/pdfs/ FDIC-Insurance-Coverage-Fact-Sheet.pdf (accessed June 16, 2014).

11. Investopedia Staff, "How Bitcoin Works," *Forbes,* August 1, 2013, www.forbes.com/sites/ investopedia/2013/08/01/how-bitcoin-works/ (accessed August 28, 2013); Joshua Brustein, "Bitcoin May Not Be So Anonymous, After All," *Bloomberg,* August 27, 2013, www.businessweek.com/ articles/2013-08-27/bitcoin-may-not-be-so-anonymous-after-all (accessed August 28, 2013); Robin Sidel, "New York Opens Probe of Bitcoin Practices," *The Wall Street Journal,* August 12, 2013, C3; Kavya Sukumar, "Government Eyes Regulation of 'Bitcoins,'" *USA Today,* August 26, 2013,

www.usatoday.com/story/news/ politics/2013/08/26/bitcoin-virtual-currency-regualtions/2702653/ (accessed August 29, 2013).

12. "NACHA Reports More Than 18 Billion ACH Payments in 2007," The Free Library, May 19, 2008, www.thefreelibrary.com/NACHA+ Reports+More+Than+18+Billion+ ACH+Payments+in+2007.-a0179156311 (accessed June 16, 2014).

13. "From the Vault . . ." Ohio Commerce Bank, Winter 2012, http://website-tools.net/ google-keyword/site/www. ohiocommercebank.com (accessed June 16, 2014).

14. Rhonda Abrams "Strategies: More Small Firms Look at Mobile-Pay Options," *USA Today*, May 15, 2013. www.usatoday.com/story/money/ columnist/abrams/2013/05/03/small-business-mobile-payments/2131029/ (accessed June 12, 2014); Jon Swartz and Brett Molina, "Take a Stand, and Deliver Digital Cash Register," *USA Today*, May 14, 2013. http://usatoday30.usatoday. com/MONEY/usaedition/2013-05-15-Square-Stand-turns-iPad-into-digital-cash-register_ST_U.htm (accessed July 22, 2013); Square Up, https://squareup.com/stand (accessed July 15, 2013); Christina Chaey, "Square's Stand iPad Register Comes to Apple and Best Buy Retail Stores," *Fast Company,* www. fastcompany.com/3014027/fast-feed/ squares-stand-ipad-register-comes-to-apple-and-best-buy-retail-stores (accessed July 22, 2013).

15. JPMorgan 2013 Annual Report, p. 10.

16. "CSI Pennsylvania," *CFO Magazine,* March 2008, p. 92.

17. David Reilly, "Banks Need Just One Things to Spur Lending: Borrowers," *The Wall Street Journal*, July 29, 2012, http://online.wsj. com/article/SB10000872396390 444840104577553291982001720.html (accessed July 23, 2014); Laura Marcinek, "Biggest U.S. Banks Shrinking Loans as Regional Lenders Fill Gap," *The Washington Post*, June 26, 2012, http://washpost. bloomberg.com/Story?docId=1376-M5ZC211A74E901-

6TCC18E25KL8I48S7VK 3O1C45O (accessed July 31, 2012); Alan S. Blinder, "How Bernanke Can Get Banks Lending Again," *The Wall Street Journal*, July 22, 2012, http://online.wsj.com/article/SB100 00872396390444873204577537212 738938798.html?mod=googlenews_ wsj (accessed July 23, 2014); Bruce Bartlett, "The Fed Should Stop Playing Banks Not to Lend," *The New York Times,* July 31, 2012, http://economix.blogs.nytimes. com/2012/07/31/the-fed-should-stop-paying-banks-not-to-lend/ (accessed July 23, 2014); Rachel Streitfeld, "Small-Business Owners, Hit by Recession, Seek Remedies," CNN, December 6, 2009, www. cnn.com/2009/US/12/06/small. business.recession/index.html (accessed July 23, 2014); Small Business Administration, "Small Business, Big Impact!" www.sba. gov/offices/headquarters/ocpl/ resources/13493 (accessed July 23, 2014); "The Lure of Shadow Banking," *The Economist,* May 10, 2014, www.economist.com/news/ leaders/21601826-shadow-banks-helped-cause-financial-crisis-better-regulated-they-could-help-avert-next (accessed July 23, 2014).

## Chapter 16

1. Matt Krantz, "A Cloud over Credit-Rating Firms," *USA Today*, September 16, 2013, 4B; Chris Isidore, "S&P: U.S. Lawsuit Is Retaliation for Downgrade," *USA Today*, September 4, 2013, http:// money.cnn.com/2013/09/04/news/ companies/sandp-downgrade-lawsuit/ (accessed December 9, 2013); Christopher Alessi, Roya Wolverson, and Mohammed Aly Sergie, "The Credit Rating Controversy," *Council on Foreign Relations*, October 22, 2013, www. cfr.org/financial-crises/credit-rating-controversy/p22328 (accessed December 9, 2013).

2. Kate O'Sullivan, "Going for the Other Green," *CFO*, September 2011, pp. 52–57; Carlye Adler, "Thinking Big," *Time,* May 3, 2011, http://bx.businessweek. com/carbon-markets/ view?url=http%3A%2F%2Fc.

moreover.com%2Fclick%2Fhere. pl%3Fr4627673218%26f%3D9791 (accessed September 26, 2011); Method, "Biodiesel Fleet," http:// methodhome.com/greenskeeping/ biodiesel-fleet/ (accessed June 18, 2014).

3. Calculated by Geoff Hirt from Apple's annual reports and website on June 16, 2014.

4. Issie Lapowsky, "Paul Graham on Building Companies for Fast Growth," *Inc.,* September 2013, www.inc.com/magazine/201309/ issie-lapowsky/how-paul-graham-became-successful.html (accessed September 16, 2013); Y Combinator, http://ycombinator.com/ (accessed September 16, 2013); Paul Graham, "A New Venture Animal," March 2008, http://paulgraham.com/ ycombinator.html (accessed September 16, 2013); Sean Ellis, "Y Combinator Hatches Brilliant Entrepreneurs," *Start Up Marketing,* December 2, 2008, www.startup-marketing.com/y-combinator-hatches-brilliant-entrepreneurs/ (accessed September 16, 2013); Ryan Mac, "Top Startup Incubators and Accelerators: Y Combinator Tops with $7.8 Billion in Value," *Forbes,* April 30, 2012, www.forbes. com/sites/tomiogeron/2012/04/30/ top-tech-incubators-as-ranked-by-forbes-y-combinator-tops-with-7-billion-in-value/ (accessed September 16, 2013); Andy Louis-Charles, "Ignore Y Combinator at Your Own Risk," *The Motley Fool,* April 28, 2009, www.fool. com/investing/general/2009/04/28/ ignore-y-combinator-at-your-own-risk.aspx (accessed September 16, 2013); Josh Quittner, "The New Internet Start-Up Boom: Get Rich Slow," *Time,* April 9, 2009, http:// content.time.com/time/magazine/ article/0,9171,1890387-1,00. html (accessed September 16, 2013); Drew Hansen, "What's the Secret Behind Y Combinator's Success?" *Forbes,* February 18, 2013, www.forbes.com/sites/ drewhansen/2013/02/18/whats-the-source-of-y-combinators-success/ (accessed June 18, 2014).

5. Joshua Kennon, "Should You Invest in an IPO?" About.com, http://

beginnersinvest.about.com/od/ investmentbanking/a/aa073106a.htm (accessed June 18, 2014).

6. Andrew Ackerman, Scott Patterson, and Robin Sidel, "J.P. Morgan Set to Agree to Big Fine for 'Whale,'" *The Wall Street Journal*, September 17, 2013, A1, A6; Robin Sidel, "Dimon Stays Upbeat in Firm's Dark Days," *The Wall Street Journal*, October 2, 2013, pp. C1, C2; Robert W. Wood, "JP Morgan Chase's $13 B Settlement—And Whale-Sized Tax Deduction," *Forbes*, October 22, 2013, www.forbes. com/sites/robertwood/2013/10/22/ jp-morgan-chases-13b-settlement-and-whale-sized-tax-deduction/ (accessed October 22, 2013); Aruna Viswanatha, "J.P. Morgan to Pay $100 Million in Latest 'London Whale' Fine," *Reuters*, October 16, 2013, www.reuters.com/ article/2013/10/16/us-jpmorgan-cftc-idUSBRE99F0JW20131016 (accessed October 28, 2013); Dan Fitzpatrick, Jean Eaglesham, and Devlin Barrett, "Two Charged in J.P. Morgan 'Whale' Trades," *The Wall Street Journal*, August 14, 2013, http://online.wsj.com/ news/articles/SB10001424127887 3248238045790122550859130222 (accessed October 28, 2013); Tom Schoenburg, Dawn Kopecki, and Laurie Asseo, "JPMorgan Reaches Record $13 Billion Mortgage Settlement," *Bloomberg,* November 19, 2013, www.bloomberg.com/ news/2013-11-19/jpmorgan-settlement-announced-by-u-s-justice-department-1-.html (accessed June 18, 2014).

7. Vincent Ryan, "From Wall Street to Main Street," *CFO Magazine*, June 2008, pp. 85–86.

8. Morningstar website, http:// corporate.morningstar.com/US/ asp/home2.aspx?xmlfile=7083. xml (accessed June 18, 2014); ChicagoMag.com, June 2006, www.chicagomag.com/Chicago-Magazine/June-2006/The-Quiet-Billionaire/ (accessed June 18, 2014); Jody Clarke, "Joe Mansueto: The Simple Idea That Made Me $1bn," *MoneyWeek,* September 4, 2009, www. moneyweek.com/news-andcharts/

entrepreneurs-my-first-millionjoe-mansueto-moneyweek-45135. aspx (accessed May 12, 2010); "FAQ: The Morningstar Rating for Stocks," Morningstar, http://news. morningstar.com/articlenet/article. aspx?id=4982#anchor3 (accessed June 18, 2014); Morningstar, "About Morningstar, Inc.," https://corporate. morningstar.com/us/documents/ UserGuides/AboutMorningstar. pdf (accessed June 18, 2014); Morningstar, *Morningstar Inc. Fact Sheet* (Chicago: Morningstar Inc., May 2014); Morningstar, "Who We Are," http://corporate. morningstar.com/US/asp/subject. aspx?xmlfile=177.xml (accessed June 18, 2014).

9. Phil Izzo, "Congratulations to Class of 2014, Most Indebted Ever," *The Wall Street Journal*, May 16, 2014, http://blogs.wsj.com/numbersguy/ congatulations-to-class-of-2014-the-most-indebted-ever-1368/ (accessed June 16, 2014).

10. Halah Touryala, "$1 Trillion Student Loan Problem Keeps Getting Worse," *Forbes*, February 21, 2014, www.forbes.com/sites/ halahtouryalai/2014/02/21/1-trillion-student-loan-problem-keeps-getting-worse/ (accessed June 16, 2014).

11. Federal Student Aid an Office of the U.S. Department of Education, "Interest Rates for New Direct Loans," July 1, 2014 https://studentaid.ed.gov/About/ announcements/interest-rate (accessed June 16, 2014).

12. Sam Frizzle, "Obama Looks to Reduce Student Loan Payments," *Time*, June 9, 2014, http://time.com/2847507/ student-loan-debt-barack-obama/ (accessed June 16, 2014).

13. Maria Shriver, "Life Ed: How to Manage Student Loan Debt," *NBC News*, June 12, 2014, www. nbcnews.com/feature/maria-shriver/ life-ed-how-manage-student-loan-debt-n129521 (accessed June 16, 2014).

14. Jill Jackson and John Nolen, "Health Care Reform Bill Summary: A Look at What's in the Bill," *CBS News,* March 21, 2010, www. cbsnews.com/8301-503544_162-20000846-503544.html (accessed May 30, 2012); "Patient Protection and Affordable Care Act," *Federal Register 75* (123), June 28, 2010, www.gpo.gov/fdsys/pkg/FR-2010-06-28/html/2010-15278.htm (accessed June 18, 2014).

15. Richard Rubin, "Wealthy Clintons Use Trust to Limit Estate Tax They Back," *Bloomberg,* June 16, 2014, www.bloomberg.com/news/2014-06-17/wealthy-clintons-use-trusts-to-limit-estate-tax-they-back.html (accessed June 18, 2014).

# Glossary

## A

**absolute advantage** a monopoly that exists when a country is the only source of an item, the only producer of an item, or the most efficient producer of an item.

**accountability** the principle that employees who accept an assignment and the authority to carry it out are answerable to a superior for the outcome.

**accounting** the recording, measurement, and interpretation of financial information.

**accounting cycle** the four-step procedure of an accounting system: examining source documents, recording transactions in an accounting journal, posting recorded transactions, and preparing financial statements.

**accounting equation** assets equal liabilities plus owners' equity.

**accounts payable** the amount a company owes to suppliers for goods and services purchased with credit.

**accounts receivable** money owed a company by its clients or customers who have promised to pay for the products at a later date.

**accrued expenses** all unpaid financial obligations incurred by an organization.

**acquisition** the purchase of one company by another, usually by buying its stock.

**administrative managers** those who manage an entire business or a major segment of a business; they are not specialists but coordinate the activities of specialized managers.

**advertising** a paid form of nonpersonal communication transmitted through a mass medium, such as television commercials or magazine advertisements.

**advertising campaign** designing a series of advertisements and placing them in various media to reach a particular target market.

**affirmative action programs** legally mandated plans that try to increase job opportunities for minority groups by analyzing the current pool of workers, identifying areas where women and minorities are underrepresented, and establishing specific hiring and promotion goals, with target dates, for addressing the discrepancy.

**agenda** a calendar, containing both specific and vague items, that covers short-term goals and long-term objectives.

**analytical skills** the ability to identify relevant issues, recognize their importance, understand the relationships between them, and perceive the underlying causes of a situation.

**annual report** summary of a firm's financial information, products, and growth plans for owners and potential investors.

**arbitration** settlement of a labor/management dispute by a third party whose solution is legally binding and enforceable.

**articles of partnership** legal documents that set forth the basic agreement between partners.

**Asia-Pacific Economic Cooperation (APEC)** an international trade alliance that promotes open trade and economic and technical cooperation among member nations.

**asset utilization ratios** ratios that measure how well a firm uses its assets to generate each $1 of sales.

**assets** a firm's economic resources, or items of value that it owns, such as cash, inventory, land, equipment, buildings, and other tangible and intangible things.

**Association of Southeast Asian Nations (ASEAN)** A trade alliance that promotes trade and economic integration among member nations in Southeast Asia.

**attitude** knowledge and positive or negative feelings about something.

**automated clearinghouses (ACHs)** a system that permits payments such as deposits or withdrawals to be made to and from a bank account by magnetic computer tape.

**automated teller machine (ATM)** the most familiar form of electronic banking, which dispenses cash, accepts deposits, and allows balance inquiries and cash transfers from one account to another.

## B

**balance of payments** the difference between the flow of money into and out of a country.

**balance of trade** the difference in value between a nation's exports and its imports.

**balance sheet** a "snapshot" of an organization's financial position at a given moment.

**behavior modification** changing behavior and encouraging appropriate actions by relating the consequences of behavior to the behavior itself.

**benefits** nonfinancial forms of compensation provided to employees, such as pension plans, health insurance, paid vacation and holidays, and the like.

**blogs** web-based journals in which writers can editorialize and interact with other Internet users.

**board of directors** a group of individuals, elected by the stockholders to oversee the general operation of the corporation, who set the corporation's long-range objectives.

**bonds** debt instruments that larger companies sell to raise long-term funds.

**bonuses** monetary rewards offered by companies for exceptional performance as incentives to further increase productivity.

**boycott** an attempt to keep people from purchasing the products of a company.

**branding** the process of naming and identifying products.

**bribes** payments, gifts, or special favors intended to influence the outcome of a decision.

**brokerage firms** firms that buy and sell stocks, bonds, and other securities for their customers and provide other financial services.

**budget** an internal financial plan that forecasts expenses and income over a set period of time.

**budget deficit** the condition in which a nation spends more than it takes in from taxes.

**business** individuals or organizations who try to earn a profit by providing products that satisfy people's needs.

**business ethics** principles and standards that determine acceptable conduct in business.

**business plan** a precise statement of the rationale for a business and a step-by-step explanation of how it will achieve its goals.

**business products** products that are used directly or indirectly in the operation or manufacturing processes of businesses.

**buying behavior** the decision processes and actions of people who purchase and use products.

## C

**capacity** the maximum load that an organizational unit can carry or operate.

**capital budgeting** the process of analyzing the needs of the business and selecting the assets that will maximize its value.

**capitalism (free enterprise)** an economic system in which individuals own and operate the majority of businesses that provide goods and services.

**cartel** a group of firms or nations that agrees to act as a monopoly and not compete with each other, in order to generate a competitive advantage in world markets.

**cash flow** the movement of money through an organization over a daily, weekly, monthly, or yearly basis.

**centralized organization** a structure in which authority is concentrated at the top, and very little decision-making authority is delegated to lower levels.

**certificates of deposit (CDs)** savings accounts that guarantee a depositor a set interest rate over a specified interval as long as the funds are not withdrawn before the end of the period—six months or one year, for example.

**certified management accountants (CMAs)** private accountants who, after rigorous examination, are certified by the National Association of Accountants and who have some managerial responsibility.

**certified public accountant (CPA)** an individual who has been state certified to provide accounting services ranging from the preparation of financial records and the filing of tax returns to complex audits of corporate financial records.

**checking account** money stored in an account at a bank or other financial institution that can be withdrawn without advance notice; also called a demand deposit.

**classical theory of motivation** theory suggesting that money is the sole motivator for workers.

**codes of ethics** formalized rules and standards that describe what a company expects of its employees.

**collective bargaining** the negotiation process through which management and unions reach an agreement about compensation, working hours, and working conditions for the bargaining unit.

**commercial banks** the largest and oldest of all financial institutions, relying mainly on checking and savings accounts as sources of funds for loans to businesses and individuals.

**commercial certificates of deposit (CDs)** certificates of deposit issued by commercial banks and brokerage companies, available in minimum amounts of $100,000, which may be traded prior to maturity.

**commercial paper** a written promise from one company to another to pay a specific amount of money.

**commercialization** the full introduction of a complete marketing strategy and the launch of the product for commercial success.

**commission** an incentive system that pays a fixed amount or a percentage of the employee's sales.

**commitee** a permanent, formal group that performs a specific task.

**common stock** stock whose owners have voting rights in the corporation, yet do not receive preferential treatment regarding dividends.

**communism** first described by Karl Marx as a society in which the people, without regard to class, own all the nation's resources.

**comparative advantage** the basis of most international trade, when a country specializes in products that it can supply more efficiently or at a lower cost than it can produce other items.

**competition** the rivalry among businesses for consumers' dollars.

**compressed workweek** a four-day (or shorter) period during which an employee works 40 hours.

**computer-assisted design (CAD)** the design of components, products, and processes on computers instead of on paper.

**computer-assisted manufacturing (CAM)** manufacturing that employs specialized computer systems to actually guide and control the transformation processes.

**computer-integrated manufacturing (CIM)** a complete system that designs products, manages machines and materials, and controls the operations function.

**concentration approach** a market segmentation approach whereby a company develops one marketing strategy for a single market segment.

**conceptual skills** the ability to think in abstract terms and to see how parts fit together to form the whole.

**conciliation** a method of outside resolution of labor and management differences in which a third party is brought in to keep the two sides talking.

**consumer products** products intended for household or family use.

**consumerism** the activities that independent individuals, groups, and organizations undertake to protect their rights as consumers.

**continuous manufacturing organizations** companies that use continuously running assembly lines, creating products with many similar characteristics.

**contract manufacturing** the hiring of a foreign company to produce a specified volume of the initiating company's product to specification; the final product carries the domestic firm's name.

**controlling** the process of evaluating and correcting activities to keep the organization on course.

**cooperative (co-op)** an organization composed of individuals or small businesses that have banded together to reap the benefits of belonging to a larger organization.

**corporate charter** a legal document that the state issues to a company based on information the company provides in the articles of incorporation.

**corporate citizenship** the extent to which businesses meet the legal, ethical, economic, and voluntary responsibilities placed on them by their stakeholders.

**corporation** a legal entity, created by the state, whose assets and liabilities are separate from its owners.

**cost of goods sold** the amount of money a firm spent to buy or produce the products it sold during the period to which the income statement applies.

**countertrade agreements** foreign trade agreements that involve bartering products for other products instead of for currency.

**credit cards** means of access to preapproved lines of credit granted by a bank or finance company.

**credit controls** the authority to establish and enforce credit rules for financial institutions and some private investors.

**credit union** a financial institution owned and controlled by its depositors, who usually have a common employer, profession, trade group, or religion.

**crisis management (contingency planning)** an element in planning that deals with potential disasters such as product tampering, oil spills, fire, earthquake, computer virus, or airplane crash.

**culture** the integrated, accepted pattern of human behavior, including thought, speech, beliefs, actions, and artifacts.

**current assets** assets that are used or converted into cash within the course of a calendar year.

**current liabilities** a firm's financial obligations to short-term creditors, which must be repaid within one year.

**current ratio** current assets divided by current liabilities.

**customer departmentalization** the arrangement of jobs around the needs of various types of customers.

**customization** making products to meet a particular customer's needs or wants.

## D

**debit card** a card that looks like a credit card but works like a check; using it results in a direct, immediate, electronic payment from the cardholder's checking account to a merchant or third party.

**debt to total assets ratio** a ratio indicating how much of the firm is financed by debt and how much by owners' equity.

**debt utilization ratios** ratios that measure how much debt an organization is using relative to other sources of capital, such as owners' equity.

**decentralized organization** an organization in which decision-making authority is delegated as far down the chain of command as possible.

**delegation of authority** giving employees not only tasks, but also the power to make commitments, use resources, and take whatever actions are necessary to carry out those tasks.

**demand** the number of goods and services that consumers are willing to buy at different prices at a specific time.

**departmentalization** the grouping of jobs into working units usually called departments, units, groups, or divisions.

**depreciation** the process of spreading the costs of long-lived assets such as buildings and equipment over the total number of accounting periods in which they are expected to be used.

**depression** a condition of the economy in which unemployment is very high, consumer spending is low, and business output is sharply reduced.

**development** training that augments the skills and knowledge of managers and professionals.

**digital marketing** uses all digital media, including the Internet and mobile and interactive channels, to develop communication and exchanges with customers.

**digital media** electronic media that function using digital codes via computers, cellular phones, smart phones, and other digital devices that have been released in recent years.

**direct investment** the ownership of overseas facilities.

**directing** motivating and leading employees to achieve organizational objectives.

**discount rate** the rate of interest the Fed charges to loan money to any banking institution to meet reserve requirements.

**discounts** temporary price reductions, often employed to boost sales.

**distribution** making products available to customers in the quantities desired.

**diversity** the participation of different ages, genders, races, ethnicities, nationalities, and abilities in the workplace.

**dividend yield** the dividend per share divided by the stock price.

**dividends** profits of a corporation that are distributed in the form of cash payments to stockholders.

**dividends per share** the actual cash received for each share owned.

**double-entry bookkeeping** a system of recording and classifying business transactions that maintains the balance of the accounting equation.

**downsizing** the elimination of a significant number of employees from an organization.

**dumping** the act of a country or business selling products at less than what it costs to produce them.

## E

**e-business** carrying out the goals of business through utilization of the Internet.

**earnings per share** net income or profit divided by the number of stock shares outstanding.

**economic contraction** a slowdown of the economy characterized by a decline in spending and during which businesses cut back on production and lay off workers.

**economic expansion** the situation that occurs when an economy is growing and people are spending more money; their purchases stimulate the production of goods and services, which in turn stimulates employment.

**economic order quantity (EOQ) model** a model that identifies the optimum number of items to order to minimize the costs of managing (ordering, storing, and using) them.

**economic system** a description of how a particular society distributes its resources to produce goods and services.

**economics** the study of how resources are distributed for the production of goods and services within a social system.

**electronic funds transfer (EFT)** any movement of funds by means of an electronic terminal, telephone, computer, or magnetic tape.

**embargo** a prohibition on trade in a particular product.

**employee empowerment** when employees are provided with the ability to take on responsibilities and make decisions about their jobs.

**entrepreneur** an individual who risks his or her wealth, time, and effort to develop for profit an innovative product or way of doing something.

**entrepreneurship** the process of creating and managing a business to achieve desired objectives.

**equilibrium price** the price at which the number of products that businesses are willing to supply equals the amount of products that consumers are willing to buy at a specific point in time.

**equity theory** an assumption that how much people are willing to contribute to an organization depends on their assessment of the fairness, or equity, of the rewards they will receive in exchange.

**esteem needs** the need for respect—both self-respect and respect from others.

**ethical issue** an identifiable problem, situation, or opportunity that requires a person to choose from among several actions that may be evaluated as right or wrong, ethical or unethical.

**eurodollar market** a market for trading U.S. dollars in foreign countries.

**European Union (EU)** a union of European nations established in 1958 to promote trade among its members; one of the largest single markets today.

**exchange** the act of giving up one thing (money, credit, labor, goods) in return for something else (goods, services, or ideas).

**exchange controls** regulations that restrict the amount of currency that can be bought or sold.

**exchange rate** the ratio at which one nation's currency can be exchanged for another nation's currency.

**exclusive distribution** the awarding by a manufacturer to an intermediary of the sole right to sell a product in a defined geographic territory.

**expectancy theory** the assumption that motivation depends not only on how much a person wants something but also on how likely he or she is to get it.

**expenses** the costs incurred in the day-to-day operations of an organization.

**exporting** the sale of goods and services to foreign markets.

**extrinsic rewards** benefits and/or recognition received from someone else.

## F

**factor** a finance company to which businesses sell their accounts receivable—usually for a percentage of the total face value.

**Federal Deposit Insurance Corporation (FDIC)** an insurance fund established in 1933 that insures individual bank accounts.

**Federal Reserve Board** an independent agency of the federal government established in 1913 to regulate the nation's banking and financial industry.

**finance** the study of money; how it's made, how it's lost, and how it's managed.

**finance companies** businesses that offer short-term loans at substantially higher rates of interest than banks.

**financial managers** those who focus on obtaining needed funds for the successful operation of an organization and using those funds to further organizational goals.

**financial resources** the funds used to acquire the natural and human resources needed to provide products; also called capital.

**first-line managers** those who supervise both workers and the daily operations of an organization.

**fixed-position layout** a layout that brings all resources required to create the product to a central location.

**flexible manufacturing** the direction of machinery by computers to adapt to different versions of similar operations.

**flextime** a program that allows employees to choose their starting and ending times, provided that they are at work during a specified core period.

**floating-rate bonds** bonds with interest rates that change with current interest rates otherwise available in the economy.

**franchise** a license to sell another's products or to use another's name in business, or both.

**franchisee** the purchaser of a franchise.

**franchiser** the company that sells a franchise.

**franchising** a form of licensing in which a company—the franchiser—agrees to provide a franchisee a name, logo, methods of operation, advertising, products, and other elements associated with a franchiser's business in return for a financial commitment and the agreement to conduct business in accordance with the franchiser's standard of operations.

**free-market system** pure capitalism, in which all economic decisions are made without government intervention.

**functional departmentalization** the grouping of jobs that perform similar functional activities, such as finance, manufacturing, marketing, and human resources.

## G

**General Agreement on Tariffs and Trade (GATT)** a trade agreement, originally signed by 23 nations in 1947, that provided a forum for tariff negotiations and a place where international trade problems could be discussed and resolved.

**general partnership** a partnership that involves a complete sharing in both the management and the liability of the business.

**generic products** products with no brand name that often come in simple packages and carry only their generic name.

**geographical departmentalization** the grouping of jobs according to geographic location, such as state, region, country, or continent.

**global strategy (globalization)** a strategy that involves standardizing products (and, as much as possible, their promotion and distribution) for the whole world, as if it were a single entity.

**grapevine** an informal channel of communication, separate from management's formal, official communication channels.

**gross domestic product (GDP)** the sum of all goods and services produced in a country during a year.

**gross income (or profit)** revenues minus the cost of goods sold required to generate the revenues.

**group** two or more individuals who communicate with one another, share a common identity, and have a common goal.

## H

**human relations** the study of the behavior of individuals and groups in organizational settings.

**human relations skills** the ability to deal with people, both inside and outside the organization.

**human resources** the physical and mental abilities that people use to produce goods and services; also called labor.

**human resources management (HRM)** all the activities involved in determining an organization's human resources needs, as well as acquiring, training, and compensating people to fill those needs.

**human resources managers** those who handle the staffing function and deal with employees in a formalized manner.

**hygiene factors** aspects of Herzberg's theory of motivation that focus on the work setting and not the content of the work; these aspects include adequate wages, comfortable and safe working conditions, fair company policies, and job security.

## I

**identity theft** when criminals obtain personal information that allows them to impersonate someone else in order to use their credit to obtain financial accounts and make purchases.

**import tariff** a tax levied by a nation on goods imported into the country.

**importing** the purchase of goods and services from foreign sources.

**income statement** a financial report that shows an organization's profitability over a period of time—month, quarter, or year.

**inflation** a condition characterized by a continuing rise in prices.

**information technology (IT) managers** those who are responsible for implementing, maintaining, and controlling technology applications in business, such as computer networks.

**infrastructure** the physical facilities that support a country's economic activities, such as railroads, highways, ports, airfields, utilities and power plants, schools, hospitals, communication systems, and commercial distribution systems.

**initial public offering (IPO)** selling a corporation's stock on public markets for the first time.

**inputs** the resources—such as labor, money, materials, and energy—that are converted into outputs.

**insurance companies** businesses that protect their clients against financial losses from certain specified risks (death, accident, and theft, for example).

**integrated marketing communications** coordinating the promotion mix elements and synchronizing promotion as a unified effort.

**intensive distribution** a form of market coverage whereby a product is made available in as many outlets as possible.

**intermittent organizations** organizations that deal with products of a lesser magnitude than do project organizations; their products are not necessarily unique but possess a significant number of differences.

**international business** the buying, selling, and trading of goods and services across national boundaries.

**International Monetary Fund (IMF)** organization established in 1947 to promote trade among member nations by eliminating trade barriers and fostering financial cooperation.

**intrapreneurs** individuals in large firms who take responsibility for the development of innovations within the organizations.

**intrinsic rewards** the personal satisfaction and enjoyment felt after attaining a goal.

**inventory** all raw materials, components, completed or partially completed products, and pieces of equipment a firm uses.

**inventory control** the process of determining how many supplies and goods are needed and keeping track of quantities on hand, where each item is, and who is responsible for it.

**inventory turnover** sales divided by total inventory.

**investment banker** underwrites new issues of securities for corporations, states, and municipalities.

**investment banking** the sale of stocks and bonds for corporations

**ISO 9000** a series of quality assurance standards designed by the International Organization for Standardization (ISO) to ensure consistent product quality under many conditions.

**ISO 14000** a comprehensive set of environmental standards that encourages a cleaner and safer world by promoting a more uniform approach to environmental management and helping companies attain and measure improvements in their environmental performance.

## J

**job analysis** the determination, through observation and study, of pertinent information about a job—including specific tasks and necessary abilities, knowledge, and skills.

**job description** a formal, written explanation of a specific job, usually including job title, tasks, relationship with other jobs, physical and mental skills required, duties, responsibilities, and working conditions.

**job enlargement** the addition of more tasks to a job instead of treating each task as separate.

**job enrichment** the incorporation of motivational factors, such as opportunity for achievement, recognition, responsibility, and advancement, into a job.

**job rotation** movement of employees from one job to another in an effort to relieve the boredom often associated with job specialization.

**job sharing** performance of one full-time job by two people on part-time hours.

**job specification** a description of the qualifications necessary for a specific job, in terms of education, experience, and personal and physical characteristics.

**joint venture** a partnership established for a specific project or for a limited time.

**journal** a time-ordered list of account transactions.

**junk bonds** a special type of high interest rate bond that carries higher inherent risks.

**just-in-time (JIT) inventory management** a technique using smaller quantities of materials that arrive "just in time" for use in the transformation process and therefore require less storage space and other inventory management expense.

## L

**labeling** the presentation of important information on a package.

**labor contract** the formal, written document that spells out the relationship between the union and management for a specified period of time—usually two or three years.

**labor unions** employee organizations formed to deal with employers for achieving better pay, hours, and working conditions.

**leadership** the ability to influence employees to work toward organizational goals.

**learning** changes in a person's behavior based on information and experience.

**ledger** a book or computer file with separate sections for each account.

**leveraged buyout (LBO)** a purchase in which a group of investors borrows money from banks and other institutions to acquire a company (or a division of one), using the assets of the purchased company to guarantee repayment of the loan.

**liabilities** debts that a firm owes to others.

**licensing** a trade agreement in which one company—the licensor—allows another company—the licensee—to use its company name, products, patents, brands, trademarks, raw materials, and/or production processes in exchange for a fee or royalty.

**limited liability company (LLC)** form of ownership that provides limited liability and taxation like a partnership but places fewer restrictions on members.

**limited partnership** a business organization that has at least one general partner, who assumes unlimited liability, and at least one limited partner, whose liability is limited to his or her investment in the business.

**line of credit** an arrangement by which a bank agrees to lend a specified amount of money to an organization upon request.

**line-and-staff structure** a structure having a traditional line relationship between superiors and subordinates and also specialized managers—called staff managers—who are available to assist line managers.

**line structure** the simplest organizational structure, in which direct lines of authority extend from the top manager to the lowest level of the organization.

**liquidity ratios** ratios that measure the speed with which a company can turn its assets into cash to meet short-term debt.

**lockbox** an address, usually a commercial bank, at which a company receives payments in order to speed collections from customers.

**lockout** management's version of a strike, wherein a work site is closed so that employees cannot go to work.

**long-term (fixed) assets** production facilities (plants), offices, and equipment—all of which are expected to last for many years.

**long-term liabilities** debts that will be repaid over a number of years, such as long-term loans and bond issues.

## M

**management** a process designed to achieve an organization's objectives by using its resources effectively and efficiently in a changing environment.

**managerial accounting** the internal use of accounting statements by managers in planning and directing the organization's activities.

**managers** those individuals in organizations who make decisions about the use of resources and who are concerned with planning, organizing, staffing, directing, and controlling the organization's activities to reach its objectives.

**manufacturer brands** brands initiated and owned by the manufacturer to identify products from the point of production to the point of purchase.

**manufacturing** the activities and processes used in making tangible products; also called production.

**market** a group of people who have a need, purchasing power, and the desire and authority to spend money on goods, services, and ideas.

**market orientation** an approach requiring organizations to gather information about customer needs, share that information throughout the firm, and use that information to help build long-term relationships with customers.

**market segment** a collection of individuals, groups, or organizations who share one or more characteristics and thus have relatively similar product needs and desires.

**market segmentation** a strategy whereby a firm divides the total market into groups of people who have relatively similar product needs.

**marketable securities** temporary investment of "extra" cash by organizations for up to one year in U.S. Treasury bills, certificates of deposit, commercial paper, or eurodollar loans.

**marketing** a group of activities designed to expedite transactions by creating, distributing, pricing, and promoting goods, services, and ideas.

**marketing channel** a group of organizations that moves products from their producer to customers; also called a channel of distribution.

**marketing concept** the idea that an organization should try to satisfy customers' needs through coordinated activities that also allow it to achieve its own goals.

**marketing managers** those who are responsible for planning, pricing, and promoting products and making them available to customers.

**marketing mix** the four marketing activites—product, price, promotion, and distribution—that the firm can control to achieve specific goals within a dynamic marketing environment.

**marketing research** a systematic, objective process of getting information about potential customers to guide marketing decisions.

**marketing strategy** a plan of action for developing, pricing, distributing, and promoting products that meet the needs of specific customers.

**Maslow's hierarchy** a theory that arranges the five basic needs of people—physiological, security, social, esteem, and self-actualization—into the order in which people strive to satisfy them.

**material-requirements planning (MRP)** a planning system that schedules the precise quantity of materials needed to make the product.

**materials handling** the physical handling and movement of products in warehousing and transportation.

**matrix structure** a structure that sets up teams from different departments, thereby creating two or more intersecting lines of authority; also called a project-management structure.

**mediation** a method of outside resolution of labor and management differences in which the third party's role is to suggest or propose a solution to the problem.

**merger** the combination of two companies (usually corporations) to form a new company.

**middle managers** those members of an organization responsible for the tactical planning that implements the general guidelines established by top management.

**mission** the statement of an organization's fundamental purpose and basic philosophy.

**mixed economies** economies made up of elements from more than one economic system.

**modular design** the creation of an item in self-contained units, or modules, that can be combined or interchanged to create different products.

**monetary policy** means by which the Fed controls the amount of money available in the economy.

**money** anything generally accepted in exchange for goods and services.

**money market accounts** accounts that offer higher interest rates than standard bank rates but with greater restrictions.

**monopolistic competition** the market structure that exists when there are fewer businesses than in a pure-competition environment and the differences among the goods they sell are small.

**monopoly** the market structure that exists when there is only one business providing a product in a given market.

**morale** an employee's attitude toward his or her job, employer, and colleagues.

**motivation** an inner drive that directs a person's behavior toward goals.

**motivational factors** aspects of Herzberg's theory of motivation that focus on the content of the work itself; these aspects include achievement, recognition, involvement, responsibility, and advancement.

**multidivisional structure** a structure that organizes departments into larger groups called divisions.

**multinational corporation (MNC)** a corporation that operates on a worldwide scale, without significant ties to any one nation or region.

**multinational strategy** a plan, used by international companies, that involves customizing products, promotion, and distribution according to cultural, technological, regional, and national differences.

**multisegment approach** a market segmentation approach whereby the marketer aims its efforts at two or more segments, developing a marketing strategy for each.

**mutual fund** an investment company that pools individual investor dollars and invests them in large numbers of well-diversified securities.

**mutual savings banks** financial institutions that are similar to savings and loan associations but, like credit unions, are owned by their depositors.

## N

**National Credit Union Administration (NCUA)** an agency that regulates and charters credit unions and insures their deposits through its National Credit Union Insurance Fund.

**natural resources** land, forests, minerals, water, and other things that are not made by people.

**net income** the total profit (or loss) after all expenses, including taxes, have been deducted from revenue; also called net earnings.

**networking** the building of relationships and sharing of information with colleagues who can help managers achieve the items on their agendas.

**nonprofit corporations** corporations that focus on providing a service rather than earning a profit but are not owned by a government entity.

**nonprofit organizations** organizations that may provide goods or services but do not have the fundamental purpose of earning profits.

**North American Free Trade Agreement (NAFTA)** agreement that eliminates most tariffs and trade restrictions on agricultural and manufactured products to encourage trade among Canada, the United States, and Mexico.

## O

**offshoring** the relocation of business processes by a company or subsidiary to another country. Offshoring is different than outsourcing because the company retains control of the offshored processes.

**oligopoly** the market structure that exists when there are very few businesses selling a product.

**online fraud** any attempt to conduct fraudulent activities online.

**open market operations** decisions to buy or sell U.S. Treasury bills (short-term debt issued by the U.S. government) and other investments in the open market.

**operational plans** very short-term plans that specify what actions individuals, work groups, or departments need to accomplish in order to achieve the tactical plan and ultimately the strategic plan.

**operations** the activities and processes used in making both tangible and intangible products.

**operations management (OM)** the development and administration of the activities involved in transforming resources into goods and services.

**organizational chart** a visual display of the organizational structure, lines of authority (chain of command), staff relationships, permanent committee arrangements, and lines of communication.

**organizational culture** a firm's shared values, beliefs, traditions, philosophies, rules, and role models for behavior.

**organizational layers** the levels of management in an organization.

**organizing** the structuring of resources and activities to accomplish objectives in an efficient and effective manner.

**orientation** familiarizing newly hired employees with fellow workers, company procedures, and the physical properties of the company.

**outputs** the goods, services, and ideas that result from the conversion of inputs.

**outsourcing** the transferring of manufacturing or other tasks—such as data processing—to countries where labor and supplies are less expensive.

**over-the-counter (OTC) market** a network of dealers all over the country linked by computers, telephones, and Teletype machines.

**owners' equity** equals assets minus liabilities and reflects historical values.

**P**

**packaging** the external container that holds and describes the product.

**partnership** a form of business organization defined by the Uniform Partnership Act as "an association of two or more persons who carry on as co-owners of a business for profit."

**penetration price** a low price designed to help a product enter the market and gain market share rapidly.

**pension funds** managed investment pools set aside by individuals, corporations, unions, and some nonprofit organizations to provide retirement income for members.

**per share data** data used by investors to compare the performance of one company with another on an equal, per share basis.

**perception** the process by which a person selects, organizes, and interprets information received from his or her senses.

**personal selling** direct, two-way communication with buyers and potential buyers.

**personality** the organization of an individual's distinguishing character traits, attitudes, or habits.

**physical distribution** all the activities necessary to move products from producers to customers—inventory control, transportation, warehousing, and materials handling.

**physiological needs** the most basic human needs to be satisfied—water, food, shelter, and clothing.

**picketing** a public protest against management practices that involves union members marching and carrying antimanagement signs at the employer's plant.

**plagiarism** the act of taking someone else's work and presenting it as your own without mentioning the source.

**planning** the process of determining the organization's objectives and deciding how to accomplish them; the first function of management.

**podcast** audio or video file that can be downloaded from the Internet with a subscription that automatically delivers new content to listening devices or personal computers.

**preferred stock** a special type of stock whose owners, though not generally having a say in running the company, have a claim to profits before other stockholders do.

**price** a value placed on an object exchanged between a buyer and a seller.

**price skimming** charging the highest possible price that buyers who want the product will pay.

**primary data** marketing information that is observed, recorded, or collected directly from respondents.

**primary market** the market where firms raise financial capital.

**prime rate** the interest rate that commercial banks charge their best customers (usually large corporations) for short-term loans.

**private accountants** accountants employed by large corporations, government agencies, and other organizations to prepare and analyze their financial statements.

**private corporation** a corporation owned by just one or a few people who are closely involved in managing the business.

**private distributor brands** brands, which may cost less than manufacturer brands, that are owned and controlled by a wholesaler or retailer.

**process layout** a layout that organizes the transformation process into departments that group related processes.

**product** a good or service with tangible and intangible characteristics that provide satisfaction and benefits.

**product departmentalization** the organization of jobs in relation to the products of the firm.

**product layout** a layout requiring that production be broken down into relatively simple tasks assigned to workers, who are usually positioned along an assembly line.

**product line** a group of closely related products that are treated as a unit because of similar marketing strategy, production, or end-use considerations.

**product mix** all the products offered by an organization.

**product-development teams** a specific type of project team formed to devise, design, and implement a new product.

**production** the activities and processes used in making tangible products; also called manufacturing.

**production and operations managers** those who develop and administer the activities involved in transforming resources into goods, services, and ideas ready for the marketplace.

**profit** the difference between what it costs to make and sell a product and what a customer pays for it.

**profit margin** net income divided by sales.

**profit sharing** a form of compensation whereby a percentage of company profits is distributed to the employees whose work helped to generate them.

**profitability ratios** ratios that measure the amount of operating income or net income an organization is able to generate relative to its assets, owners' equity, and sales.

**project organization** a company using a fixed-position layout because it is typically involved in large, complex projects such as construction or exploration.

**project teams** groups similar to task forces that normally run their operation and have total control of a specific work project.

**promotion** an advancement to a higher-level job with increased authority, responsibility, and pay.

**promotional positioning** the use of promotion to create and maintain an image of a product in buyers' minds.

**psychological pricing** encouraging purchases based on emotional rather than rational responses to the price.

**public corporation** a corporation whose stock anyone may buy, sell, or trade.

**publicity** nonpersonal communication transmitted through the mass media but not paid for directly by the firm.

**pull strategy** the use of promotion to create consumer demand for a product so that consumers exert pressure on marketing channel members to make it available.

**purchasing** the buying of all the materials needed by the organization; also called procurement.

**pure competition** the market structure that exists when there are many small businesses selling one standardized product.

**push strategy** an attempt to motivate intermediaries to push the product down to their customers.

## Q

**quality** the degree to which a good, service, or idea meets the demands and requirements of customers.

**quality control** the processes an organization uses to maintain its established quality standards.

**quality-assurance teams (or quality circles)** small groups of workers brought together from throughout the organization to solve specific quality, productivity, or service problems.

**quasi-public corporations** corporations owned and operated by the federal, state, or local government.

**quick ratio (acid test)** a stringent measure of liquidity that eliminates inventory.

**quota** a restriction on the number of units of a particular product that can be imported into a country.

## R

**ratio analysis** calculations that measure an organization's financial health.

**receivables turnover** sales divided by accounts receivable.

**recession** a decline in production, employment, and income.

**recruiting** forming a pool of qualified applicants from which management can select employees.

**reference groups** groups with whom buyers identify and whose values or attitudes they adopt.

**reference pricing** a type of psychological pricing in which a lower-priced item is compared to a more expensive brand in hopes that the consumer will use the higher price as a comparison price.

**reserve requirement** the percentage of deposits that banking institutions must hold in reserve.

**responsibility** the obligation, placed on employees through delegation, to perform assigned tasks satisfactorily and be held accountable for the proper execution of work.

**retailers** intermediaries who buy products from manufacturers (or other intermediaries) and sell them to consumers for home and household use rather than for resale or for use in producing other products.

**retained earnings** earnings after expenses and taxes that are reinvested in the assets of the firm and belong to the owners in the form of equity.

**return on assets** net income divided by assets.

**return on equity** net income divided by owners' equity; also called return on investment (ROI).

**revenue** the total amount of money received from the sale of goods or services, as well as from related business activities.

**routing** the sequence of operations through which the product must pass.

## S

**S corporation** corporation taxed as though it were a partnership with restrictions on shareholders.

**salary** a financial reward calculated on a weekly, monthly, or annual basis.

**sales promotion** direct inducements offering added value or some other incentive for buyers to enter into an exchange.

**savings accounts** accounts with funds that usually cannot be withdrawn without advance notice; also known as time deposits.

**savings and loan associations (S&Ls)** financial institutions that primarily offer savings accounts and make long-term loans for residential mortgages; also called "thrifts."

**scheduling** the assignment of required tasks to departments or even specific machines, workers, or teams.

**secondary data** information that is compiled inside or outside an organization for some purpose other than changing the current situation.

**secondary markets** stock exchanges and over-the-counter markets where investors can trade their securities with others.

**secured bonds** bonds that are backed by specific collateral that must be forfeited in the event that the issuing firm defaults.

**secured loans** loans backed by collateral that the bank can claim if the borrowers do not repay them.

**securities markets** the mechanism for buying and selling securities.

**security needs** the need to protect oneself from physical and economic harm.

**selection** the process of collecting information about applicants and using that information to make hiring decisions.

**selective distribution** a form of market coverage whereby only a small number of all available outlets are used to expose products.

**self-actualization needs** the need to be the best one can be; at the top of Maslow's hierarchy.

**self-directed work team (SDWT)** a group of employees responsible for an entire work process or segment that delivers a product to an internal or external customer.

**separations** employment changes involving resignation, retirement, termination, or layoff.

**serial bonds** a sequence of small bond issues of progressively longer maturity.

**small business** any independently owned and operated business that is not dominant in its competitive area and does not employ more than 500 people.

**Small Business Administration (SBA)** an independent agency of the federal government that offers managerial and financial assistance to small businesses.

**social classes** a ranking of people into higher or lower positions of respect.

**social needs** the need for love, companionship, and friendship—the desire for acceptance by others.

**social network** a web-based meeting place for friends, family, co-workers, and peers that lets users create a profile and connect with other users for a wide range of purposes.

**social responsibility** a business's obligation to maximize its positive impact and minimize its negative impact on society.

**social roles** a set of expectations for individuals based on some position they occupy.

**socialism** an economic system in which the government owns and operates basic industries but individuals own most businesses.

**sole proprietorships** businesses owned and operated by one individual; the most common form of business organization in the United States.

**span of management** the number of subordinates who report to a particular manager.

**specialization** the division of labor into small, specific tasks and the assignment of employees to do a single task.

**staffing** the hiring of people to carry out the work of the organization.

**stakeholders** groups that have a stake in the success and outcomes of a business.

**standardization** the making of identical interchangeable components or products.

**statement of cash flows** explains how the company's cash changed from the beginning of the accounting period to the end.

**statistical process control** a system in which management collects and analyzes information about the production process to pinpoint quality problems in the production system.

**stock** shares of a corporation that may be bought or sold.

**strategic alliance** a partnership formed to create competitive advantage on a worldwide basis.

**strategic plans** those plans that establish the long-range objectives and overall strategy or course of action by which a firm fulfills its mission.

**strikebreakers** people hired by management to replace striking employees; called "scabs" by striking union members.

**strikes** employee walkouts; one of the most effective weapons labor has.

**structure** the arrangement or relationship of positions within an organization.

**supply** the number of products—goods and services—that businesses are willing to sell at different prices at a specific time.

**supply chain management** connecting and integrating all parties or members of the distribution system in order to satisfy customers.

**sustainability** conducting activities in a way that allows for the long-term well-being of the natural environment, including all biological entities; involves the assessment and improvement of business strategies, economic sectors, work practices, technologies, and lifestyles so that they maintain the health of the natural environment.

**T**

**tactical plans** short-range plans designed to implement the activities and objectives specified in the strategic plan.

**target market** a specific group of consumers on whose needs and wants a company focuses its marketing efforts.

**task force** a temporary group of employees responsible for bringing about a particular change.

**team** a small group whose members have complementary skills; have a common purpose, goals, and approach; and hold themselves mutually accountable.

**technical expertise** the specialized knowledge and training needed to perform jobs that are related to particular areas of management.

**test marketing** a trial minilaunch of a product in limited areas that represent the potential market.

**Theory X** McGregor's traditional view of management whereby it is assumed that workers generally dislike work and must be forced to do their jobs.

**Theory Y** McGregor's humanistic view of management whereby it is assumed that workers like to work and that under proper conditions employees will seek out responsibility in an attempt to satisfy their social, esteem, and self-actualization needs.

**Theory Z** a management philosophy that stresses employee participation in all aspects of company decision making.

**times interest earned ratio** operating income divided by interest expense.

**Title VII of the Civil Rights Act** prohibits discrimination in employment and created the Equal Employment Opportunity Commission.

**top managers** the president and other top executives of a business, such as the chief executive officer (CEO), chief financial officer (CFO), and chief operations officer (COO), who have overall responsibility for the organization.

**total asset turnover** sales divided by total assets.

**total quality management (TQM)** a philosophy that uniform commitment to quality in all areas of an organization will promote a culture that meets customers' perceptions of quality.

**total-market approach** an approach whereby a firm tries to appeal to everyone and assumes that all buyers have similar needs.

**trade credit** credit extended by suppliers for the purchase of their goods and services.

**trade deficit** a nation's negative balance of trade, which exists when that country imports more products than it exports.

**trademark** a brand that is registered with the U.S. Patent and Trademark Office and is thus legally protected from use by any other firm.

**trading company** a firm that buys goods in one country and sells them to buyers in another country.

**training** teaching employees to do specific job tasks through either classroom development or on-the-job experience.

**transaction balances** cash kept on hand by a firm to pay normal daily expenses, such as employee wages and bills for supplies and utilities.

**transfer** a move to another job within the company at essentially the same level and wage.

**transportation** the shipment of products to buyers.

**Treasury bills (T-bills)** short-term debt obligations the U.S. government sells to raise money.

**turnover** occurs when employees quit or are fired and must be replaced by new employees.

## U

**undercapitalization** the lack of funds to operate a business normally.

**unemployment** the condition in which a percentage of the population wants to work but is unable to find jobs.

**unsecured bonds** debentures or bonds that are not backed by specific collateral.

**unsecured loans** loans backed only by the borrowers' good reputation and previous credit rating.

## V

**value** a customer's subjective assessment of benefits relative to costs in determining the worth of a product.

**venture capitalists** persons or organizations that agree to provide some funds for a new business in exchange for an ownership interest or stock.

**viral marketing** a marketing tool that uses a networking effect to spread a message and create brand awareness. The purpose of this marketing technique is to encourage the consumer to share the message with friends, family, co-workers, and peers.

## W

**wage/salary survey** a study that tells a company how much compensation comparable firms are paying for specific jobs that the firms have in common.

**wages** financial rewards based on the number of hours the employee works or the level of output achieved.

**warehousing** the design and operation of facilities to receive, store, and ship products.

**whistleblowing** the act of an employee exposing an employer's wrongdoing to outsiders, such as the media or government regulatory agencies.

**wholesalers** intermediaries who buy from producers or from other wholesalers and sell to retailers.

**wiki** software that creates an interface that enables users to add or edit the content of some types of websites.

**working capital management** the managing of short-term assets and liabilities.

**World Bank** an organization established by the industrialized nations in 1946 to loan money to underdeveloped and developing countries; formally known as the International Bank for Reconstruction and Development.

**World Trade Organization (WTO)** international organization dealing with the rules of trade between nations.

# Photo Credits

# Name Index

Page numbers followed by n refer to notes.

# Company Index

# Subject Index

Boldface entries denote glossary terms and the page numbers where they are defined.